TECHNIQUE

IN

TRANSITION

TECHNIQUE

IN

TRANSITION

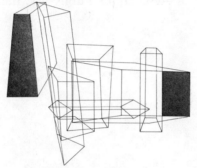

Robert Langs, M.D.

A

JASON ARONSON, INC.

New York • London

to
Richard G., Bob S.,
Tom S., Tony W., Richard Z.—
individually and collectively,
very special

Classical Psychoanalysis and its Applications

A Series of Books edited by ROBERT LANGS, M.D.

ACKNOWLEDGMENTS

Chapter 2: A version of this paper, "Day Residues, Recall Residues, and Dreams: Reality and the Psyche," was published in the *Journal of the American Psychoanalytic Association*, Vol. 19, pp. 499–523, 1971.

Chapter 3: A version of this paper, "A Psychoanalytic Study of Material from Patients in Psychotherapy," was first published in the *International Journal of Psychoanalytic Psychotherapy*, Vol. 1, No. 1, pp. 4–45, 1972.

Chapter 4: A version of this paper, "The Patient's View of the Therapist: Reality or Fantasy?" was first published in the *International Journal of Psychoanalytic Psychotherapy,* Vol. 2, pp. 411–431, 1973.

Chapter 5: "The Patient's Unconscious Perception of the Therapist's Errors" was first published in *Tactics and Techniques in Psychoanalytic Therapy, Vol 2: Countertransference*, edited by Peter L. Giovacchini, pp. 239–250, 1975.

Chapter 6: "Therapeutic Misalliances" was first published in the *International Journal of Psychoanalytic Psychotherapy*, Vol. 4, pp. 77–105. 1975.

Chapter 7: "The Therapeutic Relationship and Deviations in Technique" was first published in the *International Journal of Psychoanalytic Psychotherapy*, Vol. 4, pp. 106–141, 1975.

Chapter 8: This paper, "Misalliance and Framework in the Case of Dora," will appear in modified form under the title, "The Misalliance Dimension in the Case of Dora," in the volume *Freud and His Patients,* edited by Mark Kanzer and Jules Glenn, New York; Jason Aronson. The present version was published under the title, "The Misalliance Dimension in Freud's Case Histories: I. The Case of Dora," in the *International Journal of Psychoanalytic Psychotherapy,* Vol. 5, pp. 301–317, 1976.

Chapter 9: This paper, "Misalliance and Framework in the Case of the Rat Man," will appear under the title, "The Misalliance Dimension in the Case of the Rat Man," in *Freud and His Patients,* edited by Mark Kanzer and Jules Glenn, New York: Jason Aronson.

Chapter 10: This paper, "Misalliance and the Framework in Freud's Case of the Wolf Man," is a modified version of a paper to appear under the title, "The Misalliance Dimension in the Case of the Wolf Man," in *Freud and His Patient,* edited by Mark Kanzer and Jules Glenn, New York: Jason Aronson.

Chapter 11: "Framework, Misalliance, and Interaction in the Analytic Situation" comprises three contributions to the *International Encyclopedia of Psychiatry, Psychology, Psychoanalysis, and Neurology*, edited by B.B. Wolman: "Psychoanalytic Situation: The Framework," Vol. 9, pp. 220–225; "Therapeutic Misalliance," Vol. 11, pp. 146–150; and "Psychoanalytic Interaction," Vol. 9 pp. 189–195. New York: Aesculapins Publishers, 1977.

Chapter 12: The paper, "On Becoming A Psychiatrist," was first published under the title, "On Becoming a Psychiatrist: Discussion of 'Empathy and Intuitition in Becoming a Psychiatrist,' by Ronald J. Blank," in the *International Journal of Psychoanalytic Psychotherapy*, Vol. 5, pp. 255–279, 1976.

Chapter 13: This paper, "Transference Beyond Freud," was first published in *The Unconscious, Vol. II,* a volume devoted to the planner Tbilissi Symposium, edited by Leon Chertok and published in 1978. Its title there was "Transference Beyond Freud: Reality and Uncosncious Processes."

Chapter 14: "Validation and the Framework of the Therapeutic Situation" is reprinted with permission from *Contemporary Psychoanalysis,* Vol. 14, 1978 pp. 98–14, Journal of the William Alanson White Psychoanalytic Society and the William Alanson White Institute, New York. Its full title in that publication is "Validation and the Framework of the Therapeutic Situation: Thoughts Prompted by Hans H. Strupp's 'Suffering and Psychotherapy.'"

Chapter 15: "Some Communicative Properties of the Bipersonal Field" was first prepared for the volume *Do I Dare Disturb the Universe? A Festschrift for Wilfred Bion,* edited by James Grotstein, and to be published by Jason Aronson, Inc., New York. The paper has also been published in the *International Journal of Psychoanalytic Psychotherapy,* Vol. 7, pp. 89–161, 1978, and in *The Listening Process,* by Robert Langs, New York: Jason Aronson, 1978.

Chapter 16: "Reactions to Creatavity in Psychoanalysts" was first published in the *International Journal of Psychoanalytic Psychotherapy,* Vol. 8, pp. 189–207, 1978. It was written in response to the paper, "Transference and Countertransference," by Harold Searles.

Chapter 17: This paper, "The Adaptational-Interactional Dimension of Countertransference," is scheduled to appear in *Contemporary Psychoanalysis,* Vol. 14, 1978. It is included in a volume sponsored by the William Alanson White Psychoanalytic Society, entitled *Recent Studies in Countertransference,* edited by Lawrence Epstein, Ph.D., and Arthur H. Feiner, Ph.D., Jason Aronson, Inc., in press.

Chapter 18: "Dreams in the Bipersonal Field" was prepared under the title "Dreams in Psychotherapy" for the book, *The Dream in Clinical Practice,* edited by Joseph Natterson and to be published by Jason Aronson, Inc., New York.

Chapter 20: "Interventions in the Bipersonal Field" is scheduled to be published in *Contemporary Psychoanalysis,* Vol. 15, 1979.

As a rule, however, theoretical controversy is unfruitful. No sooner has one begun to depart from the material on which one ought to be relying, than one runs the risk of becoming intoxicated with one's own assertions and, in the end, of supporting opinions which any observation would have contradicted. For that reason it seems to me to be incomparably more useful to come back to dissentient interpretations by testing them upon particular cases and problems.

—Freud, *From the History of an Infantile Neurosis*

CONTENTS

PREFACE

There must indeed be compelling reasons to publish one's collected papers. The relative unavailability of published and pending contributions viewed as important by a wide audience, the need to present an integrated unfolding of crucial additions to the literature, an increasing demand for an opportunity to study the work of a given analyst—these are among the more general of such reasons. Each appears to apply now, I must say with all humility, to my work.

Still, I had resisted a collection such as this for some time, and did not agree to it until I felt that there was an additional and very special reason for this volume: the completion of a critical period of transition in my conception of the therapeutic interaction, and therapeutic and analytic techniques. It is, then, this sense of having passed through a series of meaningful transitions—from basic classical psychoanalytic thinking and technique to various phases of what I would term a classical psychoanalytic conception and technique from an adaptational-interactional viewpoint—that to my mind justifies this book.

The nature of these transitions and some of their implications are described in my first chapter, while the remaining chapters present in chronological sequence a series of papers that begins with an essentially classical viewpoint and culminates in a group of papers that define the essential aspects of the interactional view and technique. There is, I believe, a very meaningful transition portrayed in this unfolding, and it is one I invite the reader to experience, to struggle with, and to grow and develop through. It is, as I say, the raison d'etre of this volume, far more than the specific contributions to both psychoanalytic methodology (a much neglected avenue of creativity) and psychoanalytic clinical theory and technique.

I am especially indebted to Jason Aronson for his long-standing support and his great interest in publishing my work. Michael Farrin provided extremely helpful editing, and quite effectively functioned to oversee the production of this volume, while Sheila Gardner was responsible for much of the essential secretarial work involved. Still, I must express my greatest appreciation to my students and supervisees, who, as I have mentioned so often before, have with great fortitude and honesty, and with an intense desire to learn, presented the seemingly endless streams of clinical material that provided the clinical data for the papers in this volume. It was, indeed, their struggles with their patients and with the travails of learning psychotherapeutic technique that afforded me a very special and humbling opportunity to observe and conceptualize. I am extremely grateful for their faith in my teaching efforts, for the moments of pain that we shared, and for the personal growth afforded all of us. It is my special hope that the most positive aspects of these experiences are reflected in these pages, to a point where the reader, too, might work them over and grow.

Robert Langs, M.D.
New York, New York
July 1978

Chapter One

Technique in Transition

[1978]

This initial chapter is an overview and commentary on the clinical work and postulates reflected in the papers presented in this volume. They were written over the relatively brief span of seven years, and yet contain, I believe, a series of interrelated transitions in conception and technique with far-reaching consequences for both the patient and the therapist or analyst (the distinction between therapy and analysis will not be especially considered in this volume since it is not particularly relevant to the areas under study; I will use the terms *therapist* and *analyst* interchangeably except where the distinction seems necessary.

When I first embarked upon the clinical investigations represented here, I tended to minimize the differences between my thinking and techniques and those of the accepted classical clinical norms prevailing—in regard to both psychoanalysis and psychoanalytically oriented psychotherapy. However, I soon established a clearly distinctive approach to insight psychotherapy, one so basically at odds with the usual tenet—that such work should be undertaken primarily around conflicts and issues outside the therapeutic relationship—that it no longer either made sense or did justice to my position to attempt to see it merely as a variation of the classical view. As regards analysis proper, it is still possible to characterize my concepts as a continuation of the prevailing orthodoxy, but even here it has become evident that my approach constitutes more a departure from current practice than an extension of it.

Many factors played a role in this transition. One important dimension has been the gradual development of a basic clinical psychoanalytic methodology, a concern rather neglected in the psychoanalytic literature. Allusions to methodology tend to conjure up images of detail, obsessiveness, lack of imagination, peripheral necessity, and even sterility. This is a most unfortunate penumbra of associations, since in actuality the development of a valid psychoanalytic clinical methodology is, on the one hand, an inevitable consequence of creativity in this area and, on the other, an absolute essential for further innovation.

In the present chapter, I shall trace out the development of my thinking, both in terms of my reformulations of the nature of the therapeutic interaction and other clinical issues, and in regard to the slow evolution of a basic clinical methodology. For several years, I had considered the presentation of contrasting clinical positions as a means of clarifying and illustrating some of my own hypotheses. In the course of reading and rereading some of the major books on psychoanalytic technique, and the occasional paper on the listening process, I saw an opportunity to compare my own thinking and techniques with those of established psychoanalysts, both classical and Kleinian. I did not avail myself of the opportunity for a number of reasons: first, such an approach constitutes a form of critical or negative teaching which has always seemed of questionable value because of its destructive connotations; second, there are many limitations in attempting to evaluate another analyst's presentation; third, I was loath to be openly critical of analysts who have had the courage to forthrightly present their own clinical work in the hope of helping others learn from what they themselves have exposed; fourth, in terms of the importance of presenting material and ideas through which the analyst and therapist might learn, experience has shown me that it is quite easy for a reader to disclaim any resemblance to an analyst whose work is under criticism, regardless of how similar his own work might actually be; fifth, and finally, I have always preferred to present my own supervisory material and to work with it in a positive and constructive spirit, rather than to occasion suspicions of secondary motives and grandiosity.

I say all this by way of introducing the particular theme with which I shall initiate this overview. I plan to make but a single exception to my disinclination to invidious comparison: I will take myself, at least during the period of my early writings, as a representative classical psychoanalyst, and will use those papers as a means of characterizing a particular and popular conception of the psychoanalytic process and interaction. I shall do so not only as a means of establishing the similarities and differences in my clinical thinking then and now, but also as part of an effort to engage the reader in a delineation of his own technique at the present time—some of it through the recognition of attributes shared with those defined in these early papers. This will, I hope, make it possible to involve the reader in a way that will enable him to join me in criticisms of this technique, and in a gradual transition toward a new and more valid approach.

TWO EARLY PAPERS

To provide a brief background, I had, in the decade prior to the day residue–recall residue paper (chapter 2), completed my psychoanalytic training at the Downstate Psychoanalytic Institute and had spent almost ten years engaged in psychoanalytic research at both the Albert Einstein College of Medicine and the Research Center for Mental Health at New York University. I had published investigations of earliest memories and manifest dreams and, by myself and with a variety of coauthors, also published a series of investigations into the psychological effects of the altered state of consciousness produced by d-lysergic acid. I had the good fortune to work with Morton Reiser, Robert Holt, George Klein, and many other sophisticated, analytically oriented psychologists at the Research Center, and learned something of the need for openness, skepticism, the questioning of accepted tenets, and investigative metholdology. While virtually all the publications that resulted from the work of these years had a bearing on the clinical situation, none of the investigations dealt specifically with the therapeutic experience and process.

When in 1963 I began my work as a supervisor of psychotherapy at Hillside Hospital, I became intensely interested in the therapeutic process and gradually shifted my orientation to a more directly clinical vantage point. My first paper along these lines was an investigation of day residues, recall residues (incidents that prompt the remembering of forgotten dreams), and dreams, studied as a model of the relationship between reality and psyche (chapter 2). For some time, I had been intrigued by this relationship, especially the interplay between reality and fantasy (a term I use to imply pathological fantasy, pathological unconscious fantasies, memories, and introjects in particular). I shared with Freud (1918, 1926) an uncertainty as to the relative influence of actual early childhood traumas, as compared to very early unconscious fantasy formations, on the psychopathology and development of the individual, and I was puzzled about their respective roles in neurotic anxiety, conflicts, and symptom formation. I was aware of the work of those analysts before me who had struggled with these problems, and was aware especially of the contributions of Arlow (1963, 1969 a, b) in these areas.

In the belief, then, that there was more to be learned regarding the interplay between reality and the psyche, I pursued the study of day and recall residues. Though hardly the focus of the paper, a leitmotif emerged that has been carried through in one form or another throughout all my subsequent work. The study entails an essentially adaptive approach, and the concept of the interplay between reality and fantasy is the forerunner of the extensive adaptational-interactional considerations that characterizes my later endeavors. The investigation proved to be a fateful beginning.

To characterize the conception of the analytic situation and of analytic technique reflected in this initial paper: there is an idea of an interwoven totality in which current day residues, manifest dreams, latent dream content, and genetically significant past experiences have a kind of equipotential; there is no special accent or basic way of organizing the material. The paper implies that the day residue may well provide the key to the unconscious fantasies and memories contained in the dream, but it leaves considerable room for other approaches to the latent content. It is recognized that day residues themselves have manifest and latent content, but the basic structure of these precipitants is repeatedly formulated in terms of outside relationships that have seemingly evoked important intrapsychic conflicts, and unconscious fantasies and memories; except for special situations, these residues are viewed in a way that lacks a consistent and immediate connection on some latent level to the analytic interaction.

The apparent modifications of repressive defenses, the unfolding of dynamically meaningful material, and the communication of unforeseen genetic connections seem to justify such an approach and to imply that, quite often, there is no need to link the material to the current analytic interaction. Genetic explanations and transference displacements and distortions prevail, while projections from the patient onto the analyst constitute the main dynamism of the so-called transference relationship. These views seemed correct for both the analytic and psychotherapeutic situations, and implied that in the former setting the analyst could make important interpretations outside the transference (to use the term as I used it then, to allude to the patient's relationship to the analyst); where psychotherapy was concerned, this idea was almost universally accepted.

Thus, most of the day residues discussed in that paper center around major outside traumas and only occasionally are the links developed between (1) the network of day residue, manifest dream, and latent dream content and (2) the analytic relationship. Such links as are developed are universally characterized in terms of transference. As a result, the presentation takes on the following quality: a crucial day residue in an external relationship evokes a variety of intrapsychic stirrings, some of which subsequently become attached to the analyst or therapist as transference. In this sense, the analyst's main contribution is his availability as a so-called object for the patient's transferences, a position that is predicated on his creation of a secure analytic situation within which he functions as a participant observer. The stress is placed on the patient's projections and displacements from past and present objects onto the analyst. The introjective mode is almost entirely disregarded. Even in the vignette related to a specific day residue derived from the analytic relationship itself, the precipitant is seen in terms of a confrontation with unconscious rage based entirely on a transference projection and distortion and a seemingly valid interpretation by the analyst.

It is also of interest that in one of the vignettes related to a recall residue, the analyst appears to misrepresent a communication from the patient by mistakenly suggesting that the patient was undressed in his dream. The implications of this possible error—in terms of a pathological projective process in the therapist which might evoke an introjective response in the patient—are not discussed, nor is it seen as a factor in the recall of the previously repressed, latent sexual dream. The prevailing projective model of the patient's relationship to the analyst is maintained: this emergence is conceptualized, once again, in terms of projections and distortions based on an existing erotic transference derived largely from the patient's intrapsychic pathological fantasies and memories.

While the day residue-recall residue paper includes analytic material, the second paper of this period (chapter 3) is a study of material from patients in psychotherapy. Before touching upon the intimations of transition in the latter paper, I would like to further characterize the conception of psychoanalysis and psychotherapy reflected in these two presentations. To state this in terms of the analytic situation (I will bypass the debate regarding the differences and similarities between analysis and therapy; see chapters 9, 10, 14, 15, and 19; see also Langs 1967b), the analyst creates the conditions for the unfolding of the patient's transference neurosis or transference expressions. The central motivating factor in the treatment situation and in the patient's communications is his intrapsychic anxieties, conflict, fantasies, and memories, and the analyst, while a participant, is essentially a passive, neutral, and flexible figure toward whom these fantasies are projected and displaced. The stress is on the analytic relationship far more than on interaction. The relationship is termed *the transference* because the analyst's central function is to receive and interpret the patient's distorted and distorting fantasies and their underlying meaning. There is room in this conception for an occasional gross error and countertransference-based input, which is seen mainly as a deterrent to the unfolding of the patient's transference syndrome on its own terms, as in need of direct acknowledgment and correction with the patient, and as a possible means of productive analytic work if the repercussions for the patient are fully analyzed. Also recognized is the possibility of direct pressures on the analyst to respond in some inappropriate manner, viewed in terms of unconscious efforts by the patient to repeat his past rather than remember it, but transference expressions are conceived of primarily in terms of conscious fantasies about the analyst or about obvious displacement figures—fantasies that are seen as essentially distorting and pathological, and as deriving in the main from the patient's unconscious conflicts, fantasies, and memories (see Langs 1976b).

If we take this as a model of the analytic situation, we may note that the ground rules are, in general, taken for granted. There is virtually no reference to them in either of these initial works, a very striking observation when one considers that the second paper investigated all available material from a group of ten patients in three hundred sessions of psychotherapy. While there is mention there of absences and latenesses, it is assumed that the ground rules are part of a silent backdrop that requires little specific attention or comment. While not stated explicitly, the general attitude of such an approach is one of flexibility in respect both to deviations in technique and to the basic analytic contract, with some recognition that, as a rule, these gross modifications should be clarified as to their unconscious meanings for the patient—i.e., they deserve some analytic attention.

It is beyond the scope of this discussion to more fully characterize the model of the analytic relationship assumed in these two early papers. Having established some of the main attributes—which will serve later as a point of contrast once certain basic transitions in conception and technique have been made—I will turn now to some other important features of the second paper. Following the dream study, I became almost totally absorbed in the investigation of the psychoanalytic and psychotherapeutic situations, relationships, interactions, and experiences. I began to record my extensive supervisory experiences and from the outset was greatly aided by the many candid presentations from my supervisees—to whom, for their crucial role in the development of my thinking, I am especially grateful. I saw a place for a new, empirically grounded work on psychoanalytically oriented psychotherapy, and began to review the literature and to outline the projected volumes (Langs 1973a, 1974).

It was during this period that I wrote the second paper, having become intrigued with a controversy over whether dreams had a special place in analytic work (see Greenson 1970, Waldhorn 1967). I was especially impressed by the fact that those who participated in the debate—whether in print or by word of mouth—relied on subjective impressions rather than on the development of definitive or, at the very least, specific data. I knew too that this approach was characteristic of almost all psychoanalytic writings: the use of single cases and unvalidated impressions prevails. I therefore thought it important to attempt in my paper what is undoubtedly a crude investigative study of specific material from patients in psychotherapy, evaluating the data as best I could for manifest and latent communications, and determining the type of material that best served to convey both conscious and unconscious meanings.

In addition to the conclusions of this study, which were not unexpected, several very special rewards issued from this empirical approach—the first of what I believe to be many insights that have accrued through the use and development of an improved methodology. Without a doubt, the most important of these was the generation of the concept of the *primary adaptive context*—the *adaptive context,* as I later termed it. As I recall, this came about when I began to sift the material from the three hundred sessions under investigation. I had a basic understanding of derivatives, of unconscious fantasies and memories, of latent content and of the relations and differences between manifest and latent themes. I had received virtually no formal teaching or training in this area, though my work with dreams had provided me both a useful model and the general tools needed to search for unconscious meanings and functions.

In the dream paper, I had found that the day residue was often the crucial organizer through which the unconscious meanings took shape and could be recognized. In evaluating other types of communications—conscious fantasies, descriptions of recent events, the patient's behaviors, etc.—I found that, globally, I could identify a series of meaningful surface indicators of problems, conflicts, and resistances quite readily; on the other hand, the material appeared confused and difficult to decipher for specific unconscious fantasies and memories. The confusion was resolved, however, when I extended the day residue concept to a search for reality precipitants in every sequence of material. These precipitants turned out to be major adaptive tasks confronting the patient; it was soon evident that some of these tasks evoked relatively realistic and nonpathological responses, while others set off a sequence of unconscious fantasies and memories, almost all of which were essentially related to the patient's pathology and inner anxieties and conflicts.

As the work continued, it happened that it was only in those situations where it was possible to identify the primary adaptive task that I could subsequently define the specific unconscious fantasies and memories contained in derivative and disguised form in the manifest material. Here I sensed a concept of great importance—the first major transition in my conceptualization and technique—and I spent considerable time refining it, though I as yet had no idea as to how absolutely vital it would prove to be. In retrospect I see it as undoubtedly the single most important concept I have developed, though of course it can be viewed as an extension and derivative of Freud's (1900) monumental discovery of the day residue for the dream.

The primary adaptive task concept not only provided a means of systematically identifying unconscious fantasies and memories, but also made it possible to recognize material in which such derivatives are radically unavailable. I was able to state in that paper that patients manifest characteristic communicative styles in regard to the material with which they express their unconscious fantasies and memories, and that these styles are differentiated with respect to the availability of derivatives in the material. Thus emerged yet another theme to which I would repeatedly return, and which culminated in what I consider to be another major transition, one reflected in the communicative properties paper (chapter 15).

It seems to me, as I look back on the efforts I made in this area, that, to this day, the idea that there are some patients who communicate few analyzable derivatives has not taken hold in classical psychoanalytic thinking. Much of this stems from a basic failure to develop the details of the listening process, and to reach a consensus regarding the properties of derivative communication. Ultimately, it is my belief that such major blind spots stem from shared countertransferences, and from a prevailing dread of the psychotic part of the personality—a position that I have adopted not lightly, but only after compelling and repeated observations along such lines.

But there was more to the primary adaptive task concept: it was an adaptational conceptualization that immediately prepared the way for an essentially adaptational-interactional approach to the analytic experience. It made the search for the adaptive context an urgent necessity, and established that context as the key to the unconscious meanings of the patient's material. I began a transition in conceptualizing the patient's communications that soon allowed access to the introjective mode and the patient's unconscious perceptions. The concept also fostered a careful study of the functional adaptational context for the patient's expression of pathological unconscious fantasies and memories (and perceptions), an aspect of the now burgeoning interrelated transitions that soon led me to concentrate on the details of the therapeutic interaction.

The treatment of material in isolation was no longer excusable (though to this day it remains a very common practice), nor could one in good scientific conscience settle any longer for general unconscious fantasies rather than those specific for a given patient at a given moment. I was able to state in this paper that it was the primary adaptive task that gave new meaning to repetitive fantasies, thereby preparing the way for recent discussions of the *functional capacity* of the patient's associations (see chapter 19; see also Langs 1978).

In addition to considerations of the extent to which patients reported detectable and analyzable derivatives, this clinical study alerted me to the frequency with which the therapist's behaviors, formulated at this point largely in terms of his confrontations and interpretations, served the patient as the primary adaptive task in the material that followed. It was in this context that I suggested that certain types of material, such as acting out, represented the living out of transference and real reactions and fantasies related to the therapist—the forerunner of a far more thorough investigation of transference and nontransference responses by the patient. Yet despite these gains I still located many primary adaptive tasks outside the therapeutic relationship and concluded that the main work of psychotherapy was to be done in that realm.

One last point: this second paper presented my first definitive effort to develop a psychoanalytic methodology, there in respect to the detection of derivatives of unconscious fantasies and memories. A relatively systematic approach to the understanding of material from patients was initiated; in addition, in this study, as well as in the dream paper, there is an implicit concept of validation, though it is neither discussed nor elaborated.

THE TECHNIQUE BOOKS

The next two years or so I spent writing *The Technique of Psychoanalytic Psychotherapy* (Langs 1973, 1974, a two-volume work which provided a number of important transitional ideas to the efforts that followed. In regard to the listening and validating processes, it included an extended version of the paper last discussed, in which an elaborative effort was made to investigate the listening process and the means through which therapists detect derivatives of the patient's unconscious conflicts, fantasies, and memories as they pertain to the core of the psychopathology. To the concept of the primary adaptive task I added the notion of the *therapeutic context*—the indicators of difficulties and resistances within the patient that tend to call for interventions from the therapist. This was seen as a second-level organizer of the patient's material, which would first be developed in terms of the primary adaptive task as a means of detecting the unconscious derivatives; only then, as a way of determining the unconscious meaning of a given symptom, resistance, or the like, would it be reorganized around the therapeutic context.

In another section of the technique books, I offered, in an attempt to develop definitive clinical criteria for the validity of the therapist's interventions, an extended discussion of confirmation and nonconfirmation—my first such elaboration. It is of some interest that these chapters were developed essentially around the therapist's verbal interventions—his confronting and interpretative endeavors. While there was some discussion of the validation of nonverbal interventions and of the prevailing atmosphere of the therapeutic situation, there was no specific attention to the validation of deviations in technique and modifications in the ground rules—a position that once again reflects the prevailing attitude, both then and now.

In my delineation of the patient-therapist relationship, I made consistent use of the primary adaptive task concept. This led to an essentially adaptational-interactional approach to transference, a term that I still used in reference to most of the patient's relationship with the therapist. There were, however, discussions of the realistic aspects of the patient's relationship to the therapist, his responses to the therapist's errors, and a delineation of the therapeutic alliance.

To be a bit more precise, this approach to so-called transference soon made it abundantly clear that many intrapsychically significant reactions within the patient occurred in fact in response to the therapist's behaviors and interventions. It was also evident that these actions and verbalizations by the therapist could be positive or negative; constructive or destructive; necessarily or unnecessarily hurtful; within the framework of valid interventions or based on technical errors. Thus began my rather extensive investigations of the nature of the therapist's interventions, an exploration that soon led me to a detailed consideration of the unconscious communications they contain. This work had its inevitable counterpart in a reevaluation of the patient's experience of the therapist's interventions, and included a recognition that the patient often perceives the underlying implications of the therapist's interventions in a manner that is essentially nondistorted and veridical. It was here that the concept of the patient's unconscious perception of the therapist's interventions, and especially of his errors, first arose. I had begun to define the much neglected introjective side of the patient's relationship to the therapist, though I was far from fully appreciating its many ramifications.

In these volumes, the concept of dyadic relationship soon gave way to a stress on interaction. Much of this was first developed through a study of the therapeutic alliance—precisely that aspect of the therapeutic relationship, as viewed by classical psychoanalysts, to which both patient and therapist make basic contributions. Thus, the consideration of the alliance dimension further reinforced my interactional approach. In addition, it called for a study of the pathology of the alliance sector, and led to the concept of *anti-therapeutic alliances* or, as I prefer to term them, *therapeutic misalliances* (see chapter 9).

In restudying the therapist's relationship with the patient, I again made use of an adaptational approach. In that way I discovered that many regressions and symptoms within the patient are therapist-evoked (i.e., primarily introjective in nature) and based on errors in intervening, which as I described them there, occurred primarily in the interpretive sphere. (I soon distinguished two basic areas of intervening: the interpretive sphere and the management of the ground rules or framework.) This delineation provided another vantage point for the investigation of the realistic and distorted or fantasied responses to the therapist, and soon made it necessary to develop this distinction in regard to every significant communication and response from the patient.

In the technique books, and in the papers that followed soon after its publication, a growing number of insights and transitions were derived from an understanding of the therapist's errors and the patient's reactions to them. Focusing on this relatively neglected problem led me, more broadly, to become increasingly concerned with the immediate interaction between the patient and the therapist or analyst, and its unconscious ramifications—both introjective and projective. In fact, once I had zeroed in on this interaction, it proved impossible to ever fully depart from it; whatever outside considerations required attention and analysis, there proved always to be some link to the therapeutic interaction. However, the full realization of that important clinical observation did not materialize for some time.

In these two volumes, I also afforded a tremendous amount of space to an investigation of the ground rules of psychotherapy—their establishment and the analysis of their infringements. The scope of these two chapters attests to the frequency with which issues in this area arose in the course of psychotherapy. The basic approach was to advocate a definitive therapeutic contract, with only exceptional modifications in the basic agreement. Thus, within the prevailing principle of flexibility, my empirical investigation of the ground rules appeared to indicate that their alteration is often based on countertransference factors and unresolved transference elements; the data suggested that changes in the basic pact could lead to sectors of misalliance and to resistances within the patient.

There is little doubt that many viewed my initial position in this respect as relatively rigid and preferred a more open and flexible approach, though this could be maintained only by reinterpreting or ignoring the dozens of vignettes that I presented in that volume, all of which indicated the risks of modifications in the ground rules. The two chapters, then, are an extensive exposition of the formal nature of the ground rules of psychotherapy, the kinds of issues that arise when patients or therapists alter these basic tenets, and the need to analyze their repercussions consistently. There is a tone that suggests that modifications in the ground rules are feasible, that their implications must be analyzed, but that a sensitive therapist can do this kind of work without impairing the essential unfolding of the therapeutic experience.

Thus, despite a recognition of the difficulties that arise through many unneeded alterations in this basic contract, I had only begun my investigation of the functions of these tenets and their role as unconscious communications from the therapist. Therefore, I could only suggest that they are best adhered to, rather than breached, and that the latter course calls for definitive therapeutic work. It is interesting too that I presented these ground rules as an extension of a discussion of the initial contact with the patient, and before the two chapters on understanding the communications from patients—a reflection of the manner in which the therapeutic contract was to some degree divorced from the dynamic unfolding of the therapeutic experience.

Two final aspects of the technique books deserve mention: first, the offer of a detailed study of the therapist's interventions based on a consideration of their formal characteristics, including initial consideration of erroneous interventions and some of their consequences; second, the presence of a section in the chapter of transference in which I discuss the means of identifying transference manifestations. It is here that a first effort was made to develop criteria through which a therapist could decide whether a trauma external to the therapeutic relationship or internal to it was evocative of any particular transference response—transference being defined there as the patient's total relationship to the therapist, including both realistic and distorted elements. This was the beginning of an effort to define the relevant issues and to resolve a continued sense of confusion as to where the patient's own unconscious focus lies—within or without the therapeutic relationship—and, of course, as to where the therapeutic work needs to be done. It is also of interest that in this chapter there is a section on transference as interaction, but it is very brief and refers primarily to the patient's basic manner of relating to the therapist.

A PERIOD OF CLARIFICATION
AND GRADUAL TRANSITIONS

The two papers that followed the technique books, "The Patient's View of the Therapist: Reality or Fantasy?" (chapter 4) and "The Patient's Unconscious Perception of the Therapist's Errors" (Chapter 5), are, in the main, specific extensions of some of the more unique considerations of the therapeutic relationship developed in those volumes. Stimulated primarily by my continued clinical studies, and supported by the writings of Greenson, Wexler, and Searles (see Langs, 1976b), I attempted in 13 the first of this pair of papers to establish the basic need for the therapist to monitor—for both conscious and unconscious allusions and images related to himself— the manifest and latent content of the patient's materials.

By making use of an in-depth understanding of the adaptive context, especially in regard to the therapist's own interventions or failures to intervene, it became increasingly clear that much of what the patient said about outside relationships and experiences unconsciously had a significant (disguised) bearing on the therapeutic interaction. As adumbrated in the technique books, it was suggested that once it was determined that the material from the patient unconsciously alluded to the therapist, it was essential to make the added assessment of the extent to which, unconsciously, the material contained veridical perceptions as opposed to fantasy-based distortions. It was also pointed out that this determination relied on the therapist's self-knowledge and on clues provided in the associations from the patient. The latter is a resource that had been neglected almost entirely by previous analysts.

The recognition in this and the following paper that the patient unconsciously perceived the therapist's errors and, further, unconsciously attempted to call them to the therapist's attention, and to even correct him, proved to be the beginning of an extensive investigation of the patient's positive and negative responses to erroneous interventions, especially of what ultimately proved to be the patient's unconscious curative efforts on the therapist's behalf under these circumstances—a concept first delineated by Little (1951) and extensively developed by Searles (1965, 1975). This was also the initiation of a broad investigation of the patient's valid conscious and unconscious functioning within the therapeutic relationship, a much neglected area crowded out by considerations of the patient's pathological and distorted functioning. This is one dimension of the implicit, but prevalent model of the patient as sick and the therapist as healthy; the therapist as healer and the patient as being healed; and the therapist as interpreter and the patient as the recipient of insight—all prejudged characterizations of the therapeutic interaction which prove, upon empirical observation, to be the case only under certain conditions, while the reverse may also occur, and does so far more often than is presently realized.

These papers also include an effort to define the techniques needed to deal with the realistic elements in the patient's transferences and the distorted aspects of the patient's essentially valid responses. There is, however, still a sense of caution in regard to the extent to which such work should characterize psychotherapy.

In the unconscious perceptions paper, I attempted to develop specific clues of the unconscious perceptions of the therapist's errors in the material from patients, and saw the rectification and analysis of responses to errors as a prime therapeutic task and context. In both of these papers, I accept the basic technical premise of Greenson (1972), of directly acknowledging one's error and analyzing the patient's responses; in later work, I viewed this measure as a modification of the therapist's anonymity and stated a preference, where possible, for the *implicit* acceptance by the therapist or analyst of his errors (with obvious errors, such as lateness by the therapist, this is less an issue than with errors in interpreting that are unconsciously detected by the patient, and which should be more implicitly acknowledged).

In terms of transitions in technique, these two papers led me both to stress the extent to which the patient is unconsciously and exquisitely sensitive to the therapist's conscious and unconscious communications, including his mistakes, and to indicate a basic technical need to continuously monitor the material from the patient for his unconscious perceptions of the therapist's errors and his responses to them. In this way, my own sensitivity to the unconscious communications and interaction between patient and therapist was greatly enhanced, and this area became a dimension of the therapeutic interaction which I could then investigate in great detail. These efforts also reinforced the basic sequential methodology that I began to develop in the technique books.

By and large, the recognition of the unconscious meanings of the patient's material depended upon my capacity as a supervisor to evaluate and identify the unconscious communications contained in the therapist's interventions, and the specific nature of his errors. Thus, after listening to the material from the patient, and then assessing the unconscious meanings of the therapist's responsive interventions, we could both listen to the patient's subsequent reaction to the intervention not only for validation or its absence, but also for what I later termed the patient's *commentary* on that intervention—his unconscious evaluation in its broadest sense. In fact, what had first clued me in to this area was my repeated observation that my conscious formulations of erroneous interventions were dramatically echoed in derivative form in the patient's responsive associations. Once sensitized, I soon began to take every intervention by the therapist, whether in the interpretive realm or in response to issues relating to the ground rules, as the focal point and organizer—more precisely, as the adaptive context—for the patient's reactions. By not treating these responses as essentially transference-based and as inherently reflecting distorted fantasies, and by developing, rather, a growing recognition of their many valid components, my image of the patient was gradually changing from that of someone who was virtually always sick, distorting, misunderstanding, responding inappropriately, and the like, to that of an individual with enormous unconscious, valid, and creative, sensitivities that were eventually marred by distorting and pathological extensions. In this way, I began to appreciate the tremendous unconscious resource that each therapist and analyst has in his patient, and my search for a fuller understanding of the therapeutic interaction began to focus on the therapist's unconscious communications on the one hand, and on the patient's unconscious responses on the other—a source of insight that served me extremely well.

At the point at which I wrote these two papers, I was able to define the patient's remarkable unconscious perceptiveness and to demonstrate clear-cut unconscious efforts to correct the therapist—that is, to help him rectify his error by redirecting the therapeutic work. Almost all of this took place on an unconscious level, and in understanding this I was able to avoid the limitations of those who studied and worked with the therapist's errors primarily in terms of the patient's conscious reactions. I had not yet made what appears to be the final transition in this particular sequence, namely, to understand the patient's responses in terms of definitive unconscious curative efforts on the therapist's or analyst's behalf, though I did so in a single moment upon hearing the title of Searles's 1975 paper: "The Patient as Therapist to His Analyst" (see chapter 9).

Some of the limitations in my understanding at this time derived from my continued difficulty in fully defining the nature of the therapeutic interaction and from the attributes of the approach to therapy that I had been taught: however much they interacted, the patient and therapist were seen as relatively separate entities and the influence of the therapist's errors were largely a matter of unconscious perception—rather than introjection and introjective identification (definitive interactional mechanisms), as I was later to conceptualize the matter.

Still, the groundwork for a more careful appreciation of interactional factors and mechanisms was laid in these two papers, especially through the repeated observation that the errors of the therapist and their implications are unconsciously perceived by the patient and are often communicated through references to having himself behaved badly or done something wrong. In addition, there is a quality to these clinical observations that suggests that the patient unconsciously, but constantly, monitors the communications from the therapist, both his silences and his interventions. This implies the presence of an intense and continuous unconscious interaction between patient and therapist, in which unconscious communications play the central role. In that respect, these investigations led me to focus more and more on the unconscious communicative realm, an effort that persists to this very day.

One final implication of these two papers will be noted: with errors as the point of departure, it was becoming clear that quite often the therapist on some level repeated in actuality earlier traumatic experiences to which the patient had been a party. Implicit to this observation is the concept that allusions to genetic material is not a basis on which transference and nontransference can be distinguished. In addition, errors are actualities; they entail actual repetition and therefore clearly take precedence in terms of the patient's experience in the therapeutic interaction and in regard to interpretive and corrective interventions. All of this led me to investigate the influence of all actualities on the therapeutic experience and process of cure. I was quickly coming to realize that such realities were filled with unconscious meanings and implications for both patient and therapist or analyst. It was, however, some years later that I characterized the most crucial dimension of analysis or therapy in terms of developing insight into the unconscious meanings, present and past, of the actualities of the therapeutic interaction. Yet, with an appreciation of the ramifications of these actualities, a basic technical measure was developed: the *rectification of disruptive actualities*, here stated primarily in terms of the therapist's interpretive interventions, though this soon would be applied to his management of the ground rules as well (see chapter 10).

In the unconscious perception paper, in addition to noting the patient's efforts to correct the therapist, I began to identify his unconscious fantasies about why the therapist had erred—the immediate forerunner to recognizing the patient's unconscious efforts to cure the therapist. The connection between errors and what I had termed *iatrogenic syndromes* (Langs, 1974) was further developed, and it became evident that symptoms within the patient could receive important contributions from the therapist—an idea that presages the transition to the bipersonal field conception. At this point, while still focusing in psychotherapy on the patient's outside life in terms of a primary line of communication unmarred by the therapist's errors, the growing evidence for the frequency of the therapist's mistakes was as I noted, leading me to focus more attention on the therapeutic interaction itself.

The two papers I have just discussed were written in 1974, along with the initial versions of the next five papers (chapters 6-10). At the time, I had begun to explore further implications of the concept of the adaptive context. I developed a basic clinical definition of unconscious fantasies and memories as the working over of an adaptive context in some displaced form. On this basis, I could more clearly determine that certain patients reported analyzable derivatives, by which I now meant that in a given session or over several sessions, unconsciously, they would communicate the adaptive context as well as meaningful indirect communications related to that context. In addition, the less communicative patients could now be divided into two groups: those who would report material seemingly rich in meaning and derivatives, but without the adaptive context that would, indeed, provide definitive meaning; and those who would report a series of seemingly crucial adaptive contexts, without the accompanying meaning-laden derivative associations. Initial observation suggested that these styles were based on factors within both the patient and the therapist or analyst, and therefore within the therapeutic interaction; among the latter, the conditions of the ground rules began to take on a growing importance.

The concept of sectors of therapeutic misalliance, with its extensive interactional implications, attracted my continued attention. I began to outline a book which I never actually produced, in which I planned to investigate further the therapeutic alliance, therapeutic misalliances, the ground rules, and the curative and destructive aspects of the therapeutic interaction. My efforts in preparing this volume turned in two directions: first, since I wished to write again regarding psychoanalytic technique, and had not attempted a comprehensive review of the literature for the empirically founded technique books, I felt a responsibility to now carefully investigate the literature for all detectable forerunners of the concepts I was developing. I began to read avidly, to dictate summaries of the relevant papers, and soon became absorbed in this endeavor; the result was the two-volume work published in 1976, *The Therapeutic Interaction*.

While this undertaking was gathering force, I continued to study my clinical material. In addition to the five papers that were eventually published, I wrote four more: a pair on the patient's and the therapist's efforts to drive each other crazy—an extension of the basic paper by Searles (1959)—written as a means of offering a basic model for the actual hurtful and destructive efforts of each participant to the therapeutic dyad and as a continuation of my investigations of the actualities of the therapeutic experience; and a second pair, on the individual and mutual influence of both patient and therapist on the flow of derivatives of unconscious fantasies in analysis. These two papers were the forerunners of the communicative properties paper (chapter 15). Though none of these manuscripts reached a point of development and completion that seemed to justify publication, and were put aside, I continued to be concerned with their main themes; they have not been published here because they are now superseded by later papers in which the key concepts are undoubtedly more clearly and effectively stated.

Turning now to the published papers, the one on misalliance (chapter 6) represents a continued focus on the actualities of the unconscious interaction between patient and therapist. Interaction and reality now come to the fore. There are also some initial references to the patient's introjective identification with unconscious traits and implications derived from the therapist's interventions, and direct references to the importance of the therapist's contributions to the patient's defenses and maladaptive responses. The concept of *misalliance cure* is introduced as a form of symptom alleviation based on shared defenses or inappropriate gratifications, rather than on insight and adaptive structural change; the need to examine the material from the patient for the unconscious basis for symptom relief (or intensification) thereby became an essential component of the technical approach. It is this stress on actuality that distinguishes these considerations from some prior studies of transference/countertransference interactions (studies which were extremely rare), and the concept of realities limiting to therapeutic outcome, realities of which patient and therapist might both be unaware, is established.

reflects a transition from a focus on transference as expressed through fantasies to transference expressed as unconscious efforts to actually repeat past pathogenic interactions—a central motive in the patient in respect to his attempts to create sectors of misalliance. However, the therapist too is seen as a possible initiator of misalliances, and unneeded deviations in technique and technical errors are stated as the primary means through which this may occur. This concept has broader importance in that it suggests that alterations in the ground rules can hae a basic effect on the nature of the therapeutic alliance and on the means through which symptom resolution is being sought and effected—it is a limiting reality (see below).

Mention is made also of the three interrelated means of symptom resolution, a subject reconsidered in my paper on validation and the framework of the therapeutic situation (chapter 14.) Having developed a clearer conception of the cognitive and interactional realms, as I would later term them, I suggested that symptom resolution occurs (1) through cognitive insights derived from the therapist's interventions; (2) through curative interactions inherent to the adoption of sound principles of technique and in the therapist's maintenance of the ground rules and boundaries of the therapeutic situation; and (3) through the inevitable positive identifications with the therapist that are derived on the basis of the two former types of experience.

Misalliances are seen as pathological circular interactions, a concept I have recently elaborated in terms of *spiraling interactions* (Langs 1978), in which it is sometimes difficult to identify initiator and respondent. It becomes important here to recognize the role of unconscious set and evocation, as well as the imposition of traumatic actualities upon the subject—a theme explored earlier in the dream paper and the books on technique.

It is in this paper that the patient's unconscious efforts to modify sectors of therapeutic misalliance are seen not only in terms of attempts to correct the therapist, but also in respect of their broader curative implications. The concept of the patient's unconscious interpretations to the therapist is introduced into my writings (although I later discovered this same concept beautifully stated by Little, in her 1951 paper). In addition, my concept of supervision was established in terms of the use of the patient as the resource for insights into the therapist's errors and their basis—a tool that can be used by the therapist himself, and which suggests the aphorism that the patient unconsciously is the supervisor par excellence for the therapist—a point later explicitly made in a paper on supervision (chapter 19). Finally, the need to rectify misalliances before other types of therapeutic work can be effective is pointed up and my preference for the implicit acknowledgment of errors is stated.

The paper on the therapeutic relationship and deviations in technique (chapter 7) began as an extension of the work in this area in the technique books. It had become increasingly clear through both my supervisory experiences and a review of the literature that there was virtually no careful empirical study of the effects of deviations in technique, and that virtually no effort had been made to distinguish valid deviations from those that essentially constitute erroneous interventions; more broadly, there was little appreciation of the many functions and implications of the ground rules. The prevailing attitude, as I indicated before, was to view the ground rules as a kind of unobtrusive backdrop for the therapeutic experience, and as a means of safeguarding the transference. My clinical investigations revealed, however, that the therapist's management of what I began to call the framework and boundaries of the patient-therapist relationship (a three dimensional metaphor, borrowed from Milner [1952] that proved quite fruitful) unconsciously conveyed important information about his own intrapsychic state and his capacity to manage his inner conflicts, and that these efforts influence the patient's ongoing, continuous incorporative identifications with the therapist. It became evident also that the therapuetic field, which at that time I conceptualized largely in terms of the person onto whom the patient projects his intrapsychic fantasies and with whom he interacts, was considerably influenced by the management of the frame. The function of the framework as a basic means of establishing the therapeutic hold is also established, and the paper formed the basis for my 1976 encyclopedia article on this subject (chapter 11) and for my elaborate discussion of the nature and functions of the ground rules in both *The Bipersonal Field* (1976a) and *The Therapeutic Interaction* (1976b).

At the time, there was an extensive interplay between my reading of the literature and my clinical observations (see chapter 15). I stressed how the management of the ground rules can be influenced by countertransference problems, but was struggling here with the problem of the functions of the ground rules and their influence on the nature of the patient's and the analyst's communications, and on the entire therapeutic interaction.

In rereading this paper, I sensed a need (a *preconception*—Bion 1962) for some type of field concept with which to establish a more readily understood metaphor for the therapeutic experience. Without it, there is a continued struggle to precisely identify the pervasive influence of the ground rules. Still, it was possible to offer an extensive summary of the implications of the establishment and maintenance of the ground rules of the therapeutic situation, and to place analytic work in this sphere on a par with the analysis of the patient's verbal associations and behaviors.

It is here too that the role of actuality once again came to the fore. As realities, the adherence to or deviations in the ground rules contain crucial unconscious communications and, in addition, influence the nature of all other communications between patient and therapist— and thereby the entirety of their therapeutic work. Without exception, the empirical evidence indicated that deviations in the ground rules had disruptive and negative effects upon the patient and his introjective identifications with the therapist, and on the therapeutic alliance and analytic work. Even in emergency situations, their invocation, while essential, was often based on countertransference-based-inputs, and negative residuals were in evidence. The stress again was on the unconscious implications of these interventions, a consideration that had been remarkably neglected by those who had written on the subject.

It was in this paper that I placed the therapist's management of the framework on a par with his interpretive interventions. Both could now be taken as interrelated basic interventions, in need of consistent evaluation as to unconscious meaning and communication. Further, each could be treated as the adaptive context for the material that followed from the patient, and his responses seen as extensive commentaries on the deviation, with both valid and distorting elements (the forerunner of the concept of *transversal communications*; see chapter 19 and Langs 1978c).

The misalliance and ground rules papers, then, were at the heart of a very crucial transition, one which entailed a shift from a relatively isolated and intrapsychic conception of the patient in the therapeutic experience, to a basically interactional conception. The papers documented also a shift from the view that flexibility in the establishment and maintenance of the conditions of treatment was an inherent virtue, to one that stressed the need to maintain a secure framework as the basic means of providing the patient a sense of safety and hold, an essentially ego-integrating therapeutic setting, and a set of conditions under which he could verbally and interactionally communicate the expressions of his inner illness—a rigorous, rather than rigid, position.

There is, far more than I had initially realized (even though I had stated it), an enormous and deep need within both patient and therapist to modify the basic ground rules of the treatment situation (see chapter 7 for details). This unconscious investment in deviations is so enormous that I was put under constant pressure to modify my views and position. In the face of these efforts, often very personal and quite disruptive, I was virtually forced to validate my findings again and again (see also Langs 1978: Preface). What I ultimately termed *validation through Type Two derivatives* (chapters 14, 19; Langs 1978), the essence of psychoanalytic confirmation, was the means through which I not only confirmed my observations and my understanding of their implications, but also further expanded my understanding of the entire subject.

A PERIOD OF REWORKING AND CLARIFYING

The three papers on the misalliance dimension in Freud's case histories, of Dora, the Rat Man, and the Wolf Man (chapters 8–10), were, in part, responses to the criticisms of my writings on the framework. I had become convinced that the present-day ground rules had some very basic human and therapeutic functions, a position supported by the paper by Bleger (1967)—a unique study of the functions of the psychoanalytic frame. (I believe that it was his use of that term that first called it to my attention.) The frame metaphor itself continued to prove useful—despite its nonhuman qualities—in that it provided the ground rules a functional set of qualities that previously had been lacking.

It occurred to me that if there was any truth to these beliefs, I could use the present-day ground rules as a template and apply them to the case material offered by Freud. Each time he deviated from those standards, I would evaluate the material from the patient as a commentary on his intervention, and assess its unconscious meanings. It is true that I hoped to find confirmation for my position, but as always I tried to remain open to corrective influence and new insights.

I was quite pleased and amazed to find repeated validation in Freud's material of the concepts I had developed from my own clinical observations. For me, it provided convincing evidence of the universality of these basic tenets, and of the importance of their functions.

In addition to the discussions offered in these papers, I have continued to reflect on the implications of my findings. I would now add the following: First, I would characterize Freud's genius in this area as his remarkable ability to define a set of ground rules that embody many crucial implications and functions, despite the fact that he himself never adhered to them (for the statement of a position quite different in some ways from my own, see Lipton 1977).

Second, these case histories suggest that Freud discovered transference through the actual observation of essentially nontransference communications from his patients. By this I mean that my evaluation of the available material indicates that Freud was quite unaware of his unconscious interaction with his patients (a point developed by many others; see especially Kanzer 1952), and that the unconscious communications contained in Freud's interventions, both interpretive and in regard to the management of the framework, apparently included many countertransference-based inputs of which his pateints were unconsciously perceptive, and to which they responded with extensive introjective processes. Much of the material from these patients, including the genetic revelations, I would view as essentially nontransference reactions, actual repetitions of past traumas, with extensions into transference. On an unconscious level, there are many perceptive truths in the responses of Freud's patients to his alterations in the frame. In fact, there is, as I have noted elsewhere (Langs 1976b), considerable support for the thesis that while the discovery of transference was one of Freud's most ingenious efforts, it served a defensive function for him; it was unconsciously utilized to deny the immediate impact of the current analytic interaction and Freud's communications to his patients—a misapplication that is pervasive to this day. Freud's belief that his patient's responses were primarily fantasy-based, displaced from the past, and projected onto the therapist has a rather striking counterpart in his revision of the seduction hypothesis: early childhood seductions were no longer seen as founded in reality, but as based in fantasy formations—a position that Freud never entirely accepted himself (for example, see Freud (1918). The shift was from reality to fantasy, and from introjection to projection, and while this move opened enormous vistas related to inner mental life, it led to a significant neglect of the patient's introjective experiences in analysis. It also served as a barrier against an understanding of the many ramifications of reality, particularly the unconscious implications of the current analytic interaction and of the

analyst's interventions—often enough, the expressions of his unconscious countertransference fantasies.

A MAJOR TRANSITION TO THE
INTERACTIONAL SPHERE

In the period that followed the writing of this group of papers, I
explored many new avenues, generating a wide range of unsaturated
preconceptions in need of saturation (Bion 1962). In my clinical
studies, my vantage-point became essentially adaptional-interactional,
affording many insights. In my reading, in addition to gaining
historical perspective, I was in search of a new language that could help
me conceptualize my observations in the interactional sphere. Because
the view prevailing among classical psychoanalysts of the patient's
relationship to the analyst was expressed primarily in terms of
transference and intrapsychic fantasies, I found little help there,
though Loewald (1960) and a few others did, in a rather limited way,
attempt to investigate this very realm (see Langs 1976a).

When I finally began reading the Kleinian literature, however, I
found, to my surprise, that its emphasis was basically interactional. I
soon learned that this derived from Melanie Klein's formulation of the
presence of object relatedness from birth onward. As a result, both
projective and introjective processes were consistently considered,
though in their studies of the analytic interaction there was nonetheless
a relative neglect of the patient's introjective experiences.

As a classical analyst, my first extended exposure to the term
projective identification, in the paper on insight by the Barangers
(1966), was a frightening, shocking, and perplexing experience. At the
time, the concept was current almost exclusively among the Kleinians,
and though in the course of my own classical psychoanalytic training
and reading I had seen it occasionmally in passing, I had never
seriously considered it. I remember that at first I could see no need for a
term beyond projection or introjection, and felt almost totally
confused by the combined term: projective identification. Still, I had
some respect for those who postulated it as the basic mechanism in the
analytic interaction and had some sense of the term's potential
significance. The papers by Malin and Grotstein (1966) and Hanna
Segal (1967), provided some necessary clarification, and soon I began
not only to sense the actual presence of projective identification in the

therapeutic interaction, but to find it extremely useful as a concept. Bion's (1977) extensions of the concept which I was struggling to comprehend and had only begun to grasp, appeared then more promising than immediately meaningful. Nonetheless, the term seemed to provide the key to the interactional experiences I was attempting to understand, and it soon became basic to my view of the unconscious communicative interaction between patient and therapist or analyst.

At the same time, the Barangers' bipersonal field concept (1966) led me to organize and unify many previously disparate observations and postulates related to the therapeutic interaction—the concept served as a crucial selected fact (Bion 1962). It solidified the adaptational-interactional approach and provided a metaphor through which both intrapsychic and interactional processes could be fully considered. The field needed a frame in order to maintain its definition, its communicative qualities, and to sustain a viable therapeutic process; in this way, the functions of the ground rules and their management came to be more fully defined.

At the same time, the view of the patient and the therapist within a field, and a consideration of all the phenomena within the therapeutic interaction in terms of vectors from each participant, produced a thoroughly interactional conception of the therapeutic experience. Adapting an unbiased approach, it was possible to study both the patient's and the therapist's projective identifications, and to recognize that the latter took the form, when pathological, of errors in technique and mismanagements of the frame. Interventions were seen as interactional products developed within the patient—in his own way—and within the therapist as an amalgam of communications from the patient and of his own inner experiences; this allowed additional details of the validating process to be outlined. All of this served as a major step in the transition from essentially classical psychoanalytic and psychotherapeutic techniques to a neoclassical approach, if you will, in which a greater totality—intrapsychic and interactional—is taken into account, and a spiraling sequence of both projective and introjective processes in both patient and analyst could be recognized and explored.

In terms of my writing, I had devoted the bulk of my efforts in 1975 and 1976 to the abstracting of over five hundred references related to the therapeutic and analytic situations and interactions, and to a comprehensive critique and discussion of the major issues. As stated in my preface to *The Bipersonal Field* (Langs 1976a), I found it unthinkable as a clinician to publish a major two-volume work on the analytic interaction (*The Therapeutic Interaction,* 1976b) filled with what I believed to be major new conceptions and formulations, which was divorced entirely from clinical material. I therefore cast about in search of clinical data to illustrate the basic postulates I had developed through this interplay between clinical observation and my reading of the literature. Ultimately, I selected at random five taped supervisory seminars, revised them to some extent in terms of some last-minute addenda to my thinking, and offered *The Bipersonal Field* to the profession.

I have always viewed that book essentially as the product of a sensitive tuning in on the unconscious processes within and between therapist and patient, and especially on the resources of the latter. It had been meant as a clinical companion piece to *The Therapeutic Interaction* and was offered with full awareness that it would seem to be a major leap (though it was the culmination of a series of transitions) from my previous classical position. I had very much underestimated the resistances and countertransferences of my audience (though I allow full room for valid criticism and the almost certain need for revision), and while the book was praised in many quarters, it evoked intense mistrust, especially among classically trained psychoanalysts.

It was only a couple of years later, when I turned to the listening process (Langs 1978), that I realized that there did exist many basic, cognitive reasons for the difficulties many therapists and analysts had in evaluating and responding to *The Bipersonal Field.* Few readers took the trouble to study both of the 1976 books together—admittedly, an enormous undertaking—and as yet, there are few signs that many therapists and analysts have even attempted to comprehend the adaptational-interactional viewpoint there expounded. While the papers written subsequent to these volumes involved refinements and expansions of this new clinical position, they constituted as well a gradual series of attempts at clarifying a number of thorny issues raised by the two works.

The first of these endeavors is reflected in the three encyclopedia articles prepared in 1976 on the therapeutic interaction, therapeutic misalliances, and the framework (chapter 11). They offer rather succinct summaries of my view of the therapeutic interaction at that time.

The paper on becoming a psychiatrist (chapter 12) was a response to a clinical presentation, through which I was able to further demonstrate the clinical application of the concepts of projective identification and the validating process—an element of the psychotherapeutic and psychoanalytic situations that I had discussed in some detail in the opening part of the synthesis section of *The Therapeutic Interaction*. Addressed again the interactional aspects of countertransference, and reviewed and elaborated my basic thinking regarding such topics as therapeutic misalliances, misalliance and framework "cures," the distinction between transference and nontransference, and other related issues.

The transference beyond Freud paper (chapter 13) was likewise a kind of mopping-up operation in which selected aspects of the literature on transference—used in its broadest sense—were specifically considered in terms of the interplay between reality and unconscious processes. It was written during what soon proved to be a creative pause, one that came to an end under pressure of several commitments and as a result of the continuous reworking of clinical observations and concepts.

A MAJOR TRANSITION

This phase began when I was asked to respond to a paper by Hans Strupp (1978) on suffering in psychotherapy, and to contribute a paper to a Bion festschrift. In terms of my own ongoing clinical investigations, I was still concerned with many facets of the communicative interaction, and was quietly searching for new methodological or conceptual means which might expand my understanding.

The first step in what followed is reflected in the validation and framework paper (chapter 14), in which I presented again my conception of the nature and functions of the framework, the underlying basis for symptom alleviation, and the influence of countertransference. However, the most crucial contribution to what followed is the distinction presented there for the first time between the manifest content of the patient's material—his associations and behaviors—and its latent content. I had often pondered the different types of latent content, and had written on the subject in the technique books (1973a).

In a moment of insight, I now realized that there are essentially two types of derivatives that can be formulated from the patient's material. The first, which I termed *Type One derivatives* (see chapters 14, 15, 17–19, and Langs 1978), are inferences readily made from manifest content itself. I had long been aware of the availability of such inferences, and that patients themselves often supplied them to the therapist, primarily as resistances, especially when associating to dreams. I also knew that therapists made abundant use of such inferences, and I found empirically that, almost always, an intervention offered to the patient on that basis was isolated and intellectualized, without any central dynamic meaning, and was responded to in a manner that did not constitute validation. It was evident that many therapists and analysts work almost exclusively with manifest content and Type One derivatives, and I could not avoid the realization that this did not constitute valid therapeutic work as I had come to define it.

These were difficult ideas to present convincingly, but the entire situation changed when I realized that such formulations could be distinguished from inferences made from the manifest content that were organized around a specific adaptive context—*Type Two derivatives*. Almost immediately, it became clear that a valid interpretation began with a specific adaptive context and organized the patient's manifest associations as derivative communications indirectly related to that adaptive context—as meaningful derivatives whose form and meaning were shaped and available only through knowledge of that context. While it was evident also that Type Two derivatives could take the form of unconscious fantasies or unconscious perceptions (and introjects), the key insight lay in distinguishing these two types of inferences derived from the patient's manifest material.

The communicative properties paper (chapter 15) followed quickly upon this particular conceptualization. This paper is, for me, quite special to my mind represents an order of creativity only hinted at in my previous work. I had always felt that my extensive discoveries and rediscoveries, much of these presented as new formulations and serviceable as selected facts (as concepts that organize previously known experiences in new and unique ways—Bion 1962), had derived essentially from my capacity to tune in on the unconscious communications from patient and therapist.

The communicative properties paper, in which I delineate three major communicative styles in patients and therapists or analysts, and three major types of communicative bipersonal fields, is a conception that was not arrived at through this tuning-in process, but which required a new level of insight on my part. For me, its special creativity is attested by the manner in which these formulations serve to clarify and explain many problems that had previously perplexed me and for which I had only partial answers, if any.

The communicative properties paper began with the realization that certain patients communicate Type Two derivatives that are eventually available for interpretation in terms of both resistance and content. As I have mentioned, I had known for some time that there are patients who did not associate in this manner, who, as I said, either repressed or obliterated the adaptive context in the presence of seemingly rich associations, or embedded themselves in realities and trivia, or even significant adaptive contexts, without conveying meaningfully related indirect associations.

In reconceptualizing, I at first thought of these patients as possibly representing a defensive form of the Type A style (a style characteristic of patients who communicate both the adaptive context and derivatives, and who use symbolic communications; see chapter 15 and Langs 1978). However, it soon became evident that this was not the case; their resistances were neither readily analyzable nor expressed in derivative form. Instead their associations were flat and empty, or rich without organizing meaning; they served as impenetrable barriers— they functioned to destroy meaning rather than to convey it. Manifest content and Type One derivatives prevailed. This realization opened up the conception of the Type C field, which, much to my amazement, proved to be an extremely common communicative style in both patients and therapists.

I had only to identify the third communicative style and field, that in which interactional pressures and efforts at action and discharge prevail—the Type B field—to complete a classification which, to this point, has proven extremely serviceable. While Khan (1973) in particular had written in his own way of Type A and Type B fields, only Bion (1977) had offered observations and formulations relevant to a Type C field—a field designed for lies and falsifications, for barriers and destruction of links between patient and therapist. This latter field is studied in some detail in this paper and is, I believe, an important area for future research.

To suggest the extent to which the conception of three communicative fields served as a selected fact to resolve my own personal uncertainties, I will offer two illustrations. First, I have already alluded to my conviction that patients have distinctive communicative styles. The tripartite configuration presented in this paper seems fully to describe, and to begin to conceptualize, these styles and some of the factors in their development. I am well aware of the lack of specific genetic data and hope to eventually fill that particular void, but the clinical utility of this classification has already proved itself many times over.

Second, from the very beginning of my clinical and research career, I have, as I mentioned, been interested in dreams and all their ramifications. It was more than evident that certain patients virtually never report a dream, while others report them rarely, often in a form that is quite realistic and to which meaningful associations are either entirely absent or quite sparse. I had long wondered as to why certain patients remember and report their dreams, while others do not, and why the dreams of some are quite analyzable, while others' are totally obscure. For many years I had periodically returned to this clinical problem and attempted to develop a pertinent hypothesis; I had never succeeded.

Now, however, at almost the very moment the three communicative styles concept was crystallized, it became evident that it is the Type A patient who remembers his dreams and associates meaningfully, while the type B patient seldom recalls dreams and, when he does, uses them as a means of projective identification and discharge so that associations usually do not yield meaningful interpretable insights in terms of content. The Type C patient, of course, is the nondreamer, or the patient whose dreams are embedded in realities. The category includes those whose associations to dreams are essentially nonmeaningful and nonrevealing. It was, for me, a remarkable experience suddenly to have a functional hypothesis for a dilemma that had occupied me for some twenty years (see chapter 18).

The communicative properties paper served me in yet another important way. It proved to be a culmination of, and a justification for, my long investigations of the nature and functions of the framework. It quickly became evident that a Type A field can exist only in the context of a secure frame, and that alterations in the framework are, as a rule, a function of and tend to further evoke, the Type B and Type C communicative modes. The framework could now be seen as an essential determinant of communicative style, and of the nature and function of language and behavior within the therapeutic situation.

This paper was the realization of a major transition in technique. The papers that followed, by and large, took the form of sorting out the implications of these new discoveries, for countertransference (chapter 17), dreams (chapter 18), supervision (chapter 19), and interventions (chapter 20). Before touching upon these final contributions, I must mention the paper on responses to creativity (chapter 16) and the book on the listening process (Langs 1978), developed while writing this last group of papers.

The creativity paper is another contribution with special meaning for me. In some ways, it might well have served as a foreword to this volume. It constitutes an effort on my part to help each of us get in touch with our destructive impulses toward the innovator, and to help us toward efforts at resolving destructive barriers erected against the turmoil involved in learning and growth. In writing that paper, I was reminded of Winnicott's (1947) cogent comment to the effect that every psychoanalytic paper is in part an effort to complete the unfinished business of one's personal analysis. One may broaden that aphorism by stating that every valid contribution to the psychoanalytic literature is an attempt to resolve a segment of the collective countertransference-based blind spots and misconceptions of the field. For a writer as prolific as myself, Winnicott's comment is certainly a cause for thought and humility, though I must add that whatever working through is represented in my writing, it is fully counterbalanced by a sense of satisfaction and peace in other respects.

I mention all of this because the creativity paper, while appropriately prompted by the astounding rejection of a remarkably innovative paper by Harold Searles (1978), also turned out to be a personal attempt to understand what appears to me to be essentially irrational and nonscientific objections to my own work (as distinguished from scientifically based criticisms, which should and must always exist, to which I am consistently open, and which can only further the growth of the field and of myself personally).

My limited investigation of the literature on reactions to creativity, and the thinking through of a series of ideas that I had been mulling over for some time in this regard, ideas that were sharpened and expanded in response to the fate of Searles's paper, led to the formulations developed in that presentation. And while all of my papers have been, for me, therapeutic to some degree, and have certainly greatly enhanced my capacities as a therapist and analyst, this particular contribution helped me resolve a series of repetitive conflicts and concerns that were interfering with my freedom to continue to grow and develop.

In the volume on the listening process (Langs 1978), I explicitly stated an additional and crucial thesis pertinent to my present conception of the therapeutic situation: that an empirical, in-depth examination of the communications from the patient indicates that his crucial derivatives and pathology-related communications pertain, in some way, to the therapeutic relationship in terms of unconscious fantasies, memories, introjects, and perceptions, including their current interactional dynamics and past genetic connections. While in no way disregarding the realities of major traumas in the patient's outside relationships, I mean to imply in this tenet that some link always exists to the patient's relationship to the therapist and the current therapeutic interaction, and that therefore, though analytic work related to the unconscious pathological dynamics evoked by outside adaptive contexts is necessary, the interpretive work is incomplete without the delineation and analysis of this connection. To put this another way, the essence of analytic and therapeutic work is the complete analysis of the interaction between patient and therapist so that the unconscious meanings and communications so contained are understood in depth, as they relate to the patient's psychopathology, to the actual inputs from the therapist and their distortions, and to the patient's significant genetic past. In a word, the key to therapeutic work is in the unconscious meanings and functions of the current interaction between patient and therapist.

The final four papers, then, constitute efforts to clarify the details of my present adaptational-interactional, bipersonal field conception of the therapeutic interaction. The investigation of countertransference (chapter 17) is an interactional study, defining such inputs in terms of the therapist's erroneous interventions as they stem from contributions by both patient and therapist—viewing them as products of the bipersonal field. The influence of countertransference on the analyst's management of the frame, his holding and containing functions, and his role as the interpreter of the patient's communications is also detailed, as is the effect of countertransference on the communicative properties of the bipersonal field.

The paper on dreams in the bipersonal field (chapter 18), written for a volume being edited by Joseph Natterson, is a detailed study of the dream as a product of the therapeutic interaction—as both an intrapsychic and interactional phenomenon—and it considers the insights into dreams derived from previous studies of the bipersonal field and from the communicative properties paper.

The contribution on supervision (chapter 19) represents an effort to redefine the supervisory situation and process in terms of the bipersonal field concept and my growing understanding of the communicative interaction between patient and therapist—as well as between supervisor and supervisee. Originally prepared as a limited contribution to a volume on supervision. It is published here as a separate paper dealing with selected issues relevant to this topic, as a means of offering some new perspectives on the definition of the supervisory situation and on supervisory techniques. Discussions of the communicative properties of the supervisory bipersonal field and of the patient as the unconscious supervisor for both the supervisee and his mentor perhaps best characterize the type of thinking developed in this piece.

Finally, the paper on interventions (chapter 20), is an attempt to complete the cycle from the listening process to the therapist's interventions. While in itself it is a prelude to a more extensive investigation, it is unique in deriving its formulations from direct empirical observations, and in offering a classification of interventions based primarily on a study of the unconscious communicative interaction between patient and therapist. The result is the delineation of six interventions, three of which are somewhat unique to the literature, and the exclusion of several commonly utilized noninterpretive interventions. It is, for the moment, the final expression of the insights derived from this last transition.

CONCLUDING COMMENTS

Having traced out a series of minor and major transitions, it seems appropriate to conclude by attempting to characterize my present conception of the psychotherapeutic and psychoanalytic situations and techniques. The ground rules, originally seen as a basic agreement between patient and analyst (or therapist), have taken on three-dimensional and critical human qualities. They are seen as an expression of the analyst's functioning and as essential to a number of his basic responsibilities to the patient, including his capacity to hold the patient, to offer inherent ego support, to contain projective identifications and other disturbing processes and contents, and to establish a relationship and field within which the patient's neurosis can be both expressed and analyzed. The special role of the framework in establishing the analytic situation and the boundaries between the two participants, and in determining the nature, function, and meaning of the communicative interaction, is critical. The analyst's management of the framework reflects the state of his own intrapsychic balances and needs, and the establishment, management, and rectification of the frame, as well as his interpretive analytic work in this sphere, are basic to the process of cure.

The therapeutic relationship itself is viewed in terms of a continuous communicative interaction, both conscious and unconscious, with vital projective and introjective components, which becomes the central vehicle for analytic and psychotherapeutic work. This is so because of the patient's unique investment in the analytic relationship to a point where all his communications have some special bearing on the analytic transactions and experience, and because the analyst is a consistent participant who makes continuous inputs derived from both his valid, noncountertransference functioning and from his unresolved countertransferences; the latter, which are ever-present, create an opportunity in the present analytic situation for the patient to reexperience and rework his past pathogenic relationships.

It is the analysis of this continuous communicative interaction, in terms of its current unconscious meanings and genetic counterparts, with its interacting vectors from both patient and analyst, that is at the heart of analytic work. The patient's relationship with the analyst has both transference and nontransference elements, and while the former are expressions of his unresolved psychopathology, the latter are manifestations of the many healthy and curative aspects of his personality. The patient unconsciously but continuously monitors the communications from the analyst, and responds in terms both of valid unconscious perceptions and introjections, and of pathologically defensive and distorting elements. The analyst too responds both validly and inappropriately to the patient's every communication, though hopefully the vast majority of his efforts are preponderantly in the former sphere.

This conception of the analytic interaction takes into account conscious and unconscious intrapsychic contents and mechanisms of both patient and analyst, as well as the conscious and unconscious interaction and the interactional mechanisms that play a role. It is a bipersonal field concept within an adaptational-interactional framework. The basic technical precept is to view the analytic dyad in terms of a spiraling interaction in which the patient's communications become the adaptive context for the therapist's interventions, and these interventions in turn become the adaptive context for the patient's responses. While unconscious set, interpretation, and evocation is fully considered, each reaction to the prevailing adaptive stimulus is explored in terms of Type Two derivatives with both realistic and distorted elements, and as essential commentaries on the unconscious communications contained in each particular context. In varying proportions, mixtures of health and psychopathology infuse every response of both patient and analyst.

In essence, then, there has been a basic transition in my view of the framework of the analytic situation, and of the transactions within the bipersonal field within which it occurs. Both the cognitive and interactional realms are taken into account, and the stress is on the continuous communicative—projective and introjective—interaction between patient and analyst. The implications for technique are far-reaching, and have been outlined in this chapter; they are discussed in detail in the papers in this volume.

To conclude now, in the spirit of vitality so necessary to growth, I can only hope that this book will prove to be another way station along the road to a continuing series of transitions that will end only with the completion of my career as a therapist and analyst. It has in no way been an easy journey; it has been filled with anxiety, periods of turmoil, enormous external pressures, and much pain and grief. I have long ago learned quite well that these are the inevitable accompaniments of discovery, innovation, and personal growth, as are the periods of resolution, synthesis, peace, and support. But with each transition, there also has been, by and large, a greater sense of integration, comfort, and competency, a sense of peace that makes all the rest well worth having experienced.

It is my hope that the reader too will approach this book in the spirit of openness to learning and transition, and with a capacity to tolerate the inevitable temporary pain and chaos which must accompany it. If this work helps any of its readers to embark upon or continue such a journey, these papers will have more than served their purpose. And if in some small way they also contribute to transitions that extend beyond the scope of this present work, it will have truly fulfilled its function as a creative work.

REFERENCES

Arlow, J. (1963). Conflict, regression and symptom formation. *International Journal of Psycho-Analysis* 44:12–22.

———— (1969a). Conscious fantasy and disturbances of conscious experience. *Psychoanalytic Quarterly* 38:1–27.

———— (1969b). Fantasy, memory, and reality testing. *Psychoanalytic Quarterly* 38:28–51.

Baranger, M., and Baranger, W. (1966). Insight in the analytic situation. In *Psychoanalysis in the Americas*, ed. R. Litman, pp. 56–72. New York: International Universities Press.

Bion, W. (1962). Learning from Experience. In W. Bion, *Seven Servants*. New York: Jason Aronson, 1977.

———— (1977). *Seven Servants*. New York: Jason Aronson.

Bleger, J. (1967). Psycho-analysis of the psycho-analytic frame. *International Journal of Psycho-Analysis* 48:511–519.

Freud, S. (1900). The interpretation of dreams. *Standard Edition* 4/5.

———— (1918). From the history of an infantile neurosis. *Standard Edition* 17:3–122.

———— (1926). Inhibitions, symptoms and anxiety, *Standard Edition* 20:77–175.

Greenson, R. (1970). The exceptional position of the dream in psychoanalytic practice. *Psychoanalytic Quarterly* 39:519–549.

———— (1972). Beyond transference and interpretation. *International Journal of Psycho-Analysis* 53:213–217.

Kanzer, M. (1952). The transference neurosis of the Rat Man. *Psychoanalytic Quarterly* 21:181–189.

Khan, M. (1973). The role of illusion in the analytic space and process. *The Annual of Psychoanalysis* 1:231–246.

Langs, R. (1973). *The Technique of Psychoanalytic Psychotherapy,* Vol. I. New York: Jason Aronson.

———— (1974). *The Technique of Psychoanalytic Psychotherapy*, Vol. II. New York: Jason Aronson.

—————— (1976a). *The Bipersonal Field.* New York: Jason Aronson.

—————— (1976b). *The Therapeutic Interaction.* 2 vols. New York: Jason Aronson.

—————— (1978). *The Listening Process.* New York: Jason Aronson

Lipton, S. (1977). The advantages of Freud's technique as shown in his analysis of the Rat Man. *International Journal of Psycho-Analysis* 58:255–273.

Little, M. (1951). Counter-transference and the patient's response to it. *International Journal of Psycho-Analysis* 32:32–40.

Loewald, H. (1960). The therapeutic action of psycho-analysis. *International Journal of Psycho-Analysis* 41:16–33.

Malin, A., and Grotstein, J. (1966). Projective identification in the therapeutic process. *International Journal of Psycho-Analysis* 47:26–31.

Milner, M. (1952). Aspects of symbolism in comprehension of the not-self. *International Journal of Psycho-Analysis* 33:181–195.

Searles, H. (1959). The effort to drive the other person crazy: an element in the aetiology and psychotherapy of schizophrenia. *British Journal of Medical Psychology* 32:1–18.

—————— (1965). *Collected Papers on Schizophrenia and Related Subjects.* New York: International Universities Press.

—————— (1975). The patient as therapist to his analyst. In *Tactics and Techniques in Psychoanalytic Therapy,* Vol. II, ed. P. Giovacchini. New York: Jason Aronson

—————— (1978). Concerning transference and countertransference. *International Journal of Psychoanalytic Psychotherapy* 7:165–188.

Segal, H. (1967). Melanie Klein's technique. *Psychoanalytic Forum* 2:197–211.

Strupp, H. (1978). Suffering and psychotherapy. *Contemporary Psychoanalysis* 14:73–97.

Waldhorn, H. (1967). Reporter. Indication for psychoanalysis: the place of the dream in clinical psychoanalysis. Monograph II, The Kriss Study Group of the New York Psychoanalytic Institute, ed. E. Joseph. New York: International Universities Press.

Winnicott, D. (1949). Hate in the countertransference. *International Journal of Psycho-Analysis* 30:69–74.

Chapter Two

Day Residues, Recall Residues, and Dreams: Reality and the Psyche

(1971[1970])

The relationship between reality experiences and intrapsychic life in the development of the individual, in the evolution of psychopathological phenomena, and in ongoing experiencing and functioning is only recently receiving careful scrutiny in psychoanalytic writings. One early model of the dilemmas posed by the relationship between inner and outer experiences is the well-known crisis in Freud's thinking with regard to the abundance of reports from his patients of childhood seductions. Freud first conceived of these experiences as real, but subsequently viewed them as fantasies, a step which proved critical in his formulation of unconscious processes and fantasies. Sadow (Sadow et al. 1968) has recently reviewed the evolution of Freud's thought in this area and concluded that the seduction hypothesis is currently largely in disuse. The present study of the relationship between the dream and reality will lead us to reconsider this conclusion.

In another vein, Rapaport (1960), in a brilliant, lengthy, and largely theoretical paper, has reviewed the conceptualization of the role of external reality in psychoanalytic theory. He pointed out that, initially, the psychoanalytic theory of motivation was primarily an instinctual drive theory. In this context, reality was considered essentially in terms of the presence or absence of an object through which drive gratification could be achieved. As a result, there was a relative neglect of the role of reality as a cause, albeit a nonmotivational cause, of behavior, as well as of its role in such matters as the building and nurturing of structures, the development of controls, and learning in general.

Along more clinical lines, Arlow (1963, 1969a, b) has discussed the relationship between reality and fantasy, and has reformulated aspects of their interdependence. He pointed out that current reality situations can reproduce earlier traumatic experiences, creating fresh repetitions of infantile conflicts. This may stimulate the reemergence and activation of repressed instinctual wishes and unconscious fantasies. On the other hand, unconscious fantasies themselves create sets or attitudes which color the person's interpretation and response to life events. He stated (1969a):

> There is a mutual and reciprocal effect of the pressure of unconscious fantasy formations and sensory stimuli, especially stimuli emanating from the external world. Unconscious fantasy provides the "mental set" in which sensory stimuli are perceived and integrated. External events, on the other hand, stimulate and organize the re-emergence of unconscious fantasies. [p. 8]

Kanzer (1958) has discussed the fluctuating relationship between the inner and the outer as it unfolds within and around the psychoanalytic session. Erikson (1950), Hartmann (1939, 1956), Hartmann, Kris, and Loewenstein (1946), Niederland (1959), Piaget (see Wolff 1960), and White (1963), among others, have also discussed aspects of this problem.

My purpose is to further the study of the relationship between external reality and inner mental life through an exploration of aspects of the relationship between the dream and reality. This is done first by a reconsideration of the relationship between the dream and its day residues, the real events of the day of the dream which prompt its formation; and secondly, by a study of the relationship between the dream and what I refer to as its "recall residues," those reality events in the day following the dream which prompt the recall of a previously forgotten or repressed dream. I present a review of the pertinent literature out of which my own reformulations emerge. I then present a series of hypotheses and illustrate them with clinical material; and finally, I briefly discuss their implications.

THE LITERATURE

Very little has been added by Freud or others to the conceptualization of the role of the day residue in dream formation since Freud's own initial and lengthy discussion of this topic in *The Interpretation of Dreams* (1900). Very early in this work, Freud wrote: "I must begin with an assertion that in every dream it is possible to find a point of contact with the experiences of the previous day" (p. 165).

Freud used the well-known Dream of the Botanical Monograph to illustrate the relationship between a series of day residues and the manifest and latent content of dreams. It was his contention that there were two groups of residues: those related to the manifest content (usually an indifferent event), and those related to the latent content, discoverable only through the analysis of the dream (usually a psychically important event). The work of dream distortion and censorship accounted for the manifest dream's reference to seemingly indifferent events. As Freud (1900) reiterated so often, "our dream-thoughts are dominated by the same material that has occupied us during the day ..." (p. 174). Freud further suggested that there are conscious and unconscious links between the two groups of day residues. Clarification of the distortions introduced by the dream work is essential for the discovery of the connections between seemingly indifferent day residues and the true stimulus for a dream in the unconscious. Dreams also are "under a necessity" to combine suitable multiple residues into a unity.

According to Freud (1900), there are four sources of dreams:

> a recent and psychically significant experience... represented in the dream directly, or... several recent and significant experiences which are combined into a single unity by the dream, or... recent and significant experiences... represented in... the dream by a mention of a contemporary but indifferent experience, or... an internal significant experience (e.g. a memory or a train of thought)... *invariably* represented... by a mention of a recent but indifferent impression. [p. 180]

(He later added somatic stimuli to this list.) He emphasized that recent material is used to mold the dream because it is currently active and "worked up into a wish-fulfillment" (p. 228). The repressed, unconscious meets the day residues halfway and uses them to satisfy wishes corresponding to the event; the residue becomes a vehicle by which the repressed enters consciousness and evades the censorship. "And the anxiety which is attributed to the dream would really have arisen from the day's residues" (p. 274).

In Chapter Seven, Freud (1900), discussing dream processes metapsychologically, classified the types of thought impulses which persist in sleep:

> (1) what has not been carried to a conclusion during the day owing to some chance hindrance; (2) what...is unsolved; (3) what has been rejected and suppressed during the daytime....(4) a powerful group consisting of what has been set in action in our *Ucs.* by the activity of the preconscious in the course of the day; and finally (5)...impressions which are indifferent and have for that reason not been dealt with. [p. 554]

"Preconscious excitations must find reinforcement from the *Ucs.*," he wrote, adding that the preconscious day residues must, however, "find a connection in some way or other with an infantile wish which was now unconscious and suppressed," for the former "to be received into a dream" (pp. 555-556).

Freud admitted that "there is a whole class of dreams the *instigation* to which arises principally or even exclusively from the residues of daytime life," although "the *motive force* which the dream required had to be provided by a wish" (pp. 560-561).

He conceived of the daytime thought as the "entrepreneur" of the dream, while the unconscious wish provides the "capital"; both are indispensable. Usually "an unconscious wish is stirred up by daytime activity and proceeds to construct a dream" (p. 561.)

Freud next turned to the question of why the day residues, now reduced in importance compared with the unconscious wish, are nevertheless essential ingredients in the formation of dreams. The theory or neuroses provided the answer: unconscious ideas are incapable of becoming preconscious as such, and can exercise an effect only by establishing a connection with an already preconscious idea, "transferring" its intensity onto it, and using it as a "cover."

Some refinements of these ideas appeared in Freud's metapsychological discussion of dreams (1917). There he wrote that

> observation shows that dreams are instigated by residues from the previous day—thought-cathexes which have not submitted to the general withdrawal of cathexes.... Thus the narcissism of sleep has from the outset had to admit an exception at this point, and it is here that the formation of dreams takes its start. [p. 224]

Day residues, according to this formulation, are known to us in the shape of latent dream thoughts, and are preconscious ideas belonging to the system Pcs. They must be reinforced by unconscious instinctual impulses if a dream is to follow. This is facilitated by a reduction in the censorship between the Pcs and Ucs during sleep. The repressed portion of the system Ucs does not surrender its cathexes in sleep, and it may be through links with this part of the Ucs that day residues retain their cathexes. There follows the "decisive step in dream-formation: the preconscious dream-wish is formed, which *gives expression to the unconscious impulse in the material of the preconscious day's residues*" (p. 226).

In *The Ego and the Id* (1923) Freud discussed dream interpretation, but his ideas regarding day residues were not modified to any significant extent by the structural hypotheses. He offered the now familiar analogy, of dreams "from above and from below." The former are thoughts from the previous day which obtain reinforcement from the repressed. The latter "are provoked by the strength of an unconscious (repressed) wish which has found a means of being represented in some of the day's residues" (p. 111).

Freud warned us against making too much of this distinction. In the same paper, he noted that occurrences within an analysis become some of the most powerful day residues. He also discussed technical approaches to the analysis and interpretation of a dream. In his original comments on this subject he had stated (1900), "I am able, on occasion, to begin a dream's interpretation by looking for the event of the previous day which set it in motion; in many instances, indeed, this is the easiest method" (p. 165).

In *The Ego and the Id* (1923), and later in *The New Introductory Lectures* (1933), Freud again suggested the value of beginning the exploration of a dream by asking for the day residues. In the latter work he wrote of the associations to the day residues that "if we follow these connections, we often arrive with one blow at the transition from the apparently far remote dream-world to the real life of the patient" (p. 11).

In *An Outline of Psychoanalysis*, Freud (1940) offered his final comments on the sources of dreams, couched this time in structural terms.

> Either, on the one hand, an instinctual impulse which is ordinarily suppressed (an unconscious wish) finds enough strength during sleep to make itself felt by the ego, or, on the other hand, an urge left over from waking life, a preconscious train of thought with all the conflicting impulses attached to it, finds reinforcement during sleep from an unconscious element. In short, dreams may arise either from the id or from the ego. [p. 166]

To summarize briefly, Freud thought that every dream is prompted by one or more experiences of the dream day. These events are related to intrapsychic life and dreams in two major ways: first, a repressed, infantile, unconscious fantasy or instinctual drive from the id seeks out external experiences as vehicles through which it may gain disguised gratification in a dream; and second, a reality experience may, through the ego, stir up unconscious, infantile fantasies which then seek discharge expression in the dream. Usually, both processes work together.

Few since Freud have considered this topic. One of the first emendations to his ideas was presented by Bergler and Jekels (1940), who specifically discussed the role of the superego in prompting dreams and in the selection of day residues. They stated: "The residue is, among other things, the reproach in direct or symbolic form, to the ego by the ego ideal ... " (p. 409). The superego, they noted, directs the selection of day residues because of guilt and in order to reproach the ego. Bergler (1943) later added a related function of the day residue, stating that it "serves the purpose of contradicting the reproach of the conscience which is contained in every dream" (p. 355).

Sharpe (1937) discussed the "present-day stimulus of the dream," in her book, *Dream Analysis.* Much of her thinking follows that of Freud. Sharpe felt that no stimulus for a dream is insignificant;

seeming trifles in reality turn out to have psychic significance. She used day residues in analyzing dreams and demonstrated how, on occasion, "the stimulus of the dream was the meaning of the dream." She found these residues helpful in elucidating dreams and in giving dream interpretations "life and cogency." She found that "many a baffling dream, many an obscure analytic hour, become clear once we have found a stimulus in connection with a present-day event where the patient either consciously or unconsciously has been himself the cause of provocation, or wished to be so" (p. 162).

The analysis itself, either through material evoked or through the analyst, is a constant stimulus for dreams. The quest for these stimuli should be borne in mind, but not irrespective of all other problems.

Kanzer (1955) has discussed the communicative function of the dream and the dreamer's need to communicate with others in reality through dreams. "The urge to communicate, therefore, arising out of the dream may be seen as a continuation of a tendency within the dreamer to establish contact with reality, as represented by the day's residues" (p. 260).

In another vein, Bernstein and Glenn (1969) have recently demonstrated how conscious and unconscious masturbation fantasies may be the day residues for dreams. Leveton (1961), on the other hand, has presented observations on a related concept, the "night residue," a term which refers to the memory of a dream as it is carried into the waking state of the day following the night of the dream. In a sense, then, it is the obverse of the day residue. Leveton stressed the continuity of psychic life and discussed the ways in which the waking ego must deal with the "ego stress" represented by the night residue; he wrote:

> A further possibility arises from the fact that the night residue like the day residue, forms a bridge between sleep and wakefulness. It is the peculiar quality of the day residue that it relates to, or has contact with, a repressed wish without itself being repressed, and can serve as a point of attachment for drives seeking expression and part gratification in dream formation. The night residue is in a similar position at the other end of sleep/waking. [p. 514]

Lastly, Arlow (1969a), in his recent discussion of unconscious fantasy and conscious experience, suggested that a closer examination of day residues would indicate that they "enter the structure of a dream precisely because they are characterized by a high degree of consonance with unconscious fantasy activity" (p. 9).

Virtually all of Freud's rather sparse comments on the subject of forgetting dreams and the conditions under which forgotten dreams are recalled are found in *The Interpretation of Dreams* (1900). He observed that dreams tend naturally to be forgotten as the day progresses. Although he recognized that differences between daytime and dream thinking might account for this forgetting, he preferred to emphasize the dynamic aspects. His main thesis was that dreams are forgotten because, on awakening, the forces of censorship and resistance which were modified, weakened, and more readily bypassed during sleep, are reinstated in full strength. Freud noted that the analysis of resistances will often lead to the recall of forgotten dreams, since the forces which account for resistances are the same as those which cause the forgetting of dreams.

The waking recall of forgotten dreams, usually in response to some reality stimulus, has been discussed in some detail by Kanzer (1959), who observed that such recollections often occur when the patient is "engaged in some type of automatic action after awakening and while preparing for the routine and special activities of the day." At such times, there is an altered state of consciousness and a meaningful experience, both of which facilitate the recall of the dream. The latter is usually related to the content of the dream and often involves bodily functions, their expressions and control. The recall residue may be an experience identical with an element in the manifest dream (e.g., one patient recalled a dream about teeth while brushing his teeth) or may relate to the latent content of the dream as revealed by the analysis of the dream (e.g., a dream recalled while taking a shower was of putting on a bear rug and being in a play; urinary exhibitionism was a major latent theme).

Analysis reveals links between recall residues, day residues, manifest dream, and latent dream contents. In one instance described by Kanzer, the day and recall residues were related to virtually identical experiences. Kanzer also noted that recall residue experiences are habitual for certain patients. Anal derivatives are important in the withholding and production of such dreams and their residues, but other instinctual-drive derivatives also play a role.

Lewin (1953) emphasized oral factors in the remembering and forgetting of dreams. He equated the forgotten dream with the lost breast, and observed that associations to the forgetting of dreams are often oral in nature. Lewin viewed the recall of a previously forgotten dream as the equivalent of the continuation of sleep at the nurturing breast.

Both Kanzer and Lewin discussed the important role of the transference in the recall of forgotten dreams. Whitman (1963) also explored this factor and in an experimental setting, he and his associates (Whitman et al. 1963) demonstrated the influence of the listener to the dream on the subject's reporting or omission (due either to repression or conscious suppression) of dreams. The subjects reported different dreams from the same night to an experimenter and to the therapist; embarrassment and anxiety regarding fantasies directed toward each of these men were important determinants in this selection. In his theoretical discussion, Whitman (1963) accounts for the forgetting of dreams on several levels: in terms of the censorship between the topographical agencies of the mind; structurally, in terms of the ego's work in overcoming countercathectic barriers at different levels of consciousness; by considering the demands of reality, once awake, which interfere with the turning inward necessary for the recall of a dream; and by reference to the differences between the primary and secondary process modes of thinking which make the former more alien in the waking state.

FORMULATIONS AND CLINICAL MATERIAL

I begin this section with a series of conceptualizations or hypotheses regarding the relationship between day and recall residues as representative of reality, and the dream as representative of intrapsychic functioning. These will be stated largely in structural and adaptive terms, with reference to other metapsychological frameworks where relevant, and are followed by clinical material which will illustrate and elaborate upon them.

1. Day residues derive from reality experiences which are a significant part of an ongoing interaction of the psyche and reality. Day residues and dreams in their manifest and latent aspects form an interwoven totality of a genetically significant past and the present,

and of meaningful experience and conscious and unconscious fantasy. Further, any part of this totality may at any given moment serve or represent instinctual drives, superego expressions, and ego functions, including defenses and adaptations. The total personality constantly fluctuates in the use it makes of each element of this network over any period of time.

2. There are two major, though overlapping, types of day residues: those sought out actively by the ego in the service of any or all of the psychic macrostructures and/or the instinctual drives, and those imposed upon the total personality by significant real events.

3. Because of their strategic position in the interplay between reality and the psyche, and between the past and the present, day residues are important reference points in the analysis of dreams.

4. Recall residues refer to another dimension of the interplay between reality and intrapsychic functioning, and they share many features with day residues. They, too, may be sought out by the ego in its effort to recall dreams as part of its constant endeavor to work through and resolve ongoing conflicts, or they may be imposed on the ego by a strongly charged reality event, often a perceptual experience, closely related to the content of a repressed dream.

Several corollaries follow:

a. In those situations where day residues are sought out by the total personality, the ego is conceived of as functioning actively as part of its ongoing efforts to adapt and cope with demands from within and without. Under such conditions, the ego may utilize focal as well as incidental experiences in order to construct a dream. Such residues may relate to manifest or latent dream content. Here, the ego operates primarily in the service of its integrative, synthetic, and adaptive functions, and is guided by present concerns in the light of important genetic events. These important experiences and fantasies from the past are a constant unconscious factor in the selection of day residues. The ego utilizes such reality experiences and events as vehicles for defensive operations, gratification, or resolution of conflict on both reality and fantasy levels, and dreams are, of course, related to, and an expression of, the latter.

b. When reality events of sufficient psychical meaning are imposed upon the total personality, we may conceive of them as traumatic or gratifying experiences which have significance for the individual in the present as well as in terms of his meaningful genetic past. Further, such experiences generate anxieties and conscious and unconscious fantasies which must be dealt with and mastered by the ego. The formation of a dream with its manifest and latent content is a significant part of these attempts at mastery.

c. Recall residues highlight the role of reality in the subtle alterations of ongoing intrapsychic balances which ultimately determine the level of defensive countercathectic barriers.

d. Interventions and experiences within the psychoanalytic situation are among the more crucial sources of reality factors which contribute to both day and recall residues.

The following excerpts are derived from a number of supervisory situations and case reports. In the first, a young married man in analysis reported the following dream:

> He is in a large white room with his daughter, who is injured and bandaged. Some people seem concerned and ask the patient about what happened. The patient feels neglected.

What prompted his dream? The patient's niece, his brother's daughter, had just had open heart surgery, a circumstance which imposed upon the patient's total personality a complex, traumatic experience and day residue which had, for him, important genetic referents. It was an event that evoked a multitude of fantasies and anxieties that had to be mastered. As part of his attempts at mastery, the patient had actually selected certain incidental experiences related to his visit to his niece in the hospital, with which he built the manifest dream. The latent content of the dream referred, of course, to the niece's surgery, and associations revealed a first genetic link: the birth of twin sisters when the patient was six. Fantasies directed toward them in the present and past centered around the patient's feelings of neglect, an intense sense of rivalry and envy, and hostile, bodily destructive wishes toward his new rivals. Links between the day residues and the manifest and latent dream content are evident.

The complexities of the patient's response to this event became clearer, however, in subsequent sessions. Analysis of resistances led to the lifting of repressive forces directed against the recall of additional fantasies and experiences. First, his mother had once been hospitalized for a miscarriage. This, of course, introduced additional fantasies of bodily damage to women, touched upon certain pregnancy fantasies and the related anxieties within the patient, and led eventually to a series of oedipal fantasies. Second, he reported a previously unrevealed fact: when he was four years of age he had been hospitalized for diphtheria and had nearly died. This introduced his conflicts about his own body image, body damage, and death, which were crucial to his present neurosis, and the material also hinted at a number of transference fantasies which were clarified much later in his analysis. Repression had been directed here both at a multiplicity of day residues (e.g., the many current discussions of his own hospitalization which he had initially failed to report) and at the recall of the crucial genetic experiences. Together, these day residues, the crucial past events, and the related past and present fantasies formed the deepest available level of latent content of the dream.

In this instance, symbolization and the dream work correspond closely to the defenses directed against the recall of the day residues and the actual biographical event of the patient's hospitalization. Further, one can readily observe here a hierarchy of defenses, as well as a hierarchy of fantasies, each element serving as a revelation as well as a screen (see Gill 1963) in this network of present reality, past experience, conscious and unconscious fantasies, and manifest and latent dreams. The role of instinctual drives, superego promptings, and ego functions may be inferred readily and will not be detailed here.

My next example is an excerpt from the analysis of a twenty-seven-year-old woman who at the time of the dream was confronted with several really difficult situations: her mother was ill and probably needed gallbladder surgery; her sister's husband had had an acute heart attack, but at the time of the dream, some ten days after his hospitalization, he seemed to be doing well; and the patient was anticipating her comprehensive examination for her doctorate in history. She had postponed the examination because of acute unresolved anxiety and was becoming increasingly disturbed as it approached. In this trying period, she dreamed:

> I was on an operating table ... my appendix had been taken out ...
> they were placing a plastic tube into the wound and it seemed

foreign ... somehow, the intern had pushed it in too far. I was then with friends ... I had a knife in my hand ... but it was rubber and couldn't harm anyone. I'm at a jail ... there's somebody locked up and he is provocative ... I go to attack him but I don't hurt him. He tells me that I'm too destructive and that it's unnecessary. A sick old man is trying to push me into one of the cells ... but I fight him off.

Her associations were first to the traumatic events I have already described. Next, she turned to the day residues which her ego had unconsciously selected for working through the anxieties and fantasies evoked by these experiences. She recalled a novel that she had been reading in which a woman has a dream of killing her entire family, but awakens to find that they have not been harmed. Her cousin, a young man two years her junior, had recently been seductive, and she had rejected his advances because of her aunt, who would have been critical of any liaison between them. She then spoke of her congenital harelip, which made her uncomfortable in seeking a job, since she worried about the possible need for additional plastic surgery. Lastly, she mentioned her hostile relationship with her brother and sister when they were children, and her feeling at times that she could murder her mother, who constantly nagged her about getting married—at times, the rage was intolerable.

I will cite certain inferences from this rich network of day residues, dream, and associations, in order to illustrate the theses being developed here. The life experiences of her mother's illness, her brother-in-law's heart attack, and her pending examination were imposed upon her total personality and were selected for working through by her ego, prompting attempts at mastery and adaptation. The brother-in-law's heart attack, for example, evoked a series of fantasies and memories centered around her rivalry with her brother, including the wish to murder her brother and the undoing of this wish because of fears of punishment through bodily damage. With these and other related fantasies stirred up, the ego selected the day residue of the woman who had dreamt of murdering her family as a vehicle for the gratification of the murderous wishes in the dream fantasy, made possible in part through the use of displacement away from herself. As a day residue and association to the dream, this reference to the novel has a more symbolic, primary process–like structure and is closely related to the latent content of the dream and the dream wish. In this context, the day residue of her concern for her brother-in-law's survival served to screen and defend against her murderous feelings and the latent dream thoughts and day residues related to these latter impulses. Similarly, in the manifest dream itself, there is a struggle between overt murderous aggression, its condemnation, and its undoing.

The patient's focus on the events related to the brother-in-law's heart attack also served to displace and screen sexual fantasies related to a mother transference and to her mother directly. These impulses had heightened the patient's own bodily anxieties, fostered by the real anxieties regarding her examination and possible plastic surgery. These anxieties in turn prompted her superego to direct the ego to seek out an experience of renunciation (refusing her cousin's recent seductive overtures) as an appeasement of the mutilating mother and attacking father.

This analysis, which could be expanded considerably, should suffice to document the complexities of the interaction of various day residues. Each residue has its own manifest and latent content, conscious and unconscious meanings, and may serve both to screen and to permit drive discharge. This interaction extends into that between the various day residues and the manifest and latent dream contents.

A subsequent session brought out additional repressed aspects of this hierarchical network. After the patient and the analyst had worked on various implications of these events, the patient received notification of the date of the oral examination for her doctorate, and that night she had a vague dream of being hospitalized for cancer. This led her back to her two earlier dreams and she now reported a previously repressed day residue for those dreams: she had read a report on the Attica prison uprising which had been critical of the prison officials for the killing of prisoners. With this revelation, prompted by the modifications in defenses by means of both working through in therapy and new reality residues, the patient went on to realize that she was terrified of her oral examination because she dreaded the questions she would be asked and which she experienced as destructive attacks; she feared losing control and the possibility of either verbally or physically attacking her examiners or running away from the examination room. This led her back to her anxieties about her plastic surgery and her desperate need to reassure herself that she would survive the procedure (represented in the dream by the operation and the undoing of her murderous attacks).

At this point the analyst linked these anxieties and fantasies to her plastic surgery as a young child, a time when she thought she was going to die. She responded with the revelation of a recurrent, previously unreported fantasy—that of needing an amputation and being totally helpless on the operating table. She then remembered that her major symptom, anxiety and an experience of a lump in her throat, had its onset when her closest girlfriend had part of a finger amputated (note here the reference to a sister and mother displacement). This coincided in time with an experience in which a friend of hers had been hit by a car while walking with the patient, and had sustained minor injuries. These associations provided genetic ties to the repressed day residue of the Attica prison officials who harmed their prisoners and the latent meaning of the old man who tries to push her into the jail cell—the driver of the car had been an old man.

The two dreams, then, along with their day residues, represent a series of hierarchically layered fantasies and conflicts, of great genetic importance, currently activated and revived in this patient by ongoing life events and unresolved aspects of her past and present inner and external life. The dream and the day residues clearly form a unity in which the various fantasies and conflicts are expressed, reacted to, and defended against. Meaningful interpretation of the function and meaning of any given element can be made only through the patient's associations and an understanding of the total context. Further, these elements can have real meaning only in relationship to each other, so that the intrapsychic fantasies must be related to reality, and reality, in turn, to fantasy.

Several shorter clinical vignettes will highlight selected aspects of the connection between day residues and dreams. The first will demonstrate the relationship between day residues and infantile experiences and fantasies. It is drawn from the analysis of a man at the time his wife had given birth to their first daughter. His initial reaction was marked by an inexplicable sense of resentment toward his wife. During this time, he dreamed:

I had a sharp knife ... it had two points ... my mother and sister
were there ... my sister was blind ... I drop the knife.

Associations were to his mother's delight regarding the birth of a
granddaughter and to a childhood experience in which as a boy scout
he had been severely cut by a knife. This memory screened experiences
of having seen his mother's genital area. The patient's fantasy in
childhood had been that she had been castrated and deprived of her
penis, and it was now linked to his viewing his daughter's genitalia. Just
as his own hostile and castrating wishes toward his mother, which had
been intensified with the birth of a sister when he was four years old,
had been dealt with by alternating periods of hostility and
oversolicitude, in the dream he seems involved with blinding the sister
and with disassociating himself from that experience. In his childhood,
he had had intense fears of being blinded, which were related to his
image of his father as a powerful castrater—an image reinforced by the
fact that his father worked as a butcher. There was also an anxiety
provoking identification with this image of his father, and throughout
his life the patient attempted to control his explosive temper and his
impulses to verbally attack others. Further, with this session as a day
residue, that night the patient dreamed of being slashed in a holdup, a
dream of talion punishment for the wishes of the previous day.

The level of cathectic investment in a given fantasy or conflict, and in
the components of the fantasy itself, is in a constant state of
fluctuation. Day residues influence these cathexes. Thus, it was only
when this patient actually had a daughter that the instinctual drives
directed toward his mother and sister pressed pass the repressive
barriers. On other occasions, day residues may heighten or reinforce
repression. Such residues may also be sought out as compromises
between expressive and repressive forces.

Events within the analytic situation are the source, conscious and
unconscious, of important day residues. These are derived from all
aspects of the analytic situation: direct and incidental sensory
stimulation; the content of the patient's associations; the analyst's
behavior and his interventions or lack of them; the transference and
other conscious and unconscious fantasies; the reality aspects; and the
nonverbal communications between analyst and patient.

Because the variations are infinite, I will confine myself to a single example. The vignette is drawn from the analysis of a young woman who had been brought up in an overpermissive household with a father who had been extremely critical and attacking. There had been much open hostility between him and the patient. At the time of the analytic experience to be reported, the father had just died. The patient's initial reaction was an intense reaction-formation against the rage she felt toward her father, and displacement of this rage onto her husband and then onto her analyst—a male. Following a session in which the analyst confronted her with the evidence of her unconscious rage at him in terms of her father transference, she reported this dream:

> I meet you at a museum and you are very fatherly. We sit together holding hands.

The dream had been prompted by the analyst's confrontation, and associations led to further interpretation of the denied rage toward him as related to her unresolved hatred of her father. The associations hinted at the defensive use of this hostility as a means of covering over underlying sexual fantasies and longings, but these were not interpreted. In the next session she reported another dream:

> Father was making love to a strange woman; I am watching.

The day residue for this dream included the analyst's interpretation, which had identified unconscious sources of the patient's hostility and pointed to their defensive functions. This had modified repressive barriers to the point where the patient began to feel some sense of longing for closeness with her father. When (based on earlier material and this dream) the analyst pointed out the patient's denied sexual fantasies toward her father and the possibility of having observed him in intercourse, she recalled a previously repressed, recurrent fantasy of having relations with her father, and a previously unreported memory of having observed him once with an erection in his bedroom.

In this instance there is again a multilayered interaction between present reality, important genetic events, and the analytic situation, including the transference, the fantasy, and the dream. Reality imposed upon the patient a current trauma which was related to critical early childhood traumas, and the patient attempted now, as then, to defend herself against both the rage and the sexual longings directed at her father. The defenses are at first pointed in all directions: at the day residues, the dreams, and the fantasies about the father. With extensive analytic work the defenses were modified, and day residues which more and more clearly reflected the undisguised unconscious fantasies were incorporated into her dreams. This process culminated in the report of the repressed fantasy of having sexual relations with her father and the repressed memory of having seen his erect penis.

Day residues serve defensive as well as gratifying purposes, Just as the dream may be used as a resistance, so may the day residues. A woman in analysis had a long dream of her mother and sister in which they wander around a small town in a dense fog, parading up and down the streets, and ending up in a theater where there was considerable activity. The dream was reported during a period of great resistance which related to erotic transference fantasies with an underlying homosexual tone, based on longings for her mother. The patient spent the particular session searching for day residues, finding a multitude of them, never focusing, and avoiding her unconscious fantasies.

My observations on recall residues are intended to supplement those of Kanzer (1959), who emphasized the libidinal and altered-state aspects of this pehenomenon. Most of the recall residues I have observed have consisted of sensory elements within a reality experience which are identical with, or very similar to, an element of the manifest dream. They are therefore usually visual in nature, although they may relate to any sensory modality (Kanzer 1959). More rarely, the link between the event prompting recall of the dream and the dream itself is referrable to the latent content of the dream. Most often this latent content seems to emerge in the course of a psychoanalytic session, where either an interpretation or the natural fluctuations in the content of the patient's associations lead to the recall of a previously forgotten dream. Let us turn to some illustrations.

A young man was in analysis with a young male analyst who saw his patients in his office at a hospital center. Upon entering the consultation room and viewing a particular ashtray which lay on the table behind the couch, the patient recalled dreaming that he had given the analyst an ashtray as a gift. The sight of the ashtray as he entered the analytic session, with its concomitant intrapsychic shifts in defenses and the mobilization of transference fantasies, led to the recall of the dream. Associations indicated that this was a father-transference dream revolving around a fantasy that the analyst's recent move to a new and more spacious office had signaled his promotion at the medical center, a promotion achieved through his superiors' recognition of his successful work with the patient; the promotion was his gift to the analyst. Analysis related this to the patient's own castration anxieties and his wish for a powerful phallus. The recall of the dream was part of his ego's attempt to deal with these fantasies, which were active at the time.

An intervention by another male analyst during the analysis of a young man served to modify strong countercathexes directed against homosexual transference fantasies and led to the recall of a repressed dream. The patient had been initially silent in the session and then reported this dream:

> I was sitting silently with two of my male friends. There was a pretty wild scene around me. They kept staring at me as if I were someone special, but I really wasn't dressed for the occasion.

Associations related to his friends and to the way the patient dressed, but circumvented the transference implications of the dream. The analyst used the patient's initial silence in the session and other associations to interpret his wish to withdraw from the analysis in order to avoid wild inner feelings and fantasies that he was unprepared to handle and which he feared might expose him—much as in his dream he wasn't dressed. The patient responded that he had in fact been dressed in the dream, but very poorly for the occasion. With the reference to being undressed, however, he suddenly remembered a forgotten dream:

> I was performing fellatio on a fellow I had just met in a bar who had a mustache just like you [the analyst]. He was very excited and I tried to withdraw.

The patient acknowledged the dream as an undisguised reference to his fantasies of sexual involvement with the analyst, fantasies he had been preoccupied with in recent weeks. In this instance, the analyst's reference to being undressed, as well as his interpretation of the patient's wishes and defenses against them, served to lift the repressive barriers directed against the more undisguised dream. The relatively disguised dream here served to screen the less disguised one.

A woman in analysis, in the course of free associating, was talking of wanting to fondle her young male analyst's genitals, and she suddenly recalled a forgotten dream of her father in bed. Further material clarified her voyeuristic and sexual fantasies about the analyst, which were based on a father transference.

The same patient demonstrated how reality, instead of prompting the recall of a forgotten dream, may foster the repression of a dream and the fantasies it expresses. She was awakening from her night's sleep and recalling a dream about a train winding through the mountains, when her son came into the bedroom. Seeing him, she forgot the rest of the dream. Associations suggested that the dream's manifest and latent content related to highly conflicted fantasies of capturing her analyst's and son's penises as displacements from her father and brother. Seeing him prompted repression of what probably were relatively undisguised expressions of these wishes.

The context of the recall residue often provides clues to the latent content of the remembered dream. For example, a man in psychotherapy was sitting in a clinic waiting room when he recalled an unremembered dream of a garbage truck: the nature of his current thoughts about his therapist and therapy were unmistakable.

Repressive barriers fluctuate throughout the day because of inner and outer promptings. A married man in analysis dreamed that he had fought with his brother. Assocations led from his feeling that his brother was unduly critical to some similar feelings in his relationship with his analyst, a man. He continued, saying that on his way to the session, he had passed a man with a beard while driving in his car and had suddenly remembered this dream:

A man with a beard [the analyst had a beard] is inviting Al [a close friend of the patient] to come into a steam room with him.

He had not remembered this dream upon waking, but had met Al for lunch, at which time the patient remembered the dream only to repress it again. The experiences of approaching the analytic session and seeing the man with the beard had mobilized his transference fantasies and created the Gestalt within which the dream could once again be remembered.

For the following dream, the day residue and the recall residue were apparently identical (see Kanzer 1959). A man in analysis was, with considerable resistance, exploring a series of early experiences characterized by seductive play with his brother. On television he had seen some male ballet dancers and had found himself mildly stimulated. The show had prompted the recall of a forgotten dream in which he was invited to dance with a handsome ballet master. Associations connected it to his brother's seductiveness in childhood. The previous day, while thinking about this theme from his analysis, he had seen an advertisement for the same television program, which he then utilized as a seemingly innocuous day residue for the manifest dream. This screened the more anxiety provoking day residues related directly to the homosexual experiences discussed in the analytic session, which, in turn, formed the latent dream content. Repression had been modified to permit the development of the dream, reinstituted in the forgetting of the dream, and bypassed with the aid of the perceptual stimulus—all at a time when he was working through these experiences and his fantasies and anxieties about them.

One last variation concludes this clinical presentation. A young man in psychotherapy awakened and could not remember dreaming. As he began to consider the day ahead of him, he realized it was to be an extremely unpleasant one, with particularly traumatic prospects. He then shifted his thoughts and spent considerable time desperately trying to recall a dream from the previous night. He finally recalled one which was quite lengthy and full of obvious references to his childhood. He used his dream both in his therapy session and throughout the day to defensively distract him from, and deny, his worries that day, along with their present and genetic implications.

DISCUSSION

The observations presented here indicate that day residues, recall residues, and the dreams to which they relate are best viewed as a totality modeled upon the total relationship between the organism and its environment. In such a continuum, any point may initiate trauma or gratification, drive or defense. External reality may initiate a reaction within the person; or the person, with his intrapsychic strivings and conflicts, may seek out reality and fantasy for resolution, gratification, or defense.

Arlow (1963) has developed a comparable model for symptom formation. Current reality, in his conceptualization, may regressively reactivate an instinctual wish from childhood so that it prompts gratification in fantasy if the reality itself is frustrating; or the reality situation may correspond to an earlier trauma and therefore lead to a repetition of the original conflict; or, lastly, the real situation may foster the projection of an intrapsychic conflict or unconscious fantasy onto it. Arlow also noted that unconscious fantasies create a set through which reality is interpreted, while life events stimulate fantasies which find discharge in part through dreams.

The present observations with regard to day and recall residues offer concrete data regarding this interplay of reality and unconscious fantasy and other intrapsychic phenomena. The pressure of unconscious fantasies to find means of discharge and resolution prompts the ego to scan reality and select day residues to serve as vehicles for such discharge, both in reality and through dreams. On the other hand, particularly charged reality experiences impose themselves upon the ego and stimulate the total personality to react. The response includes fantasy formation as well as other adaptive behavior, including dreaming.

The actual variations are many. A day residue may be a frustrating experience or one of gratification; a new trauma or one fraught with implications from the past; a source of anxiety, guilt, or conflict, or the resolution of these; and an instigator of fresh, or the recreator of past, conscious or unconscious fantasies. Imposed upon the ego or sought out by it, these realities lead to dream formation as part of the total organism's efforts to gratify, synthesize, resolve, and adapt.

Recall residues, and the conditions under which they occur, are a further facet of the ongoing interplay of reality and inner mental life. Here too, unconscious fantasies may prompt the ego to seek out experiences which facilitate the recall of repressed dreams as part of its ongoing efforts to cope. On the other hand, reality may impose experiences which overwhelm countercathectic barriers and prompt the recall of such dreams.

In this context, it is easy to understand why clarification of day and recall residues of dreams play a vital part in their analysis and interpretations. Such elements are often crucial in reviving unconscious fantasies and linking them to ongoing and past concerns presently on the surface of the mental apparatus.

The observations presented here are also relevant to the psychoanalytic conceptualization of the total relationship between reality and the psyche. I cannot deal further with this complex topic here, except to indicate again that any model of this relationship must consider the total relationship between the two in terms of both past and present. This leads us to a reassessment of Freud's thinking regarding infantile seductions. In essence, we can see that Freud was actually correct in both of his formulations regarding the role of reality in the formation of neuroses: real seductions do occur on many levels, while unconscious fantasies are also constantly being created and revised from both experiencing and imagining. Together, interacting, and creating a totality, they lead to the anxieties and conflicts out of which neuroses develop.

REFERENCES

Arlow, J. (1963). Conflict, regression, and symptom formation. *International Journal of Psycho-Analysis* 44:12–22.

———(1969a).Unconscious fantasy and disturbances of conscious experience. *Psychoanalytic Quarterly* 38:1–27.

———(1969b). Fantasy, memory, and reality testing. *Psychoanalytic Quarterly* 38:28–51.

Bergler, E. (1943). A third function of the "day residue" in dreams. *Psychoanalytic Quarterly* 12:353–370.

Bergler, E. and Jekels, L. (1940). Instinct dualism in dreams. *Psychoanalytic Quarterly* 38:28–51.

Bernstein, I., and Glenn J. (1969). Masturbation and the manifest content of dreams. In *The Manifest Content of the Dream,* The Kris Study Group of the New York Psychoanalytic Institute, Monograph III, ed. B. Fine, E. Joseph, and H. Waldhorn pp. 101–109. New York: International Universities Press.

Erikson, E. (1950). *Childhood and Society.* New York: Norton.

Freud, S. (1900). The Interpretation of dreams. *Standard Edition* 4/5.

——— (1917). A metapsychological supplement to the theory of dreams. *Standard Edition* 14:219–235.

——— (1920). Beyond the pleasure principle. *Standard Edition* 18:3–64.

————— (1923). The ego and the id. *Standard Edition* 19:3–66.

————— (1933). New Introductory lectures on psycho-analysis. *Standard Edition* 22:3–182.

————— (1940). An outline of psycho-analysis. *Standard Edition.* 23:141–207.

Gill, M. (1963). Topography and systems in psychoanalytic theory. *Psychological Issues* Monograph 10. New York: International Universities Press.

Hartmann, H. (1939). *Ego Psychology and the Problem of Adaptation.* New York: International Universities Press, 1958.

————— (1956). Notes on the reality principle. *Psychoanalytic Study of the Child* 11:31–53.

—————, Kris, E., and Loewenstein, R. (1946). Comments on the formation of psychic structure. *Psychoanalytic Study of the Child* 2:11–38.

Kanzer, M. (1955). The communicative function of the dream. *International Journal of Psycho-Analysis* 36:260–266.

————— (1958). Image formation during free association. *Psychoanalytic Quarterly* 27:465–484.

————— (1959). The recollection of the forgotten dream. *Journal of the Hillside Hospital* 8:74–85.

Leveton, A. (1961). The night residue. *International Journal of Psycho-Analysis* 42:506–516.

Lewin B. (1953). The forgetting of dreams. In *Drives, Affects, Behavior,* ed. R. M. Loewenstein, pp. 191–202. New York: International Universities Press.

Niederland, W. (1959). The "miracled-up" world of Schreber's childhood.

Rapaport, D. (1960). On the psychoanalytic theory of motivation. In *The Collected Papers of David Rapaport,* ed. M. Gill, pp. 853–915. New York: Basic Books, 1967.

Sadow, L., Gedo, J., Miller J., Pollock, G., Sabshin, M., and Schlessinger, N. (1968). The process of hypothesis change in three early psychoanalytic concepts. *Journal of the American Psychoanalytic Association* 16:245–273.

Sharpe, E. F. (1937). *Dream Analysis.* London: Hogarth Press.

White, R. (1963). Ego and reality in psychoanalytic theory. *Psychological Issues.* Monograph 11. New York: International Universities Press.

Whitman, R. (1963). Remembering and forgetting dreams in psychoanalysis. *Journal of the American Psychoanalytic Association* 11:752–774.

———, Kramer, M., and Baldridge, B. (1963). Which dream does the patient tell? *Archives of General Psychiatry* 8:277–282.

Wolff, P. (1960). The developmental psychologies of Jean Piaget and psychoanalysis. *Psychological Issues* Monograph 5. New York: International Universities Press.

Chapter Three

A Psychoanalytic Study of Material from Patients in Psychotherapy

(1972[1971])

This article reports a study of the "material" of psychotherapy, the communications from patients out of which we build our formulations and interpretations and through which we ascertain confirmation or the lack of it. The inception of a new journal devoted to psychoanalytic psychotherapy seems a particularly apt occasion for a reconsideration of this most basic dimension of the treatment situation. Such an exploration has value for several important reasons. First, this aspect of therapy seems to be taken for granted and virtually ignored in the psychoanalytic literature; as I hope to demonstrate, we all have much to learn from a careful look at the material offered by our patients and our methods of working with it.

Second, studies of this kind can shed light on an important current controversy in regard to communications from patients in psycho-analysis (Greenson, 1970). In this dispute Greenson, Waldhorn (1967), and others have debated whether dreams are indeed "the royal road to the unconscious" and whether they hold a special place among the materials of analytic sessions. This issue can, of course, be broadened to relate to all communications from patients: which are most and least fruitful in understanding and analyzing the emotional problems of our patients and their unconscious roots? An exploration of this question with psychotherapy patients can serve as an initial attempt to specifically study this problem.

A third reason for a more careful assessment of the material of psychotherapy sessions is the need to update our clinical techniques in keeping with our current psychoanalytic understanding of psychopathology and symptom formation (see especially Schur 1953, Arlow 1963) and of the technique of psychotherapy itself (Wallerstein 1969). There is a great gap here, one that can be bridged by studies such as the one presented in this article.

In all, then, our ability to listen to our patients, to glean the conscious and unconscious content of their communications, and to time our interventions properly can benefit from a fresh look at the contents of psychotherapy sessions. This study treats three hundred sessions drawn from ten patients who were in twice-weekly, psychoanalytically oriented psychotherapy. The specific data consists of notes written after each session. The exploration is presented entirely as a pilot venture, and its many pitfalls and limitations are acknowledged at the outset. This survey is, at best, merely one step better than general clinical impressions. There are no controls, and there is no way to gauge the effects of biases, particularly those introduced by my own unconscious predilections, blocks, or tendencies to distort. While I consciously attempt to keep these to a minimum and to listen to the material from patients presented to me without preference and with a willingness to allow them to "direct" me to the pertinent communications of each session and to record all highlights accordingly, there is clearly no way to validate this claim. I have, however, been particularly interested in searching out unconscious meanings from every type of communication from patients and, therefore, feel that a study of this kind is a reasonable endeavor, which has every chance of producing a meaningful sampling of these communications and what they contain on every level available in psychotherapy. This is true despite the added problem that the assessment of these materials—my ratings of their contents and their internal validation by the patient's further associations—is, of course, also open to bias and lacking in outside reliability and validation.

On the positive side, however, is my effort to open up new avenues of understanding and to document tentatively an aspect of psychotherapy previously uncharted. Thus, although this is a preliminary study, it is one of considerable promise for enhancing psychotherapeutic theory and technique and for offering many leads.

THE MATERIALS OF THE STUDY

The patients for this study consist of ten randomly selected cases whom I am supervising in psychotherapy at this time. There are eight women, five adult and three adolescent, and two adolescent young men. Diagnostically, they include three borderline patients, two patients primarily with neurotic symptoms, and five patients with character disorders—one with eczema. All were in an uncovering type of psychoanalytic psychotherapy. From supervisory notes, which run about a paragraph per session, and which were intended to define and highlight the major communications and interventions of the session, thirty consecutive sessions from each patient were studied and rated. These notes were almost all written before the study itself was carried out. They were derived from all phases of therapy, from quite near the outset to the final sessions of treatment. The intention was to provide a broad sample of patients and sessions.

The notes were reviewed for sequence and for manifest and latent content. The categories for communication are listed in the table below. There are two main types of communication: those related to the behavior of the patient within the session, and those derived from his verbalizations. These in turn were divided into two types: *indicators* and *content*.

Indicators are communications that inform the therapist that a significant neurotic problem exists, without conveying the unconscious meaning of the problem or the underlying fantasies. They relate primarily to the manifest content or surface of the material. Indicators may pertain to impaired ego functioning, resistances, neurotic symptoms and conflicts, and characterological disturbances, though they do not offer information as to the specific unconscious fantasies and genetics involved. Thus, indicators tell us something is amiss, without telling us the underlying unconscious meaning and basis. Examples are absences; empty ruminations; inappropriate anger, anxiety, or depression; thoughts of leaving treatment; symptoms; and other manifestations of this kind.

Content refers primarily to latent meaning or to the breakthrough of previously repressed fantasies or memories. The category relates to unconscious fantasies in all their dimensions: specific genetic and current traumatic experiences, unconscious conflicts, unconscious derivatives of the macrostructures (id, ego, and superego), and the adaptational resolution of these neurosogenic forces. It also includes fantasies which underlie resistances and ego dysfunctions. This category, then, is ultimately related to the unconscious intrapsychic facets of the neurosis and its specific fantasied representations.

The material of each session was rated in regard to types of communication, and the elements were classified as either indicators of difficulty or specific unconscious content. These ratings were tabulated; trends related to the kinds of material, which most and least often reflected indicators and content, were developed; and an evaluation was made of just how these dimensions of the material were detectable. In addition, individual differences in styles and means of communicating were surveyed briefly.

These, then, were the methods of the study. Before presenting the findings, however, I must make one brief, but important and difficult, detour. It is impossible to present the result of a study of this kind without establishing the framework in which it was carried out. Space limitations will permit only a condensed set of statements for this purpose, and this will inevitably prove unsatisfactory and incomplete, since it must touch upon many controversial concepts and issues. Despite these risks and limitations, I want to orient the reader with a brief resumé of the psychoanalytic understanding of the structure of neurotic disturbances, focusing primarily on the problem of symptom formation. I lean heavily on the writings of others who have specifically studied this problem. Freud (1926), Schur (1953), and Arlow (1963, 1969) will be my main sources; in addition, see Langs (1971).

The following seem most pertinent to the development of a neurosis:

1. The groundwork for the development of neurotic symptoms is laid down largely during infancy and childhood. This evolves from two main dimensions in the child's adaptive problems:
   a. The first is related to the inevitable and natural development and maturation of the child, prompted by inner strivings and environmental responses and pressures. Each early phase (oral, anal, phallic, oedipal) poses tasks related to the

FREQUENCY OF CATEGORIES SCORED FOR THREE HUNDRED SESSIONS*

	Current Events & Behavior	Acting Out	Symptomatic Acts	Acting Out of Transference Reactions	References to Therapy, Therapist	Rumination	Flight & Absences	Slips of the Tongue	Affective Disturbances
Total Sessions	239	78	6	53	154	193	114	3	126
Indicators	61	36	1	32	41	3	14	0	34
Range	2–15	0–6	0–1	1–13	2–9	0–1	0–7	0	0–14
Content	67	24	4	2	30	6	1	3	3
Range	1–12	0–13	0–2	0–1	0–8	0–5	0–1	0–2	0–1

	Neurotic Symptoms	Physical Symptoms	Creative Works of Others	Recent Memories	Childhood Memories	Conscious Fantasies	Manifest Dreams	Dream & Associations
Total Sessions	36	37	12	98	50	186	102	91
Indicators	35	30	0	24	5	27	18	9
Range	0–11	0–14	0	0–6	0–2	0–12	0–7	0–7
Content	1	1	12	58	45	124	75	75
Range	0–1	0–1	0–3	1–12	0–15	1–28	2–16	2–16

*Three hundred sessions were scored, but there were fifteen absences.

expressions of instinctual drives (sexual and aggressive), in which ego and superego development and response play an ever-increasing role. Aberrant endowment, inner disturbances, or disruptions emanating from the crucial (usually parental) objects in the environment (for example, chronic overstimulation, overgratification, deprivation, or other disturbances in retating to, or rearing, the child) create intrapsychic disturbances and conflicts, which must then be resolved by the ego. Once sufficient maturation has occurred for structuralization of the psyche into id, ego, and superego, intrapsychic conflict takes the form of struggles between these agencies as evoked by inner changes, external events, and resultant internal stirrings. These conflicts may lead to symptom formation or may create vulnerabilities, fixations, personality disturbances, and unconscious sets which influence the later development of the person.

b. The second childhood factor in symptom formation relates to acute (less repetitive) traumas and their extended consequences. Events, such as the birth of a sibling, the death of a parent, or a surgical procedure, generate considerable anxiety, intrapsychic conflict, and need for adaptation. These events are particularly likely to evoke pathogenic, forbidden instinctual drive expressions which represent dangers to the person, and these pose a great burden for the ego's defenses, synthetic powers, and capacity to adapt and sublimate. Here, too, successful or unsuccessful resolution may follow, but, regardless, one is left with an unconscious set and vulnerability for later experiencing.

2. As the child grows, these nuclei of intrapsychic disturbances and drive-related conflicts are reworked whenever life situations, or inner stirrings caused by later maturation and development, evoke their conscious or unconscious (derivative) recollection. There are therefore many versions of the intrapsychic representations of these pathogenic traumas and the efforts toward their resolution. Each is represented by a specific and complex unconscious fantasy-memory, which includes derivatives of the relevant traumatic event, instinctual drives, superego promptings, and specific anxieties, and the ego's defenses and attempts at adaptation in reality or fantasy, undertaken each time the problem has arisen.

3. As long as the ego's attempts at mastery, defense, sublimation, and appropriate discharge are successful, symptoms do not appear. It is only when these defenses fail that a new attempt at resolution is necessary; at such times, symptoms may occur.

4. In adulthood a symptom may arise (though it can, of course, occur earlier) when some reality experience or major inner change repeats or touches upon the earlier, traumatic childhood situation. This experience disrupts the previous equilibrium of the intrapsychic solution and evokes a new version of the intrapsychic conflict. We are dealing here ultimately not with a reality problem or conflict, but with an intrapsychic one in which unconscious factors play a crucial and major role.

   The later events that prompt symptom formation are actually assessed by the ego largely in terms of the past traumas; technically, the ego regressively assesses the present situation and the instinctual drives it evokes, and judges it to be a danger situation. This regressive assessment of danger leads the ego to experience anxiety. The anxiety is a response, then, to a regressive assessment of a regressive instinctual drive, evoked by the current situation as it is linked to the past. It is the instinctual drives that are the ultimate source of danger, though they become so primarily through the external dangers entailed in their gratification. Such dangers include the loss of the object or its love, castration and its equivalents, and the internal danger of superego condemnation and punishment. The anxiety prompts fresh efforts at defense and adaptation. It is when these efforts fail to be entirely successful that a symptom will appear.

5. The symptom is a compromise formation in which the traumatic reality, the regressively reactivated, forbidden id wishes, the regressively responsive superego derivatives, and the requisites of the ego are all satisfied. A given symptom may emphasize one or another aspect of this total conflict, but all parties are served nonetheless.

6. The entire situation—past and present—is expressed in the form of a *repressed, unconscious fantasy*. Such fantasies find expression in disguised derivatives which take many forms, such as behavior, conscious fantasies, dreams, and the symptom itself. These unconscious fantasies, then, are the crucial expression of the intrapsychic conflict, its genetics, and the ego's attempts at

resolution, and are therefore the key to the understanding of the symptom. Not all unconscious fantasies are pathogenic, nor need all such repressed fantasies be made conscious to achieve therapeutic goals, particularly in psychotherapy, in which this quest must, of necessity, be limited.

7. By discovering the repressed, unconscious meaning of the symptom, we can make conscious the dimensions of the conflict involved and permit a reassessment and a new working through of each aspect. In this way, new resolutions and adaptations, which are less costly to the total person, can evolve; the symptom, then, is no longer needed.

8. Four additional concepts must be noted briefly:

   a. In its efforts to maintain the however-costly equilibrium gained through symptom formation and to avoid a reawakening of the intrapsychic conflict with its attendant pain, forbidden instinctual drives, and superego response, the ego develops secondary defenses in order to avoid an awareness of the pertinent unconscious fantasies. These are a major aspect of the resistances in therapy, which must themselves be resolved before the central, symptom-evoking intrapsychic conflict and its derivatives can be. These resistances, and those arising from other sources which will not be detailed here, are also based, in part, on unconscious fantasies.

   b. In addition to symptoms which evolve out of conflict, there are those which develop primarily from ego dysfunctions and regressions. While conflict-related factors play a role here too, these ego disturbances deserve separate consideration. They, too, develop out of disturbed endowment and environment. They include disturbances in defensive operations, object relationships, capacity for delay, reality testing, and the like, and are reflected, in part, in a person's character structure and in the specific way he attempts to resolve and adapt to his intrapsychic conflicts. They merit separate attention in psychotherapy and should be modified during it, leading to a strengthened ego. Space does not permit further discussion of this complex topic.

   c. Characterological disturbances are less ego-alien and more ego-syntonic than symptoms and are reflected in the lifestyle and the recurrent modes of defense, instinctual discharge, and behavior of the patient. Such disturbances also reflect, in part, unconscious fantasies of a complex nature. The delineation of these disturbances is a complex topic which I will not pursue further here.

d. The extent to which symptoms and character disturbances can be analyzed and revised in an uncovering type of psychoanalytic psychotherapy, such as that utilized with the patients in this study, is a limited one. I will not discuss here the complex issue of the distinction between psychoanalysis and psychotherapy and the differences in what each can achieve (Wallerstein 1969), but will only point out that the latter is considerably more limited in many ways, of which I will note only its scope, goals, accomplishments, and the amount of unconscious fantasy material available to it. This study, however, is based on the premise that, despite such clear and multiple limitations, certain focal and relevant unconscious material can emerge in psychotherapy and permit a meaningful degree of analysis and resolution. In fact, it is these very difficulties in working in psychotherapy that call for studies of this kind, which can enhance our ability to detect repressed and latent fantasies from such patients and work with them when they are available.

This summary is too long and condensed, yet far too sketchy and incomplete, and full of important unresolved issues. It will nonetheless, have to serve as a general orientation, and I will now turn to the results of my study.

THE MATERIAL OF PSYCHOTHERAPY SESSIONS: THE ROLE OF CONTEXT

The first finding of my survey is that specific communications do not stand by themselves and cannot be understood separately. It is, of course, well known that the *sequence* of associations reveals links and meanings which go beyond the immediate content of the material. Such sequences occur over a series of sessions or within a given session and will be illustrated repeatedly in the clinical vignettes of this paper. The use of sequential clues is also related to the problem of establishing the *context* in which the material of any given session is unfolding. It is this aspect of sequence on which I want to focus here.

Context proves to be a critical key to the understanding of the repressed unconscious fantasies expressed in the material from patients. This is because the context defines the problem with which the patient is dealing, the reality event (or internal upheaval) which has prompted the patient's adaptive response, behaviorally and intrapsychically. It is only when we know the central problem at hand that we can attain a true understanding of what the patient is communicating. At times this is relatively easy to do (for example, after a major trauma), and at other moments this can be quite difficult, since it is often defensively and unconsciously concealed by the patient. Context, then, is a concept akin to the day residues of dreams, and its usage is modeled on the relationship between day residues and the dreams they prompt (Langs 1971).

A briefly summarized session from the material of my study will illustrate these observations and develop them further. (All illustrations in this article, unless otherwise noted, are drawn from the three hundred sessions surveyed. Each patient is identified by two initials and will be labeled by the same initials throughout the paper.)

Mrs. A.H., a middle-aged married woman with five children, began this session with a dream. She is in an operating room, under anesthetic. As she awakens within the dream she sees a nurse and a doctor. They have a huge and grotesque syringe with a long needle and are going to give her an injection. They have trouble finding a vein and repeatedly puncture her arm, at which point she actually awoke. In the session, she went on to talk about death, funerals, and being embalmed. She had had an episode of blood-tinged diarrhea the night of the dream and again after awakening from the dream. She was having many problems with her children and was angry at her teenage daughter, who kept walking into the bedroom without knocking. She had been furious and had screamed at her. The patient had had a fight with her husband, who left the house and went to a bar. The dream reminded her of her mother's death and of her sense of guilt in not visiting her at the hospital often enough; still, her mother had said that seeing her had given her a sense of peace. She had continued almost daily to wear the dress that she had worn to her mother's funeral, and had done so for several weeks after that event. The injections reminded her of an intravenous anesthetic that she had received during an abortion.

In reviewing this session, we can first consider the kinds of communications this patient is offering, since this will soon be our focus. There is a manifest dream and indirect associations. There are recent and more distant recollections, as well as references to the behavior of the patient and others. There is also a conscious fantasy about punishment and a reference to somatic symptoms. What do these all add up to?

We can sense references to rage and punishment, to death and separation, and to pregnancy and loss. But we cannot really define the specific issues and conflicts the patient is dealing with or the specific unconscious fantasies which are involved. The main problem the patient is dealing with is unclear and without it we cannot define the situation or really understand the material.

If I were to indicate (as an exercise, since this is not actually the case) that this patient was in the process of terminating her therapy, how would you conceptualize this material? You might say that the termination was unconsciously being equated with being harmed by the doctor and with the death of her mother, and even with an abortion; and you could add that it was evoking guilt-ridden rage and longings to remain united with the therapist-mother, expressed through her unconscious fantasies of union through impregnation. The symptom at hand, the bloody diarrhea, would therefore represent the gratification of her wish for a child from the therapist-father (an aspect of the material that I will not especially pursue) and the punishment for the wish; it would be a regressive somatic representation of this wish and of the feared termination. It would also represent rage against the deserting, hurting mother-therapist and talion punishment for fantasies of attacking her-him. Although not the actual context of this session, it is of interest that such fantasies (with some modifications) did indeed prevail during a later attempt at premature termination by this patient.

If I were to say (again, as an exercise) that the patient was considering divorce because of her husband's cruelty and abandonment, we would clearly conceptualize and interpret the material and symptoms in still another way, focusing on the conflicts with her husband and their intrapsychic repercussions. Thus we would think of the rage at her husband as central and displaced onto her mother, and as prompting longings for the latter. The separation anxiety and related pregnancy fantasies, and the image of the abortion, would then be a reaction to thoughts of leaving her husband, and the transference implications would have to be understood in this context.

Actually, this patient's mother had recently died and there was little question but that this was the central problem for the patient at this time and the theme of this session. If I had mentioned that the patient had been discussing her loss in the previous session, you would have been alerted to this area immediately. In that session Mrs. A.H. had described in considerable detail her mother's death due to a bowel cancer.

The context, then, was established by reference to the previous session and to what at the moment was psychologically the most important reality trauma. The richness of the material—the conscious reactions and the unconscious fantasies contained in the associations—now become apparent.

Briefly, in her manifest dream Mrs. A.H. puts herself in her mother's place and suffers her symptoms and surgery. Her subsequent associations (and those from the previous session) reveal the latent content of the dream and the intrapsychic conflicts and unconscious fantasies the patient is struggling with. Thus, she wants to be with her mother and undo her loss—to die with her and as she did. She is also angry with her, and this is reflected in the displacement of her rage onto her husband and children.

Of particular note—because this leads us to one genetic factor—is the anger at her daughter for coming into the bedroom. This reality event is brought into the sessions to express an unconscious source of the patient's rage at her mother and one of the unconscious fantasies related to her symptoms: her mother had often brought her into her bed and stroked her body at times when her father was absent. The patient had been both stimulated and guilt-ridden, and had fantasied murderous, punishing retaliatory attacks by her father. The memory of the abortion also touches upon unconscious childhood fantasies of wanting her father's child (expressed more clearly in material from later sessions), dread of attack and punishment from her mother, and yet wishes to be one with him. One specific regressive unconscious fantasy related to the wish to swallow up her father's penis and have it inside of her. Her superego evokes guilt for this wish and extracts punishment. The pain she experiences both in her dream and in her symptoms reflects both of these aspects of the intrapsychic conflict, as well as regression, somatization, and a repressive response on the part of her ego. Lastly, the patient fantasies impregnation by the therapist in terms of a father transference. She also puts herself in her mother's place and expresses the unconscious fantasy that her doctor had been responsible for her death and that she is similiarly endangered in her therapy. Later material bore these formulations out in considerable detail.

I have attempted to give the reader a feeling of the complex, overdetermined nature of a symptom and to illustrate the factors delineated in the previous section. The role of context as the key to understanding the unconscious aspects of the material is now hopefully clearer as well.

Contexts may be repressed or even consciously concealed, and without such knowledge the material from a patient remains a hodgepodge lacking any central organizing theme. We then either recognize that we do not understand the material or fall into the error of interpreting aspects of the material in isolation. The latter will usually lead not to contextual, emotional insight but to empty intellectualizing. A second vignette is relevant:

Mrs. A.H. began this session by describing how her husband, a businessman, had been caught in a financial squeeze and had anxiously gone to the bank to raise additional funds. She was in a panic, even though it seemed evident that the loan would be forthcoming. She had diarrhea and dreamt on the previous night that her two sisters were discussing her mother, saying that she seldom did all that she had promised to others. She associated: her mother had been quite wealthy and could have provided the funds her husband needed. Her father now had the money and was difficult to deal with. She went on to recall some question of her mother's involvement with another man and the tubercular illness that she had had when the patient was an infant. Her sisters, who were considerably older than the patient, had taken care of her, but the patient wondered whether they had criticized her mother, who had been hospitalized briefly. They had tended to blame poor hygiene for her illness. The patient reviewed her adolescent years, during which her mother denied the impact of her absence; she thought her mother's attitude really rather absurd.

The session seems prompted by the husband's financial crisis and its intrapsychic repercussions for the patient: her longings for her mother, who could rescue her and her husband; her rage at her mother for her absence and possible unfaithfulness; and some implied concerns regarding her husband's ability to handle the business situation. There is little that is specific or revealing in regard to the unconscious fantasies evoking the gastrointestinal symptoms.

The session is of interest in light of the following hour. In that session the patient revealed that she had inadvertently not mentioned an incident which had occurred prior to the previous hour. One of her girlfriends had seen her husband having a drink with a young woman at a local restaurant. In this context the session described above had quite another focus and central meaning. In fact, the past had been used here to conceal the present; she had used her mother to screen feelings and fantasies regarding her husband. The most active and meaningful conflicts and unconscious fantasies actually related to her spouse. Associations in the second session were to fears of finding out that her husband was having an affair, her dread of confronting him, and her anxieties lest others would be talking about him. They revealed her rage, her wishes to publicly humiliate her husband, and her death wishes toward him. The sister in her dream had also been suspected of having had an affair. The bowel symptoms actually related to fantasies of defecating on and soiling her husband, in an uncontrolled release of aggression. In the correct context, the unconscious conflicts and fantasies became clear and specific.

I will crystallize some tentative but pertinent inferences drawn from these observations and the many others of which they are typical:

1. Specific communications of both a verbal and behavioral nature within a given session can be properly understood on all available levels—conscious and unconscious, past and present, and reality issues and intrapsychic conflict—only if the correct context is ascertained.
2. Context is defined as the central problem with which the patient is dealing—the primary adaptive task.
3. Context in regard to neurotic problems, as distinguished from those that are real, refers most often to some reality event (day residue) which evokes intrapsychic anxiety, conflict, conscious and unconscious fantasies, and efforts at resolution. More rarely, major intrapsychic reactions are evoked by biochemical, hormonal, and other inner changes.
4. Context is the key to the detection of unconscious fantasies, since it provides the crucial information regarding the nature of the intrapsychic conflict and the task with which the ego is confronted. It is therefore the major unconscious organizer of the material and provides the hidden focus of the associations.

5. As with any aspect of the total intrapsychic conflict, the context may be repressed and kept unconscious in a defensive effort at warding off anxiety. These defenses must be worked through. The context may then be directly revealed by the patient or may have to be detected from the latent content of the patient's associations. It is crucial to be aware of the lack of context at any given moment in treatment, and to seek it out or wait for it to emerge.
6. In assessing the patient's ego functioning, context is again a crucial factor. Only through such knowledge can we assess the exact defenses in use, the degree to which the intrapsychic and behavioral response is appropriate or a reflection of malfunctioning, and ascertain the cost to the total personality for a particular adaptive effort.
7. Ascertaining the correct context may change a disjointed, confused session into a readily intelligible one, full of latent meaning. Shifting contexts also play an important role in bringing new, previously repressed or unavailable fantasies and memories into the material on a manifest or latent level. Similarly, new contexts play a role in giving new meaning to familiar conscious fantasies and memories.

With the session, the basic model and sequence is, of course, material from the patient; understanding by the therapist of the manifest and latent content (unconscious fantasies) and the ego functioning reflected in this material; intervention by the therapist; and response by the patient—confirmation or failure to confirm. In this paper I will focus primarily on the first two of these steps: the material from the patient and its conceptualization by the therapist. This will necessitate the neglect of many related dimensions, particularly the role of the therapist's interventions, in determining the productions which come from patients. The problem is so broad, selectivity is inevitable.

THE SPECIFIC CONTENTS OF PSYCHOTHERAPY SESSIONS: NONVERBAL BEHAVIOR

I will begin the report of the specific results of this study with a source of data which, though at times crucial, can only with relative infrequency be used. I speak of the patient's nonverbal behavior within the session. This refers, for example, to rhythmic movements, playing with or pulling hair, biting or picking at fingernails, getting up from the chair, pacing, sitting away from the therapist, not looking at the therapist, and unusual forms of dress. It may also include silences and instances of acting in—disturbed behavior directed toward the therapist. As is true of any communication, such behavior, especially when deviant, expresses derivatives of conscious and primarily unconscious fantasies which are related to the neurosis.

In regard to the in-session behavior recorded in this study, there were two adolescent girls (Miss A.D. and Miss A.F.) who pulled at their hair and bit their nails in many of their sessions. On several occasions, mostly outside this period of study, these symptomatic behaviors were inquired into and explored. At no time did they produce, directly or indirectly, utilizable material (that is, either directly meaningful thoughts about the habit or subsequent associations, or shifts in the sequence of the material that illuminated the meaning of the behavior). All other patients in this study sat relatively comfortably throughout the session, and, though each had minor habits, little was made of them.

On one occasion Miss A.D. wore an outfit, a suit and tie, which strikingly resembled a man's clothing. In the context of her grandfather's death and hints in the verbal material that she had responded in part with a powerful unconscious identification with him and wishes to undo his loss, this apparel was referred to in the interpretation of these fantasies to the patient. While the clothing fit the rest of the material, its meaning was not specifically confirmed by her subsequent response and associations.

Miss A.F., who had eczema as a child and continued to suffer from excoriating rashes, would often scratch herself during these sessions. Questioning and listening revealed nothing meaningful in regard to this behavior during the period of this study. Sometime later, however, when she described a dream of being clawed at by a strange animal, and associated to fantasies of attacking someone or being attacked herself, the scratching in the session helped relate these fantasies to the transference.

In the main, then, behavior within sessions serves as indicators of conflict and fantasies and at times offers some hint of their latent content. These indicators are most often not productive when explored and do not often lead to meaningful associations or insights. Their relative insignificance is reflected in their virtual absence from my supervisory notes. They are best observed in silence by the therapist, and reference to them is best reserved for a time when other material readily relates to them; then they can be tied in. Although they provide important clues to the therapist, such habits, discussed and analyzed or not, are difficult to modify and usually are of little consequence, except for those which form major resistances and must therefore be dealt with until modified.

Thus, although all communications have a manifest and latent content, there are added factors which determine both the extent to which the latent content is detectable and the related empirical problem of the degree to which the material is interpretable in a manner useful and meaningful for the patient.

THE SPECIFIC CONTENTS OF PSYCHOTHERAPY SESSIONS: COMMUNICATIONS IN PATIENT VERABLIZATIONS

References to current events and behavior. I will begin my survey of the verbalizations of the patients within the sessions with a category that includes all references to current events and behavior on the part of the patient and others, unless it is related to acting out or acting in (which were treated as separate categories). This was, of course, a substantial part of the content of most of the sessions and was the single most frequent score (see above table).

A little over half the time, the content of these descriptions, understood in proper context, appeared to be meaningful either as surface indicators of emotional problems and ego dysfunctions or as reflectors of important latent, repressed unconscious fantasies. The content was one of the most important sources of the former and a moderately important source for the latter.

The patients varied in the extent to which such material was central in their sessions, but most spoke a good deal of such events. The exceptions were patients who spent considerable time, at certain junctures in their therapy, describing dreams and their associations to them and talking about their early childhood experiences.

The frequent use of this category of material to communicate unconscious fantasies should alert us to the need to listen carefully to descriptions of routine events for such derivatives, as well as for reflections of aspects of the patient's ego functioning. It warns us, too, to be wary of simpleminded listening to reality events and problems, without searching for latent meaning by considering both the broader context of the communication and the sequence of associations in which it is embedded. For six of the patients in this study, this type of communication was a major source of insight. This was particularly true of patients who were prone to shut off their inner fantasy life and dreams, and who preferred to focus on actions and behavior. One must, with such patients, tune in on the unconscious derivatives expressed in their descriptions of life events.

These findings provide an initial demonstration of the problem of manifest and latent content quite well. For some patients, descriptions of daily events are strongly immersed in reality and described in a manner, sequence, and context that reveals virtually no latent content. These patients defensively seal off their inner life and focus on real problems and conflicts without their intrapsychic repercussions. The derivatives of their repressed fantasies are well hidden. One must be particularly alert to detect latent implications in their material, and the interpretation of such content is quite difficult and usually meets with strong resistances. Other patients by contrast, communicate available latent content through many channels, including daily events. Derivatives of their repressed fantasies are readily detectable and interpretable, their availability shifting largely with momentary resistances and fluctuations. I will now illustrate the uses of this category of material.

Mrs. A.A. was upset when her therapist found it necessary to change her hour; the new time was inconvenient and was prompting feelings of vulnerability. In one session, in this context, she spoke at length of a tutor who had worked with her daughter and who had suddenly begun to miss appointments. Mrs. A.A. was angered by this unexpected inconsistency. This material, a displaced indicator of unresolved fantasies about her therapist's shift in the hour, served to provide clues as to the underlying unconscious fantasies.

Mrs. A.J.'s daughter had recently entered psychotherapy. In the context of describing her dread of her own fantasies and impulses, Mrs. A.J. spoke at length of her daughter's current problems, of her fears for her, and of a friend whose father had been placed in a state hospital. Her own anxiety and fears of going crazy were the main latent, unconscious content.

This depressed patient, for the first time in her life, had spent an evening with her husband that she had actually enjoyed immensely. There was no reactive guilt or depression, and in fact, for the first time, she had not found a reason to spoil the evening or to attack her husband. This was a significant indicator of major intrapsychic changes in this patient, who previously would spoil every pleasant interlude in her life.

The same patient described being at a party where she had seen two homosexuals who were quite open in their affection for each other. In context, this description reflected the patient's unconscious but emerging struggle with her own homosexual fantasies.

Acting out and symptomatic acts. There is, of course, a vast literature on acting out and considerable discussion of symptomatic acts. Here, I want to discuss the frequency with which these serve as indicators of problems and vehicles for the expression of unconscious fantasies, and the manner in which acting out often reflects some degree of ego impairment, though one must not forget the important role that trial through action plays for some patients. Briefly, I define acting out as any alloplastic living out of an intrapsychic conflict which involves an extended piece of behavior. Such behavior expresses unconscious fantasies and is usually detrimental to the patient and others. Symptomatic acts, on a continuum with acting out, are generally more circumscribed pieces of behavior, less consciously rationalized and more ego-alien than acting out, and usually, though not always, less harmful to the patient and others. For this study I treated acting out of transference fantasies and reactions to therapy separately.

In this group of patients, there were six instances of symptomatic acts and seventy-eight incidents of acting out (along with fifty-three incidents of acting out of transference reactions, with which this category merges). Such behavior constituted a rather frequent mode of expression. A population heavily weighted with borderline patients and adolescents would, of course, be prone to such behavioral expressions of problems and fantasies. Four of the six symptomatic acts revealed unconscious content related to neurotic symptoms; about half of the acting out served as indicators of problems, and another third yielded unconscious fantasies. Thus, acting out served as a prominent indicator of difficulties, particularly in regard to ego impairments, and was a less useful source of unconscious material. For only two patients in the study did acting out prove to be an important source of unconscious fantasies, and for one other it was a major indicator of difficulty. Overall, only these three patients showed significant tendencies to use this mode of expression recurrently in a readily meaningful manner. Of course, all behavior and communications have manifest and latent meaning. It is hopefully clear by now that I am dealing in this study with available and detectable derivatives of repressed fantasies.

In dealing with acting out, one must not only search out the unconscious meanings through an understanding of the context and content of the behavior, but must also address oneself to the impairments in controls, inability to delay, and difficulties in handling sexual and aggressive impulses. Acting out also often reflects major resistances to the uncovering work in therapy. I will illustrate briefly.

Mrs. A.A. had recently had a miscarriage; she decided not to attempt to get pregnant again. She spent the day with a friend who had recently given birth. In this context, she forgot to take her birth control pills. This proved to be a reflection of her unconscious wish for another child.

Mrs. A.B., in response to her father's hospitalization and the resultant uncovering in her therapy, began to recall a group of memories related to the birth of a sister when she was four, which had evoked sexual fantasies regarding her father that had later been repressed. At this point, she drove quite recklessly and received a ticket for speeding. This overdetermined act had many latent meanings. Briefly, it was, in part, an acting out of an attempt to disrupt therapy by creating a crisis and having her husband remove her from it. It was also an expression of her hope to injure herself and to evoke responses in her parents and husband which would include their anger, and yet enable her to create distance, especially between herself and her father, who had always been infuriated when his children took ill or were hurt. Her poor controls were also apparent. On a deeper level, the central unconscious fantasy which subsequently emerged was that she viewed the birth of her sister as a mutilating attack on her mother for which her father was held responsible (her mother had had a rather protracted postpartum illness and depression; the patient had also dreamt of a man chasing her with a pitchfork). Her own wish was to expose her father, to be attacked and impregnated by him, and to attack and mutilate him in return. Guilt over this wish evoked a need for punishment also reflected in her behavior.

Mr. A. E. had missed several days of work without calling after the first day, knowing quite well that his job would be in jeopardy and that being fired would create a hassle with his parents (he had been a chronic behavior problem and had lost several part-time jobs in the past). The context was the therapist's pending vacation, which the patient was experiencing in terms of his father's desertion of the family for about a year when Mr. A. E. was about two years of age. His parents had discovered his absence from work because of a telephone from his boss to his home, and they had fought bitterly with the patient, who then left home overnight. As might be expected in a case of acting out, the patient denied that he was at all affected by either his therapist's vacation or his father's past absence. Associations indicated that he was determined to prove his capabilities to survive without his therapist or parents, in the face of a panicky and homicidal response to their leaving (he had had a nightmare of going on a murderous rampage and was quite frightened of losing control). This complex sequence of acting out expresses rage and denial and hints at important unconscious fantasies. There is also an acting out of transference fantasies, since it is evoked partly by the therapist's vacation; it is directed against both of his parents, especially his father and his therapist.

Acting Out of Transference Fantasies and Reactions to Therapy; References to the Therapist and Treatment. This category includes both behavior and conscious fantasies. The acting out refers here to behavior that is primarily evoked by, and directed toward, the therapist and treatment. In addition, other references to therapy and the therapist were scored separately, forming a second group of items in this category (see above table).

This type of acting out includes absences, living out of transference and real reactions and fantasies related to the therapist, and attempts to disrupt treatment. It was not a major mode of communicating latent content and unconscious fantasies for any patient in this study; only two such scores were made. As an indicator of problems, three patients used acting out of responses to therapy and the therapist with some frequency; for the entire group, it was the third most frequently used means of communicating the presence of problems, though not their specific content. As you would expect, such behavior most often reflected serious resistances against therapy and reactions to pending vacations and terminations. When these scores are combined with those related to references to the therapist and treatment, this kind of material proved to be a major indicator of problems and resistance, but only moderately important as a conveyor of unconscious content.

Absences occurred with only three patients. (1) Mr. A. E. used absence three times to express his response to his therapist's pending vacation, indicating unconscious anger and the wish to desert him first, though not more specific unconscious fantasies. Previous material suggested that this behavior reflected his unresolved unconscious conflicts and fantasies regarding his father's absence in his childhood, including his rage at him, but exploration in the context of these absences did not produce new data. His tendency to act out and deny inner fantasies at such times was a recurrent pattern.

(2) Miss A. F., an adolescent, missed two sessions when ill with a flare-up of acute dermatitis and fever. While these episodes were indicators of problems with her parents and resistances to treatment, at this point (early in her therapy) associations revealed little of the specific latent meaning of these absences.

(3) Miss A. G., an adult, was consciously doubtful about treatment and strongly resistant. Her six absences (several due to illness) were a poorly controlled reflection and acting out of her wish to terminate; they were also used to express some displaced rage against her fiancé. Beyond this, however, the specific unconscious meanings of these missed sessions did not unfold at this time, despite the necessary focus on them. Much later in her therapy, through material related to other situations that this patient avoided, the depressive aspects of her absences became clearer (that is, as depressive feelings and fantasies mounted, she tended to withdraw into her bedroom and to totally isolate herself; beyond this, the unconscious meanings of these situations are still not clear).

References to the therapist and treatment were the fourth most frequently scored category. It must be remembered, however, that three patients were terminating their therapy. Actually, three others were considering termination, and many of the other scores related to pending vacations, to absences, and to thoughts of quitting. As such, they were, of course, frequent indicators of resistances, though they less often provided direct associational clues to their unconscious meaning (the context was more helpful in this regard). For only two patients was this category a particularly important contributor in regard to latent fantasies.

This is in keeping with my overall clinical experience. The focus of psychotherapy is usually on the life problems of the patient. The relationship with the therapist in its real and transference manifestations is hopefully set in a positive tone through a strong therapeutic alliance, providing a relatively silent background to the treatment. At times of vacations, termination, some unusual event related to therapy, major resistances, and countertransference problems, this relationship will tend to come more into focus. Beyond these, work with transference is usually confined to negative transference problems which impede treatment; a true transference neurosis generally does not appear during psychotherapy. One must, of course, be on the alert for such material and the resistances and unconscious fantasies it reflects. It is crucial to ascertain the context in which such communications appear, in order to correctly interpret and resolve the relevant unconscious transference fantasies and resistances. Such work may, of course, be vital to the continuation of therapy and, more rarely, to the resolution of the neurosis.

References to treatment also include, to some extent, all indications of rumination, avoidance, and flight from the material of the sessions. Rumination is a common defense-resistance and must be assessed for underlying content. Its low scores in this study reflect its nondescript usage by these patients, so that it provided few clues to the specific problems and unconscious fantasies at hand. If the context in which the rumination occurs, and the underlying meaning or the latent material it covers, are not discernable, the therapist will often confront the patient with the fact that he is ruminating, thereby referring to it as a general indicator of resistance. One hopes to enable the patient then to modify this defense and reveal both the underlying fantasies on which it is based and the material that it covers.

The results of the study, then, show that rumination or flight were common occurrences in these sessions. Although they serve always as general indicators of resistance, they seldom were specific enough to be scored as such in this study. Only rarely were they analyzable in terms of specific underlying fantasies. Clearly, they are major roadblocks, which merit direct confrontation in an effort to get the patient either to explore the underpinnings of his resistance or to get back to his central anxieties and conflicts. Some vignettes will illustrate:

A common indicator of resistances to treatment was acted out by Mrs. A.I., who came thirty minutes late to a session because she had become confused about the time of her hour. She was having thoughts of leaving treatment, and a dream she reported in the session readily revealed the unconscious fantasies that prompted this behavior and the discussion of her doubts about treatment. She dreamt that she was looking at her father's mutilated leg. The context related to Mrs. A.I.'s work in treatment with her mutilating responses to her father's nudity in her childhood, and her own feelings of bodily disfigurement. She had felt frightened and humiliated by this material, and sought to flee these revelations and their implications for her.

Mr. A.E., in response to an absence occasioned by his therapist's illness, came to his session rather inebriated. He had dreamed of a murderer stalking the streets, revealing the unconscious anxieties involved in this behavior. He was attempting to provoke his therapist, to keep his distance, and to prevent the emergence of unconscious fantasies and memories.

Miss A.F., a patient in the first months of her therapy, described, in what seems another response to an interruption caused by illness in the therapist, conversation with another patient in the therapist's waiting room. This is an indicator of transference fantasies and longings, but exploration produced no further workable associations and latent content. A month later, in the face of a pending midwinter vacation, she inadvertently tripped over her feet while entering the therapist's consultation room (a symptomatic act); again, nothing developed in her associations, though her hostility toward the therapist seemed clearly indicated. Lastly, in the session preceding this vacation there had been an intensification of her eczema. Associations related to fantasies of hemorrhaging and needing hospitalization, thereby exposing the therapist's failure to help her. She would make him suffer somehow. She had fantasies of being knifed in the hallway of her apartment building and imagined the blood pouring from her. This provided one of the first opportunities to interpret this patient's eczema as expressing the unconscious wish to be attacked and penetrated by, as well as to attack and bloody, the therapist—thereby gaining revenge for his leaving her. This also entailed both a punishment for her forbidden instinctual wishes and an effort to evoke guilt in the therapist for leaving her.

Mrs. A.A. illustrates a more infrequent type of transference fantasy for psychotherapy, one apparently not evoked by the therapist's behavior, but arising primarily out of inner need. As noted, she had been wishing for a child. Subsequent efforts to become pregnant had failed. She fantasied meeting the therapist at a restaurant, developed anxiety coming to her session, and wondered what happened between the therapist and his other woman patients. She asked her minister if he had any children. She was depressed and thought of suicide. Interpretation of her wish for a son from her therapist, based (from other material) on a father transference, was amply confirmed.

Slips of the Tongue. Slips of the tongue were quite rare in these sessions. Three were recorded, and each of these reflected unconscious fantasies. Several others were not recorded in the notes since they led nowhere, though they were indicators of some kind of disturbance. This reflects my general experience that these phenomena—while fascinating, sometimes useful to the therapist in understanding the patient, and interesting structurally as compromise formations (Yazmajian 1965)—are seldom useful in producing insight for the patient in psychotherapy and often may not be worth pursuing. A good rule of thumb is that slips to which the therapist can readily associate, which he can understand as to unconscious meaning, and which he feels will prove truly meaningful for the patient are worth exploring and interpreting; the others are best left alone and not brought into particular focus. If subsequent material clarifies the meaning of an unclear slip, it can be referred to when making an interpretation of the relevant material. Often, however, pursuit of slips of the tongue leads to intellectualization and speculation, which detracts from the main themes and problems of the session. To see how slips of the tongue can, however, reflect important unconscious fantasies, consider these examples:

Mrs. A.A., in the session just described (in which she discussed the therapist's relationship with his other patients and was struggling with unconscious fantasies of being given a child by him), spoke of going to her "therapist-uh-gynecologist" for a checkup. The slip alluded to fantasies of sexual contact with the therapist.

Mr. A.E., whose father had abandoned his family when the patient was a child, had been taking "downers" on and off from some time. He had attempted to abstain, but had a violent fight with his father over some seemingly trivial matter. In describing the battle, the patient spoke of wanting to "kiss-uh-kill" his father. His associations clarified the slip in terms of the patient's need to defend against murderous thoughts toward his father, the fear of losing him again, and underlying homosexually tinged longings for closeness.

Affects and neurotic symptoms. Affective disturbances and inappropriate affects are a type of symptom, and they are an important potential dimension of each session. Reported only moderately often by these patients, they served almost entirely as indicators. Most often, the references were to anxiety, rage, and depression. Patients tended to report consistently a specific single kind of affect during the period of study. Two patients often utilized reports of affect as indicators of problems; for the rest affect was an aspect of self-experience which either was seldom described or infrequently led to insight into unconscious material. Of course, reports of overwhelming panic or depression are crucial indicators and often reflect impaired or even collapsing ego functioning. These rare experiences serve as a reminder that even infrequently used indicators or vehicles of unconscious content may, in a given context, be the critical communication from the patient.

Other neurotic symptoms were rarely reported by these patients during the period of study. Mrs. A.A. experienced hysterical numbness of her legs, and Mrs. A.C., Mrs. A.H., Mrs. A.I., and Mrs. A.J. reported depressive symptoms. While these symptoms were all ultimately analyzed to some extent, during the period of the study they served almost entirely as indicators of regression or, through their diminution, of improvement. The understanding of the unconscious meaning of the symptom came, of course, from other sources.

I will illustrate briefly:

Mrs. A.A. reported anxiety and numbness in her right leg. The context was the birth of her friend's son and a visit to see the acquaintance. She fantasied that she was driving with this friend and that she was unable to brake the car so that they had an accident in which the friend was killed. She then thought of her brother, whose wife had recently had a child. The anxiety had been evoked by her unconscious rage at her sister-in-law for having given birth, and the death wishes this had evoked. The leg symptoms led back to her grandmother's stroke when the patient was a child, and ultimately to death wishes directed at her mother and punishment for them. (Further unconscious fantasies related to this overdetermined symptom will not be detailed here.)

Mrs. A.I., in exploring her bodily anxieties in her therapy, recalled her fear of closed spaces. She dreamt of a male cousin who stood in the corner of a small room; as she approached him, he darted out and cornered her. Over several sessions, she more and more clearly linked this cousin to her brother and recalled bathing with the latter as a child. She had thought of having an affair and had fantasies of being raped. Associations led to her father and to repressed derivatives of primal scene experiences. This overdetermined symptom related, at this time, to fantasies of being raped and mutilated; she had once imagined her mother to have suffered similarly at the hands of her father. The fear of closed spaces related to these rape and primal scene fantasies, and included the talion punishment for her incestuous fantasies. Fantasies of impregnation and the destruction of the fetus, based on her mother's response to being pregnant with the brother, were also involved.

Physical symptoms. References to fleeting physical symptoms were quite common and often not recorded in these notes; more critical physical symptoms were quite rare, except in the case of the eczema patient, and Mrs. A.H., who was prone to diarrhea and abdominal cramps. Although serving primarily as indicators during the period of the study, such symptoms must be analyzed for their latent, unconscious meaning with patients who tend to somatize. One must be alert to the context in which these symptoms appear, their timing, and the material in which they are embedded. Both the unconscious fantasies that determine these symptoms and the ego's tendency to express such fantasies somatically must be dealt with in such cases. I will confine myself to a brief vignette:

Mrs. A.H. had an episode of blood-tinged diarrhea (repeated medical checkups had not revealed significant pathology). Material over several sessions led to a dream of an underground explosion and fire. Associations were to the birth of her brother, and the explosion and fire were interpreted by her therapist as related to fantasies of being pregnant and getting rid of the fetus. This was verified when she recalled that she had had similar pain during her last pregnancy (a confirmation via a repressed, once-conscious experience). Her fear of these fantasies and her tendency to express them somatically was also noted.

Creative works of others. References to story lines from movies, television shows, books, persons in the patient's life, and even creations of the patient himself deserve separate mention. These references were another relatively rare form of expression; there were only twelve such reports in this study. But, when they are referred to, they almost always have been selected to express important repressed unconscious fantasies stirring within the patient. This was true with all the instances recorded here and is in keeping with my overall clinical experience. I will illustrate:

Miss A.F., who no longer lived at home, remained close enough to continually battle with her parents, whom she wished to destroy and who she felt wished to destroy her. She scratched intensely as she described provoking her parents in various ways. She had "killed" her chances for promotion on her job in order to hurt them. She had once had an acute attack of eczema after seeing a movie in which a girl was raped and stabbed. The mutually murderous dimensions of her own unconscious fantasies and her struggle with her parents were reflected in this precipitate. This was further elaborated when a movie, in which a young girl experienced a bloody abortion, prompted an acute episode of eczema.

Mr. A.E. had reported in a session before the period under study, a story of a child who was eventually killed after having been abandoned by his parents—a derivative of his fears of not surviving when his father left him as a child. This had led to his first actual recollections in therapy of his previously repressed childhood separation from his father. During the study period, he returned to therapy after his therapist's vacation and reported a dream, which, in part, was about a boy who falls safely from a tree. He had provoked his boss by not completing certain assignments, and complained that the boss kept bugging him. Associations linked this behavior to his father, who was, among other things, in a business related to gardening and tree maintenance. The dream reminded the patient of the story of Jack and the Beanstalk, which he had recently heard being read to his young nephew. As a reflection of this patient's unconscious sexual fantasies toward his mother in the absence of his father, and of his fear of punishment at his father's hands, this fairy tale served admirably as a derivative and expression.

Recent Memories. Memory material related to both recent and childhood events and fantasies were scored moderately frequently and both were major sources of unconscious fantasy content. Recent memories were also not uncommon as indicators of resistances and neurotic difficulties and, therefore, are an important source of meaningful data in sessions. For half of these patients, they indeed served as major reflectors of unconscious fantasies, and virtually every patient used this material to convey repressed fantasies at one time or another.

Often, recent recollections that contain important derivatives are repressed and emerge after the working through of resistances, or they appear after additional traumas heighten the conflicts related to the events recalled. Such remembering often serves to confirm an interpretation and to enhance insight through further, meaningful revelations. In addition to their utility for ascertaining unconscious fantasies, these memories reflect, and can be used to assess, the patient's recent levels of ego functioning. The following vignettes indicate how such material can reflect manifest and latent content, depending on the context in which they are embedded:

Mr. A.E. had been having rectal pain and delayed attending to it until he had developed insight into his fear, in the present, of being attacked by men, a fear traced out to his father, and until he had worked through part of his anxiety-provoking homosexual fantasies. The details of his rectal pain, his responses to it, and his thoughts about it, all confirmed aspects of this unconscious and unresolved conflict with his father.

Mrs. A.J. had a son who was recently divorced and having other apparent difficulties. She was deeply depressed and, after working through resistances to therapy, produced material indicating that she wished to restore her intense involvement with her son, which was a current version of an unresolved, ambivalent tie to her mother. Interpretations of this led to the recollection of many relatively recent experiences with her mother—such as the patient's obtaining a new job, which led to a battle between her husband and her mother—and of occasions when her mother had abandoned her. She also recalled a time when her mother stopped talking to her because she had dated a young man who was not of the patient's religion. The patient had been enraged and had wished that her mother would drop dead; similiar unconscious fantasies regarding her son prevailed.

Miss A.D., who had been denying any sense of loss or anxiety over termination, reported a dream in the last session of her therapy. In it, her sister returned from a trip abroad only to leave suddenly again; the patient is upset and looks for her. Associations led to her sister's trip and to the support she got from a friend with whom she traveled and could discuss her problems. The manifest dream in this context was directly interpreted to the patient as reflecting her upset over termination. She then reported a second dream, in which her mother was ill in the hospital. She wanted to visit her mother, and her fiancé left her because of it. Next, for the first time in treatment, she reported that her mother had actually been hospitalized when she was eight. She was vague about it. Her mother had bled vaginally and had had surgery, and only later had the patient learned that she had nearly died; the doctor had been blamed for the downhill course. She denied any feelings about these events. The unconscious equation between separation and death, the unresolved negative transference—the unconscious fantasy that the therapist had harmed her in some way—and her own unconscious anxieties about herself and termination were all reflected in these memories and dreams.

Early childhood memories. Recollections of early childhood experiences and, more rarely, childhood fantasies and dreams were an important source of unconscious fantasy content and occasionally served as indicators of problems. Every one of the fifty scores for this category had meaning; forty-five related to repressed fantasies. Two of the patients in this study, each just beginning her therapy, had no such references in their material, while one patient, by contrast, spoke of her early childhood in a good half of her sessions. The rest varied with from two to seven references to their childhood in the thirty sessions studied. Obviously, those who alluded to their childhood did so in a very meaningful manner. Recollections of early childhood material occurred primarily at significant periods of working through and insight.

In the example below, note how various types of material follow upon one another and build sequences through which expressions of the unconscious fantasies are conveyed, each element of the fantasy expressed in a different form of communication:

Mrs. A.A. was working through her wish for a child, which had been traced back to her longings for a child from her father and to her desire to give him the child that her mother had never given him after the mother had had a miscarriage. At this time she dreamt of being in bed with her uncle, who in the dream wants to have intercourse with her.

She suddenly feels guilty and leaves. It was clear to her that the manifest dream was one of renunciation and she felt it was an expression of some resolution (after considerable working through) of her incestuous longings. Association confirmed this and its basis, in part, in anger and disappointment in her father. She then remembered a previously repressed childhood memory of seeing her father in bed with her mother; there was every indication that they were having intercourse and the patient felt both frightened and stimulated by what she had seen. Working through this experience, and its current effects on her relationship with her husband, led to a series of sessions in which she related a dream in which her father and brother had been injured and were dying; she vented rage at both for past and present hurts. During this time the patient left her own bedroom door ajar and her children came into the room just as she and her husband were preparing to have relations. The patient next remembered a period in early childhood when she and her parents lived with her grandmother and shared a bedroom. She remembered a time when her mother had been sick in bed for several weeks and recalled seeing bloodied menstrual pads. She realized that this memory probably related to additional observations of parental intercourse and to fantasies that her father was damaging her mother. Her view of intercourse as a mutual attack unfolded, as did a long series of early childhood fantasies in which the patient is kidnapped, raped, and abused, and in which her rescuers are usually killed rather than helpful—all of this emerging from repression. There was a dream of eating an ice cream pop that led to fellatio fantasies and wishes to devour her husband's-father's penis. These guilt-ridden fantasies were related to punishment for her desires for, and against, her father, and led to a conscious fantasy (in the present) that she would develop gangrene of her leg. Working through this rich network of material at this crucial point in her treatment enabled this patient to resolve her anxiety and hysterical throat symptoms.

Conscious fantasies. These are not be confused with unconscious fantasies. The former are in awareness and the latter are not, though they may (and should) become conscious to some extent during treatment. This is, in fact, one goal of therapy. Conscious fantasies may, therefore, contain disguised derivatives of unconscious fantasies, though, as seen here, they are by no means the only such derivatives.

Conscious fantasies may serve as the starting point for the search for unconscious expressions and, actually, often do so in therapy. They are another kind of manifest content that can be either meaningful or defensive, depending on the context in which they appear and the structural balances which went into the creation of the fantasy. Thus, early in therapy, they are largely manifest screens, which are well disguised, though they reflect underlying fantasies which are themselves unconscious. Then, as the therapeutic work proceeds, the patient becomes aware of less disguised derivatives of these repressed fantasies. In this way, previously unconscious fantasies become conscious. The degree to which a given conscious fantasy reflects relatively disguised or relatively undisguised unconscious content can only be assessed through an understanding of the context of the material, the moment in therapy, a knowledge of what has been previously repressed, and an understanding of the patient's intrapsychic conflicts, symptoms, and genetics.

As for the data from this study, conscious fantasies were among the three most frequent types of communications from these patients. They were used only moderately often as indicators, although they proved to be the single largest source of latent, unconscious fantasy content. On the whole, such conscious fantasy material proved meaningful about two-thirds of the time.

In this group of patients, these fantasies—seldom exceeded by another source of data—served as a primary vehicle for communicating unconscious material for seven of the ten. The three exceptions were Miss A.D., who used dreams primarily for the expression of unconscious fantasies (both manifest dreams and their latent content reached through associations); Miss A.G., whose conscious fantasies were highly defensive and who revealed more of her unconscious thoughts through her behavior and her recent memories than through any other means; and Mr. A.C., who used his current behavior and acting out mainly to reflect his strongly guarded and rarely revealed unconscious fantasies, and with whom conscious fantasy material was highly repetitive and defensive. In regard to this last patient, later work with his defenses and resistances led to the emergence of considerable unconscious material, primarily through the vehicle of manifest dreams (and less so, because of some continuing degree of defensiveness, through the associations to them). This uncovered previously unreported, repressed fantasies.

I have already alluded to many conscious fantasies, particularly in the last vignette regarding Mrs. A.A. One additional example follows:

Mr. A.C. lived with a married sister and avoided leaving her house for any extended period of time. His manifest dreams seldom led to meaningful associations, but they hinted at frightening, incestuously tinged sexual impulses toward woman and homosexual fantasies toward men. As efforts were being made to define these fantasies by modifying the repressive barriers, so that he could bring them into consciousness, the patient began to report conscious fantasies that intruded into his awareness. These were prompted by his first efforts to vacation with a friend. They included a fantasy of having intercourse with his friend's sister and of his friend's brother playing with his penis. These fantasies for the first time gave specific content to the instrinctual drives which prompted his phobic stance.

Dreams—manifest content, associations, and latent content. My discussion of conscious fantasies is applicable to dreams. Dreams are, in a sense, conscious fantasies experienced in an altered state of consciousness and remembered in the waking state (Langs 1969). Failure to understand the implications of this fact has led to confusion in conceptualizaing the role of work with manifest dreams in psychotheapy (and also in psychoanalysis). Association to dreams, and the context in which the dream is experienced and reported, are also important in understanding the latent meaning of dream communications. Dreams can serve as indicators of problems and as reflectors of both unconscious fantasies and ego functioning.

Manifest dreams, then, are not unconscious fantasies. They are best viewed as a special kind of conscious fantasy. They must, therefore, be assessed and understood in their context and through the associations to them. But this does not mean that the associations to the manifest dream and their implications are, therefore, the only meaningful aspects of dream material.

This can be best clarifed by recognizing three levels of possible work with dreams. The first is with the manifest dream alone, devoid of context or associations. This level is usually studied in a research setting and is used appropriately there (Langs 1966, 1967, 1969). It is virtually never used clinically, however, though it may be resorted to, if context and associations are lacking, at a time when the manifest content of a dream indicates some inexplicable, but important and urgent, conflict or problem. For example, the unexpected and seemingly inexplicable appearance of suicide or murder in a manifest dream calls for inquiry and comment at any time, even if associations and context are lacking, though we virtually always should have related material from the patient on hand with which to work.

The second level of work with dreams is with the manifest dream within the specific context in which it is reported. Some patients, such as Mr. A.C. and Miss A.G. in this study, for long parts of their psychotherapy simply do not associate to their dreams or do so sparingly or with little enlightenment. Almost all patients do this at some time in their treatment. In such sessions one attempts to ascertain the crucial content of the dream through the context (often ascertained through the detection of the day residues of the dream, the reality events that precipitated it; see Langs 1971) and previous understanding of the patient. One can thus rightfully interpret the dream, if an unconscious fantasy has been revealed in this way. At times, the manifest dream in context directly reveals a previously repressed fantasy or memory, which can be pointed out to the patient without additional material. At other times, by using the context and day residues, the therapist can detect a latent fantasy expressed in disguised form in the manifest dream, which, of course, can also be interpreted to the patient. Further, manifest dreams in context (as is is true, also, of conscious fantasies and memories) are important reflectors of conscious and unconscious superego promptings and derivatives, and of various aspects of ego functioning, including object relationships and defensive operations. Dreams in context can therefore be used to work with many aspects of functioning and fantasizing. Let me emphasize, however, that one can justify interpretive utilization of the manifest dream in context alone only when every effort has been made to obtain all possible associations.

The third level of work with manifest dreams includes the associations to the dream and is directed toward an understanding of the dream work and associated latent content. These associations are of two kinds: direct and indirect. The former refers to the thoughts which come to the patient's mind as he thinks of the whole dream and of any of the elements of the dream. These, which may be quite revealing or quite defensive, are assessed in context and in light of the day residues. The latter, indirect associations, consist of all of the other material of the session, which is not directly derived from responses to the manifest dream. This material may provide clues to the context of the dream and the conflict with which it deals. On the other hand, this material may reflect strong defenses against the unconscious, latent content of the dream and a flight from it on all levels.

Associations to dream elements are among the most important avenues of unexpected insights in psychotherapy. Often they lead to latent content that could never have been anticipated by the therapist from the manifest dream alone or in context. Yet, more often, the associations are specific and essential elaborations of unconscious trends, to which the therapist has already been alerted from the manifest content of the dream in context, and which lead then to specific interpretations of the currently pertinent unconscious aspects of the material.

Thus, we can expect that manifest dreams with, and at times without, associations are important sources of insight into unconscious dimensions, major sources of confirmation of interpretations, and vital contributors of new threads and avenues in the work of treatment. The results of the present study bear this out. There were 102 dreams reported by these patients and meaningful associations to 91 of these. In all, they were a relatively frequent source of meaningful material and, while they served only occasionally as indicators of problems, they were a major source of unconscious content. This was equally true of manifest dreams per se, of manifest dreams understood in context, and of the latent content of these dreams as revealed through associations.

For half of these patients, both manifest and latent dream content served as a primary vehicle of unconscious fantasies. For all, at some time, these communications proved meaningful. For most of these patients, use of dreams corresponded to the report of conscious fantasies unrelated to dreams. As I have already illustrated, meaningful work with dreams also often led to the lifting of repressive barriers and to the emergence of previously unreported, early recollections and other significant unconscious material. Since I have illustrated work with dreams and their associations in my previous vignettes, I will add only a few examples here:

Mrs. A.J. dreamt of coming to her session without her bra. Termination was approaching and she had recently described her husband's sexual problems. She had no direct associations and the rest of the session was filled with trivia. We can be certain, in this context, that sexual fantasies were stirring in the transference. Later sessions revealed genetic aspects of the latent content of this dream; she had bathed with her brother well into childhood and had never worked out her sexualized attachment to him.

Mr. A.C. was anxious about taking a vacation with a boyfriend for the first time. In connection with his job, he also spent time at an attractive female cousin's apartment. He then dreamt of performing fellatio on a man with a huge penis. He went on to ruminate about his feelings of sexual inadequacy. Despite inquiries, there were no direct associations to the dream, nor did he relate the dream to those two events. Yet one could make the valid interpretation, from the context of the manifest dream and the sequence of the material, that the patient fled contact with women by turning to men homosexually in search of a seemingly indestructible phallus, and then in turn feared such wishes.

Mrs. A.I. dreamt that something was wrong with her leg; she had accidentally cut it off and had replaced it with a false limb. She reported the dream after discussing her displeasure with her body. The dream was prompted by her having been to the podiatrist for a problem with a bunion. She had also attended a friend's son's briss (circumcision) that day. She remembered having a friend whose foot had to be amputated after an automobile accident. She then thought of her small breasts, which she had had enlarged surgically, and her upset over early traumatic sexual experiences. She recalled seeing her parents having intercourse and her childhood fantasy that conception occurred when the man urinated in some special way into the woman's anus. She denied having seen her father's penis, but recalled childhood dreams of being chased by men with huge spears. She recalled having read that criminals used to be subjected to amputation. In the next session she spoke of having her nose fixed, of her menstrual period which had come that week, and of feeling damaged.

This is a complex network of manifest dream, associations, and latent content (Langs 1969, 1971). One can detect many unconscious fantasies in this material, all relevant to the patient's neurotic disturbances related to her body image. The early traumas that evoked some part of these disturbances are revealed, as are later consequences. The main unconscious fantasy seems to be her unconscious image of herself as a woman, damaged and punished because of her incestuous wishes for her father. She sees herself as a "castrated man" and fantasies reparation of her "lost penis" through surgery. In fact, she later further acted out these pursuits in a manner anticipated by the dream and her associations to it.

INDIVIDUAL DIFFERENCES IN STYLES OF COMMUNICATING

I will conclude my presentation with some brief comments regarding individual differences in how these patients communicated in their sessions. Each patient tended to have his own style of conveying unconscious material. Some patients, primarily defensive and resistant, revealed very little of their repressed, unconscious fantasies. This was particularly true of three patients in this brief study: Mr. A.C., Miss A.D., and Miss A.G. Two of them, Mr. A.C. and Miss A.G., communicated many indicators of problems, but little latent content; the other patient revealed the least of any subject on all levels. These same three patients also tended to report few conscious fantasies, and two of them described relatively few dreams. They all seemed to communicate more through reports of their behavior, current life events, and acting out.

Those patients whose material was richest in detectable unconscious content—Mrs. A.I., Mrs. A.H., Mrs. A.B., and Mrs. A.A., in that order—tended to report many dreams, along with their associations to them, and many conscious fantasies and childhood memories. They were more oriented toward their inner fantasy life and early childhood. Although one of them, Mrs. A.I., was also involved in a considerable amount of acting out related to treatment (because she was struggling against what was emerging in her therapy), these four patients, as a group, tended to score low on acting out of all types.

Most of the patients in this study, however, showed mixed styles of communicating, affected in part by consistent interpreting of acting out and other detrimental behavior. Thus, they would act out, then dream or report a conscious fantasy, and then shift to an early recollection as insight developed. An overall, long-term trend toward diminished acting out and increased communication of inner fantasies, dreams, and early memories tended to occur as treatment went on and resistances were analyzed. This occurred, in part, because the patient's controls were enhanced and his tolerance for anxiety and unconscious expressions was increased. In the main, however, a patient's style of communicating remained relatively stable over the four months studied here.

CONCLUSIONS

The present study has demonstrated that every aspect of the material from patients may serve as indicators of problems or resistances and as the vehicle through which specific unconscious fantasies emerge. It has also shown that all communications from patients have manifest and latent content. Some communications, which some patients tend to utilize almost exclusively, are defensively restricted to conscious, manifest content, through which little latent, unconscious content is detectable. Associations here are reality oriented, related to real conflicts and problems, and secondary processes predominate. Other communications, which other patients tend to utilize frequently, are rich in detectable, unconscious fantasy derivatives and latent content.

Material varied according to the patient's capacity to indicate problems and to express derivatives of repressed fantasies. The major sources of indicators of problems and resistances were: references to treatment and to the therapist, acting out of transference fantasies, the descriptions of the daily events of the patient's life, reports of acting-out behavior, and references to disturbances in affects.

The major sources of latent unconscious fantasy content, on the other hand, were: conscious fantasies, manifest dreams in context without significant associations, manifest dreams with associations that revealed the specific latent content of the dream, and the description of daily life events. Recent and childhood memories were important secondary sources of repressed fantasies.

The study also has revealed individual differences in style of communicating, in the specific kinds of material used to indicate problems and to convey unconscious fantasies, as well as the extent to which inner fantasy life was revealed at all.

It is hoped that this lengthy presentation, with its illustrations of technique, the use of context, and the ascertaining of unconscious fantasy material, will prove illuminating and clinically useful. Hopefully, too, it will lead to both improved clinical work and further research, ultimately contributing to the enhancement of the technique of psychoanalytically oriented, insight psychotherapy.

REFERENCES

Arlow, J. (1963). Conflict, regression, and symptom formation. *International Journal of Psycho-Analysis*, 44:12–22.

———— (1969). Unconscious fantasy and disturbances of conscious experience. *Psychoanalytic Quarterly,* 38:1–27.

Freud, S. (1926). Inhibitions, symptoms, and anxiety. *Standard Edition* 20:77–175.

Greenson, R. (1970). The exceptional position of the dream in psychoanalytic practice. *Psychoanalytic Quarterly* 39:519–549.

Langs, R. (1966). Manifest dreams from three clinical groups. *Archives of General Psychiatry* 14:634–643.

———— (1967). Manifest dreams in adolescents: a controlled pilot study. *Journal of Nervous and Mental Diseases* 145:43–52.

———— (1969). Discussion of: dream content in psychopathologic states. In *Dream Psychology and the New Biology of Dreaming,* ed. M. Kramer, pp. 397–403. Springfield, Ill. Charles C Thomas.

———— (1971). Day residues, recall residues, and dreams: reality and the psyche. *Journal of the American Psychoanalytic Association* 19:499–523. [Chapter 2, this volume]

Schur, M. (1953). The ego in anxiety. In *Drives, Affects, Behavior,* ed. R. Loewenstein, pp. 67–103. New York: International Universities Press.

Waldhorn, H. (1967). Reporter, Indications for psychoanalysis: the place of the dream in clinical psychoanalysis. The Kris Study Group of the New York Psychoanalytic Institute, Monograph II, ed. E. Joseph, New York: International Universities Press.

Wallerstein, R. (1969). Psychoanalysis and psychotherapy. (The relationship of psychoanalysis to psychotherapy: current issues.) *International Journal of Psycho-Analysis* 50:117–126.

Yazmajian, R. (1965). Slips of the tongue. *Psychoanalytic Quarterly* 34: 413–419.

Chapter Four

The Patient's View of the Therapist: Reality or Fantasy?

(1973)

Recent studies of the patient-therapist and patient-analyst relationship have made it clear that there are significant dimensions to it that go beyond the transference responses of the patient to the therapist (Greenson 1965, 1967, 1971, 1972, Greenson and Wexler 1969, and Langs 1973, 1974, 1975a). The present paper will focus on one issue raised by these discussions, namely, the extent to which the patient's conscious and unconscious perceptions of, and reactions to, the therapist are based on his intrapsychic fantasies and memories, and the extent to which they are based on realistic and essentially accurate perceptions. The importance of this distinction for the technique of psychotherapy and psychoanalysis will also be considered.

Searles (1965), in his various studies of the patient-therapist relationship during the analysis of schizophrenics, has explored the issue of the veracity of the patient's conscious and unconscious perceptions of the analyst, noting the frequent kernel of truth in these impressions. In a series of recent papers, Greenson has addressed himself to the nontransference dimensions of the patient-analyst dyad. He noted the importance of the relatively rational working alliance between these two persons, a partnership that is realistically directed toward the resolution of the patient's emotional problems and symptoms (Greenson 1965) and then, in part with Wexler, ventrued into a study of other nontransference interactions between patient and analyst (Greenson 1967, 1971, 1972, Greenson and Wexler 1969). He discussed those situations in analysis where the patient correctly and largely consciously perceives his analyst's interfering character traits, human failings, and errors, and suggested that such realities must be recognized and acknowledged, along with the analysis of their intrapsychic repercussions. In recent publications of my own (1973, 1974, 1975a), I have extended these principles and focused on their relevance to the technique of psychotherapy, and studied in particular those technical errors of which the therapist—and patient—are initially unaware. The means by which these deviations by the therapist can be detected in the latent content of the material from the patient, based on his unconscious perceptions of the therapist, were also described and discussed.

In the present paper, I will develop the implications of these studies that direct us to constantly monitor and assess the associations from the patient for conscious, and especially unconscious, fantasies about and perceptions of the therapist, and to carefully determine their sources in reality and fantasy, past and present. Correct formulations and interventions can evolve only after such an assessment has been made.

CLINICAL MATERIAL

Mrs. A. initially entered family therapy with her husband and two children, but found her therapist inconsistent, seemingly overinterested in the fee, and not helpful. She then sought similiar treatment with a second therapist—a male—who asked her in their first telephone conversation to consult with him alone; he then arranged one-to-one weekly therapy for her. She had a moderate character disorder with phobic and obsessional features. In her initial session, to which she was late, she used a diary to detail her family problems, though she spontaneously reported her own symptoms of fears of death, of heights, of closed spaces, of trains, and of losing control and behaving impulsively.

In her third session, after confrontation with several resistances, she spoke of a dream described to her by her brother-in-law, in which he came upon an intruder who reminded him of his father and recalled his death. When her avoidance of her own inner life was noted, she recalled dreaming that she was on a plush train which reminded her of the inside of a coffin. She was wearing a huge ring on her finger and her son was with her. The train was speeding along recklessly, in and out of tunnels. She turned to her son and said that she did not know why the train had not crashed; he replied that they had already been dead for some time.

Her associations revolved around an out-of-town wedding that she refused to attend without her husband, since it involved a journey by train. The therapist commented that there also seemed to be allusions to her fear of therapy—which is a kind of trip—especially without her husband present. Mrs. A. agreed as her session ended.

In her next hour, she said that she felt her therapist saw her as meek and that she is not. At work, she had been unfairly put down by one of her bosses; only later did she set her—that is, him—straight. When asked what her slip brought to mind, she said that her therapist seemed to believe that she was hostile toward men. It could be true, but she doubted it; she loved her son and husband. She again spoke of how often she felt criticized at work, and the therapist said that she felt similarly put down by him. Mrs. A. replied that she had not thought of it, but it was true. Her father was always critical of her in her childhood; nothing she did was ever good enough for him. She was often uncomfortable with strange men.

She had not spoken of sex as yet, she noted, and she went on to say that she had mixed feelings about her sexual relationship with her husband. Only once had she reached orgasm, and as a rule she was quite tense and afraid that one of her children would come into their bedroom during relations. Something embarrassed her: sometimes when she was with a man she would have fantasies in which she imagined his penis and had the impulse to touch it. She also occasionally had fantasies of affairs, but had always been faithful to her husband. She thought of some of the dishonest things that her husband had done, and stated that she herself was always honest.

Briefly, after a session of resistances, she began the hour after that by describing her former dentist, who had been overtly seductive. She had dreamt of being in the house in which she grew up as a child. She is with a girlfriend when a man suddenly appears and begins to expose himself to them, threatening to attack and rape the patient. She yells to her friend to escape. Associations were to acute attacks of abdominal cramps that she had as a child when upset with her parents. Her mother was often aloof and selfish, but her father would try to mediate their disputes. She had forgotten what the therapist's fee was. Her girlfriend had told her of a friend who had been seduced by a dentist. The girlfriend in her dream was someone she had admired; the patient had read a book about homosexuality. The therapist pointed out that the dream and the references to the dentist suggested some underlying fears of therapy. Mrs. A. said that she feared being judged and criticized; her family therapist had once said that she was dumb.

Very briefly, in the next hour she reported a lengthy dream of being in her old house and seeing her father leave her son's bedroom. As he goes off, he doubles over with abdominal pain, but then is all right. Her daughter leaves and one of a pair of twin Siamese cats goes with her. The other cat runs off and is attacked mercilessly by a huge cat, though he—or she—is not killed. Associations were to a recent illness suffered by her father, her ill-defined fears of being attacked, her father's warnings about the dangers of strange men, her claim that she had never had any sexual thoughts about her father, and her feelings that her husband was weak at times, unlike her brother, who was strong and helpful.

I selected this material from Mrs. A. as a starting point for my discussion because she was in treatment with a sensitive therapist, and had just begun her therapy so that his influence was at a minimum; she also tended to produce derivatives that clearly related to her unconscious fantasies about and perceptions of her therapist. If we focus on the problem of distinguishing the nature of her therapist-related images, what can we ascertain? I would note the following:

1. We may succinctly define primarily transference material as those associations which largely reflect displacements onto the therapist from childhood relationships and experiences; secondarily, this may include projections of the patient's own fantasies (Kernberg 1968) and displacements from more recent relationships (Greenson 1967, Langs 1973, 1974).

In monitoring this vignette for primarily transference manifestations, we are immediately impressed by the patient's initial fears of the therapist, and her wish for an additional companion and protector.

Her manifest dreams in the adaptive context of the beginning of her therapy (Langs 1973, 1974), and her associations to them, reflect increasingly less disguised derivatives of sadomasochistic, erotic transference fantasies of being seduced, attacked, or raped by her therapist, fantasies that were interpreted upward to her (Loewenstein 1957) and in terms of their resistance aspects (Langs 1973, 1974). Their roots in Mrs. A.'s earlier relationships with her brother and father are suggested from her associations, although specific memories are not included. There is also evidence of the projection by Mrs. A. of her own erotic fantasies and impulses onto the therapist (it is actually she who is exposing herself on some level to the therapist) and of displacements from her previous therapist onto her present one. This latter is also one dimension of her pre-formed transference expectations (Langs 1973, 1974).

2. Can we be confident that these are essentially transference fantasies, conscious and unconscious, and that no important perceptions of the therapist are involved? To answer this, I would note the following.

After a detailed assessment of the therapist's subjective awareness revealed no aberrant fantasies, and scrutiny of the patient's associations vis-à-vis the therapist's interventions did not point to errors of which he was not aware (Langs 1973, 1974, 1975a), it seems safe to state that there is no gross or subtle basis in the therapist's behavior for believing that the patient's images of him as seductive are essentially founded on communications from him. While his concern and warmth might be misperceived in such a way by the patient, it is important to be clear that he has not, as far as we can ascertain, behaved inappropriately to his role as a psychiatrist; in this sense, he had not evoked these fantasies in Mrs. A.

These primarily transference fantasies are not, however, without their reality precipitants (Langs 1974). Among these more neutral day residues, many of which are inevitable and part of the therapeutic milieu that is designated to promote expressions of the patient's inner life, are the beginning of the therapy itself, the intimate isolation of the patient and therapist in the sessions, and the therapist's "analytic" stance—along with the fantasies and memories that they stirred up for Mrs. A. In addition, her recent experiences with her internist contributed to her reactions to her present therapist. In all, however, her own past experiences, memories, intrapsychic conflicts, conscious and unconscious fantasies, character structure, drives, and defenses, were the primary contributors to her initial reactions to the therapist.

3. To identify a fantasy about, or reaction to, the therapist as primarily transference, we must be able to identify "neutral" precipitants, whether evoked by the therapist or not. In addition, we must be able to refute with certainty any appropriate level of truth to the patient's unconscious or conscious claim that she correctly perceives the therapist in the manner spelled out through her associations.

4. Two of Mrs. A.'s images of the therapist that do not relate to his being seductive toward her lent themselves to a different assessment regarding the mixture of fantasy and reality.

(a) Mrs. A.'s associations, which reflect an unconscious image of the therapist as critical, are based on his actual confrontations with her resistances, in which he mainly pointed out to her that she did many things without reflecting upon them, and that she took flight from her inner thoughts and feelings by embedding herself in outside realities. These insight-directed interventions were experienced by her as criticisms. A review of these remarks showed no apparent hostility, though they did imply benign criticism of a kind necessary in many "neutral" interventions. With this as the reality precipitant, Mrs. A.'s perception of, and fantasies about, the therapist were strongly influenced by her father's unreasonably critical attitude toward her in her childhood—the transference aspect.

The recognition of the reality precipitant and a full evaluation of its meanings—explicit and implicit—on all levels is essential in differentiating reality perception from fantasy in Mrs. A.'s unconscious reactions to the therapist. Should he have decided to intervene in more detail regarding her feeling criticized by him, he would have had to define the distortions involved in her perception of his comments (the adaptive context) and pointed out that her view of him was greatly influenced by her relationship with her father, thereby analyzing a fragment of the transference. To be correct, the therapist's intervention when he has actually been inadvertently and unnecessarily critical would be quite different, in that he would acknowledge the insensitivity, and analyze the patient's reactions from there.

(b) Not all unconscious perceptions of the therapist are negative or related to his errors and failings. Thus, the allusion to Mrs. A.'s wish for a stronger man, made at the end of the last session presented above, reflects her unconscious recognition—in reality—of the therapist's strength in intervening in a helpful manner. Such veridical perceptions are nonetheless influenced by unconscious fantasies and memories, and elaborated upon accordingly. There is, of course, no need technically to point out such a positively toned perception to the patient; to do so would be self-aggrandizing, seductive, and interfering.

With this first vignette, then, I have traced out several unconscious images of the therapist that were latent in Mrs. A.'s associations. The first task was to discover their precipitants in reality, especially in regard to the therapist's behavior, correct or incorrect. In this way we could then determine to what extent the image was primarily accurate and only secondarily influenced by the patient's intrapsychic set— fantasies and memories—and to what extent it was not in keeping with the actual nature of the reality precipitant and therefore primarily a reflection of the patient's intrapsychic fantasies—transference. Only when clear distortions of the day residue, which is assessed in depth for its unconscious meanings, are in evidence can the therapist correctly interpret the patient's associations as primarily reflecting transference fantasies. Under these circumstances, such interventions, when properly timed and stated, are usually strongly confirmed by the patient, and lead to insight, inner change, and a strengthening of the therapeutic alliance (Langs 1973). As we shall see, patients are unconsciously in tune with the validity of the therapist's interventions and will react in a variety of ways when he is in error regarding the reality of the patient's communications about him (Langs 1973, 1974, 1975a).

Now let us turn to the less frequently studied situation where the therapist's difficulties contribute significantly to the patient's image of him; the matter of the patient's correct unconscious perception of the therapist becomes crucial and must be recognized when the latter intervenes (Langs 1973, 1974, 1975a).

Miss B. was a college student in therapy twice weekly because she could not get herself organized and tended to have difficulties in her social relationships; she had a moderate, mixed character disorder. She had been in treatment for about six months when at Christmas time she offered a gift of a water color to her therapist. Exploration of the offer, which was refused, occupied several sessions during which the patient, in turn, refused to accept the sketch back. Her associations revealed that it represented an expression of inappropriate sexual longings for union with the therapist, revealed primarily through the report of an expression of love from a girlfriend who had offered a gift to the patient, to which Miss B. had reacted with anxiety and uncertainty. The patient eventually accepted the gift back, and her associations indicated a great sense of relief regarding the therapist's integrity.

In the next two weeks the patient reported making new and constructive relationships, including a new boyfriend who was not a destructive person, as her previous boyfriends had been. As this unfolded, there were very few derivatives of unconscious fantasies and intrapsychic conflicts in her sessions. She mentioned that she was not having relations with her new boyfriend because of some gynecological problems; she had visited the gynecologist with her mother at the latter's insistence.

In the first of two sessons to be condensed here, the patient began by saying that she had very little to say. Her college graduation was on her mind (it was to occur that June at the same time as the termination, set at a year by clinic policy, of her psychotherapy). Her mother's overinvolvement with her medical problems was discussed, and she ruminated about how she tried not to hurt her mother. Her present boyfriend was of a different religion from herself and she was afraid to tell her parents. She got along with him better because there was no sex and a lot of hassles were avoided. She had been rapping with a group of her girlfriends and discussing her problems with them, but holding back on anything important. The therapist said that this kind of withholding was also going on in treatment, referring particularly to her references to going to the gynecologist, which she had kept quite vague. The patient acknowledged her indefiniteness and described a vaginal and bladder infection, remarking that she was generally uncomfortable discussing things of this kind in her sessions. The therapist asked her how she felt about it and she said that she was glad to have the infection so that she could avoid arguments about sex with her boyfriend. She then recalled a dream about her beau in which she was lying with him on the grass and hugging him, but they were not having relations; in it, she felt distant. The therapist asked if there was more to the dream and then asked what had precipitated it. The patient said that she had called her boyfriend, and went on to describe how she tended to be a very physical person with both men and women. She had often wondered what it would be like to have sex with another woman and she was frightened of these feelings.

In the next hour, the patient said that she felt well. She was getting along nicely with her boyfriend, but a married man at work was flattering her and behaving very seductively. She had spent the day with her boyfriend and there was no sex; it had been very gratifying. Her parents had been bothering her and she was trying to avoid them. She had called the girlfriend who had referred her for her psychotherapy and planned to see her. The married man at work undoubtedly wanted a relationship with her, and just being able to tell the therapist about it made her feel that the burden was off her.

The therapist asked if there was anything specific that she felt relief about and, when the patient said no, he went on to allude to the fact that Miss B. had mentioned in the previous session that she had sexual feelings toward women. In response, the patient described a discussion with a girlfriend about these feelings, and added that she had talked to the married fellow at work about the same kind of thoughts. She felt that this was not where her problems were and that she had other sexual problems that were more important. For example, she likes being close to her father, but he gets very physical and hugs her, and then she pushes him away. She had once been involved in a drug addict treatment center, and a young man came in so badly messed up that she impulsively kissed him. She thought that she was crazy to do it. She realized that she had been having sexual feelings toward the married man who was coming on so strongly toward her. He had commented that she had better watch out when she was alone with him. When she talked to the therapist, he also looked at her in a strange and sexual way; this reminded her of her sexual feelings toward that married man. There was an older woman at work who seemed to have problems similar to that of the patient; she guessed that they fitted together. The therapist told the patient that the hour was up and she suddenly remembered that she was planning to miss the next two sessions.

Miss B.'s main unconscious images of her therapist, as revealed in the latent content of her associations, are that he is being seductive and that he shares with her some type of sexual difficulty. Links to her father are apparent, but can we consider this to be transference in the usual sense—a distortion of the present relationship with the therapist based on the past relationship with her father? Has this therapist been therapeutically neutral and nonseductive, or is there evidence that he has been unduly curious regarding the patient's sexuality at a time when other matters appear to be more pertinent? To answer these critical questions, let us formulate this material.

In following this patient in supervision, the main theme initially seemed to be early, distant derivatives of the patient's intrapsychic conflicts regarding the anticipation of termination of her psychotherapy that coming June. It is not uncommon for patients in clinics, who know that they will be faced with a forced termination, to begin to develop their fantasies about it with the turn of the new year, much as this patient was doing (Langs 1973, 1974). This might also account for her gift to the therapist and some of her defensiveness in the subsequent sessions.

However, rather than allow these derivatives to develop or the patient's associations to cluster around some other central theme or adaptive context, the therapist inquired into her sexual difficulties. While there were undoubtedly potential or actual intrapsychic conflicts related to them, there were very few indications that the patient was currently preoccupied with this theme or ready to explore it in her therapy. Her associations after describing her gynecological problem suggest that the patient felt bothered by the therapist for bringing it up. Her reference to herself as being physically inclined may well have been a response to an unconsciously perceived seductiveness in the therapist, and the references to homosexuality could very well have been a defensive flight from the erotized transference that had been evoked by the therapist's inquiry. Certainly we must recognize that this patient was quite sensitive to the therapist's questions and was being defensive regarding sexuality as well. Previous sessions had indicated that she was prone to develop erotic responses to the therapist; this was based genetically on earlier experiences with, and reactions to, her father and their consequent intrapsychic repercussions. Thus, any hint of inappropriate sexual curiosity and seductiveness on the therapist's part would be expected readily to evoke this type of reaction in her. Despite this, some version of similar fantasies is not uncommon in such circumstances in most patients.

The theme of being seduced by an older man, an apparent displacement from the therapist, developed early in the following session. At the same time, Miss B.'s concern about the termination of her therapy seems to be reflected in her searching out the girlfriend who had referred her to treatment, and her interest in the married man could have reflected her search for a replacement for the therapist. Again, long before any central theme seems to have jelled, the therapist introduced the patient's reference to homosexual feelings. While it proved to be true that the patient had been concerned with these feelings, she soon denied that this was her central problem and unconsciously corrected the therapist by pointing to her incestuous problem with her seductive father. While this may have been partially defensive, it seems likely that the therapist's continued hasty interest in the patient's sexual feelings and fantasies had evoked a somewhat justified unconscious identification between himself and the patient's seductive father. The unconscious, accurate perception that the therapist was being seductive stirred up past memories, fantasies, and conflicts from her relationship with her father, and evoked defensive efforts at pushing him away.

While these connections to the therapist were being formulated in supervision and still seemed somewhat speculative, the final set of associations from the patient made her disguised reference to the therapist unmistakable. Thus, the patient utilized a model of therapy in which physical contact—a kiss—was the mode of cure, and then directly stated to the therapist that she felt that he looked at her sexually. Miss B. ended that hour by telling her therapist that she would be missing two sessions; this was done in a way that reflected its use as a massive defensive flight from the therapist. This is a not uncommon outcome when technical errors of the therapist are unconsciously perceived by the patient and are not recognized and analyzed by the therapist (Langs 1973, 1974).

While projection of the patient's own sexual fantasies regarding the therapist was undoubtedly involved in her perception of him, it appeared to me in supervision, even before the patient unconsciously indicated her perception of it, that this therapist was actually being overcurious about the patient's sexual problems, disregarding her other difficulties.

Thus, an assessment of the therapist's interventions suggests an actual undue interest in the patient's sexual material, something that the patient is justified in perceiving as seductive. Primarily, then, this is an unconscious perception rather than a fantasy, though the fantasied elaborations of this veridical view of the therapist, as well as its projective elements and links to past figures, lie entirely within the patient.

Technically, in intervening here regarding Miss B.'s erotic reactions to her therapist, one would be incorrect in describing them as basically unprovoked fantasies, thereby denying the therapist's contribution to them and the reality of his behavior. Such a stance essentially denies the interaction involved, holds the patient irrationally responsible for her fantasies, denies their adaptive aspects, and denies the grain of truth (Freud 1937, Niederland 1959) in the patient's imagery. The negative consequences of such an attitude are extensive and undermine the therapeutic alliance and atmosphere (see below and Langs 1973, 1974, 1975a).

On the other hand, were the therapist to acknowledge his inadvertent curiosity about Miss B.'s sexual problem—without adding more as to its basis within himself—and then proceed to interpret her erotic response to it as reflected in her attraction to the married man, her fear of losing control of her sexual impulses, her fear of the therapist losing control, and her defensive flight to homosexual fantasies, he would have done a relatively accurate and complete interpretive job. Such an intervention correctly identifies the adaptive context or precipitant that evoked Miss B.'s reactions (Langs 1973) and, from there, defines the intrapsychic conflicts and fantasies stirred up within her, as well as her means of adapting to them.

Note too the important difference between relatively unprovoked erotic fantasies toward the therapist which are based primarily on experiences with, and fantasies about, her father, and strongly provoked erotic fantasies based on behavior by the therapist that actually resembles the father's seductiveness. In the former, distortions and intrapsychic fantasies predominate and disturb adaptive functioning. In the latter, accurate perception and similarity prevail, and this may initially prompt reality-attuned adaptive responsiveness, though it often is ultimately more disruptive than the first situation. Thus, distancing oneself from a seductive therapist is adaptive, and such a defense can be correctly understood only if the stimulus for it is known. However, most often the discovery of actual similarities between a seductive father and a trusted therapist leads to regression, symptoms, and a break in the therapeutic alliance. In fact, as I have shown elsewhere (Langs 1973, 1974, 1975a), when regressions occur in therapy, one prime consideration is the patient's unconscious perception of, and reactions to, the therapist's errors. Let us consider another brief vignette:

Mrs. C. was a social worker who had been in twice-weekly psychotherapy for about seven months when she became preoccupied with the termination of her treatment, some four months ahead. In this context, the patient had acted out and had an impetuous affair, after which she had felt degraded and depressed. In the sessions in which this behavior was reported, there were further associations to the therapist's ending treatment and to the patient's deep sense of loss, rage, and need for repair. Despite abundant derivatives, the therapist had not interpreted any aspect of the patient's acting out; instead, he presented—as he had often done previously—confrontations to the patient which sounded critical and seemed irrelevant to her main conflicts.

In the following hour, the patient again brought up the end of her therapy and then went on to speak about a nurse on the ward where the patient worked. She hated this nurse because she never checked up on her patients' acting out and tended to be critical at other times. She never told this nurse any of her feelings because she was afraid of her retaliation and of the possible effects it might have on the patients they shared. She saw the nurse as a superficial person who never heard what her patients communicated to her, and who insisted instead on saying what she herself had on her mind. The patient's mother was like that and she resented her for it. The therapist connected this with the patient's resentment of her mother with whom she lived, and who kept the television in her bedroom so that family members who wanted to watch it had to go into her room—a problem that had come up in an earlier session. The patient said that she felt strange lying in her mother's bed and that she had also felt odd while sitting on her girlfriend's bed. She had discussed her father, who was detached and demanding, with this girlfriend. She had also discussed her sessions with her friend, and told her that she was afraid of the therapist and afraid that he might not like her or might suddenly reject or leave her. Somehow, Mrs. C. felt depressed that nothing she did had helped her patients.

In the next hour, the patient reported that she had dreamt that all her Librium tablets had dissolved and that she felt strange about it. She spoke of how she had not taken medication for a long time, but went on to say that she was now thinking of resuming. She wondered if treatment was helping her and whether she should continue with it, and went on again to talk about the ways in which her father had never given her anything. Fantasies of her parents' deaths were described, especially a daydream in which she saw her father get out of his car and be hit by another vehicle.

In this brief vignette, the patient's associations cluster latently around insensitive, nongiving, self-centered persons—including herself—who fail to meet the needs of others. The allusion to herself as a displacement from, and disguised representation of, the therapist is a not uncommon means of conveying unconscious fantasies about the therapist. Genetic links to both of the patient's parents are included, and the therapist dealt with the material in terms of Mrs. C.'s conflicts with her mother.

An assessment of the actual clinical situation, however, indicates that the therapist was being accurately though unconsciously perceived by this patient, and that his behavior was, in reality, reminiscent of her parents. These images are therefore accurate, with elaborations based on past experiences and inner fantasies; they are not primarily transference distortions. The patient's unconscious perception of the therapist as someone who spoke repeatedly with superficial and insistent critical comments that were largely idiosyncratic, rather than derived from the material from the patient herself, was a very apt commentary, and one that had been made repeatedly to him in supervision.

In this context, we can understand why the therapist's intervention regarding the patient's conflicts with her mother was not confirmed and did not alleviate the mounting negative feelings in the patient toward her therapy and therapist.

Of note here is the revelation of some of the unconscious motives and fantasies that prompt patients almost always to maintain their negative perceptions of the therapist on an unconscious level, rather than making conscious allusion to them (Langs 1975a). Mrs. C. alluded to intense fears of harm and retaliation; such fears are especially strong and even realistic in patients who unconsciously recognize their therapist's ongoing insensitivities and errors. Modification of such perceptions of the therapist is feasible only if he correctly identifies their source, alters his own behavior, and analyzes the patient's reactions in these contexts.

I shall conclude the clinical presentation with a condensed vignette. Mrs. D. was a social worker who was in twice-weekly psychotherapy because of a faltering marriage, depression, and episodes of anxiety.

She had been in treatment for about six months when she missed two sessions because of illness. In the session upon her return, she ruminated about her sickness and wondered if it was related to the Easter holiday, which was also the anniversary of her father's death. She spoke again about his fatal illness and then recalled her own tendencies to develop physical symptoms when she was in grade school; several obsessional fears of losing her notebooks had developed at that time. She also spoke of her repulsion when she saw people who were severely injured physically. She herself had a scar on her face which made her self-conscious and which she tried to hide with her hair; the injury had occurred when she was four years old and had accidentally run into a door while being chased by her sister. At the end of the hour, the therapist escorted Mrs. D. to the door and she suddenly started to fall. The therapist supported her by the arm and assisted her back to her chair. The patient said that her leg had fallen asleep, and she sat until she recovered sensation in the leg and then left.

She began the next session by saying that she was puzzled by having fallen during the previous hour; she related it to the themes of illness that she had been discussing and reviewed them once again. Her mother wanted her to be big and strong, and she tried to live up to that. She recalled being terrified of elevators and heights because her mother had once told her about a girl whose foot was caught in an elevator door and was seriously injured. She was very upset with her mother for many years because she would repeat this story and terrify the patient. This led to a series of fantasies of being physically injured and to a description of her fear of heights, in which she emphasized her dread of losing control and impulsively jumping out a window. She had seen a lot of destructive things done in her home, and felt that somehow she was able to free herself from them and to function better than many of her friends who had grown up in similar environments. The therapist commented that the patient felt that her mother had harmed her, but that actually she only brought out fears the patient already had.

Briefly, in the next hour the patient said that she felt considerably better, and discussed at some length her social work supervisor, who made many comments which seemed to her very inappropriate and even silly. In the past she would be upset by these comments, but now she felt strong and reassured herself that the supervisor had serious problems. Her associations eventually shifted to her childhood and to an aunt who had become psychotic, threatening to harm others. In grade school, the patient bit her nails and some horrible stuff was put on them to stop her. In many ways, her mother had been punitive and had done a poor job. The therapist emphasized the patient's rebelliousness.

In the next hour, the patient said that she had not really been in touch with her actual feelings and had really been very anxious the previous session. She described a series of additional current symptoms and felt that it had a lot to do with keeping her feelings buried inside of her. She then criticized her supervisor and spoke of quitting her job. She turned next to her parents and the difficulties that they had in being sensitive to her feelings, and how it made her feel that her life was hopeless. At the end of this hour, as the patient was leaving, her leg fell asleep again and she began to fall once more. This time the therapist responded by suggesting that she sit in her chair and withdrawing to his own seat. The patient recovered and left.

In the next hour, the patient said that she was still bothered by what had happened the day her foot first fell asleep. She spoke of her difficulty in expressing anger and the way in which she ran away from things and avoided them. Her former husband had taken her children driving, and they had returned saying that he had bragged that he had had his license taken away and that he had been terribly reckless. When rumination followed, the therapist pointed out to the patient that she apparently had been quite upset when he had held her as she fell several sessions back. She had been speaking about how her mother had frightened her and held her tight, of how she held back her anger, of how she had felt misunderstood, and of her thoughts of leaving treatment. He suggested that all of these were related to his having grabbed her arm. The patient said that actually she had been extremely pleased that the therapist had sat down when at the end of the last session her leg had fallen asleep once again. She had felt terribly weak and helpless after he had grabbed her the earlier time.

In the next few sessions, the patient reported a series of vignettes involving professional people with whom she was in contact; she had abundant criticisms regarding their lack of insight, their failure to recognize their own shortcomings, and their tendency to control and manipulate patients. The therapist suggested that these derivatives in some way related to himself, but did not connect them specifically to his having touched the patient. Mrs. D. then suddenly decided to take a two-week vacation and felt extremely guilty over violating their agreement. She was afraid that the therapist would be angry with her and went on once again to criticize her supervisor for not knowing what was going on in her department. The therapist related this material and the patient's decision to take a vacation to his own breaking of the rules of treatment, but the patient disagreed with him, stating that he always behaved correctly and did no wrong. The therapist directly alluded to having touched the patient a month earlier and Mrs. D. then responded that she had always been terrified of being touched. When she was a child, her father would touch her and she would have frightening sexual fantasies. It was a crazy fear, but one that she held on to intensely. The therapist suggested that she had been thinking a great deal about craziness in other professionals and that perhaps she had seen his grabbing her to support her as a crazy act on his part. The patient agreed that she might have had such a thought, and went on to state that she had been having fantasies recently of marrying a psychiatrist. She wanted somebody who would be honest with her and with whom she could be honest. Her fears seemed to have been excited when she had been touched by her therapist because it made her experience him as a man as he held on to her. She was afraid of his becoming real and felt that she had to respond by becoming unreal herself.

The vignette reminds us that the distinction between reality and fantasy, and transference and nontransference, can at times—less often than realized, however—be difficult to establish. It also brings up the gray areas that pertain to the boundaries of the relationship between patient and therapist (Langs 1973, 1974). While it would appear more appropriate for the therapist to allow the patient to find her own way to the door upon leaving her sessions (and thereby help with the transition from a dependency on him to her independent existence outside of treatment), the fact that the therapist instinctively went to the aid of his patient as she fell to the floor can hardly be considered an insensitive extension of the boundaries of the patient-therapist relationship. While it is certainly preferable that the therapist not touch his patient, an emergency such as this might have merited the therapist's behavior. On the other hand, it might well have been that the patient would have been able to handle the situation entirely on her own and therefore should have been left to her own devices. Thus, some question must remain regarding the propriety of the therapist's behavior, although the situation is one that might well have justified his emergency response.

The main technical error, however, was that the therapist failed to explore the patient's reaction to this deviation in the following sessions. The material from the next hour should have been viewed in the context of the incident and the therapist could have readily interpreted the patient's view of him as a frightening person, one who was himself losing control, as well as her own fears of losing control in response. Over the next couple of sessions, the patient's unconscious perception of the therapist's insensitivity and lack of insight into his own behavior was apparent. It is striking that it was not until the therapist instinctively refused to repeat his behavior when the problem arose a second time (we may note here the patient's unconscious seductiveness) that the patient was able directly to indicate that she had been disturbed by his former behavior. This was feasible, in part, because the stimulus for her response was one that was readily available to conscious recognition. By this time, the problem had been disucssed in supervision and the therapist, after mastering strong inner resistances, was able to interpret a number of the patient's fantasies and reactions to his behavior, and to have them confirmed and elaborated upon. However, in the sessions that followed, he consistently avoided any further specific reference to his having touched the patient, despite the indications that the derivatives in the material from the patient continued to relate to this behavior which was so important to her. Only when Mrs. D. acted out by planning a vacation did he reluctantly make the specific interpretation that her reactions were still related to his having touched her. At that point, the patient was able to reveal the important genetic links and meanings that his behavior had had for her, and the thinly disguised sexual fantasies toward the therapist that it had evoked in her. The therapist reported that toward the end of this hour the patient seemed considerably relieved, and that he had felt that he had shared a significant experience with her.

We see here the positive outcome of correct interventions based on the acknowledgment of the truth in the patient's unconscious perceptions of, and fantasies about, the therapist, and the preceding disruptive influence of the therapist's failure to work along these lines. The therapist's countertransference difficulties were apparent in his failure to interpret Mrs. D.'s reactions to his touching her despite abundant derivatives of them in her associations and repeated supervisory discussions regarding the need for such interventions. Ultimately, it was his ability to resolve conflicts within himself which had previously prompted him to be silent with the patient in this area, his growing subjective awareness that something was amiss, his crucial ability not to repeat his behavior, and his ultimate freedom to understand the patient's communications that enabled him to intervene correctly.

An interesting postscript to this clinical interlude occurred about three months later, when Mrs. D. was deciding whether to terminate her therapy or to continue with it privately at her therapist's office, since he was leaving the clinic in which she was being seen. In one session at this juncture, Mrs. D. several times expressed concern about the fee that she would be charged if she were to become a private patient of the therapist, stating that she was afraid to consider such a step seriously since it might be too costly for her. She also spoke of rich women who dress up for their private therapy sessions, and of doctors who were mainly concerned about their fees and not about their patients.

The therapist elected not to clarify his fee to her, and in supervision this was considered to be an insensitivity on his part; it was felt that the therapist must clarify this issue, since the patient needed the information in order to assess the realities of what would be available to her. The therapist said that he had missed entirely the repeated questions about his fee.

Mrs. D. began her next session by saying that she was angry with the therapist, but did not know why. In a family discussion, her mother had said that she had often felt that Mrs. D. was not her child; the patient commented in her session that her mother had never understood her. She had dreamt that she was in the therapist's office and told him that she felt faint. He comes over to her and squats beside her, saying that everything would be all right; then he returns to his chair. In associating, Mrs. D. spoke of not wanting to be alone and again asked the therapist why she should continue her therapy. In the previous session, she had felt that she had not done something right and that the therapist wanted her to say something. She wanted comfort, but feared sexualizing it. The therapist related the dream to her wish for comfort and fear of it, as in the incident when her foot fell asleep and he did *not* touch her. Mrs. D. said that it was like a mother with a child and added that there had been a couch in the office as she had dreamt of it (none was present in the therapist's office in the clinic). She then recalled several sexual dreams that she had previously reported during her therapy. In one, she is nude in her session and her mother walks in, saying: "So this is what you do in therapy."

We may formulate several aspects of this material that are relevant to this discussion. There are the apparent sexual fantasies and anxieties in the patient regarding private therapy, based in part on the incident when the therapist had touched her, though other—unknown—factors must also contribute since erotic dreams had preceded that incident. In addition, the patient rightfully resented the therapist's failure to answer her query about his fee—the unspoken words—and had responded to his insensitivity, unconsciously perceived, with a variety of reactions and fantasies. Thus, she was consciously resentful, but without knowing why; she experienced a major breach in the "mothering" offered by the therapist; and she dreamt of a time when he had extended himself beyond the usual boundaries of their relationship and then had withdrawn this contact (i.e., latently, the dream probably refers to both incidents). One technical error or insensitivity had conjured up another similar occasion from the past; the present real hurt and fantasied sexual threat (the private office) recalled a situation in which there had been both a hurt and an erotized transference gratification, and a more correct response by the therapist as well. The erotic or erotized fantasies about the therapist (Langs 1973), in this context, may be viewed as an attempt to repair the patient's sense of narcissistic hurt and as a reflection of an unconscious fantasy as to why the therapist was pushing her away from him—a possible unconscious sensitivity to the therapist's actual sexual conflicts. Such anxieties are not uncommon in beginning therapists, especially in connection with seeing a clinic patient privately without the "protection" of the clinic; patients are not alone in this regard.

In all, then, we can see that Mrs. D. was continuously and unconsciously in tune with her therapist's behavior and its implications, and was responding to it with her own genetically determined fantasies. The working through of the conflicts that this situation had evoked was feasible only through self-change within the therapist, the recognition of the adaptive stimuli to which the patient was reacting, and a careful distillation of the reality and fantasy elements involved.

DISCUSSION AND CONCLUSIONS

The main implications of these clinical observations may be summarized as follows:

1. Among his many clinical tasks, the therapist must monitor the manifest and latent content of the patient's associations for conscious and unconscious allusions—images—related to himself.

2. When the material offers imagery likely to refer to the therapist (see Langs 1973, 1974, 1975a), he must then carefully distill the fantasied and reality elements contained in it.

3. To do this precisely, he must first use a variety of sources through which he can assess the reality elements. These include (a) his subjective awareness of his ongoing feelings and fantasies toward the patient and of the nature of his interventions—or failures to intervene—and their explicit and implicit meanings; and (b) the clues provided in the associations from the patient.

4. If he is prepared to discover realistic underpinnings and precipitants for the patient's fantasies about him and to find that these apparent fantasies contain many accurate unconscious perceptions of him, the therapist will find a constant flow of accurate perceptions of himself reflected in the communications from the patient. These can direct him to the kernels of truth in the patient's material and to a more accurate assessment of his interaction with the patient.

5. Once the reality stimuli are properly identified, the fantasy elements can then be ascertained.

(a) In those situations where the day residues—adaptive stimuli— are relatively "neutral" and intrapsychic fantasies and projections from within the patient are maximal, the therapist's interpretations will emphasize the transference elements and their genetic basis. In these situations, he will also explore the patient's defenses and the distortions in his perceptions, and allude to other ego dysfunctions when they are present, doing so in the framework of the patient's adaptive efforts.

(b) In those situations where the therapist's nonneutral or traumatic and technically erroneous behavior has been correctly and unconsciously perceived by the patient, his interventions will begin, as a rule, with an acknowledgment of the veracity of the perception and will refer to the way it served as a stimulus for the patient's responsive fantasies and conflicts, including the consequences of any actual resemblance between the therapist and a hurtful parent or other person. Such interventions are essential to the restoration of a proper therapeutic atmosphere and alliance. Once the therapist has acknowledged his contribution to the situation, however, the patient's responsibility for his reactions must be recognized and subsequently analyzed (Langs 1973, 1974). The therapist must also modify any aberrant and technically incorrect and insensitive behavior on his part for his interpretations to be effective.

6. I have not attempted to place in perspective the overall role of work with perceptions of, and fantasies about, the therapist in psychotherapy, a subject I have more fully explored elsewhere (Langs 1973, 1975a). The observations presented here do not imply that such material should be the overriding preoccupation of psychotherapy, though judicious consideration is always indicated. This is especially true when the unconscious perceptions of the therapist relate to his errors and human failings; the analytic resolution of such problems has the highest priority among the indications for the therapist's interventions.

In conclusion, this paper has presented clinical material to illustrate the vital importance of assessing the patient's material for reality and fantasy regarding the therapist. As one develops a sensitivity to this task, it is remarkable to learn how unconsciously perceptive patients are of their therapist, especially of his errors and countertransference reactions. The therapist can then use these perceptions most constructively as a guide toward better insight into himself, and to more empathic, accurate, and helpful interventions with his patients. In doing this, his ability to specifically identify the precise mixture of reality and fantasy, distorted and accurate perception, and present and past in the patient's communications will prove invaluable in his therapeutic work.

POSTSCRIPT 1978. Several years after the publication of this paper, upon reading my discussion of the ground rules and framework of the therapeutic situation (Langs 1975b), Mrs. A.'s therapist offered an addendum to this material. He stated that after the first session with this patient, she lacked transportation home. As a result, she asked to use the therapist's telephone to call for a taxicab, and was permitted to do so. The incident seemed trivial to the therapist and was never mentioned in supervision or alluded to again on a manifest level by the patient. It was only when he had begun to appreciate the implications of the ground rules and boundaries of the therapeutic relationship that he recalled the experience and began to wonder how it influenced the material that he had presented to me and which I had reported in this paper.

There is little doubt that had I had this information, I would have offered a distinctly different discussion than presented in this paper, and it is likely that I would have not at all made use of this vignette as an illustration of primarily transference-based responses in a patient. However, I must stress that I am making this statement now, at the time when I am in the process of reviewing these papers to assemble them for the present volume. It may very well be that at the time of writing this paper, I would have, indeed, still made many of the formulations presented in the current text. I suspect I might have added, however, that permission to the patient to use the telephone muddled the distinction between reality and fantasy in evaluating both the sexual material from this patient and the allusions to the existence of dangers within the treatment situation. There is no doubt that, first, I would have formulated this material as now presented somewhat differently today than at that time, and, second, that in the present I would have an entirely different assessment to offer. In it, I would stress the manner in which the therapist's permission to allow the patient to use his telephone modified the frame in a dangerous, destructive, and seductive manner that in some way repeated similar behaviors on the part of the patient's parents and siblings, especially her father.

I will not offer a more detailed evaluation of the derivative material from this patient in the adaptive context of her use of the therapist's telephone, but prefer instead to suggest to the reader that he complete his consideration of all of the papers presented here. Once finished, he might wish to return to this particular material and to reformulate it for himself. This would provide a special opportunity to understand the full significance of the many details of the therapeutic interaction, especially as they relate to the framework; many of these indeed, are, excluded from consideration and even notice in the usual case presentation. Nonetheless, these relatively ignored deviations in technique have far-reaching effects on the patient and the therapeutic process—and on the therapist as well.

REFERENCES

Freud, S. (1937). Construction in analysis. *Standard Edition* 23:256–269.

Greenson, R. (1965). The working alliance and the transference neurosis. *Psychoanalytic Quarterly* 34:155–181.

————(1967). *The Technique and Practice of Psychoanalysis,* Vol. 1. New York: International Universities Press.

————(1971). The "real" relationship between the patient and the psychoanalyst. In *The Unconscious Today,* ed. M. Kanzer. New York: International Universities Press.

————(1972), Beyond transference and interpretation. *International Journal of Psycho-Analysis* 53:213–218.

————, and Wexler, M. (1969). The non-transference relationship in the psychoanalytic situation. *International Journal of Psycho-Analysis* 50:27–40.

Kernberg, O. (1968). The treatment of patients with borderline personality organization. *International Journal of Psycho-Analysis* 49:600–619.

Langs, R. (1973). *The Technique of Psychoanalytic Psychotherapy,* Vol. I. New York: Jason Aronson.

————(1974). *The Technique of Psychoanalytic Psychotherapy,* Vol. II. New York: Jason Aronson.

————(1975a). The patient's unconscious perception of the therapist's errors. In *Tactics and Technique in Psychoanalytic Psychotherapy, Vol. II: Countertransference,* ed. P. Giovacchini. New York: Jason Aronson. [Chapter 5, this volume]

————(1975b). The therapeutic relationship and deviations in Technique. *International Journal of Psychoanalytic Psychotherapy* 4:106–141. [Chapter 7, this volume]

Loewenstein, R. (1957).Some thoughts on interpretation in the theory and practice of psychoanalysis. *Psychoanalytic Study of the Child* 12:127–150.

Niederland, W. (1959). The "miracled-up" world of Shreber's childhood. *Psychoanalytic Study of the Child* 14:383–413.

Searles, H. (1965). *Collected Papers on Schizophrenia and Related Subjects.* New York: International Universities Press.

Chapter Five

The Patient's Unconscious Perception of the Therapist's Errors

(1975[1973])

There is currently a growing interest in the psychoanalytic literature regarding the role of the therapist's errors in technique and his human failings in the psychoanalytic and psychotherapeutic situations (Greenson 1965, 1967, 1971, Langs 1973). It is the purpose of this presentation to contribute to our understanding of this subject, especially as it relates to errors of which the therapist is unaware. I will approach the subject in the following way:

1. By presenting clinical material which will demonstrate some of the most common manifestations of the patient's conscious and—far more frequently—unconscious perception of the therapist's errors.

2. By utilizing these clinical observations as a means of cataloging indicators in the associations from patients that the therapist has made a mistake, thereby facilitating their recognition by him.

3. By discussing the technique of handling such errors with the patient, including the consequences of the therapist's failure to detect his mistakes and correct them.

Briefly, this study is primarily the outcome of my work as a supervisor of insight-oriented psychoanalytic psychotherapy. Material from twice-weekly therapy of patients suffering from character disorders and borderline pathology was presented in weekly supervision. At various points in such presentations, I identified specific, major errors in technique and predicted their consequences based on the nature of the error and the patient's character structure and psychopathology (Arlow 1963, Langs 1973). Among the responses to such errors, one group included derivatives of the patient's unconscious awareness of the therapist's mistake, including the patient's fantasies about why the therapist had erred.

This study is based in part upon many fine papers on countertransference in the psychoanalytic literature (see Cohen 1952, Orr 1954, Greenson 1967, Langs 1973). Errors in technique may be based on inadequate training, faulty conceptualization of the material from the patient, an incorrect theoretical framework, the use of unsound technical measures, and unresolved personality difficulties within the therapist—countertransference problems (Greenson 1967, Langs 1973). These last may manifest themselves as acute traumatic interventions, or failures to intervene, or they may be expressed as chronic and recurrent disturbances in the therapist's stance. Elsewhere (Langs 1973), I have investigated this matter in some detail and have termed the patient's responses to the therapist's errors *iatrogenic syndromes,* a label which emphasizes the therapist's role in evoking the patient's response, while acknowledging the patient's responsibility as well.

These errors by the therapist may be detected by him through his subjective awareness (Cohen 1952, Langs 1973), and by the patient's immediate association following the therapist's error (Langs 1973). While patients occasionally are able to express their awareness of these mistakes directly to the therapist, in almost all of the several hundred clinical situations I have observed in which such errors were made, the patient's response was essentially unconscious and expressed through disguised derivatives and displacements.

This paper will focus on one source of detecting mistakes made by therapists, namely the patient's immediate associations following the error. It will be limited further to one specific type of response—associations which center around the patient's unconscious awareness that the error has been made and his unconscious concept of the error. Some other types of responses to the therapist's mistakes have been presented elsewhere (Langs 1973). These include such reactions as ruptures in the therapeutic alliance; various forms of acting in against the therapist; premature termination of treatment; erotic responses to the therapist; acute symptoms and symptomatic regression of all kinds; and major and minor episodes of acting out. In general, a patient's responses to errors in technique will include a mixture of these reactions in various sequences.

CLINICAL MATERIAL

While I have not formerly collated my findings from the more than 800 clinical vignettes that I have documented from my supervisory work, some general impressions will be helpful as an orientation for the vignettes which are to be presented (Langs 1973). By and large, the identification of major errors in technique proves to be consistently feasible so that well over 90 percent of those behaviors and interventions of the therapist identified in supervision as clearly incorrect were followed by ample validation in the subsequent material from the patient. Since most of the therapists were relatively inexperienced, errors in technique were rather frequent and averaged at least one for every two sessions presented to me. In response to these errors, at least 90 percent of the time the patient did not express any direct conscious awareness or belief that the therapist had made a mistake, but instead responded strongly and unconsciously, and expressed his reaction through derivatives. The main exceptions to this were those situations in which the patient directly disagreed with the therapist's intervention and went on to present material that supported his disagreement, and then eventually offered derivatives related to the correct area in which the therapist should have intervened.

The exact nature of the patient's response to these errors in technique depends on a number of factors. These include the nature of the error, the rapidity or slowness with which the therapist detects it, his ability to modify and correct it, and the extent to which he is able to explore the patient's conscious and unconscious reactions. On the patient's part, contributions are made mainly from his past and present relationship, his character structure and psychopathology, his ongoing relationship with the therapist, and his current life situation. To illustrate some of these points I present the following vignettes:

Mr. A. was a young man who was divorced and living alone. He came into therapy because he was depressed and had not been able to mobilize himself to find employment, to develop new relationships with women, or to visit his children, who lived with his remarried wife. He tended to withdraw from others and to smoke a good deal of marijuana; at times he took other drugs as well. He was diagnosed as a narcissistic personality disorder and was being seen in twice-weekly psychotherapy.

He had been in treatment for about two months when he began to think about seeing his children again. With this in mind, he contacted his wife and in their conversation she mentioned the possiblity of her present husband's adopting their children so that they could take his name. The patient was noncommittal, and in his sessions after the call he ruminated about whether he really wanted to see his children at all, and how being detached from them was fine with him. To see them again would just be a hassle. Yet, he spoke of receiving a call from his parents and missing them, a unique feeling for the patient. Associations led to his search for relief by taking drugs and his fears of "cracking up." The therapist remained relatively silent, saying only that the patient seemed to want something from him.

In the following two sessions, the patient requested psychotropic medication and spoke about leaving the area. He thought of writing notes to the therapist and retreated into marijuana smoking. He had suicidal fantasies, and an intense sense of depression and despair. The therapist pointed out the patient's wish for immediate relief, and Mr. A. spoke of his mounting sense of anxiety and of a boss he once had whom he hated and blamed for his suffering on the job. He felt terribly misunderstood by him, and was eventually fired. When the patient ruminated further about blaming others for his suffering, the therapist pointed out how he dumps things onto others and assumes it is their problem rather than his. The patient demanded medication and began to fall silent during hours, stating that he had nothing to say. The therapist pointed out his anger over not being given enough in treatment, and the patient went on to talk about his rage at his insensitive wife, who had never returned his last call; it made him feel like "crap." He then went on to speak at length of his guilt for ruining his children's lives, of his wish not to be just a "once-a-week father," and of his rage at his wife for her affair with her present husband while still married to the patient.

The patient was late for the next session and felt very depressed. He talked about how uncomfortable he felt when things came up in treatment, but could not specify what it was about. He was feeling frightened of people and felt that it was hardly worthwhile getting up that morning for his session. The therapist said that his lateness seemed related to his doubts about therapy.

He began the following hour by asking about a picture of the therapist's children which was on his desk. He thought about his brother and sister, and the ways in which he had failed them, of a vague sense of guilt, and of how he could not look at a picture of his parents in his own apartment. Once again, he thought of running away. The therapist picked up the reference to the picture of his children and to the theme of guilt, and said that he wondered if the patient wasn't feeling guilty about his children. The intervention surprised Mr. A., who then spoke of his concern about seeing them again and messing up their lives. He reviewed in some detail the ways in which he had failed them and how terrified he was to start up with them again, fearing that he would explode. He was furious with his wife and her present husband for their contribution to the situation. The therapist intervened again and spoke of the patient's rage and of the manner in which the patient blamed others for his troubles, pointing out that he seems to be doing this with his wife and her husband rather than facing the fact that he himself had been paralyzed into inaction. In response, the patient said that he was confused and that treatment was a very painful journey that was hurting him a great deal.

He had been on a bus the other day, when a man got on and was putting money into the coin box. It dropped to the floor several times. The patient laughed loudly, causing everyone on the bus to look at him. The patient then noticed that the man had a cane and he felt like "crap." Nevertheless, he continued to laughed to himself.

He fell silent and remembered a time in his childhood when he sat with his grandfather and put chalk into rags that he then used to beat up children he didn't like. During those years, he would have nightmares that there was a gorilla in his closet and he would never go into a dark room. He remembered a time from his early twenties when he roomed with a fellow who was a criminal. They would have relations with women together and he remembered that once this friend had nearly killed a girlfriend. The friend had held up a medical supply house, looking for drugs, and had been shot in the process. He had been in psychotherapy with a doctor who had a beautiful office; the patient had once gone there with him. The doctor would stare at his friend and they both thought that the psychiatrist was crazy. Because of that experience, the patient had hesitated a long time before seeking therapy himself.

Mr. A. began the next session by talking about how he had idealized his father and now was disillusioned. He spoke about putting walls around himself and again alluded to his feeling disappointed. He had been under the influence of drugs since the last session and had refused to share his apartment with a friend who was leaving his wife and children. He had little else to talk about. The therapist commented that something he had done in the previous session seemed to have turned the patient off, suggesting that this was reflected in the reference to the blind man; perhaps he had missed something and this had frightened the patient. Mr. A. responded that he would like things to be good for himself, and he began to speak again about his children and the times that he had felt close to and happy with them. He was afraid that they might not know him or might hurt him if he reached out to them again. He went on in considerable detail about the painful conflicts that he was feeling over whether to see them again and whether to maintain his position as their legal father.

In discussing this vignette, one must identify the therapist's errors, since they form the fulcrum for the patient's responses. These errors fall into two groups, one set related to the patient's problems with his children and the other pertaining to his relationship with the therapist. As to the first of these, I believe there were two main mistakes, which stemmed from difficulties the therapist had in being empathic and in recognizing the patient's great suffering regarding his children. As soon as the patient began to talk about the possibility of losing his children, I suggested in supervision that this was a very important problem and adaptive task (Langs 1972, p. 73) for this patient, and that it would evoke significant realistic and intrapsychic conflicts. The patient's main defenses of denial and withdrawal into drugged states were also quickly identified. The balance of the material then centered around various feelings of guilt, depression, and rage, and the accompanying conscious and unconscious fantasies related to the patient's struggles regarding the possible loss of his children. This included strong expressions of longings to be with them and to undo his own destructiveness toward them.

In this context, the therapist's early interventions regarding the patient's tendency to blame other were not only insensitive to his plight, but were also accusatory and hostile. In response, the patient's depression intensified and he began to question his therapy and to demand medication. His recollection of a boss who did not understand him is an early expression of the patient's unconscious perception of the therapist's failure to recognize his suffering; the reference to being fired is probably a derivative of the patient's thoughts of leaving treatment.

It is rather typical, in response to errors of this kind, for patients to express some rage, to regress and question treatment, to indicate some of the unconscious fantasies about the therapist's insensitivity, and to then return to important intrapsychic conflicts. Mr. A. did just this by getting back to the problem he was having with his wife and children, and by doing so with considerably more affect and pain. His wishes to be a good father may also be viewed, in addition to realistic aspects, as a fantasy expressing some longing to have an understanding therapist-father. When the latter did not respond either with an empathic statement or with some effort to explore the patient's conflicts, the patient spoke about his wife's present husband, who had cuckolded him; this reflects some of the patient's mistrust of the therapist, who remained out of touch with him. The therapist, despite supervisory discussions, was having difficulty referring specifically to the patient's conflicts about his children, and the patient seemed to feel confused.

Then, in the most dramatic session of this series, the patient once more brought up the subject of his children by alluding to the therapist's picture of his own children. Again, the patient spoke at length about his children and his guilt over being a poor father. The therapist correctly intervened by referring to this guilt. It is interesting that the patient expected the therapist to ignore these communications, and then went on to add some new material about the intensity of his desires to see his children again. It was at this point, after the patient had spoken about his rage at his wife and her present husband, that the therapist made his most dramatic error. It consisted of an incorrect intervention in which he once more criticized the patient for blaming others and directly faulted the patient for the difficulties which he currently found himself facing. The therapist seems here to have been insensitive again, and to have a strong unconscious need to deter the patient from talking about his children and his longings to be close to them.

The nature of this disturbing intervention was discussed with the therapist, and the prediction was made that the patient would react with derivatives expressing considerably rage and mistrust. This was borne out by the reference to the blind man and to the patient's own difficulties in seeing and understanding; it is a poitnant communication.

The patient went on to speak of his latent destructiveness. In my previous work (Langs 1973), I found that it is extremely common for patients to become self-accusatory when they are furious with their therapist. The reference to the patient's senseless attacks seems admirably suited to communicate his perception of the therapist's inappropriate, senseless criticisms. Mr. A.'s other associations suggest a terrifying image of his relationship with the therapist.

During the last session presented here, the therapist attempted to correct his error. The patient was talking about his disillusionment in therapist-displacement figures, this time referring to his father. When the therapist finally acknowledged his error of the previous session, he did so without specifically referring to his failure to understand the patient's grief about the situation with his children. The therapist was vague, but he discussed in some detail the patient's reactions and fantasies to his insensitivity and failure to perceive the patient's distress. He admitted that his attitude had been unjustifiably critical. In response, the patient spontaneously began to talk again about his children and the conflicts that were plaguing him. In a manner not evident until now, the patient described fears that he would explode, and said that he felt much as he had as a child, when he had been sick in bed and his doctor had laughed at him for having such a small penis. His father, he went on, had been a destructive man who would do anything for his son, even cut his own arm off, and who had begged the patient not to be like him. Yet his father laughed at the doctor's remark and the patient had been deeply mortified. After these comments, the patient returned to the exploration of his problems with his children and to some of the intrapsychic difficulties that had prevented him from being an adequate father.

It is noteworthy that even this incomplete effort at acknowledging and correcting a series of errors in technique was successful in reestablishing a positive therapeutic atmosphere and alliance. It enabled the patient to express one last unconscious fantasy regarding his perception of the therapist's recent behavior, namely that of his deep sense of inadequacy and humiliation. Following this, the patient was able to return to the exploration of inner conflicts.

I will not similarly trace out this therapist's failure to respond adequately to Mr. M.'s search for care and gratification of dependency needs in his relationship with the therapist. This was an ongoing difficulty in this therapy, and the many self-accusations regarding poor fathering refer, on this level, to the frustrations with the therapist; fantasies of rage in this connection are the counterpart of the patient's guilt over his children. The blindness, then, is not only the therapist's failure to interpret properly to the patient, but also a deeper failure to recognize his needs and demands for help and care. Let us now consider the following vignette:

Mrs. B. was in psychotherapy for multiple phobic symptoms and depressions; she had been seen twice weekly for about six months. Prior to the last session before the therapist's vacation, the patient, who had been informed of the temporary cessation of treatment, had wandered from the waiting room. The therapist searched and found her outside the hospital talking to other patients; she returned with him.

The patient began the hour by saying that she had been thinking that she should not come to her session because she would get too upset. She reported a dream in which a little child fell from a window in her apartment. Her associations were to a cousin who had had premonitory dreams of something happening to a child, after which a serious accident or injury had occured. Other associations, which touched upon themes of separation, suggested that the dream was related to the therapist's pending vacation. They were not interpreted. The therapist's extension of the boundaries of the relationship between himself and the patient, as reflected in his going outside to find her, was also not alluded to.

The patient began the first session after the therapist's vacation by stating that she had been thinking about her treatment, but had reached no conclusions. She dreamed that afternoon while napping that the therapist was screaming at her that she is always late and keeps missing her appointments. She associated her dislike of tardiness and added that in the dream the therapist was actually standing in front of the clinic yelling across the street at her. She then discussed moving because of her husband's business commitments, and spoke of her mother's destructiveness—she had not watched her children carefully.

The patient's unconscious perception of the therapist's lack of reference to his finding her for the previous hour (in my opinion, an error) is conveyed in the dream. In the dream, the patient returned to the therapist's seemingly innocuous deviation in the ground rules of therapy and the boundaries of their relationship (Langs 1973). Unconsciously, the patient felt that the therapist was angry over her lateness and therefore came to get her. Most likely the dream reflects the patient's own anger regarding the therapist's seductiveness.

During the two following sessions her associations focused upon derivatives of erotic feelings toward the therapist. He had been provocative prior to the reported sessions, so her eroticized responses could not be attributed specifically to his error in pursuing the patient.

Thus, Mrs. B. alluded to the therapist's deviation in technique in an almost undisguished fashion, but dissociated it from the precipitating incident and the context to which it referred. As a result, she was able to maintain repression of the incident and the fantasies that it had evoked in her, and because the therapist similarly repressed the incident, its consequences were not explored or resolved.

The next patient was in twice-weekly psychotherapy for about five months when her therapist took a three-week vacation. The material before and immediately after this vacation, which later proved to be linked in her mind to the pending forced termination of her therapy, indicated that the patient had had a very intense reaction to the separation, which she denied directly but expressed through acting out and other derivatives. For example, the patient returned to her home for the first time in years and took a number of articles from her parent's mementos, even though they did not belong to her. She also got involved in a long battle with her present boyfriend, a divorced man, over the possibility of his leaving her, and expressed a tremendous need for him. Expressions of rage regarding a number of people who had deserted her earlier in life appeared. She also had a severe depression with suicidal feelings. The therapist had not connected any of these behaviors or feelings to his vacation; instead, he focused upon her difficulties with her boyfriend. The pervasiveness of derivatives related to the therapist's vacation, however, indicated that this was technically incorrect.

Soon after the therapist returned, the patient spoke about how well the therapist looked. She also expressed a strong need for his help. She described an argument with her boyfriend; she had become completely disorganized when they had attempted to discuss the issues involved. She went to a party with him on the night of the quarrel and attempted to make him angry by completely ignoring him. At the party, she met a nice man who was friendly but who had no idea of what was going on. She thought of leaving the party with him, but left alone; her boyfriend stayed on with another girl. She later went to his apartment, only to find him with the girl from the party. She created a terrible scene. The man she had become involved with on the night of the party had seen a psychiatrist, and had told her that some of them were pretty crazy. She felt that her therapist was helping her, but wanted him to tell her how she could keep her boyfriend.

Here, the themes of remaining in the dark, and of being nice but not knowing what was going on, were very apt descriptions of this warm and concerned therapist, who did not recognize the need to interpret the patient's maladaptive separation reactions to his vacation. Once again, the direct reference to a psychiatrist, and especially to psychiatrists who have problems of their own, confirmed the prediction made in supervision that the patient was indeed talking about her awareness of the therapist.

DISCUSSION

Technical errors and the patient's adverse reactions to them often cause the therapist to feel anxious and guilty. Errors in technique and even failures to respond humanely will occasionally occur during any treatment. The goal is to minimize their frequency and to develop means by which the therapist can recognize his mistakes and correct them with the patient, resolving within himself those difficulties which prompt him to make repetitive errors (Greenson 1972, Langs 1973). While it is clear that there is no substitute for adequate training in psychoanalysis and psychotherapy, and for a personal psychoanalysis, it is useful to attempt to develop systematic ways of recognizing such errors. The primary vehicle for such recognition has always been the therapist's subjective awareness of these mistakes, for which his own analysis sensitizes him considerably (Cohen 1952, Langs 1973).

A second means of detecting technical errors is to recognize the patient's unconscious communication of his reactions to the therapist's error. I have described the indicators of such mistakes in some detail in my previous work (Langs 1973) and have attempted here to isolate one specific form that such material takes.

It is generally known that unconsciously the patient is exquisitely sensitive to the therapist's conscious and unconscious communications, including his mistakes. As a result, it behooves every therapist to be sensitive to all of the patient's communications which refer to conscious and unconscious fantasies about the therapist, the therapeutic alliance, and the therapeutic atmosphere. While I am not suggesting the psychotherapy should focus on such communications or make them the primary area for the work of treatment, I believe it is essential to the maintenance of a sound therapeutic alliance to remain in touch with this level of the patient's communications. By maintaining such observations, it becomes easier for the therapist to examine his own technique when he detects disturbances from the patient that suggest some technical error.

I will now list and briefly discuss the main implications of the findings presented here:

1. Among the general indicators of technical errors are ruptures and disturbances in the therapeutic alliance; acting in, such as lateness, absence, and premature termination; the appearance of regressive symptoms, acting out, and somatic and psychological symptoms (Langs 1973).

2. There are some recurrent themes in the patient's manifest and latent associations which should alert the therapist to the possiblity that he has made an error in technique. Such themes often reflect a sensitive, unconscious awareness of the nature of the therapist's error:

(a) Included here are themes of blindness, failure to be helpful, sensitive, or understanding, and of being mistreated, frightened, seduced, or attacked.

(b) Among the displacements and disguises commonly used by patients to express such feelings and fantasies, parental figures and persons who are in the healing professions are commonly used, as are teachers and other authority figures.

(c) It is also extremely common for patients to become self-critical and self-attacking over failings and disturbances which they have discovered in the therapist.

3. When the material from the patient directs the therapist to review his technique, and he becomes aware of a technical error, the following general principles may be used in dealing with it:

(a) The therapist should review the patient's material subsequent to the error and formulate it as a manifest and latent response to the error.

(b) The therapist should recognize that *the analysis of the patient's reaction to the error must take precedence over all other therapeutic work, since it is essential to the restoration of a proper therapeutic alliance (Langs 1973). Should there be another crucial problem in the session, he must deal with both his error and the patient's pressing difficulty.* If there is no urgent outside conflict, he should then focus on his error and its consequences until the patient has analyzed and worked through his reponses.

(c) As the patient's subsequent associations permit, the therapist should eventually acknowledge his error in simple words, as the starting point for his intervention. This is best done as the material from the patient fosters a discussion of the error and, as it generally will, relates to it on a latent level.

In acknowledging the error, the therapist should not go beyond a simple recognition of it to the patient and, at times, a comment to the effect that the patient can be assured that he is endeavoring to understand its basis within himself. It is inappropriate for the therapist to discuss the inner sources of his mistake.

(d) Having acknowledged the error as the starting point for interventions, the therapist should then go on to detail the patient's conscious and unconscious fantasies and conflicts which it evoked. It is often helpful if the material recalls childhood situations and relationships. References to acting out and to other behavior prompted by the therapist's error should also be discussed.

Although acknowledging his error, the therapist neither blames nor condemns himself or the patient for what has happened. He acknowledges that he is human and will inevitably make mistakes. The patient will respond and much can be learned from the interaction.

Finally, the therapist wants to be in tune with the patient's reaction to his acknowledgment of the error.

4. I want to note certain pitfalls. It is important to be specific regarding both the error and the patient's reactions in fantasy and behavior. It is also crucial that the therapist not overemphasize his mistakes, nor refer to them more than the patient's response requires. Each patient needs an intact therapist, and repetitive errors damage the image of the therapist and the patient's basic trust in him. Should these

incidents occur too often, it may prove necessary to refer the patient to a colleague—a matter I will not pursue here (see Greenson 1969, Langs 1973).

5. I have been impressed with the fact that the frank acknowledgment of an error in technique, and the exploration and working through of the patient's reaction to it, can provide a unique and growth-promoting, insight-producing experience for both patient and therapist. In addition, these errors, when correctly understood and resolved, can lead to some of the most human and moving experiences possible between patient and therapist. Thus, an error should not be seen as a terrible faux pas, or as dreaded failure, but as a human inevitability which can be turned into a productive, therapeutic experience.

REFERENCES

Arlow, J. (1963). The supervisory situation. *Journal of the American Psychoanalytic Association* 11:576–594.

Cohen, M. B. (1962). Countertransference and anxiety. *Psychiatry* 15:231–243.

Greenson, R. (1965). The working alliance and the transference neurosis. *Psychoanalytic Quarterly* 34:155–181.

———(1967). *The Technique and Practice of Psychoanalysis*, Vol. 1. New York: International Universities Press.

———(1971). The "real" relationship between the patient and the psychoanalyst. In *The Unconscious Today,* ed. M. Kanzer, New York: International Universities Press.

———(1972). Beyond transference and interpretation. *International Journal of Psycho-Analysis* 53:213–218.

———and Wexler, M. (1969). The nontransference relationships in the psychoanalytic situation. *International Journal of Psycho-Analysis,* 50:27–40.

———(1970). Discussion of "The nontransference relationships in the psychoanalytic situation." *International Journal of Psycho-Analysis,* 51:143–150.

Langs, R. (1973). *The Technique of Psychoanalytic Psychotherapy,* Vol. I. New York: Jason Aronson.

Orr, D.W. (1954). Transference and countertransference: a historical survey. *Journal of the American Psychoanalytic Association,* 12:621–670.

Chapter Six

Therapeutic Misalliances

(1975[1974])

This paper will study aspects of the psychopathology of the patient-analyst and patient-therapist relationships[1] and the therapeutic alliance, and in particular the efforts by either the patient or the analyst—or both—to effect a *therapeutic misalliance*. If we briefly define the therapeutic alliance as the conscious and unconscious agreement—and subsequent actual work—on the part of both patient and analyst to join forces in effecting symptom alleviation and characterological changes through insight and inner structural change within the patient, then therapeutic misalliances constitute interactions that are designed either to undermine such goals or to achieve symptom modification, however temporary, on some other basis. I believe that there are inherent needs in both patient and analyst to both create and resolve therapeutic misalliances in every analytic and psychotherapeutic situation, and that the recognition, analysis, and modification of these propensities and actualities is a first-order therapeutic task. In this paper I want to define therapeutic misalliances, to discuss their development, recognition, and resolution in analysis and psychotherapy, and to explore the main technical considerations which evolve from these observations.

While there had been occasional passing references to deviant alliances in the literature (see Corwin 1972 and Greenacre 1959 for examples), I believe that the first extensive and explicit use of the term *therapeutic misalliance* (alternately, *antitherapeutic alliance* to delineate its dimensions as a deviant search for "cure" that is opposed to insight) appeared in my two-volume work *The Technique of Psychoanalytic Psychotherapy* (Langs 1973b, 1974). In general, this area has been studied under the rubrics of transference and countertransference gratification, resistance, mutual acting out, and acting in—topics which still merit further study in themselves. As I shall demonstrate, the concept of therapeutic misalliances overlaps with each of these but goes beyond them as well, enabling us to develop aspects of these and other problems in technique that have otherwise been relatively neglected. In particular, this concept is especially relevant to the adaptive and interactional aspects of the patient-analyst dyad, including the mutual influence of patient and analyst upon each other, and the realistic and intrapsychic consequences of the relationship for both participants. While not all disturbances in the therapeutic alliance take the form of misalliances (there may be primarily unilateral impairments in the alliance, so that the mutuality inherent in the concept of misalliance is missing), it seems advisable to make a special study of these particular interactions, since they are basic to many disturbances in the analytic situation and are probably the single most common dimension to stalemated or failed analyses. The concept also highlights the analyst's contributions, however large or small, to such impasses or temporary difficulties in the treatment situation.

Actually, the concept of therapeutic misalliance has been implicit in many of the more extensive studies of the patient-analyst relationship, including those which focused on the therapeutic (or working) alliance dimension of it. (Freud 1915, Fenichel 1941, Greenacre 1959, 1971, Tarachow 1962, Greenson 1965, 1967, 1971, 1972, Greenson and Wexler, 1969, Friedman 1969, Myerson 1973, and Langs 1973a, 1973a, b, 1974, 1975a), and it is reflected in Freud's case histories as well (1905, 1909, 1918; see Langs, in press, for a discussion of this topic). As background for the present study, I shall confine myself to succinctly defining the concept of the therapeutic alliance and to describing some of the main indirect allusions to therapeutic misalliances in the literature (for a fuller resume of the subject of the therapeutic alliance see Zetzel 1956, 1958, 1966–1969, Stone 1961, 1967, Greenson 1965, 1967, Dickes 1967, Friedman 1969, Binstock 1973, and Langs 1973b, 1974).

To be brief, we may view the patient-analyst (and patient-therapist) relationship as an interaction based on the respective intrapsychic needs and sets, evocations and reactions—and adaptive responses—of each party. It has primarily realistic (nontransference—see Greenson and Wexler 1969, Greenson 1971, 1972, and Langs 1973a, b, 1974, 1975a) and primarily unrealistic or fantasied (transference) dimensions that readily intermix—intrapsychically and interactionally—for both participants. These two polarities are weighted differently for each, however; the latter are disproportionately greater in the patient (Racker 1968). It is out of this matrix that we isolate for study those facets, conscious and unconscious, that constitute the therapeutic alliance—the pact between that part of the patient that is motivated to cooperate with the analyst and is seeking adaptive and appropriate symptom relief, and that part of the analyst which is competent to offer it to him through his professional empathy with the patient and his relatively neutral interventions that are geared toward interpretations. Founded on both a basic mother-child relatedness (Zetzel 1958, Greenacre 1959, Stone 1961, 1967) and more mature relationships (Stone 1961, Greenson 1965), the therapeutic alliance is an agreement between the mature ego sectors of both parties (Sterba 1943) to work in consort toward the goals of treatment. However, there are also more primitive ego and id contributions to this pact (Friedman 1969) which must be well neutralized and sublimated to contribute positively to the alliance.

The therapeutic alliance has conscious and unconscious, explicit and implicit components (Myerson 1973, Langs 1973b, 1974), and is shaped by the needs and ego functions of both patient and analyst, especially by the latter's ground rules, personality, stance, work style, and interventions. It is these that guide the unfolding of this alliance in the direction of work toward inner structural change for the patient, based on a variety of communications from the analyst that are soon understood on some level by the patient.

Efforts toward therapeutic misalliances arise primarily out of unresolved intrapsychic conflicts—inappropriate instinctual drive needs, and superego and ego disturbances—and prior disturbed object relations and interactions experienced by either patient or analyst, which prompt either to seek gratifications and defensive reinforcements in their relationship that are not in keeping with the search for insight and inner change. The factors which lead to such efforts are on a continuum with those that contribute to a viable therapeutic alliance, and they intermingle; we are therefore faced with a delicate and sensitive issue. It is one that may be described in still another way: transference and countertransference inevitably contribute to and may interfere with alliance; when they do so, they must be detected, analyzed, and resolved (Zetzel 1958, Greenson 1965, Friedman 1969, Myerson 1973, Langs 1973b, 1974). It is in this realm that transference and countertransference fantasies influence reality and contribute to the ongoing adaptive efforts of each party to the therapeutic relationship. It is here that fantasy and memory are translated into actualities, gross or subtle—e.g., maladaptive conflict "resolutions" and pathological unconscious identifications—that are experienced as resistances and the search for alternative solutions to the patient's neurosis. If the resolution of such efforts is not given precedence in the analysis, little else will be accomplished; failure to detect and modify actual misalliances undermines the work toward more lasting adaptive solutions to the patient's conflicts—structural and characterological change based on insight and constructive identifications (Fenichel 1941, Langs 1974).

Elsewhere (Langs 1973b, 1974, 1975a), I have discussed in detail the manner in which misalliances arise, especially from efforts by the patient to act out primarily transference-based fantasies and from unneeded deviations in analytic or therapeutic technique and technical errors on the part of the analyst that serve as expressions of his countertransference problems (Langs 1975b). Far more subtle means of generating and maintaining misalliances also exist, though not all misalliances stem from transference and countertransference problems. They may arise primarily through extraneous sources, such as third parties to treatment (insurance companies, supervisors, etc.), manipulative nontransference motives for therapy (e.g., court remands), and personal noncountertransference needs in the analyst (e.g., a candidate's needs with a patient whom he is analyzing to fulfil his requirements at an analytic institute). Such situations may impose limiting realities on the analytic outcome and may effect unmodifiable sectors of misalliance—aspects I will discuss in a later paper (Langs 1975b).

Sectors of misalliance offer, in the realities of the therapist's involvement, an image of him that interferes critically with the three basic and interrelated avenues of sound symptom resolution: positive identifications with the therapist based on his behavior within his therapeutic role; curative interactions in which the therapist's interpretations and maintenance of the boundaries replace living out and misalliance (Racker 1968); and the development of cognitive insights based on the interpretations of the therapist. This latter is itself based on a maximal opportunity for the patient to project his intrapsychic fantasies onto the therapist and on the patient's experience of the therapist as a sound figure whose interpretations have a constructive impact on him.

These introductory considerations were first developed empirically from clinical observations of analytic psychotherapy (Langs 1973a, 1974a) and psychoanalysis. It was reassuring to find in studying the literature that many others had made similar observations, though they were conceptualized in somewhat different terms. Freud, for instance, was well aware of such occurrences and the dangers they entail. This is most apparent in his paper on transference love (1915), where he warns analysts against accepting transference love as a conquest of the patient; he developed the rule of abstinence in this context. Should there be compliance by the analyst, "the Patient would achieve *her* aim, but he would never achieve *his*" p. 165). Nor, Freud goes on, must the analyst actively repulse this transference love; he should "treat it as something unreal" (p. 166; see also Tarachow 1962) and analyze it. Then Freud refers to those women with whom attempts to analyze the erotic transference will not succeed. "These are women of elemental passionateness who tolerate no surrogates. They are the children of nature who refuse to accept the psychical in place of the material, who, in the poet's words, are accessible only to the logic of soup with dumplings for arguments" (pp. 166–167). In the terms being presented here, their sole wish is for a misalliance with their analyst. Throughout his writings, Freud emphasized that gratifications of this kind preclude successful analytic work.

Nunberg (1926, 1955) observed that patients have narcissistic and magical concepts of "cure" through fulfillment of their infantile wishes and through a different kind of work than that expected by their analysts. His presentations provide considerable clinical material related to inevitable efforts by patients to create misalliances. Fenichel (1941) put this concept succinctly: "In what is called 'handling of the transference,' 'not joining the game' is the principal task. Only thus is it possible subsequently to make interpretations" (p. 73)—in essence, avoiding a misalliance is fundamental for interpretive work). Throughout her writings on technique, Greenacre (1971) shows a sensitivity to the problem. In one notable allusion, she refers to the importance of the preservation of the patient's autonomy by the analyst. She therefore counsels against the use of active support or manipulation which impair the analytic result and weaken the patient's ego. "The therapeutic alliance is thus insidiously diluted with ingredients of a narcissistic alliance" (Greenacre 1959, p. 487). Corwin (1972) also studied narcissistic alliances.

Tarachow (1962) writes: "*The task of setting aside the other as a real object I regard as the central problem* in the theory of the treatment process" (p. 377). This problem arises out of the mutual object need of the patient and the analyst; rather than gratify these needs, the latter imposes a therapeutic barrier by interpreting and not participating in reality. This promotes experessions of unconscious fantasies in the patient's free associations and the development of the transference neurosis. The analyst must be capable of renunication, especially of his wishes for fusion with the patient. The slightest alteration in the analyst's behavior calls for self-scrutiny; collusion (i.e., misalliance) with the patient has usually been involved.

Greenson's discussion of the working alliance (1965, 1967) alludes to aberrations in this alliance which clearly reflect therapeutic misalliances; he emphasizes that analytic efforts in this area must take precedence over all other aspects, including work related to the transference neurosis. Inherent in the modifications of the misalliances described by Greenson was the recognition of the analyst's participation in the aberrant interaction with the patient, and the need for the analyst to modify his contributing behavior as well as to analyze the sources for the difficulty with the patient. In describing one such misalliance, Greenson noted: "The analysis of this transference resistance, however, was ineffectual, partly because the first analyst worked in such a way as to justify the patient's infantile neurotic behavior and so furthered the invasion of the working alliance by the transference neurosis" (1965, pp. 166–167).

Friedman (1969) studied a paradox within the patient-analyst relationship: transference is the major motivating factor in analysis and yet the prime weapon—resistance—that the patient uses to combat these efforts, and to try to gain actual fulfillment of his neurotic needs. Similarly, the emphasis on the therapeutic alliance as a compact between the mature and relatively autonomous parts of the egos of both patient and analyst presents the paradox that such an alliance, to be effective, must also rely on contributions from instinctual needs and entail some degree of gratification of these needs. In traversing the fine line between offering the patient too little and too much gratification, the danger of participating in misalliance is ever present.

In another vein, Myerson's studies of the analytic modus vivendi (1969, 1973) describe ways in which certain patients attempt to work in analysis with either too little or too much involvement with the analyst, thereby limiting analytic progress. He states that the prime task with such patients is the disruption of these deviant modi vivendi (i.e., efforts toward misalliance) through various types of interventions, some of which are noninterpretive.

Kanzer (1975) calls into question the common tendency in analysts who deal technically with aberrations in the therapeutic alliance to suggest noninterpretive interventions. His contention that such measures are antitherapeutic suggests that these techniques actually foster new sectors of misalliance, rather than constructively modifying the original problem in the alliance. My own observations support those of Kanzer (see Langs 1973b, 1974, 1975b; and see below).

There are, of course, many descriptions of misalliances in the literature on countertransference problems (for a partial bibliography, see Langs 1974). Space will not permit a survey of this aspect here except to note that Searles (1965) and Racker (1968) have been especially sensitive to this kind of problem; the latter's profound studies most clearly foreshadowed the findings to be presented here. In particular, Racker's paper (1968 [1957]) on the meanings and uses of countertransference (for him, defined as all of the analyst's reactions to his analysand) documented the occurrence of "vicious circles" in which the analyst enters the patient's neurosis and thereby cannot interpret it. Racker emphasized the role of the analyst's self-observations in preventing misalliances and demonstrated repeatedly how reactions in the analyst that complement the patient's neurotic needs preclude a proper understanding of the patient. In one pertinent statement among many, he wrote (1968, p. 152):

The transference, insofar as it is determined by the infantile situations and archaic objects of the patient, provokes in the unconscious of the analyst infantile situations and an intensified vibration of archaic objects of his own.... the analyst, if not conscious of such countertransference responses, may make the patient feel exposed once again to an archaic object (the vicious circle), and...in spite of his having some understanding of what is happening in the patient, the analyst is prevented from giving an adequate interpretation.

Lastly, in quite a different vein, Glover's early paper (1931) on the therapeutic effects of inexact interpretations may be viewed as one of the first psychoanalytic studies of therapeutic misalliances. Briefly, Glover defined an inexact interpretation as one in which the specific fantasy system on which a symptom is based is not uncovered; a related fantasy system is instead interpreted to the patient. He described the manner in which the patient may seize upon the inexact interpretation and convert it into a displacement-substitute that is sufficiently remote from the real sources of the patient's anxiety as to afford him considerable symptom relief. He also noted that such improvement occurs at the cost of refractoriness to deeper analysis. In addition, Glover described a variety of defenses, suggestions, offers of sanction, and other efforts toward providing the patient the kind of displacement systems commonly offered by nonanalysts. In the terms defined within this paper, Glover was, indeed, exploring a variety of therapeutic misalliances and their effects.

Overall, the literature reflects the inevitablity of efforts toward misalliance, major or minor, the infinitely varied forms that such endeavors may take, and the prime importance of their detection, analysis, and modification. It is, however, relatively lacking in specific discussions of the means of detecting misalliances, the techniques related to their resolution, the special efforts of the patient toward modifying them, and the mutual influence of patient and analyst upon each other in creating, maintaining, and altering misalliances. Some clinical data will enable us to clarify these and other aspects of this problem.

CLINICAL MATERIAL

Every patient who seeks psychoanalysis or psychotherapy will attempt on some level to effect a therapeutic misalliance with his analyst or therapist. The direction of these efforts is the product of his past history, character makeup, unresolved intrapsychic conflicts and symptoms, current life situation, and responses to the analyst and the analytic situation.

It is characteristic of such efforts that they tend to re-create pathogenic and unresolved infantile relationships and traumas, and unmastered conflicts—along with efforts at adaptive and maladaptive mastery. They represent attempts to gratify infantile and unfulfilled pathological fantasies directly with the analyst. Simultaneously, they defend the patient against anxiety and guilt, intrapsychic conflicts, unresolved unconscious fantasies, and the threats posed by the relationship with the analyst. Patients try to involve the analyst in living out complex, pathological, unconscious fantasies and relationships, usually as an alternative to their verbal communication in derivative form.

It is one of the analyst's tasks in the opening phase of psychoanalysis to detect expressions of the patient's—and his own—wishes for a misalliance with him (Nunberg 1926). Throughout the subsequent therapy or analysis, the therapist remains alert for such a development at any juncture, especially at times of difficulty and at termination— the latter being a very common period for needs of this kind to occur in both participants. In general, the patient's efforts may appear in derivative or direct form in his associations, or may be attempted through some behavior and actual effort to engage the analyst in this type of involvement. These efforts need not be grossly acted out, but are often reflected in the manner and content of the patient's free associations and in his general analytic modus vivendi (Myerson 1969, 1973). While these intentions and fantasies, which are initially strongly related to the patient's unconscious motives for seeking analysis and to what has been termed *the pre-formed transference* (Langs 1974), contain the potential for misalliance, they also prove to be a rich source of analyzable material if the analyst does not consciously or unconsciously join in the misalliance. The analyst or therapist may have unresolved needs for a misalliance with his patients in general, or with a specific patient, that are mobilized upon his beginning a new therapeutic venture. The underlying motives are similar to those already described for the patient, with some specific additional aspects related to his role as analyst, and they reflect a variety of countertransferences and counterresistances to his patient.

The intermingling of the sources of misalliances is such that an unconscious circular interaction is characteristic. Both patient and analyst are attempting to adapt to their own inner needs and to the stimuli emanating from the other person. One of them may initiate a move toward misalliance or may respond to some cue from, or reaction by, the other; in turn, the second one will unconsciously participate or resist, or may communicate his own need for a different type of neurotic relationship, to which the first will then react. Unconscious evocation of, reaction to, acceptance of, resistance against, attempts to intensify, and attempts to rectify the area of misalliance occur in quick succession on both sides.

As previously noted (Langs 1974), misalliances may be classified as mutually narcissistic, sadomasochistic, exhibitionistic-voyeuristic, seductive, and infantilizing. However, such terms tend to offer a classification that fails to reflect the specific nuances and richness of these interactions; a deep, dynamic clinical description and formulation promises to offer a more precise picture.

In this spirit, then, let us move directly to a vignette drawn from the opening phase of a psychotherapy; as we will see, the principles and concepts to be derived from it are fully applicable to the psychoanalytic situation as well.[2]

Dr. Z. presented a patient, Mr. A., to me in supervision. Mr. A. was a man in his fifties who sought therapy for recurrent moderate depressions and failures to advance in his work despite apparent strong abilities. He served as a consultant to an electronics firm and was concerned that his contract would not be renewed. His wife was depressed and currently in therapy. Of note regarding his past history is the fact that his parents had both died in an automobile accident when the patient was in his late teens; he had dissipated his inheritance in the years that followed and was currently worried about finances. Diagnostically, he was assessed as an obsessive character disorder with depression.

In his first sessions, Mr. A. spoke repeatedly of his financial worries and of his failure to provide his wife with security, closeness or an adequate sexual relationship. He envied the younger men who always appeared to replace him in his work. He tended to withdraw whenever he was under stress. When others failed, he always felt better.

Mr. A. detailed his current realistic problems in this manner over several hours, and the therapist asked occasional questions about them. When the patient then revealed that he was currently having joint sessions with his wife's therapist, Dr. Z. asked him how he felt about it, but otherwise did not explore or deal with it. In his associations, Mr. A. spoke of not wanting to hear about his wife's problems and of how he lacked family ties. His brother hated Mr. A.'s wife and never spoke to either of them; Mr. A. allowed his guilt to plague and inhibit him. He alluded to a previous psychotherapy in which the therapist unnecessarily reduced his fee and which got nowhere. That therapist had also seen his wife and had been overtly seductive; Mrs. A. had stopped seeing him when she caught him in an error—a contradiction—and he asked her to leave. When the therapist asked further about this past therapy, Mr. A. spoke of his anger over his wife's seductiveness with other men; he did not trust her. He would end up having to fix things himself.

In the next few hours, allusions to the sessions with his wife's therapist, which are soon discontinued at that therapist's request, were intermingled with recollections of his parents' deaths, in which his own hostility toward them was hinted at. He then recalled primal observations from his childhood, his attachment to male friends, and vaguely wondered if he was homosexually attracted to a cousin who had understood and helped him as a teenager. Later, he spoke of a cousin who had had a nervous breakdown and of how two therapists were too much to handle. His guilt immobilized him and he preferred to be left alone; maybe hypnosis would help him. He never committed himself.

I shall pause here to describe the relevant supervisory discussions and formulations. In brief, Mr. A. consciously sought help for his depression, guilt, and need to fail. Unconsciously, he initially indicated that a misalliance in which the therapist would fail would temporarily reassure ("cure") him. His associations suggested that he would also accept a situation of mutual withdrawal in which his hostile and sexual impulses were covered over (and somewhat gratified) as another sector of misalliance. This became especially clear when his associations revealed that the other therapist was protecting Mr. A. from experiencing, and therefore facing, his unconscious homosexual fantasies toward his present therapist.

Despite supervisory discussions, the therapist chose to ignore the emerging derivatives of Mr. A.'s unconscious fantasies and did not deal with the evident resistances embedded in the deviation in technique—the sessions with the second therapist (Langs 1975b). Unconsciously, he communicated to the patient his own wishes to avoid both closeness with Mr. A. and meaningful material and interaction, and his preference for focusing on realistic problems in which intrapsychic conflicts and disturbing affects and fantasies were relatively ignored.

Mr. A. and Dr. Z., each prompting and responding to the other, rather quickly and unconsciously had arranged a ruminative intellectualizing, reality-focused, fantasy-avoiding misalliance of major proportions. Despite supervisory comments, the therapist did virtually nothing to modify his position. Soon Mr. A., who had unconsciously perpetuated the misalliance, also initiated unconscious efforts to modify it. Such curative endeavors by patients toward their analysts and therapists have been described previously by Little (1951), Searles (1965), and myself (1973a, 1975a). More recently, Searles (1975) in an extensive study of the curative work of his schizophrenic and neurotic patients toward himself as their analyst, has suggested that they reflect a basic human need that arises in the infant in his earliest relationship and symbiotic experiences with his mother.

Empirically I have found that patients are exquisitely sensitive to and unconsciously perceptive of their therapist's errors, and that they respond by efforts to correct and assist the therapist at such moments. Their unconscious communications at such junctures bear the hallmark of sound confrontations and interpretations; they express ideas and formulations remarkably parallel to my own thinking and direct interventions with their therapists in supervision. Upon reflection, the underlying principle is a sound one: if the therapist is blocked or unhelpful in his therapeutic work, his cure must take precedence so that he can ultimately help the patient.

In a well-run treatment, such efforts are relatively infrequent and generally minor, though nonetheless quite important (Searles 1975). The patient's reactions at such moments are, as always, based on a mixture of valid unconscious perceptions and bona fide therapeutic efforts on the one hand, and their own intrapsychic fantasies, conflicts, and needs—including transference distortions—on the other. In emphasizing the need to recognize and implicitly make use of the patient's helpful endeavors, we must not overlook the ultimate shift of the focus of treatment to the therapy of the patient. However, the therapist who treats these efforts entirely as distortions and ignores their realistic aspects (Searles 1975) will make hurtful and insensitive interventions. Here, I shall merely attempt a preliminary sketch of patients' efforts at cure, pending more conclusive investigations.

As we have seen, Mr. A., quite early in the therapy, and well after the first sectors of misalliance had been established, spoke of withdrawing under stress and of his own failures to provide his family with a growth-promoting relationship. In part this material reflects his unconscious perception of the therapist's failings—indeed, of his need to fail—and of the misalliance; it reflects too his subsequent incorporative identification with these aspects of the therapist. While this may well appear somewhat speculative, in part because I have condensed the initial material to an extreme degree, let us follow the subsequent developments.

Mr. A. had soon revealed that he had a second therapist. In addition to reflecting his own fears of closeness and his homosexual anxieties, this is an indication of the patient's unconscious awareness of Dr. Z.'s supervisor (such communications are common among clinic patients). Perhaps Mr. A. was also suggesting that supervision might be a factor in Dr. Z's fears of the therapeutic relationship; this indeed was an impression that I had in the supervision. More important, however, it represented an effort to alert the therapist to the presence of a third (and fourth—his wife) party to the treatment, and its implicit defensive defensive and neurotically gratifying dimensions. When Dr. Z. failed to explore the situation, thereby accepting and participating in it, we can observe a variety of unconscious reactions in Mr. A.— incorporative identification, what I term *unconscious interpretations*, and further extensive efforts to "cure" the therapist.

Thus, Mr. A. alluded to the way he allows guilt to plague and inhibit him, a view—again confirmed by my supervisory observations—of an aspect of the therapist's countertransference problems. He also suggested through displaced derivatives that the therapist had an underlying hatred for him (and therefore permitted a detrimental situation to continue,while protecting himself from his anger by having an observer present); he also spoke of his own refusal to listen to his wife (the therapist who will not hear). He referred to the therapist who inappropriately reduced his fee, failed to help, was seductive, made a blunder, and sent his wife away. When these indirect allusions to the present therapist went unheeded, we hear of the patient's growing mistrust and his despairing conclusion that he will have to cure himself.

Further derivatives connect the two-therapist situation to Mr. A.'s rage at his deserting parents (the therapist) and to primal scene experiences (threesomes). There is then a strikingly condensed association that contains another unconscious interpretation, one that was exquisitely intended to bring to the therapist's awareness the underlying, interfering homosexual conflicts that prompted him to accept a third party to his relationship with Mr. A. As his supervisor, I could not have expressed such insights into Dr. Z.'s countertransference difficulties and motives for misalliance more clearly. It is evident, of course, that these associations also reflect Mr. A.'s own latent homosexual conflicts. Such condensations and multiple functions of communications from the patient are the rule.

Finally, Mr. A. went on to express his fears for his own mental integrity if the blind spot and misalliance prevailed. Simultaneously he offered a confrontation and interpretation of the therapist's anxieties: that they were based on guilt, primal scene and homosexual conflicts, and fears of being overwhelmed. Lastly, there was another reference to the therapist's striking failure to intervene—commit himself—and to another search for self-cure through hypnosis. In actuality, many of these derivatives convey unconsciously from Mr. A. direct comments that had been made in supervision to Dr. Z.

To continue more briefly with this vignette, the patient was soon told that his business contract would not be renewed. He spent many sessions ruminating about this problem and how to deal with it, and from time to time the therapist questioned him about it or pointed out an obvious aspect of Mr. A.'s concern. Soon the patient conveyed feelings that he was getting nowhere in his therapy and the therapist reported to me that he felt bored and was annoyed with his patient. In supervision, I too experienced the sessions as uninteresting and hollow. Since the therapist made no effort to deal with the resistances and misalliance that he and the patient had effected, I more strongly recommended confrontations with the patient's failure to communicate expressions of his inner conflicts (derivatives of his unconscious fantasies) and a modification of the therapist's stance: he should no longer participate in the reality focus and should confine himself to confronting and analyzing the patient's defenses and to exploring any expressions of intrapsychic conflicts that emerged. I also used Mr. A.'s unconscious interpretations to Dr. Z. to alert the latter to the underlying basis for his block.

As the therapist very tentatively began to modify his stance, Mr. A.'s associations—which had been undecipherable in connection with any type of unconscious fantasy other than those related to the misalliance—came alive again. He spoke of how he should give his son more responsibilities, and of the lack of dialogue between himself and his wife. When confronted with the lack of reference to his inner stirrings he, for the first time, told the story of the man who gets a flat and needs to borrow a jack to fix it. On walking to a house to ask for help, he is so convinced that he will be refused, and builds the scene so much in his mind, that he rings the bell and attacks the man who answers it. Mr. A. also anticipates a royal shafting wherever he goes; he becomes the good guy, and then no one feels bad.

In other sessions, he spoke of his anger when his wife stirred him up, adding, however, that he wanted to take on responsibilities with her. His friend had been in therapy and had not changed; he just accepted it. His son did nothing—it was Mr. A.'s own fault for being permissive and not meddling in his problems; he was afraid he might crush his son. His own father never intervened with him, though his mother did.

As the therapist continued to explore Mr. A.'s fears of revealing himself, the patient spoke of how he pressured his inactive son to do things and to communicate. He played psychiatrist with his son but not with himself. He disliked having the same conversation with his wife over and over; his first therapist never got behind the same old reality issues. If he exposed himself to the therapist, the latter would be just like his wife and give him advice.

We see, then, that the therapist's constructive efforts to modify the misalliance were unconsciously perceived by the patient, who also appears to have positively identified with the correctly and unconsciously perceived newfound strengths of the therapist. Derivatives of Mr. A.'s own intrapsychic conflicts become available for cognitive-emotional insight through interpretation by the therapist. Thus were opened up crucial routes for the modification of misalliances and for new, constructive avenues of conflict resolution and change for the patient.

I have presented this vignette in some detail because it demonstrates in its two misalliances—the accepted third party to the therapy and the shared obsessive-avoidance defenses—many typical characteristics of these misalliances: their mutuality, and the clues whereby they can be recognized and resolved.

Subjectively, therapeutic misalliances should be considered when the therapist senses a lack of progress or depth in the therapy, or in the unfolding of the material from the patient. Beyond such cognitive awareness, the therapist may experience a range of thoughts, feelings, and fantasies: things are not right; he dislikes the patient, or has other unusual attitudes or feelings toward him; he feels used or manipulated, or that he is ineffectual as a therapist; he is aware of notably seductive or aggressive feelings toward the patient that he is unable to resolve; he cannot understand a stalemate or a regression in the patient. Subjectively experienced disturbances in his therapeutic attitudes, or any unusual manner of intervening or behaving, are clues to the presence of countertransference problems, and direct the therapist to search for their expression in the actual interaction with the patient.

Subjective clues lead the therapist to listening especially carefully to the patient's associations with the suspected misalliance in mind. A correct and sensitive subjective appraisal that leads to the identification of a misalliance should be confirmed in the patient's associations. At times, when the therapist is especially blocked, these will stimulate him to focus on his own inner feelings and fantasies. Themes of noncommunication, of manipulation, of poor parental functioning, of poor therapy of any kind, of collusion, and other misalliance-related content should alert him. The valid understanding of these associations as they relate to a misalliance or any aspect of the patient-therapist relationship should always, in turn, be confirmed by the therapist's subjective experiences and realizations (see Langs 1975a).

In this vignette, the therapist's sense of boredom and anger could have alerted him to the obsessive misalliance (not simply Mr. A.'s resistances). A review of his interventions (e.g., repeated realistic inquiries and avoidance of instinctual-drive derivatives) would have been helpful, as would other, inevitable feelings that he did not report to me. In my supervision, I detected many clues to the misalliance. Mr. A.'s multiple communications were also available.

Therapeutic misalliances foster symptom relief through pathological, shared defenses and inappropriate gratifications. They repeat and confirm the patient's neurotic fantasies, needs, and past pathogenic interactions, and the participating therapist cannot interpret and modify such pathology; he is, for the moment, an integral part of it.

Modification of misalliances entails the following steps:

1. Recognition by the therapist.
2. Modification of the therapist's participation through self-analysis, without burdening the patient, through full use should be made of the patient's unconscious perceptions and interpretations. The therapist's failure to resolve his inner conflicts will promote new versions of the misalliance.
3. Full analysis, without blame, of the patient's own needs for the misalliance, and his role in effecting it.

When a major technical error, deviation in technique, or erroneous stance by the therapist has contributed to the misalliance, the therapist in proper context may *implicitly* acknowledge his contribution—a practice that is largely misused by patient and therapist, and therefore best confined to indirect means. Basically, even if the therapist's participation was inadvertent, he should never deny his role, should tacitly accept the actuality of his contribution, and not treat the patient's perceptions of it as fantasy-based. However, this does not preclude a full exploration of the patient's involvement in the misalliance, his extensions of reality into conscious and unconscious fantasies, and his frequent attempts to misuse the misalliance to sanction his own pathology. A full analysis of the unconscious motives for seeking and maintaining a misalliance not only clears the way to a viable therapeutic alliance, but is the vehicle for vital therapeutic work.

In fact, the analytic resulution of misalliances is a moving experience for both patient and therapist, providing both an intense kind of experience that is appropriately gratifying in a way that is unique even in the therapeutic relationship. The final mutual triumph over pathological inner needs and defenses is especially satisfying.

The interaction between the patient and the therapist has alternating thrusts toward misalliance and rectification of the misalliance—restoring the therapeutic alliance. In focusing on the efforts of one or the other toward maladaptive equilibrium, we must not overlook their respective efforts toward healthier adaptations. While we tend to focus on the therapist's conscious efforts toward resolution of the misalliance, this vignette clearly indicates consistent efforts by the patient to alert the therapist to the misalliance and to help him modify it.

Having established some basic concepts and technical principles, let us now attempt to apply and expand upon them with a second vignette.

Mrs. B. was a young teacher who had sought therapy for marital difficulties. She had been in psychotherapy for several months with a woman therapist who was, at the time of the sessions to be described, in her sixth month of a pregnancy. The patient appeared to have some phobic systems, primarily a fear of driving and an anxiety that she would be physically damaged in an accident caused by another car; these symptoms had been reported in recent sessions.

The patient had missed a session because of a legal holiday and for her following hour knocked on the therapist's door fifteen minutes early; in the session itself, she spoke of feeling isolated and lonely in her marriage, and complained about her husband's incessant nagging. She recalled having had some facial moles removed when she was thirteen years of age, a procedure that included cosmetic plastic surgery as well. While her appearance had improved, the changes had intensified her anxieties and especially exacerbated a choking sensation in her throat and difficulty in swallowing. The therapist responded with a lengthy intervention, in which she related the patient's feelings of loneliness to the missed session and connected this to her coming early; in addition, she suggested that this also related to the anticipated separation that would occur at the time of her delivery. The patient responded with some general agreement.

Mrs. B. was late to her next session; she stated that she no longer felt lonely and that she was not attached to her therapist, who she felt was somehow implying that she had had feelings during her mother's pregnancy in her childhood (a sister had been born when she was five and a brother when she was eight); she rather elaborately denied any such reaction. She also complained that the sessions were exhausting her and that the therapist was too silent.

In the next hour, the patient was five minutes late but eager to talk. She had quarreled with her husband and had been angry over his attachment to his mother, stating that he did not seem to understand that she and he were a couple and that they should function as a couple. They had argued and the patient had slept alone, but then became frightened. That night she slept at her sister's house and when the therapist asked why the patient was behaving in this way now, Mrs. B. related it to being in treatment, feeling stronger, and not seeing any change in her husband. The therapist asked her to relate it more clearly to treatment and the patient reiterated what she had said. She then spoke of her difficulties in opening up in treatment and suggested that she had to work on that. The therapist made another lengthy intervention in which she attempted to link the patient's becoming more freely verbal in her sessions to her wish to leave her husband, adding that it also seemed to reflect feelings of hurt in response to the therapist's recent comments and to the missed session. The patient said that she was thinking of reducing her sessions from two to one weekly, and the therapist commented that this represented an effort to deny any need for her.

Mrs. B. said that she had felt hurt and criticized by the therapist and had thought of not coming for her session, adding that she overreacts in an unproductive way. Doing things when she was hurt would not change the problem and her husband simply would not change. The therapist seemed not to realize how frightened she was of leaving him; she added that she had her faults too, and had to accept the marriage since she could not expect anything better. The therapist made another long intervention about the manner in which the patient was feeling criticized and therefore angry with her, relating it to her conflict with her husband. The patient responded by ruminating about her exaggerated sensitivity to hurts, relating it to her father's hitting her as a child, and contrasting it to her parents' efforts to be supportive at other times.

I shall pause here to formulate the interaction between this patient and her therapist. The material begins essentially with a missed hour and with derivatives related to what is quite evidently the primary adaptive task intrapsychically for Mrs. B., her therapist's pregnancy. The associations indicate that this patient is experiencing the pregnancy as a development through which she will suffer a great loss and a rupture of the close twosome that she had been experiencing with the therapist. In addition, there is evidence of an unconscious incorporative identification with the pregnant therapist, with related bodily anxieties—the fear of being smashed by a car and being damaged bodily, and the reparative references to the plastic surgery. On the basis of the therapist's subsequent interventions, we might speculate that the allusions to the nagging husband relate to an unconscious perception of the manner in which this therapist intervenes.

In the following hour, Mrs. B.'s denial of any reaction to the therapist's pregnancy offers a genetic clue to its unconscious meaning and is apparently designed, however defensively, to alert the therapist to the fact that it is a crucial source of anxiety and conflict—the main adaptive and therapeutic context for the moment. When the therapist failed to recognize these implications, the patient complained about treatment.

In the next hour, the patient, through displaced derivatives, expressed her anger regarding the anticipated rupture of the therapeutic couple, acting out the denial of her need for her therapist in her relationship with her husband. When the therapist failed to recognize the central source of this behavior and of the underlying conflicts (her own pregnancy), the patient soon undertook unconscious efforts to alert her to this blind spot—talking about her own problems in opening up in the sessions and in being in touch, and her thoughts of canceling her hours. When the therapist responded with lengthy, apparently anxious and inaccurate interventions, the patient spoke of the manner in which she herself overreacted unproductively— a formulation that was anticipated in supervision.

Mrs. B. goes on to again express her conflicts over leaving treatment, once more displacing these reactions onto her husband. Her own devalued self-image and an incorporative identification with the impaired (pregnant and insensitive) therapist lead her to allusions to her own faults. Another generally incorrect intervention follows, and Mrs. B. speculates on her own sensitivity to hurts, an unconscious interpretation to the therapist, perhaps an unconscious perception of the therapist's excessive sensitivity, with a related genetic intervention—that the therapist's sensitivity is related to a disturbed interaction with her parents.

The sectors of misalliance between Mrs. B. and her therapist primarily involved the establishment of a somewhat sadomasochistic and intellectualized defensive interaction designed to avoid and deny the main areas of intrapsychic conflict evoked—probably for both of them—by the pregnancy.

I would view the patient's momentary feeling that she was stronger as a *misalliance cure* (for the earlier roots of this concept see Langs 1974 and Barchilon 1958) in which the patient found support and reassurance through the therapist's difficulties and mobilized her own resources because of the latter's failure. The mutual avoidance of the patient's central anxieties and conflicts afforded her momentary relief through the shared defenses. In general, then, it is important to accurately identify the underlying basis of symptom relief and to recognize the indicators of a momentarily successful "cure" through therapeutic misalliance.

The patient began the next hour by reporting that she felt better and had worked things out with her husband; it was not completely satisfactory, but she had made an effort. She went on to describe a movie that she had seen in which several people were crippled and paralyzed; she had fled the theater. She now remembered a dream from that night, one in which she was working with crippled children. On the night prior to the present session, she had dreamt of sitting in a luncheonette and hearing some children criticize her singing.

In the session, she stated that if she were crippled or handicapped like the men in the movie, she would kill herself, even though they seemed to make the adjustment. She felt that the dream meant that she could not imagine herself being damaged and that the second dream alluded to her difficulty in taking criticism as a child, something that she could handle better now. She related this to treatment and stated that it bothered her that she ruminated in her sessions; she felt guilty with her husband because she did not do the things that she should do for him—she did not give enough to him.

These communications condensed a variety of unconscious perceptions and fantasies. The dream and associations to them reflect the patient's unconscious identification with the pregnant therapist in a manner that indicates that pregnancy is seen by Mrs. B. as a potentially crippling experience that is evoking considerable anxiety in her. This material also reflects unconscious perceptions of the therapist, who did not intervene or understand these communications—that is, failed to do the things that she should have done in the sessions. Further, the associations represent another effort on the part of Mrs. B. to direct the therapist to the source of their respective conflicts and anxieties. Mrs. B. sensed, apparently correctly, that her therapist was anxious about her pregnancy and avoiding it in the treatment situation. On this basis, she offered a series of unconscious interpretations which are amalgams of her fantasies with efforts to direct the therapist to the possible sources of her anxieties. These efforts are best illustrated in the reference to the handicapped and crippled men. In this context, the flight from the theater dramatizes the therapist's own massive avoidance.

Mrs. B. began her next hour by describing minor surgery that her husband would be having; she would have to drive him home because he would be groggy (another allusion to the necessity for this patient to take responsibility for her therapy). She had had a pleasant visit with her in-laws but had been demeaned by her husband when she had reacted to his tormenting of a waitress. There was a period of silence; when the therapist inquired into it, Mrs. B. said she had been thinking of menstruation. Her periods had been irregular for the past couple of months and her gynecologist had said it was her nerves. It made her feel that there was something wrong with her and that she would not be able to have babies; she somehow connected this to her fears of accidents and damage. When she was thirteen, she had had similar anxieties.

The therapist intervened, reiterating the various themes to which the patient had alluded, and pointed out that the patient's increased anxiety undoubtedly reflected concerns about her pregnancy and delivery, and worries that she—the therapist—would be damaged. Mrs. B. responded with a broad smile; she said that she envied her therapist's Ph.D.—she actually had an M.D.—and added that she was worried that she herself would be unable to have children when she wanted them. She suddenly recalled that she had had a dream where she had delivered a baby who was fine but was taken away. She guessed that she was, after all, concerned about her therapist's pregnancy and delivery.

In this session, relatively undisguised derivatives of Mrs. B.'s unconscious fantasies, conflicts, and anxieties as they are related to the therapist's pregnancy unfold. The onset of the patient's irregular periods coincided with the recognition of the therapist's pregnancy and affords further evidence of the patient's identification with her therapist. In addition, it hints at unconscious wishes to destroy the fetus and at rage in the rivalry with the therapist, a thesis that is supported by her own fear that she would not be able to have a child, the allusion to accidents and damage, and the element of the final dream in which the baby disappears. The therapist failed to recognize these derivatives as related to specific aggressive fantasies—a failure that could form the nucleus of another misalliance, and demonstrates how a therapist's failure to resolve his contributing intrapsychic conflicts can lead to new versions of the search for unconscious collusion.

Perhaps because the patient's unconscious interventions were of some help to this therapist, she was finally able to identify some of the important meanings of these less and less disguised associations and to interpret aspects of them. Her relativity correct intervention evoked a strongly confirmatory response in the patient in the form of the recall of previously repressed dream (Langs 1974a). The dream also suggests an unconscious incorporative identification with a more positive image of the therapist, in that it portrays the patient as being capable of delivering a baby, although this is marred by the disappearance of the child—an element which undoubtedly refers to the patient's own hostile wishes, but may also be a further unconscious attempt to suggest tot he therapist that the latter's need to avoid the subject of her pregnancy was related to her own unresolved hostility toward her fetus. A further acknowledgment of the therapist's capacities is contained in the reference to her degree, although the patient again showed her hostility by mentioning a Ph.D., which, her later associations revealed, she considered lower than the M.D. the therapist had actually attained.

As with the first vignette, the material presented here strongly indicates that this patient's apparent resistances against dealing with the conflicts, fantasies, and anxieties evoked by her therapist's pregnancy were not solely evoked by intrapsychic defenses. It is clear that the therapist's own unconscious defensive avoidance of the pregnancy significantly contributed to and reinforced the patient's defensiveness. It follows, then, that the first step toward resolving this resistance was a modification of the therapist's defenses so that she could consciously acknowledge and deal with the derivatives from the patient related to her pregnancy, and would no longer unconsciously communicate to the patient her own wishes to avoid the subject.

This material also demonstrates the manner in which a patient who is faced with a seriously defensive therapist, and who also has mounting inner anxieties and distrusting fantasies, will actively attempt to cure the therapist of her difficulty in order to obtain much-needed help in return. The therapist's correct though limited intervention was subsequently confirmed by associations that included both the further modification of repressive barriers and indications of a momentary positive incorporative identification.

In retrospect, it appears that if the therapist had properly understood the communications regarding the patient's marital problems as a means of expressing Mrs. B.'s unconscious perception of her misalliance with the therapist, and if she had more sensitively monitored the patient's associations for unconscious perceptions of her own role in the stalemate that she herself had sensed, she would have been directed much sooner to her own difficulties. Discussions with the therapist suggested that her anxieties regarding her pending delivery, and her own conscious and unconscious fantasies of bodily damage, were so intense that she did indeed unconsciously share many of these disturbing fantasies with the patient and therefore utilized comparable defenses.

We see also that the therapist's difficulties in dealing with this area created pressures within the patient toward greater self-confidence and more effective communications, and therefore afforded her a momentary misalliance cure. The symptom relief obtained by the patient through these shared defenses, and through the gratification of being more in tune with her anxieties than the therapist was with hers, was short-lived, and the patient's anxieties soon returned. The subsequent material clearly reflects the fact that the patient had in no way understood her intrapsychic conflicts and anxieties as related to the pregnancy, but that she had found temporary relief through bypassing them. As her anxiety intensified, it became necessary for her to return to the specific unconscious fantasies that were disturbing her and to seek the assistance of the therapist in resolving them. In a small way, these observations provide clues regarding the vicissitudes of the identificatory processes in the therapeutic relationship as they fluctuate with the therapist's actual capacities and thereby strengthen or weaken the patient's self-image and general ego capacities. The interpretation of derivatives of unconscious transference fantasies, by contrast, offers specific cognitive insights that enable the patient to master areas of conflict.

In concluding my discussion of this vignette, I would note that the material supports the thesis that the development of a firm therapeutic alliance depends on both the nonparticipation of the therapist in a misalliance and correctly timed, pertinent interpretations. Attempts to be reassuring, to offer so-called reparative deviations in technique, and any other kind of noninterpretive intervention could only foster additional sectors of misalliance and further convey the therapist's difficulties in understanding the patient's intrapsychic conflicts. In addition, any effort to reassure the patient regarding the therapist's good intentions (Zetzel 1966-1969) or to discuss the patient's realistic concerns (Greenson and Wexler 1969) would not only reflect an insensitivity to the main source of the patient's conflicts and difficulties, but would also entail at times the conscious denial of the patient's valid, unconscious perceptions of the therapist. Such a noninterpretative stance reflects the therapist's failure to appreciate both the transference and realistic elements in the patient's communications, and their unconscious elaborations.

I am well aware of the danger of reading too much into the patient's associations. I want to emphasize that it was the striking correspondence between my own conscious assessment as a supervisor, and the unconscious perceptions and communications of the patient that led me to recognize the remarkable extent to which patients are in touch with their therapist's failings, and the extent of their endeavors to assist the therapist with them. Similarly, when in this case I formulated that the therapist had make a sound and helpful intervention, the patient's unconscious communications reflected a perception and incorporation of these positive attributes. Once this exquisite sensitivity on the part of the patient is fully appreciated, it enables the therapist to understand and predict the unfolding of many previously confusing sessions—a powerful means of understanding the patient-therapist and patient-analyst interactions.

DISCUSSION AND CONCLUSIONS

Therapeutic misalliances, as sectors of the patient-analyst relationship, are related to the intermixtures of transference and countertransference, as well as to other aspects of the patient's and the analyst's mutual attempts to adapt. They may be present in patients or analysts who appear to be working well and seem overtly to be cooperating and not acting out or acting in. They offer, however, momentary maladaptive resolutions to the patient's and/or analyst's conflicts, and foster maladaptive identifications of each with the other, undermining the therapist's effectiveness. They must, therefore, be analyzed and resolved to permit other aspects of the analytic work to unfold effectively. Yet, as inevitable expressions of the patient's pathology and of the residuals of the pathology in the analyst, these efforts at misalliance are, paradoxically, a major opportunity for effective and necessary analytic work and for growth within both participants.

Although misalliances are always embedded in the specific conflicts, character structure, and genetic history of the patient and the analyst, we may identify certain general motives for the creation of misalliances. On the patient's part, the search for misalliance stems from the hope for maladaptive relief from the anxiety and guilt related to his intrapsychic conflicts. A misalliance can serve as a major defense against closeness with the analyst and all that such intimacy represents to the patient. It may also provide him inappropriate gratification of his neurotic needs and be a means by which he repeats past interactions that fostered his neurosis and justifies its continuation. Through a misalliance, the patient also bypasses the painful process of reunciation and inner change. A misalliance can reinforce inappropriate superego sanctions and punishments, and offer a wide range of pathological defenses to the patient—as well as to the analyst. For any given moment, it may provide the patient temporary and usually unstable symptomatic relief so that he does not attempt to seek out other, more adaptive but arduous solutions to his conflicts. To the extent that misalliances gratify wishes to circumvent reasonable boundaries and to deny separateness, they also provide the patient illusions of symbiotic ties, and a false sense of omnipotence and of a right to special gratification, which can momentarily reassure him to the extent that he is not plagued by his intrapsychic conflicts. The inherent depreciation and destruction of the analyst who becomes involved in a misalliance provides the patient neurotic feelings of power and pathologically gained self-esteem.

Through a misalliance, the analyst no longer represents insight, delay, optimal adaptation, renunciation, and the process of analytic scrutiny; the patient thereby is able to unconsciously justify his abandonment of meaningful analytic work toward inner change. More broadly, the analyst is for the moment no longer a "good object" with which the patient can constructively identify, but has become instead a "bad object" who is incorporated to the detriment of the patient's self-representation and functioning. In all, the inevitable wish to maladaptively and momentarily lessen conflict, anxiety, and guilt at any cost, the universal human search for unlimited closeness and immediate discharge, and the need to repeat and master past traumatic relationships prompt these efforts toward misalliances in patients.

Despite these gains, the inherently maladaptive, destructive and inappropriately gratifying aspects of an effected misalliance will prompt the patient to make efforts to modify and renounce the collusion with the help of the analyst. Unconsciously aware of the ultimately self-defeating dimensions of a misalliance, the patient communicates his perceptions to the analyst in his efforts to find a new and healthier adaptation. In addition, he unconsciously attempts to resolve the misalliance through curing the therapist as well as himself.

In general, despite the momentary symptomatic relief that misalliances afford, they are often followed by serious regressive and acting out episodes if they are not detected and modified. Further, if the patient's efforts to modify the misalliance go unheeded and if the analyst has unresolved unconscious needs to maintain it, the patient will either abruptly terminate the therapy or will continue in the stalemated therapeutic situation in which he can maintain the inappropriate relationship and gratifications so obtained.

The analyst's inevitable residuals of unmastered anxiety and guilt, neurotic and maladaptive defensive needs, his longings for personal or magical closeness and for inappropriate gratifications, his struggles against the severe limits imposed by the analytic relationship, and his own search to repeat and master past pathological interactions prompt him to search for misalliances with his patients. Specific unresolved intrapsychic conflicts stirred up by a particular patient may prompt him to seek out a misalliance rather than to assist the patient in resolving his difficulties analytically. It should be noted, however, that the analyst's or therapist's responsibilities in this area differ from those of the patient. He must recognize and master a developing misalliance as quickly as possible, to prevent it from permanently impairing the therapeutic relationship and derailing the analytic work. While the patient, for his analysis to be successful, must be willing at some point to explore, analyze, and resolve his quest for misalliance with the analyst, the analyst carries the responsibility to resolve his inner difficulties along these lines largely on his own, tacitly accepting whatever assistance the patient consciously or unconsciously offers. He should not feel unduly guilty over a misalliance that he has evoked, but should utilize his disturbed interaction as a means of understanding the patient and his own neurotic needs.

I will conclude by briefly listing the main heuristic and technical implications of the concept of the therapeutic misalliance.

1. The misalliance concept leads directly to a study of the patient-analyst interaction and its intrapsychic consequences when impairments arise in the therapeutic alliance and in the treatment situation. This is a viable alternative to the more common focus at such moments on the patient's damaged capacities, such as an inability for mature object relationships and trust (Zetzel 1958, 1966–1969). While recognizing the importance of such factors, the misalliance concept points to the frequency with which difficulties arise from shared unconscious interactions and communications.

2. The concept of therapeutic misalliance fosters use of the adaptational-interactional viewpoint, in which the intrapsychic repercussions of the actualities of the therapeutic relationship and the behaviors of the analyst are considered, along with manifestations of the effects of transference and countertransference fantasies.

The therapist's ongoing relationship with the patient, his therapeutic stance and "hold," and his projections and communications to the patient as an actual person ("object"—Loewald 1960) contribute to important incorporative identifications into the patient's self-representations and psychic structures, and create the basic background for effective interpretive work. They are as important as the capacity of the therapist to offer meaningful insights through interpretation.

3. The misalliance concept leads to a full appreciation of the importance of the patient's unconscious perceptions of the therapist, and the kernels of reality in his relationship with the therapist. It establishes them as a constituent to be added to unconscious fantasies and memories (transference) as the main determinants of the patient's reactions to the therapist or analyst, and the main basis for neurotic symptom formation.

4. The concept also leads us to recognize the vital importance of who the analyst is, and how he behaves and structures the relationship with the patient—in addition to how and what he interprets. The therapist's needs and identity are conveyed in the way he uses the ground rules of therapy, in his maintenance of the boundaries of the relationship, and in his capacity to interpret rather than participate in a pathogenic interaction. These now become important focuses of therapy, rather than peripheral factors.

5. This concept leads to a recognition that the patient's intrapsychic resistances and pathogenic needs often find unconscious reinforcement in the responses of the therapist, and to a more careful study of the manner in which intrapsychic conflicts and defenses are, in general, supported by interactions with others.

6. This concept focuses on a facet of the treatment situation that must be analyzed first before other effective work can be done, and on an aspect of the therapist's interaction with the patient that must be modified, along with the intrapsychic basis on which it has developed; for true resolution to occur, words are not enough.

7. The concept helps to create a better perspective on the therapeutic relationship and the contributions of transference and countertransference (distortions) on the one hand, and nontransference and noncountertransference (reality) on the other. It leads, also, to a fuller appreciation of the pathological needs of both participants, and especially to the curative needs and capacities of both. It shows us, too, that in pathological interactions lie the seeds of growth and constructive change.

My emphasis on the patient's curative efforts toward his therapist is not intended to suggest that this dimension of their relationship should be prominent or central to therapy. The therapeutic situation is designed for the patient's needs and should center upon them; however, we should not neglect the potential for adaptive change available to the therapist at those moments (hopefully relatively infrequent) of need. I am aware that I have dealt briefly with many pertinent issues, but hope primarily that I have stimulated fresh considerations of the patient-analyst interaction and its role in impediments and progress in therapy. The spirit of this report is reflected in a quote from Freud (1937, p. 221): "Instead of an enquiry into how a cure by analysis comes about (a matter which I think has been sufficiently elucidated) the question should be asked, what are the obstacles that stand in the way of such a cure."

NOTES

1. I shall use the terms *therapist* and *analyst* interchangeably here because the segment of the therapeutic relationship that I am investigating is largely

(though not entirely) comparable. The clinical data that I can specifically report in this paper are drawn from analytic psychotherapy, though I have made countless comparable observations in the psychoanalytic situation as well.

2. For a variety of reasons, I have made the decision to not use material from my own clinical practice, past and present, in any of my writings. In part, this decision has derived from the observation that such use of one's therapeutic or analytic work entails serious risk of misalliance with the patient (see also Langs 1975b).

REFERENCES

Binstock, W. (1973). The therapeutic relationship. *Journal of the American Psychoanalytic Association* 21:543–557.

Barchilon, J. (1958). On countertransference "cures." *Journal of the American Psychoanalytic Association* 6:222–236.

Corwin, H. (1972). The scope of therapeutic confrontation. *International Journal of Psychoanalytic Psychotherapy* 1(3):68–89.

Dickes, R. (1967). Severe regressive disruptions of the therapeutic alliance. *Journal of American Psychoanalytic Association* 15:508–533.

Fenichel, O. (1941). *Problems of Psychoanalytic Technique.* New York: Psychoanalytic Quarterly.

Freud, S. (1905). Fragment of an analysis of a case of hysteria. *Standard Edition* 7:3–124.

————(1909). Notes upon a case of obsessional neurosis. *Standard Edition* 10:153–320.

————(1915). Observations on transference-love (further recommendations on the technique of psycho-analysis III). *Standard Edition* 12:157–171.

————(1918). From the history of an infantile neurosis. *Standard Edition* 17:3–122.

————(1937). Analysis terminable and interminable. *Standard Edition* 23:209–253.

Friedman, L. (1969). The therapeutic alliance. *International Journal of Psycho-Analysis* 50:139–154.

Glover, E. (1931). The therapeutic effect of inexact interpretation: a contribution to the theory of suggestion. *International Journal of Psycho-Analysis* 12:397–411.

Greenarce, P. (1959). Certain technical problems in the transference relationship. *Journal of the American Psychoanalytic Association* 7:484–502.

——(1971). *Emotional Growth,* Vol. 2. New York: International Universities Press.

Greenson, R. (1965). The working alliance and the transference neurosis. *Psychoanalytic Quarterly* 34:155–181.

——(1967). *The Technique and Practice of Psychoanalysis,* Vol. 1. New York: International Universities Press.

——(1971). The "real" relationship between the patient and the psychoanalyst. In *The Unconscious Today,* ed. M. Kanzer. New York: International Universities Press.

——(1972). Beyond transference and interpretation. *International Journal of Psycho-Analysis* 53:213–217.

——, and Wexler, M. (1969). The non-transference relationship in the psychoanalytic situation. *International Journal of Psycho-Analysis* 50:27–39.

Kanzer, M. (1975). The therapeutic and working alliances. *International Journal of Psychotherapy* 4:48–68.

Langs, R. (1973a). The patient's view of the therapist: reality or fantasy? *International Journal of Psychoanalytic Psychotherapy* 2:411–431. [Chapter 4, this volume]

——(1973b). *The Technique of Psychoanalytic Psychotherapy,* Vol. I. New York: Jason Aronson.

——(1974). *The Technique of Psychoanalytic Psychotherapy,* II. New York: Jason Aronson.

——(1975a). The patient's unconscious perception of the therapist's errors. In *Tactics and Techniques in Psychoanalytic Theraphy, Vol. II: Countertransference,* ed. P. Giovacchini. New York: Jason Aronson. [Chapter 5, this volume]

——(1975b). The therapeutic relationship and deviations in technique. *International Journal of Psychoanalytic Psychotherapy* 4:106–141.[Chapter 7, this volume]

——(in press). The misalliance dimension in Freud's case histories. In *Freud and His Patients,* ed. M. Kanzer and J. Glenn. New York: Jason Aronson. [Chapters 8–10, this volume]

Little, M. (1951). Counter-transference and the patient's response to it. *International Journal of Psycho-Analysis* 32:32–40.

Loewald, H. (1960). On the therapeutic action of psycho-analysis. *International Journal of Psycho-Analysis* 41:16–33.

Myerson, P. (1969). The hysteric's experience in psychoanalysis. *International Journal of Psycho-Analysis* 50:373–384.

————(1973). The establishment and disruption of the psychoanalytic *modus vivendi. International Journal of Psycho-Analysis* 54:133–142.

Nunberg, H. (1926). The will to recovery. *International Journal of Psycho-Analysis* 7:64–78.

————(1955). *Principles of Psychoanalysis.* New York: International Universities Press.

Racker, H. (1968). *Transference and Counter-Transference.* London: Hogarth Press.

Searles, H. (1965). *Collected Papers on Schizophrenia and Related Subjects.* New York: International Universities Press.

————(1975). The patient as therapist to his analyst. In *Tactics and Techniques in Psychoanalytic Therapy, Vol. II: Countertransference,* ed. P. Giovacchini. New York: Jason Aronson.

Sterba, R. (1934). The fate of the ego in analytic therapy. *International Journal of Psycho-Analysis* 15:117–126.

Stone, L. (1961). *The Psychoanalytic Situation.* New York: International Universities Press.

————(1967). The psychoanalytic situation and transference: postscript to an earlier communication. *Journal of the American Psychoanalytic Association* 15:3–58.

Tarachow, S. (1962). Interpretation and reality in psychotherapy. *International Journal of Psycho-Analysis* 43:377–387.

Zetzel, E. (1956). Current concepts of transference. *International Journal of Psycho-Analysis* 37:369–376.

————(1958). Therapeutic alliance in the psychoanalysis of hysteria. In *The Capacity for Emotional Growth,* pp. 197–215. New York: International Universities Press, 1970.

Chapter Seven

The Therapeutic Relationship and Deviations in Technique

(1975[1974])

The framework and boundaries of the patient-analyst and patient-therapist relationships are a relatively neglected but important area. It is my main thesis that the manner in which the analyst or therapist[1] establishes and maintains the ground rules and boundaries of the therapeutic setting and interaction is among the most important means through which he conveys to the patient the essence of his identity and the dynamic state of his own intrapsychic structures, conflicts, and balances. The therapist's management of the therapeutic relationship therefore influences the ongoing identificatory and incorporative processes in the patient vis-à-vis the therapist, and contributes to the nature of the analytic "field" or "screen"—the person with whom the patient interacts and onto whom he projects his intrapsychic fantasies. It therefore influences the transference dimension as well. As a result, modifications or deviations in the established ground rules and boundaries of the therapeutic setting and relationship have a wide range of deeply significant consequences, of which only a certain portion is modifiable through subsequent analytic-interpretive work in the cognitive-verbal sphere. Actual changes in the therapist's stance are essential to correct the detrimental consequences of such deviations and, further, it may prove virtually impossible to alter certain effects on the patient through any means.

Specifically defined, the ground rules and boundaries of the therapeutic relationship include the following: set fee, hours, and length of sessions; the fundamental rule of free association with communication occurring while the patient is in his chair or on the couch; the absence of physical contact and other extratherapeutic gratifications; the therapist's relative anonymity, physicianly concern, and use of neutral interventions geared primarily toward interpretations; and the exclusive one-to-one relationship with total confidentiality. While the psychoanalytic and psychotherapeutic situations may differ in the placement of the patient and the analyst or therapist, and in frequency of sessions, they nonetheless are both created with a definable set of ground rules that offer as good as possible a therapeutic situation and relationship. I shall focus in this paper on the management of these ground rules and boundaries; I shall be less concerned here with the consequences arising from the different framework of the two therapeutic modalities. For both settings, it is these ground rules and boundaries that delimit the therapeutic "hold" (Winnicott 1958) and the boundaries of the therapeutic interaction; they are experiences that, per se, offer important opportunities for identification, structure building, and the projection of intrapsychic fantasies by the patient. Further, they influence the manner in which the patient perceives and assimilates the therapist's verbal interventions.

With this as our basic definition, let us now consider the relevant literature. With the single exception of Bleger (1967), explorations of the ground rules and boundaries of the analytic relationship derive initially from the technical issue of whether ego defects or dysfunctions in the patient call for modification of the usual limits of psychoanalytic technique, i.e., for *parameters* of technique, a term suggested by Eissler (1953). From there, such exploration extends into considerations of the therapist's flexibility (A. Freud 1954a, b) and, more recently, into the degree of deprivation necessary and optimal in the psychoanalytic situation (e.g., Stone 1961) and into those deviations in technique supposedly designed to foster the therapeutic alliance (e.g., Zetzel 1966–69 and Greenson and Wexler 1969). While, as we shall see, a wide range of deviations and parameters in technique have been advocated by various writers, the specific consequences of these deviations for the therapeutic relationship and the intrapsychic conflicts and structures of the patient are virtually neglected. Most writers limit themselves to general impressions of the productivity of such maneuvers—a factor I shall discuss later in this paper.

The papers on parameters and deviations in technique raise a host of issues, only some of which are pertinent here. The most unavoidable of these important secondary problems is that of delineation of classical psychoanalytic technique (Eissler 1953, Greenson 1958). Here I shall simply offer a brief definition of the classical psychoanalytic situation as one in which a relationship between a patient and analyst is established in order to assist the patient in resolving his neurotic difficulties through constructive unconscious identifications and the greatest possible development of insight and adaptive, inner-structural change; the latter is reflected in symptom alleviation and in constructive characterological alterations. The treatment milieu is designed to foster the fullest possible expression of the patient's intrapsychic conflicts, fantasies, and memories, especially as revealed in the relationship between the patient and the analyst. Thus, it is a setting in which all efforts are made to minimize the contribution of the analyst's unresolved intrapsychic conflicts and fantasies to the unfolding interaction between himself and the patient, and, further, to offer the patient an opportunity for inevitable identifications with the analyst based on the latter's constructive manner of functioning and relating. Without digressing, I would suggest that the psychotherapeutic situation is of comparable design, though less intensely so (for details, see Langs 1973b, 1974; since the literature on deviations is founded on the psychoanalytic situation, I will base my own discussion here on that modality).

In creating a climate in which these goals can be achieved, the analyst directly and indirectly indicates to the patient the nature of their respective roles and responsibilities; he delineates a set of explicit ground rules and implicit boundaries in the relationship. In this context, the analyst develops and maintains an atmosphere of warm and growth-promoting concern (Loewald 1960, Greenson 1967), while his primary goal is to understand the patient's communications and to intervene in a relatively neutral manner, ultimately through interpretations that lead to the patient's achievement of insight into his unconscious fantasies, memories, and conflicts. Other types of interventions, such as directives, manipulations, and counterreactions to the patient's associations, fall beyond the scope of such standard technique.

Within this classical framework, *variations* in technique are inevitable (Greenson 1958); they reflect each analyst's personality, style of work, and his appropriate, limited, flexible responses to momentary clinical situations. Beyond these variations, which fall clearly within the classical psychoanalytic framework, lie minor and major *deviations* in technique. Greenson (1958), for example, refers to minor deviations as modifications in technique—necessary and temporary interruptions of the basic procedures and aims of psychoanalysis—and speaks of major deviations as measures that entail "permanent changes in the psychoanalytic method with a consequent renunciation of its results" (p. 200). *Minor deviations* in technique may therefore be defined as consciously intended or inadvertent extensions of the basic psychoanalytic stance that are within such limits for any given patient and analyst that the essential therapeutic relationship and analytic work are not significantly modified, providing that they are recognized, corrected, and the patient's reactions to them analyzed. The ultimate determination of this group of relatively benign deviations, which fall into the gray area between standard technique and extensions which modify it significantly, depends on a careful assessment of the patient's—and analyst's—total reaction to the deviation in question. As I shall show later, patients in analysis and therapy are exquisitely sensitive to these deviations and universally react to them. The issue is whether, by exploring the consequences, such a deviation can be clearly distinguished from a technical error evoked by faulty knowledge and especially by the analyst's countertransference needs, and whether it—in any case—can be worked through so that there is no lasting impairment in the analytic relationship and situation. If this is impossible, then the intervention is best designated a major deviation which has altered to some degree the analysis and its outcome. If the measure was used because of the patient's unmodifiable psychopathology, the intervention may be termed a *parameter* of technique.

Major deviations and parameters clearly transcend the boundaries of the standard psychoanalytic situation. They will usually result in a permanent modification of the patient-analyst relationship and the outcome of the psychoanalytic work. Even when indicated, these deviations always provide considerable inappropriate gratification for the patient and they may affect constructive structural change. It is here that the distinction between necessary parameters and unneeded deviations—technical errors—becomes critical. Since major deviations also generally provide the analyst with momentary gratifications which extend beyond those usually available to him in the analytic situation, the deviation itself may have countertransference-based motives which must be separated from the realistic, patient-oriented indications for the measure.

Turning now to the literature, I shall bypass here a study of Freud's deviations in technique since I have made a separate exploration of them (Langs, in press). The findings, it may be noted, are in keeping with data to be presented here: these deviations have major consequences; the distinction between deviations and technical errors or countertransference-evoked measures is often difficult; the deviations may permanently modify the patient-analyst relationship and compromise the analytic outcome; and they generally evoke strong, regressive responses in the analysand in addition to any positive consequences.

The definitive paper on the subject of parameters was that of Eissler (1953), who, following leads developed by Freud (1937), proposed that our theoretical understanding of the structure of the ego leads us to develop varieties of (deviant) psychoanalytic technique to enhance the ego's achievement of mastery. While he defined standard psychoanalytic technique as one in which interpretrations alone are made, he acknowledged the idealization of this model and attempted to modify it in a later paper (Eissler 1958). In his original presentation, he coined the term *parameter* for a technique which he defined as a deviation that is both quantitatively and qualitatively different from the basic model of psychoanalysis, which requires interpretation as an exclusive tool. He stated that such parameters are introduced only when: (1) the basic model of analysis does not suffice in the analytic situation; (2) the alteration never transgresses the unavoidable minimum; (3) its use can finally lead to its self-elimination; and (4) its effects on the patient's transference can be undone by interpretation.

However, Eissler (1953) himself acknowledged possible dangers in the use of parameters. He described three: (1) that the therapeutic process might be falsified so that obedience is substituted for structural change and for the resolution of the corresponding conflicts;

(2) that resistances might be temporarily eliminated without having been properly analyzed; and (3) that the concept of parameters might be used to cover an inability to use interpretations properly. In addition, he commented that parameters might have a lasting effect on the patient's transference—one that could not be undone by interpretation. In a later panel discussion (1958) Eissler also raised the point that an analyst might utilize a parameter when an interpretation was feasible and it was not necessary for him to be directive. He introduced the concept of "pseudo-parameters" so that he could include relatively neutral interventions other than interpretations within the framework of classical technique, and indicated that at times these might have interfering qualities, such as, for instance, a gift to the patient.

In the same panel, Loewenstein (1958) pointed out the dangers of modifying psychoanalytic technique in noting these possible consequences: that it may curtail the spontaneous productions of the patient and therefore lead the analyst to misunderstand his unconscious; that interpretation may be minimized and manipulation maximized; and that it may hamper analyzability and jeopardize the transference neurosis. His own discussion centered upon variations in analytic technique rather than clear-cut deviations, although he included several of these as well. He also noted that deviations in technique may occur in many forms, on many levels, and entail a variety of meanings.

Bouvet's (1958) presentation at this panel was based on his particular concepts of object relationships and of the distance between patient and analyst. While recognizing that deviations may be rationalized and actually stem from countertransference problems, he advocated modifications that help to modulate the distance between patient and analyst, thereby fostering the analytic work, and he noted that they must subsequently be eliminated and analyzed.

Reich (1958), in her contribution to this panel, described a special variation of technique in which she utilized strong confrontations regarding an analysand's mother in a manner which was unusual for her, and which she felt conveyed value judgments which went beyond her usual neutrality. This proved necessary with a sadomasochistic, guilt-ridden, acting-out patient who had idealized her mother and had developed an analytic impasse of acting out and acting in, which alternated with unbearable guilt. The devaluation of the patient's mother proved vital to the resolution of this stalemate.

Nacht (1958), in discussing the panel presentation, pointed out that parting from the analyst's neutrality can provide unconscious neurotic satisfactions for the patient; these may become an end in themselves and, as a result, make the transference neurosis unresolvable. On the other hand, rigid neutrality can create the same type of situation by creating a sadomasochistic couple. He suggested that with certain types of patients, after a full countertransference exploration, an abandonment of neutrality is necessary in order to establish the analyst's "presence" and at times in order to provide some type of reality to his relationship with the patient in the form of a reparative gift. He emphasized that he did not mean by this concrete gratification, but primarily a gratifying attitude. Rosenfeld (1958) sated his preference for interpretations rather than parameters.

Frank (1956) stated that every analysis includes moments of advice and injunctions, and he spoke out against ritualism in analytic technique. He described two patients, who appeared to be schizophrenic or severely disturbed, and with whom he used grossly modified analytic techniques. (I shall not examine the use of deviations with such patients here.)

Allen (1956) pointed out that the analyst's wish to "break" or change the basic rules of analysis always creates considerable conflict within him; she emphasized that such decisions should always be based on the needs of the patient's personality. In considering such changes, the analyst inevitably struggles against the introjects of his own analyst, teachers, and parents—his superego figures—and he must therefore fully analyze within himself both any inappropriate need to comply rigidly with these figures or to rebel against them. She then presented patients with whom she felt that the classical model was creating either stasis or undue emergencies; she found it useful for the progress of the analytic work to modify the use of the couch and to have the patient sit facing her at times.

Lorand (1963) pointed out that complete neutrality is a myth; advice and manipulation are part of every analytic situation. He noted that these can be excessive, reflecting countertransference problems, but presented one patient with whom such advice, in the form of a confrontation with alternatives in reality, appeared to be beneficial. He also offered two vignettes from his supervisory experiences in which deviations in technique were clearly a reflection of countertransference problems and constituted technical errors. Balint (1968) wrote of the difficulties in treating certain types of severe character disorder on borderline patients, and described in a general way the use of certain variations and deviations in analytic technique which, he felt, fostered analytic work with these patients.

Hoedemaker (1960) discussed variations in technique used primarily with delinquent and schizophrenic patients. His emphasis on setting limits as part of the standard analytic technique led him to describe situations in which he ejected patients from analysis and from his office. Stating that such limit-setting fosters healthy identifications, he yet leaves a number of unanswered questions in his discussion of the issue of deviations in technique. Similarly, Rodgers (1965) advocated the parameter of concurrent psychotherapy of the spouse of an analysand by the same analyst in order to overcome a stalemate supported by the spouse, and Calogeras (1967) sanctioned silence and nonadherence to the fundamental rule of free association with a patient who was apparently unable to adhere to this ground rule. They describe pragmatic success with these measures, but the presentations do not permit a thorough study of the reasons the parameter worked as it did—a comment that is pertinent to almost all of the presentations reviewed here.

Greenacre (1959, 1971) generally recommended adherence to basic analytic technique, emphasizing that deviations tend to undermine the patient's autonomy and to create narcissistic alliances (misalliances; see Langs 1975b). Anna Freud (1954a, b) attempted to define the dangers of both inflexibility and excessive flexibility in regard to the technical rules of analysis, and suggested that deviations in these rules are usually "necessary whenever the aspect of a case leads us to expect manifestations of transference or resistance which exceed in force or in malignancy the amounts with which we are able to cope" (1954a, p. 50).

Lastly, Stone (1954, 1961, 1967) has spoken out against rigid adherence to technical rules, including those related to anonymity and the absence of transference gratifications. In a series of complex presentations that are too detailed for full discussion here, he advocates the use of parameters and deviations in technique as long as they bring about the ultimate analytic outcome. Under these conditions they can, he states, usually be deprived of their negative effects on the transference.

While Stone (1961) was reacting primarily to inappropriate rigidities in the clinical stance of many psychoanalysts, the present paper has arisen out of repeated observations that therapists and analysts currently tend all too readily to discard or modify the ground rules and boundaries in their relationship with their patients. The concept of parameters is often used to justify countertransference-based interventions and technical errors. In the literature, these issues are discussed without the specific study of clinical data (a striking feature of the literature). Often there is a failure to recognize the far-reaching and universal effects of all variations in technique—correct or erroneous—on their patients (Langs 1973b).

In general, there have been many additional reasons offered to justify temporary deviations in technique. The purported or expected effects are too often taken at face value, while the latent and implicit content and meanings of the deviation and its consequences are ignored. Deviations have been advocated to enhance the therapeutic alliance, to express the "real" relationship between patient and therapist, to lessen the deprivation inherent in analysis and therapy, to promote the therapeutic relationship, to avoid unnecessary frustration of the patient, to avoid a trauma that the patient will not be able to tolerate, to make the therapist seem more human, and to demonstrate his flexibility. The far-reaching effects of deviations per se are relatively negelected, as is the basic psychoanalytic methodology of probing the meanings of the analyst's interventions and the patient's responses to them rather than confining one's considerations to preconceived theories or to naive, surface-oriented assessments of manifest meanings and reactions (see Kanzer 1975).

As noted, Bleger's contribution (1967) is along different lines. Taking as his starting point Winnicott's definition (1958) of the analytic setting as the summation of all of the details of management, Bleger considers the total psychoanalytic relationship and defines the frame of this relationship as non-process, made up of constants within whose bounds the process of analysis takes place. He then focuses on the silently maintained protective elements in the frame and the necessity of their ultimate analysis, relating that frame to the concept ɔf institutions that are viewed as contributing to the individual's identity. It is invariable and nonpalpable, and Bleger therefore postulates that it is related to the most primitive and undifferentiated psychic organization out of which the ego is built, and that it has a strong basis in the bodily ego and in the early symbiosis between mother and child. The frame therefore contains the symbiotic elements of the patient-analyst relationship and acts as a support and mainstay, interfering only when it changes or breaks.

Modifications in the frame may occur at the patient's behest and compliance by the analyst repeats the neurotic interaction of the patient's childhood. However, when the frame is respected, the repetition does not occur, and this brings out and makes available for analysis the most permanent elements in the patient's personality, viewed by Bleger as his psychotic core.

Bleger also suggests that the patient brings his own frame—in the institution of his primitive, symbiotic relatedness—to the analytic situation. On the one hand, the patient may attempt to have the analyst modify the frame in order to create a sense of magical union with him and to evoke a magical cure; on the other, any break or variation in the frame, necessary or unnecessary, induced by the analyst, is disruptive and creates a catastrophic situation for the patient, bringing the "non-ego" to a crisis, contradicting the fusion, challenging the ego, and compelling ego changes and defenses. Moreover, the frame may become a kind of addiction if it is not systematically analyzed, leading to a false ego development without internal stability. While the analyst must initially accept the frame that the patient brings to the analysis and the primitive symbiosis that it contains, Bleger suggests that he should not bend his own frame, since it is through that vehicle that he is able to analyze the disturbance within the patient and to transform the frame itself into useful processes for the patient. Any patient-analyst relationship outside this strict frame enables the psychotic transference to be concealed; instead, there develops a facade which he terms *the psychoanalytic character.* Since the frame is viewed as the most primitive fusion with the mother's body, Bleger feels that the psychoanalyst's frame helps reestablish the original symbiosis as a step toward modifying it. In all, then, for Bleger the psychoanalytic setting or frame—the ground rules and boundaries—contributes to the deepest levels of the patient-therapist interaction and may have profound effects on the patient.

SOME POSTULATES

This brings me now to the results of a re-examination of my own earlier observations in this area (Langs 1973a, b, 1974). It is evident to me that every patient has an identifiable, predictable, and intense response to the slightest deviation in the framework of the therapeutic relationship. A careful investigation of responses to such interventions reveals that these measures have extensive meanings and consequences for the patient, and makes clear the inherent and silent meanings of the therapeutic framework itself, as well as the implications of altering it. Before presenting additional clinical material, I shall therefore briefly list the main meanings of this framework, the basic consequences of deviations from it, and techniques for modifying detrimental consequences and fostering positive effects in such deviations.

1. The manner in which the therapist delineates and explicates the ground rules and boundaries of the therapeutic relationship significantly reflects his identity as a therapist, and his resolution and management of his own intrapsychic conflicts and inner needs.

(a) Modifications that are not specifically and clearly indicated by the therapeutic needs and pathology of the patient will reflect intrapsychic disturbances—countertransference problems—within the therapist. In so doing, they convey important unconscious meanings.

(b) This framework is the basic vehicle for the therapeutic "hold" which provides the stability, security, and boundaries necessary for the patient properly to relate and communicate in the therapeutic situation.

(c) It is also the backdrop onto which the patient projects his intrapsychic fantasies—the transference dimension—and is one factor that influences the specific timing and nature of these projections and their extensions in interactions with the therapist.

2. Proper maintenance of the framework of the therapeutic relationship provides the patient constructive interactional experiences which lead to positive, ego-enhancing, inner-structural changes through incorporative identification with the positive qualities of the therapist. Such changes are to be distinguished from the structural effects of interpretations, though they contribute to and interact with them.

3. The maintenance of proper therapeutic boundaries in response to inappropriate efforts by the patient to evoke deviations—an important type of behavioral transference expression—or in the face of the therapist's own inappropriate needs to modify them, is one means through which the therapist avoids pathogenic interactions with the patient that repeat his—and the therapist's—past pathogenic object

relationships within the therapeutic situation. This fosters experiential modification of such relatedness, the development of analyzable expression of the related unconscious fantasies and memories, and avoids therapeutic misalliances (Langs 1975b).

4. The proper maintenance of the boundaries of the therapeutic relationship is essential not only for maximal projection of the patient's intrapsychic pathological fantasies (transference), but is also vital for the greatest effectiveness of the therapist's interpretations, which will be undermined or modified if the therapist's management behavior has evoked a negative image of himself, one that fosters negative and traumatic incorporative identifications, and unconscious needs in the patient to defend himself against the therapist's communications.

5. Because they fall into the realm of behavior, the management of the boundaries of the relationship must be secure for verbal interventions to convey their intended meanings and to have their greatest insight-producing effects.

6. Deviations in technique evoke intense reactions because of their actual unconscious meanings, which are elaborated in the patient's own needs and fantasies. Such reactions may include interference with the most basic hold and necessary symbiotic ties offered by the therapist to the patient, and shifts in the more mature sectors of relatedness between the two. Deviations alter the boundaries between patient and therapist, arousing issues of failure to maintain separate identities, incest barriers, and the like. Deviations by the therapist may also reflect impairment in both sexual and aggressive, instinctual-drive-discharge management.

7. All deviations in technique, regardless of the indications for them, entail inappropriate gratifications for both therapist and patient. The extent and specific unconscious meanings of such gratification must be recognized and ultimately analyzed. Whenever a deviation in technique is undertaken without clearcut indication, the first step must be to modify the deviation in reality. Those deviations that are clearly indicated must also eventually be retracted as far as possible. Only thus can verbal analysis of the consequences of a deviation for the patient be carried out to the fullest.

8. Deviations in technique may reflect and evoke modifications in the psychoanalytic relationship and process that are lasting and unmodifiable through verbal interventions. Especially if they are not

recognized, they create sectors of therapeutic misalliance and compromise the therapeutic outcome. Even when recognized, those deviations that have been undertaken out of the therapist's countertransference needs may leave a lasting—and often incorporated— image of the therapist, derived from the patient's conscious and unconscious realistic perceptions, and from its subsequent intrapsychic extensions within himself, in terms of his own psychopathology, unconscious fantasies, intrapsychic conflicts, past and present object relationships, and other inner factors.

9. Deviations in technique of all kinds, therefore, lead to intense adaptive responses, often rather pervasive and productive on the part of the patient. The specific meaning of this material, however, can be properly understood and analyzed only if the deviation itself is recognized as the major adaptive context and organizing factor in the patient's reactions and communications, and constructive inner change will follow only if the meaning of the deviation is fully analyzed, and the boundaries to the relationship properly restored.

10. Many deviations in technique are not undertaken primarily because of the patient's needs, but are rationalizations of the extensive countertransference gratifications they offer the therapist. In so doing, therapists neglect the ego-strengthening factors and structural reinforcements that are inherent in the firm maintenance of proper and clear-cut boundaries and ground rules. Also missed are the anxiety-provoking and disruptive aspects inherent in the therapist's failure to maintain these much-needed boundaries.

11. My cumulative observations suggest—although I shall not pursue this in detail here—that deviations and parameters in techniques should be limited to clear-cut emergencies and to those relatively rare clinical situations in which the genetic basis and unconscious fantasies maintaining the patient's ego dysfunctions have been thoroughly analyzed, the therapist's countertransference has been carefully subjected to self-analysis and controlled as a disturbing factor, and a stalemate based on the patient's ego dysfunctions appears to be present. Before deviating, a full consideration of all other disturbing factors should be made, since problems within the therapist and with his technique are often more important to the stalemate than is the psychopathology of the patient.

12. Therapists who tend to deviate in technique once will tend to do so again. In addition, patients who are successful in evoking deviations

in technique from their therapists will endeavor to evoke further deviations. There is a strong tendency for patients to accept the therapeutic misalliances inherent in such deviations as a means of temporarily affording themselves symptom relief without structural change (Langs 1975b), and for therapists to maintain such misalliances for their own inappropriate reasons as well.

13. Once evoked, any deviation in technique must be a primary adaptive and therapeutic context (Langs 1973b) for subsequent listening and analytic work. Their residual manifestations must be modified so that the boundaries and ground rules are restored to the relationship, and the patient's reaction to the deviation itself and to its subsequent elimination is fully explored and resolved.

14. Unconsciously, patients will often initially accept the therapeutic misalliance evoked by a deviation in technique because of the momentary relief and the neurotic gratification which it offers, but they will also subsequently attempt to modify the misalliance and help the therapist restore the proper boundaries in seeking lasting symptom relief (Langs 1975b). In their search for ultimate conflict resolution through inner structural change, they make unconscious efforts to alert the therapist to the presence of the deviation and to their unconscious understanding of the inner basis within the therapist for the deviation he has evoked. Patients also make efforts that I have described elsewhere (Langs 1975b) as "unconscious interpretations" designed to help the therapist resolve the countertransference problems which led to his deviation. However, recognition of the detrimental consequences of an unneeded deviation in technique is primarily the responsibility of the therapist, who should assess his use of a deviation through a close study of the patient's reactions and of his own subjective state.

15. In general, then, in those circumstances where the therapist formulates the need for a deviation in technique because of some emergency with the patient, an otherwise unresolvable stalemate, or the need to respond in a human and unusual manner under extraordinary conditions, he should counterbalance his assessment of the indications for the deviation with a full anticipation of the possible negative consequences. Only such an assessment can lead to a final conclusion that will restrict deviations to those that are truly constructive to the therapeutic relationship and outcome.

This is a rather lengthy list of basic principles, and their many ramifications cannot be fully discussed in this paper. In order to illustrate their validity and to briefly discuss some of their main implications, let us turn now to a few respresentative vignettes.

CLINICAL MATERIAL

Mr. A. was a young man with a severe character disorder, in twice-weekly psychotherapy for a severe depression that followed the suicide of an older sister who had terminated her psychotherapy just weeks before her death. In addition, he was confused about his goals in life, seriously concerned about again becoming a homosexual, and disturbed over his inability to find a suitable marriage partner. His parents had had a stormy marriage and were divorced, and another sibling, a brother, was divorced and having emotional problems.

From the outset, the treatment, which I occasionally supervised, did not go well. The therapist had considerable difficulty in understanding his patient, especially his underlying conflicts and fantasies, and his interventions tended to be naive and inaccurate. The patient had responded with a great deal of open resentment, with questions about the efficacy of therapy, and with occasional absences. There was considerable evidence that he had quickly joined the therapist in a misalliance with bilateral obsessional, sadomasochistic, and latent homosexual qualities, one that he alternately accepted and attempted to modify (Langs 1975b).

In the sessions prior to those that we will study here, Mr. A. had been questioning the frequency of his hours and was worried that he would not get any help in his treatment. He had had an argument with a male cousin who had referred him for therapy and described a variety of fantasies about leaving treatment; he had been depressed. Without available derivatives, the therapist had attempted to relate this depression to the death of Mr. A.'s sister. The material actually pointed strongly both to feelings of hopelessness regarding the therapeutic situation and to rage at the therapist as the underlying factors in this symptom—an assessment that was made in supervision. In response to the therapist's intervention, the patient spoke in considerable detail of the manner in which his mother never accepted responsibility for failures in their family—a comment that reflected a rather sensitive, indirect unconscious perception of the therapist's difficulties.

In the next session, the patient described feeling exceptionally well, although the previous day had been his sister's birthday and he had been quite depressed; he had thought of calling the therapist. He ruminated about fears of becoming dependent on the therapist and about the guilt that the therapist had suggested he had experienced in regard to the death of his sister. When the therapist commented that Mr. A. seemed to have difficulties in discussing certain feelings with him, the patient complained about the therapist's coldness and likened him to a fellow with whom he had lived and with whom he had frequently quarreled. He thought of changing therapists; he felt that they were getting nowhere, and yet he feared offending the therapist. He recalled that when he got made at his father, he was beaten, and when he was angry with his mother, she would cry; as a result, he always controlled his anger with other people.

Mr. A. arrived for his next session, which was early on a Saturday morning, in the midst of a snowstorm. The therapist began the hour by asking Mr. A. how the driving had been, and the patient responded that it had been pretty bad; in turn, he asked the therapist if he had had difficulties driving to his office. The therapist said that he lived nearby, within walking distance of his office, and the patient fell silent. Next, he said that he felt quite shy. He had seen his father and had discussed his sister's suicide; he had decided not to visit his father again. He did not hate him, but rather felt sorry for him; he then thought of the snow falling on his sister's grave.

The therapist commented that he seemed preoccupied with his sister, and the patient said that he felt guilty and that he also did not want to see his mother again. With her, he gave the peace sign but inside he was full of hate. His mother had gone to the West Coast because his brother had been ill, but the situation was not serious and it was an unnecessary trip. It would have been better if she had stayed with her sister, who was quite ill, and if she had given better care to the daughter she had lost. His parents had a way of tearing their children to pieces; he then thought of the manner in which his sister had died. He was afraid that if he told his mother he didn't want to see her, she would go crazy, but felt if he didn't say something, he would go crazy.

At this point, the therapist chose to convey to the patient some information regarding his mother that he had taken from the assessment interview carried out by another therapist in the clinic in which the patient was being seen; this related to an apparent psychotic depression and hospitalization which the patient's mother had gone through after Mr. A.'s birth. The patient said that he really ought to find out more about what happened and that he had not heard from his mother for several days; she would disappear on purpose so that everybody would fear that she had killed herself. Sometimes things that he himself said led people to be afraid that he would kill himself, but he had no recollection of making such remarks. He had some fear that his mother might commit suicide and that somehow he would be blamed.

To discuss briefly the material to this point, we may identify the first deviation in technique as the therapist's revelation to the patient that he lived near the clinic—a modification in his relative anonymity. Despite this deviation's human qualities, it was predicted in supervision that it would be experienced by the patient as a homosexual gift and seduction offered as compensation for the therapist's failure adequately to intervene and as an attempt to undo his unresolved hostilities toward Mr. A. It appeared to reflect a homosexual countertransference problem in the therapist, one that existed beyond any technical confusion on his part. As supervisor, I anticipated that it would evoke homosexual longings and anxious suicidal fantasies, and that the patient would seek out further deviations in order both to gratify his own neurotic unconscious fantasies and needs, and to reinforce the defensive misalliance. Along other lines, however, he would also attempt to assist the therapist in reestablishing the boundaries of their relationship and in modifying the therapist's unresolved countertransference difficulties.

In view of these predictions, we may note that the patient had responded to the therapist's self-revelation with a period of silence and a feeling of shyness—an initial withdrawal reaction, and an effort to reestablish distance and appropriate broundaries (this may also be an unconscious suggestion to the therapist that he be less open). There followed allusions to his sister's suicide and thoughts of not wanting to see his father again. Implied here are feelings of rage toward his father who, he felt, had contributed to his sister's suicide, and a sense of compassion for him—feelings, in the present adaptive context, that are displaced from the therapist. Next comes the thought of not seeing his mother—another effort to create distance—and then the comment that the patient gives the sign of peace but is full of hate inside. This reflects in part an incorporative identification with the angry and somewhat destructive therapist. It also conveys a sensitive, unconscious recognition that the deviation in technique was meant in part as a peace offering (the therapist spoke of it to me as an attempt to further the failing therapeutic alliance), that it was an attempt by the therapist to deny his countertransference anger.

The next associations reflect the patient's unconscious recognition of the deviation as a misguided effort on the part of the therapist—as was that of his mother—to offer an expression of concern; the patient also comments that such efforts should find more appropriate expression. I consider these associations a valuable commentary, one that is generally applicable to therapists' misguided efforts to reinforce the therapeutic alliance through deviations in technique, rather than through the more appropriate channels of correct interventions leading to valid interpretations and a proper maintenance of the therapeutic boundaries. The latter avoid mutual acting out of transference-countertransference fantasies—misalliances—and their consequences. In his own way, the patient went on to describe the manner in which such unfortunate efforts only tear their patients to pieces, and how they will, in patients so predisposed, evoke suicidal fantasies and reactions, rather than constructive inner change.

It is in this latter material that we begin to see some of the specific intrapsychic elaborations and unconscious meaning that the deviation in technique has evoked in Mr. A. Despite the emphasis in this paper on the actual detrimental unconscious meanings and implications of unneeded deviations in technique—the kernel of truth—we should not overlook the manner in which these veridical perceptions and experiences are then processed through the patient's own intrapsychic pathology and adaptive resouces. Each patient will respond to deviations in technique in a manner that reflects both the broader general meanings of the deviation and their highly specific implications for him.

The next associations reflect the dilemma in which the patient is placed when faced with an unnecessary deviation in technique: on the one hand, if he attempts to reestablish the boundaries, he will create anxiety in the therapist, who has been unable to tolerate the necessary deprivation required by the therapeutic situation, and who has failed to maintain his own intrapsychic integration and to renounce his inappropriate instinctual drives. On the other hand, however, if he fails to assist the therapist in reestablishing the proper framework to their relationship, the patient himself will be under pressure. Through the perception of this disturbance in the therapist and through incorporative identification with him, this aspect of the deviation threatens the structural balances and mental integrity of the patient as well.

In keeping with my previous observation that the therapist who deviates once will be prone to repeat, we find that the therapist at this point in the session introduced information that he had obtained from an extratherapeutic source—the assessment notes. This brings to the fore a third party to the therapy, bypasses the patient's associations, and is introduced solely in terms of the therapist's need to present it. On the basis of my discussion with this therapist, I speculated that this was an attempt to deflect the focus away from the patient-therapist interaction and an unconscious effort to create a situation in which the patient, rather than himself, would be disturbed. Mr. A. responded with a reference to his mother's disappearance and her intention that others be concerned with her suicide. This may be viewed as an unconscious perception of the therapist's insensitivities; it also conveys the patient's own suicidal feelings and hostility toward the therapist. Mr. A's subsequent allusion to his not remembering something that he was purported to have said may be viewed as a response to the therapist's use of material that was drawn from outside sources. As the session ended, we sense the patient's mounting rage at the therapist and the possibility of its being turned inward.

Briefly, in the following hour, the patient began by saying that his mother had turned up and seemed to be well. The cousin who had referred Mr. A. to therapy had exposed himself to the patient, and this had led Mr. A. to feel dominant; the cousin had confessed a whole series of personal troubles that he was having with his wife and daughter. The therapist suggested that this reflected Mr. A.'s concern over the fact that he—the therapist—had revealed something about himself in the previous hour. The patient heartily agreed, adding that he felt that the therapist was in love with him in the previous hour, as if they were two women; he had felt that he was about to become the dominant one because the therapist was losing his objectivity. Mr. A.'s associations then went on to his concerns about becoming a homosexual and a fantasy of being dominated homosexually by a huge black man who had become his lover. He had thought of calling the therapist soon after the previous hour because he was in a panic over his mother's absence, but he was afraid he would evoke a panic in the therapist.

We see from this material that the patient's view of the deviations in technique contains some validity and some intrapsychic elaboration. In response to the therapist's correct intervention, Mr. A. revealed his impression that the therapist was involved homosexually with him, that he had lost his objectivity, and that he had reacted out of anxiety. These conscious and unconscious interpretations are clearly shaped by the patient's own homosexual anxieties and conflicts; they cannot, however, simply be dismissed as reflecting them since there is considerable evidence that the deviation in technique has indeed reflected the therapist's own unresolved homosexual countertransference.

In the next hour, Mr. A. reported that he had clarified the facts of his mother's early illness. He recalled being teased by a delivery man as a child and spoke of a childhood injury that had been misdiagnosed by a doctor who had believed that there had been some brain damage, although this was subsequently ruled out. He recalled a few sessions with a psychiatrist during his college years in which the therapist directed him to avoid his father and told the patient that he was retarded. He then spoke of his mother's concerns; she had arranged for the patient to have a nevus removed although it turned out there was nothing wrong with it.

In this session, we may recognize unconscious attempts by the patient to alert the therapist to his technical errors and erroneous deviations in technique, and to call to his attention his need to manipulate and to underestimate the patient's capacities. In addition to the themes of doctor's mistakes and of unnecessary therapeutic measures, the material reflects an incorporative identification with the therapist, who is behaving in a somewhat incompetent manner.

The hour had been concluded with an allusion to how the patient himself had been a likable and bright little child. This reflects, in part, Mr. A.'s continued mixed image of the therapist. It is based largely on the fact that the latter had made a correct intervention, but had not been able to follow it up with additional interpretations and with a specific reestablishment of the proper boundaries of the therapeutic relationship.

The patient began the next hour by telling the therapist that he had confessed some of his homosexual fantasies to his cousin, who seemed more favorably inclined toward him after that revelation. The patient had dreamt that his mouth was stuffed with sand and that someone's head was cut off. The therapist immediately asked for thoughts about the dream and whether there was any additional content to it, and Mr. A. said that it reminded him of fellatio and of a teenage homosexual experience. The stuffed head reminded him of his need to keep his feelings back; he then spoke of some suicidal feelings that he had had some months ago. The therapist said that he was trying to express his feelings and the patient agreed, adding that he did not want to kill himself. He remembered getting attention when he was injured in his childhood.

In the following hour, the patient spoke of how strange the early Saturday morning session seemed, and he reviewed the events that led to his sister's suicide. The therapist intervened and suggested that the patient was afraid of going crazy and was trying to disrupt his relationships by revealing his homosexual conflicts to his cousin. The patient disagreed, stating that it was all right to be crazy and that one should accept his imperfections. He then told the therapist that he had joined a choir and had been singing a great deal, asking the therapist if he had a good voice and inquiring into the therapist's religion. He also wondered if treatment could be extended beyond the one-year deadline established by clinic policy and said that he had thought of calling the therapist, but had been afraid that the therapist would be angry.

In these two sessions, the relationship between the material and the deviation in technique is less clear. The associations reflect the patient's unconscious awareness of the homosexual misalliance, and suggests both a wish to participate in it, and rage at himself and the therapist because of it. There appears to be a fear of losing control and a dread of excessive guilt that might evoke a suicidal reaction. Finally there are a number of additional efforts by the patient to extend the boundaries of the relationship and further to modify the therapist's anonymity; the therapist neither complied nor attempted to confront or interpret these efforts.

The patient began the next hour by asking the therapist if he was a psychiatrist, since he was so young. The therapist explained his status as a trainee in the clinic, and the patient said that he had really wanted someone older, who could be the ideal mother he had never had. The therapist intervened, stating that the patient seemed to feel that he was not an ideal therapist; Mr. A. agreed that this was so. He was wondering if he could seduce the therapist and saw the therapist as being very much like his mother, who would get upset when others revealed themselves. He could remember wanting to sleep with his mother and using girlfriends to cover over these wishes. He was afraid there would be a crisis in treatment and he would have to leave it even though he shouldn't do so.

In this hour, we discover that the therapist had not resolved the countertransference problems that had prompted him to reveal information regarding himself and that quite without rational purpose he had revealed his status in the clinic. The patient responded with disappointment; he saw the therapist as a poor mother and as someone who could be seduced. He then offered an unconscious interpretation to the effect that the therapist was upset when his patients revealed thoughts about themselves, thereby suggesting that the therapist's self-revelations were unconsciously designed to deflect focus from these disturbing revelations from his patient. This latest deviation in technique, one that the patient sought out, is also unconsciously viewed and interpreted to the therapist by the patient as an incestuous seduction, based on unresolved incestuous conflicts in the therapist. These interventions to the therapist are, of course, once again intermixed with the patient's own intrapsychic fantasies and conflicts. These seductive deviations evoked thoughts of flight from therapy, accompanied by wishes to remain.

In the next hour, the patient began by saying that he was furious that the therapist told him when to end their sessions. He was also furious with his cousin, who had revealed additional personal facts about his life. Mr. A. had had a dream in which he was in a small town and being hassled by the police. There was a black man in a fancy foreign car and the people wanted him to go on the radio. There also was a black boxer who had been on television as an entertainer, and the patient asked him for a ride out of town to West Virginia. The man agreed but said that he was going to Alaska. They were on the road and there was a huge oil truck behind them that honked to pass them. The patient felt that the people from town were after them. The truck passed and the car broke down; the man said that it was all right to go fishing. They pulled off the road and did so.

In his associations, the patient recalled a time that he and a homosexual friend had been briefly put into jail for petty thievery. He spoke of some foreign students who were extremely incompetent and knew nothing about anything; they thought he was a snob because he looked down upon them, but he felt that it was realistic since he had more experience.

The therapist pointed out that the patient seemed to be angry at him, since he had told him that he was a trainee at the clinic, and that the patient viewed him as incompetent. The patient said that he had been wondering how competent the therapist actually was and that he felt that in therapy he had to do most of the work. Nonetheless, he felt that the two of them could grow together and he wanted to stay with the therapist beyond the one-year limit. He had the impression that the therapist did not read enough, and recalled a fantasy of screaming at the therapist and calling him names. He somehow saw the therapist as overintellectual, unfeeling, of a different religion than himself, and as a momma's boy; he felt guilty telling the therapist these things and was afraid of hurting his feelings.

It is of interest that the patient begins this hour by expressing anger over the way in which the therapist established one of the boundaries of treatment—the length of the session. From this, we see that the boundaries of the therapeutic relationship and setting are very much on his mind, and next we learn again of his anger toward those who reveal too much about themselves. Lacking extensive associations to the dream, we may speculate that it reflects the patient's unconscious perception of the therapist's need to exhibit himself, perceptions and acceptance of the homosexual misalliance offered by the therapist through the deviation, and a sense of absurdity regarding the therapeutic situation in which the therapist was having difficulty in maintaining the boundaries. In addition, we see that the therapist's deviations offered a momentary "misalliance cure" (Langs 1975b) in that the patient felt, appropriately to some extent, that he was more competent than his therapist and that he was in a position to teach a great deal to the therapist so that they could grow together. It is in this context that he wanted to yell at the therapist and then confronted him with some of his difficulties, indirectly suggesting that they were based in part on the therapist's conflicts with his mother.

Mr. A. was late to the next hour and said that his brother was feeling better but was on tranquilizers. The patient had planned a business trip for the following week, one that would interrupt the therapy; he had not told the therapist because he felt that he would be annoyed and ask him to stay. He asked the therapist his diagnosis and speculated that he was manic-depressive. He liked the idea of that diagnosis because he could do anything he wanted. He asked the therapist if he like traveling and the therapist, in turn, asked the patient for his thoughts. Mr. A. spoke of leaving the area and treatment; he thought of going to Australia, where people were closer, and of finding a girlfriend. The therapist spoke of Mr. A.'s wish to be close to people, including himself, and of the difficulty that Mr. A. seemed to be having in taking a trip that would entail two missed sessions. The patient said that he would like to be closer to the therapist and would like to get to know him because the therapist's failure to answer his questions made him feel that it wasn't a human relationship and that he was being put in a box without any concern. He told the therapist to enjoy sleeping late while he was away and then missed the next two hours.

To discuss this hour, we may suggest that the patient attempted to establish boundaries on his own, by missing two sessions, in part to fend off his seductive therapist and in part out of his fears of his own reactions to the therapist. Mr. A.'s speculation as to his underlying illness is an unconscious reflection of his concerns about the therapist, and the subsequent association to using the diagnosis as an excuse for doing anything that he wants to do tentatively touches upon the therapist's status as a trainee who can justify behaving carelessly. His further associations indicate that the missed hours are an acting out of fantasies of termination, and the hour concludes with a mixture of the patient's longings to join the therapist in a latent homosexual misalliance and his continued wishes to establish reasonable boundaries—the box—as well. It is of interest that the patient complained that the therapist did not answer his questions, while the latent material indicates that he had been deeply disturbed by the fact that the therapist had, indeed, done so.

Very briefly, upon his return the patient began his hour by expressing a fear that the therapist would not be there. He spoke of a movie that he had seen while he was away, in which an extremely self-centered man promiscuously made love to many different women. The therapist commented that the patient seemed conflicted about returning and was afraid of getting too close to him, and Mr. A. agreed, saying that he had had an image during his absence of begging the therapist not to seduce him. He directly asked if the therapist intended to seduce him and stated that he did not want another lover, but that he just wanted someone who understood him and knew what conflicts about homosexuality are like. The therapist intervened, telling the patient that his sexual feelings toward him had apparently intensified because of the self-revelations he had made, adding that this seemed to be interfering with his talking in the sessions and with others. Mr. A. responded that his homosexual feelings did seriously interfere with his relations with men, and he illustrated this with a man he had met on his trip.

In the next hour, the patient felt considerably better and expressed gratitude toward the therapist, stating that for the first time he could see the therapist as a real person who understood him. He had told his cousin of his homosexual fantasies toward the therapist and this had terrified the cousin, who was afraid of such things. He then went on to describe how he had once tried to seduce a very close friend, who had refused him, and he then spoke further about the death of his sister.

This material begins with a further unconscious perception of the therapist's difficulties and emphasizes the seductive aspects of his deviations in technique. The patient's actual fear of being seduced strongly reflects his own psychopathology, including some degree of difficulty in reality testing and his extensive homosexual conflicts. On the other hand, his statement about not wanting another lover—the therapist—but just someone who understands him, is a poignant expression of the specific need of every patient in psychotherapy: inappropriate love repeats past neurotic interactions and reinforces the neurosis; reasonable "love" in the form of concern offers a positive identification; but only insightful understanding leading to interpretations can promote lasting, adaptive, inner change based on conflict resolution.

In this session, the therapist made a sensitive and correct intervention which the patient confirmed to some extent in his recollection of his meeting with another man during his trip. In the following hour we then see the indications of a positive incorporative identification with the therapist, who was now viewed as attempting to establish appropriate boundaries—a close friend who refused to be seduced. The patient remains concerned that the therapist is frightened of his own and the patient's homosexuality. We see, too, that he continues to struggle with his own anxieties regarding the therapist's self-revelations, and the unconscious homosexual perceptions and fantasies they had stirred up within him.

Before drawing together some general inferences from this material about both psychotherapeutic and psychoanalytic technique, I shall supplement this vignette in two ways: by offering a brief summary of reactions to deviations in technique in patients presented elsewhere and by offering a brief vignette from the psychoanalytic literature to establish the fact that comparable responses occur in patients in psychoanalysis when their analysts deviate from the basic ground rules. The following vignettes typify the material already presented in my book, *The Technique of Psychoanalytic Psychotherapy* (Langs 1973b, 1974):

Mr. S.W. (1973b, pp. 539–551) was advised by his therapist that his homosexual fantasies and anxieties were being stirred up by sharing a bedroom with his mother, and it was suggested to him that he sleep elsewhere. The following themes were most striking in this patient's reaction, one that occupied him over a period of many weeks: fears of excessive dependency; the therapist as a god who must be refuted; a dream in which his father is dead and that, in context, reflected murderous wishes toward the therapist, who was attempting to control the patient; references to lying; an allusion to how people intruded into his bathroom and permitted him no privacy in his house; his father looking at his pubic hair; mutual exhibitionism with his sister; references to the fact that the therapist could be missing something; a homosexual attraction to a co-worker which led to direct homosexual fantasies about the therapist; anger at his father who told him what to do; a dream of someone who killed everybody, which was directly associated to the therapist's telling this patient what to do. Further themes included a homosexual advance made by the patient to someone else and additional intense homosexual fantasies toward the therapist; a fantasy of the therapist attempting homosexual penetration but being impotent; fantasies of mutual fellatio; having intercourse with a woman since he could not have relations with the therapist; and a revelation that the patient had fantasied that the therapist was telling him not to be interested in women, but to be interested in him.

We begin to see common themes in the patient's unconscious perceptions of unneeded deviations in technique, their unconscious meanings, and the manner in which they are then elaborated upon in the patient's own psychopathology. With Mr. S.W. this included extensive latent homosexual conflicts and their vicissitudes.

Mrs. H.Y. (Langs 1973b, pp. 202–204) reacted to her therapist's holding her up as she fell while leaving a session with unanalyzed associations to the manner in which her mother had frightened her regarding heights and bodily injury, references to a psychotic uncle, threats of leaving treatment, missed sessions, direct and indirect allusions to the therapist's being unaware of things, a repetition of the falling behavior, to which the therapist did not respond with assistance, allusions to her own problems with anger and the ways in which she avoids problems, and references to her husband as a reckless driver.

In contrast, Miss B. (Langs 1973b, p. 417), whose therapist did not accept a gift, reacted to the establishment of these boundaries by developing a new relationship that was far less destructive than her previous relationships had been. In brief, this last response reflects the kinds of positive incorporative identifications that follow from the appropriate maintenance of the ground rules and boundaries of the therapeutic relationship, a subject I will not pursue in any detail in this paper.

A paper by Gudeman (1974) describes a clinical vignette pertinent to this presentation. In brief, the material relates to a married woman, the mother of two children, who came to analysis because of frigidity and a poor marriage. In her analysis, there was an initial flood of instinctualized material and a description of her kleptomania after her grandfather died, her masturbatory practices, and the recall of a seduction by an older man in her early adolescence; though no sexual intimacy had occurred, the patient had felt guilty, since she had contributed to what had happened.

While in the opening months of the treatment, following the description of the death of her grandfather, the patient came early to a session carrying a bouquet of flowers. While the analyst saw that she was living out the wish for a wedding, he accepted the flowers with some discomfort and said nothing immediately. He knew that the acceptance of the gift could enhance the erotic components of the "transference," but he felt that rejection of it would mobilze separation, anxiety and anger beyond the patient's ability to understand and analyze. He also viewed the gift as a possible harbinger of fragile ego boundaries and a reflection of significant regressive potential. His goal in accepting the gift was to foster the therapeutic alliance and to prevent undue regression.

In the session, after giving her gift, the patient spoke of wanting to be loved by her analyst and wanting him to be her father. She wanted to know his first name and the analyst responded that it would be of most use to talk about these feelings and not always useful to give him a present, although she might want to do so. The patient was angry when the analyst did not give her a pat on the head.

Later on, when her husband was away, the patient brought her children to the waiting room. At another time, she gave her analyst tobacco as a present, having had a gynecological examination on the previous day. Other material demonstrated that the patient had set up a triangular situaiton in which the analyst was the loving, good person who could provide her gratification, while the husband was seen as withholding and hostile.

After nine months of treatment, the patient took a one-week vacation (we are not informed as to whether she was held responsible for these sessions). Then, a month after the analyst's summer vacation, the patient brought in a request from her husband that the analyst write a letter justifying a vasectomy for him because of his wife's emotional illness. In associating to this request, the patient said that she preferred that it be done, since it would eliminate the problem of her being a woman or having her own tubes tied. The analyst eventually indicated that there was no psychiatric basis for such a letter and that he would not write it. The patient responded by saying that she could then have another child and cut it into little pieces. She felt pleased and disappointed, as if the analyst had taken something away from her. She probably thought that she could get him to write the letter and felt that her husband would be cross with her but would survive.

Soon after, the patient dreamt that she was in a bathroom where there were toilets for deaf and blind people. She felt exposed and there was a younger man being seduced by an older woman. She came to the analyst's office and the analyst told her, "That's it," and the patient sat up and they ended up talking. An intervention that the dream indicated that the analyst was not hearing or seeing something led to associations about her not getting away with the vasectomy request, but little else.

There followed fears that the analyst would abandon her and then a phone call from her husband because the patient was disturbed. In the next session, she appeared psychotic and, in a disorganized way, she spoke of taking a knife to herself, of her father beating her, of her grandfather teaching her to masturbate, of lies, of being seduced by the analyst, of masturbating, of blaming the analyst, and of secrets. The analyst became more active and in subsequent sessions, the patient brought in a long biographical sketch, and she spoke of dead babies and being raped by her father and everyone. When the patient did not respond well one particular session, the analyst called her by telephone and had her return that day, seeing her in the sitting position. He described to the patient his sense of confusion and medicated her, and over the following several days the patient became calmer.

In confining my discussion of this vignette to the question of deviations in technique, we can see that central to this patient's psychotic episode was a series of deviations in technique, rationalized by the analyst on the basis of promoting the therapeutic alliance and the wish to avoid so-called undue regression, that apparently remained relatively unanalyzed with the patient. They evoked in her intense wishes for erotic gratification from the analyst, desires to modify a number of other boundaries in the relationship, and the offer of further gifts to him. The sequence culminated in the request that the analyst justify the vasectomy for the husband, and when the analyst now modified his stance and attempted to establish that particular boundary, a psychotic episode followed.

In dealing with the dream that was reported at this time, the analyst chose to allude to the possible representations of his deafness and blindness, but apparently missed the other communications (both perceptions and fantasies), thereby confirming the very unconscious perception that he was attempting to clarify. As we have already seen, the dream contains elements characteristic in communications from patients when they are adapting to deviations in technique. It was undoubtedly prompted by the change in the therapist's stance, which the patient perceived as a reflection of his own unconscious guilt and anxieties regarding the extent to which he had permitted the patient to seduce him. In a manner that is typical of reactions to technical errors of this kind (Langs 1975a), the patient dreamt of deaf and blind people, alluding to the analyst who had missed the implications of his erroneous interventions—here the deviations in technique. The patient feels exposed, in part because of an incorporative identification with the analyst who exposed himself, and the manifest dream (we have few associations) reflects her unconscious perception of her having seduced the analyst, who then suddenly tells her the analysis is at an end. A subsequent association alludes to seduction and to her great confusion over the boundaries between herself and the analyst.

We may speculate that the dream is an effort to communicate the patient's unconscious interpretations of the basis of the analyst's behavior in his bodily anxieties and erotic countertransference. Most striking in this situation is the analyst's abrupt shift in his management of the boundaries of the analytic relationship, and this is reflected in the manifest dream in the shift from exposure and seduction to the words "that's it" and the patient's sitting up in the session. The analyst's confusion—which he later directly acknowledged to the patient—is reflected in the patient's psychotic confusion. Here, both incorporative identification and the patient's own pathology played a role.

It seems clear that rather than enhancing this patient's therapeutic alliance, reality testing, and self-boundaries, and rather than assisting this patient to avoid disruptive regression, the deviations in technique significantly contributed to the patient's potential for disturbance in each of these areas. Once again, we see that this patient's regressive reaction, her sense of fusion with the analyst, and her guilt over seducing him and being seduced by him, were all intensified by the analyst's failure to provide appropriate boundaries and to indicate his own ability to maintain appropriate limits to their relationship. While this reaction certainly reflects the patient's own psychopathology, it seems likely that it would have emerged in a more gradual and manageable fashion, and in the context of a viable therapeutic alliance, if the analyst had not permitted the patient to seduce him into modifying the boundaries of their relationship and had, instead, adhered to the ground rules and extensively analyzed the patient's wishes to modify them.

DISCUSSION AND CONCLUSIONS

In concluding, I will briefly highlight the main implications of these observations and suggest some important areas of further study.

1. The manner in which the therapist or analyst establishes and maintains the ground rules and boundaries of the therapeutic

relationship is an important manifestation of his identity, the state of his controls, and his capacity for renunciation, for managing his own intrapsychic conflicts, for handling the stirrings within himself evoked by the patient, and for avoiding pathogenic interactions. Modifications of these boundaries and ground rules often stem from unresolved countertransference problems and reflect difficulties that are unconsciously detected by the patient. Even when deviations are invoked in emergency situations, or when a ground rule is altered for some other real reason, they generally provide the therapist—and the patient—with inappropriate gratifications and repetitions of pathogenic object relationships of which the therapist must be aware since this too will be unconsciously perceived by the patient.

2. The therapist's maintenance of the ground rules and boundaries of the therapeutic relationship is an area of activity that is constantly monitored by the patient and is utilized as a basis for unconscious, incorporative identification. Constructively handled, it provides a basis for positive and adaptive inner change that supplements the patient's endeavors to achieve conflict resolution and symptom relief through cognitive insight based on the therapist's interpretations. In addition, the proper maintenance of these boundaries is essential to give the patient the best opportunity to project his intrapsychic fantasies and to attempt to enact his past pathogenic object relationships in his interaction with the analyst in a manner that can be recognized and analyzed. Modifications in these boundaries lead to significant contaminations of the patient's intrapsychic projections, and to a situation in which the pathological introjects, unconscious fantasies, and past object relationships are repeated and justified in the therapeutic relationship, rather than frustrated and not confirmed in reality so that they can be analyzed primarily in terms of the patient's unconscious conflicts, fantasies, and memories.

3. The idea that deviations in technique are necessary to foster the therapeutic alliance appears to be based on a naive treatment of the subject, one that fails to recognize the extensive unconscious meanings and implications of these deviations. Such an attitude overlooks the manner in which firm, analytically justified maintenance of the ground rules offers to the patient a structured framework and secure image of the therapist through which a strong and viable therapeutic relationship can be established. In this context, it is to be noted that, empirically, deviations in technique of all kinds often stem from

uncontrolled anxieties in the therapist and from doubts regarding his capacity to analyze the patient; further, the patient unconsciously recognizes such sources of deviations and reacts strongly to these unconscious meanings.

4. Clinically, the ramifications of unneeded deviations in technique are unconsciously perceived by the patient, who attempts to alert the therapist to the unconscious meanings of the deviation, to offer— interpret—to the therapist his ideas as to the neurotic difficulties that have prompted the therapist to undertake these deviations, and to assist the therapist in restoring the proper boundaries of the therapeutic relationship. On the other hand, the hope of sharing inappropriate defenses and of finding momentary gratifications and symptom relief through the misalliance engendered by the acceptance of the therapist's deviations in technique will lead the patient to accept these deviations and seek out others. However, as the guilt and anxiety mount, in response to the unconscious awareness of the mutual corruption in the lack of boundaries and in reaction to its hidden, forbidden meanings, the patient will react by ultimately terminating the treatment or interrupting it temporarily, withdrawing from the therapist in some other way, and acting out in keeping with the model offered by the therapist. Other, contrasting efforts are made to reestablish the necessary boundaries in the hope of some ultimate benefit from the treatment.

With considerable unconscious perceptiveness, patients recognize that deviations in technique tend to promote undue surrender and loss of autonomy; reflect inappropriate and destructive mothering; have exhibitionistic and seductive implications; reflect a lack of barriers, including those that range from separateness of self and object to the incest barrier; are unconscious attempts at seduction; are inherently destructive toward the patient; reflect some degree of loss of control in the therapist; and often serve to conceal underlying sexual and aggressive conflicts in the therapist—to name but a few of the kinds of communications latently inherent in these measures. The appearance of such themes in the material from patients should prompt the therapist to examine his management of the ground rules and boundaries of the therapeutic relationship for any gross or subtle modification in his stance.

5. Technically, a deviation in technique, however minor, that has been evoked by a patient or offered by the therapist, calls for the following measures:

(a) Identification of the deviation and modification of the therapeutic stance so that the deviation is not continued unnecessarily, and it is made clear to the patient, implicitly or explicitly, that the boundaries will be restored and maintained. Without the modification of the deviant situation in reality, all other therapeutic endeavors will be of no avail.

(b) A full exploration and analysis of the patient's reaction to the deviation and to the reestablishment of the boundaries. During such an analysis, it is generally not advisable for the therapist to directly acknowledge that his deviation was in error, but his attitude should *implicitly* reflect his awareness that the deviation was inappropriate and that the patient's perceptions of this aspect of the deviation are not fantasy but have significant kernels of realistic perceptiveness in them. The advice that the therapist acknowledge his errors to the patient has generally been based on a wish to appear human and fallible to the patient when it seems appropriate. This stance overlooks the deviation in boundaries that such an explicit acknowledgment entails, and the consequences thereof. This is a complex issue that deserves fuller study; my present observations suggest that implicit acceptance of appropriate responsibility is the most helpful therapeutic attitude for the patient.

The therapist must carefully and sensitively separate the patient's valid perceptions of the implications of the deviation and the therapist's unconscious need for it from the extension of these perceptions into the patient's fantasies. In addition, he should try to understand how the deviation in technique was perceived by the patient as a loss of control, an acting out, and a failure to maintain inner and outer boundaries on the part of the therapist. Failure to analyze the implications of these nonverbal aspects will prompt a negative incorporative identification and acting out on the part of the patient, who will often attempt to misuse the therapist's countertransference problems as an inappropriate sanction for his own acting out. In addition, the specific working through of these aspects of the deviation in technique fosters the reestablishment of the patient's own inner and outer boundaries and controls.

(c) The therapist should be prepared for derivatives related to deviations in technique to appear in the patient's associations and his adaptive responses for some time following such an incident; he should also be prepared for their reemergence throughout the subsequent treatment and especially at the time of termination. Continued analytic work with the repercussions of such deviations will reveal their genetic and current dynamic unconscious meanings for the patient. It will enable an assessment of the extent to which the deviation did in reality repeat the pathogenic behavior of, and interaction with, early significant figures, and the extent to which the patient used the stimulus of the deviation as a source of more distorted transference fantasies. Clearly, reactions to deviations in technique cannot be viewed simply as transference responses, but must be undersatood in terms of the mixture of reality and fantasy involved.

6. The marked productivity of patients following deviations in technique can now be understood to reflect the traumatic impact that such deviations have on them and the intense adaptive efforts that they make in response. Such efforts include attempts to cure the therapist of his own intrapsychic conflicts as reflected in the unneeded deviation (Searles 1975, Langs 1975), attempts to rectify the actual therapeutic situation, and efforts to readapt to the intrapsychic conflicts and memories stirred up by the deviation in technique.

7. The present findings suggest that deviations in technique should be restricted to emergency situations and to the use of parameters that are truly necessitated by ego dysfunctions in the patient. They point to a need to reevaluate the indications for deviations in technique and parameters, and should promote extensive self-scrutiny by the therapist when he is considering or has made a modification in technique. In addition, these observations suggest that even in those emergency situations where deviations prove necessary for the patient, their unconscious ramifications are extensive and require considerable subsequent analysis and modification.

Tentatively it would appear that many of the therapeutic crises that prompt therapists to deviate in their technique are evoked by an interaction between the patient's psychopathology and that of the therapist. These data suggest that the therapist's initial stance at such times should center on an effort to understand the specific percipitants of the crisis and on self-analytic work toward modifying his own contribution, as well as the basic use of correct interpretations to the patient. This not only provides the patient cognitive insight, but affords him an actual experience in which the therapist does not repeat the past pathogenic interaction, but instead detaches himself from it and is capable of interpreting it (Racker 1968). The danger of mutual acting out and misalliance through deviations should, if at all possible, be considered before they are invoked. The therapist should engage in considerable self-scrutiny and in a reassessment of his interaction with the patient and of his understanding of the material; he should preferably restrict the use of deviations to those situations where he is unable to detect any countertransference difficulties and there is an emergency need, such as a suicidal or homicidal patient. In doing so, the deviation should be kept to the absolute minimum and modified in reality as quickly as possible, with a full analysis of all the dimensions of the experience (Eissler 1953).

8. Technically, the therapeutic stance used when the deviation is entirely necessary and justified is different from those situations in which the deviation proves to have been unneeded and in large measure a product of the therapist's countertransference. In the former situation, the inappropriate gratifications afforded to both patient and therapist can be analyzed as inevitable side effects of an essential technical measure, while in the latter situation the neurotic gratifications and the repetition of past neurotic object relationships is the central contributing factor and must be recognized as such.

9. The counterpart of these findings regarding deviations in technique is the postulate that the present ground rules and boundaries of the therapeutic relationship in adult psychoanalysis and psychotherapy offer an optimal therapeutic hold and setting for the patient. The finding that patients are exquisitely sensitive to the seemingly most trivial alterations in the boundaries and ground rules—e.g., a necessary change of hour—also attests the importance of this dimension of the therapeutic relationship.

10. The present findings should, however, not be construed as a brief for therapeutic rigidity or misconstrued as a basis upon which to advocate a lack of humanity and concern in the psychotherapist or analyst. To the contrary, it is intended to help the therapist become aware of the major ramifications of any deviation in technique so that these factors can be considered along with other dimensions when such a measure is contemplated. These observations prepare the therapist who has expressed human concern or other controlled, noninterpretive reactions to the patient for those consequences that he might not otherwise have anticipated. They can serve to remind us that the most meaningful expression of the therapist's or analyst's humanity in the

treatment setting lies in his usual attitude of concern and in his capacity to offer the patient a correct interpretation, especially at a moment when he has not participated in a neurotic interaction with the patient. Without deviating, the therapist who wishes to be appropriately supportive can respond to emergency situations with implicit concern, an increased rate of intervening, and by affording the patient a model of someone who is reasonably involved, interpretively helpful, and also has the capacity to maintain necessary limits. Many who have written on the subject of deviations in technique have failed to appreciate the powerful supportive dimensions inherent in nondeviant analytic technique and seem to underestimate the power of a correct interpretation that emanates from an analyst who is not involved in a misalliance or embroiled in a countertransference conflict.

11. These findings also remind us of the powerful inner forces that move the therapist or analyst toward deviations in technique and misalliances, ranging from deep personal needs to deny one's own limitations and mortality to the search for specific countertransference-based neurotic interactions, gratifications, and defenses (Langs 1975b).

12. Finally, this study also emphasizes the importance of the distinction between reality and fantasy in the therapeutic relationahip (Langs 1973a). It is insufficient to explore and analyze the content of the patient's reactions to deviations in technique in terms of his intrapsychic fantasies, without recognition of their basis and stimulus in reality and the actual, nonverbal meanings and effects of these deviations on the patient. Here, the distinctions between interpretation and management, free association and interaction, fantasy and actuality, and verbal interaction and nonverbal communication became pertinent. Who and what the therapist is becomes as important as what he says. The culmination of analytic work in insight gained from the analyst's interpretations does not thereby lose status, but is supplemented by another important dimension of technique: the management of the analytic relationship.

NOTES

1. The area under study in this presentation is largely comparable for psychotherapy and psychoanalysis, and I shall therefore use the term

therapist generically to allude to both the psychotherapist and the psychoanalyst, and reserve the latter two terms when referring specifically to a psychotherapeutic or psychoanalytic situation. I have not included material from my own psychotherapeutic and psychoanalytic practice because of a decision to not use these sources in my writings. Among the many reasons for this decision is the empirical discovery that such use of one's clinical experience, past and present, significantly modifies the framework and boundaries of the therapeutic situation. It is, in effect, a deviation in technique that has all the consequences, more or less, of the deviations described in the body of this paper. Since some degree of deviation is already inherent in the supervisory situation and in material published by others, I shall use vignettes drawn from these sources to develop the theses offered here.

2. Upon completion of this paper, I came across Milner's (1952) intriguing comments, made in the context of a study of symbolism and child analysis, regarding the frame that demarks the reality that prevails within the psychoanalytic situation from that which exists outside of it. She views the frame as essential to the creation of the transference illusions—a suggestion that clearly relates to the ground rules and boundaries discussed in this paper.

REFERENCES

Allen, S (1956), Reflections on the wish of the analyst to "break" or change the basic rule. *Bulletin of the Menninger Clinic* 20:192–200.

Arlow, J., and Brenner, C. (1966). Discussion of papers on the psychoanalytic situation. In *Psychoanalysis in the Americas,* ed. R. Litman. New York: International Universities Press.

Balint, M. (1968). *The Basic Fault: Therapeutic Aspects of Regression.* London: Tavistock Publications.

Bleger, J. (1967). Psycho-analysis of the psycho-analytic frame. *International Journal of Psycho-Analysis* 48:511–519.

Bouvet, M. (1958). Technical variations and the concept of distance. *International Journal of Psycho-Analysis* 39:211–221.

Caloteras, R. (1967). Silence as a technical parameter in psychoanalysis. *International Journal of Psycho-Analysis* 48:536–558.

Eissler, R. (1953). The effect of the structure of the ego on psychoanalytic technique. *Journal of the American Psychoanalytic Association* 1:104–143.

—— (1958). Remarks on some variations in psychoanalytic technique. *International Journal of Psycho-Analysis* 39:222–229.

Frank, J. (1956). Indications and contraindications for the application of the "standard technique." *Journal of the American Psychoanalytic Association* 4:266–284.

Freud, A. (1954a). Problems of technique in adult analysis (with discussion by several others). *Bulletin of the Philadelphia Association of Psychoanalysis* 4:44–69.

—— (1954b). The widening scope of indications for psychoanalysis, discussion. *Journal of the American Psychoanalytic Association* 2:607–620.

Freud, S. (1937). Analysis terminable and interminable. *Standard Edition* 23:209–254.

Greenacre, P. (1959). Certain technical problems in the transference relationship. *Journal of the American Psychoanalytic Association* 7:484–502.

—— (1971). *Emotional Growth,* Vol. II. New York: International Universities Press.

Greenson, R. (1958). Variations in classical psycho-analytic technique: an introduction. *International Journal of Psycho-Analysis* 39:200–201.

—— (1967).*The Technique and Practice of Psychoanalysis,* Vol. 1. New York: International Universities Press.

—— (1972), Beyond transference and interpretation. *International Journal of Psycho-Analysis* 53:213–217.

——, and Wexler, M. (1969). The non-transference relationship in the psychoanalytic situation. *International Journal of Psycho-Analysis* 50:27–39.

Gudeman, J. (1974). Uncontrolled regression in therapy and analysis. *International Journal of Psychoanalytic Psychotherapy* 3:325–338.

Hoedemaker, E. (1960). Psycho-analytic technique and ego modification. *International Journal of Psycho-Analysis* 41:34–45.

Kanzer, M. (1975). The therapeutic and working alliances. *International Journal of Psychoanalytic Psychotherapy* 4:48–68.

Langs, R. (1972). A psychoanalytic study of material from patients in psychotherapy. *International Journal of Psychoanalytic Psychotherapy* 1:4–45. [Chapter 3, this volume]

——(1973a). The patient's view of the therapist: reality or fantasy? *International Journal of Psychoanalytic Psychotherapy* 2:411–431. [Chapter 4, this volume]

————(1973b). *The Technique of Psychoanalytic Psychotherapy,* Vol. I. New York: Jason Aronson

————*(1974). The Technique of Psychoanalytic Psychotherapy,* Vol. I. New York: Jason Aronson.

———— (1975a). The patient's unconscious perception of the therapist's errors. In *Tactics and Techniques in Psychoanalytic Therapy, Vol. II: Countertransference,* ed. P. Giovacchini. New York: Jason Aronson. [Chapter 5, this volume]

———— (1975b). Therapeutic misalliances. *International Journal of Psychoanalytic Psychotherapy* 4:77–105. [Chapter 6, this volume]

———— (in press). The misalliance dimension in Freud's case histories. In *Freud and His Patients,* ed. M. Kanzer and J. Glenn. New York: Jason Aronson. [Chapters 8–10, this volume]

Loewald, H. (1960). On the therapeutic action of psycho-analysis. *International Journal of Psycho-Analysis* 41:16–33.

Loewenstein, R. (1958). Remarks on some variations in psychoanalytic technique. *International Journal of Psycho-Analysis* 39:202–210).

Lorand, S. (1963). Modifications in classical psychoanalysis. *Psychoanalytic Quarterly* 32:192–204.

Milner, M. (1952). Aspects of symbolism in comprehension of the not-self. *International Journal of Psycho-Analysis* 33:181–195.

Nacht, S. (1958). Variations in technique. *International Journal of Psycho-Analysis* 39:235–237.

Racker, H. (1968). *Transference and Countertransference.* London: Hogarth Press.

Reich, A. (1958). A special variation of technique. *International Journal of Psycho-Analysis* 39:230–234.

Rodgers, T. (1965). A specific parameter: concurrent psychotherapy of the spouse of an analysand by the same analyst. *International Journal of Psycho-Analysis* 46:237–243.

Rosenfeld, H. (1958). Contribution to the discussion on variations in classical technique. *International Journal of Psycho-Analysis* 39:238–239.

Searles, H. (1975). The patient as therapist to his analyst. In *Tactics and Techniques in Psychoanalytic Therapy, Vol. II: Countertransference,* ed. P. Giovacchini. New York: Jason Aronson.

Stone, L. (1954). The widening scope of indications for psychoanalysis. *Journal of the American Psychoanalytic Association* 2:567–594.

———— (1961). *The Psychoanalytic Situation.* New York: International Universities Press.

———— (1967). The psychoanalytic situation and transference: postscript to an earlier communication. *Journal of the American Psychoanalytic Association* 15:3–58.

Tarachow, S. (1962). Interpretation and reality in psychotherapy. *International Journal of Psycho-Analysis* 43:377–387.

Winnicott, D.W. (1958). *Collected Papers.* London: Tavistock Publications.

Zetzel, E. (1966). The analytic situation. In *Psychoanalysis in the Americas,* ed. R. Litman, New York: International Universities Press.

Chapter Eight

Misalliance and Framework in the Case of Dora

(1976[1974])

In past decade or so, there has been growing interest in developing a well-rounded and comprehensive understanding of the patient-analyst relationship. Among the many issues that have been explored in the course of these endeavors, one segment will be considered here on the basis of a restudy of one of Freud's case histories, that of Dora (Freud 1905a). My focus will be on problems in the establishment and maintenance of the therapeutic alliance, and the development of a particular type of disturbance in sectors of this alliance that I have termed *therapeutic misalliances* (1974, 1975b, 1976a, b). In particular, the contribution of deviations in the basic ground rules and boundaries of the analytic situation and their relationship to the development of sectors of misalliance will be explored. It will be my main hypothesis that modifications in the basic framework of the analytic relationship evoke intense responses in the patient, and that these characteristically offer him a basis for potential sectors of misalliance with the analyst. It will be my goal to return to Freud's case histories in search of support or refutation of this hypothesis, and to examine the implications of my findings. In order to concentrate on this task, it will be necessary to bypass many other contributing factors to the material that I will study, and I will be able only briefly to counterbalance my focus on misalliance with references to the indications of positive segments of therapeutic alliance between Freud and his patients (Kanzer 1952, 1975, Zetzel 1966).

We may broadly define the therapeutic alliance as the conscious and unconscious agreement, applied in subsequent actual work, on the part of both patient and analyst to join forces in effecting symptom alleviation and constructive characterological changes through insight and inner structural change on the part of the patient. In contrast, therapeutic misalliances constitute interactions that are designed either to undermine such goals or to achieve results on some other basis (Langs 1975b). Therapeutic alliances and misalliances constitute a continuum, and, at any given moment, one or the other may predominate. While often difficult to distinguish, this differentiation is important since sectors of misalliance entail transference gratifications, shared defenses, and mutual acting out, even though they represent mutual and misguided efforts at cure. The determination of the presence of a misalliance is based on a careful and repeated scrutiny of the patient's associations and behaviors, and the analyst's subjective awareness. This type of assessment—which I have termed *the validating process* (Langs 1976a, b)—is repeatedly carried out during the course of an analysis and it serves as an indicator of the direction taken by the analytic work at a given moment. The recognition of misalliances is important in that their development undermines sectors of the basic psychoanalytic work and compromises aspects of the outcome of the analysis. It is therefore essential that they be resolved if insight and structural change are to be maximally achieved for the patient. In fact, the development of sectors of misalliance are inevitable in any analytic experience, and their recognition and analytic resolution are among the most insight-producing and growth-promoting experiences for the patient—and, at times, for the analyst as well.

While investigating therapeutic misalliances, it was found empirically that they are often based on deviations in the analyst's usual stance and on errors in technique (Langs 1973b, 1974, 1975b, c, 1976a, b). These findings led to a reconsideration of the framework of the psychoanalytic relationship and of the indication for, and complications evoked by, deiviations or parameters of technique (Langs 1975c).

The attempt was made to establish the distinction between valid deviations from those that prove detrimental to the analytic process and are, therefore, best classified as technical errors. Related to this problem is the issue of how to best establish and maintain the therapeutic alliance (Stone 1961, 1967, Greenson 1965, 1967, 1971, 1972, Greenson and Wexler 1969, Arlow and Brenner 1966, Zetzel 1956, 1958, 1966–1969, Heimann 1970, Kanzer 1975, Arlow 1975, Langs 1975b, c, 1976b).

In brief, my own clinical observations have indicated that the therapeutic alliance is best maintained and developed through a firm though not rigid adherence to the basic ground rules of analysis and through a sensitive maintenance of the psychoanalytic framework. This includes the establishment of a sound therapeutic stance and the use of interpretations; in general, noninterpretive measures of all kinds prove determental and are the source of misalliances.

In this context, I attempted (1975c, 1976b) to define the present, empirically derived optimal ground rules of the psychoanalytic situation. I included the following: set fees, hours, and length of sessions; the fundamental rule of free association with communication occurring while the patient is on the couch; the absence of physical contact and extratherapeutic gratifications; the analyst's relative anonymity and the use of neutral interventions geared primarily toward interpretations; and the exclusive one-to-one relationship with total confidentiality. I found that in most clinical situations— including the treatment of adolescents—it was more therapeutic to adhere to these basic ground rules under any conditions short of an emergency, and to offer interpretations to the patient rather than deviate. Further, all modifications of these ground rules, even when prompted by necessary human responsiveness or an emergency situation, universally evoked intense responses in the patient. If these went unrecognized and unanalyzed, they tended to have deterimental effects on the analysis and on the patient.

These earlier findings were not considered a brief for rigidity, but they indicate the importance of the framework of the analytic relationship and the great influence on the patient of any modification in this basic area. It was concluded that the manner in which the analyst establishes and maintains the boundaries and framework of the analytic relationship reflects important aspects of the management of his own intrapsycic state and fantasies, including their countertransference aspects. Further, the proper management of the framework implicitly offers the analyst as a constructive figure for the most viable and uncontaminated unfolding of the patient's transference projections and neurosis—and their interpretation and modification. On the other hand, impairments in the management of the framework and unneeded deviations in technique tend to inappropriately gratify and offer maladaptive defenses to both patient and analyst, promoting pathogenic interactions and identifications. I concluded that the present ground rules and boundaries of adult (and adolescent) psychoanalysis contain within them an optimally viable and valid basic hold for the patient (Winnicott 1965) and a corresponding setting for the unfolding of the analytic work.

With these observations and hypotheses in mind, I restudied Freud's case histories. I reasoned that if my main conclusions were valid, and if these basic tenets had stood the test of time and could be viewed as fundamentally sound, it would also be possible to look to the past and apply the current ground rules of analysis to Freud's work—despite the fact they did not represent his own framework. In this way, I would have an opportunity to test hypotheses developed from current clinical observations and possibly develop further insights concerning them. Thus, I proposed to use the current set of ground rules as a template to be applied to Freud's work, so that each time he intervened in a manner that did not fit with the present framework I would observe the consequences of the "deviation" and its repercussions for the patient.

In taking this backward look and applying current standards to Freud's work, I recognize the extent to which he experimented with the ground rules and maintained a consistent search for more effective therapeutic principles. It would be difficult to delineate a consistent set of rules by which Freud worked, and I will not attempt to do so here. Further, his case histories in no way incorporated a detailed account of Freud's analytic technique or of the sessions with his patients. We are therefore faced with a number of limitations to this exploration, and yet it seems possible to benefit from Freud's early ingenious efforts to develop a viable psychoanalytic technique and to learn from the mistakes he inevitably made. Thus, despite the inherent difficulties, the attempt to test current hypotheses based on a retrospective study of Freud's material offers an unusual opportunity to ascertain the extent to which the management of the framework of the psychoanalytic relationship meaningfully contributes to the therapeutic experience of the patient. With these idea in mind, let us now consider Freud's analysis of Dora (1905a).

THE CLINICAL MATERIAL

In studying the case of Dora for misalliances, I am not embarking upon an entirely original research. Erikson (1962) utilized aspects of this analysis to develop his conceptualization of reality and actuality both in the analytic situation and for the individual in his life. In attempting to demonstrate that actuality—defined as "the world verified only in the ego's immediate immersion in action" (p. 453)—differed for Dora and Freud, Erikson was studying a dimension of misalliance from his own vantage point. Before comparing his findings with my own, however, I will present some pertinent clinical material.

A review of Freud's paper on Dora indicates that there were two main "deviations"—by present definition—and one related minor one in analytic technique utilized by Freud and two types of misalliances which developed between himself and Dora, formed partly on the basis of these deviations. Specifically, Freud had treated Dora's father for syphilis and also knew her father's sister and brother; in addition, Freud knew Herr K., the man who had attempted to seduce or marry Dora and who also had referred Dora's father to Freud. Freud's presentation suggests that Dora's father spoke to him directly about her prior to the analysis and that he communicated with Freud after the analysis had been completed, and possibly did so during the three months in which the analysis was in progress as well. In these ways, Freud did not maintain the one-to-one relationship with Dora that many analysts would currently establish (Langs 1973b), and these various third parties to the analysis—directly and indirectly—appear to have become important factors in the outcome of the analytic experience.

A second area of deviation related to Freud's special interest in Dora's sexual material—a modification in neutrality—while a third and more minor "deviation" occurred when Freud experimented with Dora by pointing to a book of matches that he had brought into his consultation room; the role that this maneuver played in the analysis will be discussed presently.

In this context, then, the first sector of misalliance between Dora and Freud related to the manner in which she entered analysis. Her father brought her to Freud with the evident intention that the latter should actively intervene on the father's behalf so that Dora would no longer press him to give up his affair with Frau K. As Dora's father gave Freud a history of her problems, he said: "Please try and bring her to reason" (Freud 1905a, p. 26).

Dora, for her part, apparently entered analysis in order to convince Freud that her assessment of the situation with her father was correct and in all likelihood she also hoped to persuade Freud to intervene for her with her father so that he would give up his mistress (Erikson 1962). Thus, Dora began treatment in the hope of establishing a misalliance in which Freud would help her to manipulate her father and disrupt his relationship with Frau K. As additional evidence that this was among Dora's motives for seeing Freud, we may note that she had threatened suicide and was first brought to Freud for analysis after a quarrel with her father on this very subject.

Dora was also suffering from a multiplicity of hysterical symptoms and wished to find symptomatic relief from these maladies. In all likelihood, this contributed to segments of a viable therapeutic alliance with Freud that fostered the development of the positive aspects of their therapeutic endeavors. However, in addition to possibly being prepared to resolve her inner conflicts and symptoms through the analytic efforts developed by Freud, it appears that Dora also hoped to alleviate these difficulties through the special assistance she sought from him. Thus it seems likely that Dora's conscious and unconscious motivations for analysis, and her conscious and unconscious fantasies related to the means through which she would find symptomatic relief, contributed to sectors of both alliance and misalliance with Freud. This is typical of patients entering analysis, and much depends on the analyst's response.

For his part, Freud was aware of Dora's intended misalliance and while he did not specifically interpret and analyze it, rather early in the analysis (p. 42) he pointed out to Dora that her illness was intended to detach her father from Frau K. In so doing, he added that she would recover if this were achieved, but that he—Freud—hoped that her father would not yield in the face of Dora's symptoms, since this would provide her a most dangerous weapon. This intervention preceded by a short time the appearance of Dora's first dream which conveyed her intentions of terminating her analysis. Freud's comment may have contributed to these intentions, since he was, in effect unconsciously indicating to Dora his unwillingness to participate in her intended misalliance, doing so without providing her insight into the meanings of the misalliance and without offering—however indirectly— alternative methods of resolving her difficulties. In a sense, this may be seen as an early effort by Dora to effect a *misalliance cure* (Langs 1975b, 1976a,b)—noninsightful symptomatic relief effected with the help of Freud. The latter's comment indicates the extent to which he sensed the power of such "cures" and recognized them to be antianalytic. This interaction and the areas of developing misalliance should, however, become clearer after we have outlined Freud's apparent contributions to them.

Freud was, of course, interested in helping Dora alleviate her hysterical symptoms through insight into the unconscious fantasies on which they were based. However, he also indicated in his presentation that there were other motives which prompted his interest in Dora, and these had the potential for creating sectors of misalliance that could also disturb the analysis. They are evident in one of Freud's pivotal statements (p. 31): "I was anxious to subject my assumptions [regarding sexuality] to a rigorous test in this case." As we know, Freud had recently written *The Interpretation of Dreams* (1900) and was learning to apply his new theories about dreams and neurosis clinically. Furthermore, he was working on his "Three Essays on the Theory of Sexuality" (1905b) and was therefore most eager to test out his hypotheses regarding infantile sexuality in his clinical work with his patients. As Freud himself later stated (1912), therapeutic zeal and vested interest of this kind can prove disruptive to an analysis—in our terms, can create misalliances. Erikson (1962) has written of these concerns as part of Freud's quest for genetic truth. Erikson contrasted it with Dora's search for historical truth, as related to her then current realities and to the fidelity of those close to her; this served as a means of establishing her identity as a young woman.

Let us now briefly follow some of the highlights of Dora's analysis, with a focus on the threads woven out of Freud's "deviations" and the potential efforts toward misalliance of both Freud and Dora. The first communications from Dora—as reported by Freud in his paper— alluded to an attempt at seduction by Herr K. when she was fourteen years of age; this had preceded by two years the scene at the lake with

Herr K. during which he had proposed to her. The latter incident had prompted Dora to rupture her relationship with her and intensified her efforts to separate her father from Frau K. In an earlier experience, Harr K. had arranged to be alone with Dora and had kissed her, evoking a reaction of disgust. Dora was frightened and Freud considered this an abnormal reaction; he very quickly brought out her awareness of erections in men.

From the vantage point we have taken, it would appear reasonable to formulate the hypothesis that Freud's personal acquaintance with Dora's father and Herr K. contributed to a very early and intense erotization of her relationship with Freud, one that was communicated in a relatively thinly disguised form in this first communication. If we remember that Dora's father had turned her over to Herr K. as a kind of payment for his relationship with Frau K., we can immediately recognize a very striking parallel between that situation and Dora's initial relationship with Freud. While it is true that Freud failed throughout this analysis, as he readily acknowledged and discussed, to interpret Dora's transference (i.e., primarily genetically—or intrapsychically—based) feelings and fantasies toward him, the additional fact that Freud was closely identified in reality with Dora's father and Herr K. undoubtedly contributed to her conscious and unconscious perception of this relationship (Langs 1973a). It would therefore be difficult and incorrect to attribute this initial relationship with Freud, as well as the subsequent rather pervasive, erotized one, entirely to transference factors. There were strong kernels of reality at the roots of Dora's inner responses to Freud that were embedded in the latter's relationships with these two men and in the actual stance that Freud took with Dora in the analysis. His ready acceptance of sexuality and his very early emphasis (intervening and questioning) in this area undoubtedly heightened Dora's belief that Freud was in some ways not unlike her father and Herr K. Freud's intense interest in specific sexuality—amounting to a relaxation of his neutrality—seems to have contributed to a misalliance with Dora which she (unconsciously?) perceived very strongly in sexual terms (Langs 1975a).

This delineation of the role of possible unconscious perceptions of Freud and of the interactional dimension of Dora's responses to him help to clarify her ongoing intrapsychic conflicts and unconscious fantasies. A patient's reactions to the analyst are always a mixture of reality—as it exists and is perceived—and fantasy, of transference and nontransference. Only by specifying the actual nature of the ongoing interaction with the analyst, and especially the implicit and explicit meanings of his interventions and failures to intervene, can one establish the components of reality and fantasy in the patient's reaction to him. (Langs 1973a, 1975a, 1976a, b).

The relative neglect of reality factors in the patient-analyst relationship (see also Greenson 1972) and of nontransference elements was not only characteristic of Freud's technique at the time of his analysis of Dora, but persists to the present day. Freud tended to neglect the interaction between himself and his patients, and the precipitants of primarily transference reactions therein. With Dora, he was quite slow to recognize the transference reactions in her communications, and he tended to quickly link them to genetic material without a full appreciation of the implications for his current relationship with his patient (Kanzer 1966). We can still learn a great deal from the consequences of these oversights in Freud's work with Dora.

To return more specifically to my discussion of this analysis, the case history indicates that Dora expressed other concerns that were related to the manner in which she entered analysis and to the fact that Freud knew her father. She spoke of how a governess had pretended affection for her while in reality preferring her father; eventually she dropped Dora. This may be an indirect representation of her concerns in her relationship with Freud. She may even have fantasied that Freud's primary allegiance was to her father and that there was an unholy alliance between the two. For her part, the patient continued to attempt to prove that the scene by the lake had been a reality and not her fantasy, and Freud concluded—undoubtedly conveying this to Dora—that she was being completely truthful. As a possible reward for this affirmation, Dora told Freud that she believed that her father was impotent and acknowledged her awareness of fellatio. Freud then quickly interpreted Dora's love for her father and for Herr K., but she denied being attracted to the latter. It was in this context that the first dream was reported.

In it, a house is on fire and Dora's father is standing beside her bed and wakes her. She dresses quickly but her mother wants to stop and save her jewel case; her father says, "I refuse to let myself and my two children be burnt for the sake of your jewel case" (p. 64). They hurry downstairs and as soon as Dora is outside, she wakes up.

This dream had first been dreamed three times at the lake after Herr K.'s attempt to either seduce or propose to her. It is striking that in his analysis of this dream, while Freud alluded to the concept of day residues, he neglected the task of determining the *specific* day residues for this dream—the adaptive tasks or stimuli which had prompted it (Langs 1973a). Since they undoubtedly included major precipitants from Dora's ongoing relationship with Freud, this suggests that Freud had a blind spot for Dora's feelings toward him—the so-called transference—since the dream, even retrospectively to Freud, very clearly conveyed Dora's thoughts of fleeing the analysis and her fantasies that she was once more in danger sexually with Freud as she had previously been with Herr K. (a repetition of the initial theme of the analysis).

The manifest dream itself and certain of Dora's associations illuminate the theme of misalliance in that her mother wanted to save her jewel case, but her father wanted to save his children. The associations to the jewel case related to Dora's virginity, which she has felt had been threatened by Herr K.; she apparently felt similarly threatened by Freud. While the unfolding genetic history provided clues as to the development of the intrapsychic fantasies and needs within Dora that prompted her to sexualize her relationship with Freud and to respond to this technique in an erotic manner, our main efforts here will continue to focus on the generally ignored contributions made by Freud to these sexual anxieties and fantasies, and to the misalliance with which Dora was concerned. In this regard, the dream seems to reflect Dora's anxiety regarding Freud's intense interest in her sexual fantasies, his close association with her father and Herr K., and her responsive determination to flee the analytic situation.

The continuum and intermixture of alliance and misalliance is suggested by the apparent dual roles in which Freud was placed in this dream: seducer and protector. This provides evidence that in addition to the sector of misalliance between Freud and Dora, there were important areas of alliance and continued hopes in the patient that Freud would rescue her from her plight, both inner and outer. Further, the manifest dream was concerned with alerting and adaptive responses to danger. On this basis, and in keeping with Dora's subsequent associations, we may also postulate that the dream was prompted by unconscious perceptions of the misalliance and was reported to Freud as part of an effort to call it to his attention and to assist him in resolving it (Langs 1975b, 1976a). It therefore appears that Dora was attempting to save her analysis at the very juncture that she was thinking of abandoning it—a response that is characteristic of patients faced with sectors of misalliance with their analysts.

Dora's associations to this dream eventually led to the fact that Herr K. had taken the key to her bedroom and had left her unprotected from his intrusions. Freud interpreted her intentions to escape from Herr K.'s persecution, but did not develop a comparable theme for her relationship to himself. Eventually, the anxieties were traced to her feelings toward her father, who actually was the middleman in both situations. Freud was also able to point out that Dora was frightened by her readiness to submit sexually to Herr K. and needed to flee him because of this—though he again did not allude to the analysis.

It was in this context that Freud attempted his experiment of placing matches where Dora could see them from the couch. When she could see nothing, Freud pointed to the matches and examined how fire was tied to fears of bed-wetting, and they went on to establish that she had indeed a bed wetter in her childhood. Here Freud's interest in the genetic truth and in sexuality deflected him from verbalizing Dora's current anxieties and fantasies, although his behavior did demonstrate an unconscious appreciation of some of the current stimuli for her fantasies and associations. Unconscious perceptiveness of this kind is often evident in otherwise deviant or erroneous interventions by analysts (Langs 1976a). In addition, Freud was unconsciously acting out something akin to Dora's very fear of an uncontrolled analytic situation—fire—thereby sharing this fantasy with her. It is of interest, in view of my finding that deviations in technique almost always evoke attempts by analysands to evoke further deviations (1975c), that Dora later responded with two symptomatic acts of her own—the hiding of a letter from Freud, thereby playing secrets with him, and playing with a reticule during a session. This latter reflected her masturbatory fantasies and, undoubtedly, her mounting sexual anxieties in the analytic situation and her unconscious perception of Freud's behavior. We may view Freud's use of the matches and Dora's behavior with the letter and reticule as a sector of misalliance in which nonverbal communication and acting out—actually, acting in—was permitted in lieu of verbal communication.

Freud's experiment led to a most revealing addendum to the first dream: Dora had smelled smoke. Freud then connected the dream to himself, since he was prone to use the phrase, there can be no smoke without fire; yet when she directly objected to this intervention, Freud appears to have dropped it. It may well be that here both he and she shared a defensive misalliance—a displacement away from their relationship. Freud did, however, return to this area in a small way when he interpreted Dora's wish to yield to Herr K. and to have a kiss from him, suggesting that she also wished to be kissed by himself. In this context, Freud later made the general comment that transference fantasies cannot be proven—something that seems to reflect his skepticism and difficulties in this area.

Freud then adds that the dream had actually been reported when he and Dora had been working on the topic of masturbation. He next reports that Dora knew of her father's syphilitic diagnosis by virtue of the fact that she had heard her father talking about it after he had seen Freud. She had connected this illness with her father's loose behavior and we can see again how Freud was, for Dora, undoubtedly identified with her father and with his style of life. Freud did attempt then tentatively to suggest to Dora that perhaps he himself reminded her of Herr K., but he did not consider the possibility that his behavior, in being similar to that of Herr K., was a factor. There is a general tendency in the psychoanalytic literature on so-called transference phenomena to ignore this latter aspect (Langs 1974, 1976b).

The second dream, one far more complex than the first, begins with Dora being in a strange town and then going into a house where she finds a letter from her mother that refers to Dora's having left without her parents' knowledge. She learns that her father is dead and asks about a hundred times, "Where is the station?" receiving the answer, "Five minutes." She sees a woods and then asks a man who replies, "Two and a half hours more." She refuses his company and then sees the station that she is seeking in front of her, but cannot reach it. She feels anxious and then is at home where a maid opens the door and replies that her mother and the others are already at the cemetery.

As indicated by Dora's associations and Freud's analysis, this dream had many allusions to the scene at the lake as well as to Dora's plans to terminate her analysis. Freud delineated three unconscious fantasies in the latent content of this dream: revenge on her father, defloration by force, and waiting until a goal is reached. Associations led to pregnancy fantasies and to sexual curiosity.

In the third session in which this dream was being explored, Dora announced her intention to terminate at the end of the hour. Her associations indicated that, in doing so, she was identifying with a governess toward whom Herr K. had made advances and who had succumbed, only to be rejected later by him. Despite her anger, the girl had waited around, hoping that Herr K. would pursue her, although he never did. Still ignoring the "transference" implications of this dream and associations, Freud used it to finally convince Dora that she had been deeply hurt by Herr K., who had used similar language in approaching both Dora and the governess. Freud added that it was this hurt that had prompted her to flee from Herr K.—all the while secretly hoping that he would pursue her and convince her that his intentions were sincere. In a sense, by accepting Dora's decision to terminate and by not analyzing the meanings of this decision, Freud enabled Dora to reenact the incident with Herr K.—with one important modification: she was now the aggressor and Freud was the victim. This type of shared acting out of conscious and unconscious fantasies is another common form of misalliance.

In his discussion of the analysis, Freud indicated his awareness that Dora was attempting to have him ask her to continue and to thereby provide her the substitute gratification she longed for. In stating this, he was alluding to another kind of misalliance that Dora sought to live out with Freud, one in which she would spurn him and he would ask her to remain. This would have entailed the bilateral enactment of another unconscious fantasy related to the experience with Herr K., and, while Freud did not gratify this misalliance, he also did not interpret it. In all, Dora lived out her revenge on both her father and Herr K., as well as undoubtedly some direct hostility toward Freud, in terminating in the manner she did.

Freud emphasized that his failure to master the transference was an important factor in Dora's abrupt termination, although he did not ascribe to it the prime importance that he gave to his failure to explore Dora's homosexual fantasies. He did state, however, that "owing to the readiness with which Dora put one part of the pathogenic material at my disposal during the treatment, I neglected the precaution of looking out for the first sign of transference" (p. 118). He then goes on to say that Dora "kept anxiously trying to make sure whether I was being quite straightforward with her, for her father 'always preferred secrecy and roundabout ways'" (p. 118). We see here Freud's own awareness that his special interest in Dora's sexual material had contributed to his neglect of the transference; his comments also seem to reflect his unconscious realization that Dora had strongly identified him with her father, although he does not trace this to the role that her father played in introducing Dora to him. We see that, to the very end, this "deviation" in technique contributed to Dora's transference and nontransference fantasies, and to the premature interruption of her analysis; Freud's overriding interest in having her confirm his theories of infantile sexuality is also reaffirmed here as a source of misalliance and flight.

In concluding his presentation, Freud describes Dora's return visit some fifteen months after her termination. As Erikson (1962) emphasized, Freud stated that he immediately knew that she was not in earnest, thereby reflecting some difficulty that remained within him regarding his relationship with her. In that last interview, Dora described how five months after termination, at the time of the death of one of Herr and Frau K.'s children, she had confronted everyone and was vindicated. Her visit to Freud, however, related to a facial neuralgia that she had developed after she had apparently read of Freud's promotion to professor. Without considering why she returned to see him at the time she did, Freud "forgave" Dora for not letting him cure her more fully and the interview ended.

Erikson (1962) suggested that Dora's vengeance seemed to Freud to be acting out, and that this assessment may have been a factor in his feeling that she was not interested in pursuing further analysis with him. Further, to extend Erikson's discussion of the importance of establishing a sense of fidelity so as to assist Dora in affirming her feminine identity, we can see that Freud's involvement with Herr K. and her father impaired both his image as a person with whom his patient might identify in a more healthy manner and as the analyst who might help her achieve a sense of identity based on a strong sense of fidelity. As Erikson noted, Dora's first dream assigned to her father the role of a hoped-for protector, a role that she has no doubt transferred to Freud, but then had difficulty in maintaining.

DISCUSSION

To summarize, the case of Dora suggests that Freud's "deviation" from present technique, through which he accepted a patient under the circumstances of having previously treated her father and having known the man who had attempted to seduce her, along with his continued contact with this patient's father during and after the analysis, violated the one-to-one quality of the analytic relationship. In doing so, it threatened the sense of confidentiality necessary for a proper analytic atmosphere and confounded Dora's image of Freud. This deviation in technique runs like a clear thread throughout the analysis and is directly related to the premature termination enforced by Dora, who fled Freud in a manner very similar to her flight from Herr K. The material strongly suggests that she was never able to sufficiently differentiate Freud from her father and Herr K., and was never clear as to Freud's motives for seeing her and as to the underlying basis for his interest in her sexual fantasies.

This special interest, which modified Freud's neutrality, prompted a second sector of misalliance between him and Dora, and placed undue emphasis on the patient's sexual associations and on the efforts to search out the genetic dimensions of her infantile sexual life. This was perceived by Dora as strongly seductive and quickly linked to her father and Herr K., and was further reinforced by the fact that Freud had made the diagnosis of her father's syphilitic infection. Dora was also unable to overcome the suspicion that Freud was directly involved in a misalliance with her father and carrying out the latter's wish to deter her from disrupting his relationship with Frau K. or that Freud was to serve as a new potential substitute lover.

From the material available to us, it is unclear how effective interpretations of Dora's conscious and unconscious perceptions of Freud's tendencies toward misalliance would have been, since their realistic core could only be partially modified through the necessary first step of rectification (Langs 1973z, 1974, 1975b, 1976a). Clearly, when such interpretations were not offered, Dora terminated her analysis, possibly because of her uncertainty regarding Freud's intentions and because of her own temptations to submit to the potentially erotic misalliance.

For her part, Dora intended another kind of misalliance with Freud, one through which she could prove the veracity of her contentions. While a good deal of her initial communications to Freud unfolded along these lines, when he indicated his belief in her and his hopes that she would not use her symptoms as a weapon against her father, Dora seems to have shifted her focus to her own sexual anxieties and fantasies, and to her response to the erotic stirrings evoked in part by Freud. When these were not interpreted to her and her fears of losing control sexually apparently mounted, she terminated her analysis to protect herself—another latent meaning of her first dream.

In all, then, major unanalyzed "deviations" in technique in the case of Dora proved central to the premature termination of this analysis. They contributed to an exhibitionistic-voyeuristic and erotized sector of misalliance which went uninterpreted and was resolved only through Dora's premature termination. It may well be that when Dora realized that she could not gratify her intended manipulative misalliance with Freud she terminated in order to do the job herself— something she accomplished several months later.

The determination of reality and fantasy in Dora's relationship with Freud is very complex (Langs 1973a, 1976b). Because of Freud's acquaintance with Dora's father and Herr K., her erotic fantasies toward Freud had a significant kernel of truth to them, although they were not founded on directly seductive behavior by Freud. On the other hand, the latter's intense interest in Dora's sexual material readily lent itself to the development of conscious and unconscious fantasies of sexual interest in his patient.

As I have shown elsewhere (1973a,b, 1974, 1975a, 1976a), patients are exquisitely sensitive to the slightest deviation in technique and to any undue interest in a particular area on the part of the analyst. Such responses are based on conscious and, more usually, unconscious perceptions of this interest which are largely veridical—though never totally undistorted—and extensions of these realities into intrapsychically determined fantasies on the part of the patient are the rule. It is also not uncommon (it seems to have been the case with Dora) for certain patients to retreat, regress, and to become momentarily less communicative—except in regard to the deviation itself—when faced with modifications in the framework of the analytic situation (Langs 1975c, 1976a in press a, b, Viderman 1974), especially when these are unrecognized and unanalyzed with the patient. Thus, Dora's second dream and the associations to it seem far more confused then in the case of the first dream, though both manifestly and latently reflect a variety of conscious and unconscious fantasies (related to the analytic experience) with which she was struggling.

I would speculate that both Freud and Dora engaged in unconscious efforts to modify the sectors of misalliance—respective, unconscious attempts at cure (Langs 1975b, 1976a). Freud's use of the matchbook may have unconsciously conveyed his recognition that the analytic interaction was a major source of anxiety and disturbance for Dora, even though his manifest use of this measure was primarily for reconstruction. Dora's first dream may be viewed as an unconscious effort to alert Freud to the misalliance and to her unconscious perceptions of her analyst's apparent difficulties with her—an effort to awaken Freud to these problems. Along with her associations, this dream also became the vehicle through which she attempted to communicate to Freud her unresolved "transference" fantasies and possibly her unconscious perceptions of his unresolved countertransference difficulties as well. Freud's capacity to benefit from these unconscious efforts by Dora found their ultimate fulfillment in his recognition of the role of transference fantasies and resistances in her—and in all—analysands, though he failed to make this discovery before she left. The universal unconscious capacity of patients to teach and "cure" their analysts (Langs 1976 a, b) thereby found a most exquisite expression.

We see, then, that misalliance and alliance tend to intermix and that patients—as well as analysts—have the unconscious need to both maintain and resolve them. Early efforts toward misalliance are inevitable in patients; their analysis and modification by the analyst, who does not participate in them or who is capable of their rectification and interpretation should they occur, offers a significant therapeutic experience for both patient and analyst.

Finally, I wish to note that the study of Viderman (1974), which I discovered after completing this paper, offered, in part, a similar though more general approach to some of the issues discussed here. Viderman suggests that Freud failed to establish a clearly defined "analytic space" for Dora's analysis and that he did not create "classical conditions" for her treatment. He argues that the analysis ended prematurely because Freud's and Dora's words did not resonate, or accrue meaning, in this poorly demarcated clinical situation and that an unresolvable resistance was established. Thus he views Dora's premature termination as largely a consequence of Freud's failure to establish clear-cut ground rules and boundaries for her analysis. My own observations support this aspect of Viderman's position.

SUMMARY

Using as a template the ground rules and boundaries of the patient-analyst relationship, as they are generally established in contemporary adult—and in some quarters, adolescent—psychoanalytic practice, the case of Dora has been studied as to deviations from current standards as set by Freud at that time. Three such deviations were identified and their consequences investigated in an effort to demonstrate that such modifications of the analytic framework contributed to sectors of therapeutic misalliance between Dora and Freud. The intrapsychic repercussions of the misalliances for Dora were investigated, and an effort was made to describe both her participation in them, as well as her—and Freud's—unconscious efforts to modify them. The consequences of Freud's failure to consciously recognize these sectors of misalliance and to modify them in actuality, as well as to analyze their implications for Dora, were considered, as was their influence on Dora's premature termination of her analysis.

REFERENCES

Arlow, J. (1975). Discussion of Mark Kanzer's "The therapeutic and working alliances." *International Journal of Psychoanalytic Psychotherapy* 4:69–73.

Arlow, J., and Brenner, C. (1966). Discussion of Elizabeth R. Zetzel's "The analytic situation." In *Psychoanalysis in the Americas,* ed. R. Litman, pp. 133–138. New York: International Universities Press.

Erikson, E. (1962). Reality and actuality. *Journal of the American Psychoanalytic Association* 10:451–474.

Freud, S. (1900). The interpretation of dreams. *Standard Edition.*

——— (1905a). A fragment of an analysis of a case of hysteria. *Standard Edition* 7:1–122.

——— (1905b). Three essays on the theory of sexuality. *Standard Edition* 7:125–243.

——— (1912). Recommendations to physicians practicing psychoanalysis. *Standard Edition* 12:109–120.

Greenson, R. (1965). The working alliance and the transference neurosis. *Psychoanalytic Quarterly* 34:155–181.

—— (1967). *The Technique and Practice of Psychoanalysis,* Vol. 1. New York: International Universities Press.

—— (1971). The "real" relationship between the patient and the psychoanalyst. In *The Unconscious Today,* ed. M. Kanzer, pp. 213–232. New York: International Universities Press.

—— (1972). Beyond transference and interpretation. *International Journal of Psycho-Analysis* 53: 213–218.

——, and Wexler, M. (1969). The non-transference relationship in the psycho-analytic situation. *International Journal of Psycho-Analysis* 50:27–40.

Heimann, P. (1970). Discussion of "The non-transference relationship in the psychoanalytic situation." *International Journal of Psycho-Analysis* 51:145–147.

Kanzer, M. (1952). The transference neurosis of the Rat Man. *Psychoanalytic Quarterly* 2:181–189.

—— (1966). The motor sphere of the transference. *Psychoanalytic Quarterly* 35:522–539.

—— (1975). The therapeutic and working alliances. *International Journal of Psychoanalytic Psychotherapy* 4:48–73.

Langs, R. (1973a). The patient's view of the therapist: reality or fantasy? *International Journal of Psychoanalytic Psychotherapy* 2:411–431. [Chapter 3, this volume]

—— (1973b). *The Technique of Psychoanalytic Psychotherapy,* Vol. I. New York: Jason Aronson.

—— (1974). *The Technique of Psychoanalytic Psychotherapy,* Vol. II. New York: Jason Aronson.

—— (1975a). The patient's unconscious perception of the therapist's errors. In *Tactics and Techniques in Psychoanalytic Therapy, Vol. II: Countertransference,* ed. P. Giovacchini. New York: Jason Aronson. [Chapter 5, this volume]

—— (1975b). Therapeutic misalliances. *International Journal of Psychoanalytic Psychotherapy* 4:77–105. [Chapter 6, this volume]

—— (1975c). The therapeutic relationship and deviations in technique. *International Journal of Psychoanalytic Psychotherapy* 4:106–141. [Chapter 7, this volume]

—— (1976a). *The Bipersonal Field.* New York: Jason Aronson.

—— (1976b). *The Therapeutic Interaction.* 2 vols. New York: Jason Aronson.

————— (in press a). The Misalliance dimension in Freud's case histories. II. The Rat Man. In *Freud and His Patients*, ed. M. Kanzer and J. Glenn, New York: Jason Aronson.]Chapter 9, this volume[

————— (in press b). The misalliance dimension in Freud's case histories. III. The Wolf Man. In *Freud and His Patients*, ed. M. Kanzer and J. Glenn, New York: Jason Aronson. [Chapter 10, this volume]

Stone, L. (1961). *The Psychoanalytic Situation*. New York: International Universities Press.

————— (1967). The psychoanalytic situation and transference: postscript to an earlier communication. *Journal of the American Psychoanalytic Association* 15:3–58.

Viderman, S. (1974). Interpretation in the analytic space. *International Review of Psycho-Analysis* 1:467–480.

Winnicott, D.W. (1965). *The Maturational Processes and the Facilitating Environment*. New York: International Universities Press.

Zetzel, E. (1956). Current concepts of transference. *International Journal of Psycho-Analysis* 37:369–376.

————— (1958). Therapeutic alliance in the psychoanalysis of hysteria. In E. Zetzel, *The Capacity for Emotional Growth*, pp. 182–196. New York: International Universities Press, 1970.

————— (1966). /Additional "notes upon a case of obsessional neurosis." *International Journal of Psycho-Analysis* 47:123–129.

————— (1966–1969). The analytic situation and the analytic process. *The Capacity for Emotional Growth*, pp. 197–215. New York: International Universities Press.

c

Chapter Nine

Misalliance and Framework in the Case of the Rat Man

(1974)

The present paper is an effort to continue the investigation of sectors of misalliance between Freud and his patients, and their relationship to deviations in technique as measured by the template of current psychoanalytic standards. The Rat Man case (Freud 1909) is unique among Freud's writings in two respects that are pertinent to this study: a summary of each of the first seven sessions of the analysis is available in the published presentation of the case, and further, through some unusual circumstance, Freud preserved the notes for the first three months of the analysis; these were subsequently published in Volume X (pp. 253–318) of the Standard Edition. This material therefore presents us a rare opportunity to view aspects of Freud's technique as he practiced it in 1907. In fact, this material is so rich that it will be necessary to be highly selective and focus almost exclusively on what is relevant to the main theses of this paper. The present study can be supplemented by the papers of Zetzel (1966), Kestenberg (1966), Grunberger (1966), and (especially) the careful investigation of the relationship between the Rat Man and Freud presented by Kanzer (1952), a study which foreshadowed many of the findings and formulations presented here.

In Freud's interaction with the Rat Man there are two types of deviation from current classical technique. The first concerns the nature of the interventions that Freud made and, in general, reflects deviations in Freud's neutrality, level of activity, and degree of anonymity. The second includes specific deviations in technique, such as feeding the Rat Man and lending him a book. Here, I will more briefly review the first group of "deviations" or variations in technique, since they have been rather thoroughly considered by Kanzer (1952), and will focus more extensively on the relatively unexplored second group.

Sectors of misalliance may be initiated by the patient or analyst; most often they derive from a circular interaction between the two. If we first examine the Rat Man's initial communications to Freud, we can identify their potential for misalliance; we will then be able to investigate Freud's responses to these efforts and to follow the subsequent interaction.

THE PUBLISHED PAPER

While the Rat Man's conscious wish was to be relieved of his obsessional symptoms through treatment by Freud, he very quickly revealed in his initial communications an unconscious wish for misalliance which had several meanings. His first words upon beginning his analysis alluded to a friend who gave him consistent moral support by reassurances that he was not a criminal and that his conduct was irreproachable. In the Rat Man's earlier years, a student had reassured him but had subsequently betrayed him, using his relationship with the Rat Man to get close to the latter's sister.

In this way, the Rat Man revealed an unconscious motive for treatment related to his wish to obtain direct reassurance from Freud in a manner that would bypass the analysis of the unconscious fantasies on which his obsessional—and other—symptoms were based. In addition to this aim, the material reflects the potential for a homosexual transference with active and passive, and, as later borne out, masculine and feminine, sadistic and masochistic features. Any effort by the Rat Man to gratify these transference fantasies and wishes in his relationship with Freud could form the basis for a Sector of misalliance—unconscious shared efforts to achieve symptom relief through means other than insight. In addition, in the third session of the analysis, when Freud was attempting to directly reassure the Rat Man, the latter revealed a conscious wish to obtain a certificate from Freud to the effect that he should be permitted to live out the requirements of his obsessions in order to maintain his state of health. Further, by anticipating Freud's betrayal, the Rat Man showed not only his mistrust of his analyst, but also his intense masochistic wishes to be harmed or wronged.

In all, then, these various deviant motives for treatment, and the search for transference gratifications that they entailed, created strong potentials for sectors of misalliance with Freud. Transference expressions are both maladaptive efforts at self-cure (Freud, as quoted in Ferenczi 1909), and the communications that make insight feasible through the interpretations of the analyst. Much will therefore depend on the analyst's responses to the patient's attempts to directly gratify his transference wishes; any conscious or unconscious compliancy by the analyst will establish a sector of misalliance. In this context, we may now examine the manner in which Freud responded to his patient and trace out their subsequent interaction for data related to modifications in the frame of the analysis (as measured by present standards), sectors of misalliance, and the patient's unconscious perceptions of, and primarily nontransference reactions to, Freud.

At first Freud listened. The Rat Man's associations went to his early sexual history, manifestly because he had read some of Freud's writings. The first image was one of the Rat Man as a child creeping under his governess's skirt, a memory that may reflect his unconscious view of the analysis. Similarly, his reference to telling his mother of his erections and his feeling in childhood that his parents knew his thoughts presumably contain fantasies about his analytic relationship. The hour culminates in a thought that through his voyeurism something might happen—for example, that the Rat Man's father might die.

In the second session, the Rat Man began to tell the well-known story of the rat punishment and the cruel captain. He became agitated and asked Freud to spare him, walking around the office. Freud stated that he could not grant such a wish and, as the Rat Man had difficulty in describing the punishment, joined in with guesses such as impalement and a reference to the rat's boring into the anus of its victim. As Kanzer (1952) noted, Freud had very quickly joined the Rat

Man in acting out on some level the very torture and interaction that was so disturbing to the patient. In our terms, Freud had joined in a sadomasochistic, homosexual misalliance with the Rat Man, one that would afford the latter gratification on many levels and evoke further reality-based—primarily nontransference—responses to Freud based on these actualities. This was most striking when the Rat Man called Freud "Captain," which Freud did not analyze but rather responded to with reassurance. Other versions of this sadomasochistic and mutually defensive sector of misalliance appeared in later sessions, especially in Freud's intellectual explanations and the Rat Man's challenging and questioning responses (Kanzer 1952).

The fifth session contained a great deal of this intellectual interplay and ended with Freud's expression of a good opinion of the Rat Man. The consequences of this seductive "deviation" in technique (as defined by present standards) are striking: in the next hour, the Rat Man spoke again of his fear that his parents could guess his thoughts and alluded to his love of women—undoubtedly as a defense against the homosexual anxieties and fantasies stirred up by Freud's remarks. An allusion to his father's death followed, with the comment that the sister of a friend whom he knew as a child would then be kind to him. This association, which seems to express defensive hostility toward Freud, may also reflect the Rat Man's unconscious perception of Freud's focus on his death wishes against his father (Langs 1975a), an aspect of the material that may well have received undue attention in Freud's interventions.

Freud responded by suggesting a suicidal fantasy to the Rat Man, who was not convinced by it, and who insisted upon his love for his current lady friend. When Freud became theoretical, the Rat Man became agitated and defended his love for his father. After considerable arguing, Freud escaped the current situation by a reconstruction related to the Rat Man's childhood hostilities toward his father. This was characteristic of Freud's technique at the time, in that he consistently avoided the day residues and current precipitants of his patient's transference reactions; nor did he note any realistic perceptions and reality-based reactions to himself (Kris 1951, Kanzer 1952). It was in this setting that, in the following session, Freud made the comment to the Rat Man that, since his disturbing impulses were from his childhood, the Rat Man was not responsible for them. The Rat Man was extremely dubious of this unconsciously sought reassurance—and sector of misalliance—and Freud attempted to prove it to him.

It is here, however, that the initial report of the analysis ends, although there are isolated allusions to the analytic work in the subsequent discussions presented by Freud. In particular, the Rat Man is described at one point as walking around the room after Freud had pressured him about his hostility toward his father. At this time, the Rat Man said that he should be turned out and expressed a fear of being beaten by Freud. In addition to the transference elements, these communications reflect accurate conscious and unconscious percep- tions of the aggressive elements in Freud's technique. It was this material that led directly to the rat ideas and to the overdetermined series of derivatives related to the unconscious meanings that rats had for the Rat Man. While his associations clearly reflected both transference meanings and unconscious perceptions of Freud (the nontransference element) that contributed to the revelations and underlying implications of the rat fantasies, their analysis was made almost entirely in symbolic and genetic terms. Thus, it appears likely that these constellations of distorted and perceptive responses to Freud, including their contribution to sectors of misalliance, contributed to the expression of the Rat Man's nuclear pathogenic unconscious fantasies.

Thus, the reported case material indicated that Freud participated with the Rat Man in several sectors of misalliance that bypassed the quest for insight and inner change. These centered around a homosexual misalliance in which sadomasochistic fantasies were acted out on some level, and also included unconscious attempts by the Rat Man to obtain sanctions and reassurances regarding his disturbed ideas and behavior, and Freud's offering of such.

The case report raises an important additional issue. The data suggests that at the junctures of "technical deviations" by Freud, such as the moment when he expressed a positive opinion of his patient, there was a striking outpouring of material rich in unconscious fantasy content. However, a proper understanding of this content could be made only if the adaptive context—Freud's remark—was thoroughly appreciated (Langs 1973b). Both Kanzer (1952) and Zetzel (1966) have made particular note of the productivity of the Rat Man in regard to derivatives of unconscious fantasies, emphasizing that this indicates a viable therapeutic alliance and a strong therapeutic atmosphere. While this may be the case, as I have shown elsewhere (Langs 1974, 1975c, 1976), deviations in technique and the development of misalliances are among the most certain sources of productive material from patients. Stimulated by the extensive unconscious meanings of such alterations in the otherwise secure and safe boundaries of the patient-analyst relationship, unconscious fantasy activity and communication are utilized as a prime means of adapting to such traumas. Thus, in assessing such material, the precipitant and context must be recognized in order to properly evaluate its sources and meanings. In this way, deviations and momentary sectors of misalliance can lead to productive analytic work—though only if they are identified and the analyst's actual contributions to them are rectified as they are being worked through with the patient (for a different but related viewpoint, see Viderman 1974).

In tracing the effects of Freud's "deviations" and his possible countertransference-based interventions, and the sectors of misalliance to which they contributed, it has been necessary to bypass the indications of significant sectors of a viable therapeutic alliance between Freud and the Rat Man. In addition to the signs of sincere, mutual respect, there is a quality to the meaningful and analyzable unfolding of the Rat Man's associations that indicates its secure presence. In addition, the frequency with which the Rat Man appears to have genuinely confirmed many of Freud's interventions points in this direction. Admixtures of sectors of alliance and misalliance in varying proportions are characteristic of all analytic work. Insightful cure will intermix with misalliance cure (Langs 1975b), and the basis for symptom modification must therefore be investigated in terms of its antecedents and underlying basis. As might be expected, the insight cure generally proves far more stable and adaptively useful for the patient than does the misalliance cure. The data offered by Freud do not, however, offer a basis sufficient to specify the contributions from each of these spheres to the Rat Man's improvement. There is evidence in both directions; however, Freud's more constructive work with this patient should not be overlooked in the course of our study of his "deviations" and the sectors of misalliance that they helped to create. Freud's original case records will afford us an opportunity to obtain some specific additional data pertinent to these issues, so let us turn to them directly.

THE ORIGINAL CASE RECORD

This record starts with the eighth session, since the previous hours had been presented in the published report. The notes begin with a reference to a bad day (apparently, a bad session) in which resistances predominated after Freud asked to see a photograph of the Rat Man's Lady. The patient thought of leaving analysis as an alternative to the surrender of his secrets. His next communication refers to a prayer by which he protected himself and others from harm, and he then recalled an experience in a mental hospital where he wanted a room next to a young lady with whom he was having an affair. He had wished that the professor who held this room would be gone; subsequently, the professor had a stroke and died. The request for the photograph would be a deviation in current standard analytic technique—our template— and the consequences are clear: resistance, thoughts of leaving analysis, fear of surrender, magical protection against the seducer, and death wishes.

As the notes proceed, there are frequent descriptions of struggles between the Rat Man and Freud. The patient would not reveal his lady's name and Freud actively persuaded him to do so. A little later on, Freud made some apparently gratuitous comments including a speculation that the Rat Man's lady had been seduced by her stepfather. This led to a period of intensified masturbation by the Rat Man and requests by him to be dismissed from the analysis. When Freud responded by attempting to explain transference, a forty-minute struggle ensued during which the patient was angered by Freud's forcefulness. There followed a series of blatant sexual fantasies which involved Freud and his family—undoubtedly in part as a response to Freud's aggressiveness and seductiveness. Some analytic work then proved feasible with this material, momentarily turning the sector of misalliance based on modifications in Freud's neutrality into positive therapeutic endeavors; but, when Freud eventually reassured the Rat Man regarding his frightful fantasies, the patient specifically described his mistrust of Freud. The material during this period also indicated that the Rat Man and some of his family knew members of Freud's family.

THE POSTCARD

It was in December of the analysis that Freud described several specific "deviations" in technique. The session of December 8, for example, began with an allusion to a rendezvous between the Rat Man and a dressmaker which ended in premature ejaculation. The Rat Man became depressed and this was reflected in "transferences in the treatment." There were references to each of the Rat Man's parents as related to their son's coarseness, and a pursuit of the "transference" led to material about a relative who would set the Rat Man up in business if he would marry one of his daughters. Freud apparently interpreted these associations in terms of the genetics of the Rat Man's illness, missing the likely tie to a later-reported "deviation" that had already occurred: a postcard that Freud had recently sent to the Rat Man. The latter responded with great irritation with Freud, expressed by direct insults. He accused Freud of picking his nose, refused to shake hands with him, thought that a filthy swine like Freud needed to be taught manners, and added that the postcard that Freud had sent to him, which had been signed "cordially," was too intimate.

Ignoring the implications of this "deviation" in technique, Freud continued to relate this material to the genetics of the Rat Man's choice of a love object. The Rat Man responded with a fantasy that "Frau Prof. F. should lick his arse" and by picturing Freud's daughter with two patches of dung in place of eyes. Freud's symbolic translation of the Rat Man's love of his daughter for her money was a continuation of his disregard for the current precipitants in his relationship with the Rat Man for the latter's dreams and fantasies. It was in this context that the Rat Man referred to standing up against his mother's complaints about the money he had spent.

From there, the material goes to the theme of the rats, and Freud noted that the Rat Man avoided relating this theme to his mother. One meaning evoked at this time had to do with laughing at his father, whose lack of education greatly embarrassed the Rat Man. His father was spendthrift while his mother was able to economize. The Rat Man referred to the way in which he secretly supported a friend, and Freud saw this as an identification with his father, who had behaved in the same way with their first lodger. While his father seemed to be a kindly man, the Rat Man was ashamed of his simple and soldierlike nature.

We may pause here and offer an alternate formulation of this material (see also Zetzel 1966). The entire sequence seems to have been evoked by Freud's cordial postcard, which apparently had a strong homosexual meaning for the Rat Man and evoked considerable anxiety, erotic fantasies, and anger. The postcard fostered fantasies that Freud wished to be more personally involved with the Rat Man and to have him as member of his family. As an apparent defense against this seductiveness, the Rat Man became quite enraged with Freud and attacked him for his attempts to become too intimate. The mixture of defensive fury and wishes for gratification are reflected in the fantasy that Frau Prof. F.—obviously a representation of Freud's wife ultimately connected to Freud himself—should lick his "arse." The dream or fantasy of Freud's daughter with the patches of dung in place of eyes is to be viewed here as—among its many meanings—a reflection of the Rat Man's unconscious perception of Freud's blindness to the interaction between the two of them. As I have shown elsewhere (Langs 1974, 1975a, 1975c), it is particularly in situations where the analyst has made a technical error or has deviated from the usual and appropriate boundaries of the therapeutic relationship, and has in addition failed to recognize and acknowledge his deviation, that the patient unconsciously perceives the error as well as the analyst's failure to recognize it. In this context, allusions to blindness and failures to perceive are extremely common—a finding that is remarkably borne out in this material. These communications may also be viewed as efforts by the Rat Man to alert Freud to his blind spot and to "cure" Freud of the difficulties he was having in understanding his patient. Characteristically, attempts to maintain misalliances are accompanied by efforts to modify them; this is generally true of both patient and analyst (see Langs 1975b, 1976).

It may be noted once again that I am putting aside other contributions to the sequence I have just analyzed. For example, the Rat Man's anger at Freud also probably related to the hours that he had missed because of Freud's vacation and to the envy of the women whom he seems to have fantasied to have been with Freud. This may well have been another determinant of the material related to the Rat Man's mother, and other contributions to this sequence could also be developed. Central to the ideas I am attempting to develop from this clinical material, however, is the striking similarity between the sequence of the Rat Man's associations and behaviors following the receipt of the postcard and reactions of patients currently in psychoanalysis to comparable alterations in the framework of the analytic relationship (Langs 1975c, 1976). It is also rather typical that a patient responding to such behavior on the part of his analyst avoids direct references to the deviation, embeds it indirectly in his associations, and accepts the inappropriate gratifications and misalliance generated by it. Only later will he unconsciously attempt to modify the misalliance through further tangential references to the deviations and its consequences, with communications designed to indicate the disruptive effects of the misalliance. Finally, it should be remembered that the Rat Man's specific intrapsychic responses to this deviation were clearly determined by his own inner conflicts and unconscious fantasies; each patient responds to his analyst's efforts to create sectors of misalliance in keeping with his own needs and character structure.

The next communications touch upon the Rat Man's mother's inappropriate attitude toward money and the patient's ability to stand up against her. References to poor mothering are also extremely common when the analyst has deviated, and we must therefore suspect that the Rat Man's ability to stand up to his mother evolved in part as a reaction to Freud's unconscious and inadvertent seductiveness, and the Rat Man's defenses against it. The references to the Rat Man's father's lack of education and lack of understanding may be viewed as another indication of the patient's unconscious perception of Freud's failure to understand the current interaction, and his efforts to help Freud modify this problem.

In all, then, it is remarkable to find that the notes written by Freud permit an understanding of the Rat Man's response to an extension of today's usual boundaries between patient and analyst in terms entirely in keeping with formulations derived from more current studies of such modifications in the framework of the analysis (Langs 1973b, 1974, 1975c, 1976). Once again we see that such occurrences are extremely productive of associations replete with derivatives of unconscious fantasies (and perceptions) but they can be properly understood and analyzed only with a clear appreciation for the correct adaptive context and precipitants for the material (Langs 1973a). It also seems clear that there are inherently sound safeguards in the specific tenets which constitute today's ground rules and boundaries— the frame—of the psychoanalytic relationship and situation. The sensitivity of the Rat Man to alterations in this frame, which to some extent was not that of Freud at the time, appears to support such a thesis.

THE FEEDING

It was at the end of this month that Freud began a session with the note that the Rat Man "was hungry and was fed." Let us first detail the sequence that preceded this experience and the reactions that followed, after which we will be able to formulate the repercussions of this particular "deviation"—a direct, noninterpretive gratification of the patient.

In general, in the preceding sessions the Rat Man was concerned with his anger at his father in a way that suggested "transference" reactions. It is notable that the Rat Man had been upset by the illness of Dr. Pr., the physician who had taken care of both his father and himself (in the session following the hour of December twenty-eighth Freud alluded to an interruption in the analysis because of the death of Dr. Pr.; there is some confusion regarding the date of this session). In this earlier hour, there were fantasies of Pr.'s death and of both killing him and keeping him alive—an allusion to the Rat Man's fantasies of omnipotence. Dr. Pr. was then connected to the death of the Rat Man's sister, Katherine, since he was the physician in attendance at the time; this brought the Rat Man to what undoubtedly was one of the major traumas in his early childhood and a focal point of his neurotic illness—a factor that Freud had some difficulty in exploring and crystallizing (Zetzel 1966). The Rat Man's guilt over his sister's death was linked to the death of a dressmaker who had committed suicide when the Rat Man had spurned her. This then led to an account of the beginning of the Rat Man's obsessional thinking, in which his father's death and his relationship with the lady played a prominent role. There were allusions to suicidal fantasies and intense self-reproaches, particularly because of thoughts that his lady was a whore. The theme of religion emerged (while unclear, it appears that the Rat Man's parents were Jewish, and that his mother had been adopted by a Jewish family) and the struggle with the temptation to marry a Jewish woman was mentioned. His oath to not masturbate in his teens and the incidents in which he would open the door for his dead father while exposing himself in a mirror were reported at this time. This latter material was disconnected and unintelligible to Freud, who attempted to explain it in terms of the Rat Man's defiance of his father by masturbating. This was only partially confirmed and the associations in this sequence ended with a reference to an earlier incident, in which the Rat Man had spied upon a naked girl and felt guilty.

It was thus that the hour of December twenty-eighth began with the feeding. The Rat Man then continued his story of his stay at Unterach, where the voyeurism had occurred and where he had, he now added, suddenly decided to make himself slimmer through long bouts of running which included stepping to the edge of a steep precipice and having the fantasy of jumping over. Next came mention of his service in the army and a fantasy of how he could measure his love by examining his response to the question: if his father collapsed, would he fall out of rank to help him? His father's death was mentioned, as was a lieutenant who was a bully and who struck his men with the flat of his sword. The issue of standing up to such a man and the fear of being horsewhipped came next, and the patient described fantasies of challenging him to a duel. Then came a reference to his father's superior, an officer who had been extremely nasty until the time the patient's father armed the Jews of a particular town with spades to clear the snow for the army train; this officer had then praised the patient's father, who was, however, critical of such praise.

The next associations alluded to the Rat Man's compulsion to talk at Unterach and to his obsessions of counting and protecting, including magical efforts to protect his lady from illness and to understand every syllable spoken to him. The counting anxiety in thunderstorms pointed to a fear of death, and the running in the sun had a suicidal quality to it—factors which Freud pointed out and which were confirmed by the Rat Man. There followed further memories of suicides in his family, including one that occurred over an unhappy love affair. The Rat Man himself had sworn that because of his mother he would never kill himself, even if disappointed in love. At this point, Freud noted that the suicidal fantasies must have been self-punishment for his having during his rage, wished his lady friend—his cousin—dead. Freud then gave him Zola's *Joie de Vivre* to read, apparently because the hero of this novel was perpetually occupied with thoughts of his own and other peoples' deaths. It was in this context that the Rat Man described his obsessional experience with the stone that might have overturned his lady's carriage—an incident in which he had moved the stone and then returned it to the position where it might do damage.

It was, as I noted, in the following hour that the reference to the interruption owing to the illness and death of Dr. Pr. occurred. This led to rat wishes and hostile thoughts, and to the fantasy of Dr. Pr. sexually assaulting his sister Julie. Freud considered this to represent the Rat Man's envy over medical examinations and did not relate it to either the feeding or the loan of the book. The Rat Man's father had hit Julie when she was ten and said that she had an arse like a rock. Freud apparently interpreted the Rat Man's rage against his father, but noted that there was no confirmation of this intervention. Instead, a "transference" fantasy was reported: "Between two women—my wife and my mother—a herring was stretched, extending from the anus of one to that of the other. A girl cut it in two, upon which the two pieces fell away (as though peeled off)." The only associations to this fantasy were that the Rat Man disliked herring intensely and that when he had been fed by Freud recently, he had left the herring untouched. The girl was one whom the Rat Man had seen on the stairs and had taken (apparently correctly) to be Freud's twelve-year-old daughter.

The following hour began with a reference to an invitation from his sister to go to a play with her. This invitation angered him and he wished upon her the rat torture. In the face of the Rat Man's rumination, Freud was very active and attempted to link the rat fantasy to the patient's earlier episode with anal worms. In doing so, Freud attempted to connect the story of the herring to enemas given at that time, once again devoting himself to genesis at the expense of the current interaction. Much of this went unconfirmed and the reader could profitably turn directly to this material to see the many new associations that reflect the Rat Man's unconscious fantasies and perceptions in interaction with Freud. I will confine myself to some very striking allusions. There was a reference to a cousin who had shown the Rat Man a large worm in his stool, to which he reacted with disgust. While Freud was attempting to interpret fantasies of the Rat Man to the effect that his masturbation had caused his sister's death, the patient continued to allude to exhibitionistic material, such as actually showing his mother an erection, and to voyeuristic recollections of nude girls.

At this point, homosexual memories of mutual exhibitionism and voyeurism were reported. Reference to a recent episode of diarrhea was connected with the herring episode (the material in the remainder of the sessions recorded by Freud repeatedly returns to the incident of his having fed the patient and its repercussions). This theme was further developed through an image of the Rat Man being caught with his pants down and a reference to the girl, viewed indirectly as a prostitute, who had cut the herring in half. This led to allusions to pubic hair, and Freud offered some apparently extraneous comments about the way in which women at that time gave no care to their genital hair—a possible countertransference reaction. Freud's house was seen as one that was run by two women, and the Rat Man reported a fantasy that two women had prepared the meal that Freud had fed him.

In the next hour, there were allusions to prostitutes and Jewishness; homosexual play with a brother was reported, as was a series of sexual fantasies which Freud linked to the Rat Man's mother. In the experiences with his brother, the latter's penis had come into contact with the Rat Man's anus. Then, in the following hour, the Rat Man reported a fantasy of kicking Freud's child, which was again related by him to the herring. Next came the fantasy of impregnating his own sister and the thought that Freud had made a profit from the meal he had served the Rat man, since the latter had lost time and the therapy would last longer. The Rat Man also felt that he should pay an additional fee for the meal. Embedded in this material was a fantasy that linked the fee for the meal to a bridegroom's offer that a waiter have the first copulation with his wife and be paid for it. Here, the Rat Man said that whenever Freud praised any of his ideas he was very pleased, but that a second voice went on to say, "I shit on it."

In the next hour, the Rat Man reported a dream that he went to the dentist to have a bad tooth pulled. One was extracted, but it was not the right one. Further, in a subsequent session, there were references to a young girl cousin who had been inappropriately touched under her bedclothes by a doctor.

The Rat Man's responses demonstrate and confirm a wide range of previously reported observations and formulations based on contemporary clinical material (Langs 1973a, 1974, 1975a, b, c, 1976)). Once again I will stress the consequences of the deviations and their contributions to the unfolding of this material, and I will not attempt to establish the manner in which this source of the patient's conscious and unconscious fantasies and perceptions of Freud interdigitated with other stimuli for this sequence. I would stress at the outset, however, that it is characteristic for patients to be directly and, more frequently, indirectly preoccupied with the impact of a major deviation in the framework for long periods of time, especially when it has gone unnoticed and unanalyzed.

To select the main points relevant to the hypotheses under exploration in this paper, the material suggests that the Rat Man's moment of hunger occurred at a time when he was dealing with some very traumatic memories and some very disturbing feelings toward Freud. Some of this may have been evoked by the apparently seductive postcard sent by Freud to the Rat Man, the effects of which had remained unanalyzed. Since Freud's focus at this point in his technique was on the genetic roots of symptoms and so-called transference fantasies, he almost entirely overlooked the current precipitants of the Rat Man's reactions toward him and had no extensive clinical experience in distinguishing his patients' primarily intrapsychically determined fantasies about him (transferences) from their conscious and unconscious realistic, veridical perceptions (nontransferences) (Langs 1973a, 1976).

The feeding provided obvious transference gratification and was the basis for a sector of misalliance which disturbed the Rat Man to some extent, although he participated in and accepted gratification from it. This generous and seemingly supportive measure, which transgressed the usual current boundaries of the patient-analyst relationship, was responded to in a wide variety of ways; there are a number of indications that it evoked intense anxiety in the Rat Man and considerable concern regarding what might further happen between himself and Freud. Thus, he had quickly responded to the feeding by alluding to suicidal fantasies developed in the context of the need to slim himself. The anxiously accepted incorporative gratification had to be rejected on some level, even at the cost of his life.

Among the many other frightening fantasies that this feeding had evoked in the Rat Man—all with clear meanings relevant to the analytic relationship—were death wishes toward his father, the mention of the lieutenant who was a bully and the fantasies of challenging him to a duel, the use of the Jews as menial help, the rejection of the the favorable comments made by his father's superior officer to him, and the ultimate linking of the suicidal fantasies to an unhappy love affair and to the need for punishment. The feeding, as this material indicates, was seen in part as a dangerous homosexual seduction and attack, to which the Rat Man reacted with great mistrust and rage.

Rather than interpreting this material, Freud responded by giving the Rat Man a second gift—that of the book. Now the Rat Man's unconscious perception of Freud's behavior became clearer and was more vividly expressed in the derivatives in the sessions. A relatively undisguised fantasy, in which the doctor who had recently died was assaulting the Rat Man's sister sexually, shows the mixture of unconscious perception with genetic—transference and fantasied—contributions that deviations of this kind usually evoke in patients (Langs 1975a, 1976). The rich imagery involved in the herring fantasy and in the Rat Man's dislike for herring reflects, among other things, the patient's dreaded wish to be seduced.

There is also considerable additional material related to the rejection of seductive invitations and continued efforts by the Rat Man to communicate his fantasies and anxieties regarding Freud's feeding of him. There is a reference to the greatest fright of his life, when he thought his mother's stuffed bird was alive. In his fantasies, the Rat Man felt that Freud was behaving like a prostitute—or using his patient as one—and was attempting to seduce him. This prompted him to defend himself against his own passive feminine wishes, which had evoked and were being further stirred up by Freud's behavior. A good deal of this material culminates in the conscious fantasy that Freud had profited inappropriately from the feeding, which was equated by the Rat Man with an offer from a bridegroom to have another person copulate with his wife. These are by no means entirely transference-based fantasies, but are clearly related to the realistic seductive overtones of the situation; they are a mixture of reality and fantasy. It is of interest that the Rat Man alluded at this time to another "deviation" from neutrality in Freud's technique, namely, Freud's praise of him. Again, he indicated his need in part to reject this praise.

As is so typical of patients involved in an unanalyzed interaction of this type, the material culminates in a dream, in which a dentist pulls a wrong tooth. The dream expresses very succinctly the Rat Man's unconscious perception of Freud's technical errors (Langs 1975a, 1976), and his continued efforts to aid Freud in resolving them.

DISCUSSION

To offer a general conclusion, this material supports the thesis that deviations in technique and extensions of the patient-analyst relationship beyond the usual boundaries—alterations in the frame—

evoke extremely significant and intense responses on a fantasied and behavioral level in all patients. The analysis of the patient's responses generally takes precedence over all other analytic work except for emergencies (Langs 1975c). In a viable analytic atmosphere with a generally good therapeutic alliance such as that created by Freud with the Rat Man, these analytic experiences can be extremely moving and meaningful. Failure to deal with this area when it is pertinent will generally leave the analytic situation in apparent chaos, and promote regressive and acting out responses in the patient. It is striking to see the number of times that the Rat Man failed to confirm Freud's interventions because they did not deal with the deviations in technique. While the Rat Man's associations were extremely productive and there are many recognizable derivatives of unconscious fantasies once the main context for this material is understood, there is little indication in these pages of a general confirmatory responsiveness on the patient's part.

Because of Freud's failure to analyze the Rat Man's responses to his extensions of the boundaries of their relationship, the Rat Man continued to express derivatives of unconscious fantasies related to these "deviations" in the month of subsequent sessions detailed by Freud. There remained within him the overriding need to adapt to these experiences and to resolve the intrapsychic anxieties and conflicts they were evoking in him.

In all, there were several sectors of misalliance created by Freud's extraanalytic behavior. Both Freud and the Rat Man shared major defenses against an awareness of the conscious and unconscious meanings of what had transpired between them, and there were some shared efforts to accomplish symptom alleviation through sanction and the gratification of the Rat Man's neurotic behavior and needs. The notes also portray the homosexual and sadomasochistic qualities in the misalliance sector which directly gratified many of the Rat Man's pathogenic unconscious fantasies, and also evoked considerable anxiety. The many allusions to exhibitionistic and voyeuristic fantasies also characterized an element of the misalliance in which Freud and the Rat Man alternately played the role of voyeur and exhibitor, as well as seducer and seduced. It was largely Freud, however, who played the active, penetrating, seductive, overgratifying role that the Rat Man invited, accepted, and then defended himself against.

Freud's "deviations" in technique and the sectors of misalliance that they generated—and the Rat Man's and Freud's efforts to perpetuate as well as modify these misalliances—contributed to the ongoing flow of the patient's associations. The presentation by Freud provides evidence that, in addition to these determinants, his valid interventions and a variety of life experiences of the Rat Man also contributed significantly to this material. All of the adaptive stimuli were processed by the Rat Man in keeping with his own intrapsychic needs, conflicts, and fantasies. A full comprehension of this material and its transference and nontransference components is feasible, however, only if the precipitants and actualities that have been identified here are recognized and understood. In this way, the derivatives of the Rat Man's unconscious fantasies find meaning both in terms of his current adaptive reactions and their genetic basis. Further, on this basis reality and fantasy, perception and misperception, can be sorted out in a way that fosters the patient's grasp of inner and outer realities and generates insight into his own intrapsychic disturbances.[1]

SUMMARY

The consequences of an extensive variety of modifications in present standard psychoanalytic technique in Freud's work with the Rat Man have been explored, especially in regard to contributions to sectors of misalliance between patient and analyst. Most of these modifications in the basic framework evoked intense adaptive responses in the Rat Man, with both transference and nontransference, fantasied and perceptive, components. The findings support the thesis that patients are extremely sensitive to modifications in the framework, and that the analysis of these reactions, and the rectification of unneeded deviations, where feasible, are prime analytic tasks.

NOTE

1. Beigler's thinking (1975) is in keeping with my observations and conclusions regarding the Rat Man. His article was published after this paper was written.

REFERENCES

Beigler, J. (1975). A commentary on Freud's treatment of the Rat Man. *Annual of Psychoanalysis* 3:271-285.

Ferenczi, Sandor (1909). Introjection and transference. In *Further Contributions to Psychoanalysis,* pp. 55-93. New York: Bruner, 1950.

Freud, S. (1909). Notes on a case of obsessional neurosis. *Standard Edition* 10:153-320.

Grunberger, B. (1966). Some reflections on the Rat Man. *International Journal of Psycho-Analysis* 47:160-168.

Kanzer, M. (1952). The transference neurosis of the Rat Man. *Psychoanalytic Quarterly* 21:181-189.

Kestenberg, J. (1966). Rhythm and organization in obsessive-compulsive development. *International Journal of Psycho-Analysis* 47:151-159.

Kris, E. (1951). Ego psychology and interpretation in psychoanalytic therapy. *Psychoanalytic Quarterly* 20:15-30.

Langs, R. (1973a). The patient's view of the therapist: reality or fantasy? *International Journal of Psychoanalytic Psychotherapy* 2:411-431. [Chapter 4, this volume]

———— (1973b). *The Technique of Psychoanalytic Psychotherapy,* Vol. I. New York: Jason Aronson.

———— (1974). *The Technique of Psychoanalytic Psychotherapy,* Vol. II. New York: Jason Aronson.

———— (1975a). The patient's unconscious perception of the therapist's errors. In *Tactics and Techniques in Psychoanalytic Therapy,* Vol. II, ed. P. Giovacchini. New York: Jason Aronson. [Chapter 5, this volume]

———— (1975b). Therapeutic misalliances. *International Journal of Psychoanalytic Psychotherapy* 4:77-105. [Chapter 6, this volume]

————(1975c). The therapeutic relationship and deviations in technique. *International Journal of Psychoanalytic Psychotherapy* 4:106-141. [Chapter 7, this volume]

————(1976) *The Bipersonal Field.* New York: Jason Aronson.

Viderman, S. (1974), Interpretation in the analytical space. *International Review of Psycho-Analysis* 1:467-480.

Zetzel, E. (1966). 1965: Additional "notes upon a case of obsessional neurosis." *International Journal of Psycho-Analysis* 47:123-129.

Chapter Ten

Misalliance and Framework in the Case of the Wolf Man

(1974)

FREUD'S CASE REPORT

In writing of the Wolf Man, Freud's primary purpose was to demonstrate the importance of the infantile neurotic factors in subsequent emotional illnesses—the Wolf Man had reported a dream from the age of four which proved to be the key to his symptoms as a child and an adult. This was an important matter for Freud, since his theory of infantile sexuality was being challenged by Adler and Jung. However, in addition to this primary purpose, Freud utilized the material to develop a series of brilliant observations of great diversity, including the first references to the concept of the primal scene, discussions of the important issue as to whether traumatic memories were essentially realities or fantasies, remarks on the development of the ego, a clarification of the libidinal developmental phases, and further observations on obsessional neurotic formations.

For our purposes, the reported case is of interest because of Freud's use of several deviations in technique, one of which would probably be defined today as a parameter—though it could not be analyzed after its actualization—evoked in response to ego pathology in the Wolf Man (Eissler 1953, Freud 1937). Both deviations arose when the Wolf Man had persisted over most of the initial three years of his analysis in remaining deeply entrenched in resistances. At a point where Freud felt that the Wolf Man's attachment to him was quite strong, he set a fixed termination date—the parameter—and also promised to relieve the Wolf Man of his constipation of many years. As Freud describes it, the Wolf Man responded with a plethora of material which permitted the analysis of his infantile neurosis as well as his adult difficulties, and this enabled him to terminate the analysis on a successful note.

While Freud had virtually nothing to say about the Wolf Man's relationship with him, we may extract some pertinent data from his case report. In doing so, the reader finds himself in the midst of a great wealth of material that seems pertinent to the Wolf Man's relationship with Freud, material that has an immediate "feel" for transference and nontransference implications. This impression was also developed by Offenkrantz and Tobin (1973), who suggested that there were problems in Freud's therapeutic alliance with the Wolf Man because Freud had a dual interest in his patient, that of research as well as that of helping him alleviate his symptoms. They felt the Wolf Man's likely knowledge of Freud's research interest in him had created a narcissistic transference which enabled the patient to continue to function, and that this narcissistic misalliance—as I would term it—was later replaced by a similar alliance with the analyst Ruth Mack Brunswick. These authors also noted the lack of "transference" discussions in Freud's case report and suggested that the wolf dream had, as one of its current day residues, the Wolf Man's awareness that Freud was presenting aspects of his case to the small group of followers with whom he met in Vienna.

Freud's discussion of the Wolf Man centers around his childhood dream and its relationship to primal scene experiences and fantasies. Central here was the Wolf Man's feminine identification and wish to copulate with his father, and the castration anxiety that this entailed. Freud noted that the Wolf Man drew a scene from this dream and that he—Freud—kept this drawing—the first allusion to a "deviation" in technique. In this context, the Wolf Man's first recorded association to the dream related to a follower of Pasteur who had inadvertently killed many sheep on the Wolf Man's grazing lands when he was a child, doing so through innoculations which, instead of being preventive, proved fatal. The Wolf Man's dread and mistrust of Freud is strongly hinted at in this association, and Freud described his awareness that a father transference predominated throughout this analysis, though the suspicious and hostile elements were not developed (Kanzer 1972).

However, in light of what was to follow, one can wonder about the reality precipitants for the Wolf Man's mistrust. Related to this aspect of the "transference"—more correctly, the patient's total relationship with Freud—are the Wolf Man's openly expressed fears that Freud would eat him up, and the patient's need to look at Freud during the first weeks of the analysis, during which he was in a sanatorium. References to coitus *a tergo*—the means of intercourse in the reconstructed primal scene—also lent itself strongly as a representation of the relationship with Freud, who noted that the wolf dream which contained this element was reported in many variations throughout the analysis. This suggests that many current day residues in the relationship between Freud and the Wolf Man prompted the repetitive communication of this particular dream (Langs 1971). In addition to the unconsciously perceptive aspects of these dreams, there were undoubtedly transference elements, including contributions from the Wolf Man's feminine identification and his identification with Christ—he was born on Christmas—particularly in the sense that Christ was permitted by his father to die. Further, in his identification with his mother, the Wolf Man imagined himself with bowel problems and bleeding, and had many blatant castration anxieties.

At termination, the Wolf Man reported that he had been born with a caul, a fact which allowed him the illusion of being a special child of fortune. The associations reported by Freud indicated that the primal scene material now expressed the Wolf Man's fantasied conditions for recovery, namely, that if he submitted as a woman to his father and gave him a child, he would be cured.

From this material, it is possible to suggest that Freud's modified parameter of setting an irrevocable termination date prompted, in part, a sector of misalliance with the Wolf Man, in which Freud became the God (father) who promised cure and who brought matters to an end (death), and in which the Wolf Man became the victim, Christ. In addition, as had occurred with the Rat Man (Kanzer 1952), it would appear that the promise of cure and the insistence of a forced termination did, in reality, gratify a whole range of passive feminine fantasies related to the primal scene dream and experience, and its intrapsychic consequences. Thus, we may speculate that the Wolf Man obtained in part a countertransference or misalliance cure (Barchilon 1958, Langs 1975a), or that he responded with alleviation of his symptoms because of a narcissistically gratifying or defiant misalliance with Freud (Offenkrantz and Tobin 1973). In addition, insight and inner change may well have played a role; here I am attempting to delineate additional facets of the Wolf Man's initial apparent recovery. In this context, the Wolf Man may be seen as having submitted in a feminine manner to Freud and as having produced a child for him—the wolf dream and its analysis—and thereby a cure in part through a misalliance and mutual inappropriate gratification (Kanzer 1972).

The case as reported by Freud does not seem to permit speculation beyond this point. If we now turn to the Wolf Man's memoirs and recollections of Freud, we may offer some additional formulations. In doing so, however, we must proceed with caution; Brunswick (1928) felt that the Wolf Man had distorted Freud's stance on several important matters—a problem to which I will return later.

THE WOLF MAN'S MEMOIRS AND RECOLLECTIONS

In his memoirs, the Wolf Man described his first experience in Russia with a therapist who was a hypnotist. This physician saw him and treated him in a very special manner, but proved uninterested in him personally and more concerned about having the Wolf Man, who was a teenager at the time, influence his family to give this psychiatrist-neurologist a large contribution of money. As Brunswick (1928) has pointed out, the Wolf Man attempted to provoke poor care from many of the physicians who treated him, but at the same time he was, in reality, often treated badly. These experiences served to generate and reinforce his intrapsychic mistrust and the unconscious fantasies on which it was based. In the context of this statement, I want to emphasize again that in attempting here to trace out some of the reality factors in the Wolf Man's psychopathology I will of necessity not attempt to counterbalance my discussion with the complementary understanding of the Wolf Man's intrapsychic pathology, which was independent of, and which then interacted with, these reality stimuli. As we now know, both the reality stimuli and the intrapsychic set and response must be known in order to fully account for any particular symptom or fantasy; historically, it is the former dimension of the Wolf Man's problems that have been relatively neglected and, because of this, it will be my main focus.

It was a Dr. D. from Russia who brought the Wolf Man to Freud; the Wolf Man was so impressed that he immediately decided that he wanted to be analyzed. According to the Wolf Man, he remained in analysis only because Freud agreed to permit him to marry Theresa, the woman he loved, although Freud said that this decision had to be analyzed before it could be consummated. The Wolf Man stated further that the analysis was at a standstill until Freud agreed to this marriage, and that he had to delay the marriage because he wanted to finish his analysis with Freud and felt that the latter would not agree to this if he acted prematurely; for him, the actual end of his analysis was tied to Freud's agreeing to the marriage. The Wolf Man indicates that Freud saw Theresa with him before the analysis ended and that he had a positive picture of her. These "deviations" which, as Kanzer (1972) described it, the Wolf Man "forced upon" Freud (it is not uncommon for patients to attempt to evoke deviations from their analysts) added to the dominant-submissive, mutual gift-giving sector of misalliance that I have already formulated as obtaining between Freud and this patient.

In addition, the Wolf Man returned to Freud some five years after he had completed his analysis. At that time, he claimed he felt fine, but Freud told him more analysis was needed. We learn from Brunswick (1928) and Jones (1955) that the Wolf Man's constipation, which Freud, true to his promise, had cured, had returned; Freud apparently felt that this was due to some unresolved transference fantasies. The additional period of analysis lasted several months and, because the Wolf Man was now relatively destitute, Freud agreed (offered?) to treat him without a fee.

In the Wolf Man's recollections of Freud are some relevant comments. His apparently valid (Kanzer 1972) image of Freud is that the latter did a considerable amount of educating and explaining. In addition, the Wolf Man was privy to a number of personal comments from Freud, such as a remark related to Freud's son's fracturing a leg and allusions to other patients by name. The Wolf Man pointed out that Freud had commented that friendliness between the patient and analyst may overstep certain boundaries and thereby interfere with analysis, but this patient's description of their relationship suggests that Freud permitted himself great latitude in extraanalytic contacts and comments with his patients. The Wolf Man felt much like a co-worker with Freud, and based this feeling on Freud's discussions with him of politics, art, and the opponents of analysis; on Freud's direct advice against his becoming a painter; and, as we learn later from Brunswick's report (1928), especially on his advice that the Wolf Man not return to Russia in 1919. Because he felt there was danger of the patient's being stuck in the "transference" with too close a tie to his analyst, Freud requested that each of his patients upon termination give him a gift in order to decrease his feelings of gratitude. Interestingly, the Wolf Man gave Freud a female Egyptian figure which he reports having seen in pictures of Freud's office taken many years later.

The multitude of deviations and extensions of the boundaries of the patient-analyst relationship described by the Wolf Man undoubtedly promoted a seductive atmosphere, a submissive and passive-feminine stance in the Wolf Man, and an unconscious image of Freud as seductive, masculine, and powerful—with reactive instinctual stirrings. With these kernels of reality (Niederland 1959), the Wolf Man's related unconscious responses cannot be considered entirely in terms of transference—i.e., displaced fantasies and projections from the Wolf Man's past; they contained important valid unconscious perceptions and were also in part meaningful adaptive responses to the actual situation with Freud. This myriad of misalliances and transference gratifications went unrecognized, uncorrected, and unanalyzed by Freud; their repercussions and influence on the Wolf Man's psychopathology and fantasy life went unmodified. The consequences of this became clearer in the analysis with Brunswick (1928) to which I now turn.

RUTH MACK BRUNSWICK'S REPORT

The Wolf Man was sent by Freud to Brunswick because of the patient's delusion that he was the victim of a nasal injury caused by electrolysis therapy performed by a Professor X. It was apparent to Brunswick (1928) from the outset that the source of the problem was an "unresolved transference" to Freud, and it is this that we will study.

As background, Brunswick (1928) reported that after his brief period of analysis in 1919, which was undertaken without a fee, as was her own analytic work with the Wolf Man, Freud collected money for the Wolf Man each spring for six years. The Wolf Man had accepted this in a dishonest manner by concealing the possession of jewels he thought of considerable worth, although they later turned out to be less valuable than expected.

In 1923, after Freud's first minor mouth surgery, the Wolf Man saw Freud and was shocked by his appearance, responding with a period of increased masturbation. A later operation was more serious, which the Wolf Man knew and was disturbed by.

In writing his own case history for Brunswick after her analytic work with him had been for the moment completed (he returned to her sporadically afterwards), the Wolf Man described a series of visits to dentists who differed in their opinions regarding his oral problems and the treatment required; one had pulled the wrong tooth. During his analysis, Freud had referred the Wolf Man to Professor X. for obstructed sebaceous glands, and in the period before his analysis with Brunswick, the Wolf Man went to several dermatologists who offered him divergent opinions as to the nature of his problem and suggested different forms of treatment. It was a diathermy treatment by Professor X., however, that left the Wolf Man scarred and delusionally preoccupied with his nose. Another treatment by Professor X. had led to the flow of blood and the feeling of ecstasy. Brunswick described the connections between the Wolf Man's concern with his nose and identifications with both his mother, who had a wart on her nose, and his dead sister, who was concerned with her pimples. There were other genetic connections which I will not trace out. Of interest to us is a dermatologist the Wolf Man consulted whose office was near Freud's. Thinking the Wolf Man a man of means, he charged him his usual fee, and the Wolf Man was elated that he was able to pay him like a gentleman rather than being treated gratis.

During the three years that these delusional symptoms were alternately exacerbating and remitting, one remission occurred after Freud had written to the Wolf Man asking him some additional questions regarding the wolf dream. In addition, this request prompted the Wolf Man to recall several new childhood memories, including an operation performed on stallions and the manner in which a sixth toe was removed from a child after birth. Soon after receiving this letter, the Wolf Man went to a dermatologist who criticized the work of Professor X. and who told him the damage would be permanent. This led to an intense depression; the obsessional-delusional thought that now preoccupied the Wolf Man was a question as to how Professor X., who was one of the most well-known dermatologists in Vienna, could be guilty of such irreparable injury to him. He wondered if this were an accident, negligence, or unconscious intention, and he hated X. as his mortal enemy. From the first, both Brunswick and the Wolf Man knew that this question, and the fantasies—and, I would add, unconscious perceptions—embedded in it, referred indirectly to Freud.

In describing the course of this five-month analysis, Brunswick initially reported that the Wolf Man's deception of Freud, and his refusal to discuss with her either his nose, the dermatologist, or Freud, proved to be early "impregnable" resistances. His first dream, which was not described in detail although many others were, was a version of the wolf dream in which there were grey wolves; they were associated with the grey police dog owned by Freud. That the Wolf Man's delusions related to Freud was unmistakable. The second dream is described more specifically. In it, the Wolf Man is at the prow of a ship carrying a bag containing his wife's jewelry and a mirror. He leans against the rail and breaks the mirror, and realizes that he will have seven years of bad luck. It had been seven years since he had been analyzed by Freud and it was suggested that the broken mirror related to his feelings that his face was damaged. The possible allusions to the Wolf Man's objections to the narcissistic misalliance between himself and Freud, and to the analysis as a mirror, were not considered.

The heart of the analysis centered around Brunswick's exploration of what she considered to be the Wolf Man's grandiosity regarding his personal intimacy with Freud and his deep suspiciousness of Freud's advice that he not return to Russia, which the Wolf Man felt had led to the loss of his fortune. When Brunswick told the Wolf Man that it was impossible for Freud to have made such explicit statements, there was little response. It appears likely, however, that Freud had indeed made comments along these lines, though how explicit they were is an open question. Gardiner (1971), Kanzer (1972), and Offenkrantz and Tobin (1973) have all suggested that there were realistic aspects to the Wolf Man's perceptions of his relationship with Freud; one cannot validly discuss his feelings entirely as transference distortions or delusions.

Getting nowhere in her attempts to devalue the Wolf Man's belief in his special relationship with Freud, Brunswick boldly informed the Wolf Man of the death of Professor X., and this led to the revelation of blatant fantasies of revenge on him, with denial regarding their connection to Freud. Brunswick then proceeded to systematically destroy the Wolf Man's belief in his favored position with Freud, using information obtained from Freud and from her own direct observations of Freud and the Wolf Man. Ignoring the many grains of truth on which the Wolf Man founded his impressions, including his idea that Freud and Brunswick had discussed him (this was true, although apparently not to the extent that he believed), Brunswick repeatedly denied his contentions. She soon provoked dreams in which she appeared indirectly in a masculine and powerful role, and in a devalued manner. The Wolf Man made threats to kill both Brunswick and Freud. Then, for reasons unclear to Brunswick, except for the fact that she felt that she had destroyed his Christ fantasy, positive dreams began to appear and the Wolf Man's delusion was eventually resolved. In this context, a dream of a doctor forcing things onto the Wolf Man appeared, and eventually he felt that he could forgo the gifts from Freud because they were not worth the passivity involved. In his final dream of the analysis, the patient is walking with the second dermatologist who treated him; the physician is speaking of venereal disease. The Wolf Man mentions the doctor who had overtreated his gonorrhea, and the dermatologist says, it was not he but another. To the very end, despite his symptomatic resolution, the Wolf Man was mistrustful and critical of physicians. While Brunswick notes that Professor X. played right into the Wolf Man's fantasies—reinforced them in reality—and that the gifts from Freud represented sexual satisfaction from the Wolf Man's father, the influence of these realitites on the Wolf Man were not traced out.

In considering the sectors of misalliance that developed between Freud and the Wolf Man, the cumulative material from many sources suggests that each of the "deviations" in technique, however benignly motivated, fostered and enhanced a series of pathogenic unconscious fantasies and identifications that interfered with a lasting inner resolution of the Wolf Man's psychopathology. These noninterpretive measures may well be the unconscious but realistic basis for the Wolf Man's belief that Freud had treated him wrongly and had left him crippled—castrated—for life. These kernels of reality were undoubtedly subsequently distorted and elaborated by the Wolf Man on the basis of his inner pathology and fantasies, but their full analytic resolution would have required a recognition of their veridical aspects. By pressuring the Wolf Man into a passive feminine position which intensified his castration anxieties and undoubtedly his fears of annihilation (note the dream of the broken mirror), Freud aggravated the Wolf Man's anxieties and conflicts in this area and thereby inadvertently contributed to the delusional symptomatology.

While that symptomatology has been previously clearly related to Freud, heretofore it has not been especially noted that there were valid elements to these beliefs, that they were the basis for a pathogenic sector of misalliance between Freud and the Wolf Man, and that they were fostered by the former's extraneous interventions. The clearest prior statement along these lines was made by Flarsheim (1972), who briefly suggested that the Wolf Man's paranoid residual transference reactions to Freud stemmed in part from the latter's forced termination of the analysis. Flarsheim relates this consequence to the generally adverse reactions in patients to any forcible technical device used to control them. More generally, Greenacre (1959) has noted that deviations in technique tend to undermine the patient's autonomies and thereby foster narcissistic and other pathological misalliances. The material from the Wolf Man clearly supports her thesis. In addiction this material supports the observations that I have made elsewhere regarding the relationship between deviations in technique, sectors of misalliance, and difficult to analyze regressive episodes in patients (Langs 1973a, 1975, 1976).

While fraught with problems, it seems of value to make a tentative effort to formulate the basis for the development and resolution of the Wolf Man's delusional symptoms. To do this, it will prove helpful to recall that in order to fully comprehend the intensification of a patient's pathological unconscious fantasies, anxieties, and disturbances in ego functioning, we must have an in-depth appreciation for the nature of the stimuli and trauma with which he is dealing (the adaptive context; Langs 1972, 1973b). In addition, we must have a full picture of the intrapsychic conflicts that these precipitants have stirred up within the patient and his available adaptive resources and shortcomings—in brief, his intrapsychic responses and their contribution to his behavioral and fantasied reactions. However, the intrapsychic components are not fully intelligible without a full recognition of the interactional aspects (Langs 1973a, 1976). A similar model of the importance of the adaptive aspects of unconscious fantasies (and transference) was implicit in Freud's comprehension of the relationship between day residues and dreams (Freud 1900, Langs 1971).

Certain stimuli are inherently traumatic and, among these, deviations and errors in technique are especially important for patients in analysis (Langs 1973b, 1975a, b, 1976). Such deviations generally entail pathological gratifications, the sharing of defenses, overstimulation, and inappropriate sanctions—in addition to any positive features they may have. They evoke, as we have seen in each of these case studies, a mixture of gratification and fear, and lead to acting out and other regressive responses. The deviant behavior fosters an image of— and an unconscious identification with—the analyst as a seductive, aggressive, and otherwise poor therapist, all elaborated intrapsychically within the patient according to his own personality, pathology, conflicts, and conscious and unconscious fantasies and memories. In all, in order to identify the transference and primarily intrapsychic elements in these reactions, we must first be able to delineate precisely the nontransference or reality aspects.

This situation is further aggravated by the analyst's unawareness of the countertransference aspects of his deviation when this is present, and his failure to recognize the relationship between the patient's pathological reactions and fantasies and his noninterpretive interventions. As a result, he is unable to correctly interpret the patient's unconscious fantasies and perceptions; he has missed his role in evoking them. Thus, he also cannot provide the patient the cognitive mastery verbalized insight might afford him. In all, both his basic "hold" (Winnicott 1958)—as expressed as effecting a secure frame and implicitly offering himself as a model of someone ("an object") who can properly manage the analytic situation and therefore his own inner state—and his ability to offer correct interpretations are impaired. Many regressive episodes and stalemates in analysis stem from such unrecognized sources.

We can speculate that a stalemate created in part by factors such as these may have existed between Freud and the Wolf Man. This was based initially on a variety of "deviations" and variations in technique—including direct advice, seeing the Wolf Man's fiancée, and discussing personal matters in Freud's life. The later forced termination, gifts, and the free analytic sessions may then have contributed to the fixity of the sectors of misalliance, and to the intensely negative perceptions of Freud as a malicious and destructive physician who had wronged him. They also fostered unresolved ambivalent fantasies and attitudes toward Freud that reflected the patient's own inner pathology as well. With the occurrence of Freud's illness and the threat of his loss, the Wolf Man's unmastered conflicts, anxieties, perceptions, and guilt seem to have intensified, as did his longings for fusion and his murderous hatred. The delusional symptom that developed at this time expressed many dimensions of the unresolved transference and, in addition, of the sectors of misalliance—the mutually fostered sense of merger and identification, the belief and extension into fantasies that he (the Wolf Man) had been damaged, the revenge on Freud turned against himself, the Wolf Man's actual need for further treatment, and the exhibitionistic-voyeuristic, sadomasochistic dimensions of the misalliance. Through the symptom, the actual contributions of Freud—nontransference and reality— are represented in disguised form, as well as their intrapsychic elaborations and other fantasied contributions from within the Wolf Man. Because of the Wolf Man's own propensities and due to the nature of the "deviations," this patient's symptom highlights the actual damage done to patients by unneeded modifications in the frame—an aspect evident also in my studies of Dora and the Rat Man. Elsewhere, I first termed such symptoms in patients, *iatrogenic syndromes* (Langs 1974)—here, iatrogenic paranoia—and, more recently (Langs 1976), *interactional neuroses or psychoses.* These designations are designed to stress the contributions from the analyst to the patient's symptoms, and from the point of view of technique, the need for rectification of such contributions in addition to the analysis of their repercussions for the patient.

Brunswick was an extension of Freud for the Wolf Man and undoubtedly represented another of his gifts—Freud had sent him to her and he was again seen without a fee. The transference and nontransference responses evoked by these realities were not analyzed in her work with the Wolf Man, but instead her efforts were designed to destroy the Wolf Man's pathological misalliance with Freud (represented as his Christ fantasy), and in all likelihood this was replaced with a more benign, less anxiety-provoking misalliance with herself (Offenkrantz and Tobin 1973). Freud may have intuitively aided in this resolution by not continuing to work with the Wolf Man and by sending him to a woman analyst. The final dream of his analysis with Brunswick seems to express this more benign but continued misalliance: the Wolf Man is walking with the second, less damaging doctor, and another is blamed for his poor work, while there is a mysterious allusion to a third doctor. In a sense, the Wolf Man perpetuated this misalliance and the imparied autonomy that it entailed in the many years that followed.

CONCLUDING COMMENTS

In attempting to trace out the negative, infantalizing, and regression-promoting aspects of Freud's template-measured "deviations" in technique and misalliances, I have not attempted particularly to counterbalance my presentation with comments related to the many positive dimensions of Freud's relationship and work with the Wolf Man. These "deviations" were undertaken within the framework of Freud's search for a viable psychoanalytic technique and a dedicated wish to help his patients resolve their neurotic—or more severe— difficulties; there is much evidence that Freud provided considerable healthy support and insight to each of his patients, including the Wolf Man. However, in regard to Freud's noninterpretive interventions, the material available to us from these case histories points more strongly to their negative effects than to their possible positive influence.

It is of special interest that Freud's parameter with the Wolf Man has been cited many times in the literature as a model deviation in technique (Eissler 1953), although, as Stone (1961) noted, it did not meet all the criteria for a parameter as defined by Eissler, since there was no opportunity to resolve the effects of the forced termination through subsequent analytic work. Thus, as both Gardiner (1971) and Brunswick (1928) noted, the forced termination left the Wolf Man with many unanalyzed feelings and fantasies toward Freud, many of which proved strongly pathogenic and contributed to the subsequent psychotic episode. The recognition of such adverse sequelae to a parameter brings with it a need to restudy their indications and clinical use (see Langs 1974, 1976).

It would provide an important chapter in the history of psychoanalytic technique to trace out the manner in which Freud's analytic framework was modified through the years so that many of the measures undertaken by both himself and Brunswick have been either considerably altered or entirely given up. It would appear that empirically it became clear to some analysts during the past fifty years that such certain gross deviations in the boundaries of the patient-analyst relationship interfered with the analytic outcome, with the image of the analyst, and with the achievement of insight and inner, structural change for the patient. Because of the many inherent human needs—pathological and nonpathological—that are gratified by such deviations for both patient and analyst (Langs 1975a), there is an ever-present pressure from many quarters within psychoanalysis to reestablish or maintain many of these "deviations" as acceptable procedure, without regard for the data available both from Freud's case histories and from more recent clinical observations. For this reason, this present restudy of Freud's technique may provide additional impetus for further careful in depth investigations of the consequences of such measures.

It is clear from each of the case histories that the "deviations" in Freud's technique, and the misalliances that he created with his patients, came up repeatedly in the direct and indirect associations from his patients. This is in keeping with the observations made elsewhere (Langs 1973a, 1975a, 1976) that patients are exquisitely sensitive to such maneuvers by their analysts and that, when they are undertaken, they must be recognized, take precedence in the analytic work, and be resolved in actuality—rectified—before analytic exploration in other areas is possible. In addition, we learn from these case histories that productivity of material is not a reliable criterion for working through and inner resolution. It becomes clear that in addition to identifying the latent content embedded in derivatives of unconscious fantasies, it is essential to identify the ongoing adaptive context for a communication, especially as it relates to the analytic interaction. We see too that the invocation of major deviations prompts strong fantasied and perceptive responses in patients (as they do in analysts, as well), and that if they are properly conceptualized and analyzed, they can evolve into productive analytic work.

Finally, these observations lend support to the formulation that the manner in which the analyst creates and maintains the analytic setting and relationship is continuously and unconsciously monitored by the patient. These ground rules and boundaries reflect crucial aspects of the analyst's identity and functioning, and deeply influence the patient's sense of security and trust, the important ongoing identificatory aspects of his relationship with the analyst, and the nature of the patient's intrapsychic fantasies, unconscious perceptions, and projections. In finding responses to these template-measured "deviations" in Freud's patients that strikingly parallel those seen in today's patients (Langs 1975a, b, 1976), we may tentatively suggest again that the present basic ground rules of analysis as earlier defined (above; see also Langs 1973b, 1975b) offer an optimal therapeutic hold, a maximal chance for an interaction designed for the inner benefit of the analysand, and the ideal setting within which his intrapsychic fantasies, pathology, and transference expressions may be safely expressed and analytically resolved and worked through.

I will conclude with a quote from Freud which describes the spirit in which this series of papers has been written and which alludes to the hopes for future studies that it may stimulate:

> As a rule, however, theoretical controversy is unfruitful. No sooner has one begun to depart from the material on which one ought to be relying, than one runs the risk of becoming intoxicated with one's own assertions and, in the end, of supporting opinions which any observation would have contradicted. For that reason it seems to me to be incomparably more useful to come back to dissentient interpretations by testing them upon particular cases and problems." [Freud 1918, p. 48]

REFERENCES

Barchilon, Jose (1958). On countertransference "cures." *Journal of the American Psychoanalytic Association* 6:222–236.

Brunswick, Ruth Mack (1928). A supplement to Freud's "History of an Infantile Neurosis." In *The Wolf-Man by the Wolf-Man,* ed. M. Gardiner, pp. 263–307. New York: Basic Books, 1971.

Eissler, K.R. (1953). The effect of the structure of the ego on psychoanalytic technique. *Journal of the American Psychoanalytic Association* 1:104–143.

Flarsheim, A. (1972). Treatability. In *Tactics and Techniques in Psychoanalytic Therapy,* Vol. I, ed. P. Giovacchini. New York: Jason Aronson.

Freud, S. (1900). The interpretation of dreams. *Standard Edition* 4/5.

——— (1918). From the history of an infantile neurosis. *Standard Edition* 17:3–122.

——— (1937). Analysis terminable and interminable. *Standard Edition* 23:211–253.

Gardiner, M. (1971). The Wolf-Man in later life. In *The Wolf-Man by the Wolf-Man,* ed. M. Gardiner, pp. 311–366. New York: Basic Books.

Jones, E. (1955). *The Life and Work of Sigmund Freud.* Vol. II. New York: Basic Books.

Kanzer, M. (1952). The transference neurosis of the Rat Man. *Psychoanalytic Quarterly* 2:181–189.

———(1972). Book Review of the *The Wolf-Man by the Wolf-Man,* ed. M. Gardiner. *International Journal of Psycho-Analysis* 53:419–421.

Langs, R. (1971). Day residues, recall residues, and dreams: reality and the psyche. *Journal of the American Psychoanalytic Association* 19:499–523. [Chapter 2, this volume]

——— (1972). A psychoanalytic study of material from patients in psychotherapy. *International Journal of Psychoanalytic Psychotherapy* 1: 4 [Chapter 3, this volume]

———(1973a). The patient's view of the therapist: reality or fantasy? *International Journal of Psychoanalytic Psychotherapy* 2:411–431. [Chapter 4, this volume]

———(1973b). *The Technique of Psychoanalytic Psychotherapy,* Vol. I. New York: Jason Aronson

———(1974. *The Technique of Psychoanalytic Psychotherapy,* Vol. II. New York: Jason Aronson.

———(1975a). Therapeutic misalliances. *International Journal of Psychoanalytic Psychotherapy* 4:77–105. [Chapter 6, this volume]

———(1975b). The therapeutic relationship and deviations in technique. *International Journal of Psychoanalytic Psychotherapy* 4:106–141. [Chapter 7, this volume]

———(1976). *The Bipersonal Field.* New York: Jason Aronson.

Niederland, W. (1959). The 'miracled-up' world of Schreber's childhood. *Psychoanalytic Study of the Child* 14:383–413.

Offenkrantz, W., and Tobin, A. (1973). Problems of the therapeutic alliance: Freud and the Wolf-Man. *International Journal of Psycho-Analysis* 54:75–78.

Stone, Leo (1961). *The Psychoanalytic Situation.* New York: International Universities Press.

Winnicott, D. W. (1958). *Collected Papers.* London: Tavistock Publications.

The Wolf-Man (1971). My recollections of Sigmund Freud. In *The Wolf-Man by the Wolf-Man,* ed. M. Gardiner, pp. 135–152. New York: Basic Books.

Chapter Eleven

Framework, Misalliance, and Interaction in the Analytic Situation: Three Encyclopedia Articles

(1977 [1976])

THE FRAMEWORK

Freud recognized the necessity for a clear-cut delineation of the framework of the analytic interaction, although he tended to take a rather flexible and even lax position in this regard, as relfected in his case histories (Viderman 1974). While Freud indicated that transgressions of these basic tenets could afford the patient inappropriate transference gratifications and thereby undermine both the therapueutic alliance and the basic analytic work, he did not specifically investigate this area.

Following Freud's initial comments, analysts tended to be relatively silent regarding the ground rules. From time to time, as illustrated by Ferenczi's well known experiments, a suggestion to modify one or another ground rule would appear based solely on general clinical impressions. The basic rules set forth by Freud were maintained, and a few additional tenets soon became standard practice; the development of the present basic analytic ground rule for adult patients remains, however, a part of the silent agreement of psychoanalysts.

In the classical psychoanalytic literature, discussions of the framework of the analytic relationship derive mainly from Freud's original papers and from the presentation of Eissler (1953) on parameters of technique. Eissler's paper introduced the subject of indications for modifications and deviations in technique, which proved to be the primary focus of most subsequent analytic papers in this area. A parameter of technique was defined as a modification in the ground rules that was necessitated by an ego defect within the patient; it was to be introduced only when absolutely necessary, kept to a minimum, eliminated as quickly as possible, and subsequently fully analyzed with the patient. An extensive body of literature followed in which virtually every imaginable type of modification in technique was suggested. With the exception of occasional clinical anecdotes, however, no specific attempt was made to carefully and analytically explore the consequences of these alterations in the ground rules, and critical analytic thinking was seldom applied.

A number of additional papers advocating both a wide range of flexibility in maintaining the framework and the use of deviations in technique have derived from the monograph by Stone (1961) and from investigations of the widening scope of psychoanalysis—the estensions of analysis for the treatment of borderline, psychotic, and narcissistic patients. The proposed basic tenet here is to the effect that stringent adherence to the framework of the analytic relationship overly frustrates the patient and that selective and carefully analyzed modifications are in order. While widely accepted in some quarters, criticisms of such techniques have also appeared. There is no evidence of a consensus on this subject in the literature to this date.

There is a second and basically different approach to the ground rules and framework of the analytic relationship, one that has appeared primarily in the British literature. It was initially most extensively presented by Winnicott (1965) and elaborated upon by Milner (1952) and others. These analysts wrote of the therapeutic functions of the framework, stressing that, especially with nonneurotic patients, the offer of a sound and secure framework is the vehicle of the therapeutic work for long periods of time. While their own clinical material, interestingly enough, was filled with modifications in the framework, they nonetheless emphasized the importance of what Winnicott termed the *therapeutic hold* in assisting the patient to develop the ego strength necessary for the analysis of his intrapsychic fantasies and conflicts. Further, it was Milner (1952) who first pointed out that it was the framework of the analytic relationship that set it apart from all other segments of reality and created the opportunity for the development of the transference illusion and, by implication, the transference neurosis. Thus, the framework appeared to have importance not only as a means of affording the patient a secure hold and a general means toward strengthening his ego, but also as an essential component of the analytic situation through which the development of an analyzable transference neurosis could unfold.

Bleger (1967), following up on Winnicott's work, defined the frame of the analytic relationship as a nonprocess that is made up of constants within whose bounds the work of analysis takes place. He focused on the silently maintained protective elements of the frame and the necessity of their ultimate analysis, and likened the frame to the most primitive and undifferentiated psychic organization out of which the ego is built. It was seen as containing the symbiotic elements of the patient-analyst relationship and as a basic support to the patient. Bleger also noted that the patient brings his own frame into the analytic relationship and that compliance with it by the analyst repeats the neurotic interactions of the patient's childhood; by contrast, establishment of the analyst's frame avoids such a repetition and makes available for analysis the disturbed elements in the patient's personality.

Viderman (1974) investigated the framework in terms of a concept of the analytic space. In the main, he suggested that the patient will test out the boundaries of this space during the initial phases of his analysis. When the analyst answers these attempts to disrupt the analytic process by progressively accentuating the specific attributes of the situation through an increasingly rigorous application of the technical rules, the relationship will be clearly delineated and the analytic space established. It is only then that the patient will actually enter into analysis and develop both transferences and a transference neurosis. Viderman indicated that the analytic space is defined by its physical and psychological components, and the rules that establish it. These include the fundamental rule and the analyst's evenly sustained attention; neutrality; benevolence; and the silence and passivity of the analyst, altered only by his interpretations. Viderman also noted that the establishment of an effective psychoanalytic space relied on the control of the analyst's countertransferences.

More recently, Langs (1975b, 1976a, b) offered a specific clinical exploration of the framework of the analytic relationship and an extensive discussion of its theoretical implications, especially in terms of the manner in which it establishes the bipersonal field within which a therapeutic analytic interaction may occur.

BASIC IMPLICATIONS OF THE FRAMEWORK

The framework of the analytic relationship is established by the ground rules of analysis. Each of these implicit and explicit tenets is essential to the therapeutic unfolding of a viable analytic interaction and to the resolution of the patient's psychopathology through a constructive analytic experience. The explicit ground rules and boundaries include the following: set fee, hours, and length of sessions; the fundamental rule of free association with communication occurring while the patient is on the couch; the absence of physical contact and other extratherapeutic gratifications; the therapist's relative anonymity, concern, and use of neutral interventions geared primarily toward the interpretation; and the exclusive one-to-one relationship with total confidentiality. Any modifications of these tenets, for whatever reason, will modify the structure of the bipersonal field within which the analytic process unfolds.

Among the meanings and functions of the framework of the analytic relationship, the following are of particular importance:

1. The framework is essential for establishing a therapeutic interaction for both participants. It serves to create a setting in which analyzable derivatives of unconscious fantasies, introjects, and conflicts will be communicated by the patient in a form that enables the analyst to validly interpret to the patient in a manner that fosters insight and inner structural change. Within a clear-cut framework, the uniqueness of the analytic relationship is established in a way that facilitates the development of the patient's transference and interactional "neuroses" in an analyzable form. The frame is essential for the so-called transference illusion, in that it guarantees the nongratification of pathogenic fantasies and wishes to the greatest extent feasible. Since modification in the framework alter these conditions and are associated with gratifications of the patient's neurotic needs and with

actual repetitions of infantile and childhood pathogenic interactions, a basically unmodified frame is crucial to constructive analytic work. Put another way, a clear-cut framework offers the patient a therapeutic container into which the patient's psychopathology can be placed for analytic modification. In this sense, the analyst himself is an especially crucial component of the framework and of the containing functions of the analytic field.

2. A secure framework offers the patient a basic psychoanalytic hold that provides him a sense of safety and ego strength, a basis for a secure object relationship, and a sense of trust—essential for his work with the analyst. It also creates a maximally uncontaminated backdrop onto which the patient projects his intrapsychic fantasies and introjects, projectively identifies into the analyst, and secures the analytic situation as a safe place in which he may regress and reveal his inner disturbances.

3. For the analyst, a clearly delineated framework secures a setting in which he can function most effectively. It offers him necessary protection against the gratification of countertransference needs and reduces the consequences of his inevitable countertransference expressions to their absolute minimum. It provides a safe setting in which he may maintain his evenly hovering attention, trial identifications, and empathic capacities with maximal effectiveness, since it assists him in safeguarding the restoration of his own self-boundaries and helps to modify his pathological counteridentifications. It also offers him an important aid in minimizing his pathological projective identifications into the patient and lessens his need to use the patient as a container for his own psychopathology. It establishes a setting in which his interpretations will have their consciously intended effects and not be undermined by contradictory behaviors and communications that stem from alterations in the framework. Lastly, in properly managing and maintaining the framework, the analyst implicitly offers himself as a figure for a positive introjective identification by the patient. This occurs because the analyst's capacity to handle the framework reflects the state of his own intrapsychic balances and controls and his ability to manage his own inner conflicts and tensions.

4. Any modification of a dimension of the framework significantly alters the implications of all other ground rules and the nature and function of the communications that take place within the bipersonal

field. Such an alteration lessens the distinction between the analytic situation and external reality and similarly blurs the therapeutically necessary differences between the patient's inner pathological reality and a healthy outer reality, the patient's pathological introjects and the actual constructive behaviors of the analyst, and the patient's "neurosis" and a "nonneurotic" surrounding field. Patients uncon - sciously test out and monitor the analyst's management of the framework, and respond with intense adaptive—behavioral and fantasied—responses to the most minimal shift in the frame. These alterations in the ground rules and boundaries are an extremely common basis for the development of misalliances between patient and analyst, and because of their actualities their analysis and realistic correction comprise a prime therapeutic task.

EFFORTS TO MODIFY THE FRAMEWORK

The Patient. Clinical evidence indicates that the patient is unconsciously aware of the role and functions of the framework and that he realizes that modifications in the frame can be used as an interactional means of supporting his intrapsychic defenses and resistances. Such efforts on his part are not only characteristic of the opening phase of the analysis, but also appear throughout the analytic experience, especially in response to the threat of necessary periods of therapeutic regression.

In this context, one quality of the framework that has been almost entirely overlooked in the literature comes into focus. The analytic hold has been likened to the mother's hold of her infant, without due recognition of the differences. Briefly, the mother's total hold is designed to foster the safety, comfort, and maturation of her child without regressive experiences which, although they inevitably occur, are not part of the essential goals of this hold. By contrast, the analytic hold is designed to produce both safety and regression, since both are essential for the resumption of the patient's maturation in analysis. By and large, *therapeutic regressions* will only occur within a secure framework, while relatively *nontherapeutic regressions* occur in response to unneeded disturbances in the framework. Because of this aspect, the patient will often attempt to modify the framework in order to protect himself from a therapeutic regression. Subsequently, when the analyst maintains the frame and analyzes the unconscious meanings of the patient's efforts to alter it, the patient responds with a positive identification with the analyst, cognitive insight into the conflicts and defenses related to the efforts to shift the frame, and a renewed dread of the analytic situation. This latter is based on his fear of regression and of the further unfolding of the transference and interactional "neuroses," to which the patient responds with both anxiety and with recognition in regard to its necessity.

The patient's fear of the regression and the related anxieties will prompt him to renew his efforts to modify the framework either unilaterally (e.g., through lateness or absence) or with the countertransference-based cooperation of the analyst (e.g., by effecting an unneeded change of hour or by not charging for an unneeded absence). As a rule, the patient will then experience momentary symptomatic relief and the therapeutic regression will be curtailed for the moment; he has effected what is best termed a *framework cure*. When the analyst has participated, this is a form of *misalliance cure*. It stems from the transference gratifications, the reinforcement of defenses, the opportunity for the patient to projectively identify his illness into the analyst who has behaved in an inappropriate manner, and the maladaptive reassurance that accrues to the patient when the analyst behaves in a manner that is in keeping with his pathological introjects and with prior pathogenic behaviors of early childhood figures. Many periods of temporary symptom relief occur on this basis; such episodes, however, are not in the service of adaptive structural change.

The Analyst. The analyst may initiate a modification in the framework when he is under the pressure of certain "realities" (e.g., an insurance form) or unconscious countertransference problems. Such modification may provide him a *framework cure* of his own countertransference difficulties, although it does so at the expense of involving the patient in a sector of misalliance and of perpetuating an unresolved countertransference problem. Thus, any consideration of a modification in the framework by the analyst should be subjected to extensive scrutiny, including a careful review of his own inner state and an in-depth consideration of the ongoing associations from the patient; these will provide clues to possible countertransference factors and demonstrate the adaptive context—the disturbing precipitant—for the analyst's ill-advised plan. As a rule, only true emergencies justify a modification in the frame, and even under such circumstances one must recognize the temporary and sometimes permanent alterations in the bipersonal analytic field that occur as a consequence.

TECHNICAL CONSIDERATIONS

Unneeded and even seemingly necessary deviations in technique and modifications of the framework are unconsciously perceived by both patient and analyst. Their identification by the analyst is crucial to their correction, and he may do so through a monitoring of the patient's associations. Patients will initially accept the unconscious gratifications and defenses offered by alterations in the framework, but will subsequently attempt to assist the analyst in restoring a therapeutic frame and in resolving the countertransference difficulties that have led to his participation in altering it. With considerable unconscious perceptiveness, the patient recognizes that modifications in the frame tend to promote undue surrender and loss of autonomy, reflect inappropriate and destructive "therapist-mothering," and reflect a loss of control and problems in internal management in the analyst. Communications of themes related to these perceptions are offered as a means of alerting the analyst. His technical response should be as follows:

1. Identification of the alteration in the framework and a full restitution of a totally secure frame.

2. A full exploration and analysis of the patient's reactions to the modification and to the reestablishment of the boundaries. As a rule, this will include *implicit* acknowledgement by the analyst of his contribution—if any—to the disturbed framework and a recognition of those aspects of the patient's reaction that are based on valid unconscious perceptions of the implications of the deviation. Beyond this veridical component, the analyst must fully analyze the extensions of these realities into distorted intrapsychic fantasies—transference— by the patient and efforts by the patient to misappropriate the modification in the framework in the service of his own neurotic needs.

3. When the analyst has participated in the modification in the framework, he must privately undertake a self-analysis in order to

resolve the underlying countertransference difficulty involved. He may also utilize the patient's conscious and unconscious therapeutic endeavors on his behalf, implicitly accepting them, without further burdening the patient.

4. The restoration of the framework and the analysis of the repercussions of its modification must take precedence over virtually all other therapeutic endeavors. Since the altered framework has impaired the therapeutic qualities of the bipersonal field, its restoration is essential for the resumption of effective analytic work. However, it is well to recognize that analytic endeavors of this kind yield important cognitive insights for both patient and analyst. They also afford the patient an opportunity to modify the negative incorporative identifications that have evolved from the analyst's unneeded modifications in the framework by offering an effectively managing and interpreting analyst as an implicit object for positive introjective identifications.

In concluding, it is to be stressed that these observations do not imply a rigid and inflexible maintenance of the frame, nor do they speak for a lack of humanity and concern in the analyst. They indicate the importance of a sound frame and prepare the analyst for those exceptional situations where modifications in the boundaries are temporarily necessary. Such incidents occur almost exclusively in the treatment of nonneurotic patients and characteristically occur only after the frame has been well secured and its management extensively tested out by the patient. Then, under rare circumstances, such as those seen with patients who have experienced early life-threatening traumas, the patient may regress to the point where he works through his suicidal and homicidal fantasies and impulses, and inherently demands of the analyst specific and limited modifications in the framework. These parameters appear to be sought as a means of concretely conveying to the patient the analyst's deep commitment to his survival, thereby enabling the analysand to modify his malignant and destructive introjects and to work toward a reintegration of his personality. Such emergency modifications of the framework should be minimal, should be extremely rare, and should be comprehensible in terms of the severe psychopathology and traumatization of the patient; they should, in addition, be rectified and analyzed with the patient as soon as he begins to emerge from his severely regressed state.

The influence of the actuality of the framework and its management on the functions, meanings, and adaptive implications of the patient's intrapsychic fantasies, and on his verbalizations to and interaction with the analyst, are brought into sharp focus through these investigations. The distinction and relationship between reality and fantasy in the therapeutic interaction is clarified. Who and what the therapist is and what he does become as important as what he says. The central role of the analyst's interpretations and the accrued insights and structural change derived from them by the patient are supplemented by the therapeutic influence of another important dimension of technique: the management of the analytic frame.

MISALLIANCE

One of the most frequent disturbances of the therapeutic alliance is best conceptualized as a result of a pathogenic interaction between a patient and analyst termed *therapeutic misalliance* (R. Langs 1975a). The therapeutic alliance is the conscious and unconscious agreement on the part of both patient and analyst to join forces in effecting symptom alleviation and characterological changes for the patient through insight and other constructive means that promote structural change and conflict resolution. Therapeutic misalliances are, therefore, interactions between these two participants that are designed either to undermine these goals or to achieve symptom modification, however temporary, on some other basis. There are strong needs in both patient and analyst to create and resolve sectors of therapeutic misalliance throughout the course of a psychoanalytic treatment; the recognition, analysis, and actual modification of these sectors of the analytic interaction are basic therapeutic tasks that are vital to the restoration of a viable analytic field.

While seldom specifically related to the therapeutic alliance, investigations of inappropriate transference- and countertransference-based gratifications, of certain types of resistances, and of mutual acting out between patient and analyst have implicitly touched upon the problem of sectors of therapeutic misalliance. Historically, Freud's writings indicate an awareness of the possibility of the development of a misalliance, based, for example, on the analyst's acceptance of the patient's transference love (Freud 1915). Freud indicated that any compliance by the analyst would enable the patient to accomplish his aim, while the analyst would never achieve his. Freud introduced the rule of abstinence in this context. Implicit in such thinking is the recognition that unconscious efforts to develop sectors of misalliance are, in part, maladaptive or misdirected efforts at "cure" or, more precisely, at symptom relief without insight.

Also, Glover (1931) described the therapeutic effects of inexact interpretations as a vehicle for noninsightful symptom relief. Searles (1965) has also indicated a variety of ways in which misalliances may develop from unanalyzed transference and countertransference problems. More specifically, Baranger and Baranger (1966) described *bastions* of the bipersonal field—split-off sectors developed through the shared defenses of patient and analyst. Racker (1968) documented the occurrence of neurotic *vicious circles* in which the analyst enters and shares the patient's neurosis and thereby cannot interpret it. Under these circumstances the analyst is repeating in some form an earlier pathogenic interaction between the patient and his parents, thereby confirming both the patient's pathological inner reality and the need for his neurosis.

More recently, Langs (1976) undertook an extensive investigation of therapeutic misalliances and stressed the importance of the recognition of sectors of misalliance, since they are disturbed actualities in the analytic interaction; they disrupt the process of analytic cure and must be modified before the verbal interventions of the analyst can have their intended effects. However, it was also recognized that the resolution of a therapeutic misalliance is an extremely common and important vehicle through which the analyst effects the cure of the patient.

THE MOTIVES FOR THE DEVELOPMENT
OF THERAPEUTIC MISALLIANCES

The patient. For the patient, the search for sectors of misalliance with his analyst stems from the hope for maladaptive relief from anxiety and guilt related to his intrapsychic conflicts and pathogenic introjects. Through the development of a misalliance, he is able to momentarily validate his distorted view of the world in a manner that justifies the maintenance of his psychopathology. In developing an interaction of this type with his analyst, the patient is able to gratify a variety of inappropriate instinctual needs and to reinforce a wide range of superego pathology. A misalliance usually includes shared interactional defenses that reinforce the patient's conflict-related intrapsychic defenses. The analyst's participation also generates a negative image that is introjectively incorporated by the patient, thereby momentarily strengthening his own pathological introjects. Further, a misalliance offers the patient an opportunity to project and projectively identify into the analyst many aspects of his own psychopathology and to thereby deny and nullify the effects of his own intrapsychic disturbances by placing them into the analyst, who then serves as a pathological container for the patient's illness.

In all, misalliances offer inappropriate symptom-alleviating gratifications related to every level of psychosexual development and to the pathology of each of the patient's intrapsychic structures and introjects. They provide maladaptive symbiotic ties and a false sense of omnipotence that can momentarily reassure the patient to the point of symptom relief. The inherent depreciation of the analyst who becomes involved in a misalliance also helps the patient to achieve these gains. Through a misalliance, the analyst no longer represents insight, renunciation, and the process of analytic scrutiny; the patient is therefore able to unconsciously justify his abandonment of meaningful analytic work. However, when the analyst does not participate, the patient's efforts toward misalliance provide him an avenue for the analytic resolution of many components of the analysand's psychopathology.

The search for misalliances represents inevitable needs within and pressures from the patient; they are one form in which he seeks actual gratification of his pathological unconscious fantasies. Their proper analytic resolution depends on two important, interrelated factors: the actual nonparticipation of the analyst, and his capacity to interpret the unconscious meanings of these efforts to the patient from the latter's behaviors and associations. In this way, the analyst offers the patient both cognitive insight and his implicit availability as a model for constructive introjective identifications. Efforts to create sectors of misalliance are an inevitable form of interactional resistance; it is only when they are not properly understood by the analyst or evoke his countertransference-based acceptance of the pathogenic interaction that the problem of an actual therapeutic misalliance presents itself.

The analyst. The analyst's motives for accepting or initiating a misalliance are not unlike those within the patient. They stem from his inevitable residuals of unmastered anxiety and guilt, neurotic and maladaptive defensive needs, and his unresolved searches for inappropriate gratification. One important factor is the analyst's reactions to the stringencies of his analytic role and the extraordinary renunciation it entails. In addition, any type of countertransference difficulty may be translated into this type of pathogenic interaction with the patient.

One must, however, recognize certain differences between the patient and analyst in this regard. It is inevitable that the analyst will, from time to time, participate in or create a sector of misalliance with his patient. However, in a well-run psychoanalysis, such occurrences should be relatively infrequent and the analyst should make every effort to recognize and modify them as quickly as possible, always endeavoring to analyze their consequences for the patient. Thus, while the patient's search for misalliances is an inherent part of the curative process, the analyst's endeavors in this direction generally are not. This does not imply that they cannot be turned toward therapeutic gain, since the recognition and modification of the analyst's participation in a misalliance can indeed provide a therapeutic experience for the patient. However, because of their detrimental consequences, every effort should be made to safeguard the patient from these experiences.

Despite the many temporary gains for both patient and analyst derived from a sector of misalliance, there are powerful motives within each of them to modify and resolve such interactions and to restore a proper therapeutic atmosphere. Before turning to these endeavors, let us consider the specific means through which misalliances are developed.

THE VEHICLES THROUGH WHICH MISALLIANCES ARE EFFECTED

The patient. The patient's attempts to create sectors of misalliance with the analyst develop along two lines: efforts to modify the framework of the analytic relationship and attempts to involve the analyst in pathogenic interactions. The former is an extremely common and relatively unrecognized vehicle for the development of misalliances. Clinical observation indicates that efforts to modify the framework of the analytic relationship are initiated by the patient primarily at moments of marked regressive and internal pressures. Often he is at a significant point in the analysis of his transference and interactional neuroses, and the inevitable resistances take the dual form of the development of some type of intrapsychic defense and efforts to create a misalliance with the analyst through some modification in the framework. The unwary analyst, often prompted by some degree of internal pressure of his own in response to the unfolding material from the patient, may participate in the modification in the boundaries. He thereby supports the patient's defenses and offers him momentary symptom relief that lessens his acute conflicts and enables him to repress the derivatives related to it. Such a development has been termed a *misalliance cure* or *framework cure* (Langs 1976b). It can be detected only by a careful utilization of the validating process through which the analyst explores the antecedents of the patient's symptom relief and, in addition, makes an in-depth assessment of the analysand's subsequent associations and his own subjective responses. Misalliance cures are an extremely common and still relatively unrecognized form of symptom relief based on a maladaptive interaction rather than on true insight and constructive inner change within the patient.

The second means through which the patient involves his analyst in sectors of misalliance is based on unconscious components of the analytic interaction through which the two share defenses and inappropriate gratifications. Included here are not only gross efforts by the patient to avoid certain topics or to evoke strikingly hostile or seductive reactions within the analyst that will gratify the analysand's transference needs, but far more subtle enactments as well. The manner in which the patient free-associates, avoids a particular topic, behaves in a subtly teasing or provocative way, and evokes other countertransference-based responses in the analyst, contains the potential for the creation of a sector of misalliance. Technically, it behooves the analyst to monitor the patient's associations and his own subjective reactions to his analysand in an effort to ascertain efforts of this type and to check out any unconscious participation on his part. His goal is detection, nonparticipation, and a full analysis of the unconscious meanings of the patient's endeavors. However, it is not uncommon for the analyst to initially and inadvertently join the patient in a sector of misalliance, after which his technical goal becomes its discovery and modification.

The analyst. For the analyst, too, there are two main ways in which he evokes or participates in misalliances with his patients: through modifications in the framework, and through countertransference-based interventions and interactions with the patient. The unconscious utilization of modifications and deviations in technique is perhaps one of the most widely and erroneously rationalized means through which analysts have created sectors of misalliance with their analysands. Because modifications in the framework alter the contents and functions of the bipersonal field, and the meanings of the patient's experiences within it, even the most necessary modifications in the framework—for example, in cases of emergency—will entail sectors of misalliance with the patient. Patients characteristically respond to analyst-initiated modifications of this type with conscious acceptance, while their unconscious communications reveal considerable opposition to the misalliance and striking efforts to modify both the analyst's need to deviate and the effects of the deviation itself.

In his ongoing interaction with the patient, the analyst has ample opportunity to develop both gross and subtle sectors of misalliance with his patients. They stem from a wide range of countertransference-based behaviors that have seductive, hostile, defensive, and provocative qualities. Erroneous interpretations also often serve as invitations to the patients to create sectors of misalliance, since they stem from countertransference problems within the analyst and tend to reveal aspects of his own pathological unconscious fantasies. In addition, they express the analyst's inappropriate needs to projectively identify his own inner disturbed contents into the patient. Here too the patient will tend to initially accept the offered misalliance and subsequently make efforts to assist the analyst in modifying it.

Sectors of misalliance may be viewed as pathological segments of the bipersonal field which are established and maintained by patient and analyst. The presence of a misalliance will disturb the therapeutic functioning of the bipersonal field. Because of the influence of this actuality on the two participants, the resolution of sectors of misalliance generally takes precedence over all other analytic work.

THE ANALYTIC RESOLUTION OF
THERAPEUTIC MISALLIANCES

Present clinical evidence indicates that both patient and analyst are unconsciously aware of the presence of a sector of misalliance, and that they make efforts to both maintain and modify it. The resolution of a misalliance depends on its conscious recognition, the alteration of the actualities that are contributing to it, the self-analysis of the analyst (without the participation of the patient) as the means of resolving the basis for his contribution to it, and a full analysis of the patient's reactions to the development of the misalliance and its working through. While the analyst has the ultimate responsibility for the interpretation and modification of sectors of misalliance, clinical observation clearly demonstrates that patients make unconscious efforts in this direction which can be of therapeutic benefit to both themselves and the analyst. As a result, in maintaining a continuous search for the presence of misalliances, the analyst may utilize both his own subjective impressions and the associations of the patient, so long as both are properly understood and placed in the correct adaptive context.

Turning first to the patient's therapeutic endeavors, if the analyst follows his analysand's associations in the adaptive context of the development of a misalliance, he will quickly recognize that the patient has unconsciously detected this area of disturbed interaction. Through a variety of displaced communications and actions, the patient endeavors to bring the problem to the attention of the analyst, to interpret the basis for the analyst's participation, and to assist the analyst in rectifying the disturbance (Langs 1976b, Searles 1975). Thus, at such times, the patient often talks about collusion between two people, the misuse of one person by another, corrupted relationships, and the like, and he will often extensively speculate regarding the motivations of the persons involved. Often, too, the patient will allude to his own participation in some type of inappropriate relationship and will offer comments regarding himself that are unconsciously designed as interpretations to the analyst. He will in addition offer himself as a model of an uncorrupted and incorruptible person in an effort to mobilize the healthy parts of the analyst. Much of this is a response to the patient's unconscious perceptions of, and introjective identification with, the analyst's inner disturbance that has formed a basis for the latter's participation in the misalliance. These efforts by the patient contain important nontransference as well as transference components and extend into his endeavors to also convey unconscious perceptions related to his own part in the misalliance; the analyst can constructively utilize these efforts in resolving the misalliance. Failure on the part of the analyst to become aware of the misalliance and the patient's efforts to modify it will generally lead to regressive and other disturbed responses by the patient, who unconsciously perceives the analyst's difficulties and becomes frustrated and enraged with his failure to modify them.

For the analyst, the detection of therapeutic misalliances relies on his utilization of a wide range of inner signals that enable him to detect unconscious countertransference disturbances and their expression in his interaction with the patient. These are supplemented by a consistent monitoring of the associations from his patient so that any disturbance prompts a search for sectors of misalliance. Once a shared defense, fantasy, or unconscious interaction has been detected by the analyst, his first technical responsibility is to modify his actual participation in the misalliance. As his patient's associations permit, he will then analyze the patient's motives for his participation in the misalliance, while *implicitly* accepting his responsibility for his own contributions. It is here that the analyst must be careful not to generate an additional sector of misalliance by inappropriate self-revelations to the patient. He must therefore implicitly accept responsibility for his participation in the misalliance without explicitly reviewing it with the patient. His own self-analysis is essential for the resolution of the countertransference problems that prompted his role in the misalliance; without such work, a new sector of misalliance will soon be developed between himself and the patient.

The unconscious development and conscious analytic resolution of sectors of misalliance is one characteristic of a viable analytic process. The analysis of the unconscious perceptions, fantasies, memories, and introjects that contributed to the patient's participation in a misalliance provides crucial insights into core genetic experiences, fantasies, and conflicts related to the patient's psychopathology. At the same time, the conscious and unconscious realization that the analyst has been able to recognize, modify, and analyze a misalliance provides the patient an important opportunity for positive identification with him. In addition, the insightful resolution of such experiences offers the analyst an opportunity for self-analytic work and gain; while such endeavors are not the basic province of the patient's analysis, their inevitable occurrence affords the analyst a special opportunity for inner change in his work with his patients. The working through of this type of shared interactional pathology is one of the most important means through which a truly viable therapeutic alliance is established and reinforced during the course of an analysis.

PSYCHOANALYTIC INTERACTION

Psychoanalytic investigations of the analytic interaction have been rather sparse, despite the considerable importance of this subject. While most psychoanalysts implicitly recognize interactional contributions to both transference and countertransference phenomena, few have recognized the totality of the analytic interaction and its implications. In the classical psychoanalytic literature, with few exceptions, explorations in this area have been restricted to the sphere of the therapeutic alliance and have stressed relatively autonomous ego functions within both participants; they have not proven to be the vehicle for a full investigation of the interactional dimension. On the other hand, the Kleinian approach, which stresses the role of object relationships in all instinctual strivings, has tended to view both transference and countertransference in interactional terms, although it has shown a relative disregard for the nondistorted and realistic contributions to these interactions.

Historically, there was an implicit interactional tone in Freud's writings on transference, especially in his last work (1938). Freud's focus was on the manner in which the patient places the analyst in the role of his superego and therefore gains an opportunity for a kind of aftereducation, in which the inner consequences of his parents' mistakes can be corrected. Earlier, J. Strachey (1934) emphasized the curative role of the processes of introjection and projection in the patient's relationship with the analyst and wrote that the patient tends to make the analyst into an auxiliary superego (and ego) onto whom he projects his introjected archaic objects, and from whom, as a new object, he accepts in turn more benign introjects. Strachey indicated that it is essentially when the analyst maintains a consistent nondeviant role as the interpreter of the patient's fantasies that he serves as a benign and corrective object for the analysand's pathological inner objects.

Subsequently, a number of analysts investigated the curative potential of the actual differences between the analyst and earlier traumatic parental figures. While, for some analysts, this implied the use of noninterpretive interventions, others stressed the importance of the analyst's adherence to his basically neutral and interpretive role as the optimal means of implicitly offering himself to the patient as a vehicle for constructive identifications.

On the other hand, studies of the analyst's countertransference reactions tended to be cast in interactional terms (R. Heimann 1950, Little 1951). Little (1951) described the patient's and the analyst's unconscious perceptions of each other and the "mirror" that the patient holds up to the analyst. She also described the analysand's unconscious responses to disturbances within the analyst, including efforts to help him to resolve his problems. She suggested that resistances within the patient are based not only on intrapsychic defenses and unconscious transference fantasies, but may also be derived from unconscious contributions from the analyst.

Racker (1968) also explored both the patient's and the analyst's reactions in terms of the pathological and nonpathological components of their interaction. He too noted the analyst's unconscious sensitivities and identifications with the patient, and explored their constructive and impaired functioning. He described the patient's unconscious awareness of the analyst's neurotic wishes, and the vicious neurotic circles that are established between patient and analyst when the former finds himself, in the actual situation, confronting a version of his own pathological internal reality.

Loewald (1960) specifically studied the role of interaction in the analytic situation. His main thesis was that in an analysis there is a resumption of the patient's ego development which is contingent upon his relationship with a new object—the analyst. He also described the introjection of the constructive interaction process that transpires between analysand and analyst.

De Racker (1961) studied the process of interpretation in terms of the interaction between patient and analyst, noting that the patient unconsciously assists the analyst in formulating his interventions. The Barangers (1966), in their investigation of insight, viewed the analytic situation as a bipersonal field with a basic asymmetry in regard to the contributions of patient and analyst. They described the basic structure of this field with stress on the mechanism of projective identification and its consequences for both participants. They also explored the dynamics of the bipersonal field, the distribution of roles between analyst and analysand, the appearance of defense mechanisms within the field, and the development of *bastions* that represent split-off parts of the field established and maintained by both participants—the interactional correlate of intrapsychic repression.

Searles (1965) described the interactional components of the analytic relationship, especially with schizophrenic patients. He described both introjective and projective processes within both participants and delineated the basic therapeutic symbiosis that characterizes the analytic interaction. He investigated the analyst's conscious and unconscious attempts to both cure and harm the patient and the patient's similar efforts toward the analyst. More recently, Searles (1975) explored the patient's curative efforts toward the analyst.

COMPONENTS AND PROPERTIES OF THE BIPERSONAL FIELD

The bipersonal field (Langs 1976a, b) is created by the physical conditions of the analyst's office, the analytic pact, the implicit and explicit ground rules and boundaries of the analytic relationship, and the respective roles and behaviors of the two participants. Any modification in the structure or framework of the field will have a profound influence on both participants and on the therapeutic qualities of the field. The field is essentially bipolar and interactional, with patient and analyst as its two nodal points; it has an *interface* that reflects the coalescence of the vectors in the field from moment to moment. Among the most important dimensions of the bipersonal field are the following:

Events or experiences. At or within any given point in the field, these reflect occurrences in the totality of the field and are determined by this totality. This indicates that the intrapsychic experiences of the patient, his free associations and behaviors, his defenses and resistances, and his insights are all products of the field; they are derived from contributions that stem from within the patient himself, the analyst, and their interaction. As a result, the analyst can draw upon the communications of the patient as a means of understanding both his analysand and himself, including his countertransference and noncountertransference contributions to the analytic process. Similarly, all experiences within the analyst reflect something of the state of and communications from the patient and can be used as a means of comprehending these processes.

The bipersonal field. When therapeutic, it has firm boundaries and is asymmetrical. The interface of the analytic interaction, therefore, receives distinctive ongoing contributions from each participant. Crucial to this asymmetry is the degree to which the analyst has resolved his countertransference dispositions, the characteristics of the patient's psychopathology, and the differences in the ground rules for each participant. It is the analyst's responsibility to contribute only minimally to the pathology of the field and to contribute maximally—though not exclusively—to the conscious curative insights and the constructive figures for identification that are placed into the field. By contrast, it is expected that the patient will contribute almost all—though not the totality—of the psychopathology of the field and that much of his comprehension will occur on an unconscious level. However, in a successful analysis, this gradually shifts toward more extensive conscious perceptiveness and understanding on his part.

The study of the curative and pathological dimensions of the bipersonal field begins without bias as to which participant is contributing most significantly for the moment to these aspects of the field. It is incumbent upon each of the participants, generally at different levels of awareness, to make determinations of the therapeutic and disrupted aspects of the field, to validate their assessment, and to then undertake the cure of the disturbing elements.

Mechanisms. A number of intrapsychic and interactional mechanisms characterize the bipersonal field. Of particular note are the following:

1. *Unconscious nonpathological and pathological fantasies, memories and introjects*—intrapsychic biases, needs, and sets. The pathological elements are the basis for distorted perceptions, communications, and reactions; these comprise the primarily transference and countertransference components of the field. These unconscious constellations are compromise formations, with contributions from the past and present, and from each psychic structure. They contribute significantly to the pathology of the field.

2. *Unconscious perceptions*—of self and others—of the patient and the analysand. Unconscious perceptions are the core of nontransference and noncountertransference functioning, true perceptiveness, and valid communication, and form a vital basis for the nondistorted components of the bipersonal field. The analyst continually assesses the unconscious communications from the patient for their veridical elements, since this is the only means through which the distinction between reality and fantasy, transference and nontransference, accurate perceptiveness and distortion can be made. Neglect of this component of the bipersonal field has led many analysts to interpret certain communications and perceptions of the patient in terms of transference distortions when they actually represent veridical unconscious perceptions of the analyst and the analytic interaction.

The patient's unconscious perceptions may be utilized by the analyst as a means of checking out his own contributions to the bipersonal field and especially as a basis for the detection of unconscious countertransference-based inputs. However, it must be kept in mind that the patient processes these unconscious perceptions in accordance with his own intrapsychic conflicts and needs; ultimately, they thereby become intermixed with distorted components. Further, the patient may communicate unconscious misperceptions whose presence can be determined only when the therapist has a very thorough knowledge of himself and the total bipersonal field. Technically, the distinction between unconscious fantasies and unconscious perceptive communications from the patient is based on the recognition of the adaptive context for his communications, and on the sorting out of the manifest and especially latent content of his associations.

3. *Projective identification* and *evocations of proxies* (Wangh 1962). These are among the major unconscious interactional mechanisms that prevail within the bipersonal field. The former refers to an interactional effort by a given person to place into another

individual his own intrapsychic contents—his conscious and unconscious fantasies, conflicts, and introjects—in order to manage them externally and to incorporate the response of the other person. It is to be distinguished from projection, which is an intrapsychic mechanism through which the patient unconsciously attributes his own inner contents and impulses to another individual without actual interactional efforts to place these contents into the other person and to have the other person experience and deal with them. Projective identification is specifically interactional, in that it is unconsciously designed to create an intrapsychic effect within the recipient. While its use stems from the earliest mother-child relationship, it is a universal mechanism that may entail fluidity of self-object boundaries or may occur in more sophisticated forms in the presence of intact boundaries. Lastly, the concept of projective identification may, but does not necessarily, imply parallel states between the patient and the analyst. Attempts to evoke proxies include mechanisms that may be subsumed under projective identification, though the concept stresses unconscious efforts to mobilize ego and superego functions and other adaptive resources lacking in the subject and sought for in the object.

Patients use projective identification within the bipersonal field as a major means of alleviating intrapsychic anxiety and conflict and of unconsciously influencing the analyst. The latter may respond by unconsciously incorporating the projective identification of the patient—projective counteridentification (Grinberg 1962)—or he may become aware of these efforts by the patient, consciously sample them, and then utilize them to understand and interpret to the patient (see Langs 1976a, b). An interaction of the first type becomes the basis for a shared pathological sector of the bipersonal field that has been termed a *therapeutic misalliance* (Langs 1976a,b) or a *bastion* (Baranger and Baranger 1966). On the other hand, the empathic and conscious processing of a projective identification of the patient by the analyst forms the basis for interpreting aspects of the psychopathology of the bipersonal field generated by the analysand. Essential here is the interpretation of both the interactional components of the analytic relationship and the patient's intrapsychic pathology as placed into the field. Such analytic work leads both to cognitive insight within the patient and to constructive introjective identifications with the analyst who has been able to adequately manage and deal with the projective identifications placed into him by the patient. These introjective processes, based on the actual responses of the analyst, are a crucial noninterpretive, interactional component of analytic cure.

Projective identifications are also used at times by the analyst. They are essentially countertransference-based and are conveyed to the patient through his errors in intervening and mismanagements of the framework. They are far more common than previously recognized and are the basis for many analyst-evoked disturbances of the field.

4. *Incorporative identification* also plays an important role in the bipersonal field. The analyst's incorporative identifications of contents and attributes of the patient, when conscious, are a vehicle for interpreting to the patient. On the other hand, unconscious and unmetabolized incorporative identifications with the analysand by the analyst are a basis for psychopathology of the bipersonal field and sectors of misalliance.

Within the patient, incorporative identification similarly may play a therapeutic or disruptive role. In regard to the former, incorporative identifications—with an analyst who can adequately manage the framework of the analytic relationship, sensitively interpret to the patient, constructively deal with the patient's projective identifications and unconscious perceptions, and essentially manage his own intrapsychic state—are the basis for considerable inner growth and modification of pathogenic introjects. These incorporative identifications enhance the patient's ego strength, including his capacity to manage his intrapsychic conflicts, states, and self. On the other hand, incorporative identifications of the disturbances within the analyst— reflected in his failures in interpreting and in managing the framework—are the means through which the patient incorporates aspects of the psychopathology of the bipersonal field to the further disruption of his inner state. These incorporative identifications with the analyst's psychopathology are the basis for the patient's unconscious efforts to modify both the pathology of the field and the intrapsychic pathology of the analyst.

PSYCHOPATHOLOGY OF THE BIPERSONAL FIELD

The bipersonal field concept implies that all disturbances within the analytic situation, and within each of its participants, have an interactional component. This means, for example, that a symptom experienced by the patient has both an intrapsychic and an interactional component and that its determinants are shared by both patient and analyst. Under unusual circumstances, in which the analyst is contributing in a major way to the pathology of the bipersonal field, a symptom experienced within the patient may have as its most central determinant the psychopathology of the analyst—though this conceptualization should not be used to overlook the additional contributions from within the patient. Similarly, countertransference-based symptoms within the analyst have both intrapsychic and interactional determinants.

Interactional resistances. By locating resistances within the analytic interaction and bipersonal field, the analyst is directed to search for both their intrapsychic determinants within the patient and his own contribution to these disturbances in communication. While it may often be the case that the major source of given resistance is that of an unconscious intrapsychic conflict, fantasy, or introject, especially in relationship to the analyst—the classical concept of transference resistance—quite often, one can detect unconscious contributions from the analyst.

The interactional neurosis. Similar considerations to those presented for interactional resistances apply more broadly to the psychopathology of the patient as it becomes centered in the course of the analysis around unconscious fantasies and perceptions of the analyst. Thus, in addition to the intrapsychically determined transference neurosis (used here in the broadest sense to include all types of transference syndromes), considerations of the bipersonal field lead to the discovery of contributions to this neurosis from the analyst and the analytic interaction. The concept of the *interactional neurosis* accounts for these contributions to the ongoing pathology of the patient. The transference and interactional neuroses thereby become the central focus of the analytic work, and the resolution of these neuroses rely not only on the analyst's capacities to formulate and interpret properly but also on his ability to resolve his own mobilized countertransference neurosis and his contributions to the neurosis of the bipersonal field—however small or large.

Sectors of misalliance and bastions. A sector of misalliance or bastion is based on the conscious or, more usually, unconscious collusion of patient and analyst to modify the bipersonal field and the analytic work, so that the central purpose is not for the moment the pursuit of inner structural change for the patient but some other means of maladaptive symptom resolution or the disregard for symptom modification entirely. Sectors of misalliance may include shared resistances and defenses, shared pathological unconscious gratifications, and shared expressions of inappropriate superego functioning. They constitute, for both patient and analyst, the repetition of earlier pathogenic interactions with significant parental figures and a verification of the pathological inner world of each participant. These sectors of misalliance may be restricted to isolated components of the bipersonal field or may undermine its fundamental therapeutic structure and functioning. They are derived from modifications in the framework and from the analyst's errors in intervening—vehicles for his contribution to the pathology of the field.

CURATIVE ASPECTS OF THE BIPERSONAL FIELD

Having located the psychopathology that disturbs the analytic relationship and each of its participants within the bipersonal field, we are in a position to study the curative efforts of both patient and analyst. These are manifested in two interdependent spheres of functioning: the interactional—with its stress on actuality and identificatory processes—and the cognitive—with its emphasis on verbalized insight and the conscius tools of adaptive mastery.

The curative efforts of the patient. While there are occasional instances in which the patient consciously recognizes a disturbance within the analyst and its contribution to the pathology of the bipersonal field, most of his interpretive and curative efforts occur on an unconscious level. They are identified by the analyst, who becomes aware of a countertransference disturbance and its influence on the bipersonal field and recognizes that this disturbance is virtually always a central adaptive task for the patient. The patient not only unconsciously perceives the difficulties in his analyst but also usually introjects these disturbances to the point that the cure of the analyst becomes the cure of an inner part of the patient. With enormous creativity, the patient offers a wide range of unconscious interpretations based on his conscious and unconscious observations of the analyst; most of these are on a general level, since the patient does not have available to him the specifics of the analyst's associational flow and life history and must rely on his unconscious perceptiveness of the wealth of implicit and explicit information derived from the analyst's behaviors.

In addition to such unconscious interpretations, often couched in terms of the patient's speculation about sources of his own difficulties, the patient will unconsciously offer himself as a constructive and well-functioning model for identification by the analyst. These curative efforts have clear-cut veridical and nontransference components, although they do in addition acquire transference meanings. Often, what begins as unconscious efforts by the patient to modify the pathology of the bipersonal field and of the analyst becomes an unconscious endeavor to maintain a sector of misalliance or to exploit the pathology of the analyst in the service of maintaining the analysand's own neurosis.

Technically, the analyst must recognize from his own subjective experiences and the monitoring of his patient's associations those moments when he has contributed significantly to the pathology of the bipersonal field and should *implicitly* utilize the curative efforts of his patient. At such times, it is vital that the framework of the field not be modified by unneeded self-revelations and acknowledgment of errors; the analyst's use of the patient's therapeutic endeavors should occur on an implicit level. In a well-run psychoanalysis, such experiences are kept to a reasonable minimum, and the goal is to resolve these disturbances as quickly as possible and to resume the major work of the treatment in terms of the inner resolution of the patient's psychopathology. This is accomplished through the self-analysis of the analyst with the implicit assistance of the communications from the patient and without burdening the patient in any additional way.

The analyst's curative efforts.   Recognition of the bipersonal field and the pervasiveness of exquisite efforts by the patient to both maintain and modify the pathology of the field leads to a profound appreciation of the extent to which the analyst should and must patiently rely on the communications from his analysand for the development of his interpretive efforts. The patient's unconscious perceptiveness and wisdom serves as the ultimate source of comprehension of the pathology of the field. Interactionally, the patient makes persistent efforts to communicate to the analyst those elements of his inner fantasy life that will enable the analyst to develop the crucial cognitive interpretations that he must offer. Each patient comes to unconsciously appreciate and develop a specific communicative relationship with his analyst and to unconsciously control the extent to which he conveys to his therapist analyzable derivatives of unconscious fantasies, memories, and introjects. Further, through efforts at projective identification and proxy evocation, the patient attempts to place into the analyst his pathological contents as a means of evoking curative responses in his therapist.

Embedded in the bipersonal field, the analyst manages and maintains the framework and pursues his efforts to comprehend the unconscious sources of the patient's psychopathology. By adhering to his basic psychoanalytic stance and by offering sensitive, well-timed interpretations, he provides the patient both cognitive insights and reparative identifications. The former serve the patient by assisting him in developing the means of cognitive mastery with which he can resolve specific intrapsychic conflicts. The latter have a more general effect in strengthening the patient's ego and in modifying his self-concept and his pathological introjects by providing him interactional experiences through which such inner changes can be achieved.

The approach to the analytic interaction in terms of the bipersonal field appears to offer a comprehensive and sensitive understanding of the analytic process. It acknowledges the depth of the analyst's involvement with his patient, while establishing an effective framework and set of boundaries for his participation. It acknowledges and utilizes the therapeutic creativity of both members of the analytic dyad and offers an opportunity to more precisely identify and resolve the factors that compromise or interfere with the cure of the patient. The intrapsychic focus of classical analysis is extended through a full appreciation of the interactional dimension, and the curative powers and opportunities of patient and analyst are significantly enhanced.

REFERENCES

Baranger, M., and Baranger, W. (1966). Insight in the analytic situation. In *Psychoanalysis in the Americas*, ed. R.E. Litman, pp.

56–72, New York: International Universities Press.

Bleger, J. (1967). Psycho-analysis of the psycho-analytic frame. *Journal of Psycho-Analysis*, 48:511–519.

Eissler, R. (1953). The effect of the structure of the ego on psychoanalytic technique. *Journal of the American Psychoanalytic Association* 1:104–143.

Freud. S. (1915). Observations on transference-love. *Standard Edition* 12:157–171.

——— (1938). An outline of psycho-analysis. *Standard Edition* 23:141–207.

Glover, E. (1931). The therapeutic effect of inexact interpretation: a contribution to the theory of suggestion. *International Journal of Psycho-Analysis* 12:397–411.

Grinberg, L. (1962). On a specific aspect of countertransference due to the patient's projective identification. *International Journal of Psycho-Analysis* 43:436–440.

Heimann, P. (1950). On countertransference. *International Journal of Psycho-Analysis* 31:81–84.

Langs, R. (1975a). Therapeutic misalliances. *International Journal of Psychoanalytic Psychotherapy* 4:77–105. [Chapter 6, this volume]

——— (1975b). The therapeutic relationship and deviations in technique. *International Journal of Psychoanalytic Psychotherapy* 4:106–141. [Chapter 7, this volume]

Langs, R. (1976a). *The Bipersonal Field*. New York: Jason Aronson.

———*(1976b). The Therapeutic Interaction*. 2 vols. New York: Jason Aronson.

Little, M. (1951). Countertransference and the patient's response to it. *International Journal of Psycho-Analysis* 32:32–40.

Loewald, H. (1960). On the therapeutic action of psychoanalysis. *International Journal of Psycho-Analysis* 41:16–33.

Milner, M. (1952). Aspects of symbolism in comprehension of the not-self. *International Journal of Psycho-Analysis* 33:181–195.

Racker, H. (1968). *Transference and Countertransference*. London: Hogarth Press.

Searles, H. (1965). *Collected Papers on Schizophrenia and Related Subjects*. New York: International Universities Press.

——— (1975). The patient as therapist to his analyst. In *Tactics and Techniques in Psychoanalytic Therapy, Vol. II: Countertransference,* ed. P. Giovacchini, pp. 95–151. New York: Jason Aronson.

Stone, L. (1961). *The Psychoanalytic Situation.* New York: International Universities Press.

Strachey, J. (1934). The nature of the therapeutic action of psychoanalysis. *International Journal of Psycho-Analysis* 15:127–159.

Viderman, S. (1974). Interpretation in the analytic space. *International Review of Psycho-Analysis* 1:467–480.

Wangh, M. (1962). The "evocation of a proxy": A psychological maneuver, its use as a defense, its purposes, and genesis. *Psychoanalytic Study of the Child* 17:451–469.

Winnicott, D. (1965). *The Maturational Processes and the Facilitating Environment.* New York: International Universities Press.

Chapter Twelve

On Becoming A Psychiatrist
(1976)

Specific investigations of the motivations for becoming a psychiatrist and of the psychiatric resident's earliest modes of functioning appear to be quite rare. Because of this, Blank's (1976) description of the psychotherapy of his first patient offers unique data with which to consider some specific issues related to the choice of psychiatry or psychotherapy as a profession. His presentation reveals not only the expressions of inner disturbances inevitably found in the beginning therapist—countertransference problems that he will spend the balance of his career endeavoring to master—but also the kernels of constructive functioning that he will hopefully develop as the basic core of his therapeutic aptitudes.

Using the material offered by Blank, with its inevitable limitations, I will discuss some of the issues every budding psychiatrist must deal with and will focus on the following selected issues (see Langs 1976a for a broader discussion of the therapist's functioning): the motivations for becoming a psychiatrist, and especially their relationship to the mechanisms of projective and introjective identification and the therapist's containing functions; the specific advantages and disadvantages that derive from the therapist's early and relatively naive functioning; the role of the validating process in psychotherapy and in testing out the subjectively identified experiences of both empathy and intuition; the means of early therapeutic "cures" and their relationship to "misalliance cures"; the distinctions between transference and nontransference, and countertransference and noncountertransference; and the functions of the framework of the psychotherapeutic situation.

While I know of no precedent for this attempt to utilize a specific description of a therapeutic interaction as a means of developing observations related to the problems and motives in becoming a psychiatrist, this study has as its heritage a wide range of investigations related to the analyst's nonconflicted (noncountertransference-based) and conflicted (countertransference-based) functioning (see Langs 1976a for details). More specifically, there have been several notable general discussions of the motivations for becoming a psychoanalyst and the traits that best serve this profession. Among the most well known of these efforts are the papers of Sharpe (1930), Fleming (1961), and Greenson (1966, 1967). Greenson in particular attempted to define the central genetic experiences and intrapsychic conflicts that contribute to the choice of psychoanalysis as a profession, and he stressed the role of pregenital sadistic drives and various pregenital and oedipal libidinal conflicts, the contribution of primal scene experiences, the role of various defensive maneuvers, and aspects of identification with the mother. Along different lines, Olinick (1969), in his study of empathy and regression in the service of the other, suggested that a powerful motivation in becoming a psychiatrist derives from a rescue fantasy involving a depressed mother—a thesis that seems especially relevant to the material we shall discuss. All of these authors emphasized the importance of the mastery of such underlying conflicted constellations in the effective functioning of a therapist. With this as a general background, I will now turn to the data offered in Blank's paper (1976).

THE MOTIVATIONS FOR BECOMING A PSYCHIATRIST

Opportunities to projectively and introjectively identify. Of all the motives related to the wish to be a psychiatrist, I should like to focus on two interrelated determinants: the therapist's wish for opportunities to projectively identify[1] aspects of his own inner conflicts, unconscious fantasies, and introjects into his patients; and, contrariwise, his wish to have the opportunity to receive—introjectively identify with— pathological projective identifications from his patients. Related to these motives are the therapist's wishes to have the patient serve as a container for the former's contents and, in addition, to serve as a receptacle for the pathological contents of the patient (Bion 1962, 1963). These motivations may be adaptive or maladaptive, pathological or nonpathological, openly expressed or defended against, and well managed or sublimated on the one hand, or poorly managed and unsublimated on the other. Before discussing this dimension further, I will turn to selected material in Blank's presentation that relates to these ideas.

In this context, it is of interest that Blank first met his patient while she was receiving an intravenous infusion. She was somewhat older than he and was frustrated and depressed. The therapist's first intervention was offered at their second meeting and in response to the patient's expression of a strong wish to die; he told her firmly that he would not allow her to die.

Here we see one type of effort at projective identification that is characteristic for many therapist initiates: the need to intervene without permitting the development of derivatives related to the patient's unconscious fantasies, and to do so by placing manifestly good contents into the patient. Such an intervention reflects the rather characteristic ambivalence seen in beginning—and even more experienced—psychotherapists in regard to unconscious fantasies and introjects. The selection of psychiatry as a profession relates to the wish to delve into the unconscious fantasies of others and, interactionally, to accept these unconscious contents from the patient into oneself. However, the dread of the primitive aspects of unconscious fantasies and introjects and of the internal damage they will generate often prompts strong defenses within the therapist against such expressions. This leads to many premature interventions and other efforts to shut off the patient's unconscious communications.

In terms of my central thesis, such an intervention unconsciously appears to express several trends within the therapist. First is the unconscious need to place good, hopeful, and controlled contents into the patient. However, by making this effort prematurely, the therapist surrounds these good qualities with his own anxiety, so that the projective identification has both positive and negative, helpful and disturbing, aspects. In addition, the intervention serves to disrupt the flow of associations and unconsciously conveys to the patient the therapist's refractoriness toward being a container for more pathological contents. We may note that Blank's comment came after the patient began to talk about her deteriorating marriage and sexual relationship with her husband—material that may have generated some anxiety within the therapist. Since the patient responded to the intervention with feelings of hopelessness and emptiness, she may have unconsciously detected the therapist's difficulties. While this may seem speculative, it should be noted that patients are extremely sensitive to this component of the therapeutic interaction (Langs 1976a).[2]

Next we learn that Blank found himself lingering at the hospital hoping to see a repetition of the previous night's events, during which the patient had made a suicide attempt that had necessitated efforts at resuscitation. Among other implications, we see here an intense wish, expressed in a seemingly countertransference-based form, to have an opportunity to directly contain the patient's sickness, so that we may suspect a pathological need to do this. In general, such pathological needs are extremely common among neophyte psychiatrists. These wishes may prompt the therapist to intervene incorrectly and to unconsciously provoke the patient into regressive episodes that the therapist can readily submit to introjective identification and work over within himself.

While we have no data in regard to Blank's unconscious communications to the patient, we learn next that the patient did indeed attempt to strangle herself once again. The therapist's comments in this context afford an opportunity to demonstrate the distinction between projection and projective identification, mechanisms often used by psychiatrists in their interaction with the patient. Blank indicates that he was aware that the patient had aroused in himself a rescue fantasy that he later found to be her dominant mode of social interaction with him. However, this unilateral suggestion overlooks his evident parallel needs. Thus the focus on the patient's need to be rescued is here in part a defensive projection. This could extend into a projective identification in the therapist's interaction with the patient—i.e., into an actual interactional effort—if he were to communicate to the patient his wishes to rescue her, and there is some evidence that this did in fact occur.

Blank next describes his active efforts in response to the problem he found upon going to the patient. He reacted with a strong appeal, made physical contact with her, and observed her exposed breasts. He had violated a taboo set by his patient's husband, and she responded with a prolonged period of breath-holding, and with further clawing at her throat. Once the patient's respiration had returned, the decision was made to treat her with an ice pack.

The patient then responded by speaking about her grandfather and expressing her love for him, and then her hatred for someone else; she was directly unresponsive to the therapist. Next, the therapist turned to hypnosis to bring the patient out of her dissociated state, and he was amazed to find her responsive. The patient was amnesic and pleaded that she be allowed to die, stating that she felt empty, and then talking of her father, whom she feared she had let down in his dying years and again of her love for her dead grandfather. She expressed the concern that the therapist could not help her, and he responded with the reassertion of his determination not to allow her to die.

In his discussion, Blank indicates that he felt quite protective toward the patient and that he had become aware of her strong symbiotic needs. He suggests that he responded empathically to her and with intuition as well, although he notes the danger of projecting aspects of his own past relationships and interactions onto the present situation in the name of empathy (Shapiro 1974). He viewed himself as identifying with the patient's lack of control and suggested that his empathy led him to offer her the firmest controls available. Blank also expresses a fear of losing control of the situation and acknowledges an aspect of omnipotence in his rescue tactics.

For our purposes, we see in this interaction a situation in which the patient offered herself as an unconscious container for aspects of the therapist's own need for symbiosis and fusion, and for the patient to into the patient his own symbiotic needs and possibly his own fears on some level of suicidal impulses. For her part, the patient attempted to projectively identify into the therapist aspects of her own self-destructiveness, to which the therapist responded by modifying the classical boundaries of the therapeutic relationship (Langs 1973, 1976a)—in making physical contact with the patient, observing her breasts, offering her an ice pack, wiping her brow, and then, finally, hypnotizing her. These measures appear to make evident the therapist's own need for symbiosis and fusion, and for the patient to serve as a container for his own inner disturbances.[3]

Throughout this interaction we observe efforts by the therapist to project—that is, intrapsychically attribute to the patient—and to projectively identify—interactionally place into the patient—aspects of his own inner needs and difficulties. Similarly, we see his repeated efforts to evoke regressive responses in her and his mixed reaction to their occurrence in that he very abruptly responds to these regressive communications with directives that indicate his refractoriness about containing them. The patient generally responded to this with disillusionment followed by a mobilization of her own resources.

I would therefore suggest that in this particular initial interaction, the patient's abrupt recovery reflects the development of a therapeutic misalliance (Langs 1975a) that was both mutually seductive and hostile, and which gratified the symbiotic needs of both participants, thereby evoking what I have termed a *misalliance or framework cure* (Langs 1976a). This constitutes momentary symptomatic recovery based on bilateral unconscious collusion that creates *bastions*—split-off sectors of denied and repressed contents within the bipersonal therapeutic field (Baranger and Baranger 1966, Langs 1976a). This relief also stems from gross modifications of the framework which undo the buildup of the patient's pathological intrapsychic fantasies and anxieties. It appears that these vehicles were the primary modality of symptom alleviation in this case. My general clinical experience indicates that this is characteristic of beginning therapists.

The wish to and fear of containing the patient's inner contents. In this connection, two aspects of this material deserve specific discussion. The first relates to the unconscious motives on the part of the psychiatrist as these pertain to his wish to work with unconscious fantasies and introjects—inner contents that are usually viewed in terms of frightening, regressive, primitively sexual and aggressive material. As Greenson (1966) has noted, much of this relates to the child's curiousity regarding the contents of his mother's body, and undoubtedly such voyeuristic interests derive from a variety of specific individual experiences, intermixed with unconscious fantasies drawn from all levels of development.

The characteristic conflicts regarding the exploration of the patient's primitive inner contents are evident in the presentation by Blank. We see both his intense curiosity about his patient's fantasies and his defensiveness; the latter is reflected in efforts to obliterate their communication. It seems likely that the patient introjectively identified with the therapist's fear of her inner contents, and that this is another aspect of the mobilized misalliance cure which enabled this patient to seal off her symptoms. This struggle is handled in a not uncommon manner by invoking the concept of supportive treatment as a means of justifying the obliteration of the patient's unconscious fantasies and introjects. Accompanied with this rationalization is the decision not to do insight psychotherapy and not to offer so-called deep interpretations.[4]

It is quite common for those psychiatrists who dread their patients' inner contents to arrive at a similar rationalization that supports their turning away from any type of insight therapy. The early months in his training provide crucial interludes during which the therapist may choose to allow the patient to speak, or may consciously or unconsciously decide to shut off avenues related to the latter's unconscious communications. Throughout the paper we see Blank interrupting the patient with some type of general and surface intervention at precisely those moments when she initiates movement in the direction of her inner struggles. These defenses are a factor in the disillusionment of many psychiatrists in regard to psychoanalytic psychotherapy and psychoanalysis.

In addition, when the therapist avows some struggle with his aggressive impulses with this patient, there is also strong evidence for an overlooked intense erotic countertransference—his examination of the patient and observation of her breasts, his difficulty in recognizing the patient's erotic transference and nontransference responses, his interruptions of the patient each time she approached communications related to himself, his fear of her becoming too dependent on him, and his final "gifts" to her. The therapist's unconscious defenses against his own erotic and hostile countertransferences led him to obliterate the communication of the patient's unconscious fantasies lest they approach these areas—especially the sexual. Put another way, it would appear that because of his own unresolved intrapsychic conflicts, the therapist was especially refractory about containing the contents of the patient's erotic fantasies and her essentially valid unconscious perceptions of the therapist in this area.

These data illuminate the choice of insightful or noninsightful therapeutic modalities by the early psychiatric resident. They clarify common rationalizations for advocating so-called supportive therapy that is actually, in part, designed to obliterate the patient's unconscious contents. There is a concomitant failure to acknowledge the supportive aspects of sound, sensitive interpretations (Langs 1973, 1976c). This initial interaction also demonstrates the manner in which patients may invite projective identification by the therapist by offering themselves as containers for particular kinds of pathology that especially threaten the treating psychiatrist. The anticipation of this type of experience also motivates the therapist's choice of profession.

The wish to exclusively possess the patient. Another motive for becoming a psychiatrist relfected in this material is the desire for exclusive possession of the maternal and paternal objects, especially the preoedipal and oedipal mother. Stalemates in long-term psychotherapy and analysis are not infrequently based on the failure to resolve such unconscious wishes. In the material from Blank, these relatively unresolved wishes appear to be reflected in his decision not to allow her any visitors, and in his evident rivalry with the patient's husband for total possession of her. In addition, the therapist's response to the patient's initial suicidal gesture and respiratory difficulties seems to reflect wishes to totally possess and fuse with her. The material suggests symbiotic longings as well as later oedipally based wishes. These possessive needs are a factor in the therapist's overidentification with, and excessive needs to introject from, his patient. They are also reflected in the therapist's threat to commit this patient should she wish to leave the hosptial prematurely.

The resolution of the countertransference-based aspects of these motives is also evident. Blank develops some self-awareness in this area and ultimately informs the patient that he will not rescue her and that she will have to take care of herself. This is then reinforced when he apparently scolds her for behaving like a little child and for testing out whether he cared and would protect her. His display of anger and upset became the medium through which he was able to establish boundaries between himself and his patient that he was otherwise unable to effect. The patient's unconscious perceptions of the therapist's symbiotic and oedipal needs may well have been reflected in her failing to have her menstrual period; in this way she seems to have lived out fantasies of impregnation that were evident to the therapist, although apparently not interpreted to the patient.

The final expression of these needs for fusion and possession appears in the therapist's sessions with the patient after she left the hospital, while her subsequent therapist was on vacation. We can detect Blank's sadness in giving up his patient, but we also find indications that he has resolved his more primitive longings for fusion. In these final moments, he conveys his needs for this patient on a more object-related and oedipal level, to which the patient apparently responded favorably. One may theorize that she found considerable relief through her perceptions of these changes in him.

EMPATHY AND INTUITION; PROJECTION AND PROJECTIVE IDENTIFICATION

Validating seemingly empathic and intuitive experiences. Both Beres and Arlow (1974) and Shapiro (1974) have addressed themselves to the need to utilize what I have termed the *validating process* (Langs 1976a) to verify the therapist's empathic and intuitive experiences (see Langs 1976c for a full review of these topics). In brief, these authors described empathy as an emotional form of knowing through a temporary identification with the patient, while intuition, according to the former authors, tends to involve the more cognitive aspects of immediate knowing. To these aspects of empathy and intuition I would add the contributions of projective and introjective identification through which the therapist places int othe patient aspects of his own inner contents in order to have the patient work them over (in part as efforts to evoke proxies; see Wangh 1962, Langs 1967a), and through which the therapist interactionally takes into himself aspects of the patient's contents for simila processing. These mechanisms may have adaptive and maladaptive aspects, and the distinction between empathy and intuition as valid processes on the one hand, and projections, projective identifications, and introjective identifications on the other, is by no means absolute. These latter processes are the basis for aspects of empathic and intuitive functioning, so that the validating process must be utilized to determine the extent to which the therapist is involved in their pathological use and the extent to which these are utilized in the service of understanding and interpreting to the patient.

Blank's presentation offers concrete data regarding the failure of many therapists to undertake efforts at validation in response to subjective experiences within themselves that they identify as empathic and/or intuitive. Such a validating process actually must include a careful exploration of the therapist's own subjective reactions and a continued assessment of the patient's associations for fantasied and perceptive responses in the context of the empathic or intuitive experience and the conclusions derived from it. The material from the patient following a valid empathic or intuitive response will almost always broaden the therapist's understanding of that response and will usually include allusions to helpful figures. In addition, the patient will generally be working over aspects of his own unconscious fantasies, conflicts, and affects as related to the areas in which the therapist is responding empathically and intuitively, and the patient will add specific, additional, previously repressed contents to the initial, more blurred, empathic or intuitive experience of the therapist (Langs 1974).

It appears that at this particular stage of his development, Blank generally did not apply such a validating process to his intuitive and empathic experiences. It is evident from the psychoanalytic literature (Langs 1976c) that the consistent use of validating measures is relatively rare even among psychoanalysts, and that much work remains to be done in establishing the validating process as the cornerstone of psychoanalytic methodology. In addition, Blank's presentation reveals the readiness with which empathic and intuitive subjective experiences can actually constitute pathological projections, introjective identifications, and projective identifications.

empathy intuition and countertransference. In general, Blank attempted to work largely in advance of and without the full use of his patient's associations. In representative fashion, he somewhat narcissistically relied on his own inner responses without broad efforts at validation; he thereby often fell into difficulty. This involves not only cognitive problem, but reflects difficulties in containing and working over—metabolizing—the patient's sickness and his need to place his own difficulties into the patient.

The first indications of a brief for empathic response appear when the author states that he empathically identified with the patient's utter lack of control and thereby instituted the firmest of controls. He also states that this led to intuitive action and justified his intervening on the basis of the danger of the patient's possible suicide. Because there was some ground for the therapist's assessment of this patient's difficulty with controls, we cannot view his excessive measures as entirely deriving from his own needs. Instead, this interlude demonstrates how patients lend themselves to the therapist's projections and projective identifications. The degree to which the therapist had actually responded empathically here, and the extent to which his responses constituted a projection and even a projective identification, cannot be fully determined from the data.

It can be pointed out, however, that the concerns about loss of control were utilized in part as a major defense against the recognition of intense aggressive—and especially sexual—unconscious fantasies that seem to have been present in both patient and therapist. Thus, the therapist's empathic response in terms of the lack of control and his efforts to institute general controls were designed in part to shut out specific sexual and aggressive contents and, in addition, to prevent their emerging in the patient's associations—and possibly even in the therapist's subjective awareness. The therapist indicates his own fear of losing control of the situation, without referring to the specific underlying unconscious fantasies—a common oversight. This type of defensiveness appears throughout the therapeutic interaction. Here, the empathic functioning is restricted to a nondescript and general issue as a means of shutting out more specific sexual and aggressive fantasies, and such an approach is reinforced by shutting off the patient's associations and by disregarding the validating process. Similarly, Blank's intuitive responses also served in part the mutual defensive needs of the patient and himself and, in effect, generated a misalliance that afforded some controls and relief to each of them, while bypassing the search for more insightful adaptations.

The fear of interpreting. In a not uncommon way, Blank and her supervisor decided to approach the patient without deep interpretations, since these were considered a threat to her tenuous hold on reality. The conclusion was to direct the therapist toward a more supportive role in which empathy and intuition would play a particularly significant part. This seems to reflect a common misconception among therapists regarding the consequences of valid interpretations, viewing them as disturbing to a patient's equilibrium and to his reality testing. Such a concept is based on a failure to appreciate the importance of the capacity to differentiate internal from external reality testing. On this basis, interpretations, when offered in a valid and sensitive manner, with due respect for the patient's fragile ego, actually enhance the patient's capacity for reality testing rather than disrupting it. In addition, this misconception is related to another mistaken view that ego dysfunctions are inherent or innate within the more disturbed patient, and that disruptive unconscious fantasies, memories, and introjects do not significantly contribute to these malfunctions. Clinical evidence indicates that this too is far from the case, and that sensitive interpretations can help to resolve inner disturbances that disrupt the patient's functioning, including reality testing.

The data in the presentation by Blank indicate that these misconceptions tend to be based in part on a fear of the patient's inner world—unconscious fantasies and introjects—and the parallel fear of these aspects of the therapist's inner self. Because of these shared anxieties and avoidances, such a so-called supportive approach actually constitutes a basic therapeutic misalliance in which there are shared defenses against the respective unconscious fantasies and introjects of both participants. Such work, as Blank's paper demonstrates, helped the patient to massively mobilize sufficient defenses or resources to reconstitute her functioning. However, such a "misalliance cure" (Langs 1975a, 1976a) did not help the patient to resolve her inner conflicts and the underlying basis for her suicidal attempts and severe inner pathology.

These therapeutic decisions to be somewhat supportive and less interpretive led to a so-called empathic and intuitive attempt to let the patient be honest with the therapist. Blank saw this as based partly on a denial of his own countertransference anger, which the patient had consciously perceived. As a result of this countertransference difficulty—and the apparently concealed erotic countertransference—there was actually a distinct failure in the therapist's empathic responses to his patient. However, Blank appears to have gradually become aware that he was projecting certain aspects of his own inner difficulties onto the patient and that he was directing his efforts to offer her structure as a means of trying to contain his own aggressive—and he later adds erotic—countertransference impulses. Eventually he realized that he was struggling with his own guilt and fear of the patient's suicide, and that he was adopting an inappropriate and omnipotent stance because of these worries. Here he acknowledges his countertransference problems as they contributed to his threat to commit the patient when she was ready to leave the hospital prematurely. He also notes that the patient nonetheless responded well to this enforced structure, despite the fact that it was based on his own countertransference anxiety. Here again the therapist's empathic capacities seem actually to have failed him and to have been disrupted by his needs to project onto and projectively identify into his patient. However, Blank's gradual recognition of his countertransference problems suggests a crucial initial movement toward mastery—a point to which I will return later.

The role of unrecognized countertransferences. Blank then offers two vignettes through which he details what I view as the resolution of a misalliance and shared bastion of the bipersonal field established between himself and his patient. These were related to the erotic unconscious fantasies and unconscious perceptions of the patient regarding her therapist, and therefore to her unconscious and conscious erotic transference and nontransference reactions to him. In addition, the vignettes involve the resolution of the therapist's blind spots in this area and possibly some inner working through of his won erotic countertransference.

In this context, Blank reports a session that followed the patient's first leave outside the hosptial. In that hour, she vividly described her erotic fantasies toward her previous therapist. Blank invokes his empathic capacities to point out to the patient that she had not gotten over her feelings toward this previous therapist, despite her belief that she had done so. The author later recognized that he had experienced a general empathic failure to understand the patient, and that intially he had disregarded the associations from the patient that strongly suggested the presence of erotic feelings toward himself. As he worked over this blind spot, Blank came to the conclusion that the patient was concerned with developing toward himself the same feelings of attachment she had experienced with her previous therapist. He then specifically acknowledges efforts to defend himself against both sexual and hostile feelings that he was unconsciously experiencing from the patient, but he did not extend this insight fully into a comparable blind spot in regard to his own sexual and hostile countertransferences.

This sequence is of general interest because it characterizes the work of many psychiatrists who quickly become disillusioned with insight psychotherapy, and it revealed aspects of the basis for this reaction. We see an effort to work empathically without support on the cognitive level and without sufficient use of the patient's specific associations. This vignette reminds us of the dangers of working empathically and intuitively without the full use of the contents of the patient's associations and without a full utilization of the validating process. And the vignette also reveals something of the unconscious basis for these restrictions: the patient was moving toward specifically indicating feelings of love and wishes for marriage in her relationship with her present therapist, and she was hinting at strong sexual fantasies toward him. These responses were evidently mobilized by her separation from the therapist and undoubtedly had other precipitants in earlier sessions with him. Because of the dangers of the patient's and therapist's erotic feelings, we see the therapist attempting to maintain a displacement onto the previous therapist—another bastion of the bipersonal field in which the erotic transference and countertransference is split off and displaced onto the previous therapy and denied in the current interaction.

We see here too the common fear of the patient's erotic feelings toward the therapist, one that is in general far more intense than fear of the patient's aggression. These anxieties mobilize intensive defensive efforts by the therapist; unrecognized, they may lead him away from insight therapy.

Blank's failure to fully recognize and rectify his erotic countertransference, and the related anxieties and defenses, created a situation in which he in part utilized the patient's sickness as a container for his own countertransferences and as a means of projecting, and probably projectively identifying, his inner fantasies into the patient. This too

The defensive use of so-called empathic and intuitive experiences. As we observe this interaction, it becomes evident that the so-called use of empathy and intuition can actually serve as a defense against the specific cognitive awareness of derivatives of the patient's unconscious fantasies and perceptions. We also see that it is often difficult for the therapist to conceptualize the specific ways in which his empathy and intuition are failing him wihtout the use of cognitive material, so that we come to the conclusion that the beginning therapist who feels a need to rely on his empahty and intution is at a great disadvantage in his interaction with the patient. The outcome of these failures in empathy, intuition, and cognitive understanding culminated in the session under study with the patient's dissociation and with her abrupt ending of the hour. In part, these responses confirm the present assessment of the therapist's problems.

In the second detailed session, the author describes an "Aha experience" through which he felt he had empathically recognized that the patient was afraid of becoming symbiotically attached to him. He also indicates that he felt he intuitively understood what the patient was experiencing and describes an intervention in regard to the patient's wishes to be rescued by him that was offered on the basis of those inner experiences. However, this empathic response was not subjected to the validating process. Thus, while it seems to have had a valid component, it also served as another defense against the patient's and therapist's erotic fantasies toward each other. As a result, the patient did not confirm this intervention, though she seemed less upset. This relief may be viewed in terms of the defensive misalliance offered to the patient and the unconscious communications in the therapist's interventions. These latter were to the effect that the therapist was beginning to resolve his unconscious countertransference fantasies and that he would attempt to subject the patient less intensely to them. Thus, while the specific unconscious fantasies within the patient and the therapist were not made conscious or interpreted, the therapist unconsciously indicated some degree of resolution of his countertransference difficulties. This appears to have offered the patient yet another sector of misalliance cure, based on the therapist's indications to the patient that he no longer wished to possess her.

In the termination phase, the therapist again attempted to utilize his empathic responses. On that basis, he essentially scolded the patient for her behavior, and she responded by apologizing. Here again we find the use of empathy and intuition in the service of obliterating the patient's threatening communications, which at this point again had to do with her feeling toward the therapist. Her hostility was condensed with a continued need to defend herself against her own and the therapist's erotic fantasies, leading to the wish to disfigure herself. These shared defenses against the erotic components of their relationship I have elsewhere (1976a,c) termed *interactional resistances,* while I have considered the patient's symptoms under such conditions to be an expression of an *interactional neurosis* (or psychosis) since they express inputs from both patient and therapist.

Threatened by this regression and by the fear that he had failed, the therapist spoke based on his own subjective feelings. He indicated to the patient that she seemed to be testing him to see if he really cared and would protect her, and he told her that she was upsetting the staff and himself by her behavior. It would appear that the patient was then able to mobilize her own adaptive resources once she had experienced the sense of helplessness that the therapist projectively identified into her, and that the result of the interaction had been the evocation of a proxy (Wangh 1962) in which the patient developed adaptive resources that were failing within the therapist. As a general principle, erroneous interventions contain efforts by the therapist to projectively identify into, and evoke proxies from, the patient.

Confirmation of the shared and unresolved erotic problems, and the failures of both patient and therapist to contain the sexual aspects of their interaction, may well lie in the patient's delayed menstrual period. I have postulated (1976a) that spillage into the somatic sphere occurs in the context of failures to contain. Unconscious fantasies of impregnation were evident to the therapist, but were not interpreted; instead, physiological confirmation of the absence of the pregnancy was effected. Similarly, there was a referral back to the original female therapist without an analysis of the underlying factors, including its role as a defense against the erotic elements of this interaction. Lastly, in the post-hospitalization interviews, the therapist provided the patient with birth control pills as a possible final uninterpreted means of denying his sexual fantasies toward her and of asking her to contain and deny her sexual fantasies toward him.

In summary then, we discover that the therapist's subjective use of empathy and intuition was basically an effort to avoid specific hostile and erotic feelings within his patient and himself. These so-called empathic responses had strong defensive components, and served as a means of managing disturbing unconscious fantasies and interactions through the creation of bastions and sectors of therapeutic misalliance that afforded both patient and therapist strong defensive backup and a modicum of unconscious hostile and erotic gratification. Nonetheless, embedded in these defensive and inappropriately gratifying uses of so-called empathy and intuition were islands of constructive efforts. It is characteristic to find contained in essentially unsound and countertransference-based interventions such nuclei of unconsciously helpful intentions. It is these latter that must be expanded if a therapist is to be appropriately gratified in his work.

The data indicate that the patient's improvement occurred not through insight and consequent structural change, but largely through the therapist's projective identifications into her of his own concerns about controls, and his own unresolved hostile and erotic counter-transferences. The patient responded to these evocations of proxies by developing ego and probably superego responses as a means of coping with these shared difficulties. Theoretically, such misalliance cures and evocations of proxy within the patient are likely to be relatively unstable, although it is possible that there could be structuralization of these changes and long-lasting symptom relief. However, we must be reminded that symptom alleviation through insightful interpretations is far less risky. This avenue would provide the patient the specific cognitive means for resolving her intrapsychic conflicts, and offer her positive introjective identifications with a nonanxious and truly helpful therapist.

OTHER COMMON PROBLEMS FOR THE BEGINNING PSYCHIATRIST

Unneeded modifications of the frame; framework cures. It is not uncommon for beginning and more experienced psychiatrists to repeatedly modify the framework of their therapeutic relationship and not specifically explore and interpret the repercussions of these measures (Langs 1975b). Here, such modifications ranged from Blank's physical examination of the patient, his viewing her breats, his use of adjunctive measures including cold packs, hypnosis, and medication, and his interviews with the husband. Elsewhere I have indicated that those modifications in the frame are often, however justified, a reflection of unmanaged countertransferences, and my previous discussion suggests that this thesis appears to be confirmed in Blank's material.

In addition, I will comment on one effort by the patient to effect what I have termed a *framework cure* at a moment of mounting anxiety in both participants—an intensification of the pathology of the bipersonal field (Langs 1976a). This occurred in the interview after the patient's first outside pass, one that was videotaped by the therapist—another modification in technique. It was evident that the patient at this time was experiencing an intensification of her own—and possibly the therapist's—erotic fantasies. When she expressed derivatives of these fantasies and perceptions in alluding to her relationship with her previous therapist, Blank indicated his incapacity to contain this material as it related to himself by intervening in regard to his predecessor. The patient responded by wondering if the therapist was angry with her. This seems to reflect a perception of the therapist's anxieties and his reactive anger in the fact of her erotic fantasies. It also expresses a mobilization of her own hostility in the face of her fears of her own erotic fantasies, as well as her responsive anger to the therapist's failure to understand her. The therapist then modified his neutrality and anonymity by denying the anger, and the patient responded by feeling insecure and with a crushing feeling of depression. She subsequently dissociated and then asked if the hour could be ended, to which the therapist readily agreed.

This interaction demonstrates some of the risks of the therapist's countertransference difficulties and of his failures to be truly empathic when it comes to specific erotic and hostile fantasies. The patient unconsciously perceives the therapist's difficulties and attempts to protect herself, experiencing a type of depression that is rather characteristic at such moments. It is just this type of danger that is involved in offering the patient a sector of misalliance in which erotic fantasies are to be split off. It appears that, when the patient recognized that neither she nor the therapist could contain or manage the shared erotic fantasies that were intensifying within the bipersonal field, the patient resorted to a termination of the session as a means of alleviating the mounting mutual anxiety. It is this that I have termed a *framework cure* (1976a) in order to designate a type of misalliance cure in which mounting intrapsychic conflict and anxiety is temporarily resolved through a modification in the framework of the therapeutic relationship. In addition, the material suggests that many modifications in technique undertaken by this therapist were designed, however rationalized, to afford a similar type of momentary symptom alleviation.

Distinguishing Transference and Nontransference

Another common problem suggested by Blank's presentation relates to the distinction between transference and nontransference components in the patient's responses to the therapist (Greenson 1972,

Greenson and Wexler 1969, Langs 1974, 1976a, b), and the therapist's defensive use of the concept of transference (Szasz 1963, Langs 1976a). Blank alludes several times to his relationship with the patient as interpersonal, without attempting to sort out the transference and nontransference components of his patient's relationship to him. He implies that the patient experienced a symbiotic and maternal transference with him, and there are allusions to transference-based anger experienced by the patient toward the therapist and to the patient's concern for the therapist's health that has been displaced from past relationships.

This material provides an opportunity to discuss certain common misuses of the term *transference*. Many therapists think of the patient's relationship to the therapist as transference, and fail to continuously search for and identify nontransference elements in this relationship and in the patient's communications, except in terms of the so-called real relationship between the patient and the therapist. For example, even though Blank acknowledges his own errors in technique, there is the repeated implication that the patient was essentially distorting her reactions to him and perceiving him primarily in terms of past relationships, rather than for the most part reacting to him validly and in keeping with the present interaction. Such a conception will not only lead to erroneous interventions and especially to failures to appreciate the patient's unconscious perceptiveness, but will also prevent the therapist from becoming aware of the extensive consequences of his countertransferences in his relationship with the patient. Often, the concept is used to blame the patient and to make him fully responsible for regressive episodes and other disturbances in the therapeutic interaction, and as a means of denying the therapist's contributions to such interludes.

A closer examination of the material indicates, for example, that the patient's dread of being overly attached to her therapist stemmed not only from her own pathological inner needs, but in a very major way from the therapist's communications to her—e.g., his decision to offer her long-term hospitalization, to refuse her visitors, to examine her physically and become otherwise involved with her, his insistence that he would not let her die, his threat to commit her should she wish to leave the hospital prematurely, his initial lingering and waiting for the patient to regress after his first interview, and finally his strongly protective stance. For this reason, an identification of the symbiotic component of the patient's relationship to the therapist would have to include a scrutiny for both transference and nontransference aspects, and include a full recognition of the therapist's contribution to the patient's reactions. It is for reasons such as this that I have advocated the use of the concept of the bipersonal field as a dyadic situation into which both the patient and therapist place pathological and nonpathological contributions (Langs 1976a). On this basis, any fantasy within the patient is examined for contributions from each participant, and transference and nontransference components are separated out; there is always an admixture of the two.

Blank's interventions, with their unconscious sexual and aggressive components, contributed to the patient's hostile and erotic fantasies as well. The patient's responses to them included both valid unconscious perceptions of these interventions as well as intrapsychic elaborations and distortions from within herself. On this basis, we might suspect that the patient's discussion of her love and marital wishes toward her previous therapist, which she was now attempting to renounce, contained not only erotic transference elements but also erotic nontransference components in that they related to unconscious perceptions and introjective identification of the therapist's sexual longings for the patient. The patient's efforts at renunciation appear to stem from her appreciation that the therapist was making attempts in this direction—a positive introjective identification—and her own needs for resolution as well. In this context, the therapist's failure to understand the patient's communications in that hour may have prompted the dissociated state within the patient because her unconscious perceptions of the therapist failed to indicate further resolution or a resurgence of his erotic countertransference.

My emphasis here, however, is on the need to separate transference from nontransference components in this patient's communications—and unconscious fantasies about, from unconscious perceptions of, the therapist. As I have indicated elsewhere (1976a,b) patients will, of course, elaborate their unconscious perceptions of the therapist in keeping with their intrapsychic needs and will always distort and color these perceptions, but this does not negate their valid core.

The constructive elements in countertransference-based interventions I will conclude my discussion with a consideration of the positive aspects of this therapeutic experience. My prior work (1976a) has indicated that in every technical error and every therapeutic misalliance, no matter how predominant the psychopathological contribution from each participant, there are nuclei of adaptive efforts and positive therapeutic intentions. This observation appears first in his overidentification with the patient and in his extraordinary protective efforts. The positive nucleus here is his determination to rescue the patient to seduce her in a positive sense that offers her a feeling of being attractive and a hope for life, and to redeem her from her fate of death. The patient apparently unconsciously perceived these aspects of the therapist's work, along with their more destructive components, when she responded to his initial frantic therapeutic efforts with expressions of both love and hate. She seems to have experienced the therapist's countertransference-based need for a symbiotic tie with her both positively and negatively, welcoming it one moment and dreading it the next. Even the therapist's decision not to allow the patient any visitors and to thereby totally possess her had within it a significant wish to protect and cure.

It should be noted, however, that each of these positive nuclei were surrounded by significant countertransference difficulties, and were often overshadowed by these elements. As a result, it seems likely that the therapeutic interaction was in constant danger of being overwhelmed by the therapist's countertransference-based contributions to it. It is these uncertain and tenuous but helpful nuclei that often sustain patients who are in treatment with therapists who avoid interpretations and the comprehension of the patient's unconscious fantasies and perceptions. The resultant therapeutic experience is not unlike that of the patient described: there is an erratic clinical course that is often difficult for the therapist to understand because he is obliterating some of the most significant contributions to these developments.

The slow and uneven mastery of countertransferences. In the case of Blank, we soon learn that the therapist's empathic responses—here referring to relatively uncontrolled and defensive uses of empathy—were being "dismantled by reason." The therapist began to recognize his wish to be the omnipotent rescuer and recognized some of his countertransference based anger and erotic feelings. Blank indicates his belief that his errors enabled the patient to expreience anger toward him and that this kept her within the bounds of reality and away from a dissociated state—his own communication that within his errors there was something useful for the patient. More and more the therapist was becoming aware of his blind spots and difficulties with the patient. Despite this, he still theatened her with commitment, thereby again expressing a countertransference difficulty within which was contained a need to protect the patient from her self-destructiveness. It may well be that in this way he was undoing something of his own unconscious hostility to the patient as well.

In the first session presented by Blank we see a further awareness of some aspects of his countertransference difficulties and an effort to struggle with them. The patient's dissociated state is then seen as the product of the bipersonal field and the therapist acknowledges his contribution to the patient's psychopathology, thereby implicitly indicating his awareness that this was an interactional syndrome (Langs 1976a).

While the therapist's need to deny both the patient's and his own erotic fantasies toward each other is prevalent in the first vignette, in the second vignette Blank begins to recognize that the patient is dealing with feelings toward him. While, as I noted earlier, this neophyte therapist had the characteristic difficulty of separating the transference and nontransference components of the patient's reactions toward him, and while he also continued to avoid her specific erotic and aggressive fantasies, we see a dramatic bit of personal growth in his capacity to explore the patient's relationship with him.

The patient apparently picks up the unconscious communications from the therapist that the therapeutic relationship should be explored in terms of dependency and she accordingly confines her efforts to this level. The avoided bastion concerning the analysis of the therapeutic relationship was modified, but only to a limited degree. At this juncture, instead of interpreting the specific unconscious fantasies and perceptions with which the patient was struggling in her relationship with him, Blank focuses on the issue of rescue fantasies and indicates to the patient that she must take care of herself. The latter responds both quizzically and with relief, after which she is left less depressed.

This session was seen as decisive in that the therapist was able to consciously verbalize aspects of the patient's fantasies toward him, however incompletely. He was also able to refute his wishes to rescue and protect her. Using his own native abilities (as Blank put it), he had unconsciously let the patient know that he was renouncing his symbiotic, erotic, and hostile countertransferences toward her, and that he expected her to mobilize her own resources. The patient's positive response could well be viewed as amounting to a countertransference cure (Barchilon 1958) in that she then lived out the therapist's wishes. It could also be seen as a transference cure (Oremland 1972) in that she responded favorably as a result of a transference-based wish to please the therapist. My own preference, however, is to term this a *misalliance cure* (Langs 1975a, 1976a) in that it occurs with a minimum amount of insight and with the unconscious participation of both patient and therapist. This cure utilizes projective identification inasmuch as the therapist placed some of his capacity to renounce into the patient and she introjected and benefited from it. In addition, it included an effort to evoke proxies of adequate functioning based not only on incorporative identifications of the therapist, but on the mobilization of adequate functioning in the patient.

However, the situation then deteriorated somewhat because neither patient nor therapist was able to resolve the specific sources of the disturbances in the therapeutic relationship. A compromise was worked out by returning the patient to a female therapist. The unsatisfactory aspects of this resolution are reflected in the patient's wish to burn her face so as to make herself ugly and affording her husband no cause to be jealous of other men's attention toward her. This is the patient's unconscious perception and fantasy of solving a sexual problem through manipulation.

In the face of mounting tension, the therapist then made what he terms an interpretation to her. We may note that this intervention reflects the common difficulty in conceptualizing the nature of an interpretation as a comment that should allude to the patient's unconscious fantasies and perceptions. The term is often used in a way that also fails to recognize that such an intervention grows out of the therapeutic interaction. As a result, so-called interpretations may contain much that comes from the therapist rather than the patient; the concept may be utilized as a cover for the former's countertransference difficulties.

Blank's comment comes across as a way of scolding the patient and as a means of further denying his countertransferences. As is characteristic of erroneous interventions, there is a projective identification into the patient of both the therapist's renunciation and his disturbance over her regressive behavior. The patient responds by mobilizing her own empathic capacities and more adequate ego functions, thereby apologizing and integrating. Later when Blank recognizes that his intervention probably was not an interpretation, he once again resorts to the appellation of empathy and takes pride in the honesty of what he communicated to the patient.

The post-hospitalization session reveals a continued need in the patient to support the therapist, whom she apparently saw as threatened and attached to her. In the context of the therapist's growing capacity to renounce his overinvolvement with her, he engages in an intellectualized discussion of the nature of psychotherapy and attempts to remind the patient that it should take place in a unique environment. This is an extremely important concept that the therapist seems to have intuitively arrived at; here, his *unconscious intuition* was mobilized in a most adaptive manner. He was of course alluding to the fact that without a unique environment with a specific framework, the patient's intrapsychic fantasies cannot unfold within the therapeutic relationship in a safe and analyzable manner (see Langs 1976a). The therapist was appealing to the patient to accept the necessary renunciations entailed in maintaining a secure framework for psychotherapy with adequate interpersonal boundaries. While Blank candidly acknowledges some of the pain that he is having in his work with the patient, he now offers symbolic substitutes for himself in suggesting that the patient internalize and take her psychotherapeutic work with her.

Here we see an effort to place a positive introject in the patient. While this is a relatively well-managed and controlled partly countertransference-based response, it nonetheless reveals disturbances within the therapist, who is having difficulty in working out his own separation from the patient; it reflects his need to keep a part of himself within her. The final offers of medication, however justified, also may reflect a need by the therapist to place parts of himself into the patient. It is extremely common for therapists to experience intense separation anxieties in terminating their patients, and many deviate unnecessarily at such moments in a countertransference-based effort to manage their own inner disturbance (Langs 1974,1975b).

The session ends with a mutual expression of sadness and appreciation, and then a final hour occurs in which all therapeutic work is avoided. The therapist expresses his great state of happiness and views himself as a father sending off his favorite daughter to college. In doing so, we see further indications of his growing capacities for sublimation and control: this fantasy is a far cry from his initial direct and possessive interventions. At the same time, in expressing his favoritism toward the patient and in offering her the birth control pills as an added measure of protection, not surprisingly we see possible continued reverberations of his erotic countertransference and his failures to completely master it.

In all, there is evidence of considerable growth in the therapist, and I strongly suspect that his patient's improvement derived in part from her unconscious recognition that she had been of help to this therapist. The therapist's capacity to *implicitly* accept and utilize the patient's unconscious therapeutic efforts toward him can have strong positive effects on the patient. The patient also introjectively identified with the improved functioning of the therapist and thereby was able to reinforce her own adaptive ego functioning.

We cannot help but feel a deep sense of empathic identification with the therapist's long struggle and ultimate conviction that he had been a help to this patient, and with his growing self-esteem and positive feelings about his therapeutic abilities. While in no way wishing to undermine this growing sense of security, it is also crucial that it be based on sound clinical observations and that the therapist develop an ability to appreciate the basis for his patient's clinical improvement. Failure to establish a validating process in this regard will lead to many puzzling disappointments and to the therapist's discouragement. It is for those reasons that I have stressed the contributions of misalliance cure and of the patient's therapeutic efforts toward the therapist, since there was ample reason to view this as part of the basis for this patient's improvement. There was little in the clinical data to indicate that her symptom resolution occurred on the basis of cognitive insights and secure positive introjective identifications based on the therapist's interpretive ability. The material, however, demonstrates the extent to which the patient can incorporate good aspects of the therapist in the face of may technical errors and actual failures of empathic and cognitive capacities.

The choice of insight-oriented or noninsightful *therapeutic work*. In concluding, we may note the manner in which this material has illuminated the motivations and conflicts of the beginning psychotherapist and the influences on his choice of insight-oriented versus noninsightful therapy. Having had the good fortune to be able to cure a patient through sublimated and unsublimated love may well encourage the therapist who believes that his interpretive interventions have contributed to this outcome to search further for such techniques. On the other hand, such a cure may prove frightening and confusing to the therapist and he may turn away from more insightful work. In addition, should the patient not respond favorably to this type of therapeutic endeavor, or should he or she quickly relapse, the anxiety and guilt evoked the therapist's countertransference difficulties may prompt him to move away from the intimate one-to-one therapeutic relationship involved in insight-oriented treatment.

Perhaps the most important aspect of this therapist's development is reflected in the indications of his capacity to benefit from the therapeutic efforts of, and interactions with, his patient, and his developing ability to modulate and control aspects of his countertransference difficulties. Movement in this direction can provide the therapist the strength necessary to face both his own inner fantasy life and that of his patient. Such progress can provide him the courage to move toward greater use of insight psychotherapy and to better handle his patient's unconscious fantasies and perceptions about himself. It becomes clear that the therapist's response to the therapeutic interaction and to the intense intrapsychic pressures that it creates for him is a crucial determinant in his future development. If he is unable to bear the stirrings, and the projections and projective identifications, effected by the patient's behaviors and associations, he will become more and more defensive and will endeavor to shut out both the patient and his inner awareness of himself. He will be loath to become a container for the patient's sick contents, since their specific aspects disturb him. He will also be prone to project and projectively identify his own difficulties into the patient, and to seek the therapeutic modalities that will justify these countertransference needs. On the other hand, a growing tolerance for the patient's unconscious fantasies and perceptions, and for his projective identifications, provides the strength through which the further development of an interest in analytically oriented psychotherapy can unfold.

Blank's presentation can profitably take every psychotherapist back to his earliest work. It provides us a humbling reminder of the anxiety and difficulty that each of us faced in our first therapeutic encounter, and in retrospect may help us to remember many countertransference difficulties that were mobilized in that first therapeutic experience. It gives us pause to assess the extent to which we have indeed mastered these early anxieties and countertransference difficulties, and helps us recognize that the struggle to maintain such mastery and to enhance it is part of our everyday therapeutic work.

In terms of empathy, there is a bit of Dr. Blank in every therapist, and we can share with him both the limitations of the resolution of his countertransference difficulties and the many moving indications of his budding efforts to master the problems facing every therapist. We are reminded of the human condition—the psychotherapist's condition—and of the fact that it is an eternal struggle to the last moment of which it best can be said that there are those who achieve relative mastery and there are those who are less fortunate.

NOTES

1. Throughout this paper, I will use the term *projective identification* to refer specifically to actual interactional efforts by a given subject to put into a particular object aspects of his own inner state, so as to externally manage them and to evoke adaptive responses for reintrojection. Projective identification is to be contrasted with projection in that the latter is essentially an intrapsychic mechanism, while the former is interactional; both range from primitive to sophisticated forms. The term *identification* is applied in an unusual manner in the term *projective identification;* it refers to the subject's continued attachment to—his identification with—the contents that he has externalized and to his efforts to evoke an identification in the object. *Introjective identification* refers to the complementary interactional process within the object who takes in contents that have been projectively identified into him by the subject, and who then processes these contents according to his own intrapsychic needs. *Containing functions* refers to the totality of these intaking processes and their inner "metabolization" by the object (see Langs 1976a for full details).

2. Because of the limitations in the data available, speculations are inevitable, and confirmation of hypotheses, though feasible within limits, will

be less elaborate and specific than possible in the clinical situation. In my discussion, I will bypass the therapist's possible use of noninterpretive efforts to develop the therapeutic alliance with his patient, and will focus instead on the basic contributions of valid interpretive work to creating an insight oriented alliance (see Langs 1976c). Many pertinent issues related to Blank's material will, of nexessity, be bypassed in this discussion.

3. Here I will not consider the important issues raised by the contributions of ward policy, supervisors, and other "cultural" pressures on Blank's decisions and techniques. These often serve as sanctions for countertransference-based expressions in the therapist. A consideration of their role is beyond the scope of this discussion, as is the issue of the accepted boundaries of the therapeutic relationship and the therapeutic setting under consideration as compared to the classically defined framework for psychoanalysis and psychoanalytic psychotherapy (for relevant explorations, see Langs 1973, 1975a,b, 1976a,b).

4. Here again it will be necessary to bypass a host of additional factors in this decision.

REFERENCES

Barchilon, J. (1958). On countertransference "cures." *Journal of the American Psychoanalytic Association* 6:222–236.

Beres, D., and Arlow, J. (1974). Fantasy and identification in empathy. *Psychoanalytic Quarterly* 43:26–50.

Bion, W.R. (1962). *Learning from Experience.* New York: Basic Books. Reprinted in W.R. Bion, *Seven Servants.* New York: Jason Aronson, 1977.

——— (1963). *Elements of Psycho-Analysis.* New York: Basic Books. Reprinted in W. R. Bion, *Seven Servants.* New York: Jason Aronson, 1977.

Blank, R. (1976). Empathy and intuition in becoming a psychiatrist: a case report. *International Journal of Psychoanalytic Psychotherapy* 5:237–252.

Fleming, J. (1961). What analytic work requires of an analyst: a job analysis. *Journal of the American Psychoanalytic Association* 9:719–729.

Greenson, R. (1966). That "impossible" profession. *Journal of the American Psychoanalytic Association* 14:9–27.

—— (1967). *The Technique and Practice of Psychoanalysis.* Vol. 1. New York: International Universities Press.

—— (1972). Beyond transference and interpretation. *International Journal of Psycho-Analysis* 53:213–217.

Greenson, R. and Wexler, M. (1969). The non-transference relationship in the psychoanalytic situation. *International Journal of Psycho-Analysis* 50:27–39.

Langs, R. (1973). *The Technique of Psychoanalytic Psychotherapy,* Vol. I. New York: Jason Aronson.

—— (1974). *The Technique of Psychoanalytic Psychotherapy,* Vol. II. New York: Jason Aronson.

—— (1975a). Therapeutic misalliances. *International Journal of Psychoanalytic Psychotherapy* 4:77–105. [Chapter 6, this volume]

—— (1975b). The therapeutic relationship and deviations in technique. *International Journal of Psychoanalytic Psychotherapy* 4:106–141. [Chapter 7, this volume]

—— (1976a). *The Bipersonal Field.* New York: Jason Aronson.

—— (1976b). The misalliance dimension in Freud's case histories. I. Dora. *International Journal of Psychoanalytic Psychotherapy* 5:301–317. [Chapter 8, this volume]

—— (1976c). *The Therapeutic Interaction.* 2 vols. New York: Jason Aronson.

Olinick, S. (1969). On empathy and regression in the service of other. *British Journal of Medical Psychology* 42:41–49.

Oremland, J. (1972). Transference cure and flight into health. *International Journal of Psychoanalytic Psychotherapy* 1(1):61–75.

Shapiro, T. (1974). The development and distortions of empathy. *Psychoanalytic Quarterly* 43:4–25.

Sharpe, E.F. (1930). The technique of psycho-analysis. *International Journal of Psycho-Analysis* 11:251–277.

Szasz, T. (1963). The concept of transference. *International Journal of Psycho-Analysis* 44:432–443.

Wangh, M. (1962). The "evocation of a proxy": a psychological maneuver, its use as a defense, its purposes and genesis. *Psychoanalytic Study of the Child* 17:451–472.

Chapter Thirteen

Transference Beyond Freud

(1978 [1977])

Transference, as is well known, is the central therapeutic vehicle for psychoanalysis. Similarly, its investigation is perhaps the single most fruitful means of clarifying the functioning of the human mind, especially the unconscious processes that prevail there. The discovery of transference proved crucial to the conception and elaboration of Freud's theory of the mind, and proved to be the wellspring for his insights into the nature of the psychoanalytic process—his basic clinical theory. Similarly, subsequent investigations of transference (here defined as the patient's total reactions to the analyst; see Langs, 1976b) have offered a major tool for refining our conception of the analytic interaction and for developing fresh insights into clinical processes.

In keeping with this tradition, the present paper will offer a discussion of transference and the related unconscious processes as developed by psychoanalysts after (and occasionally simultaneously with) Freud. Because I have elsewhere (Langs 1976b) presented a comprehensive survey of these writings and because of the necessity of providing a special focus for the present paper, I shall concentrate this discussion on what seems to be one of the most crucial elaborations of, and addenda to, Freud's writings in this area—the interplay between the patient's unconscious transference fantasies and external reality. This will lead to a special investigation of the interaction between patient and analyst.

In his relatively sparse clinical writings (see especially Breuer and Freud 1893–95, Freud, 1905, 1912a,b, 1913, 1914, 1915, 1920, 1940; see also Langs 1976b), Freud documented his discovery of transference and derived a series of implications for psychoanalytic technique from this monumental finding. In brief, Freud suggested that transference is based on unconscious fantasies and memories, and he saw it as the central distorting factor in the patient's relationship with the analyst. Displacement onto the analyst from early important figures was viewed as the central psychic mechanism, and interpretations of these displacements—and reconstructions—as the definitive vehicle of symptom resolution and cure. Resistances to the analysis of transference and the function of transference as a resistance were discovered, as was the crystallization of the transference neurosis. A special issue involved the patient's propensities to act out his unconscious transference fantasies, either directly with the analyst or with others; such behaviors, while meaningful, served mainly as a resistance to the recollection of the crucial memories on which the unconscious transference fantasies were based.

As an outgrowth of his consideration of the important problem of acting out, in a brief section of *Beyond the Pleasure Principle* Freud (1920) stressed his finding that the patient will actually revive earlier unwanted situations and painful emotions "in the transference"—i.e., in his relationship with the analyst—endeavoring to evoke reactions in the analyst comparable to those of earlier figures and to gratify his infantile fantasies and instinctual drive wishes. It is here, then, that the interactional dimensions of transference were first specifically recognized.

It is generally overlooked that Freud, despite his overriding intrapsychic focus, approached a second dimension of interaction in his final comments on transference in *An Outline of Psychoanalysis* (1940), a book written some years after Strachey's landmark comments (1934) on this subject, to which Freud did not directly refer. In this work, Freud noted that the analyst is placed by the patient in the role of his superego, and he stated that this provided a kind of aftereducation for the analysand that would modify the detrimental influences of his parents—so long as the analyst maintained his interpretive role. Here, although Freud did not specifically elaborate, the curative aspects of an unconscious component of the analytic interaction was defined, a process in which identification and introjective identification are the salient mechanisms.

On the whole, analysts who have investigated transference on the basis of Freud's key discoveries can be divided into two groups: first, those who elaborated upon the intrapsychic dimensions of transference, such as the nature of unconscious transference fantasies, the delineation of the transference neurosis, the mental mechanisms involved in transference, the classification of transference responses, the manifestations of transference in different diagnostic groups, and the nature of transference resistances; for these analysts, interpretations and reconstructions of unconscious transference fantasies and memories are seen as the central vehicle of analytic cure. The second group have tended to stress the nature of unconscious processes and mechanisms as they prevail within the analytic interaction, deriving their writings more from Strachey (1934) than from Freud (1940), and, with notable exceptions (see below), have been followers of Melanie Klein rather than classicists; these analysts, while acknowledging the importance of interpretation, have stressed the curative potential of projective and introjective identifications, especially identificatory processes within the patient derived from his relationship with the analyst. It is these studies, in which the influence of actuality and interaction on the patient's intrapsychic and unconscious processes is considered, that I shall now explore; remarkably, a careful consideration of reality factors will prove extremely illuminating in regard to unconscious mechanisms.

INITIAL INTERACTIONAL STUDIES

As early as 1909, Ferenczi stressed the role of introjection in the phenomenology of transference. He postulated that through introjection the neurotic takes into his ego large segments of the outer world, making them the object of his unconscious fantasies. There is a consistent search for persons who will serve as objects for introjection, a mechanism that operates unconsciously and which also involves self-taught attempts by the patient to cure himself.

It remained for Strachey (1934), in his investigation of the nature of the therapeutic action of psychoanalysis, to more fully delineate the role of both projection and introjection in the psychoanalytic situation. It was Strachey's main thesis that an introjection of the analyst into the patient's superego based on the former's actual traits and behaviors was basic to the resolution of the latter's symptoms—a thesis later extended by Rosenfeld (1972) to include modifications in the ego and in internal objects, good and bad parts of the self.

Strachey described what he termed *the neurotic vicious circle*, in which the patient projects an id impulse or superego fantasy and subsequently reintrojects it essentially unmodified from the external object. In order to break such a vicious circle, there must develop a benign circle based on positive introjections. Thus, in the analytic situation, the patient tends to make the analyst into an auxiliary superego onto whom he projects his introjected archaic objects, and from whom, as a new object, he in turn accepts introjects.

Significantly, this process is based on real and contemporary considerations that enable the patient to differentiate benign introjects from the analyst from the destructive introjects that comprise the original superego. Further, these modifications require first, that the analyst maintain a basically interpretive stance and in no way endeavor to behave like the patient's good or bad archaic objects—an effort that that will confirm the patient's inner fantasies rather than enabling him to modify them; and second, the use of "mutative interpretations" which are offered when the patient has actively invested id energies toward the analyst. Through such an intervention the analysand becomes aware that these energies are directed toward an archaic fantasied object and not toward a real one—the analyst as he is actually behaving.

These formulations indicate that Strachey viewed both interpretation and introjective identification as essential to the resolution of the patient's neurosis, although he did not attempt to distinguish their respective functions. However, Strachey called to our attention the importance of the actual object relationship with the analyst and of the nature of the unconscious interaction between analyst and analysand; he saw the actual behaviors of the analyst as crucial, since any correspondence to the patient's pathological inner objects would vitiate the effectiveness of his interpretive efforts. Here, then, we find that the resolution of a transference neurosis entails considerably more than the interpretation of unconscious fantasies. The realities of the analyst's demeanor, his adherence to the basic ground rules of the analytic situation, and his ability to tolerate and interpret fantasies directed toward him all play a vital role.

SOME LATER INTERACTIONAL STUDIES

Strachey's paper paved the way for many investigations of what we may now term *the interactional component of transference*. It generated a shift from thinking of transference solely as an intrapsychic phenomenon to a recognition of a strong interactional dimension. Ultimately, it led to the distinction of two basic forms of transference (Langs 1976a,b): classical transference, in which the primary mechanism is displacement from past figures onto the analyst; and interactional transference, in which the main mechanisms active in the analytic exchange are those of projective identification and introjective identification—with genetic factors playing a secondary role (Langs 1976a,b). Let us now turn more definitively to this latter form of transference.

While a number of Kleinian writers have discussed the role of projective identification (first defined by Klein in 1946) and introjective identification in the analytic interaction (see Langs 1976b), the most definitive presentations appear to have been those of Malin and Grotstein (1966), Segal (1967), and myself (1976a). Malin and Grotstein afforded projective identification a central role in the analytic interaction. They carefully defined the term, which has been a source of considerable confusion both because of the nature of the mechanisms involved and because the word *identification* is used in an unusual manner. Thus, these writers—and later both Segal and myself—suggested that transference can be viewed only in terms of a transference-countertransference interaction, since transference is inseparable from the analyst's reactions.

Malin and Grotstein defined transference as the patient's conscious and unconscious relation with the analyst based on all prior and current object relations, internal and external, beginning with the primary relationship with the breast-mother that has subsequently been internalized. In this context, projective identification is defined as an early primitive mechanism through which the infant splits off hidden bad internal parts, and omnipotently places them into the object, usually the mother. It is a mental mechanism that matures with later development, though its earliest expressions occur before self-object differentiation; its later forms occur within the context of clear object relatedness and constitute basic interactional efforts to place parts of one's inner self—structures, fantasies, and introjects—into others, so as to manage intrapsychic disturbances outside of oneself (see also Segal 1967). Thus, while projection is essentially an intrapsychic mechanism in which parts of the inner self are attributed to others without direct interactional pressures toward the object (see Langs 1976a,b), projective identification constitutes an actual interactional effort to psychologically place some aspects of one's inner self and contents into an external object.

We can see, then, that the term *identification* in projective identification refers both to an effort by the subject to evoke an identification in the object and to the fact that the subject remains identified with the projected parts that are placed into the object. It should be noted, however, that the object may or may not accept the projective identification and is free to process the contents and to reproject them into the subject according to his own intrapsychic needs and defenses. Recently (Langs 1976a,b), in an effort to clarify the concept, I suggested the term *interactional projection* for projective identification in order to stress the actualities involved.

Introjective identification is the complementary process through which the object incorporates into his own self-representation, self, and inner world the projective identifications of the subject. In the analytic situation, the Kleinians have stressed the role of the patient's projective identifications. I have attempted a more balanced view (1976a,b) which considers pathological projective identifications (in keeping with the function of any defense, this mechanism may take pathological and nonpathological forms) initiated by either the patient or the analyst—leading as a rule to a sequence of projective identification, introjective identification, reprojection, and reintrojection.

One other facet of this process has come under special scrutiny, especially by Bion (1962, 1963, 1965, 1970; see Grinberg et al. 1977, Langs 1976a,b)—that of the relationship between the container and the contained. This metaphor, initially developed by Bion, alludes to the contents that are projectively identified as the contained, while describing the object who incorporates these contents as the container. In the analytic interaction, one important function of the analyst is to contain the patient's pathological projective identifications, accepting them consciously into himself and metabolizing them into understanding and interpretations to the patient.

Failures in this process, especially those in which the analyst unconsciously introjects aspects of the patient's pathology and becomes involved in a noninsightful exchange of projective and introjective identifications, have been described by Grinberg (1962) as projective counteridentifications. Bion (1962) too has described disturbances in the containing function, such as compression and denudation—which deprives the contained contents of their meanings—and he has also suggested that pressures from the contained may lead to a disintegration of the container—and the reverse. Bion (1970) defined three types of links between the container and the contained: commensal, in which there is coexistence without mutual influence or in which two objects share a third for mutual benefit; symbiotic, in which one object depends on another for mutual benefit; and parasitic, in which envy plays a characteristic role and there is destruction of both objects. In a later work (Langs 1976a), I attempted to define clinically the manifestations of disturbances in containing functions, especially as they pertain to the countertransference difficulties of the analyst.

Returning to our focus on the subject of transference, these studies and the conceptions derived from them are relevant in a number of ways. First, they offer one means of recognizing the intensity with which unconscious transference fantasies and memories are expressed directly in the interaction with the analyst. Second, in regard to analytic technique, they call for an appreciation of the actualities of the unconscious interaction between patient and analyst, and for the need to interpret not only displacements from earlier figures, but also the nature of the actual interactional efforts by the patient toward the analyst in the current situation. Third, they indicate that in addition to his interpretative functions, the analyst has an important role as a container for the patient's projective identifications, and that the patient's experience of this actual containing capacity has a curative potential—in addition to the interpretations so derived. Fourth, they point to the danger of unconscious interactional vicious circles of projective identification, introjective identification, reprojection, and reintrojection. When this occurs on an unconscious level for both participants so that conscious insight is not achieved, it will also constitute actual interactional confirmation of the patient's inner pathology. In this respect, it is not only interpretive insight that leads to inner change for the patient, but the actual experience of the analyst's containing capacities and his ability not to be drawn into pathological vicious circles with the patient—an occurrence which only tends to confirm the patient's pathological inner mental life and to repeat in some derivative form the pathogenic behavior of earlier parental figures (see Racker 1968). Thus, these papers demonstrate the great influence of external realities, especially those within the analysis, on the patient's transference constellations, and point to the possibility of interactional modification of transference-related pathology.

CLASSICAL FREUDIAN STUDIES OF THE ANALYTIC INTERACTION

There has been a gradual but unmistakable trend among classical analysts toward recognizing interactional aspects of transference. A major contribution was offered by Loewald (1960), whose main thesis was that there is a resumption of ego development in analytic treatment which is contingent on the relationship the patient has with the new object—the analyst. The latter not only interprets transference distortions, but also implies aspects of undistorted reality which the patient grasps and subjects to the process of identification, especially in the context of such transference interpretations (see the earlier contribution by Strachey 1934). Loewald also suggested that the development of various adaptive ego functions within the patient is dependent upon his interaction with the analyst and can occur only in the favorable environment that becomes increasingly internalized by the analysand.

In two more recent papers (Loewald 1970, 1972), this author elaborated his basic position, viewing the analytic relationship as creating a matrix that provides a psychic field for the development of the patient. His stress was on interactional processes and the patient's internalization of such processes, rather than on external events and phenomena. Considerable emphasis was placed on the parallels between this interaction and the mother-infant matrix, and on the manner in which the patient ultimately differentiates himself out of this interactional field with the analyst into a separate psychic sector.

Another notable contribution was offered by Wangh (1962), who described a form of transference interaction which he termed *the evocations of a proxy,* in which the patient, mainly for purposes of unconscious defense, attempts to mobilize in the analyst libidinal and instinctual drive needs, threatening superego reactions, and a variety of self-experiences and ego functions that the patient himself does not wish to experience, utilize, or acknowledge, or that he is unable to generate—the analyst thereby serving as a proxy. This mechanism, which appears to be identical with certain forms of projective identification, is unconsciously designed to evoke adaptive responses in the analyst which the patient may then reintroject, strengthening his own adaptive resources and resolving his own intrapsychic conflicts. Wangh emphasized the extent to which these efforts constitute interactional pressures on the analyst, and he suggested that an unresolved symbiotic phase contributes significantly to its utilization. In addition to stressing the importance of interactional expressions of transference, Wangh's contribution highlighted the adaptive aspects of interactional projection, an element often overlooked by the Kleinian group.

Another avenue for the study of transference and interaction developed when analysts began to recognize important differences in the manifestations and management of unconscious transference fantasies in patients with various clinical diagnoses (see Sandler et al. 1973, Langs 1976b). There was a growing recognition that borderline and psychotic patients manifested relatively more primitive and action-oriented transference expressions than those seen with neurotics, and that patients with narcissistic pathology showed a distinctive and often difficult to handle form of transference (see also Kernberg 1975, 1976, Kohut 1971, 1972, 1977). Further, the more impaired the patient's ego functions, the greater his difficulty in managing these transference expressions and the more they were either strongly denied or intensely concentrated in wishes for direct gratification and interactional pressures on the analyst. Many aspects of transference were clarified through investigations of these relatively more primitive forms, and this is especially true of the interplay between transference and reality.

Among the many analysts who investigated this area, the work of Winnicott (1958, 1965), Searles (1965), Kernberg (1975, 1976), and Kohut (1971, 1972, 1977) is perhaps the most outstanding. Winnicott stressed the importance of the analysts's actual hold of the patient—his basic mode of relating, his management of the ground rules, his steadiness and reliability—in promoting both transference regression and analysis. In relatively nonneurotic patients there is a need to experience the analyst in a special way that thaws earlier environmental failures and provides a current opportunity for the resumption of the patient's arrested psychic development. Rather than reviving the memory of dependence, these patients respond to the analytic situation with actual dependence and rely on the analyst's ability to create a proper environmental setting. The setting therefore becomes an essential vehicle for the patient's progress, especially during the period of regressed dependence, and offers an opportunity for the patient's true self to meet current versions of early environmental failures and to modify the false self that had been previously developed in response to such failures.

In regard to transference, then, Winnicott stressed the central contribution of early failures in "good enough mothering" in creating pathological forms of transference which are then expressed directly in the analytic interaction. Further, while acknowledging the ultimate importance of interpretive efforts, Winnicott saw the actual good enough behavior of the analyst, especially in offering a secure hold for the analysand, as crucial to the resolution of these transference-based disturbances.

It becomes clear that those analysts who have afforded a significant role to the analytic interaction have done so in regard to both its role as a vehicle for the patient's transference expressions and the importance of the analyst's actual handling and management of these derivatives. While interpretation of unconscious transference fantasies, and especially of their direct expression in the analytic interaction, remains a sine qua non, considerable importance is placed on the actualities of the analyst: who he is; how he conducts himself; his basic relationship with the patient; his capacity to tolerate and introject the patient's interactional pressures and projective identifications; his ability to consciously metabolize them toward interpretation; his interactional failures based on countertransference problems; and his basic assets and limitations as a human being. Two fundamental but interrelated vehicles of conflict resolution, growth, and adaptation are thereby identified within the analytic experience; specific cognitive insights based on definitive interpretations, and ego-enhancing growth based on unconscious introjective identifications derived from the valid functioning of the analyst.

Searles (1958, 1959, 1965, 1972) offered an extensive series of studies of transference manifestations in schizophrenic patients which he felt were applicable to the study of transference in all patient populations. His basic approach was interactional, and he showed a special sensitivity to the role of reality as a precipitant for transference reactions, as an unconsciously incorporated element in transference manifestations, and as a factor in the actual interaction between patient and analyst. Thus Searles (1972) demonstrated the extent to which the patient's psychotic transference manifestations incorporate unconscious perceptions of the analyst, including aspects of the latter's own inner state of which he may himself be unaware. Technically, such a situation can be successfully analyzed and resolved only if there is an actual modification of the dissociated urges within the analyst—an important consideration that demonstrates how an appreciation of realities is vital both for the delineation of distorted and pathological unconscious fantasies and for their analytic resolution (see below).

Searles also described in considerable detail the patient's unconscious introjection of both pathological aspects of the analyst and those that are nonpathological and constructive. He paid considerable attention to the actual analytic interaction—*the therapeutic symbiosis,* as he termed it—and described a variety of pathological and nonpathological forms. For example, Searles (1959) identified a form of transference reenactment in which the schizophrenic patient creates in actuality a struggle in which either he or the analyst, or both, attempt to drive the other crazy. Throughout these considerations, Searles stressed the role of identificatory and projective processes, and conceptualized transference as essentially one component of a transference-countertransference interaction.

Along different lines, Sandler (1976) studied classical transference from an interactional vantage point. He suggested that on the basis of his unconscious transference fantasies the patient actually attempts to manipulate or prod the analyst into behaving in a particular way that is related to needs, gratifications, and defenses derived from early relationships—a restatement and elaboration of the early ideas of

Freud (1920). Sandler viewed these efforts as endeavors to actualize in some disguised way unconscious images and fantasies in the analytic interaction, and as a means of imposing both interactions and roles onto the analyst. He also suggested that the analyst should be open to controlled responses to these role evocations by adopting an attitude of free-floating responsiveness which would permit a sensitivity to these transference-based efforts, a controlled response in which mutual acting out does not occur, and the opportunity to interpret these endeavors. Many of these efforts are quite subtle and call for considerable sensitivity on the part of the analyst.

SOME RECENT APPROACHES TO THE INTERPLAY BETWEEN REALITY AND TRANSFERENCE

I will conclude this survey by presenting the highlights of two current approaches to selected dimensions of transference: investigations of the relationship between transference and reality, and explorations of transference as it unfolds within the interactional field with the analyst—the bipersonal field. The first group of studies has included investigations of both the reality antecedents of transference responses and their realistic consequences, especially in the interaction with the analyst. They have led to a stress on the clinical importance of distinguishing primarily transference-based reactions from those that are primarily nontransference-based; and they have led analysts to more clearly separate the distorted and valid components in the patient's responses to the analyst.

As for the reality precipitants of transference responses, recent investigations (see especially Searles 1965, Greenson 1971, 1972, and Langs, 1973a, b, 1974, 1975a,b,c, 1976a,b) have demonstrated that in addition to his neurotic functioning and transference responses, the analysand has a capacity for considerable nontransference-based and valid functioning within the analytic relationship. He is remarkably, though as a rule unconsciously, sensitive to and perceptive of the unconscious elements in the analyst's communications, including the latter's personality and character, his errors in interpreting, and his mismanagements of the ground rules. This capacity for unconscious perception is central to the analysand's nontransference reactions to the analyst in a manner that is comparable to the role of unconscious fantasies and memories in his transferences. However, these studies have also shown that the patient's unconscious perceptiveness and appropriate responses to the analyst's traumatizing behaviors, attitudes, and interventions will, as a rule, eventually extend into the transference realm because of subsequent distortions based on the patient's own pathological inner needs. Similarly, every essentially transference response is based on some reality precipitant and contains a kernel of valid perceptiveness and responsiveness within it.

In my own investigations of the specific stimuli for transference reactions (Langs 1973a, 1974, 1976a, b), I stressed the importance of the interactional approach to transference and commented especially on the need to distinguish traumatic-pathological attitudes and interventions by the analyst from those that are essentially constructive and nonpathological, however hurtful to the patient. Through such a distinction one can more carefully clarify the transference and nontransference components in the patient's associations and behaviors. Technically, in those situations where the analyst's behavior has been largely countertransference-based, rectification of the actual error in technique, modification of the underlying countertransference problem, and implicit acknowledgment of the patient's valid perceptions were seen as important components to the analyst's response to the patient—elements which are, on the whole, unnecessary when the analyst has not behaved traumatically and the patient's reaction is essentially founded on his own intrapsychic pathology.

In regard to the realistic consequences of transference-based communications and behaviors from the patient, it is striking that analysts were quite slow to discover the actual impact and consequences of such behaviors, especially on the analyst. While Freud (1915) had indeed commented that the patient's transference love may express a wish to destroy the analyst's authority, so long as transference was seen primarily as belonging to the realm of fantasy and as an illusion, and the analyst viewed primarily as a screen rather than an active participant in the analytic experience, there was little appreciation for the effects of transference expressions on the analyst.

Searles (1959, 1965) was among the first to recognize that at times, based on unconscious transference fantasies and memories, the analysand makes actual efforts to hurt the analyst—for example, by attempting to actually drive him crazy or to otherwise harm and threaten him. Searles also recognized that these transference-based repetitions of past pathogenic interactions contain within them the hope for an interpretive and nonparticipating response in the analyst, and therefore for the cure of the patient's neurosis or psychosis.

Remarkably, it was not until 1972 that Bird offered an initial specific discussion of actual harmful intentions by the patient toward his analyst. Bird pointed out that these efforts are more successful than is generally recognized. He suggested that transference-based resistances are often used as weapons against the analyst and constitute attacks upon him, as may stalemates and negative therapeutic reactions. He described the actual destructive elements in the patient's behavior that are designed to injure the analyst, noting that they are considerably more than mere mental respresentations of hostile fantasies, wishes, and reactions. Bird also indicated that it is essential to differentiate transference-based attacks on the analyst from retaliations on the analyst for his actual, often unconscious, attacks on the analysand.

Writing both before and after Bird, I attempted (1973b, 1974, 1976a,b) to delineate the destructive elements in both erotized and aggressivized—instinctualized—transferences, and to define various unconscious efforts by the patient to inappropriately seduce or attack the analyst based on his transference-based needs. Interactionally, I viewed these disruptive efforts as an attempt to create sectors of therapeutic misalliance. In contrast to the therapeutic alliance, which is designed toward insight and inner structural change, misalliances are designed to maintain and gratify the patient's neurosis, and to involve the analyst in a countertransference-based participation in such endeavors. I too stressed the patient's positive wishes to be analyzed and cured contained within these destructive efforts, and went on to elaborate upon the harmful elements in the patient's interactional projections or projective identifications—aspects that create intense stresses for the analyst.

It is a most revealing aspect of the history of the psychoanalytic study of transference—and more broadly, of the analytic relationship—that the last aspect of transference to be clearly defined entails the patient's unconscious efforts to help or cure his analyst. While there are, as a rule, noncountertransference contributions to such efforts, Little had as early as 1951 identified both the patient's great unconscious sensitivity to the analyst's difficulties and the analyand's offer of countertransference interpretations when these problems prevail.

In 1958, in the context of a study of the schizophrenic's vulnerability to his therapist's unconscious processes, Searles noted the possibility that the patient may respond with therapeutic efforts toward his therapist. These endeavors are based upon the patient's introjections of his therapist's problems and constitute unconscious efforts toward therapeutic help.

It was not, however, until 1975 that Searles wrote specifically and extensively on this subject—the patient as therapist to his analyst. Searles suggested that innate among man's most powerful endeavors is an essential psychotherapeutic striving toward others, beginning with the infant in his relationship with his mother. He further stated that the patient is ill because these strivings have been frustrated and unduly mixed with components of hate, envy, and competitiveness, and therefore repressed—thereby becoming an aspect of transference. Transference itself, in this context, is viewed as an expression of both the patient's illness and of unconscious attempts to cure the doctor. Involved here is a genuine concern about whether the analyst grows and thrives as a result of the patient's therapeutic ministrations to him, and the entire effort relies on the patient's unconscious sensitivity and introjection of flaws within the analyst.

My own investigations (1975, 1976a) further—and independently— confirmed and developed the observations and concepts offered by Searles. For example, I delineated the patient's unconscious perceptions of his therapist's errors (1973a, 1974), and defined efforts by the patient to help the therapist correct these errors and the underlying problems on which they are based. Among the means of effecting the cure of the therapist I identified the patient's *unconscious interpretations* to the analyst, indirectly communicated interventions that bear all the earmarks of interpretive work, though they are offered without the patient's awareness.

Interactionally, I stressed the extent to which the therapist's countertransference difficulties are expressed in both misinterventions and mismanagements of the frame, and how these constitute pathological efforts at projective identification by the analyst which the patient then, as a rule, introjects and metabolizes. Under these circumstances, the pathological introjects will blend into the inner disturbances within the patient—his transferences—and the consequent self-curative response is the equivalent of unconscious efforts to cure the analyst.

These investigations of the antecedents and consequences of transferences have demonstrated the importance of an interactional approach, and the extent to which transferences are indeed both influenced by and have an influence on reality. This realization is also implicit in the essentially interactional approaches to the analytic relationship to which I now turn.

A full interactional conception of transference requires a three-dimensional concept of the analytic situation itself, the field within which the analytic interaction occurs. In this way it is recognized that transferences are not isolated intrapsychic elements, but are in an open and continuous interaction with the influences from the surroundings, especially the analyst—countertransference in its broadest sense. Considerable understanding of transference and of the relevant analytic techniques have accrued through the work of such analysts as the Barangers (1966), who defined the bipersonal field of the analytic interaction (see also Langs 1976a), and Viderman (1974), who wrote of the analytic space.

In brief, the Barangers saw the bipersonal analytic situation as a basically asymmetrical field that is primarily two-person oriented, although triangular relationships are also introduced. The field is structured according to three configurations: the analytic contract; the nature of the manifest associations of the patient; and the unconscious fantasies of both patient and analyst that determine the emergence of this material, including their fantasies about the analytic situation itself and their concept of cure. The analyst, they stated, exerts a continuous influence on the patient's unconscious transference fantasies and their communication, since all such fantasies must be defined in terms of contributions from both participants—even where the patient is the preponderant contributor, as in transference. The bipersonal field concept therefore calls for a careful study of the ground rules since they define the field and its communicative properties (see Langs 1976a,b); any manifestation within the field, such as transference, must be investigated in terms of the properties of the entire situation and the contributions of both participants.

Interactionally, then, the analytic pair will tend to create within their relationship a repetition of their own unresolved neurotic pasts. In a properly structured bipersonal field, the pathological contributions from the patient will predominate; however, both the patient and analyst must be cured through interpretations. Insight thus becomes a process of comprehension of unconscious aspects of the field which reduces the pathology of the field and rescues the respective pathological parts—transferences—of each participant. Insight and interpretation (see also de Racker 1961) are interactional processes, and resistances which interfere with these curative efforts also have interactional dimensions. For example, the Barangers described "bastions," which are split-off aspects of the field created by both patient and analyst that divide the communication between the pair. This split-off sector will enclose the patient's transference resistances and the analyst's unconscious resistances and interfere with the communication between them; it can be modified only through resolution of the pathology of both participants. In this way, the concept of *transference neurosis* is supplemented by that of *interactional neurosis* (Langs 1976a), and that of *transference resistance* by that of *interactional resistance;* the second term in each pair pertains to the interactional components of the patient's disturbance and the relevant unconscious contributions of the analyst.

CONCLUDING COMMENTS

It is remarkable to discover that Freud had anticipated virtually every major area of study related to transference. Historically, in keeping with Freud's basically intrapsychic conception of transference, most early investigators offered elaborations of this dimension. By and large, classical psychoanalysts have maintained this intrapsychic focus, and while they have slowly developed a supplementary understanding of interactional influences and consequences that have a bearing on transferences, they still accord the interactional elements a secondary position. Despite this limitation, these analysts have shown a growing sensitivity to the interactional aspects of transference. Their approach calls for an adaptational-interactional approach to transference so that this important intrapsychic constellation is properly viewed within the totality of the external influences that help shape it.

It is the Kleinians who have most clearly stressed the influence of unconscious transference fantasies and memories on the immediate object relationship between the patient and his analyst, and who more sensitively defined a variety of basic transference-based interactional mechanisms, especially those of projective and introjective identification. One difficulty with the Kleinian approach has been its biased focus on the patient's transferences and pathological projective identifications to the relative exclusion of the analyst's pathological countertransferences and his own pathological projective identifications. While I have in this presentation focused on transference and thereby on the patient's pathological contributions to the analytic interaction, I have elsewhere (1976a,b) placed considerable emphasis on the need to recognize that in the actual analytic experience, to the extent that every analyst remains open to the influence of unresolved countertransference difficulties, he too may initiate important disruptive processes within both that interaction and his patient. A careful appraisal of the communications from the patient and of the inner state of the analyst, one that includes a search for both fantasied and realistic elements, is an essential part of the analyst's continuous therapeutic work. As I have described elsewhere (1976b), this calls for the ongoing use of the validating process, through which virtually every communication from the patient—as well as from the analyst—is assessed in depth. So long as we maintain our basic psychoanalytic methodology, with its stress on an extensive use of the validating process and on unconscious processes and communication, we can be assured of further refinements in our conception of transference and of a progressive broadening of our ideas concerning the patient-analyst relationship. Among the important consequences of such developments will be further refinements in analytic technique, and a deeper understanding of the essentials of human nature.

REFERENCES

Baranger, M., and Baranger, W. (1966). Insight in the analytic situation. In *Psychoanalysis in the Americas,* ed. Robert E. Litman, pp. 56–72. New York: International Universities Press.

Bion, W. R. (1962) *Learning from Experience.* New York: Basic Books. Reprinted in W. R. Bion, *Seven Servants.* New York: Jason Aronson, 1977.

———(1963).*Elements of Psycho-Analysis.* New York: Basic Books. Reprinted in W. R. Bion, *Seven Servants.* New York: Jason Aronson, 1977.

————(1965). *Transformations*. New York: Basic Books. Reprinted in W. R. Bion, *Seven Servants*. New York: Jason Aronson, 1977.

————(1970). *Attention and Interpretation*. London: Tavistock. Reprinted in W. R. Bion, *Seven Servants*. New York: Jason Aronson, 1977.

————(1977). *Seven Servants*. New York: Jason Aronson.

Bird, B. (1972). Notes on transference: universal phenomenon and the hardest part of analysis. *Journal of the American Psycho-Analytic Association* 20:267–301.

Breuer, J., and Freud, S. (1893–1895). Studies on hysteria. *Standard Edition* 2:255–305.

Ferenczi, S. (1909). Introjection and transference. In Sandor Ferenczi, *Sex and Psychoanalysis*. New York: Robert Bruner, 1950.

Freud, S. (1905). Fragment of an analysis of a case of hysteria. *Standard Edition* 7:3–122.

————(1912a). The dynamics of transference. *Standard Edition* 12:97–108.

————(1912b). Recommendations for physicians practicing psycho-analysis. *Standard Edition* 12:111–120.

————(1913). On beginning the treatment (further recommendations on the technique of psychoanalysis I). *Standard Edition* 12:121–144.

———— (1914). Remembering, repeating, and working-through (further recommendations on the technique of psycho-analysis II). *Standard Edition* 12:145–156.

———— (1915). Observations on transference-love (further recommendations on the technique of psycho-analysis III). *Standard Edition* 12:157–171.

———— (1920). Beyond the pleasure principle. *Standard Edition* 18:3–64.

———— (1940). The technique of psycho-analysis. From: An outline of psycho-analysis. *Standard Edition* 23:173–182.

Greenson, R. (1971). The "real" relationship between the patient and the psychoanalyst. In *The Unconscious Today*, ed. Mark Kanzer, pp. 213–232. New York: International Universities Press.

———— (1972). Beyond transference and interpretation. *International Journal of Psycho-Analysis* 53:213–217.

Grinberg, L. (1962). On a specific aspect of counter-transference due to the patient's projective identification. *International Journal of Psycho-Analysis* 43:436–440.

Grinberg, L., Sor, D., and deBianchedi, E. (1977). *Introduction to the Work of Bion*. New York: Jason Aronson.

Kernberg, O. (1975). *Borderline Conditions and Pathological Narcissism*. New York: Jason Aronson.

—— (1976). *Object Relations Theory and Clinical Psychoanalysis*. New York: Jason Aronson.

Kohut, H. (1971). *The Analysis of the Self*. New York: International Universities Press.

—— (1972). Thoughts on narcissism and narcissistic rage. *Psychoanalytic Study of the Child* 27:360–400.

—— (1977) *The Restoration of the Self*. New York: International Universities Press.

Langs, R. (1973a). The patient's view of the therapist: reality or fantasy? *International Journal of Psychoanalytic Psychotherapy* 2:411–431. [Chapter 4, this volume]

—— (1973b). *The Technique of Psychoanalytic Psychotherapy*, Vol. I. New York: Jason Aronson.

—— (1974). *The Technique of Psychoanalytic Psychotherapy, Vol. II*. New York: Jason Aronson.

—— (1976a). *The Bipersonal Field*. New York: Jason Aronson.

——(1976b). *The Therapeutic Interaction*. 2 vols. New York: Jason Aronson.

Little, M. (1951). Counter-transference and the patient's response to it. *International Journal of Psycho-Analysis* 32:32–40.

Loewald, H. (1960). The therapeutic action of psycho-analysis. *International Journal of Psycho-Analysis* 41:16–33.

—— (1970). Psychoanalytic theory and the psychoanalytic process. *Psychoanalytic Study of the Child* 25:45–68.

—— (1972). Freud's conceptions of the negative therapeutic reaction, with comments on instinct theory. *Journal of the American Psychoanalytic Association* 20:235–245.

Malin, A., and Grotstein, J. (1966). Projective identification in the therapeutic process. *International Journal of Psycho-Analysis* 47:26–31.

deRacker, G. (1961). On the formulation of the interpretation. *International Journal of Psycho-Analysis* 42:49–54.

Racker, H. (1968). *Transference and Countertransference*. London: Hogarth Press.

Rosenfeld, H. (1972). A critical appreciation of James Strachey's paper on the nature of the therapeutic action of psychoanalysis. *International Journal of Psycho-Analysis* 53:455–461.

Sandler, J. (1976). Countertransference and role-responsiveness. *International Review of Psycho-Analysis* 3:43–47.

Sandler, J., Dare, C., and Holder, A. (1973). *The Patient and the Analyst: The Basis of the Psychoanalytic Process.* New York: International Universities Press.

Searles, H. (1958). The schizophrenic's vulnerability to the therapist's unconscious processes. *Journal of Nervous and Mental Diseases* 127:247–262.

—— (1959). The effort to drive the other person crazy: an element in the aetiology and psychotherapy of schizophrenia. *British Journal of Medical Psychology* 32:1–18.

—— (1965). *Collected Papers on Schizophrenia and Related Subjects.* New York: International Universities Press.

—— (1972). The functions of the patient's realistic perceptions of the analyst in delusional transference. *British Journal of Medical Psychology* 45:1–18.

Segal, H. (1967). Melanie Klein's technique. *Psychoanalytic Forum* 2:197–211.

Strachey, J. (1934). The nature of the therapeutic action of psychoanalysis. *International Journal of Psycho-Analysis* 15:127–159.

Viderman, S. (1974). Interpretation in the analytic space. *International Review of Psycho-Analysis* 1:467–480.

Wangh, M. (1962). The "evocation of a proxy": a psychological maneuver, its use as a defense, its purposes and genesis. *Psychoanalytic Study of the Child* 17:451–469.

Winnicott, D.W. (1958). *Collected Papers.* London: Tavistock Publications.

—— (1965). *The Maturational Processes and the Facilitating Environment.* New York: International Universities Press.

Chapter Fourteen

Validation and the Framework of the Therapeutic Situation

(1978[1977])

As a psychoanalyst accrues experience as a therapist and teacher, he comes to recognize that his basic commitment to the clinical psychoanalytic and psychotherapeutic situations carries with it a number of peripheral important areas of interest and even concern. Thus, in addition to his basic responsibilities to his patients, the psychoanalyst may find himself embroiled in debates and constructive efforts in such areas as the social impact of emotional illness and the broader problem of the psychological dimensions of culture and society; the narrower field of the political and organizational structure both of psychoanalysis itself and of communication among psychoanalysts; and the basic clinical methodology of the psychoanalytic therapist and researcher. This kind of widening scope of the analyst's activities confronts him with situations in which his basic clinical methodology and expertise cannot guide or fulfill either his own needs or those with whom he deals on these "alien" grounds. He must then both face his limitations as a clinician in an unfamiliar field, and search for new and more appropriate guides and insights if he is to contribute meaningfully in these broader areas.

My own preference has been to work within the clinical psychoanalytic and psychotherapeutic situations, and to endeavor to broaden my understanding of these special, bipersonal fields. This has proven to be such a complex and challenging endeavor, and its mastery so elusive, that I have concentrated my efforts on documenting and validating clinically the ideas that I have derived from my own work with patients, and especially from my supervision of the work of others. Thus, while I fully recognize a responsibility for analysts to broaden their endeavors beyond the narrower clinical situation, my own struggles with clinical methodology and the comprehension of the therapeutic situation have made me wary of entering fields which would, of necessity, require new guidelines and techniques. For similar reasons, I have refrained from purely theoretical, hypothetical, or speculative discussions, even as they pertain to the clinical situation, viewing them as an almost impassable jungle despite my recognition that such free-wheeling, undisciplined, and even imaginative discussions could lead to the development of important concepts and issues that could lead ultimately to new hypotheses that could then be validated in the clinical situation.

Dr. Strupp's paper, "Suffering and Psychotherapy" (1978), raises important issues both at the clinical core of psychoanalysis and in regard to its wider purview. And while, as I have indicated, it would be my preference to deal with these problems through a shared investigation of relevant and definitive clinical data, since his own presentation is devoid of such material, I will respond in kind. Further, my comments must be highly personal and selective; Strupp's presentation raises so many basic controversies that it will be possible here to deal only with those that seem most pressing for current-day psychoanalysis.

There appear to be four major areas for discussion in response to the Strupp presentation. First and foremost, I am prompted to consider the nature of psychoanalytic methodology and especially the role of the validating process in the clinical analytic and psychotherapeutic situations. Without the establishment of a sound methodology there can be no meaningful discussion of psychoanalytic issues. Second, there is the problem of the nature and functions of the ground rules of the psychoanalytic and psychotherapeutic situations—the *framework*, as I prefer to term it (Langs 1976a,b). Here, too, it seems impossible to develop a discussion of specific ground rules without a full understanding of the overall role of the framework and its relevance to the therapeutic relationship and interaction. Third, we must consider again the basis for symptom relief during a therapeutic experience, and reassess current thinking in this area. And, finally, I was led to a number of thoughts regarding the role and influence of countertransference—used here in one special broad sense, to refer to all *pathological* elements within the psychoanalyst as expressed in any area of his professional functioning—on the investigation and understanding of these three major dimensions of the therapeutic situation.[1]

METHODOLOGY AND THE VALIDATING PROCESS

Were it not for an appreciation of the continuing influence of segments of individual and shared countertransference-based blind spots in all analysts, one might feel astonished at the neglect of psychoanalytic methodology and clinical validation. My own efforts to develop a bibliography in this area (1974, 1976b) revealed but five references, of which the summary of Brenner's (1955) panel presentation on the validation of psychoanalytic interpretations proved the most clinically relevant—despite the fact that the full paper has never been published. However, in two works of my own (1974, 1976b), I attempted first, a clinical study of validating and nonvalidating responses to the therapist's interventions, and second, a synthesis of the requisites in this regard, based on a study of the psychoanalytic literature and my own clinical experience. My focus was on confirmation within the clinical setting, and I omitted a consideration of the broader, and in some ways more difficult, issue of the valid presentation of psychoanalytic ideas in more theoretical presentations—although the former is clearly the more basic, and the latter a matter of more general scientific methodology, considerations for logic, a recognition of the nature of evidence, and the like.

It seems self-evident that we must have a psychoanalytic methodology if we are to generate sound psychoanalytic ideas. It is well known that psychoanalytic concepts and observations are open to the influence of distorting countertransferences within the observer, and because of this, psychoanalysis has a special need for a methodology that can be as free of such influences as humanly feasible. There is a need too for a constant awareness of possible countertransference-based effects and for a system of observation that can help in their detection.

In writing here of analytic methodology, my stress is not only on analytic research, but on the day-to-day work of the practicing analyst or therapist. The literature abounds with papers and discussions which manifest a total disregard for methodology, and which at times show an apparent neglect of logic and sensibility (see Langs 1976b; these generalizations, in terms of the critique being offered here, must be understood as impressions already documented in previous works and open to validation by the reader). Without belaboring the consequences of this trend, I would like to outline the basis for an essential clinical psychoanalytic methodology, stressing its function as a means of evaluating contributions to the literature (see Langs 1976a,b for similar presentations that have stressed the function of the validating process in the clinical situation itself).

As a basic minimum, every clinical contribution to the psychoanalytic literature should be founded upon the following validating process:

1. It should be based on a series of clinical observations drawn from the psychoanalytic or psychotherapeutic situations. It is preferable that these observations involve more than one patient; validating single case data are to be considered useful, but tentative.[2]

2. Within the clinical situation, the following validating sequence is essential: material from the patient, intervention by the therapist, validation from the patient—and, secondarily, from the therapist (see Langs 1973b, 1976b).

3. The formulations by the therapist should be developed primarily from the patient's associations and from his own intuitive, empathic, and other subjective responses. These elements will lead to silent hypotheses which should receive initial, tentative confirmation from the patient's ongoing associations before the therapist has intervened. With the coalescing of themes from the patient and indications of confirmation, the therapist then intervenes with a comment geared ultimately toward an interpretation. He is then silent and seeks further confirmation from his continued subjective reactions, and especially from the patient's subsequent associations.

4. Clinical validation should occur in two spheres: cognitive and interactional-identificatory. In regard to the first area, true confirma-

tion constitutes the revelation of previously repressed material which helps to reorganize the previous associations, sheds unforeseen light on the material, and provides truly original insights into the patient's current anxieties, conflicts, and inner mental life. In this sense, therefore, direct agreement (which is an aspect of *primary confirmation*—the patient's initial response to an intervention) in no way constitutes validation; similarly, direct disagreement does not represent nonconfirmation. The assessment of the extent of validation is based on the patient's *secondary confirmatory responses*, that is, his subsequent associations, which are viewed entirely in the context of the therapist's intervention. In this respect, it is also to be stressed that the patient's responses to interventions are not confined to the fantasy realm, but include unconscious perceptions and valid conscious, and especially unconscious, commentaries.

In the interactional-identificatory realm, derivatives of a positive introjective identification should appear in the material from the patient subsequent to a valid intervention. Such responses are based on an unconscious introjection of the therapist's valid functioning as reflected in his insightful interpretive efforts. Should these fail to appear or should derivatives of a negative introjective identification appear, nonconfirmation is suggested.

There are many facets of the validating process that cannot be considered in detail here (for a more complete discussion, see Langs 1976b). However, it should be understood that both the manner in which the therapist understands the patient's communications, as they form the basis for his intervention, and his way of listening for validation depend largely on his understanding of the implications of the patient's associations. As reflected in the literature and in clinical case presentations, there appear to be three levels on which the patient's associations can be organized: first, solely in terms of the *manifest content* of his communications. Here, the so-called therapeutic work is done within the confines of the patient's conscious feelings, thoughts, perceptions, fantasies, emotions and affects, and the like. Second, there is the development of what I term *Type One derivatives*. Here, the therapist acknowledges the presence and importance of derivatives of unconscious fantasies—and, I would add, perceptions and introjects—in the patient's associations, and recognizes that they form the intrapsychic basis for the patient's emotional disturbance—his maladaptive symptoms or characterological disorder; his psychopathology. However, Type One derivatives are confined to inferences made by a knowledgeable therapist from the manifest content of the patient's associations. They are implicit contents present in disguised form that are detected from a knowledge of the patient, of symbols and matters of representability, and of unconscious mechanisms including defenses and the like. They may be exemplified by a patient who talks about a teacher or another doctor; such an association is formulated as a disguised and displaced reference to the therapist. At this level, the patient's specific associations are understood as reflecting—both representing and concealing—the patient's unconscious contents in a fairly static, relatively nondynamic manner (see also Langs 1975a, 1976a,b).

The third level of conceptualizing the associations from the patient requires the organization of the material around an adaptive context (Langs 1973, 1976a,b)—the inner, or more usually outer, intrapsychically relevant stimulus for the patient's reactions and communications. Such an organization reveals *Type Two derivatives,* unconscious contents detectable only when ordered around the adaptive stimulus. Here, once the therapist identifies an adaptive context, all the patient's material is organized around it and is seen as reflecting a series of unconscious fantasies, memories, perceptions, and introjects, all mobilized by the adaptive stimulus. Type Two derivatives are therefore only truly comprehensible with the knowledge of the adaptive context; and conversely, it is the awareness of the adaptive context that enables the therapist to identify as derivatives of unconscious contents a wide range of manifest associations that would not otherwise be understood in this way. In clinical practice, the vast majority of the adaptive contexts that serve as organizers for Type Two derivative responses in the patient involve the therapist and therapeutic interaction, and their unconscious meanings fall into the realm of primarily transference (distorted) and nontransference (nondistorted) reactions. Further, by organizing the patient's associations around an adaptive context, the derivative responses of the patient take on dynamic and adaptive meaning. The patient's associations are viewed in the light of the ongoing therapeutic interaction, and, overall, his unconscious responses are not seen in terms of isolated unconscious fantasies or introjects—a view that leads to isolated and intellectualized interpretations of primitive and other mental contents—but are instead seen as an inherent part of the patient's adaptive reactions—an approach that leads to integrated and affectively meaningful interpretations of unconscious derivatives.

An example of a Type Two derivative can be seen when a patient associates to a teacher who had seemingly inappropriately kept the patient's child after school. In an adaptive context of the therapist's pending vacation, this association would be hypothesized to represent derivatives of an unconscious fantasy-wish to remain with the therapist, and possibly a fantasy of being punished for unconscious wishes to possess the therapist. In an adaptive context of a situation in which the therapist extended the patient's session, these associations would be suspected of representing an unconscious perception of the therapist's inappropriate need to detain and possess the patient. Subsequent associations are an essential means of clarifying and extending these formulations; in addition, the self-knowledge, capacity for knowing reality, and ability to comprehend the unconscious implications of the therapist's own interventions are also vital to the understanding of, and analytic work with, Type Two derivatives.

If we think of the validating process in terms of the level at which the material from the patient is formulated, we might suggest that those therapists who confine themselves to manifest contents are *not* dealing with unconscious processes and should *not* be considered as functioning as psychoanalytically oriented therapists. Their observations are not based on psychoanalytic methodology and their conclusions can have little bearing on psychoanalytic theory and practice. While more could be said in regard to such observations, I will not pursue the topic further here.

Formulations, interventions, and efforts at validation based on Type One derivatives appear to be the prevailing psychoanalytic methodology as reflected in the clinical literature to date. Such efforts are, however, quite limited in that they rely on the therapist's capacity to intuit unconscious communications and, especially, to identify derivatives related to the patient's interaction with himself (clinical observation suggests that this is in the area of the therapeutic relationship that most interpretations and efforts at validation, as they pertain to psychoanalytic hypotheses, take place). In general, more disguised derivatives may elude detection. Further, a concomitant of work with Type One derivatives is the concept of the patient's relationship to the therapist which stresses the transference component—the patient's unconscious fantasies about the therapist—and tends to neglect the patient's more valid unconscious perceptions of the therapist, based on the underlying meanings of interventions or failures to intervene.

Use of Type Two derivatives—and such work would embrace Type One derivatives and extend to comprehending additional material as well—provides the most sensitive barometer available to analytic therapists at this time. It requires that once an intervention is made—and I refer here both to interpretations and to management of the ground rules or frame—all of the material from the patient must be organized around that intervention, and considered as responsive unconscious perceptions and fantasies, nondistorted and distorted. Work on this level brings to the fore the extent to which the therapist must be aware of the unconscious implications of his interventions—his own unconscious communications to the patient—as a basis for his assessment of the patient's reactions to them. Such self-knowledge can be enriched by the further recognition that all of the communications from the patient take place along an interface that refers on the one side to the patient himself and on the other to the therapist—the *me-not-me interface* (Langs 1976a,b); thus, all of the material from the patient can be taken as a *running commentary* upon the behaviors of the therapist—again, in terms of both valid and distorted fantasies and perceptions (Klein 1952).

Basically, then, I would suggest that every meaningful clinical psychoanalytic hypothesis be validated through responses from patients that include confirmatory Type Two derivatives in the cognitive and interactional-identificatory spheres. I am well aware that little in the psychoanalytic literature would meet such criteria, but I would also suggest that many of the erroneous ideas that exist in the field today stem in part from a failure to utilize this methodology—an omission which in turn derives in large measure from the collective countertransference problems and blind spots of psychoanalysts and analytically oriented psychotherapists. Nonetheless, the use of such a methodology would afford the therapist a far broader understanding of the implications of his interpretations and management of the ground rules, and would yield validated insights that are considerably at variance with the conclusions reached by analysts who have made use of manifest content responses and Type One derivatives alone.

I will conclude this discussion with a brief comment on presentational methodology. My proposal includes the suggestion that theoretical and clinical papers be consistently founded on data derived from hypotheses validated through Type Two derivatives. Further, it suggests that discussions on any other basis are open to conceptual limitations and countertransference-based influences to a far greater degree than under the conditions proposed here; at best, they should be seen as the distillate of limited clinical experiences which have, for the moment, not embraced the full range of unconscious implications of the material presented by patients to their therapists. Discussions of this kind must be viewed as impressionistic, biased, extremely tentative, lacking in psychoanalytic methodology, and highly idiosyncratic. This does not suggest that psychoanalysis cannot benefit from nonvalidated speculations and from undisciplined efforts at creativity or debate; we must, however, maintain a perspective on such endeavors—their usefulness and limitations. Certainly, discussions at that level have a highly tentative and uncertain cast, and by no means can such free-floating ideas be taken as clinical facts or established data. At best, such papers offer speculations and highly tentative hypotheses for more careful study based on the kind of psychoanalytic methodology I have outlined here.

THE THERAPEUTIC RELATIONSHIP AND ITS FRAME

A consideration of the function of any particular ground rule of psychotherapy or psychoanalysis, should, as I hope to have established, be founded on observations in which a valid psychoanalytic methodology has prevailed, and which have yielded a full conceptualization of the nature and functions of these ground rules, which I term the *framework of the bipersonal field* (1975b,c, 1976a,b). My recent review and discussion of the psychoanalytic literature in this ares (Langs, 1976b) indicated that on the one hand, some apparently gifted analysts had been able to generate some remarkable insights into the role of the frame in the psychoanalytic situation, while on the other hand, virtually no psychoanalytic investigator had applied definitive psychoanalytic methodology to this subject. In addition, prior to my own investigations and effort at synthesis (1975c, 1976a,b), no analyst had attempted to integrate into a unified theory the quite diverse studies and commentaries on the ground rules of the psychoanalytic situation and the analytic pact. There is also considerable evidence of a strong bias among psychoanalysts in favor of alterations in these ground rules, without clinical substantiation of the validity of the maneuvers for the patient, and without in-depth investigations of the consequences of such deviations for both patient and analyst.

In brief, it was Freud (1912b, 1913, 1915, 1940) who first attempted a delineation of a set of ground rules for the psychoanalytic experience. In his basic papers on technique, he divided his attention between an investigation of transference and its vicissitudes (Freud 1912a, 1914, 1915), and the basic ground rules of analysis, extending his comments in the latter area in a brief discussion of the analytic pact in 1940. On this basis, I have more recently suggested the following fundamental ground rules for both psychoanalysis and psychoanalytically oriented psychotherapy (1973b, 1975c, 1976a,b): set fees, hours, and length and frequency of sessions; the fundamental rule of free association; the analyst's physician-like concern, anonymity, neutrality and the use of interventions geared toward interpretation; the one-to-one relationship with total confidentiality; the use of the couch or the face-to-face modality; the absence of physical contact and the restriction of communications between the participants to the prescribed confines of the analyst's consultation room.

In defining these ground rules, Freud stressed their importance in safeguarding the transference (see also Greenacre 1954, and Greenson 1967) so that the patient's transference neurosis or syndrome could unfold on its own terms—that is, in keeping with the patient's psychopathology rather than inappropriate intrusions from the analyst. It is evident that this implies a certain degree of deprivation and suffering for the patient, and the nongratification of his unconscious transference fantasies and wishes. However, this was in no way viewed as a *deliberate* effort to have the patient experience emotional pain, but as a necessary prerequisite for a more adaptive resolution of the patient's intrapsychic conflicts and other problems—one based on their insightful resolution, rather than through other less serviceable means. In keeping with efforts by analysts to understand the underlying basis for symptom resolution, it was the consensus that such transference gratifications, expressed largely through technical errors and inappropriate alterations in the ground rules, would gratify and reinforce the patient's psychopathology and its reflections in disruptive unconscious transference fantasies, and would preclude their understanding and inner resolution.

There are, once again, many facets to these considerations that bear discussion, but I will comment briefly on only one important side issue—namely, the nature of gratifications available to the patient in the psychoanalytic and psychotherapeutic situations. In my study of the literature (1976b),[4] I found considerable confusion in this regard. To offer a brief perspective: in a well-managed psychotherapeutic relationship, the patient is afforded a wide range of appropriate gratifications that stem from the very nature of the therapeutic relationship and the therapist's approach, and from the positive qualities of the holding environment that is created through the establishment of a well-defined bipersonal field. Such satisfactions as acceptance, attention, physician-like concern, nonretaliatory responses, the placing of the patient's therapeutic interests above all, the capacity to contain the patient's material and its disruptive qualities, the ability to manage the framework and to offer valid interpretations, the ultimate achievement of symptom resolution—and much more— provide the patient a variety of nonneurotic comforts and strength in the therapeutic experience.

However, it must also be recognized, first, that the analyst may behave in ways that interfere with such reasonable and necessary gratifications, and he may even be traumatizing and distinctly hurtful to the patient. Second, the patient himself, primarily for pathological reasons, will at times seek other, more inappropriate gratifications from the therapist—much as the therapist may inappropriately seek them from the patient; collusion in this regard is viewed as a sector of *therapeutic misalliance* (Langs 1975b, 1976a,b). There are therefore a wide range of pathological or inappropriate gratifications that may accrue to a patient through countertransference-based interventions by the therapist—a dimension I will discuss further when I consider the underlying basis for symptom alleviation. The failure by many psychoanalysts to clarify the distinction between appropriate and inappropriate gratifications for the patient has generated considerable confusion in the psychoanalytic literature and in clinical practice.

With this in mind, let me return to the framework of the therapeutic situation. It is most important to recognize that each component of the frame is essential to its total composition, and that an alteration in any element of the ground rules has extensive repercussions both in regard to the manner in which the patient experiences the therapist's hold and the therapist himself, as well as the nature and meanings of the communications from both participants to the therapeutic relationship (Langs 1976a,b).

There are, of course, many implications to this conceptualization. To be selective, I would suggest that proposals to modify any component of the framework must be considered in the context of its interaction with all other components of the frame and in terms of the overall functions of the total framework. Second, the therapist who proposes an alteration in the frame has the responsibility to validate his suggestion through extensive clinical observations in which full application of the validating process, as described above, is employed. In this respect, as I have previously indicated (1976b: chapter 16), the disruptive influence of any alteration in the frame complicates and contaminates the observational process, and calls for the use of special validating procedures.

To clarify I must briefly indicate the outcome of my investigations of the framework, both clinically and in respect to my survey of the literature (see especially 1975c, 1976a,b). As I have indicated above, the first conception of the ground rules viewed them as a series of basic tenets designed largely to insure the continuation of treatment, the unfolding of the so-called transference on the patient's terms, the exclusion of maladaptive symptom resolution, and, to some extent, the continuity of the analyst's income. Without tracing out subsequent developments in detail, it soon became evident that adherence to the ground rules tended to serve as a safeguard against the intrusion of the the analyst's countertransference-based needs into the therapeutic situation and that, in addition, it provided an opportunity for the patient to express a viable and analyzable transference syndrome, including the so-called transference illusion. Despite this consensus, analysts continued to advocate a variety of alterations in the frame for an enormous range of seeming necessities, failing almost without exception to validate their proposals in anything but loose anecdotal form, if that.

Milner (1952) very early offered a view of the frame through an analogy with the frame of a painting, as the relatively stable boundary that sets off the world within its confines from the remainder of reality, and creates the special conditions within—especially those that would permit the experience and expression of the transference illusion.

Winnicott (1958, 1965) took a different and quite unique approach, one that has to this day failed to receive the extensive recognition it deserves (for exceptions see Khan 1960, 1969a,b, 1972a,b, Modell 1976, and Langs 1976a,b). In essence, he suggested that the analyst's creation of the psychoanalytic situation through the delineation and maintenance of the ground rules offered the patient a special holding environment which provides him appropriate nurturance, ego support, and strength, so that he may have the capacity to undergo the necessary therapeutic regression that will permit the analysis of his inner problems.

Bleger (1967), basing his approach on Winnicott's fundamental ideas, offered a unique discussion of the psychoanalytic frame and stressed its contribution to the necessary therapeutic symbiosis (to borrow Searles's important concept; 1965) that is fundamental to the therapeutic and analytic relationships. Viderman (1974) saw the ground rules as defining the analytic space within which the analytic interaction occurs, and viewed the framework as essential to the unconscious implications of the patient's and the analyst's communications. He noted too that every patient attempts to modify this frame and to test out the analyst's management of it, doing so largely as part of an effort to avoid the experience of the regressive transference syndrome and its analysis.

In synthesizing these and many other observations related to the frame, and in extending these concepts based on my own clinical observations, I suggested (1975b,c, 1976a,b) that the frame does indeed have several crucial and interrelated functions in the analytic and therapeutic situation. First, it provides a basic therapeutic hold and milieu for the patient, thereby offering him a general enhancement of his ego functions and capacities. Second, its sets off a distinctive therapeutic field from the rest of reality and defines the special conditions of that field, both in regard to the nature of the communications from the two participants and the analyzability of the material from the patient. The establishment and maintenance of a secure frame ensures the patient that his communications will be treated as material for analysis, explored for their conscious and unconscious implications (fantasies and perceptions), handled without retaliation or inappropriate gratification, and ultimately interpreted to provide the patient specifically adaptive insights into his inner conflicts and problems, a process that secondarily and inherently generates ego strengthening introjects of the therapist by the patient.

Such conditions generate a trust of the therapist and a sense of safety that fosters the communication of the patient's unconscious fantasies, perceptions, introjects, conflicts, and the like, in a form that is truly analyzable, both in terms of inevitable resistances as well as core unconscious contents. They safeguard the patient from the intrusion of the analyst's countertransference-based communications, which not only contaminate the unfolding of his transference constellation, but also have extensive effects on the very nature of the patient's communications, his introjects from the analyst, and the overall conditions of the bipersonal field—the therapeutic situation—itself. The ramifications of the therapist's alternations of the frame are extensive and often constitute a vehicle for the expression of his unconscious countertransference fantasies, and typically entail the projective identification into the patient of aspects of the therapist's own pathological inner mental life. In general, alterations in the frame create a bipersonal field in which action, discharge, and evacuation predominate—even with respect to the participants' verbal communications; a secure frame promotes control, management, and the production by the patient of analyzable derivatives (symbolic language and the use of illusion), and constructive, insightful interpretations by the analyst.

In this context, the patient's inevitable testing of the analyst's management of the frame may be seen to entail, in part, a testing of the analyst's relationship with his own inner world and of his capacity to manage countertransference pressures—a point adumbrated by Little (1951). Failures to appropriately maintain the frame are experienced and introjected by the patient in terms of the therapist's pathology and its specific contents, and, while inappropriately gratifying on one level, they generate negative introjects and disruptions of communication and therapeutic work on another.

Patients are extremely sensitive to the least alteration of the frame, and even in those rare instances where the patient's needs, based on an emergency of suicidal or homicidal proportion, totally justify a deviation in the ground rules, the patient will experience intrusions on his autonomy and right to decide the course of his life, and will feel manipulated—in addition to the positive elements experienced under such conditions. Unneeded deviations in the frame, which, by these standards, are extremely common in psychoanalytic and psychotherapeutic practice, are typically experienced through negative introjects as efforts by the therapist or analyst to be inappropriately controlling, as an incursion upon the patient's autonomy, as a disrespect for the patient's capacities to manage, and as both seductive and hostile.

These hypotheses, or more precisely, clinical observations, may be readily validated by all therapists who wish to seek out such verification. It is in this respect that I return to the point I began to develop earlier: such validation is clearly influenced by the conditions of the bipersonal field, and becomes especially difficult when an alteration in the frame has already been effected. Under these conditions patients are typically mistrustful of their therapists, with valid cause, and quite perceptively, although on an unconscious level as a rule, they detect a variety of countertransference problems within the therapist. These responses are not primarily transference or matters of distorted fantasy, but entail the nondistorted perception and introjection of actual countertransference-based interventions— alterations in the frame that are not in the patient's best interest and which interfere with his pursuit of adaptive inner change.

In applying the validating process to alterations in the frame, the therapist must, when faced with a situation in which he has initiated or participated in a modification of a ground rule, consider all subsequent material from the patient in the light of the deviation. It is crucial too that the therapist recognize that his patient's responses will reflect valid unconscious perceptions and understanding of the implications of the altered frame, as well as distorted fantasies. It must also be recognized that once the framework has been modified the image of the analyst has been altered, a sense of mistrust prevails, and the patient experiences a realistic danger that additional inappropriate gratifications and noninterpretive interventions will be forthcoming. Under these conditions, there is an alteration in the communicative properties of the bipersonal field and in the associations from the patient. Derivative reactions to the altered frame will be well concealed, and massive defensiveness will at times prevail. Derivatives related to other adaptive contexts will either be unavailable or will not appear in analyzable form. At best, by organizing the relatively defended material around the adaptive context of the altered frame, the therapist will have available for interpretation limited derivative responses that contain the patient's unconscious perceptions and fantasies.

Further validation of the detrimental consequences of altering the frame and of the therapeutic functions of a secure frame becomes available once the therapist has recitifed an altered frame and no longer persists in the prevailing therapeutic misalliance (Langs 1975b,c, 1976a,b). If he then continues to listen to the patient's associations in the adaptive context of the altered and now rectified frame, he will discover previously repressed derivatives that reveal additional unconscious perceptions and fantasies pertinent to the situation. The restoration of the frame fosters a more positive introjection of the therapist, a renewed sense of trust, and a restoration of the appropriate communicative properties of a viable bipersonal field.

A third and far more fruitful, less damaging means of validating the positive functions of a secure frame can be utilized under circumstances in which a patient proposes an alteration of a ground rule—or the therapist silently considers such a modification. Here, under conditions which maintain the openness of communication and a viable therapeutic alliance based on the therapist's nonparticipation in the proposed deviation, the patient will quite freely communicate the derivatives of his unconscious perceptions and fantasies as they pertain to the proposed change in the ground rules. Such material consistently reveals, largely through Type Two derivatives, the negative and pathology-reinforcing qualities of all such proposed alterations in the frame.

It is largely under conditions in which this type of methodology and efforts at validation are not utilized that therapists take an approach in which they relatively freely alter the basic ground rules of analysis. In a remarkably consistent manner (Langs 1976a), patients will consciously accept such deviations, often with considerable enthusiasm, while the derivative material consistently reveals an unconscious appreciation of the detrimental consequences of the deviation, and a sense of hurt, rage, criticism, and the like. By not applying the validating process and by failing to attend to the associations and behaviors of the patient that follow an alteration in the frame in the context of the deviation, therapists have been able to ignore their extensive consequences in the reinforcement of the patient's pathology, regressions in his symptomatology, tendencies toward acting or living out, disturbances in the therapeutic alliance and in the communication between patient and therapist, and open disruptions in the treatment situation itself.

Nonetheless, as the literature bears out, many therapists endeavor to carry out some type of psychotherapeutic experience under conditions that deviate considerably from the ground rules that I have outlined. It is further apparent, though my own clinical observations indicate that such occurrences are far more infrequent than the literature would have us believe, that at times, under these conditions, patients experience symptom alleviation. It is therefore essential that we now conceptualize the factors in such responses. I will do so based on previous investigations into this very issue (Langs 1976a,b), making use of the concepts of *misalliance cure* and *framework cure* as explanatory hypotheses (see also Langs 1975b). To help us to understand this type of symptom alleviation, I will now briefly consider the problem of symptom modification.

THE BASIS OF SYMPTOM ALLEVIATION

Here too, we are faced with a vast topic with many facets, and I will, of necessity, be highly selective. Based on my own readings (and I have not reviewed the literature in this respect in any detail), it seems to me that despite the utilization of a wide range of treatment procedures, few psychoanalysts or therapists would dispute Freud's basic conception (1926) of psychopathology, as lucidly summarized and elaborated by Arlow (1963), and as extended by countless investigators of early developmental and so-called pregenital disorders; together, they constitute a series of hypotheses that enable us to take into account the entire gamut of psychopathology, from psychosis to neurosis (see also Langs 1973b: chapter 8).

In essence, a psychopathological syndrome is based on distorting unconscious fantasies, memories, perceptions, and introjects that prompt maladaptive responses to inner and outer stimuli that are inappropriate to the consensually validated nature of the realities of these stimuli. Such unconscious processes are, in general, relatively inaccessible to alteration through subsequent conscious experience; they continue to exert their influence from within until their nature is exposed and understood by the patient, in the context of a therapeutic or other experience that in addition provides inherently corrective introjects. In the psychotherapeutic situation, such introjects are feasible only when the therapist maintains the frame and his interpretive role, and they do not occur when he deviates or attempts to be deliberately good or, as it is erroneously termed, supportive (see Strachey 1934, and Langs 1973b: chapter 16, 1976a,b). Under all such deviant conditions, the therapist's effect on the patient's inner pathology will have relatively little influence on its unconscious core, and will have distinctive qualities of unpredictability and uncertainty.

With this as a necessarily terse central formulation, how do diverse therapeutic procedures lead to symptom alleviation? First, we can see that psychoanalysis or psychoanalytically oriented psychotherapy is designed to provide the patient a secure therapeutic hold and relationship, as well as a series of insights and inevitable introjects based on interpretations derived from the communications of the patient. This work relies especially on the interpretation of Type Two derivatives, often pertaining to the therapeutic relationship, that provide the patient specific adaptive responses and inner peace in the place of previous maladaptive reactions to his intrapsychic conflicts and pathological introjects.

I would stress here that the psychotherapeutic situation, established with a secure frame and therapeutic alliance, can in actuality provide some degree of relatively immediate symptom alleviation, often considerable, to the patient. Such relief in no way precludes further therapeutic efforts, since it is seldom total and cannot be founded on the specific resolution of inner pathology. However, my own clinical observations indicate that this is a not uncommon occurrence in analysis or therapy. It can be understood—and validated—in the basic terms offered here, as a response to a maternal-like hold created by the therapist without manipulation or deviation. Further, this type of symptom alleviation is nonspecific and is founded on the general ego strengthening that derives from a relationship with a therapist who is capable of managing his own inner problems and, therefore, of maintaining a secure frame and working interpretively with the patient—without intruding, to any significant extent, the expressions of his countertransference problems into the therapeutic relationship. These nonspecific effects in no way resolve the patient's intrapsychic pathology; such resolution can be achieved only through definitive interpretations of these unconscious processes and contents, their working through, and the development of adaptive inner solutions and behaviors.

A second major basis for symptom alleviation occurs under conditions quite different from those that prevail with a secure frame and an interpretive stance by the therapist. Here, the possibilities are legion and, as a rule, entail an endless variety of modifications of the framework, including a host of noninterpretive interventions by the therapist. Validated clinical studies of a sampling of such interactions (see especially Langs 1975b,c, 1976a) indicate that such interactions are quite vulnerable to the countertransference-based needs of the therapist and that the symptom alleviation derives from shared, usually pathological, defenses, inappropriate instinctual drive gratifications, and pathological superego sanctions.

For example, a therapist's deviant behavior—as measured by the model proposed earlier—may unconsciously communicate to, and be experienced by, the patient in terms of a reinforcement of the latter's pathological defenses; this may reach a point where there is temporary symptomatic relief. Along different lines, the therapist may inappropriately gratify a variety of unconscious transference wishes— pathological instinctual drive needs—which provide the patient momentary relief, because of both the direct gratification involved and the sanction of inappropriate needs implied when the therapist satisfies them. In a variety of ways, the therapist may intrude himself into the patient as a superego figure who permits acting or living out, a variety of inappropriate satisfactions, the reinforcement of pathological defenses, and the like; in these ways, the patient feels supported in his maladaptive efforts to resolve his inner turmoil, and thereby may momentarily experience an alleviation of his symptoms.

However, symptom relief achieved on this basis tends to be quite vulnerable to new traumas and to regression, and to the cessation of the relationship with the therapist. It tends to foster a search by the patient for outside persons who will continue to play the pathological role that has been developed by the therapist. It tends to fix pathological characterological patterns and to promote acting out, the use of pathological projective identifications, and the manipulation of others. For these and other reasons, such moments of relief tend to be temporary, unpredictable, and in need of pathological reinforcement from within the patient and in his relationships with others. It therefore carries with it a requisite for a variety of necessary conditions and a sense of uncertainty that is far less likely to occur when symptomatic change has been based on the insightful, adaptive inner resolution of the patient's psychopathology.

Using the best scientific methods available to them, analysts have identified a number of such noninsightful means of symptom alleviation. Freud (1913) was the first to propose that primarily on the basis of unconscious transference fantasies, the patient could temporarily feel well, effecting a "transference cure." This thesis was subsequently investigated and clarified by a number of analysts, especially Oremland (1972). This author also studied episodes of flight into health, in which the patient, largely out of fear of the therapist and treatment, mobilizes his defenses for an early symptomatic cure. Barchilon (1958) proposed the term *countertransference* for symtomatic relief that stemmed primarily from the therapist's unconscious communication of his countertransference-based wishes as they pressured the patient to get well, largely to please the therapist or to satisfy his unconscious pathological needs, rather than through any type of insightful endeavor.

More recently, I suggested (1975b, 1976a,b) that most noninsightful cures should be termed *misalliance cures*, to indicate the unconscious and collusive participation of both patient and therapist. Using clinical material, and applying the validating process, I demonstrated how such misalliances can provide temporary symptom relief through reinforcement of pathological defenses, through inappropriate gratifications of both patient and therapist, and through pathological superego sanctions by the therapist.

A specific form of misalliance cure occurs when symptom alleviation follows upon an alteration of the frame to which both patient and therapist are party. However, *framework cures* can be effected unilaterally by either participant, and their underlying basis encompasses a number of possibilities. Thus, an unneeded alteration in the frame may provide the patient relief from the anxiety engendered by a more therapeutic hold which, while it offers support, also creates the conditions for regression and for the awareness of his disturbed inner mental life. An unneeded deviation can also be the vehicle for inappropriate sanction, gratification, and reinforcement of defense. In some form, each such deviation creates conditions in therapy that are comparable to the patient's early pathogenic environment; creates a valid image of the therapist as someone who repeats the past traumatizing behaviors of the parents; and confirms the patient's pathological introjects and unconscious fantasies. Further, when an unnecessary deviation is initiated by the therapist, since it reflects a failure on his part to manage his countertransferences the patient may feel relieved through what might best be called a "nefarious comparison" between himself and the therapist. There are clear indications in the clinical material that I have observed in supervision that when the therapist unnecessaily modifies the frame and acts under the pressure of his countertransference-based needs, the patient perceives and introjects him as weak, vulnerable, unable to manage, and often as corrupt, corrupting, and otherwise demeaned. While such perceptions and introjects generate considerable disturbance in the patient, they may temporarily enable him to find symptomatic relief through the belief that he is healthier or more stable than the therapist and somewhat better able to manage his inner problems. In addition, these perceptions and introjects create a very threatening experience of the therapist which can also prompt symptom relief as one means of escaping the dangerous therapist.

It is not my intention here to attempt to fully delineate the specific basis for symptom alleviation in various noninterpretive treatment situations. Nor have I attempted to catalogue all the possible means through which such noninsightful symptomatic changes can occur. I have merely endeavored to offer a *model* through which these problems can be approached and understood, one that needs considerable specific psychoanalytic study with careful use of the validating process. Further, it is not my wish to engage in polemics as to the best means of symptom relief for the patient. There are some patients—and many therapists—who are terrified of a secure hold and of a therapeutic regression; with these patients, at least initially, some small measure of noninterpretive relief may prove necessary, even if preliminary to more insightful work. However, such patients are actually quite rare, tend to fall toward the psychotic end of the psychopathological continuum, and must be distinguished from other patients with similar pathology who have the ego strength and inclination to do such work. By far the vast majority of patients, despite efforts at testing the frame and, at times, conscious protest, unconsciously welcome the unique opportunity to change from within which psychoanalysis or psychoanalytic psychotherapy offers; they show a great unconscious sensitivity to, and lack of appreciation for, a therapist who does not maintain the frame and offer interpretive interventions.

In addition, I have already garnered some evidence (1974, 1975a,b,c, 1976a) that indicates that adaptive inner change is not only feasible in almost all well-run psychoanalytic psychotherapies, but also offers the patient a relatively stable and lasting means of symptom resolution. By contrast, while occasional noninterpretive and noninsightful periods of symptom relief may persist, they tend to entail the maintenance of maladaptive patterns and relationships, and to leave the patient ill prepared for new stresses and tribulations. I therefore see no reason whatever to work noninterpretively with patients, to inappropriately gratify countertransference-based needs at their expense, to deliberately place negative and disruptive introjects into them, or to reinforce aspects of their psychopathology in the hope of symptom alleviation—especially when it proves far more gratifying for both patient and therapist to work within a secure frame and to generate specific insights and concomitant positive introjects based on validated interpretations.

THE ROLE OF COUNTERTRANSFERENCE

In the course of the foregoing discussion, I have made repeated references to the role of countertransference-based needs as a factor in distorted views of the therapeutic interaction, the nature and functions of the framework, and the use of deviations in technique. It is my belief, based largely on my personal experiences, my observations of students, my understanding of the material from patients as it constitutes, in part, an unconscious commentary on the therapist's countertransferences, and my reading of the literature, that countertransference—far more than any other factor—is the key to misconceptions in the views of those who debate the issues of psychoanalysis. I shall therefore conclude this paper with a few comments in this area, remarks which cannot be validated through the psychoanalytic methodology described earlier, except insofar as individual therapists look to themselves.

As Racker (1957) and many others have indicated, no analyst is ever entirely free of countertransference influences. Further, there is a tendency within each training analyst to unconsciously pass on to his analysands his own countertransference difficulties and blind spots. As a result, our field is open to shared countertransference difficulties and blind spots, and I would suggest that the history of psychoanalytic understanding, beginning with Freud, can be described, on one level, as the resolution of shared and individual countertransference influences.

I would also propose that it is countertransference, and not transference—as suggested by Freud (1905) and Bird (1972), among others—that is the hardest part of the analysis. It is in the area of countertransference that the analyst is most vulnerable, most narcissistically invested, most likely to be out of touch, and least inclined to undertake efforts at validation. While it is true that many analysts conscientiously undertake what Glover (1955) described as the analyst's necessary analytic toilet, and maintain a consistent vigilence for countertransference difficulties, the means through which such endeavors should be effected have received far less than the full discussion they deserve (see Langs 1976b).

In addition to consistent efforts at self-scrutiny and a preparedness to explore every unusual experience, impulse to act, or wish to deviate, the therapist must also continuously monitor the patient's associations for valid unconscious perceptions and introjections of his own—the therapist's—pathological fantasies, memories, and introjects, and their expression in the therapeutic interaction. Such efforts, however necessary, are wearing, and lapses are quite common. In addition, some therapists soon set aside or make sporadic use of such endeavors, and gradually ignore the possibility of countertransference-based factors in many facets of their work, failing to take them into consistent account when considering material from the patient. This attitude is even more pervasive once the therapist or analyst is removed from the therapeutic situation itself and turns, for example, to the writing of papers, and to clinical and theoretical discussions with his colleagues.

Much of this is illustrated in the attitude of students, clinicians, and writers who have considered the framework of the psychoanalytic and psychotherapeutic situations. There is extensive evidence for an inherent human need among therapists and analysts for inappropriate gratifications in interactions with their patients, whether this is considered in terms of wishes for fusion as described by Tarachow (1962), fear of aloneness, fear of separation and individuation, fear of separation and death, fear of the irrational, or unresolved needs for inappropriate instinctual drive satisfactions. Despite such urges, because of their commitment to their work and to their patients, analysts have struggled against these inappropriate needs from the beginning. They have, however, focused the vast majority of these endeavors on their interpretive work, to the point of recognizing a variety of countertransference factors in erroneous interventions— although they have done so only recently and in limited ways (see Langs 1976b).

On the other hand, to a large extent, the management of the framework has been separated from considerations of countertransference influence, and the literature on deviations in technique suggests that this has been an area of unconscious, countertransference-based collusion for many analysts, in that deviations in technique generally have been accepted without validation and without exploration of possible countertransference-based influence (for exceptions to this trend, see Langs 1975b, 1976a,b). In this context, it is well to note that a secure frame offers both support and the potential for anxiety to therapist and patient alike. A stable frame provides ego support in the form of secured boundaries, a well-defined therapeutic field, a set of relatively defined certainties for the therapeutic interaction, the outline of relatively well-defined roles, and the like. The patient himself holds the therapist to some extent, unconsciously offering support, stability, and other positive inputs from time to time.

On the other hand, a stable frame contributes to the conditions under which the patient will regress and expose primitive mental contents to the therapist, and especially relatively primitive instinctual drive wishes and needs that are directed toward the therapist himself. These expressions can evoke anxiety in the therapist, who has the responsibility to experience, contain, and metabolize them toward interpretation. However, the influence of such vectors and introjected contents can be quite disturbing for the therapist, since they tend to stir up his own unresolved vulnerabilities, pathological unconscious fantasies and introjects, and residual inner mental turmoil. In addition, the secure frame prompts a limited regression in the therapist which exposes him to potentially disruptive inner mental contents and a temporary loss of self (ego)—boundaries that are usually more repressed or well secured, and under control; this too is experienced on some level by the therapist as anxiety provoking and dangerous. It appears that these latter qualities of a secure frame, while generating potentially therapeutically useful though somewhat disruptive inner experiences for the therapist, have evoked anxieties and disturbances within many therapists that have been handled by modifications in the framework that serve as framework cures for the therapist, rather than the therapeutic needs of the patient. It seems evident that insightful mastery of these tensions by a therapist who maintains the frame and metabolizes his inner experiences for understanding both his patient and himself is a far more adaptive and serviceable means of resolving these inevitable stresses.

More broadly, we must recognize that psychoanalytic observations and discussions are also especially vulnerable to countertransference-based influences. We must resort to those safeguards available to us: the careful use of psychoanalytic methodology and of an in-depth validating process, techniques that should be revised and improved as further psychoanalytic understanding permits; the personal psychoanalysis of the psychoanalytic investigator, a process which must itself be scrutinized for countertransference and misalliance, and for the perpetuation of collective countertransference-based misconceptions—a difficult endeavor, to be sure, and one that deserves extensive separate discussion; and the unwavering determination to search for the unconscious factors in all treatment procedures. While it is true that, empirically, the surface phenomenon of symptom alleviation must be the hallmark of an effective therapeutic process, I hope I have made it evident that we must also have a commitment to investigate the underlying basis and durability of these symptomatic changes and to fully assess their meanings and implications for both patient and therapist. I therefore conclude this discussion with a brief for greater self-knowledge in therapists, for constant vigilance for countertransference-based influences in all their endeavmrs, for the use and impcovement of psychoanalytic methodology, and for meaningful dialogue undertakn with these principles as their foundation.

NOTES

1. To immediately set aside one issue raised by Strupp's presentation, I will refer here quite broadly to the therapeutic situation. I will make no effort to distinguish between the psychoanalytic and psychotherapeutic situations as they pertain to the topics I will discuss, largely because my own clinical

observations support the position that almost all the basic concepts, hypotheses, and principles to be developed in this paper apply with equal validity to both.

2. I will not here deal with valid sources of psychoanalytic formulations that lie outside the clinical situation, such as direct child observations, cultural studies, and the like.

3. In this discussion I will concentrate on the framework, and will offer relatively few comments regarding the nature of the therapeutic relationship and interaction; for extensive discussions of this latter area, see Langs (1976a,b).

4. I openly express my trepidations in commenting on an inpressionistic paper with surmises of my own. I therefore stress again that I have elsewhere fully documented the basis for my descriptions here of the literature, and the clinical data on which I have established some distinctive hypotheses that are at a variance with, or extensions of, prevailing conceptions (see Langs 1973a,b, 1974, 1975a,b,c, 1976a,b). In addition, I wish to apologize for the extensive use that I am making of my own work, justifying this approach, first, out of necessity to respond to Strupp's presentation as tersely as possible; and, second, because I have in my prior writings, especially in *The Therapeutic Interaction* (1976b), fully and directly acknowledged the contributions of other analysts to my own thinking and do not have sufficient space to document that aspect here.

REFERENCES

Arlow, J. (1963). Conflict, regression, and symptom formation. *International Journal of Psycho-Analysis* 44:12–22.

Brenner, C. (1955). The validation of psychoanalytic interpretations. Reported by J. Marmor, *Journal of the American Psychoanalytic Association* 3:496–497.

Barchilon, J. (1958). On countertransference "cures." *Journal of the American Psychoanalytic Association* 6:222–236.

Bleger, J. (1967. Psycho-analysis of the psychoanalytic frame. *International Journal of Psycho-Analysis* 48:511–519.

Freud, S. (1905). Fragment of an analysis of a case of hysteria. *Standard Edition* 7:3–22.

——— (1912a). The dynamics of transference. *Standard Edition* 12:97–108.

—— (1912b). Recommendations to physicians practicing psycho-analysis. *Standard Edition* 12:111–120.

—— (1913). On beginning the treatment (further recommendations on the technique of psycho-analysis I). *Standard Edition* 12:121–144.

—— (1914). Remembering, repeating, and working-through (further recommendations on the technique of psycho-analysis II). *Standard Edition* 12:145–156.

—— (1915). Observations on transference-love (further recommen-dations on the technique of psychonalysis III). *Standard Edition* 12:157–171.

—— (1926). Inhibitions, symptoms, and anxiety. *Standard Edition* 20:77–175.

—— (1940). An outline of psycho-analysis. *Standard Edition* 23:172–182.

Glover, E. (1955). *The Technique of Psycho-Analysis.* New York: International Universities Press.

Greenacre, P. (1954). The role of transference. *Journal of the American Psychoanalytic Association* 2:671–684.

Greenson, R. (1967). *The Technique and Practice of Psychoanalysis, Vol I.* New York: International Universities Press.

Khan, M. (1960). Regression and integration in the analytic setting. *International Journal of Psycho-Analysis* 41:130–146.

—— (1969a). On the clinical provision of frustrations, recognitions, and failures in the analytic situation: an essay on Michael Balint's researches on the theory of psychoanalytic technique. *International Journal of Psycho-Analysis* 50:237–248.

—— (1969b). Vicissitudes of being, knowing, and experiencing in the therapeutic situation. *British Journal of Medical Psychology* 42:383–393.

—— (1972a). Dread of surrender to resourceless dependence in the analytic situation. *International Journal of Psycho-Analysis* 53:225–230.

—— (1972b). The finding and becoming of self. *International Journal of Psychoanalytic Psychotherapy* 1(1):97–111.

Klein, M. (1952). The origins of transference. *International Journal of Psycho-Analysis* 33:433–438.

Langs, R. (1973a). The patient's view of the therapist: reality or fantasy? *International Journal of Psychoanalytic Psychotherapy*, 2:411-431. [Chapter 4, this volume]

—— (1973b). *The Technique of Psychoanalytic Psychotherapy*, *Vol. I*. New York: Jason Aronson.

—— (1974). *The Technique of Psychoanalytic Psychotherapy*, *Vol II*. New York: Jason Aronson.

—— (1975a). The patient's unconscious perception of the therapist's errors. In *Tactics and Techniques in Psychoanalytic Therapy*, *Vol. II: Countertransference*, ed. P. Giovacchini. New York: Jason Aronson. [Chapter 5, this volume]

—— (1975b). Therapeutic misalliances. *International Journal of Psychoanalytic Psychotherapy* 4:77-105. [Chapter 6, this volume]

—— (1975c). The therapeutic relationship and deviations in technique. *International Journal of Psychoanalytic Psychotherapy* 4:106-141. [Chapter 7, this volume]

—— (1976a). *The Bipersonal Field*. New York: Jason Aronson.

——(1976b). *The Therapeutic Interaction*. 2 Vols. New York: Jason Aronson.

Little M. (1951). Countertransference and the patient's response to it. *International Journal of Psycho-Analysis* 32:32-40.

Milner, M. (1952), Aspects of symbolism in comprehension of the not-self. *International Journal of Psycho-Analysis* 33:181-195.

Modell, A. (1976). "The holding environment" and the therapeutic action of psychoanalysis. *Journal of the American Psychoanalytic Association* 24:285-308.

Oremland, J. (1972). Transference cure and flight into health. *International Journal of Psychoanalytic Psychotherapy* 1(1):61-75.

Strachey, J. (1934). The nature of the therapeutic action of *Psychoanalytic Quarterly* 26:303-357.

Searles, H. (1965). *Collected Papers on Schizophrenia and Related Subjects*. New York: International Universities Press.

Strachey, J. (1934), the nature of the therapeutic action of psychoanalysis. *International Journal of Psycho-Analysis*, 15:127-159.

Strupp, H. (1978). Suffering and psychotherapy. *Contemporary Psychoanalysis* 14:73-97.

Tarachow, S. (1962). Interpretation and reality in psycho-therapy. *International Journal of Psycho-Analysis* 43:377–387.

Viderman, S. (1974). Interpretation in the analytic space. *International Review of Psycho-Analysis* 1:467–480.

Winnicott, D. (1958). *Collected Papers.* London: Tavistock.

———(1965). *The Maturational Process and the Facilitating Environment.* New York: International Universities Press.

Chapter Fifteen

Some Communicative Properties of the Bipersonal Field

(1978 [1977])

When a psychoanalytic investigator is struggling to develop a new perspective on disquieting clinical observations, there is often a most constructive interplay between his ill-formed ideas, his ongoing clinical observations, and his reading of the literature. Preoccupied with clinical data that momentarily defy organization, he searches for the *selected fact* (Bion 1962) that would synthesize and properly link together his still divergent conceptions and observations. The analyst may actively sift others' contributions in the hopes of discovering clues to the missing integrating elements. More often than not, however, such active efforts do not bear fruit; the problem lies fallow or repeatedly frustrates efforts at resolution, until either a moment of clinical insight develops or, through serendipity, reading undertaken for a quite different purpose provides catalytic insights that allow for the elusive solution.

This proved to be the case in regard to my efforts to conceptualize the communicative dimension of the patient-analyst interaction. In the course of many years of struggle, bits of insight, new uncertainties, further understanding, new dissatisfactions, further clinical observations, and minor clues from reading generated a seemingly endless cycle in which fragments of resolution alternated with additional clinical observations that raised new and pertinent questions. Along the way, it was the reading of Bion's *Learning from Experience,* and especially his discussion of alpha functions and of alpha and beta elements—supplemented by a study of his later works (see Bion 1977)—that provided me with a critical selected fact that finally helped to organize my experiences and ideas in a somewhat stable manner. This presentation offers a broad outline of the crystallizations that followed: it describes some basic communicative properties of the psychotherapeutic and psychoanalytic bipersonal fields[1] and suggests a major means of categorizing the overall qualities of these fields. The implications of these conceptualizations for the understanding of the analytic interaction and for the technical approach of the analyst will also receive special emphasis.

THE DEVELOPMENT OF BACKGROUND CONCEPTS

In outlining the developments that have led me to a basic classification of communicative therapeutic fields, I will sketch historically some of the major observations that contributed to these formulations. My own training as a psychoanalyst and my recent study of the psychoanalytic literature related to the analytic experience (Langs 1976c) have indicated that, on the whole, classical psychoanalysts assume the psychoanalytic experience to take place in a single type of communicative field. With few exceptions (see below) analysts in general—Freudians, Kleinians, the middle group who have followed the lead of Winnicott, and others who have attempted an integrated approach—have written an enormous number of clinical papers related to the psychoanalytic interaction and psychoanalytic technique with the inherent assumption that there is a single basic analytic model. As a result, little or no attention had been paid to the communicative style of the patient (and still less, to that of the analyst) except to suggest that certain patients who do not develop a so-called transference neurosis are essentially not analyzable (see Greenson 1967). Such a suggestion implies that the patient is unable to fit into the analyst's stereotyped communicative model and is therefore unanalyzable (for another relevant example see Angel 1971). Not all, however, of these difficult patients, generally viewed as having borderline syndromes or psychotic reactions, have been considered unsuitable for analysis, while many with seemingly less severe disturbances have, for a variety of reasons, been so considered (for a similar discussion of the trend see Giovacchini 1975).

The type of communicative field which these analysts accepted and found workable can be characterized as one in which the patient readily and verbally free associates, conveys analyzable derivatives of his inner mental world—his unconscious fantasies, memories, introjects, self-representation, and the like—and in which the analyst in response interprets relevant contents, defenses, and dynamic constellations as they have a bearing on the patient's intrapsychic conflicts and psychopathology. Disturbances in this flow and analytic work generally appear in the form of interference with the communication of derivatives (primarily those related to the analyst) and as those readily identifiable behaviors which have been termed *acting out,* or as I prefer, either *living out* or *enactments* (see Langs 1976c). These serve primarily as resistances, although they do simultaneously communicate, in some sense, unconscious contents and dynamics.

Inevitably every analyst experiences exceptions to this model. In fact, it is my current clinical impression, based on experiences directly with patients and in supervision, that exceptions are far more common than the rule. Quite early in my analytic work I was confronted with analysands whose associations did not appear to be readily interpretable. I was also struck by patients both in therapy and analysis who seemed relatively uninterested in the acquisition of cognitive insights, but who, it eventually turned out, remained in treatment for a variety of other reasons: to gain direct support against a spouse, to spend large sums of money as a means of harming a spouse or parent, to provide a cover for directly destructive intentions toward another person, to gain in the therapist a gratifying companion in an otherwise empty life, or to find a target for unbridled expressions of aggression and sexuality. (This latter type of patient has been described in the literature on erotized and aggressive transferences; see Langs 1976c.) Such analysands challenged for me the generally accepted image of analysis and the tenet that the role of the analyst was to create a secure analytic setting and therapeutic alliance within which the derivatives of the patient's transference constellation (his unconscious transference fantasies) could unfold and be analyzed.

I had observed much of this well before Bird, in a relatively isolated communication (1972), dramatically stated that at times patients attempt to harm their analysts, meanwhile, Searles (1965) was writing during this period of such matters as patient's efforts to drive their analysts crazy and the realistic impact that patients have on their analysts—including the much delayed discovery of the former's therapeutic intentions and efforts toward the analyst (see especially Searles 1959, 1975, and Langs 1975b, 1976a, b). At this time, I was painfully aware that the overidealized and unrealistic world-of-fantasy model of analysis and therapy was something of a myth, a point expressly made in the second volume of *The Technique of Psychoanalytic Psychotherapy* (1974). My understanding of the problem, however, was limited to an awareness that patients enter analysis with deviant motives and to the technical recommendation that these needs and intended or actual misuses had to be discovered, analyzed, worked through, and resolved before other analytic work would be feasible.

My perception of this aspect of the analytic situation began to change gradually as a consequence of the development of several new clinical concepts. Largely because *The Technique of Psychoanalytic Psychotherapy* (Langs 1973, 1974) was empirically derived, I had approached the study of transference within an adaptive framework, thereby reformulating aspects of the influence of the patient's unconscious transference fantasies and stressing his exquisite, unconscious sensitivity to the therapist's errors. Having already written on the relationship between day residues and dreams (Langs 1971), I found this model quite serviceable in considering the patient's reactions to the therapist, since it stressed the precipitants of these responses as on key to their understanding. I pointed out that transference responses do not occur ex nihilo, but are consistently prompted by life events, especially by occurrences within the therapeutic or analytic interaction. Redognizing the presence of many reactions in the patient derived primarily from the countertransference-based errors of the therapist, I described a series of iatrogenic syndromes (Langs 1974).

This adaptive, interactional approach crystallized while I was completing the Technique volumes, and I embodied in in the concept of the *adaptive context* (Langs 1972, 1973)—the internal or, more usually, the external reality stimulus for the patient's intrapsychic responses. The discovery of a reality precipitant for every intrapsychic reaction consolidated the adaptive dimension of my approach to understanding the patient and led to an extensive consideration of the nature of these adaptive stimuli, especially as they pertained to the therapist's interventions and failures to intervene. The principles that all of the patient's associations subsequent to an intervention bore on the analyst's communication and that the patient's responses were always a mixture, on the one hand, of valid perceptiveness and commentary and, on the other, of distorting fantasies, encouraged many new perspectives. It was soon feasible to extend these principles to the therapist's management of the ground rules—a position that led to a number of additional discoveries.

I soon realized that the patient was, unconsciously, exquisitely sensitive to the analyst's errors and I could trace the vicissitudes of his responses. I found that the clinical data readily reaffirmed and extended Searles's concept (see 1965, 1972, 1975) that the patient not only unconsciously perceives the analyst's errors, but also unconsciously introjects dimensions of the analyst's maladaptive inner world and functioning as they are unconsciously communicated through his errors. This led to studies of the patient's unconscious curative efforts toward the therapist, an insight first described by Little (1951) and then specifically elaborated upon by Searles (1965, 1975), and was counterbalanced by investigations of the positive effects of valid interventions.

While I was developing an appreciation of the complexities of the analytic interaction and of the extent of the analyst's continuous involvement and conscious and unconscious communication with the patient—aspects of the interaction which I once again found Searles (1965, 1972, 1975) especially sensitive to—my reading and clinical work prompted me to consider more carefully the analyst's demeanor, his basic attitude or stance, toward the patient. In this respect, Balint's *The Basic Fault* (1968) was especially important in that he suggested that certain types of patients require both a different mode of listening by the analyst and a different manner of relating. He referred to patients suffering from what he termed a *basic fault,* an ego defect or sector of inner mental damage derived from such disruptive preoedipal experiences as acute traumas and faulty mothering. These analysands require a response from the analyst that creates a sense of *primary love*; the analyst essentially becomes the medium through which the patient can regress, discover his basic fault, mourn it, and then progress once again. He drew an analogy to the oxygen we breathe and the water through which the swimmer swims: neither the oxygen nor the water asks anything of the recipient and yet offers essential support. For Balint, this therapeutic carriage was essential with patients for whom two-person interactions were far more important than those at a three-person level.

Here was an important indication that, in addition to his interpretations, the manner in which the analyst creates the analytic situation and relates to the analysand can have a significant influence on the analytic work and outcome. Winnicott (1958, 1965), who stressed the *holding* qualities of the analytic setting and of the analyst's stance, had suggested as early as 1956 that with certain patients the holding environment, of which the analyst is a part, would have to do all the esential therapeutic work for long periods of time. It is no coincidence that Winnicott's metaphor of the maternal-like holding functions of the analyst bears a striking resemblance to Bion's metaphor (1977) of *the container* and *the contained*, which he too applied, in part, to the analyst's functions (see below, and also Langs 1976a, b, c). Khan too (1963, 1964), in writing of the *maternal shield,* offered a metaphor for certain inherently protective, and yet noninterpretive, aspects of the analyst's relationship with his patient.

It had become increasingly clear (a) that many patients do not confine themselves to the largely verbal communication in an analyzable form of derivatives both of unconscious fantasies and of other inner contents and defenses, and (b) that the analyst's functions extend beyond his development of a safe setting and the use of verbal interventions geared toward neutral interpretations. He has an additional responsibility to create a special setting and hold for the patient, to manage the ground rules, and to maintain his hold as long as necessary. It had also become evident that there was an ever-present interaction between the patient and the analyst, much of it on an unconscious level, with continuous pressures toward both health and regression on both sides (see Searles 1965, and his concept of *therapeutic symbiosis*). Finally, with the development of the concept of the adaptive context, it was possible to study more carefully the communications from the patient and to recognize that at times his associations provided interpretable derivatives, while at other times they did not: either there were many apparent derivatives and no adaptive context in which to dynamically organize and understand them, or the adaptive context was evident, but clear-cut and meaningful derivatives were lacking (see Searles 1973b for a related discussion). Further, the production of these derivatives was not solely a function of the intrapsychic balances, contents, and state of the analysand, but was continuously influenced by ane analyst as well (Langs 1975a, b, c, 1976a, c).

I had begun to develop clinical material for a new book, and intending a rather comprehensive investigation of this area, I decided to review very carefully the relevant literature. Among many, for me truly remarkable, discoveries (Langs 1976c), I was especially drawn to a paper by the Barangers (1966) in which they discussed the development of insight in the analytic situation—*the bipersonal field,* as they termed it. While I can remember vividly my initial, utter confusion in response to their discussion of projective indentification as the major mechanism within that field—my first exposure to the term—I nonetheless found their conception of the analytic relationship in terms of a bipersonal field not only extremely attractive, but soon quite productive of additional personal insights.

The field concept led me to intensify my investigations of the ground rules of analysis, since it was evident that these tenets were, in part, the delimiting determinants of the field—both as its internal and external boundaries and, as a key factor in the very nature of the transactions within its confines. The field metaphor was supported by Milner's analogy (1952) between the ground rules of analysis and the frame of a painting: each sets off the world within its confines from the rest of reality and gives that inner world its special qualities and rules. In analysis, for example, the frame makes the transference illusion possible. In these two ways, the ground rules of analysis took on three-dimensional and human qualities and a reexamination of their functions became vital. I soon saw that since they could be viewed as the framework of the bipersonal field, their establishment and maintenance were perhaps the major factors giving the analytic field its therapeutic qualities and communicative characteristics—a point suggested by Bleger (1967) and explicitly elaborated upon by Viderman (1974).

Among the many important ideas to which the bipersonal field concept led, several are most pertinent to this presentation. The metaphor suggests that every point in the field—every communication, interaction, structure, and occurrence within and between the two members of the dyad—receives vectors from both participants, albeit in varying proportions. Thus, every communication from the patient is influenced to a greater or lesser extent by the analyst, and vice versa. Further, every point in the field is layered and thus requires equal consideration of its realistic and fantasied components. Each content and communication, with its conscious and unconscious elements, must be scrutinized for its veridical core (primarily its nontransference layer for the patient and its noncountertransference layer for the analyst) as well as for its intrapsychically distorted aspects (primarily transference for the patient and countertransference for the analyst). In addition, both intrapsychic and interactional processes and mechanisms must consistently be considered.

One can hypothesize an interactional interface along which the communications from patient and analyst take place, and then consider the vectors that determine its position and qualities: its location vis-a-vis the respective pathologies of patient and analyst; the extent to which it is fixed or mobile, in terms of the relative contributions of the patient and analyst; the degree to which its primary qualities are related to unconscious fantasies, memories, and introjects, or to projective and introjective identifications; and the degree to which it embodies what I have termed the *me-not-me* property—the manner in which the communications from each participant allude both to self and not-self. (In other words, the patient's associations consistently refer both to himself and the analyst, in terms both of valid perceptions and distorted fantasies; see Langs 1976a,c).

The bipersonal field concept directs the analyst to a consideration of the nature of the communications that take place within the field: the extent to which verbal communications prevail and maintain their intended meaning; the degree to which symbolic and illusory verbal and behavioral communication is present; the openness of the interactional flow; the presence of projective identifications; and the use of language and behavior for discharge and direct gratification rather than for insight (Langs 1976a,c). The concept also encourages a study of the defenses that exist within the field, stressing the contributions of both participants, thereby supplementing the strictly intrapsychic viewpoint of both defenses and resistances. Thus, while the Barangers (1966) had described *bastions* of the bipersonal field (shared sectors of the communicative field that are split off, repressed, and denied by both participants), I delineated various sectors of *therapeutic misalliance* (Langs 1975b, 1976a,c) which involved unconscious collusion between patient and analyst directed toward noninsightful symptom relief and other innapproperiate, shared defenses and gratifications. Similarly, I delineated *interactional resistances* that were created and shared by the two participants. This line of thought led to the recognition of *interactional syndromes:* symptoms in either participant to which both patient and analyst contribute in varying proportions—a notion that provides an interactional addendum to the concept of the intrapsychically based transference and countertransference neuroses (or syndromes).

Work on the bipersonal field interdigitated with studies of the nature of the unconscious and conscious communication between the patient and analyst. For the patient, the stress was on a balanced appreciation of his valid functioning, as compared to his pathological responses, so that both unconscious perception and unconscious fantasy received attention. The former, while most often valid, could also be distorted—*unconscious misperception.* Such perceptions form the core of the patient's introjects of the analyst—realistic nuclei which may then be surrounded by pathological, intrapsychically founded distortions. Unconscious perceptions and introjections of the therapist's countertransference-based behaviors and their underlying psychopathology may, on the one hand, be misappropriated by the patient to reinforce his own psychopathology and may, on the other, evoke both unconscious retaliation and unconscious efforts at cure (Searles 1965, 1975, Langs 1975b, 1976a,c). Valid interventions by the analyst, however, not only generate cognitive insight and the related resolution of intrapsychic conflicts, anxieties, and distorted fantasies and introjects, but they also inherently provide the patient with positive and curative introjects based on the analyst's sound functioning.

For the analyst, his manifest interventions—interpretations and managements of the frame—were seen to extend beyond their direct contents into a wide range of unconscious communications. Erroneous interventions and mismanagements of the frame were found, since they were not in keeping with the patient's communications and needs, to convey aspects of the analyst's pathological unconscious fantasies, memories, and introjects, and to constitute the projective identification into the patient of aspects of the analyst's own pathological inner mental world. Here too Bion's unique investigations of projective identification, and his specific development of the metaphor of the container and the contained (1977), facilitated the understanding of this dimension of the unconscious interaction between the patient and analyst. While heretofore the stress had been on the patient's pathological projective identifications into the analyst and on the latter's capacity to contain, metabolize, and interpret these contents (see for example, Grinberg 1962, Bion 1977, Langs 1976a,b,c), the bipersonal field concept prompted an equal consideration of the analyst's pathological projective identifications into the patient, and his use of the patient as a pathological or inappropriate container for these contents (Langs 1976a,c).

In this connection, I also recognized that projective identification could range from primitive omnipotent fantasies with almost no effort at interactional fulfillment to more mature, structuralized interactional efforts at placing contents into the dyadic partner. I suggested the use of the term *interactional projection* (Langs 1976a,c) to stress the actuality of the projective effort in projective identification and to contrast it with projection which I—and others—defined as an essentially intrapsychic mechanism. Finally, by making extensive use of Wangh's concept (1962), the *evocation of a proxy,* I was able to recognize uses of projective identification beyond its usually described role as a means of getting rid of bad inner contents, placing good contents into an object for safekeeping, and externalizing one's troubling inner representations in order to better manage them from without (Segal 1967). Wangh's work implied that projective identification also serves the subject as a means of evoking adaptive responses in the object which can then be introjected by the subject.

One final clarification helped to set the stage for the main subject of this paper—the identification of major types of communicative bipersonal fields. This took the form of clarifying the types of communications from the patient and the ways in which the analyst could organize and conceptualize this material (Langs 1978b). In essence, it was suggested that on the first level, a patient's associations could be organized around their *manifest contents.* This approach, which is essentially nonanalytic since it totally rejects all notions of unconscious process and content, confines itself to the surface of the patient's communications.

On the second level, the analyst organizes material from the patient by attending to the manifest associations, isolating various segments of this material, and imputing to each a specific unconscious meaning; I term these inferences *Type One derivatives.* Here, the manifest content is addressed in relative isolation, and the latent content—the unconscious communication—is determined by the recognition of obvious displacements, the use of symbols, the intuitive understanding of underlying meanings, and a knowledge of a given patient's communicative idiom. By and large, the distinction between unconscious fantasy and unconscious perception is ignored, and Type One derivatives are conceived of primarily in terms of the former.

A third level of organizing the material from the patient is feasible through the use of the *adaptive context* as the dynamic organizer of the patient's associations; this yields *Type Two derivatives*. The model here is that of the day residue and the manifest dream, the latent content of which is fully comprehended only with the knowledge of the dream's precipitant and related associations (Langs 1971, 1978b). Each adaptive context itself has both manifest and latent meanings. Further, most crucial adaptive contexts for the patient in analysis stem from his interaction with the analyst; as a result, a true understanding of the nature of an adaptive stimulus and of the responses it evokes (associations and behaviors) is founded on the self-knowledge of the analyst—his sensitivity to the conscious, and especially, unconscious meanings and projections conveyed in his verbal interventions, silences, and efforts to manage the frame.

Type Two derivatives, then, are always viewed dynamically and as responses to adaptive stimuli. As a rule, they imply that virtually all of the communications from the patient must, on this leel, be appended or related to the analytic interaction—those representing perceptions and introjections, as well as fantasies and distortions. At this level, many seemingly divergent and relatively undecipherable associations accrue significance in the light of the recognized adaptive context.

In all, then, my investigations of the bipersonal field had, at this point, provided me with the following tools: (1) the concepts of the adaptive context and of Type Two derivatives, means through which it became feasible to determine whether the communications from the patient constituted analyzable derivatives of unconscious fantasies and perceptions, (2) an understanding of basic interactional mechanisms and of the unconscious communications and projective efforts of both patient and analyst, (3) a comprehension of the essential role played by the framework of the analytic situation in determining the communicative properties of the therapeutic field, and (4) a conception of the dimensions of the bipersonal field itself, as created and continued by both patient and analyst.

At this juncture, there was evident need for a basic conceptualization of major types of therapeutic or communicative bipersonal fields. Through continued clinical observations, I experimented with a number of possibilities, but a satisfactory classification seemed to elude crystallization until a point at which a reorganization of my clinical observations coincide with a rereading of Bion's writings, especially a series of comments in his 1962 book, *Learning from Experience*. Much later, after the necessary concepts had been developed, I found independent confirmation of aspects of my ideas in an important paper by Khan (1973). At the time of writing this paper, I restudied a series of additional ideas in Bion's writings (1977) that, on the one hand, suggested an unconscious influence on the delineation of these fields that I had not explicitly recognized before, and that, on the other, helped to further refine my understanding of the concepts I was attempting to define. Finally, I have just now become aware of efforts by Liberman (in press) to study styles of communication in patients.

THE THREE MAJOR BIPERSONAL FIELDS

For some time, I had developed, as I have described, considerable evidence for distinctly different types of bipersonal fields. In the course of struggling with these clinical observations, I found that Winnicott's (1965, 1971) conception of the analytic setting as a type of transitional or play space within which the capacity for illusion plays a central role seemed pregnant with meaning. I could see that, in my terms, this implied the presence of analyzable Type Two derivatives, and I was aware that certain bipersonal fields possessed this quality, which others certainly did not. This, however, seemed insufficient for a full classification; the crucial variables had not emerged. Still, I had made a number of fascinating clinical observations along the following lines: as a rule, when the analyst modified the framework of the bipersonal field, the transitional-play qualities tended to diminish or disappear. This could be seen in the flatness of a patient's subsequent communications and in the relative absence of interpretable derivatives (see Halpert 1972, for an illustration). Often, under these conditions the patient would eventually make such comments as "I can no longer write or paint," or, "My child's school does not have a playground."

These observations provided further evidence of the importance of the analyst to both the patient's communicative style and to the overall communicative qualities of the bipersonal field, and placed special stress on the role of a secure framework in creating a transitional-play-illusory communicative space. Still, they did not facilitate an understanding of those fields in which these qualities were more or less absent. Under the latter conditions, it was evident that patients and perhaps analysts tended to overuse projective identification, denial mechanisms, and acting out on gross and far more subtle levels, but these findings still lacked an organizing element.

In *Learning from Experience,* Bion (1962) postulates the presence in the mind of an *alpha function,* which operates on sense impressions and raw emotions to create alpha elements that are suitable for storage and dreaming—that is, for symbolic usage (see also Khan 1973). This function is essential for memory, conscious thinking, and reasoning. It is developed in the infant through an interaction with a mother capable of *reverie* who subjects a young child's projective identifications to her own alpha functioning and returns, into the child, detoxified projective identifications which were formerly terrifying and morbid. When alpha functioning is disturbed, either because of innate factors or by attacks based on hate and envy, the infant is left with *beta elements* which are things-in-themselves, suitable for projective identification and acting out, but not for dream thoughts; nor can these elements cohere into a *contact barrier* that will enable the mechanisms of repression, suppression, and learning to occur. Beta elements essentially are objects that can be evacuated to rid the psyche of accretions of stimuli and to eject unwanted contents.

Perhaps most crucial to the development of alpha functioning and elements is the capacity of the infant to modify, rather than evade, frustration. Thus, thinking may remain at a level modeled on muscular movement and may function as a means of unburdening the psyche, largely through projective identification; here, the infant does not attempt to actualize his omnipotent fantasies of projective identification because he has an undeveloped capacity to tolerate frustration. This type of projective identification, primarily a flight from reality, is quite different from that used excessively to have the mother or analyst experience the inner contents of the child-patient. In Bion's discussion, the mother's capacity for reverie was seen as comparable to the analyst's hold and to his receptivity to the patient's projective identifications (see also Bion 1965, 1970, and Langs 1976a,c).

While these basic concepts are subjected to extensive elaboration by Bion, the outline presented here is sufficient for the purposes of this paper. Most relevant is his thesis that there are two types of communicative elements: *alpha* and *beta*. The former are suitable for symbolic usage and creative communication and may readily be seen as comparable to what I have termed *"analyzable derivatives of unconscious fantasies, memories, and introjects*—Type Two derivatives. They are one of the major organizing elements of the Type A field. In contrast, beta elements are not utilized symbolically or for the purposes of communication and cognitive understanding; they are primarily discharge products, largely projective identifications designed to lessen inner psychic tension. This concept relates to the finding that patients may free associate verbally without producing analyzable derivatives organized around meaningful adaptive contexts and without permitting valid interpretations in terms of their unconscious contents. These elements are an important factor in the Type B field. It seems evident that these discharge products require a particular type of analytic intervention, either in the form of appropriately holding and containing the patient and his projective identifications or of interpretations based on the *metabolism* (Langs 1976a) and understanding of the relevant projected contents and processes. In Bion's terms, such holding and intervening may foster the development of alpha functions and elements in a patient previously blocked in this regard and are the expression of the analyst's capacity for reverie.

One additional group of interrelated concepts almost exclusively developed by Bion (1977) pertain to the static, noncommunicative Type C field that rounds out the classification to be presented here. These brilliant and original ideas are scattered throughout Bion's (1977) four major works and may be briefly organized around four basic concepts: (1) the K-link (Bion 1962), the functions of column two of the grid, (2) the psi function (Bion 1963, 1965), (3) the phenomenon of reversible perspective (Bion 1963), and (4) his discussion of lies and the thinker (Bion 1970).

In brief, Bion (1962) postulated three types of links between objects: K (knowledge), L (love), and H (hate). The K link is "commensal" in that it involves two objects (persons) who are dependent on each other for mutual benefit without harm for either. It is growth promoting and permits both particularization and abstraction. In contrast, the –K link tends to be infused with envy and to be parasitic in that it may be destructive to both objects and interfere with growth. It is characterized by not-understanding (misunderstanding or misrepresenting) and it functions to defeat the analyst and to denude and strip of meaning all interactional elements, thus generating a worthless residue. This link destroys knowledge, has a primary quality of "withoutness", converts alpha elements into beta elements, and creates a feeling in the patient of being surrounded by the bizarre objects that represent in part his thoughts stripped of meaning and ejected.

Although Bion's (1977) development of a grid with horizontal and vertical axes designed for the classification and comprehension of the elements of psychoanalysis cannot be fully detailed here, several of its aspects are relevant. The horizontal axis provides "the definitory function of a formulation' (Bion 1963, p. 65)—that is, the use of a communication. Communications are placed into column two of this grid, the psi function, when they constitute hypotheses known to be false and maintained as a barrier against anxiety lest any other theories take their place. These communications are utilized to inhibit thought; they constitute ideas used to deny more accurate, but more frightening, ones and serve as barriers against turbulence and psychological upheaval. At times, in the form of commonsense facts, they are used to deny expressions of fantasy; their manifestations pertain to the patient's defenses and resistances. This language function cannot, however, be interpreted until the column-two dimension is apparent and has evolved. Bion (1965) suggests that the criterion for intervening relates to the analyst's capacity to experience resistances in the patient that would be evoked if an interpretation were given.

To explain reversible perspective, Bion (1963) draws upon the familiar line drawing which may be seen either as two profiles or as a vase. Through this metaphor he suggests that in the area of sensibility—the experience of the lines per se—there may be agreement between two individuals, while in the area of insensibility—the conception of what is seen—there may be disagreement. Applying this to the patient and analyst, Bion describes analytic situations in which both appear to agree on the facts, while the patient conceals an important level of disagreement that relates to the basic assumptions of the analytic relationship and situation. The patient's glib agreement is designed to conceal his lack of conviction; even when painful emotions are evident, the patient has a facile explanation for them. Basically, the patient's responses, designed to disguise the real nature of his experiences, invite interventions regarding contents that will not be confirmed. This occurs because the patient accepts interpretations on the surface, while secretly rejecting the premises on which they are based. The analyst may comprehend, but the patient does not, and views the analyst's premises as false. The debate, however, is unspoken; it derives from the patient's maintaining a point of view that is different from that of the analyst. The patient's agreement, then, serves –K and column-two functions in that it is a barrier against pain and a defense against change. Such analytic situations are stalemated; they lack real progress and are quite static. Splitting is arrested, as is the evacuation of beta elements, and action is unnecessary. The conditions are similar to those under which the patient uses an hallucination as a substitute for reality. There is a no engagement on the issues; rather than agreeing or disagreeing, the patient simply reverses the perspective and shifts his point of view. For Bion, the main factor here is the patient's impaired capacity to tolerate pain.

In his comments on "Lies and the Thinker," Bion (1970) extends and elaborates upon many of the earlier ideas outlined here. He investigates the lie and demonstrates its frequent column-two function, while noting that, at times, it may fall into his column six—an action-oriented group of communications—as well. In the former function, the lie serves as a barrier against statements that would lead to psychological upheaval, while in the latter, it may actually generate that upheaval. The lie is also studied in terms of its –K function, and its role in preventing catastrophic change. Bion notes that the patient tries to induce the analyst to accept and work with the lie in order to prevent the experience of inner disruption. The patient in analysis will often experience a conflict between the need to know and the need to deny, and the problem is complicated by their being no absolute value to either truth or lie. Bion suggests the need to investigate column two in order to see in what respects its pains compare with those of other systems. He notes that this category involves conflicts with impressions of reality. When the conflict between needing to know and needing to deny becomes acute, the patient may usher in attacks on linking in order to stop the stimulation that has led to the conflict; however, with some liars, such an aim is not detectible and they do not betray a pattern of this kind. In general, the relationship between the liar and his audience is parasitic, and the lie functions as a means of denudation.

While this highly condensed resume of Bion's ideas has undoubtedly generated some degree of confusion in the reader, I trust that the main themes are evident: (a) that certain communications may function as barriers, lies, forms of concealment, and attempts to destroy rather than generate meaning, and (b) that there are many patients who attempt to maintain a static and stalemated analytic situation through extremely subtle and difficult to detect means—this, largely in the service of preventing a dreaded psychological upheaval. The relevance to the Type C field to be described below will soon become evident.

Before completing this final introductory survey, I must openly express certain misgivings in the context of the present discussion. I have been quite concerned that the concept of beta elements and the discharge qualities of projective identifications draws upon an economic model of the mental apparatus that is open to serious theoretical and clinical questions (see the recent discussion by Wallerstein, 1977). This economic view of the mental apparatus is a throwback to Freud's earlier, topographic model, much of which is now no longer serviceable according to most writers. It may well be that such metaphors are more descriptive than theoretically meaningful, but despite repeated efforts to search for a different type of conception, I continue to find the present delineation eminently useful for clinical formulation, prediction, and interpretation. I am well aware that many analysts will believe that these descriptions of column-two functions (efforts at destruction of meaning) are merely restatements of familiar concepts related to our present understanding of defense and resistance. It is beyond the scope of this paper to establish the important distinctions and their clinical implications that I believe to be pertinent here, although I will offer initial clinical observations and ideas in this respect in my discussion of the three communicative fields. These vital clinical and theoretical issues are all unsettled, and I would welcome revision and refinement based on additional clinical observations and conceptual rethinking.

In all, then, the insights provided by Bion's discussions and my own continued clinical observations finally led me to a tripartite classification of communicative fields. While I will stress this point less here, these styles of communication seem also to be descriptive of individual propensities. I will now identify each major type of bipersonal field, and describe its principal characteristics. Although, in actual clinical situations, one finds intermixtures, my own observations indicate that a particular group of characteristics do indeed tend to predominate. Each field will be described as a bipersonal and a communicative field under the influence of both patient and analyst.

THE TYPE A FIELD

In the Type A field of symbolic communication, analyzable derivatives and symbolic interpretations of inner mental contents and mechanisms predominate. The patient's associations and behaviors convey analyzable derivatives, and the analyst offers valid interpretations of their functions, contents, and meanings. This is the communicative field in which transference as an illusion (a complex concept in itself—see Langs 1976c), the use of symbolic communication, and the broader use of illusion prevail. It has been described as an analytic play space (Winnicott 1971) or as a transitional space (Khan 1973). The patient's verbal and behavioral communications are readily organizable around significant adaptive contexts, thereby yielding derivatives of his unconscious fantasies, memories, introjects, perceptions, and self-representations (aspects of id, ego, and superego) expressed in a form that lends itself to verbal interpretation. In addition, the patient is prepared to understand the symbolic meaning of the analyst's interventions, which are themselves conveyed in this idiom. It is this type of field, as I indicated previously, that is implicitly the ideal of the classical psychoanalyst, who expects to work under these conditions and who may view patients who are unable to comply as unanalyzable—that is, because their associations appear to be uninterpretable or because they are prone to what is viewed as intractable acting out.

In this Type of bipersonal field, the communications from the patient organize primarily around adaptive responses, analyzable derivatives of unconscious transference fantasies and perceptions, and the verbal and nonverbal resistances to their expression. It is to be stressed, however, that when resistances and defenses predominate, the unconscious derivatives relevant to their nature and to the material being defended against are, in general, available in the communications from the patient. It is possible to establish the adaptive context and precipitant for these resistances. Ultimately they are analyzable in terms of unconscious meanings and defenses.

In the Type A field, a secure frame is an essential and silent element, consistently maintained while the analyst interprets the patient's communications. It therefore requires an analyst capable of securing and managing the framework—one who, in addition, has the capacity to think symbolically and utilize the transitional space as a pace both for understanding the patient's derivatives and for their synthesis into valid, sensitively timed symbolic interpretations. The patient must be capable of symbolic communication, must have a tolerance for the regression and anxiety invoked by a secure frame (Langs 1976a, 1977c), must possess an ability to use illusion and derivative expression, and must have a capacity to understand and utilize the analyst's interpretations on that level. It is my impression that Searles's description (1970, 1971, 1973a) of a workable therapeutic symbiosis refers to this type of field.

Not all analysts are capable of synthesis and symbolic communication at this level, nor are all analysts capable of securing the framework needed for a bipersonal field characterized by these communicative qualities. As will become evident, virtually all previous so-called training analyses have taken place in a field under consistent pressure to deviate from this Type A form to either the more discharge-oriented field (Type B) or the more static, noncommunicative interaction (Type C). Such analytic experiences tend to occur within bipersonal fields whose frames are modified, often extensively so since so-called training analysts are prone to nonillusory and nonsymbolic communication toward their analysands. They may use language or mismanage the frame in order to projectively identify into their analysands their own inner disturbance, thereby fostering Type B communication, or they may use cliche-ridden stereotyped interventions, unconsciously designed as falsifications and barriers, which promote the development of a Type C field. As a result, an analyst's own analysis has tended to reinforce his own greater or lesser need for either the discharge or the nonmeaningful modes of communication characteristic, respectively, of Types B and Type C interactions. Either outcome, of course, greatly influences the communicative interaction with his own patients. Often, these propensities are outside the analyst's awareness and are expressed despite his manifest intentions to secure the ground rules of each analytic situation and to create opportunities for interpreting. His actual, unconsciously determined communicative style and use of language may deviate significantly from the optimal Type A mode.

There are strong, inherent needs within both patient and analyst to shift away from a Type A communicative field toward the more direct and inappropriate gratifications and barriers against chaos that are relatively absent in the symbolic mode. It has been assumed in the classical psychoanalytic literature, so far as I can determine, that all analysts attempt to create a Type A field and that they are capable of doing so and of offering relevant interpretations within such a field. If I may be permitted a well-founded, but undocumented, thesis, I would suggest that, to the contrary, there are many classically trained analysts who are quite incapable of consistently maintaining this Type A field, and it is quite likely that this is even more the case with therapists with other backgrounds.

In brief, the analyst may be the prime mover in modifying a Type A field into Type B or C, or he may accept the latter types when patients attempt to create them. He does this through inappropriate silences, erroneous verbal interventions, and alterations in the framework of the bipersonal field that are, almost without exception, quite inappropriate. This latter is the single most overlooked vehicle both for countertransference expressions and as a means of detrimentally altering the communicative properties of the bipersonal field (see Langs 1975c, 1976a, 1976c, 1978a). In one sense, all such technical errors tend to express failures in the analyst's holding capacity, containing functions, and use of alpha function; they therefore reflect the nonsymbolic use of language and behavior for pathological projective identification and to express beta elements and thus rid the analyst of accretions of inner tension.

Characteristically, patients will respond to such efforts in kind. They will shift away from the use of alpha elements, and away from derivative and symbolic communication if this has been their communicative style, and move either toward holding the analyst and containing his projective identifications or toward the discharge of projective identifications and beta elements on their own part. In addition, patients who suffer from inadequate alpha functioning and are blocked in their use of symbolic and derivative communication will tend themselves to maintain Type B and Type C fields and be refractory toward any possible shift to a Type A field. Under these conditions, verbal interventions are virtually useless. The analyst must first *rectify* the altered frame and shift to symbolic communication; only then will his interventions have their consciously intended meanings and effects. Clearly, both self-awareness and the resolution of the underlying countertransference problems are a vital part of such work.

In this context, it should be noted first, that I have not suggested that a Type A field is characteristic of patients at the more neurotic end of the psychopathological continuum, nor will I later suggest that Type B and Type C fields are necessarily characteristic of those with more severe psychopathology—that is, borderline, narcissistic, and schizophrenic patients. While in general, it may well be that this is the general trend, I have noted many exceptions to this rule and leave the matter open to empirical study. Secondly, implicit in these ideas is the suggestion that the analyst move the patient toward the utilization of a Type A communicative mode through his appropriate management and maintance of the framework and his valid verbal, symbolic interpretations. These are essential for the Type A field itself; however, I do not wish to suggest, as implied in the classical psychoanalytic literature, that the Type A field is the only viable therapeutic field. While Khan (1973) has suggested that what I term the Type A field is optimal and has indicated that it requires a high level of maturation, my own clinical observations suggest that communicative styles are genetically and intrapsychically determined, and that effective analytic work will tend more to create interludes of symbolic communication in Type B and Type C patients, rather than, as a rule, to effect a shift to a fundamentally Type A mode (see below). In any case, it is evident that effective analytic work and adaptive, insightful, and structural inner change can accrue to a patient in types of fields other than the Type A. It is therefore my belief that further clinical research will be needed to identify the advantages and limitations of analytic work within each of the three types of fields described here.

One final point: while the Type A field is most efficacious for cognitive insight, it is also the field in which the patient and, to a lesser extent, the analyst most intensely experience their pathological and primitive inner mental contents and the related anxieties and temporary mental disorganization. While this is an aspect of a therapeutic (or analyzable) regression (Langs 1976a) with great curative potential, it is a quite disturbing experience that prompts defensive reactions. In part, then, a shift to a Type B or C field initiated by either participant has an important defensive function.

The Type B Field

The Type B field is an action-discharge field in which projective identification predominates. In it, either the patient or the analyst makes extensive use of projective identification designed to rid the psyche of distrubing accretions of inner stimuli, to make use of the other member of the dyad as a container for disruptive projective identifications, and to evoke positive proxy responses. Major contributions to the development of this type of communicative field may come from either the patient or the analyst, and often come from both.

There are patients of all psychopathological types who show deficient alpha functioning and impairment in the use of illusion and symbolic communication—failures in the expression of analyzable derivatives of inner contents and dynamisms. Such patients make extensive use of projective identification, largely as a means of denying reality and utilizing the analyst as a container for their disturbing inner contents, endeavoring to transform the analytic situation into a place of discharge and action.

In a Type B field either participant may also seek inappropriate, direct gratification of pathological, instinctual drive needs. In the patient, this usually takes the forms of direct demands for alterations in the frame and of subtle or gross efforts to obtain a variety of noninterpretive satisfactions. Should these be gratified, his use of this mode of communicating—and functioning—is reinforced.

Despite the relative absence of a contribution from the analyst that would shape the field along Type B lines, patients so inclined tend to adhere to this type of communication for long periods; their basic use of this mode is, perhaps, essentially unmodifiable. This suggests that this form of communication is a long-standing, basic personality attribute and mode of interaction. While the matter should be left open in that it may well be feasible analytically to modify the pathological aspects of Type B communication to where the patient will shift to a basic Type A mode, an equally constructive analytic goal appears to be to develop longer, more effective use of alpha functioning with more usable alpha elements, and to modify the pathological use of projective identification and efforts at discharge so that the Type B communicative mode is maintained in a less pathological form. Such a modification also implies the analyst's development of nonpathological defenses and capacities to manage his own inner mental world. Analytic experience supports Bion's (1977) concept that it is essential that the analyst have the capacities to hold the patient, to maintain a state of reverie, to think symbolically, and to contain and metabolize the patient's projective identifications toward symbolic understanding. In this way, he creates an interaction in which the patient is able to introjectively identify with these attributes of the analyst, to incorporate detoxified projective identifications, and to develop his own alpha functioning.

In a Type B field, there are actually few analyzable derivatives of unconscious mental contents, and interpretations of contents and defenses along usual symbolic lines are virtually never confirmed by the patient, either on the cognitive or introjective-interactional levels (Langs 1976a,c 1978b). The analyst must work within the communicative medium of the patient, in which projective identification and the excretion of tension producing stimuli prevail. He must therefore contain these projective identifications, metabolize them toward understanding, and offer interpretations of these interactional efforts, holding the frame steady all the while. Only the maintenance of a secure frame and interpretations of the unconscious functions of the Type B communicative style will adaptively modify its pathological meanings and uses.

As for the analyst, any alteration that he makes in the frame will express his own propensity for a Type B communicative field and pressure the patient in that direction. His own use of pathological projective identification and discharge as reflected in his verbal interventions and other behaviors will have a similar influence. All of his communications to the patient, therefore, must be scrutinized in depth for such expressions. The development of a Type B communicative field calls for *rectification* of an altered frame and a resumption of symbolic-interpretive work by the analyst. It is characteristic of patients who tend to communicate along Type B lines to momentarily shift to the communication of analyzable derivatives in response to the analyst's unneeded alterations in the framework. Such associations, however, are only relevant to the impaired frame and tend to be quite fleeting; these patients will shift to action-discharge and projective identification soon after initial efforts to convey their unconscious perceptions and introjections of the erring therapist—their unconscious efforts to cure the therapist. In general, however, it is consistent analytic work in keeping with the attributes of the Type B field, undertaken in a secured framework, that promotes the gradual shift toward a greater use of Type A communications and a lessened use by the patient of pathological projective identifications and other interactional mechanisms. Finally, it appears to me that the Type B field has many of the characteristics of the pathological symbiosis described by Searles (1971).

The Type C Field

In delineating this static, noncommunicative field I would stress at the outset that while the Type A and Type B fields reflect modes of positive communication and are designed to convey derivatives of inner mental states, contents, and mechanisms, the Type C field is designed for noncommunication, for the destruction of meaning, and for the absence of derivative expression. To the extent that such efforts destroy meaning, relevant interaction, relatedness, and positive communication they have a negative function and meaning; in this restricted and unusual sense, then, the Type C field reflects and conveys a meaningful mode of relating and interacting.

The Type C field is characterized by the pervasive absence of interpretable derivatives of unconscious fantasies, memories, and introjects and by the presence of massive defensive barriers. As a rule, the patient's communications are on a manifest content level, and there is a remarkable sense of flatness and emptiness to behaviors and associations. When an adaptive context is evident, the patient's associations do not meaningfully organize around its conscious and unconscious implications; similarly, when the patient's associations seem filled with potential meaning, there will be no adaptive context to serve as the essential organizer. Typically, these patients ruminate emptily for long periods of time or tend to report detailed, extended narratives in a form that renders their possible unconscious meanings undecipherible. Occasionally, there is a circumscribed sense of depth and metaphorical communication; at such times, these patients tend unconsciously to represent the static, noncommunicative, walled-off qualities of their communicative style and the bipersonal field within which it is embedded. Without interpretive efforts directed toward these massive defenses, the therapist or analyst almost never has material available for interpretation. The most common exception occurs only occasionally, when the patient responds to an erroneous interpretation or an unneeded modification in the framework with derivatives related to the unconscious perceptions and introjections of the therapist's communicated and projected pathology, and briefly works over these pathological introjects.

In a Type C field, patient behaviors and associations are essentially barriers, falsifications, and lies (in the nonmoral sense) designed to seal off meaningful mental contents and to maintain the therapeutic interaction and work in a stalemated state. These massive barriers differ in important ways from the defenses utilized by patients in the Type A and Type B communicative fields, and are, I believe, significantly different from the defenses described in the classical psychoanalytic literature.

For example, in a Type A field, defenses and resistances are communicated in both manifest and derivative forms; eventually the unconscious fantasies and memories on which they are based and the sector of unconscious, anxiety provoking material against which they defend are communicated indirectly by the patient and become available for interpretive analytic work. While there are moments of flatness and emptiness in such a field, the patient consistently and spontaneously shifts to derivative and in=depth communication that permits symbolic understanding and intervention.

By contrast, in a Type C field, the patient's massive defenses are, most of the time, essentially amorphous and impervious to any possible underlying meaning and derivatives. They are impenetrable barriers whose own essential meanings tend not to be communicated by the patient. Although from time to time he will indeed represent more metaphorically the nature of these defensive walls, he reveals little of the quality of what lies beyond them. Type C patients typically speak from time to time of things being meaningless, of huge brick and concrete walls, of empty vacuums and abysses, of death and coffins and graves, of entombment in metal containers such as army tanks, and of similar representative image. Most of the time, they destroy not only the positive meaning of their words and behaviors, but the basic links between themselves and their objects, including the therapist, and between their conscious awareness and their unconscious inner mental world. Their associations are filled with cliches, the commonplace, and that which is already know, and they turn the analyst's previously meaningful interpretations and formulations into noncommunication, repeating them in endless and empty detail.

Except for the remarkable studies of Bion (1970), the systematic identification of the Type C field has tended to elude analysts. Certainly, analysts in general have been aware of major difficulties in working with certain types of patients and in generating validated interpretations to them. More specifically, it seems likely that some of the narcissistic patients described by Kohut (1971, 1977) and Kernberg (1975), patients who treat their analysts as seemingly nonexistent and who generate intense boredom in these analysts, are operating within a Type C communicative field. Still, the analyst's commitment to search for truth and meaning, plus his possible need to deny his own propensities toward Type C communication, seems to have defensively delayed the delineation of this type of communicative field. Similarly, it may well be that in addition to the patient's own inherent propensities toward this type of communication, these tendencies of the analyst play a significant role in the creation of a Type C field. In the main, when this occurs the analyst mismanages the framework and intervenes on a manifest content level, or he may even use Type One derivatives (specifically, through not working with Type Two derivatives) that actually constitute psychoanalytic cliches, falsifications, and barriers, rather than meaningful interpretations.

It is, I believe, the Type C field in which reversing perspective, as described by Bion (1963), often occurs. Under these conditions, both patient and analyst are aware of the behaviors and words exchanged, and yet the analyst may attempt to ascribe meaning to communications which for the patient are meaninglessness and function as barriers. At times, of course, the reversing perspective may occur in the other direction: the patient actually communicates in derivative form while the analyst experiences defensiveness and an absence of meaning. Communications in this field often resemble the figures embedded in a field of multi-colored dots used to test individuals for color-blindness. In a Type C field, the analyst or patient may well see the numbers because he is not "colorblind," while the other is only able to see a series of meaningless dots.

Another way to conceptualize the flat and elusive quality of this field is to think of the patient's communications as reflections in a mirror. To treat such unreal images as actualities and attempt to touch them or to experience them in depth would be to fail to recognize the function of the mirror. In such a case the mirror itself is a barrier to reality, actuality, and substance. There is a significant sense of deception and invalidation when the analyst treats as actual the falsified and unreal communications of the patient. In this field the distinction between language and communication becomes evident: while language may indeed serve as a means of conveying meaning, it is clear that its main function may also be the destruction of meaning and the creation of impenetrable barriers to such meaning—that is, noncommunication.

Initial observations suggest that the type C communicative mode constitutes a massive defensiveness against what may be variously termed a psychotic core, excessive psychic pain, inner mental catastrophy, and inner disorganization. These patients—and therapists—are often quite able to function socially and within work situations as long as they can utilize these massive defensive barriers. Often well defended latent psychotics and depressives they may appear to have narcissistic character disorders and to be severely depressed or paranoid-like. As a rule, there are isolated clues to the massive underlying disturbance: either in the reported history of the patient or in an occasional early session during which there is momentary, and as a rule quite limited, breakthrough of the underlying turmoil. The extremely guarded and suspecious patients destroy the sense of meaning in any effort by the analyst to interpret unconscious contents, doing so because they dread the inner core and need to maintain their rigid, impenetrable defenses. On the other hand, because of wishes for cure and relief, they will accpet and work with interpretations related to their massive defensiveness, as long as these are well timed and affectively meaningful; it is at such moments that patients are likely to meaningfully communicate derivatives of their chaotic, pathological inner mental distrubance, thus permitting momentary periods of deeper interpretive work.

In a type C Field, the interaction is characteristically static and immobile. Very little projective identification and few analyzable derivatives are available from the patient. The field is characterized by its holding qualities. However, while the analyst's main function for long periods may well be that of securing the framework and holding the patient, these patients often show little apprecation of being held (in the analytic sense) and seem instead disconnected and detached because of the destruction of their links to the analyst on so many levels. By distinguishing these holding functions from the analyst's containing capacities, which relate to the introjection of the patient's projective identifications and other communications, we can see that there is also little for the analyst to contain and metabolize. These patients often endure ling unproductive analyses or periods of psychotherapy and often generate stalemated treatment situations. Because of these qualities of the type C patient, the analyst often feels bored, empty, undrelated, and poorly held by the patient as well. It may well be that these patients fall into the group described by Searles (1965, 1970, 1071, 1973a) as in the autistic phase of analysis. In addition to often disregarding the presence of the analyst, the patient will treat him as part of the nonhuman environment.

While I have characterized the type C Field largely in terms of the patient's needs and characteristics, it should be stressed that many analysts and therapists have comparable needs and communicative propensities that contribute significantly to the developvent of the type C Field. These propensities are mainfested in unneeded modifications in the frame which function as massive barriers to meaningful communication in derivative form, and which serve to generate interactional defenses within the patient. Through failing to interpret and through a variety of erroneous interventions, especially those that fail to utilize the adaptive context and derivative communication, these may be from both patient and analyst. Many of the narcissistic type C relatedness in their patients. Such analysts wish to be helped inappropriately by the patient. They fear placing destructive projective identifications into the patient and wish instead to maintain a static field that will reinforce their own massive barriers against the chaotic and unresolved inner mental worlds of both themselves and their patients. As Bion (1977) noted, the container may fear the contained, and the contained may fear the container: each dreading attack, denudation, and destruction. The analyst may therefore dread both containing the patient's pathological mental contents and projecting his own disruptive inner mental world into the patient. Immobilization and noncommunication are rigidly maintained as the only seemingly safe harbor.

Technically, in a Type C field the analyst must wait patiently for unconscious communications from the patient that represent the massive defensive barriers and falsifications characteristic of this mode of communication. When such material appears, often accompained by some suggestion of the dreaded underlying derivatives, the analyst is in a position to help the patient understand the presence and nature of these massive barriers and to provide hints as to the nature of the underlying contents that they serve to so massively seal off. In general, such efforts are validated largely through the additional revelation of dreaded unconscious derivatives which may then be interpreted cognitively, introjected, metabolized, detoxified, and reprojected in less disruptive form. While efforts to interpret unconscious contents directly are, by and large, doomed to failure, an approach that understands the true nature of the communicative mode of these patients and concentrates on the interpretive modification of these defensive barriers will prove effective in modifying their psychopathology and the aspects of that pathology reflected in their communicative style.

To carry out such work, however, the analyst must be capable of managing his responses to the patient's barriers and falsifications, his destruction of links, his forms of nonrelating, and his use of falsifying cliches. He must control propensities to modify the frame, to intervene erroneously based on an inappropriate need within himself to suggest meaning in its absence or to jar and stir up the rigid and stalemated Type C patient. The analyst must also be capable of full use of the validating process, lest he continue to intervene in terms of manifest content and Type One derivatives, considering the cliched and unmeaningful responses of his patient as validation. Such interactions are characteristically filled with self- and mutual-deception, and produce no true insight or inner structural change. In addition to being capable of symbolic communication, such an analyst must be able to tolerate the anxiety and dread related to experiencing the intensely primitive and horrifying inner mental world of these patients and to the threats to his own defenses against surprisingly similar inner contents. He must also analyze and resolve his dread of containing his patient's underlying, destructive projective identifications and his fear of being driven crazy by the patient—an anxiety studied by Searles (1959). He must master his dread of being attacked and even annihiliated by the patient's noncommunication and negative projective identifications, which create a void in which his capacity to think, formulate, organize—to function meaningfully and relatedly—are being attacked and destroyed by the patient's Type C style.

ADDITION RELEVANT LITERATURE

In his quite original and creative contribution, "The Role of Illusion in the Analytic Space and Process," Khan (1973) studied the constitution of the analytic space and interaction. He did this initially in terms of the analytic framework as defined by its basic taboos—motility, sight, and touch. These taboos facilitate the patient's expression of his incestuous and parricidal wishes through the word. For Khan, these taboos-in my terms, the ground rules or framework—create an area of illusion in which language may explore and express wish systems beyond mere humiliation and remorse.

Noting the importance of the increment of affect which the area of illusion provides through transference, Khan suggests that Freud (1914), in his basic study of repetition and action as compared to remembering, had stressed the distinction between (a) action as converted into language and affective expression and (b) action that involves muscular and behavioral expression. The former requires a degree of growth and a stability of personality organization for both parties, so that they may work in the area of illusion through symbolic discourse. Acting out is therefore defined as behavior that transgresses symbolic discourse and seeks concrete expression and need fulfillment. Within this framework, Khan offered two clinical vignettes—patients either unable to develop an area of illusion or with whom it was precariously held.

With one patient, he felt that he had been eliminated from the analytic space and had become a passive witness whom the patient victimized with her excruciating pain and inexhaustible demands. He found her unable to relate to her own self-knowledge or to his interpretive interventions. In a dream, the patient observed a stained-glass ceiling of a cathedral crumbling and disintegrating, a communication that Khan saw as a warning of what she was going to do to the illusional space of the analytic situation—disrupt and destroy both the illusion and its structure.

This patient had been involved in direct physical contact with previous analysts and had actually seduced one of them. Khan felt that she was perpetually either acting into language, which he noted was not symbolic discourse, or acting upon life, which constitutes the total negation of any positive experience of relating that might take place in her analysis. Her language failed to assimilate her experiences on the intrapsychic and interpersonal levels, just as her body personalized her instincts and her affects. He soon referred this patient to another analyst. In his discussion of this patient, Khan stressed her total negation of his presence, her negation of herself as a person, and her invention of the fetishistic object of her psyche with which she provoked the analyst in order to destroy rather than be cured. These factors did not allow the space of illusion in the analytic situation to crystallize; instead, the patient seemed to live in a delusional reality that she wished to shed.

The second patient described was unable to respond to the demands of a previous analyst that she should verbalize her feelings and unconscious fantasies; instead, she had traumatized her analyst, pulling her hair, and breaking up the furniture in her consultation room. Khan was able to sympathize with her incapacity to use language as an idiom either to express herself or to relate to him. He permitted open motility and limited touching of his books, and he felt that his capacity to hold her in the analytic space gradually led her to tolerate him as a separate person, distant but related. He described the development of some distance between himself and the patient and the gradual creation of an illusional space in which the patient could begin to explore language as playing. Her incapacity and rage were valid to Khan as existential facts. Crucial in the developments described in this analysis was the fact that he had not tried to intrude upon these two areas of her experience with interpretations.

Khan discussed his findings in terms of Winnicott's paper (1951) on transitional objects and phenomena in which the concept of illusion was first introduced to psychoanalysis. Khan stressed the importance of a period of hesitation, as related to playing and transitional phenomena, which provides the matrix for the emergence of the area of illusion. He noted that the concept of resistance in classical analysis takes for granted the capacity to operate in such an area, while his concept of a period of hesitation, borrowed from Winnicott (1951), connotes the emergence of a capacity which is as yet far from established as an ego function. Following Winnicott (1945), Khan also wrote of the importance of the maternal holding environment for the development of these ego functions, noting that moments of illusion develop as the mother and child live and experience together.

In concluding, Khan suggested that his first patient had made of language and mentation a frenzied existence that had a momentum all its own; neither vehicles of self-knowledge or relating, they had functioned to negate the reality of the analytic space and the analyst, as well as that of emotionality. This was seen as a usurpation of the legitimate functions of the bodily organs; illusion breaks down and fantasy generates into mentation, while language usurps the functions that belong to organs of experience and discharge—a pathogenic distortion of the ego. Khan stressed the importance of recognizing that with certain patients who have not established this area of illusion the analyst must technically endeavor to curtail his hypermentation to facilitate the emergence of this area of illusion and the period of hesitation.

It may be seen, then, that Khan has described here, to use the terms developed in his paper, his own recognition that not all patients are able to create a type A communicative bipersonal field. The particular patients that he described appear to have developed Type B and Type C communicative fields respectively, possibly, however, in part because his own responses had qualities that fosterd their specific development. His clinical observations vividly define some of the qualities of these two communicative fields, and his discussion serves to clarify aspects of their genetic basis and the distinctive analytic techniques required by each.

In a separate series of studies, most of them published in Spanish, Liberman (in press) has attempted to delineate styles of psychoanalytic dialogue that he identified in terms of both the patient's ways of offering his material and the analyst's manner of receiving and interpreting it. These styles are correlated with specific ego states, anxieties, and mechanisms of defense and are classified in terms of clinical diagnostic entities, modes of communication, and linguistic styles. The latter are described as occurring in persons looking for unknowns without creating suspense, lyrical, epic, narrative, seeking unknowns and creating suspense, and dramatic with esthetic impact. Each requires a distinctive interventional response by the analyst.

It is beyond the scope of this presentation to further describe the typology developed by Liberman and to compare it with the classification offered here. Perhaps most important for the moment is the recognition that this analyst is attempting to explore a dimension of the analytic interaction that is comparable to the area under investigation here and that his particular contribution attempts to investigate the interrelatedness of clinical diagnosis, style of defense, mode of communication, linguistic usage, and interpretive response— an endeavor that points to the rich complexities and extensive clinical importance of these studies.[2]

CLINICAL VIGNETTES

Because of my unmodifiable commitment to the total confidentiality of my own therapeutic and analytic work, it will not be feasible for me to present material from this work, even though such an approach would, due to the interactional emphasis, prove especially meaningful. I will instead offer a series of highly condensed clincal segments drawn from my supervisory experiences and trust that they will orient the reader sufficiently to discover and elaborate personally the basic concepts presented here. I do plan to offer far more elaborate and specific clinical vignettes in a series of future publications.

Case 1

Mr. A. was in psychotherapy with Dr. Z., who had also treated his brother. The early phase of this treatment was characterized by occasional family sessions, contacts with Mr. A.'s parents, a wide variety of noninterpretive interventions by Dr. Z., and frequent modifications in the basic ground rules. At one point, an emergency arose and it was necessary for Dr. Z. to take an extended vacation. Dr. Z. explained the details of the illness in one of his parents that had necessitated the trip, and the patient had responded in a rather chaotic manner with a multiplicity of questions; he missed the last session prior to the therapist's trip and two of the three initial sessions when therapy was resumed.

In subsequent sessions, the patient was rather directly demanding and provocative of Dr. Z, who attempted to interpret these reactions as a reflection of Mr. A's anger over the unexpected interruption. There was no sense of validation of these interventions: the patient tended to deny hostile feelings regarding his therapist's trip and instead behaved quite provocatively at home—to the point of evoking urgent telephone calls from Mr. A's mother to Dr. Z. This situation remained chaotic until Dr. Z. began to refuse to talk to Mr. A's parents on the telephone and interpreted directly to the patient that he seemed involved in efforts to either destroy the treatment process itself or to so disturb Dr. Z. that he would feel inordinately frustrated, angry, or disorganized. To this, the patient responded by remembering how, just prior to the session, he had fought with his mother over a petty issue, not allowing her to offer any possible compromise and refusing to even understand what he now recognized were her rather sensible arguments. He had virtually driven her up a wall.

It appears that through a variety of noninterpretive interventions and inappropriate modifications of the framework, this therapist was utilizing his patient as an inappropriate container for his own pathological projective identifications (Langs 1976a) and that his own propensity to create a Type B communicative field had reinforced the patient's tendencies in this direction. As a result, this bipersonal field was characterized by unconscious exchanges of projective identification and pathological reprojections, without insight or control in either participant. Efforts by the therapist to treat the patient's behaviors and associations as symbolic communications, based on the mistaken hypothesis that a Type A field prevailed, were met with nonconfirmation and the intensification of disruptive behaviors and projective identifications by the patient. There is evidence too that while this therapist considered his interventions themselves to be symbolic communications, they actually constituted a vehicle for pathological projective identifications on his part—a means of discharging inner tension rather than offering true cognitive insight.

Under the influence of supervision, the therapist undertook extensive efforts toward self-analysis and toward rectifying the frame. In addition, by limiting his interventions to the symbolic interpretation of the patient's pathological projective identifications, he found derivative, symbolic validation, as illustrated in the patient's recollection of his quarrel with his mother. In addition to offering cognitive insight, this interpretation provided the patient with an opportunity (a) to experience the therapist's capacity to metabolize and understand his potentially disruptive projective identifications and (b) to receive a reprojection that had been detoxified. Subsequent associations alluded to a teacher who was able to handle another instructor's class when it got out of control and included associations to the calming effect on all concerned. This positive introject also helped the patient better manage his own inner impulses and propensities toward pathological projective identification. With additional working through, his behavior calmed down considerably both in the treatment situation and at home.

The patient began a session some months later by wondering if his mother had again called the therapist. He had been anxious in a restaurant while eating with his parents, and for the first time his mother was tolerant; Mr. A felt that this reflected the direct influence of the therapist. The patient had two oral presentations pending and wanted the therapist to tell him how to manipulate his professors so that he would not have to present in front of the classes. One of the teachers might understand, but the other would be very destructive. When the therapist remained silent, the patient kept asking what he should do and demanded an answer. The therapist then intervened and noted that the patient appeared to have assumed that he, the therapist, had spoken to his mother and told her how to handle him, and that he therefore felt that the therapist should advise him about the school problem as well.

The patient now alluded to past telephone conversations between the therapist and his mother and said that on the one hand, the therapist did not like to be rude, but on the other hand, he would not violate his patient's trust. The patient had spoken to a friend (a peer with whom he had an evident latent homosexual relationship) rather extensively about his own therapy and about his fantasies of collusion between his therapist and his parents. He thought of his mother and father as weak and incompetent fools.

The therapist pointed out that the patient had very intense feelings regarding the prior contacts with his parents and seemed quite infuriated by them. Mr. A. then spoke of his trust of the therapist, but after some elaboration in this direction, he suddenly indicated that these conversations had indeed been a violation—something like his parents coming into his room and opening his drawers but finding nothing. He turned to the onset of his symptoms, which included intense anxiety when speaking in class and when eating, and wondered if he could now understand what had really happened.

In this hour, we can see continued efforts by the patient to create with the therapist a Type B field in which the discharge of tension and immediate gratification would prevail. When the therapist did not respond in kind, and implied as well that the frame was now secure in regard to the confidentiality of the treatment, the patient shifted to symbolic communication and the bipersonal field took on characteristics of a Type A field. In the adaptive context of the previous alteration of the framework and its present rectification, the patient offerred Type Two derivatives that implied an unconscious perception of the deviant therapist as one who was gratifying unconscious homosexual fantasies and defending himself against them as well, whatever additional homosexual gratification and defense the arrangements and qualities of the interaction had for Mr. A. himself. The patient also communicated his unconscious perception of himself and the therapist in this context as foolish and incompetent. With the further effort at interpretation, the patient modified his massive denial regarding the therapist's violation of his confidentiality and conveyed this realization through a simile. This constituted a symbolic representation of a type previously quite unusual for this patient. Thus, there was a growing change not only in this patient's behaviors, but also in his mode of interacting and in the form of his communication. I would view the patient's return to his initial symptoms and his renewed search for understanding as a reflection of his hope for more insightful resolution of the relevant unconscious fantasies, memories, conflicts, etc.—a hope based on the growing development between himself and his therapist of a Type A communicative field.

I would make a particular point of the patient's comment that the violation in confidentiality was something like his parents' searching his drawers and finding nothing. In addition to extensively exchanging pathological projective identifications, this patient and therapist had created interactional interludes which were quite static and empty. These occurred despite the therapist's efforts at intervening. The patient's unconscious communication here seems to stress the extent to which pathological projective identification and mutual acting out, as well as cliched interventions, are designed on one level to create voids and absence of true meaning.

Case 2

Mr. B. was in psychotherapy with Dr. Y. During the initial months, his sessions were characterized by lengthy and detailed narratives with no apparent adaptive context. He would talk of both major and sometimes seemingly insignificant problems on his job, of the details of his sexual exploits, and of a variety of problems with his male peers. Efforts by the therapist, based largely on Type One derivatives, to suggest general unconscious hostility, sexual and bodily anxieties, and competitiveness with his peers, and additional attempts to relate these themes and anxieties to the therapeutic relationship, generated both responses that were flat and nonvalidating and new lengthy tales.

Soon, the therapist became relatively silent. When the patient hinted at a possible source of anxiety, Dr. Y. suggested concerns about treatment and anxieties about becoming involved. In general, the patient rather flatly acknowledged such worries, but had little more to say. In one session during this period, the patient began his hour by describing his sense of invincibility and how readily he gets past dangers and problems. He had once been suspended from his job and had neatly manipulated his reinstatement. He had nicely evaded serving in the armed forces. After describing in some detail the relevant experiences, he alluded to an address before a meeting of the tenants in his apartment house. He was the vice president of the tenant organization, but the president, frightened because a tenant had been killed in the building, had turned the meeting over to the patient. Under these pressures, Mr. B. felt weak and forced to reveal himself. Although that night he had had some kind of homosexual dream, he denied homosexual fears and went on in some detail regarding his preference for women, noting, however, that he had had many strange fantasies about them. He concluded this hour by stating that he wanted to get to know himself better, but somehow it all seemed so pointless.

In the following session the patient went on in great detail about his job, about games and roles, about not knowing what to believe and about how disturbed he was with his way of life. His parents had never helped him discover himself and he had had to learn how to meet his own needs. Again in some detail, he described a sexual relationship with a girlfriend who seldom talked to him and who had been shocked when he revealed his secrets, including his fears of impregnating her. Sometimes he liked women that he could dominate even when he was afraid of them. The next few hours were similarly ruminative.

In assessing this clinical situation, there was evidence that both patient and therapist had initially created a Type C field in which the patient generated extended narratives without a relevant adaptive context or meaningful bridges to the therapeutic relationship. It seems likely that his use of language in these hours was designed as a barrier and falsification with which he covered underlying homosexual fantasies and perceptions pertinent to his relationship with the therapist. Unconsciously, the therapist had attempted to give these manifest associations pertinence and meaning, without however alluding to the underlying homosexual problems. His interventions had proved to serve as cliches that reinforced the patient's own facade and intensified the Type C qualities of the bipersonal field. The patient felt disillusioned and even bored at times, while the therapist felt somewhat confused and distracted, finding little to grasp in the patient's long tales.

Under the influence of supervision, the therapist became relatively silent and intervened occasionally in respect to the patient's needs for defensive obstacles. While these interventions did not sufficiently utilize the various metaphorical representations of these barriers communicated by the patient, unconsciously they sufficiently conveyed the therapist's willingness to modify the Type C field into a Type A mode so that the patient responded with the session described here.

In this particular hour, the patient described the false sense of invincibility that one can derive from impenetrable Type C field barriers. He implied, however, that such manipulations leave one vulnerable and proceeded to talk of the tenant's meeting—a situation with a background of violence in which he was forced into the spotlight. This appeared to be the patient's experience of the therapist's recent interventions, and it conveyed the therapeutic anxiety characteristic of a Type A field. Compromising but endeavoring to communicate, the patient then referred vaguely to a homosexual dream, but immediately denied homosexual anxieties. He turned to fantasies of women and yet recognized that something was awry. He went on in some detail, indicated his wish to get to know himself better, and when the therapist failed to intervene, he became disillusioned. In the following hour, there was a static and flat quality, some indirect, Type Two derivative allusions to the therapist's failure to help the patient discover himself and to an unconscious perception of Dr. Y.'s dread of containing Mr. B.'s primitive inner mental world—a dread undoubtedly shared by Mr. B. was well.

In the adaptive context of the therapist's silent listening and interventions regarding the patient's undue defensiveness, this session conveys in Type Two derivative form the patient's fear of revealing himself within the therapeutic situation and the underlying violence-related and homosexual anxieties. The patient had offered a bridge to the treatment situation, and the therapist should have interpreted that the patient was experiencing pressures in the treatment situation to reveal himself and that he sensed the background of violence and homosexual fears which the patient tried to obliterate through vagueness and a shift to thoughts about woman. In this way, the therapist would have responded with a cognitive symbolic interpretation of his own to the patient's shift toward a Type A mode of communication. In the communicative realm, this would have reinforced the patient's development of a Type A field and conveyed the therapist's capacity to contain and metabolize the patient's primitive inner mental fantasies and perceptions, his valid unconscious perceptions of the therapist's anxieties, and the symbolic mode of communication. Based on what we must postulate as his own need for massive defensiveness and noncommunication, the therapist failed to intervene, and the patient responded with relatively embedded or concealed derivatives—centered for the moment on the therapist's inappropriate anxieties and failures to contain. When the therapist was unable to understand the meanings of these latter communications, the patient shifted back to the Type C mode for several sessions.

Case 3

Mrs. C was a fifty-eight-year-old woman in treatment with Dr. X. For some months therapy had been based on a so-called supportive approach, filled with such alterations in the framework as last-minute changes in the hours, self-revelations by the therapist, and extensive use of noninterpretive interventions. There had been, however, no sense of progress, and the patient's difficulties with an insensitive husband and a drug-addicted daughter continued to plague her and to generate repeated episodes of depression.

Under the influence of supervision, the therapist, over several weeks, rectified the frame and initiated efforts to intervene, primarily on an interpretive level. The patient's sessions, which had been quite disorganized and seemingly meaningless to the therapist, became filled with affect and a unique sense of meaning.

During one hour at this time, the patient tearfully spoke of her drug-addicted daughter and her need for proper limits. She had visited another daughter and fro the first time spoken meaningfully to her and experienced a sense of warmth. The patient had felt a great sense of relief, but there had been something disquieting and strange about the experience. Together with this daughter, the patient for the first time confronted her husband regarding his drug-addicted child and he became disorganized and wanted to leave. When this daughter had been ill as a child, her husband had been unavailable. During the pregnancy with this child, the patient had nearly suffered a miscarriage but her obstetrician had put her to bed and changed her medication, thereby saving the situation.

At this point in the session, the patient asked the therapist if she should take medication. He responded that the patient was now expressing feelings she had previously suppressed and which both she and her family feared, and that now she wanted to run away from them again. Mrs. C then said she had been thinking of a vacation, but was afraid of leaving her addicted daughter in the house, since she and her friends would wreck it. The patient recalled a similar discussion early in treatment and remembered the therapist as saying it would have been better for everyone if the house had caught fire when the daughter was in it. The therapist responded that the patient was becoming quite afraid of the feelings she was now experiencing in treatment and that she had a need to generate an image of him as unfeeling and destructive. The patient ended the hour by saying that she had been afraid that the therapist would give up on her and was relieved that he hadn't; she felt that she would be able to make it someday.

In the adaptive context of the rectified frame, we may sense the therapeutic regression and anxiety developing in this patient as she shifted from a Type C to a Type A communicative field. Prior to the corrective efforts of the therapist, Mrs. C. and Dr. X had used language primarily for noncommunication, and the bipersonal field had a distinctly static quality. The therapist's seeming kindnesses unconsciously were designed to help cover over his patient's inner destructiveness and, in all probability, parallel problems within himself. They were part of an effort at creating falsifications that could conceal far more painful truths.

In a sense, then, it is no coincidence that the patient responded to the securing of the frame with the communication of Type Two derivatives related to her unconscious perception and introjection of the therapist's initial stance and its alteration. Her reference to her husband's fear of the truth and wish to flee, along with her request for medication, contains in derivative form both (a) her dread of her own inner mental world and a Type A communicative field, plus related efforts to shift back to the Type C field through the use of medication as an obliterating agent, and (b) the therapist's previous dread of these same inner contents and his reinforcement of the patient's massive defenses.

The patient's validating responses to the therapist's initial interventions, however lacking in specifics, demonstrates how the interface of the bipersonal field shifts significantly toward the pathology of the patient in the absence of countertransference-based inputs from the therapist. In derivative form, the patient communicated both her dread of inner devastation and her fear of her uncontrolled destructiveness toward her addicted daughter. It is not surprising that the patient attempted to project and projectively identify these impulses into the therapist and that, in addition, she communicated these anxieties in the form of a fabrication (however destructive the therapist's attitude had been toward both the patient and this daughter, he was certain that he had never consciously expressed a blatantly murderous wish toward either of them).

It appears that the patient wished once again to utilize the therapist in creating a misalliance and bastion through which the truth might still remain unknown. In this situation, however, it is quite evident that the patient's defenses are no longer in the form of amorphous and impenetrable barriers, but instead quite clearly reveal both the underlying nature of the defense itself and the fantasies and impulses that are being defended against. It is, as I said above, the presence of such derivatives in the face of the patient's defensiveness, and their analyzability as Type Two derivatives within a specific adaptive context, that characterizes resistances in the Type A field. Showing some appreciation for the symbolic qualities of the patient's communications, the therapist interpreted aspects of the patient's defenses and anxieties, and despite the fact that his intervention once again fell short of the specificity and depth required in this situation, the patient responded with a sense of appreciation for the therapist's perserverance, and by implication, for their shared capacity to modify the Type C field into a more hopeful, however painful, Type A mode.

Case 4

As a final illustration I will turn to the psychotherapy of Mr. D., who had been treated some years earlier in a clinic for what had appeared to be an ambulatory schizophrenic syndrome with multiple obsessions, phobias, and depression. He was now in twice-weekly psychotherapy with a private therapist who essentially had offered the patient a secure frame and hold, occasional general interpretations based on Type One derivatives, and a sense of tolerance for the patient's anxieties, along with some capacity to contain Mr. D.'s disruptive projective identifications—although these were seldom metabolized toward interpretive insights. Over many months, the patient's symptoms had gradually improved to the point where he appeared capable of confronting his dreaded phobic situations and his obsession seemed no longer horrifying, overintense, or disruptive to his functioning. It seemed evident that termination was somewhere invisibly in the air, although neither patient or therapist had as yet suggested it.

During one session at this time, the patient meticulously detailed a journey that he had taken recently by railroad in connection with his job as a salesman. He described the experience several times over and emphasized how fine he felt and how different it was from years ago when he would panic and fear being overwhelmed as the train moved along, or even worse, getting upset that it might suddenly break down stuck. His girlfriend of several years had been surprised that he had handled this particular trip so well, and the patient spent much of the final part of the session asking the therapist what he thought about what his patient had accomplished.

During the next hour, the patient described another trip in some detail. On this occasion, the train had been stuck in a tunnel, and the patient had been momentarily frightened, but then felt quite well. For a moment, he felt that it was not himself who was on that train, but this passed, as did another momentary feeling that the train was not really stuck—that nothing was happening. He then ruminated at length over earlier episodes in which he had been stuck on trains and elevators, and the type of panic and anxiety that he had experienced. He stressed the extent to which this was not present now and how this characterized him in the past, not in the present. In response to continued inquiries as to the therapist's thoughts about all of this, Dr. W. suggested that the patient seemed to have mastered his bodily anxieties and fears of disintegration. The patient felt quite reassured and repeated this therapist's formulation in several different versions.

During the next hour, the patient ruminated in some detail about how well he was feeling. He recalled a dream in which a young man, E., who had recently been fired at the patient's place of business, invited Mr. D. to undress and get into bed with him. He suggested that they perform fellatio on each other. The dream reminded him of homosexual fantasies and anxieties that he had had some years back, although, he said, he had none of these feelings in the present. He had enjoyed working with E. and would miss him. E. was very good at making up stories and at hiding from the boss, and all this reminded the patient of times when he would lock himself in the bathroom at work in order not to be disturbed. After ruminating about his job, the patient asked Dr. W. what he thought about the dream and the therapist remained silent. The patient ended the hour by ruminating further about his job.

During the next session, the patient described a battle with his girlfriend and his rage at her for always changing the subject and not facing issues. He spoke in some detail again about the firing of E. and his own concerns about suddenly losing his job. For him, it would be an unreal experience, and he would just disappear for a few weeks if it were to happen. On the other hand, he might want to come to his sessions; he would be afraid of losing the therapist's support. Here, the therapist intervened and suggested that the patient was concerned about the eventual termination of his treatment and that he had a need to put such a possibility at a distance and create barriers to the anger and turmoil it would create for him. The patient stated that he had had a strange thought that the therapist might want to end the treatment. He had had a fleeting image of going berserk but had then gotten himself under control and really didn't feel worried about it. Besides, it was too soon to end treatment, and he really didn't think that the therapist would just kick him out.

In the next hour, the patient reported a dream about a man who seemed to be chasing him out of his own apartment. There was some sense of a sexual threat, something like the danger of rape, but then the patient had found himself in an empty vault with the door closed and had felt safe and protected. The patient ruminated about a man at the bank that he mistrusted and about details of his job. He had had thoughts of changing his bank because he no longer felt appreciated as a customer, but he had really put the matter quite out of his mind. Often, when he felt conflicted, he could make his mind a blank and feel relief. The therapist pointed out that the patient had a tendency to seal himself off from dangers and to seek safety in voids; he suggested that this was reflected not only in his dream but in the way in which he was communicating in the session. The patient responded by recalling childhood fears of bombs and explosions, and by remembering fantasies about attacking his boss for firing E.—fantasies that he had forgotten until that moment. In a rather tentative way, he wondered if all this had something to do with the possibility of his treatment ending; he did feel much better and perhaps it was time to think about it after all.

This material illustrates the development of a Type C communicative field, largely based on the patient's intense need for unmodifiable barriers, an impenetrable container for his psychotic core. While the therapist appears initially to have contributed to the Type C field by attempting to interpret contents that had been communicated by the patient largely as a means of denying any difficulty and creating an impenetrable barrier to the underlying anxieties and fantasies, we see in the sequence that Dr. W. soon recognized that such interventions were not confirmed and seemed to have little effect on the patient.

In the adaptive context of anxieties regarding eventual termination, this material initially served as a distracting fabrication designed to avoid this subject and its ramifications for the patient totally. Perhaps in part because the therapist introduced bodily anxieties which the patient introjected as Dr. W.'s unconscious homosexual difficulties, Mr. D. did report an overtly homosexual dream. However, despite a few fragmented derivative associations—e.g., the firing of Mr. E.—the material remained quite flat and was without a clear-cut adaptive context (the day residue related to Mr. E.'s loss of the job actually covered the more significant concern about termination which the patient essentially avoided). The subsequent associations did not generate derivative meaning. In this session, the patient represented the Type C field symbolically through the references to hiding and locking himself in the bathroom, but the therapist failed to intervene. As a result, the following hour was quite ruminative, although the patient did eventually produce rather remote and thin derivatives related to possible termination. When the therapist intervened in this regard, the patient responded with initial validation and then denial.

During the following hour, there was a shift toward Type A

communication, especially after the therapist interpreted the patient's use of denial, emptiness, and barriers. The dream itself appears to represent fantasies and anxieties related to the possible termination of the treatment, as do the additional associations prior to the therapist's next intervention. Following that comment, the patient found a means of representing his dread of losing control of his explosive and primitive inner mental world; he then quickly reconstituted.

This sequence reflects, first, the type of underlying material that tends to be revealed by patients in a Type C field when their massive defensiveness and use of fabrication to generate nonmeaning are pointed out to them. Secondly, we see that in a Type C field dreams are quickly sealed off and that even when there are some derivative associations and a meaningful adaptive context, the patient remains rather constricted and fearful. Through the therapist's proper intervening, it appears that this patient was able to express aspects of his dreaded inner mental world and that he felt capable of managing these disruptive contents. Subsequent sessions suggest that this was not a return to rigid Type C barriers, but instead, that it represented a better degree of flexibility, a softening of his defenses, and a capacity to better manage the inner contents experienced when he momentarily modified these defenses. Earlier in treatment, such breakthroughs of explosive content were followed by repeated ruminative sessions and intense efforts at noncommunication and barrier formation, including rather striking use of denial and projection. At this point in treatment, the therapist felt that these efforts had been considerably modified in a positive direction.

Earlier in treatment, this patient had repeatedly objected to the therapist's interventions on the grounds that he—the patient—made it a practice to conceal his most important communications from the therapist for several weeks at a time. As a result, since every effort at interpretation undertaken by this therapist was actually based on accepting the patient's ruminations (essentially fabrications, or lies, designed to cover the painful underlying truths) the therapist was consistent and met with ridicule and refutation. The therapist soon became aware of the significance of this mechanism, and began to interpret its function, no longer endeavoring to interpret content. In a manner that cannot be detailed here, these efforts to deal first with the patient's communicative mode significantly modified this defense to the point that the patient was able to renounce it. During the period within which the patient maintained this mechanism, the therapist felt enormously frustrated: he was working with images that the patient would immediately make disappear by telling him that these were not his important associations, and he experienced himself as if he were under a vicious attack designed to destroy his integrity, his capacity to interpret, and perhaps even his own sanity. Whle I will not attempt to further document this therapeutic interlude, I refer to it in concluding these clinical vignettes in an effort to characterize the underlying envy and destructiveness that prevails in a Type C communicative field, the truly deceptive qualities of the patient's associations as they function to destroy meaning rather than to generate it, and the absurdity of attempting to interpret such contents in light of their true nature.

CONCLUDING COMMENTS

It is my impression that the delineation of three major communicative styles and fields has extensive clinical and theoretical ramifications. Investigations of the communicative properties of the bipersonal field not only sheds light on the intrapsychic and interactional realms, and their interplay, but also generates an additional level of conceptualization that extends beyond these two familiar spheres. I shall therefore conclude this presentation with a brief listing of some of the major implications of these concepts.

1. Basic to the conceptualization of communicative bipersonal fields is the listening process. In this respect, consistent efforts must be maintained to identify the adaptive context for the patient's associations and behaviors, and it is essential to organize this material in terms of manifest content and Type One and Type Two derivatives. In addition, one needs sensitivity to interactional mechanisms and a capacity to experience, metabolize, and understand the patient's projective identifications, validating all such experiences through the patient's verbal associations. These listening, experiencing, and organizing abilities must be applied not only to the patient's communications, but also to those of the therapist as well. In this manner, it becomes feasible to monitor fluctuations in the nature of the communicative field and to identify the main instigator for such shifts.

2. While it appears evident that the Type A communicative mode is

essential for the therapist or analyst, and represents the greatest degree of maturation for both patient and therapist, insightful therapeutic work is feasible in each communicative field. Such endeavors, however, require a symbolic interpretive capacity in the therapist, without which he will be unable to interpret the patient's unconscious fantasies, memories, and introjects as they appear in a Type A field related to the patient's intrapsychic conflicts and anxieties; neither will be able to properly metabolize and interpret projective identifications in the Type B field, nor the negation of meaning and use of amorphous barriers in the Type C Field. Inherent to such an interpretive approach is the generation of positive, ego building introjective identifications that occur quite unconsciously in the course of the therapeutic interaction. Insight and positive introjection go hand and hand, and are the essential basis of adaptive structural changes (Langs 1976a,c).

3. The intrapsychic and interactional nature of defensive formations are distinctive to each communicative field. In a Type A Field we find the array of defenses described in the classical psychoanalytic literature—repression, displacement, isolation, and the like. However, in addition to their intrapsychic basis, they are open to interactional influence in that both pressures toward, and models of, defensiveness and resistance may be offered to the patient by the therapist, generating what I have termed *interactional defenses and resistances* (Langs 1976a,c). In the Type A field, the patient characteristically expresses these resistances in a form that includes the communication of Type Two derivatives related both to the unconscious meaning and functions of the defense-resistance itself and the unconscious fantasies, memories, and introjects which are being defended against—most often in relation to the analyst. There is a sense of depth to the patient's resistances and they are essentially analyzable over a reasonable period of time.

In a Type B field, the major defenses will be interactional, with intrapsychic underpinings. They will take the form of defensive utilization of projective identification as a means of disburdening the psyche of anxiety and placing intolerable fantasies and introjects into the object—here, from patient into therapist. However, these defensive projective identifications have in common with the resistances seen in the Type A field that they serve a positive communicative function, so that the patient's behaviors and verbal associations tend ultimately to reveal the unconscious nature, meaning, and function of the defensive projective identification and the underlying contents that the patient wishes to externalize.

In a Type C field, however, the patient's defenses and resistances have a distinct sense of flatness and emptiness and are in themselves basically designed for noncommunication, absence of understanding, falsification, and impenetrability. For long periods in such therapies, there are few, if any, interpretable derivatives related to these defenses and the disturbing contents that they seal off. At best, the Type C patient will communicate occasional metaphors—Type one derivatives—with which they represent the nature of their communicative style. It is therefore not feasible to interpret these defense-resistances in depth or, as a rule, in terms of a specific adaptive context and Type Two derivatives.

4. The therapist's basic interventions are also distinctive for each bipersonal field. In the Type A field, his basic tools involve the maintenance of a secure framework and the use of interpretations and reconstructions derived largely from Type Two derivatives—unconscious fantasies and perceptions—related to the therapeutic interaction, in terms of both transference and nontransference. Such work will center upon the analysis of defenses and resistance on the first level, and core unconscious fantasies, memories, and introjects on the second.

In a Type B field, the basic tool is the acceptance and containment, metabolism and understanding, and interpretation of the patient's projective identifications in terms of their defensive and core meanings. In this field, the maintenance of a secure frame is also essential; the work proceeds from resistances to core contents as it does in the Type A field. However, while Type Two derivatives are the main material for interpretation in the Type A field, in the Type B field much of the analytic work is based on the patient's projective identifications. These interactional projections can, however, be organized around meaningful adaptive contexts and thus permit dynamic and genetic interpretations, much of it once again related to the therapeutic interaction in terms of both transference and nontransference.

In the Type C field, specific adaptive contexts are rare, as are Type Two derivatives. Much of the therapeutic work is based on the patient's projective identification into the therapist of meaninglessness, and his use of falsifications, noncommunication, and opaque barriers. The interpretive work must therefore utilize Type One derivatives in the form of metaphors from the patient related to these defensive barriers and the efforts at noncommunication; the effective interpretation of these resistances will also permit periods of interpretation and reconstruction of the emerging material.

5. It follows from this discussion that we can no longer maintain the unitary model of the course of a satisfactory psychoanalysis or psychotherapy, of the indications for termination, and of the definition of *cure*. To date, the classical psychoanalytic literature has delineated these factors in terms of the Type A field, correctly suggesting that with such patients the analytic work concentrates on the analysis of transference (and nontransference) in terms of resistances, core fantasies, memories, and introjects, current dynamics, and reconstructions of significant past experiences and responses to them. True structural change is defined accordingly and derives primarily from the cognitive insights accrued from these interpretive and reconstructive efforts, and secondarily from the positive introjections of the analyst that occur spontaneously and unconsciously in the course of such work. Termination is indicated at the point of symptom relief based on the working through of the relevant areas of conflict and disturbance and on the establishment of stabilized insight and other inner adaptive changes. Such accomplishments imply a diminution in the use of pathological defenses and an improved capacity to manage one's inner mental world.

In a Type B field, much of the analytic work is done through the metabolism and interpretation of the patient's pathological projective identifications, efforts that include the interpretation of their defensive and unconscious content dimensions. In the course of a successful treatment, there is a modification in the extent to which the patient utilizes pathological projective identifications. This is accomplished in part through the interpretation of their nature and function and in part through the introjective identification by the patient of the constructively modified projective contents as they are validly reprojected by the therapist into the patient. This interactional process generates constructive introjective identifications based on therapist introjects, process introjects, and the reception of detoxified reprojections. Overall, the therapeutic process may be seen as achieving a diminution in the use of pathological projective identifications and a modification or detoxification of the contents and inner states so projected. In addition, from time to time, there will be opportunities for the interpretation and reconstruction of symbolic communications and Type Two derivatives as well.

In all, then, the goal of analysis or therapy with these patients is symptom relief based primarily on insightful and structuralized modifications of their use of pathological projective identifications and secondarily on alterations of the related pathological unconscious fantasies, memories, and introjects. With some Type B patients, it may be feasible to shift their basic mode to Type A communication, while with others, the outcome may take the form of more frequent use of Type A communications along with a less pathological use of the Type B mode. It is to be stressed that the pursuit of cognitive insights and symbolic interpretations of the patient's use of interactional mechanisms is a sine qua non; it is fundamental to the constructive cognitive and identificatory changes that take place within this field. My initial impression is that both definitive reconstructions and specific interpretations of unconscious fantasies, memories, and introjects will be feasible somewhat less often than with Type A patients.

In the Type C communicative field, the goal is to analyze and work through the efforts by these patients to destroy meaning and communication, and to maintain their impervious barriers against a highly disturbed inner core. Interpretive efforts concentrate on the complexity of these defenses and the patient's interactional projections of nonmeaning. From time to time, as the patient begins to modify the rigidity and destructiveness of these defenses, the primitive underlying contents—unconscious fantasies, memories, and introjects—will be expressed in derivative form and will lend themselves to interpretation and reconstruction. However, as one would expect, such interventions are less common with these patients than in the other two communicative fields. Termination with Type C patients is based both on the gradual modification of their rigid defenses plus their needs to destroy meaning and falsify, and on the periodic interpretation and reconstruction of the underlying contents and processes. Both cognitive and identificatory factors are involved, but an initial impression suggests that most of these patients maintain this communicative mode throughout their treatment, albeit in a gradually less pathological form. Occasionally, there may be a major shift to the Type A form.

6. We may briefly consider the interaction between patient and analyst, or therapist, based on their individual preferred communica-

tive mode. A Type A therapist will feel adequately held and stimulated by a Type A patient and should work well in developing interpretations and reconstructions of the patient's Type Two Derivative symbolic communications. Potentially, such a therapist should be capable, with a Type B patient, of containing, metabolizing, and interpreting the patient's projective identifications, though there is a danger of countertransference-based defensiveness and other inappropriate reactions. At times such a therapist may feel and be somewhat overwhelmed by these interactional pressures. A common countertransference problem in this symbolically functioning Type A therapist takes the form of a failure to consciously recognize the patient's interactional projections and a related tendency to disregard the interactional sphere.

Finally, with the Type C patient there may be a strong sense of boredom, and a possibility of failure to understand the true nature and functions of the patient's associations. A Type A therapist may have difficulty in empathizing with a Type C patient and may have problems in recognizing the need of such a patient to destroy meanings and to erect impenetrable barriers. Such therapists may be inclined to attribute and interpret meaning where none is intended, experiencing the reversing-perspective and embedded-figure types of experiences referred to earlier in this paper. There may be countertransference-based hostility and seductiveness in Type A therapists with Type C patients, as well as efforts unconsciously designed to rupture their most frustrating defensive alignment. The implicit envy and destructiveness in the Type C form of communication may evoke countertransference-based reactions of various types within a Type A analyst. If such a therapist comes to terms with the patient's communicative mode, he can then become capable of patient and meaningful interventions when indicated.

The Type B therapist will be bored by a Type A patient, will have difficulties in interpreting and reconstructing, and will tend to use language as a means of discharging his own anxieties and as a form of interactional projection into his patient. The therapist's communicative mode will exert great pressures on the Type A patient to shift toward a responsive Type B mode or a defensive Type C form. Because virtually all therapists maintain an ideal of Type A functioning, it is often difficult to recognize one's own tendencies toward Type B communication through the discharge use of language and mismanagement of the framework that are consciously intended and mistaken as validly therapeutic. In particular, the development of a Type B mode of communication in a patient should direct the therapist toward similar propensities within himself, although in general, each therapist should undertake an extensive self-examination to determine his own communicative style and its fluctuations.

With the Type C patient, the Type B therapist is likely to feel quite bored and empty. He will tend to be prone to traumatic sexual and aggressive and other projective identifications into the Type C patient in an effort to rupture his defenses and to evoke responsive interactional projections.

A Type C therapist will be threatened by both the Type A and Type B patient. The former, with his symbolic communications and therapeutic regressive anxiety, will constitute a threat to the Type C therapist who dreads the inner mental world of both his patient and himself. These patients generate meaning and communication, and the Type C therapist will unconsciously intervene in a manner designed to destroy such meaning, to falsify, and to evoke amorphous barriers. Similarly, with a Type B patient who is generating meaningful and anxiety provoking projective identifications, the Type C therapist will be refractory in containing such projective identifications and will unconsciously endeavor to obliterate their presence. He will be greatly threatened by such interactional pressures, in that they could rupture his massive defenses and generate meaning in the face of his efforts to destroy such qualities. His own intensely sealed off psychotic core is under persistent pressures from the communications of both the Type A and Type B patient, and he will tend to respond countertransferentially in an effort to maintain his own relatively fragile equilibrium. In contrast, with the Type C patient he will feel comfortable and even interested, tending to share cliches and falsifications, as well as barriers, and to generate a typically stalemated therapeutic interaction.

In brief, a Type A patient will feel comfortable and work well with a Type A therapist. He will feel threatened and disorganized by a Type B therapist, and the experience of the therapist's pathological projective identifications will tend to evoke both unconscious curative efforts on his part and pathological interactional mechanisms as well. With a Type C therapist, he will experience a sense of emptiness and a lack of progress.

The Type B patient will find the Type A therapist who can interpret his projective identifications quite helpful, although he will make consistent efforts to evoke a misalliance in which pathological projective identifications are exchanged. With the Type B therapist, he may well feel a sense of comfort and become embroiled in a serious misalliance based on unconscious and repeated sequences of pathological projective identification and reintrojection. In the long run, however, such an interaction is destructive to both participants and may well lead to a rupture in the therapy. The Type B patient will feel little sense of relatedness to a Type C therapist, will sense the extent to which he is a danger to such a therapist, and will experience an uncertain treatment course of little valid help.

The Type C patient will endeavor to break his links or relatedness to the Type A therapist, but should such a therapist respond interpretively and empathically, he will undergo a slow development of progress and adaptive inner change. With a Type B therapist, the Type C patient will feel quite threatened and often will simply interrupt the treatment. With a Type C therapist, this patient will feel quite safe and will tend to accept the falsification and barriers offered by such a therapist. Some Type C patients, however, ultimately become dissatisfied with the stalemate and generate efforts at true communication. Should the therapist be incapable of modifying his own communicative style at such times, these patients will either become depressed and accept the stalemate or will terminate.

7. A few final comments: Dreams, symbols, and affects may appear in any of the three communicative fields. In a Type A field, all are utilized for meaningfully symbolic communication, while in a Type B field, they are in the service of discharge and projective identification rather than cognitive understanding. In a Type C field, they are designed as falsification and deceptions, and as a means of noncommunication.

Somatization seems more common in the Type B and Type C fields, especially the latter. In another vein, the genetics of communicative style, their relationship to personality, intrapsychic structure, self, and identity—all require extensive investigation. It appears too that the classical Freudians have been investigating the Type A field and it is their belief that they themselves characteristically work within the Type A mode. On the other hand, the Kleinians seems to be working a Type B field, whatever the contribution to this communicative mode made by from both patient and analyst. Many of the narcissistic patients recently described by Kohut (1971, 1977) and Kernberg, (1975) appear to function in the Type C field, and the therapeutic techniques described by Kohut have qualities of both the Type A and Type C communicative mode, while the formulations presented by Kernberg have both Type A and Type B dimensions. Finally, it appears that once a patient has been in treatment with a Type B or Type C therapist, it is extremely difficult for them to work with a Type A therapist and to tolerate the necessary therapeutic regression, symbolic communication, and anxiety required for effective analytic work in such a field.

These are but a few of the implications of the present formulations, many of which deserve extensive clinical investigation. In this context, I am reminded that there are those who feel that psychoanalysis is in a state of basic consolidation or even stalemate (see Rangell 1975), and others who find analysis to be in a state of considerable flux and creativity (see Green 1975). In addition to hoping that I have prompted the reader to take a fresh look at his interaction with his patients, I hope also to have demonstrated that there are many original and imaginative thinkers in psychoanalysis today—some of whom have been mentioned in the course of this presentation. Psychoanalysts should master their propensities for the Type B and Type C modes of communication, not only with their patients, but in their work at large, and should be capable of maintaining a Type A field in which they welcome new and even strange ideas and concepts, and tolerate the growth-promotiong anxieties and potential reorganization so contained (see Stone 1975). It is on this note that I conclude with the following:

Medium is message; medium determines message; medium must be analyzed before message.

NOTES

1. In this paper, I will not attempt to distinguish between the psychoanalytic and psychotherapeutic situations. Although in large part the ideas that will be developed have equal applicability to both modalities, I will allude primarily to the analytic experience, since most of the relevant literature is so focused. I wish to apologize for the personal historical approach I have adopted in

developing the themes of this paper; to the extent that they represent discoveries, the ideas presented here have had a very personal development and I have found no other means of doing full justice to my subject. I do, as well, offer full acknowledgement of the contributions of others (see also Langs 1976c).

2. After completing this paper, I found a study by Fiumara (1977) of the development of the symbolic function in infancy and in analysis. Many of her ideas overlap with and extend basic concepts discussed here. Fiumara's work indicates, as does that of Khan (1973), that the Type A field and mode of communication is, indeed, the most mature and optimal. Fiumara is sensitive as well to the roles of the framework and interpretations in creating conditions for possible symbolic communication, and alludes to the use of pseudosymbols and falsifications that are protective but inimical to growth.

Angel, K. (1971). Unanalyzability and narcissistic transference disturbances. *Psychoanalytic Quarterly* 40:264–276.

Balint, M. (1968). *The Basic Fault: Therapeutic Aspects of Regression.* London: Tavistock.

Baranger, M. and Baranger, W. (1966). Insight in the analytic situation. In *Psychoanalysis in the Americas,* ed. R. Litman, pp. 56–72. New York: International Universities Press.

Bion, W. (1962). *Learning from Experience.* In W.R. Bion, *Seven Servants.* New York: Jason aronson, 1977.

———(1963). *Elements of Psycho-Analysis.* In W.R. Bion, *Seven Servants.* New York: Jason aronson, 1977.

———(1965). *Transformations.* In W.R. Bion, *Seven Servants.* New York: Jason aronson, 1977.

———(1970) *Attention and Interpretation.* In W.R. Bion, *Seven Servants.* New York: Jason Aronson, 1977.

———(1977). *Seven Servants.* New York: Jason Aronson.

Bird, B. (1972). Notes on transference: universal phenomenon and the hardest part of analysis. *Journal of the American Psychoanalytic Association* 20:267–301.

Bleger, J. (1967). Psycho-analysis of the psychoanalytic frame. *International Journal of Psycho-Analysis* 48:511–519.

Fiumara, G. (1977). The symbolic function, transference and psychic reality. *International Review of Psycho-Analysis* 4:171–180.

Freud, S. (1914). Remembering, repeating, and working-through. *Standard Edition* 12:145–156.

Giovacchini, P. (1975). The concrete and difficult patient. In *Tactics and Techniques in Psychoanalytic Therapy,* ed. P. Giovacchini, pp. 351–363. New York: Jason Aronson.

Green, A. (1975). The analyst, symbolization and absence in the analytic setting (on changes in analytic practice and analytic experience). *International Journal of Psycho-Analysis* 56:1–22.

Greenson, R. (1967). *The Technique and Practice of Psychoanalysis.* Vol. 1. New York: International Universities Press.

Grinberg, L. (1962). On a specific aspect of counter-transference due to the patient's projective identification. *International Journal of Psycho-Analysis* 43:436–440.

Halpert, E. (1972). The effect of insurance on psychoanalytic treatment. *Journal of the American Psychoanalytic Association* 20:122–133.

Kernberg, O. (1975). *Borderline Conditions and Pathological Narcissism.* New York: Jason Aronson.

Khan, M. (1963). The concept of cumulative trauma. *The Psychoanalytic Study of the Child* 18:286–306.

———(1964). Ego distortion, cumulative trauma, and the role of reconstruction in the analytic situation. *International Journal of Psycho-Analysis* 45:272–278.

———(1973). The role of illusion in the analytic space and process. In *The Privacy of the Self,* pp. 251–269. New York: International Universities Press, 1974.

Kohut, H. (1971). *The Analysis of the Self: A Systematic Approach to the Psychoanalytic Treatment of Narcissistc Personality Disorders.* New York: International Universities Press.

———(1977). *The Restoration of the Self.* New York: International Universities Press.

Langs, R. (1971). Day residues, recall residues, and dreams: reality and the psyche. *Journal of the American Psychoanalytic Association* 19:499–523 [Chapter 2, this volume]

———(1972). A psychoanalytic study of material from patients in psychotherapy. *International Journal of Psychoanalytic Psychotherapy* 1(1):4–45 [Chapter 3, this volume]

———(1973). *The Technique of Psychoanalytic Psychotherapy.* Vol. 1. New York: Jason Aronson.

———(1975a). The patient's unconscious perception of the therapist's errors. In *Tactics and Techniques in Psychoanalytic Therapy, Vol 2: Countertransference,* ed. P. Giovacchini, pp. 239–250. New York: Jason Aronson [Chapter 5, this volume]

————(1975b). Therapeutic misalliances. *International Journal of Psychoanalytic Psychotherapy* 4:77–105 [Chapter 6, this volume]

————(1975c). The therapeutic relationship and deviations in technique. *International Journal of Psychoanalytic Psychotherapy* 4:106–141 [Chapter 7, this volume]

————(1976a). *The Bipersonal Field.* New York: Jason aronson.

————(1976b). On becoming a psychiatrist. *International Journal of Psychoanalytic Psychotherapy* 5:255–280. [Chapter 12, this volume]

————(1976c). *The Therapeutic Interaction,* Vols. 1 and 2. New York: Jason Aronson.

————(1978a). *Dreams in the Bipersonal Field.* New York: Jason Aronson (in press).

————(1978b). Validation and the framework of the therapeutic situation. *Contemporary Psychoanalysis* 14:98–124. [Chapter 14, this volume]

Liberman, D. (in press). Complementarity between the styles of the patient's material and the interpretation. *International Journal of Psychoanalytic Psychotherapy.*

Little, M. (1951). Countertransference and the patient's response to it. *International Journal of Psycho-Analysis* 32:32–40.

Milner, M. (1952). Aspects of symbolism and comprehension of the not=self. *International Journal of Psycho-Analysis* 33:181–195.

Racker, H. (1957). The meaning and uses of countertransference. *Psychoanalytic Quarterly* 26:303–357.

Rangell, L. (1975). Psychoanalysis and the process of change: an essay on the past, present and future. *International Journal of Psycho-Analysis* 56:87–98.

Searles, H. (1958). The schizophrenic's vulnerability to the therapist's unconscious process. *Journal of Nervous and Mental Disease* 127:247–262.

————(1959). The effort to drive the other person crazy—an element in the aetiology and psychotherapy of schizophrenia. *British Journal of Medical Psychology* 32:1–18.

————(1960). *The Nonhuman Environment.* New York: International Universities Press.

————(1965). *Collected Papers on Schizophrenia and Related Subjects.* New York: International Universities Press.

————(1970). Autism and the phase of transition to therapeutic symbiosis. *Contemporary Psychoanalysis* 7:1–20.

————(1971). Pathological symbiosis and autism. In *The Name of Life,* ed. B. Landis and E. Tauber, pp. 69–83. New York: Holt, Rinehart and Winston.

————(1972). The functions of the patient's realistic perceptions of the analyst in delusional transference. *British Journal of Medical Psychology* 45:1–18.

————(1973a). Concerning therapeutic symbiosis. *The Annual of Psychoanalysis* 1:247–262.

————(1973b). Some aspects of unconscious fantasy. *International Journal of Psychoanalytic Psychotherapy* 2:37–50.

————(1975). The patient as therapist to his analyst. In *Tactics and Techniques in Psychoanalytic Therapy, Vol. 2: Countertransference,* ed. P. Giovacchini. New York: Jason Aronson.

Segal, H. (1967). Melanie Klein's technique. *Psychoanalytic Forum* 2:197–211.

Stone, L. (1975). Some problems and potentialities of present-day psychoanalysis. *Psychoanalytic Quarterly* 44:331–370.

Viderman, S. (1974). Interpretation in the analytic space. *International Review of Psycho-Analysis* 1:467–480.

Wallerstein, R. (1977). Psychic energy reconsidered: Introduction. *Journal of the American Psychoanalytic Association* 25:529–536.

Wangh, M. (1962). The "evocation of a proxy": a psychological maneuver, its use as a defense, its purposes and genesis. *Psychoanalytic Study of the Child* 17:451–469.

Winnicott, D. (1945). Primitive emotional development. In *Collected Papers: Through Pediatrics to Psycho-Analysis.* pp. 145–156. London: Tavistock, 1958.

————(1951). Transitional objects and transitional phenomena. In *Collected Papers: Through Pediatrics to Psycho-Analysis.* pp. 229–242. London: Tavistock, 1958.

————(1956). Primary maternal preoccupation. In *Collected Papers: Through Pediatrics to Psycho-Analysis.* pp. 300–305. London: Tavistock, 1958.

————(1958). *Collected Papers: Through Pediatrics to Psycho-Analysis.* London: Tavistock.

————(1965). *The Maturational Processes and the Facilitating Environment.* London: Hogarth.

————(1971). *Playing and Reality.* New York: Basic Books.

Chapter Sixteen

Reactions to Creativity in Psychoanalysts

(1978[1977])

Harold Searles wrote his paper, "Concerning Transference and Countertransference," in late 1948 and early 1949. At the time, he was a candidate at the Washington-Baltimore Psychoanalytic Institute and a practicing psychiatrist anticipating his residency at the Chestnut Lodge Sanitorium. The paper was submitted during 1949 to two prestigious psychoanalytic journals; one responded with an unsigned form letter and rejection, while the other, also without accepting the paper, suggested that it was too broad and lengthy and that it required further research into the literature on transference phenomena. This latter journal also indicated that the paper had been carefully considered and that it had evoked interest in respect to some of Searles's ideas; they advised the author to submit other manuscripts in the future. The paper was then filed away and only brought to light in the course of a dialogue between Searles and myself (Langs and Searles, in press); it was reviewed by the Editorial Board of the *International Journal of Psychoanalytic Psychotherapy* and finally accepted for publication—some thirty years after its creation.

As I shall soon document, it is my belief that this paper is a remarkable and truly original contribution to the psychoanalytic literature. At the time it was written, its publication would have afforded Searles a striking place in the history of psychoanalytic thinking in respect to its two most fundamental conceptions: transference and countertransference. Even today, it constitutes a meaningful and unique clarification of issues related to both of these subjects, and offers clinical material, seldom specified in this context, as illustration and documentation. It is a contribution that evokes considerable thought, touches upon many basic technical and theoretical issues, and merits discussion along many important lines. To be selective, however, it seems to me that the nature and fate of this paper confronts us with two major responsibilities: first, to place the contribution itself in historical perspective; and second, to examine the intensely disturbing issue of why a contribution by an analytic candidate filled with such remarkable insights was summarily dismissed by two psychoanalytic editorial boards. In this context, I wish to state that the main objective of this discussion will be to garner preliminary evidence that directs us to the following critical hypothesis: there is on the part of each and every psychoanalyst and mental health professional a consistently mixed reaction to a creative and truly original contribution, and to its progenitor. On the one hand, there are efforts at acceptance, understanding, and support, while on the other, there are always endeavors at refutation, ostracism, and the destruction of both the concept and its proponent.

AN HISTORICAL PERSPECTIVE

Searles's paper is so rich in content that it would be possible to tease out and identify an extensive array of relatively original, seminal concepts. I will, however, for the purposes of this discussion, confine myself to briefly placing into historical perspective those ideas which are most clearly developed and which seem most significant in the context of the evolution of psychoanalytic thinking regarding the patient-analyst relationship. Those readers who wish to develop a more comprehensive appreciation of the perspectives to be outlined here should find my recent compendium of the psychoanalytic literature on this subject and the accompanying effort at analysis and synthesis of considerable help (Langs 1976b). I shall now turn to the major creative thrusts of Searles's contribution.

1. *In addition to the genetic determinants of a transference-based response by the patient, such behaviors and reactions are influenced by*

crucial factors in the immediate analytic interaction. This rather basic thesis had a number of antecedents, and touched upon an issue that has preoccupied psychoanalysts during the last three decades. It has led to investigations under such diverse headings as the therapeutic alliance, the so-called real relationship, identificatory and introjective processes both within the analytic experience and in the process of cure, and the interplay between reality and transference—to name but a few. (Throughout this discussion, my time reference for "before" and "after" will be 1949.) Among its antecedents were a wide range of comments offered by Freud (1912a,b, 1913, 1914, 1915, 1920, 1940), most of which constituted indirect and implicit suggestions that the actualities of the analytic interaction have an influence on the patient's transference expressions. Freud's most explicit comments in this regard related to the patient's effort to actualize his unconscious transference fantasies and memories in his relationship with the analyst (Freud 1914, 1920), a dimension that I will discuss below.

In particular, Strachey (1934), Balint and Balint (1939), Rioch (1943), and Thompson (1946) had, in relatively general fashion, offered earlier comments on the interplay between the realities of the analyst's office, personality, and behaviors on the one hand, and the analysand's transference reactions on the other. There is little doubt, however, that Searles's treatise would have been the most comprehensive and specific current effort to identify dimensions of the analytic interaction as they have a bearing on the patient's transference expressions. Searles's discussion included efforts to identify the precipitants of transference reactions, their basis in reality, their influence on the analyst, and their immediate intrapsychic basis. As such, the paper stands even today as a landmark contribution.

Searles's basic approach to the interplay between reality and transference contrasts with the position of most classical psychoanalysts. This is perhaps most clearly represented by Greenson (1967), who stated that the critical factor in transference is the unconscious fantasy-memory and the various intrapsychic reactions to it, while the precipitants, or day residue, are often unimportant, though occasionally they may play a notable role. Recently, there is, however, as documented in *The Therapeutic Interaction* (Langs 1976b), a distinct growing reconition among such analysts, of the intimate connections between current realities, expecially those within the analytic relationship, and transference expressions. It is quite interesting, however, that by far the most comprehensive explorations in this area were carried out later on by Searles himself and by myself (see Langs 1976b for details).

2. *In addition to the genetic determinants and displacement, a major mechanism in transference-based responses is that of projection.* This specific thesis had a major antecedent in the landmark paper by Strachey (1934), who investigated aspects of the immediate analytic interaction as it pertains to the cure of the patient. Essential to Strachey's thesis was his suggestion that the patient will project id impulses onto the analyst, and that should the analyst respond interpretively and thereby in a different fashion than an earlier pathogenic object, the patient will introject into his superego (and ego, as later noted by Rosenfeld 1972) a benign and curative introject. Searles's study, apparently undertaken without an awareness of Strachey's work, constituted a significant extension of Strachey's ideas, and in its own right, offered a number of original concepts regarding the role of projection in transference. Actually, it was not until 1952 that Melanie Klein offered a far more condensed discussion along some of the lines suggested in Searles's presentation. Historically, it is she and Strachey who have been identified as the writers who provided the core papers on this subject.

Subsequent developments extended in two directions: First, the Kleinians studied the analytic interaction extensively and soon shifted from a stress on projection to the position that projective identification—an interactional form of projection (Langs 1976a, b)—is the primary mechanism within the analytic field. Second, classical analysts, to some extent, accepted projection of inner mental contents and mechanisms onto the analyst as one dimension of transference, although interestingly enough, this concept has been acknowledged only by isolated authors, especially Sandler and his associates (1969), who termed the relevant mechanism *externalization.* Searles himself, through his investigations of the analytic interaction with schizophrenics and others (Searles 1965, 1970, 1971, 1972, 1973), has been the most careful student (among American analysts) of such projections and the complementary role played by introjective processes. His approach has clear-cut interactional implications that suggest that he stresses, as do I, projective and introjective identification (Langs 1976a,b) as the central interpersonal dynamisms of the analytic experience.

3. *Transference-based responses, whatever their form, do not occur in isolation, nor do they exist as relatively encapsulated intrapsychic formations; instead, they are evoked responses and are quite often stimulated by the behaviors and communications of the analyst.* It is here that Searles adopts what I later termed the *adaptational-interactional* conception of transference (Langs 1974, 1976a,b). Unconscious transference fantasies and the reactions based upon them are no longer viewed in terms of a closed intrapsychic system, but are seen as current adaptive responses in which both intrapsychic and interactional mechanisms—especially introjection—as well as genetic determinants, play a role.

Prior to reading this paper by Searles, I had been unable to find a truly specific precursor of my own interactional concept in this area— namely, the *adaptive context* for transference-based reactions. While I was aware that this adaptive viewpoint constituted, on one level, the adoption of Freud's model (1900) of the relationship between the day residue (adaptive stimulus) and the dream (intrapsychic response) as applied to the analytic interaction, I had been unable to find a specific explication of this crucial concept in the psychoanalytic study of transference—a definitive statement and clarification of the adaptational and introjective aspects of transference. This position immediately requires the study of the nature of the analytic interaction, and in particular, the conscious and unconscious implications of the analyst's interventions (both interpretations and management of the framework; see Langs 1976a,b) and his failures to intervene. In a sense, then, it leads to a deep appreciation of the fullness of the analyst's role in the patient's transference reactions, and in addition, demands the development of distinctions between transference and nontransference responses, so that the patient's appropriate and valid perceptions and reactions to the analyst can be separated from those that are primarily distorted. It is therefore not al all surprising that in his presentation, Searles soon turns to a more careful study of the actualities of the analyst and his relationship with the patient.

Had this paper been published when it was written, it might well have generated considerable progress in delineating the basic components of the analytic interaction, the nature of transference and nontransference, as well as the particulars of the analyst's countertransference- and noncountertransference-based responses. Searles's own subsequent publications demonstrate the extent to which this seminal paper did, indeed, lead him to one of the most extensive and careful considerations of each of these dimensions available in the psychoanalytic literature to datz.

4. *Transference-based projections are by no means simply intrapsychically based distortions, but instead tend to be founded on actual traits and behaviors of the analyst which are largely exaggerated because of the patient's intrapsychic pathological needs.* Nowhere in the prior literature had this point been explicitly stated, and it was many years before analysts such as Klauber (1968) and E. Ticho (1972) initiated investigations of such matters as the influence of the analyst's personality on the patient's transferences. Searles stresses the actualities of the analyst and the need for extensive self-awareness on his part as a basis for understanding the implications of the patient's communications. This germinal concept can be traced in Searles's subsequent writings to his most illuminating studies of the patient's unconscious perceptions of the analyst and of his extensive unconscious introjection and working over of many of the analyst's actual traits, some of which are even unknown to the analyst himself.

This early conception of a kind of exploitation by the patient of his analyst's characteristics may also be viewed as the nucleus of Searles's later investigations of the patient's actual efforts to both harm and cure the analyst. Perhaps most crucial here is Searles's recognition that transference-based perceptions and reactions are not entirely distorted but are founded on realities within the analyst. This calls for a full consideration of the analyst's conscious and unconscious communications to the patient in understanding the latter's behaviors and associations. It could have constituted another basis upon which the important distinction between transference and nontransference, and the intimately related distinction between countertransference and noncountertransference, could have been developed. In many ways, this paper would have constituted a very crucial challenge to psychoanalysts to extensively clarify and refine their conception of the analytic interaction and the respective contributions of both patient and analyst.

5. *An important factor in transference-based reactions is the effort by the patient to evoke complementary and confirmatory responses from the analyst, thereby reinforcing the patient's neurosis, pathological introjects, and his past pathogenic interactions.* It is here that

Searles completes one aspect of the adaptive sequence of which transference is a part: adaptive context, transference responses, efforts to evoke reactions in, or to influence, the analyst. Freud (1914, 1920), in considering acting out, did state that the patient attempts to re-experience his unconscious transference fantasies in the actual relationship with the analyst, but this particular thesis tended to be relatively neglected by those who followed him. Searles's comments in this area, and his clinical documentation, are quite unprecedented. While the Kleinians subsequently wrote of the influence of the patient's projective identifications on the analyst, it was not until 1976 that Sandler specifically investigated both the patient's efforts to evoke role-responses in the analyst and their usefulness in understanding the patient.

6. *Among the implications of these accumulated observations and formulations is the need to focus more carefully on the analyst's actual experiences in his relationship with the patient. It then becomes clear that the analyst is by no means merely a mirror, that he experiences a wide range of emotions in his interaction with the patient, that these are not essentially undesirable or pathological, and that often they are actually quite necessary. Further, the analyst's subjective experiences, since they are evoked by the patient, can serve as a useful means of understanding the patient, so long as one validates the formulations so derived.*

Here, while not clearly distinguishing countertransference from noncountertransference (i.e., the analyst's primarily pathological reactions to the patient from those that are essentially nonpathological), and while using countertransference in its broadest sense to include both appropriate and inappropriate reactions in the analyst, Searles specifically opens up a major avenue for the constructive utilization of countertransference experiences—an area that has received continued consideration to this day (see Langs 1976a, Segal 1977). While my own scrutiny of the analytic literature revealed that Hann-Kende (1933) seems to have been the first analyst to allude to the possible constructive utilization of the analyst's countertransferences, most historians have credited Heimann (1950) with establishing this most crucial concept. It is evident, then, that Searles, at the very least, deserved at least an equal share of this important credit. His special stress on the need to validate the information derived from these subjective experiences is also one of the first allusions to the importance of a *validating process* in evaluating the analyst's experiences vis-à-vis his patient.

In all, then, it is evident in the light of present historical perspective that this previously unpublished paper by Searles is genuinely remarkable and creative in a number of extraordinary ways. It is probably to this day the most original and insightful clinical contribution ever generated by a psychoanalytic candidate: it offers a major breakthrough directing analysts to the crucial importance of the actualities of the analytic interaction as a means of understanding its unconscious and distorted, transference-based components; it presents a strikingly adaptational understanding of transference, thereby opening up pathways to the investigation of the interplay between reality and transference; and it suggests a crucial alteration in the view of countertransference, indicating in particular that these reponses of the analyst, previously viewed entirely as unwanted and detrimental side effects, also contain important positive potentials. The refusal by two editorial boards to publish this paper creates an unmistakable demand on every analyst and therapist to examine the possible contributing factors to such an occurrence.

REACTIONS TO CREATIVITY

In considering reactions to innovative ideas in psychoanalysis, I propose to spare no one his or her necessary acknowledgment of inevitable efforts to silence and destroy both the innovation and the innovator, however strong or weak his or her additional efforts at support and acceptance. My comments will be based on discussions with currently acknowledged psychoanalytic innovators; my own personal experiences as a writer, and observations derived from my own clinical work and supervisory experiences; the reading of a small, selected group of papers in this area (Greenson 1969, Bion 1970, and Stone 1975); a host of general impressions derived from scattered sources; and, of course, my ideas regarding the fate of Searle's paper. As a result, I will not only reiterate and elaborate upon the ideas presented by Greenson, Bion, and Stone to some extent, but will also be presenting a rather diffuse mixture of observations, impressions, hunches, hypotheses, and even conclusions.This discussion is not an effort at documentation and validation, but is instead, an attempt to comment freely on an extremely vital issue within psychoanalysis in hope of generating specific hypotheses and definitive investigations, and personal change—for both myself (as it has, already, in the writing) and the reader.

Both Greenson (1969) and Stone (1975) have commented on the resistance in analysts to what the latter has termed *change in fundamental tenets of technique or theory* (p. 343). The former writer stresses the narcissistic disruption evoked by new ideas, and after considering the origin and fate of new ideas within the creative psychoanalyst himself, has studied their fate within psychoanalytic groups. Utilizing as his model an historical series of splits in the psychoanalytic movement that led to new and distinctive schools of psychoanalysis, Greenson emphasizes the manner in which the development of these new establishments tended to have a disintegrative effect on the field. They have interfered with the integration of original ideas into a central body of psychoanalytic theory and technique and have generated rigidity within disparate schools.

Stone (1975), on the other hand, has written of analysts' extraordinary investment in what he describes as a "rigidly maintained, narcissistically invested fiction of certainty" (p. 343) in the face of inevitable intellectual and other uncertainties in the field of psychoanalysis. He also examines the hostility toward the so-called malefactor who threatens the defenses on which such rigidity is based. In this regard, he explores the roles of shared group convictions, of the political struggle and authoritarianism that is so inimical to original thought, and of the general lack of humility of those in power. Most importantly, Stone expresses his belief that the hostile responses to creativity are derived, in part, from the analyst's training analysis. Here he focuses on the reporting procedures that deprive candidates of the indispensable rights of any analytic patient in regard to inviolable confidentiality and immunity from intrusion by the analyst into the analysand's extraanalytic life. He links this to the distinct tendency among analysts to displace away from themselves and their methods the reasons for therapeutic failure.

Both of these compelling papers were offered in the form of general impressions that, unfortunately, support the ease with which the psychoanalytic reader can maintain a critical defensive split: denial of one's own involvement in such destructive attitudes and behaviors, and the condemnation of others who so act. Certainly, no psychoanalytic paper can function as a curative influence on any but a minimal level; this remains the province of one's personal analysis and continued self-analysis afterwards. Nonetheless, as I have already indicated, I shall make every effort to disrupt this insidious defensive split, recognizing immediately that as I do so, I am already a disturbing innovator toward whom many will respond with hostility and renewed defensiveness. I shall, however, nonetheless move on and offer a restatement of Bion's (1970) especially creative comments in this area, ideas that he offered in the context of his study of the container and the contained as it applies to that exceptional individual he calls "the mystic" and to his relationship with the group.

Categorizing mystics as either primarily revolutionary or nihilistic, and as both creative and destructive, Bion suggests that these contradictory trends coexist within each individual creator. In a series of most illuminating comments, Bion explores the relationship between the mystic and the group—the contained and the container. He theorizes that this relationship may be commensal, symbiotic, or parasitic. In the first type of relationship, the two sides coexist in a manner that is harmless to each other; in the second, there is a growth-producing confrontation; while in the third, there is destruction to both parties—envy, as a function of the relationship, destroys both host and parasite. In the symbiotic relationship, the group is capable of both hostility and benevolence, while in the parasitic association even friendliness is seen as deadly. It is the realization that the mystic simultaneously creates and destroys that evokes these responses in the group; their reactions eventually must be modualted by the Establishment—that subgroup or function of the group that exercises power and responsibility—so that the mystic and his ideas can eventually be integrated and institutionalized.

It is now possible to restate my own thesis in Bion's terms by suggesting that every individual responds to the mystic—the creator—with a mixture of varying proportions of commensal, symbiotic, and parasitic reactions. I am also in agreement with Bion that envy is a basic emotion—a response that characterizes a fundamentally disruptive human need that can destroy the finest and most helpful qualities of a good object or creation (see Joffe 1969, for a study of the literature on this subject)—and that envy constitutes a major unconscious motive for the eradication of the mystic and his ideas.

A second major motive for destructive reactions to the psychoanalytic innovator lies in the realm of the respondent's need to protect and stablize his often fragile personal inner equilibrium, in his sense of coherence and identity, and in his overall need for inner mental balance. It is, of course, characteristic of the new idea that it disrupts the basic stability of those who address it; among psychoanalysts, this always implies an attack, in some sense, on unconscious countertransference-based fantasies and defenses. The new idea, to the extent that it is valid, has been derived to some extent by the innovator's resolution of a shared unconscious countertransference need and blind spot; his conception then challenges every other psychoanalyst and clinician to experience the related countertransference anxieties and conflicts, and to accomplish a more adaptive resolution. Each clinician will have some degree of resistance to this type of threat, and a major means of defense and of maintaining his pathological equilibrium lies in attacking or destroying the source of his discomfort—the adaptive context (Langs 1973) for his momentary or potential disturbance. It is for these and other reasons that I have suggested (Langs 1977b) that the history of psychoanalytic discovery is, on one level, the unfolding of the resolution of individual and shared countertransferences.

For similar reasons, I maintain that the psychoanalyst and the psychoanalytically oriented clinician have a special responsibility to introject and experience internally the qualities and implications of a new idea, to tolerate the inevitable internal disruption, and to benefit from the equally inevitable conflict resolution and insights that can be derived in this way. This is a process that is fundamental to his effective functioning with his patients, a point that I will soon develop from other vantage points (see below). Further, because of the individual's and group's need for the genius and new ideas—for example, as a means of adapting to continual external and internal change and challenge—such an openness is vital to the survival of the psychoanalytic practitioner and his field. It is my impression, shared with those who have considered this area, that a major factor int he decline of psychoanalysis as a respected body of scientific understanding and as a treatment modality, is based, in part, on the failure of analysts, individually and collectively, to sustain the necessary disequilibria and mastery of envy required for the slowincorporation of original ideas into its main body of knowledge and technical functioning.

It appears to me that Stone's sensitivity to the structure of the psychoanalytic situation (1961, 1975) and the important functions of its ground rules or framework (Langs 1976a,b) has led him to identify one of the most crucial factors in generating parasitic, envious, and destructive responses to creativity among psychoanalysts. My own extensive investigations in this area have unmistakably validated his position, which I will state even more broadly: Extensive and common alterations in the framework of training analyses (disruptions in neutrality, the use of noninterpretive interventions, the absence of total confidentiality, the dilution of the analyst's commitment to his analysand, alterations in the one-to-one relationship, and the like) significantly modify the communicative, introjective, and insightful properties of the bipersonal analytic field. As a result, intensely destructive introjects flourish and selected areas of conflict and pathology are split off from the analytic work and never analytically resolved. In all, every so-called training analysis is incomplete in major ways. While some of these defects can be rectified through a subsequent analysis or through extensive self-analysis, the disruptive residuals are unmistakable. In the present context, these significant remnants of psychopathology are especially evident in the failure to resolve and master envy-based reactions, a residual that promotes paranoid-like responses to creativity; in addition, they are manifested in the already described difficulties in tolerating the disquieting effects of innovative ideas.

Based on my own studies and those of Bion (1977), I would characterize the situation as follows: The framework influences not only the contents and meaning of the communications between analyst and analysand, but also serves as the fundamental basis for the analyst's crucial therapeutic (maternal-like) hold of the patient—the basic substrate of the necessary growth promoting, therapeutic symbiosis (Searles 1965, 1970, 1971, 1973, Winnicott 1965). The maintenance of the framework is also an essential expression of the analyst's containing capacities—his ability to introject the patient's pathological projective identifications, to metabolize or process them toward interpretive understanding, and to impart these interpretations to the patient, who then experiences both cognitive insight and a positive introjective identification related to the analyst's constructive understanding and containing efforts (Bion 1977, Langs 1976a, b). Disruptions in the framework inevitably reflect impairments in the analyst's holding and containing capacities—his capacity for "reverie," as described by Bion (1962) — and as a result, the analysand suffers a significant incapacitation in regard to his own holding and containing functions. It is a disruptive form of this sequence of experiences, initiated by deviations in the framework of the analysand's own analysis, that, in my opinion, generates significant difficulties in his capacity to hold and contain new ideas.

The development of the foregoing hypothesis leads me directly to the analyst's own work with his patients. In that regard, it is my thesis that the very psychopathology that interferes with the psychoanalyst's introjection, metabolism, understanding and acceptance of creative ideas, similarly disturbs his functioning as an analyst with his own patients, and further, that it is impossible to resolve countertransference difficulties in one realm without their resolution in the other. This implies that it is crucial to recognize a countertransference-based disturbance that emerges either in one's own work with patients or in response to creative ideas. The analyst should endeavor not to make use of a denial and splitting through which he states that he will maintain a vigilance to countertransference-based influences in his work with his patients and implies that he need not do so in his scrutiny of the psychoanalytic literature.

This argument becomes particularly compelling when we recognize that every genuine interpretation offered by a psychoanalyst is an innovative idea (Bion 1970). Because of this, the analyst who has a need to destroy the creative ideas of others will experience his patient's reactions to his interpretations as similar attacks on his own creativity, and will tend also to be markedly constricted in regard to the repertoire of his interpretive range. He will have difficulty empathizing with and comprehending his patient's responses to his interpretations, since he will be out of touch with the disturbing elements inherent in his valid interpretive communications, as well as his patient's inevitable envy and defensiveness. In addition, he will actually envy his own creative self-parts (Searles 1976) and experience conflict when generating interpretive interventions. To state this in still another way, to the extent that a psychoanalyst has not mastered his responses to the creative ideas of others, his functioning with his patients in his special role as interpretor must suffer.

A second and equally disruptive influence on the analyst's functioning with his patients stands related to his intolerance for new ideas. In 1951, Little ingeniously suggested that unconsciously, a patient engages in extensive therapeutic and interpretive efforts designed for the cure of the analyst whenever the latter is suffering from some type of countertransference-based difficulty in his work with his patient. My review of the literature (Langs 1976b) indicated that this remarkably innovative concept was totally ignored by subsequent psychoanalysts until the work of Searles (1965, 1975) and myself (Langs 1975, 1976a,b) extensively documented and expanded upon this much neglected and quite original clinical observation and thesis (for additional references, see Searles 1965, p. 539). Not only have analysts tended to deny, and failed to appreciate, the patient's unconscious therapeutic efforts on their behalf, but individually and collectively, they have tended to be almost totally absorbed with the patient's pathological, transference-based functioning and his destructive intentions vis-à-vis the analytic experience and the analyst—this, to the virtual exclusion of the patient's valid, nontransference-based functioning and his creative endeavors within the analytic situation. The patient as enemy, his creativity to be envied and destroyed, has insidiously dominated the psychoanalyst's view of his analysand. Relatively few analysts have acknowledged and attempted to comprehend the analysand's extensive positive functioning and potential within the analytic relationship.

The replication of the analyst's destructive responses to the creativity of other analytic innovators in his reactions to the creativity of his own patients is unmistakable. Without further developing this crucial parallel, it becomes evident that the same factors have prompted resistance and destructive reactions in both realms, and that once again, resolution of the underlying countertransferences as they apply to one sphere, goes hand in hand with resolution in the other. Further, an important and related thesis is that a major source of these problems lies in the likelihood of failures by training analysts to implicitly acknowledge and appreciate the unconscious curative efforts and creativity of their candidate analysands. As Racker (1957) so aptly described, an unconscious handing down of countertransference difficulties from analyst to analysand is one major complication and danger of every so-called training analysis. Such a heritage is offered verbally and nonverbally, directly and indirectly, consciously and unconsciously. It contributes to an analysand's intolerance for creativity through the training analyst's failures both in holding-containing and in comprehending and accepting the candidate-analysand's unconscious curative and creative thrusts on his behalf.

A number of parallels between an analyst's reactions to his patients and to innovators may be developed through a consideration of the typology of communicative styles which are revealed in the interaction between analysts and their patients (Langs 1978b). To rephrase these findings in terms of the present discussion, it is the Type A analyst who is characterized by his use of symbolic messages, indepth meaning, and efforts at insightful mastery of anxieties, conflicts and resistances; and it is he how is clearly the most receptive and productive in responding to creative thrusts—either in patients or in mystics. In contrast, the Type B analyst, who is characterized by urgent self-oriented action, discharge and riddance of disturbance, and projective identification, tends to infuse responses to creativity with envy, destructiveness, and repudiation unless the creativity provides immediate self-gratification or relief. The Type C analyst with his need for the *status quo* and his use of language for noncommunication barriers and deception, fosters responses to innovations that can reach a level at which their existence is totally denied, and any unique truths so contained are subjected to falsification and restatement as cliché, being rendered essentially nonexistent.

To state these ideas in slightly different form, it is my impression that analysts who tend to be refractory to creativity have, in general, been analyzed in predominantly Type B and Type C communicative fields, and in turn, unconsciously promote this type of communication between themselves and their patients. Other determinants of communicative style lie within the family and genetic history of each individual analyst—important influences that are beyond the scope of this presentation.

At the risk of my offering a somewhat circular argument, it deserves to be stated that the prevalence of responses to creativity that are characteristic of the Type B and Type C communicative fields strongly suggests in itself that many so-called training analyses take place with these modes of communication predominant. It seems likely too that such analyses do not, in themselves, support the creativity of the analysand, but instead tend to undermine or destroy aspects of his symbolic functioning and his use of language for illusion, play, and transition. In this sense, then, the analysand's openness to innovation and his own personal creativity are damaged in the course of his analytic experience. By contrast, an analyst capable of creating a Type A communicative field with his analysands offers an important opportunity to both himself and his patients for the tolerance and mastery of anxiety and conflict necessary to explore unconscious fantasies, memories, introjects, and the like, and so promotes both openness to creativity in others and personal originality.

I have alluded to some basic factors in the preponderance of envious and hostile reactions to creativity, but a few words must be addressed to the bases for the more positive responses of the minority. It may well be that these analysands have had a greater opportunity to experience positive and constructive holding and containment from their analysts and a more noticeable unconscious acceptance of their creative thrusts. The basic personality attributes and needs of these analysts may also play a role, as expressed, for example, in a prevailing and positive need for reparation that fosters a search for new means of undoing harm and damage. They may also have a greater than usual need—pathological or nonpathological—for potentially curative experiences of disequilibrium. Pressing personal and ideological dissatisfactions could have a similar effect. Finally, there is the possibility of the mature analyst who can tolerate anxiety, master envy, and maintain an openness to new ideas in which rational, cognitive assessment plays a major role. The latter, however, appears to be an ideal that few fully attain.

It is beyond the scope of this discussion to attempt an investigation of the many factors that influence in each individual clinician the internal balance between receptivity to, and destruction of, new ideas. This would lead to a study of creativity itself, since it can be said that openness to new ideas is, in part, a function of one's own capacity for innovation. I will instead, in keeping with my effort to identify the negative aspects of every individual's reactions to the innovator, conclude my discussion with some brief comments on the symptoms of this disruptive syndrome and its influence on the creator.

It is striking that at the very time Searles submitted his paper to two psychoanalytic journals in the United States, and was rejected, the *International Journal of Psycho-Analysis* was in the process of publishing a series of papers in which the very ideas presented by Searles would appear. The implicit notion here that the European culture had—and may still have—a greater openness creativity than we find in the United States suggests a socio-cultural avenue of investigation. In a different vein, Searles, at the time of writing his paper, was an analytic candidate, while those already published in these areas during that era tended to be relatively well-known and established analysts. The common intolerance to creativity in neophytes and younger analysts on the part of the psychoanalytic establishment (despite conscious denial and another form of splitting) is an attitude fraught with rather obvious destructive effects on both individual and collective levels.

The type and foim of creativity also influence the responses of the group and individual. There is abundant evidence that those analysts who repeat what is already known, in a manner that deceptively suggests revision while actually maintaining sameness, will find far more ready acceptance than those who generate truly original ideas. New findings within the basic framework of established thinking—findings that essentially extend present ideas rather than challenge fundamental tenets—also tend to find more open acceptance than new concepts that essentially challenge and disrupt the established order. There is evidence too that those individuals within the group who gravitate toward the Establishment have a greater investment in maintaining stability and conformity than those who remain outside of this core. This implies that leaders of psychoanalytic organizations and members of editorial boards, despite their avowed interest in promoting creativity, may well have special difficulties in this area. Their generally acknowledged failure to support and publish those who are relatively inexperienced, their rejection of unprecedented manuscripts and suppression of selected book reviews, their tendency to exclude true innovators from official programs and publications, their directives to rewrite papers in conformity with established ideas, and their many gross and subtle additional efforts to stifle creative freedom are all syptomatic of these often unrecognized problems.

On a more individual level, the decision not to read a particular writer because of his seemingly strange ideas or because he is identified with an alien group of psychoanalytic thinkers is one of the basic signs of this ubiquitous syndrome. In responses to creativity, there are also tendencies to shift from scientific refutation to personal attack, to become preoccupied with minor criticisms as a means of ignoring and destroying the valid aspects of a new concept, and to disregard all considerations of psychoanalytic methodology. There is intolerance of the necessary period of personal confusion and anxiety, plus reluctance to experience the period of sometimes painful and personal working through required for the absorption of new ideas. One commonly finds a defensive search for group solidarity and rigidity as a means of mastering the evoked anxieties, as well as personal dislike of innovative colleagues.Direct efforts are made to negatively influence the academic career and psychoanalytic practice of the innovator, even to the exercise of personal and social pressures and isolation. This cataloguing of group and individual symptoms in response to creative efforts is in marked contrast to the idealized self-image of every psychoanalyst. This discrepancy between what is said, or felt, and what is done reflects the use of splitting and denial, repression and isolation, and other defenses. In this context, it may be noted that in the long run, despite the anxieties generated by innovative ideas, their inner working over and ultimate acceptance has a distinctly therapeutic effect on the recipient.

As one would expect, attacks on his creativity evoke a variety of reponses within the creator. There is no means of determining how many potentially creative psychoanalysts have responded with depression, retreat, surrender, and conformity to individual and collective efforts to destroy their uniqueness and ideas. There are undoubtedly some innovators who cannot thrive without a significant degree of support, especially from the group with whom they are primarily identified. For them, the development of isolated and outside group support does not prove sufficient nurture to sustain their original efforts and, sadly, they succumb.

Other innovators appear to thrive in the face of adversity. Rather than participating with the group in a parasitic interaction character-ized by mutual envy and destructiveness, they make repreated thrusts toward symbiotic relatedness by modifying and reshaping their creative insights to the point where refutation by the group becomes less persistent or necessary. Ostracism by the group, once it is accepted by the innovator, provides him with a special freedom to explore and discover, unencumbered by the relative restraints created by his wish to remain strongly embedded within the group and its need for conformity. The very working through of the unconscious conflicts, fantasies, and memories evoked by the struggle between the innovator and his group, and between him and his individual friends and colleagues, may aid in the resolution of unconscious obstacles to the innovator's own creative potential. On the other hand, such isolation and withdrawal may have its pathological aspects and be unnecessarily defensive; it may deprive the innovator of constructive feedback and perspective.

It is more than evident, then, that this inevitable battle between the mystic and the group, even when it leads to the relative exclusion of the creator, can have its positive effects. It is similarly evident that a truly creative individual is virtually never without the support of some more peripheral groups and of selective persons within his own group; as a rule, some degree of sustenance is always available to him. The danger, however, of isolating the true and needed innovator from the mainstream of psychoanalytic thinking and practice has already been touched upon, and will not be elaborated here. In all, it is apparent that the insightful resolution by all parties of the inevitable anxieties and conflicts generated by the creative individual and his ideas will have a crucial and growth-promoting effect on both the creator and his audience, and, through them, on the entire field of psychoanalytic thinking and endeavor.

CONCLUDING COMMENTS

I shall conclude by reminding the reader that psychoanalysts do indeed have very special responsibilities to themselves, their patients, their field, and the world at large. There can be no justification for anything but a commitment to the truth and its pursuit, and to consistent efforts directed toward the resolution of individual and collective countertransference problems. It is unthinkable that we can be anything but appalled by the fate which this paper by Harold Searles met at the hands of his elders, and deeply concerned over his apparent initial decision never to publish this contribution.

Some, still being defensive (in reality, one cannot expect total resolution of individual and collective defenses—only efforts to approach this ideal), might suggest that Searles's original ideas were nonetheless developed by other analysts who followed him. In this way they might hope to avoid a personal confrontation with the issues and dilemmas discussed in this presentation. In many ways, that would be a most unfortunate expression of continued avoidance, and it would neglect the rejoinder that such destructiveness and suppression of creativity significantly slows down the progress of the field and harms our patients. So long as valid innovative concepts related to our clinical work are not appropriately integrated into our technique, both patients and analysts suffer unduly. Ultimately, destructive acts directed toward individual creativity will render the core of psychoanalytic thinking and practice ineffectual and obsolete. There can be no substitute for our continuous vigilance for expressions of countertransference within our own clinical work and within the field of analysis at large, especially in responding to the innovator. We must, each of us, move toward a more effective resolution of our envious, destructive responses to creativity in our patients and in our colleagues. Our individual and collective survival and growth depend on it.

REFERENCES

Balint, A., and Balint, M. (1939). On transference and countertransference. *International Journal of Psycho-Analysis* 20:223–230.

Bion, W. (1962). *Learning from Experience*. In W. Bion, *Seven Servants*. New York: Jason Aronson, 1977.

——(1970). *Attention and Interpretation*. In W. Bion, *Seven Servants*. New York: Jason Aronson, 1977.

——(1977). *Seven Servants*. New York: Aronson, 1977.

Freud, S. (1900). The interpretation of dreams. *Standard Edition* 4 and 5.

——(1912a). The dynamics of transference. *Standard Edition* 12:97–108.

——(1912b). Recommendations to physicians practicing psychoanalysis. *Standard Edition* 12:111–120.

——(1913). On beginning the treatment (further recommendations on the technique of psychoanalysis I). *Standard Edition* 12:121–144.

——(1914). Remembering, repeating, and working-through (further recommendations on the technique of psycho-analysis II). *Standard Edition* 12:145–156.

——(1915). Observations on transference-love (further recommendations on the technique of psycho-analysis III). *Standard Edition* 12:157–171.

——(1920). Beyond the pleasure principle. *Standard Edition* 18:3–64 (especially 18–23).

——(1940). An outline of psycho-analysis. *Standard Edition* 23:172–182.

Greenson, R. (1967). *The Technique and Practice of Psychoanalysis.* Vol. 1. New York: International Universities Press.

————(1969). The origin and fate of new ideas in psychoanalysis. *International Journal of Psycho-Analysis* 50:503–516.

Hann-Kende, F. (1933). On the role of transference and countertransference in psychoanalysis. In *Psychoanalysis and the Occult,* ed. G. Devereux, pp. 158–167. New York: International Universities Press, 1953, 1970.

Heimann, P. (1950). On countertransference. *International Journal of Psycho-Analysis* 31:81–84.

Joffe, W. (1969). A critical review of the status of the envy concept. *International Journal of Psycho-Analysis* 50:533–546.

Klauber, J. (1968). The psychoanalyst as a person. *British Journal of Medical Psychology* 41:315–322.

Klein, M. (1952). The origins of transference. *International Journal of Psycho-Analysis* 33:433–438.

Langs, R. (1973). *The Technique of Psychoanalytic Psychotherapy,* Vol I. New York: Jason Aronson.

————(1974). *The Technique of Psychoanalytic Psychotherapy,* Vol II. New York: Jason Aronson.

————(1975). Therapeutic misalliances. *International Journal of Psychoanalytic Psychotherapy* 4:77–105. [Chapter 6, this volume]

————(1976a). *The Bipersonal Field.* New York: Jason Aronson.

————(1976b). *The Therapeutic Interaction.* 2 vols. New York: Jason Aronson.

————(1978a). Validation and the framework of the therapeutic situation. *Contemporary Psychoanalysis* is in press. [Chapter 14, this volume]

————(1978b). Some communicative properties of the bipersonal field. *International Journal of Psychoanalytic Psychotherapy* 7:89–136. [Chapter 15, this volume]

Langs, R., and Searles, H.F. (in press). *Psychoanalytic Dialogues, IV: Concerning the Interactional and Interpersonal Realms.* New York: Jason Aronson.

Little, M. (1951). Counter-transference and the patient's response to it. *International Journal of Psycho-Analysis* 32:32–40.

Racker, H. (1957). The meaning and uses of countertransference. *Psychoanalytic Quarterly* 26:303–357.

Rioch, J. (1943). The transference phenomenon in psychoanalytic therapy. *Psychiatry* 6:147–156.

Rosenfeld, H. (1972). A critical appreciation of James Strachey's paper on the nature of the therapeutic action of psychoanalysis. *International Journal of Psycho-Analysis* 53:455–461.

Sandler, J. (1976). Countertransference and role-responsiveness. *International Review of Psycho-Analysis* 3:43–47.

Sandler, J., Holder, A., Kawenoka, M., Kennedy, H., and Neurath, L. (1969). Notes on some theoretical and clinical aspects of transference. *International Journal of Psycho-Analysis* 50:633–645.

Searles, H.F. (1965). *Collected Papers on Schizophrenia and Related Subjects.* New York: International Universities Press.

———(1970). Autism and the phase of transition to therapeutic symbiosis. *Contemporary Psychoanalysis* 7:1–20.

———(1971). Pathologic symbiosis and autism. In *The Name of Life,* ed. B. Landis and E. Tauber. New York: Holt, Rinehart and Winston.

———(1972). The function of the patient's realistic perceptions of the analyst in delusional transference. *British Journal of Medical Psychology* 45:1–18.

———(1973). Concerning therapeutic symbiosis. *The Annual of Psychoanalysis* 1:247–262.

———(1976). Jealousy involving an internal object. Presented at a conference on Borderline Disorders under the auspices of the Advanced Institute for Analytic Psychotherapy, New York.

———(1977). Concerning transference and countertransference. *International Journal of Psychoanalytic Psychotherapy* 7:165–188.

Segal, H. (1977). Countertransference. *International Journal of Psychoanalytic Psychotherapy* 6:31–38.

Stone L. (1961). *The Psychoanalytic Situation.* New York: International Universities Press.

———(1975). Some problems and potentialties of present-day psychoanalysis. *Psychoanalytic Quarterly* 44:331–370.

Strachey, J. (1934). The nature of the therapeutic action of psychoanalysis. *International Journal of Psycho-Analysis* 15:127–159.

Thompson, C. (1946). Transference as a therapeutic instrument. *Psychiatry* 9:273–278.

Ticho, E. (1972). The effects of the analyst's personality on psychoanalytic treatment. *Psychoanalytic Forum* 4:137–151.

Winnicott, D. W. (1965). *The Maturational Processes and Facilitating Environment.* New York: International Universities Press.

Chapter Seventeen

The Adaptational-Interactional Dimension of Countertransference

(1978)

It is the basic purpose of this paper to outline, discuss, and synthesize a series of clinical postulates regarding countertransference, developed through an adaptational approach to this dimension of therapeutic and analytic relationships. These postulates are based on clinical observations and an extensive review of the psychoanalytic literature (Langs 1976a,c), and were shaped with a view toward enhancing our understanding of the treatment interaction and with some stress on their pertinence to analytic and therapeutic technique.[1] The present investigation of countertransference is somewhat different than the prior explorations I have undertaken (1974, 1976a,c), in that I shall focus here almost exclusively on the interactional aspects of countertransference and shall concentrate on recent conceptions developed largely since those earlier publications—some of which have not previously been considered at all, either by myself or by others. I shall adopt an approach that concentrates on the delineation, elaboration, and clinical illustration of these postulates and, while the ideas presented here have been contributed to significantly by earlier writers, I will not provide an historical survey since I have done so in an earlier work (1976c). Without further introduction, then, I shall turn now to the basic definitions that we will need in order to define and comprehend the interactional dimension of countertransference.

BASIC DEFINITIONS

I shall proceed in outline form, offering only the essentials (the interested reader may find the elaborating literature in Langs 1973a,b, 1974, 1975a,b,c, 1976a,c, 1978a,b).

1. *The bipersonal field* (Baranger and Baranger 1966, Langs 1976a,c) refers to the temporal-physical space within which the analytic interaction takes place. The patient is one term of the polarity; the analyst is the other. The field embodies both interactional and intrapsychic mechanisms, and every event within the field receives vectors from both participants. The field itself is defined by a framework—the ground rules of psychoanalysis—which not only delimits the field, but also, in a major way, contributes to the communicative properties of the field and to the analyst's hold of the patient and containment of his projective identifications.

Communications within the field take place along an interface determined by inputs from both patient and analyst, and possessing a variety of characteristics, including, among others, psychopathology, depth, and stability. The major interactional mechanisms in the field are those of projective and introjective identification, although other interactional defenses, such as denial, splitting, the creation of bastions (split-off sectors of the field; see Baranger and Baranger 1966), and additional unconsciously shared forms of gratification and defense are also characteristic. The major intrapsychic defenses are those of repression, displacement, and the other well-known classically described mechanisms.

2. The investigation of the communicative medium provided by the frame of the field and the communicative mode of each participant is essential for an understanding of the analytic interaction and therapeutic work. The basic communications from each participant occur verbally and nonverbally, through words and actions serving a variety of meanings and functions. As a fundamental means of categorizing these communications, they can be classified as manifest content and as Type One and Type Two derivatives (Langs 1978a,b). The first term refers to the surface nature and meaning of a

communication, while a Type One derivative constitutes a relatively available inference or latent theme extracted from the manifest content. In contrast, a Type Two derivative is organized around a specific *adaptive context*—the precipitant or instigator of the interactional and intrapsychic response—and entails definitive dynamic meanings and functions relevant to that context. Further, within a given bipersonal field, every communication is viewed as an interactional product, with inputs from both participants.

3. On this basis, we may identify three basic styles of communicating and three related forms of interactional field (Langs 1978a). The Type A style or field is characterized by the use of symbolic communications, and the bipersonal field itself becomes the realm of illusion and a transitional or play space. In general, the patient's associations can be organized around a series of specific adaptive contexts, yielding a series of indirect communications that constitute Type Two derivatives. These latent contents and themes fall into the realm of unconscious fantasy, memory, and introject on the one hand, and unconscious perception on the other. For the development of a Type A field, both patient and analyst must be capable of tolerating and maintaining a secure framework; in addition, the analyst must have the ability to offer symbolic interpretations of the patient's communications.

The Type B field or style is one in which action, discharge, and the riddance of accretions of psychic disturbance is central. The primary mechanism in this field is that of projective identification and living (acting) out, and both language and behavior are utilized as means of discharge rather than as vehicles for symbolic understanding.

While the Type A and Type B fields are positively communicative, each in its own way, the essential characteristic of the Type C field is the destruction of communication and meaning, and the use of falsifications and impervious barriers as the main interactional mode. Here, language is used as a defense against disturbed inner mental contents. The Type C field is static and empty, and is further characterized by the projective identification of both emptiness and nonmeaning, finding its only sense of meaning in these efforts to destroy communication, links, and meaning itself. While resistances in the Type A field are characterized by the availability of analyzable derivatives, and those in the Type B field are amenable to interpretation based on the defensive use of projective identification, defenses and resistances in the Type C field have no sense of depth and possess a persistent, amorphous, and empty quality.

4. Within the bipersonal field, the patient's relationship with the analyst has both transference and nontransference components. The former are essentially distorted and based on pathological, intrapsychic unconscious fantasies, memories, and introjects, while the latter are essentially nondistorted and based on valid unconscious perceptions and introjections of the analyst, his conscious and unconscious psychic state and communications, and his mode of interacting. Within the transference sphere, in addition to distortions based on displacements from past figures (genetic transferences), there are additional distortions based on the patient's current intrapsychic state and use of interactional mechanisms (projective distortions). Further, nontransference, while valid in terms of the prevailing actualities of the therapeutic interaction, always includes important genetic components—though essentially in the form of the actual repetition of past pathogenic interactions (for details, see Langs 1976c).

The analyst's relationship with the patient is similarly constituted in terms of countertransference and noncountertransference. The former entails all inappropriate and distorted reactions to the patient, whatever their source, and may be based on displacements from the past as well as on pathological projective and introjective mechanisms. Factors in countertransference-based responses range from the nature of a particular patient, the quality and contents of his communications, the meaning of analytic work for the analyst, and interactions with outside parties—other patients and others in the analyst's nonprofessional and professional life.

The noncountertransference sphere of the analyst's functioning entails his valid capacity to manage the framework, to understand the patient's symbolic communications and offer meaningful interpretations, and a basic ability to contain, metabolize, and interpret symbolically the patient's projective identifications. There are a wide range of additional aspects of the analyst's valid and noncountertrasnference-based functioning which will not be detailed here (see Langs 1976c).

INTERACTIONAL POSTULATES REGARDING COUNTERTRANSFERENCE

Postulate 1: As a dimension of the bipersonal field, countertransference (as well as noncountertransference) is an interactional product with vectors from both patient and analyst.

Among the many implications of this generally accepted postulate, some of which have not been specifically identified and discussed in the literature, I will consider those most pertinent to psychoanalytic technique and to the identification and resolution of specific countertransference difficulties. In this context, it is well to be reminded that countertransference-based interventions and behaviors are often not recognized as such by the analyst, due largely to the fact that countertransference is itself rooted in unconscious fantasies, memories, introjects, and interactional mechanisms. The adaptive-interactional approach to countertransference greatly facilitates their recognition and resolution.

This initial postulate implies that each countertransference-based response from the analyst has a specific and potentially identifiable adaptive context. While this stimulus may reside in the personal life of the analyst or in his work with another patient, it most often entails stimuli from the relationship with the patient at hand and is, as a rule, evoked by the communications from that patient. Any unusual feeling or fantasy within the analyst, any failure by the patient to confirm his interventions (whether interpretations or management of the framework), any unusual or persistent symptom or resistance in the patient, or any regressive episode in the course of an analysis should alert the analyst to the possible presence of countertransference factors.

The interactional approach proves to be of special value in these pursuits in three important ways: (1) by establishing the finding that the patient's communications and symptoms may be significantly derived from the countertransferences of the analyst; (2) by indicating that through the process of introjective identification the patient becomes a mirror and container for the analyst, in the sense that the patient's communications will play back to the analyst the metabolized introjects derived from his countertransference-based interventions (and his valid, noncountertransference-based interventions as well); and (3) by directing the search for the form and meaning of countertransferences to the sequential interaction of each session.

If we consider these sequential clues first, we may recognize that the immediate precipitant for a countertransference-based reaction can be found in the material from the patient that precedes the erroneous intervention (inappropriate silences, incorrect verbalizations such as erroneous interpretations, and mismanagements of the framework). While there is often a broader context to the countertransference-based intervention in the ongoing relationship between the analyst and his patient, and while there may be, as I have noted, additional inputs derived from relationships outside of the immediate bipersonal field, clinical experience indicates that these immediate adaptive contexts provide extremely important organizing threads for the detection and comprehension of the underlying countertransference fantasies. When dealing with a countertransference-based positive intervention (as compared to silence, which I would consider a negative intervention), it is, of course, the last of the patient's associations that prompts the analyst's response. If this communication is viewed within the overall context of the patient's material, and understood in terms of manifest and latent content, and if all of this is addressed in interaction with the manifest and latent content of the analyst's erroneous intervention, the amalgam provides important and immediate clues as to the nature of the analyst's underlying difficulty.

Thus, the interactional sequence for a countertransference-based response is (1) adaptive context (especially the stimulus from the patient at hand), (2) the analyst's erroneous reaction (positive or negative intervention, whether interpretation or management of the frame), and (3) response by the patient and continued reaction by the analyst. If countertransferences are to be understood in depth, they must be organized around their specific adaptive contexts, so the analyst may understand himself in terms of Type Two derivatives, including both unconscious fantasies and perceptions. Without such an effort, he would be restricted to an awareness of the manifest content of his erroneous intervention or to readily available inferences—both fraught with possible further countertransference-based effects.

This sequence also implies that the analyst may recognize the presence of a countertransference difficulty at one of several junctures—as the patient is communicating disturbing material, while he is intervening, or after he has intervened—and that this recognition may be based either on his own subjective reactions or on subsequent communications from the patient. Much has already been written regarding subjective clues within the analyst who has a countertransference problem, while less consideration has been given to those leads available from the patient; let us now examine these latter more carefully.

The bipersonal field concept directs the analyst to the investigation of his countertransferences when any resistance, defense, symptom, or regression occurs within the patient or himself. Since the adaptational-interactional view considers all such occurrences as interactional products, it generates as a technical requisite the investigation of unconscious factors in both participants at such moments in therapy. As a rule, these disturbances, when they occur within the patient (to take that as our focus), will have unconscious communicative meaning. In the presence of a prevailing countertransference-based communication from the analyst, they will reflect the patient's introjective identification of this disturbance, his unconscious perceptions of its underlying basis, and his own realistic and fantasied metabolism of the introject. The patient's reactions to the disturbed intervention from the analyst may include exploitation, the creation of misalliances and bastions, and use of the intervention for the maintenance of his own neurosis (a term used here in its broadest sense), as well as unconscious efforts to detoxify the introject and cure the analyst.

In terms of the patient's associations and behaviors following an incorrect intervention, the interactional model directs us to the intervention itself as the adaptive context for the patient's subsequent association. In this way, the patient's material can, as a rule, be treated as Type Two derivatives in response to the particular adaptive context. I term these associations *commentaries* on the analyst's intervention, in that they contain both unconscious perceptions and unconscious fantasies.

It is here that we may identify a particular hierarchy of tasks for the analyst, based in part on the recognition that this discussion implies that the patient's associaitions always take place along a *me–not-me interface* (Langs 1976c, 1978a) with continuous references to self and analyst. Thus, valid technique calls for the monitoring of the material from the patient for conscious and unconscious communications related to the analyst before establishing those related to the patient; actually, the one cannot be identified without an understanding of the other. In addition, in both spheres—self and analyst—the analyst must determine the patient's valid perceptions, thoughts, and fantasies before identifying those that are distorted and inappropriate; here too, the identification of one relies on a comprehension of the other. Ultimately, of course, these determinations have as their most essential basis the analyst's self-knowledge, and especially his in-depth understanding of the conscious and unconscious meanings of his communications to the patient.

In the adaptive context, then, of the analyst's interventions, the patient's responsive associations are an amalgam of unconscious perceptions of the manifest and latent qualities of the intervention, on the one hand, and, on the other, their subsequent elaboration in terms of the patient's valid and distorted functioning. Thus, in addition to determining whether such associations truly validate the analyst's intervention by providing genuinely new material that reorganizes previously known clinical data (i.e., constitutes a *selected fact*, as Bion, 1962, has termed it) and evidence for positive introjective identification, the analyst must also consider this material in terms of the patient's experience and introjection of his communication—valid and invalid. This introjective process takes place on the cognitive level as well as in terms of interactional mechanisms. The analyst must therefore be prepared to recognize that both cognitive-symbolic communications and projective identifications are contained in his interventions; in fact, he must be prepared to recognize his use of interventions as facades, clichés, falsifications, and barriers as well (see below).

This interactional approach enables the analyst to make full use of his patient's conscious and unconscious resources, and of the analysand as an unconscious teacher and therapist. The analytic bipersonal field is not, of course, designed primarily for such a use of the patient, but these occurrences are inevitable in every analysis, since countertransferences can never be totally eliminated. In addition, in actuality, these experiences often have enormously therapeutic benefit for the patient (see Searles 1975), so long as the analyst has not deliberately misused the analysand in this regard, and is in addition capable of understanding and responding appropriately to the patient's curative efforts. In this respect, it is essential that the analyst make silent and unobtrusive use of his patient's introjection of his countertransferences and of his additional therapeutic efforts on his behalf, responding without explicit acknowledgment and with implicit benefit. This latter implies the analyst's ability to follow the patient's leads and benefit through efforts at self-analysis based on the patient's unconscious perceptions and therapeutic endeavors; it also requires a capacity to actually rectify—correct or modify—any continued expression of the countertransference difficulty and to control all, if not most, subsequent possible expressions. In addition, it may entail the analyst's *implicit* acknowledgment of an error in technique and a full analysis of the patient's unconscious perceptions and other responses in terms that accept their validity—work that must in addition address itself eventually to the patient's subsequent distortions, and to the pathological misappropriations and responses to these countertransference-based difficulties within the analyst.

Postulate 2: The analyst's unconscious countertransference fantasies and interactional mechanisms will influence his three major functions vis-à-vis the patient: his management of the framework and capacity to hold the patient; his ability to contain and metabolize projective identifications; and his functioning as the interpreter of the patient's symbolic associations, projective identifications, and efforts to destroy meaning. A complementary postulate would state that the analyst's countertransferences can be aroused by, and understood in terms of, not only the patient's associations and behaviors, but also in terms of the analyst's responses to the framework of the bipersonal field, and to the holding and containing capacities of the patient.

While some analysts, such as Reich (1960) and Greenson (1972), have questioned the invariable relationship between technical errors and countertransference, my own clinical observations clearly support such a thesis. However, virtually the entire classical psychoanalytic literature prior to my own writings (see especially 1975b,c, 1976a,c, 1978a) considered as the sole vehicle of countertransference expression the analyst's erroneous verbal interventions, especially his errors in interpreting. A number of Kleinian writers, especially Grinberg (1962) and Bion (1962, 1963, 1965, 1970) have also investigated countertransference influences on the analyst's management of projective identifications and on his containing functions. A full conceptualization of possible avenues of countertransference expression would include all these areas, as well as the analyst's management of the ground rules and his capacity to hold the patient.

As we have already seen in the discussion of the first postulate, the adaptational-interactional view helps to deepen and render more specific our understanding of the interplay between countertransference and the analyst's interpretive interventions. Not unexpectedly, it leads us to include missed interventions and inappropriate silences among the expressions of countertransference, and provides us extensive means for identifying, rectifying, and interpreting the patient's responses to these errors. Much of this has been discussed above, tends to be familiar territory for most analysts, and has been considered rather extensively in prior publications (see especially Langs 1976a,c); I will therefore restrict myself here to a consideration of those aspects of this postulate that have been relatively disregarded.

Perhaps the single most neglected arena for the expression of the analyst's countertransferences is that of his management of the ground rules—the framework of the bipersonal field. In part, because virtually every analyst has to this day been analyzed within a bipersonal field whose framework has been modified, the influence of countertransferences on the analyst's management functions has been virtually ignored by all. Nonetheless, I have garnered extensive evidence for the basic and necessary functions of a secure framework (Langs, 1975c, 1976a, 1978a), demonstrating its importance in creating a therapeutic hold for the patient, in establishing the necessary boundaries between patient and analyst, and in affording the bipersonal field its essential open and symbolic communicative qualities.

However, the maintenance of a secure framework requires of the analyst a tolerance for his patient's therapeutic regression and related primitive communications, a renunciation of his pathological and countertransference-based needs for inappropriate gratification and defenses, and a capacity to tolerate his own limited regression and experiences of anxiety, which are inevitable under these conditions. Thus, because the management of the frame is so sensitively a function of the analyst's capacity to manage his own inner state, and to maintain his psychic balance, his handling of the framework is in part a direct reflection of the extent to which he has mastered his countertransferences. Further, because of the collective blind spots in this area and the sanction so implied, analysts will tend to monitor their verbal interventions for countertransference-based influences, while neglecting to do so in regard to their management of the frame. Clearly, any alteration in the framework can provide the analyst countertransference-based and inappropriate gratifications, as well as defenses and nonadaptive relief from anxiety and other symptoms; all possible deviations in the frame should therefore be explored for such factors (see Langs, 1975c).

Interactionally, one of the analyst's basic functions is to receive contain, metabolize, and interpret the patient's projective identifications (interactional projections) and other interactional inputs. Due to underlying countertransferences, an analyst may be refractory to such containment and impervious to both the patient's communications and his interactional efforts. Much of this is based on what Bion (1962, 1970) has described as the container's dread of the contained, and which he has characterized as fears of denudation and destruction. An analyst may indeed dread the effects on himself of the patient's communications and projective identifications, and may respond on a countertransference basis with nonlistening, with distancing or breaking the link with the patient (Bion 1959),or by undertaking active efforts to modify the patient's disturbing communications and projections—often through the use of irrelevant questions, distinctly erroneous interpretations, and sudden alterations in the framework.

A second form of countertransference-based disturbance in the analyst's containing function may occur in regard to the processing or metabolizing of the patient's projective identifications (see Langs 1976b). Grinberg (1962) has termed this *projective counteridentification*: a situation in which the analyst receives a projective identification, remains unconscious of its contents, meaning and effects, and inappropriately and unconsciously reprojects the pathological contents back into the patient—either directly or in some modified but not detoxified form. Bion (1962) has termed this containing function the capacity for *reverie*, and has stressed the importance of the detoxification of dreaded and pathological projective identifications, leading to reprojections back into the patient that are far more benign than the original projective identifications. In my terms, this detoxification process entails the appropriate *metabolism* of a projective identification, the awareness in the analyst of its conscious and unconscious implications, and the symbolic interpretation of these contents in terms of defense-resistance functions and the revelation of pathological introjects. In this regard, countertransference-related anxieties, introjects, and disruptive fantasies may disturb the metabolizing and detoxifying process within the analyst, and may render him incapable of becoming aware of the nature of the patient's projective identifications and unable to interpret them. Under these conditions, he will, as a rule, pathologically metabolize the introject in terms of his own inner disturbance, and reproject into the patient—

through verbal interventions and mismanagement of the framework—a more terrifying and pathological projective identification than that which orginated from the analysand.

A third type of containing pathology entails what I have described as a pathological need for introjective identifications—a countertransference-based need to inappropriately and excessively contain pathological introjects (Langs 1976a,b). This tends to be expressed through provocative interventions—whether interpretive or in respect to the frame—that are unconsciously designed as intrusive projective identifications into the patient, intended to evoke responsive pathological projective identifications from the analysand. These analysts have a hunger for pathological expressions from their patients, and find many means of inappropriately disturbing their patients and generating ill-timed pathological projective identifications.

The analytic bipersonal field is designed for the cure of the patient, and for the analytic resolution, through cognitive insight and implicit positive introjective identifications, of his psychopathology. It has proved difficult for analysts to accept that a valid and secondary function of the same bipersonal field—valid only so long as it is, indeed, secondary—is that of the analytic resolution of more restricted aspects of the analyst's psychopathology. This idea is often misunderstood to imply a belief in the use of the patient and the analytic situation as a primary vehicle for the cure of the analyst. Despite explicit disavowal of such intentions, the recognition that this will inevitably be a second-order phenomenon is viewed as exploitation of the patient, rather than as a relatively silent and actually indispensable benefit that will accrue to the well-functioning analyst. In the course of overcoming the many resistances against accepting this postulate—more precisely, a clinical observation—it has become evident that this attribute is an essential component of the bipersonal field, and that it is unlikely that the analyst could function adequately in its absence. Without it, it would be virtually impossible for him to master the inevitable anxieties and disturbances that will occur within him, as interactional products, in the course of his analytic work with each patient. Their inevitable presence has not only a potential therapeutic effect on his behalf, but also renders him a far more effective analyst for his patients.

The basic framework—the ground rules—of the psychoanalytic situation provides a hold, appropriate barriers, and the necessary communicative medium for analyst as well as patient. This hold affords him a valuable and appropriate sense of safety, a means of defining his role vis-à-vis the patient, assistance in managing his inappropriate impulses and fantasies toward the patient (his countertransferences), and insures the possibility of his use of language for symbolic interpretations (it is therefore essential to his interpretive capacities).

Just as certain aspects of the analyst's behavior and stance are essential dimensions of the framework, the patient too offers a hold to the analyst. Such factors as the regularity of his attendance at sessions, his being on time, his payment of the fee, his complying with the fundamental rule of free association, his listening to and working over the analyst's interpretations, and his own adherence to the ground rules and boundaries of the analytic relationship contribute to a holding effect experienced by the analyst. Further, the patient will inevitably serve as a container for the analyst's projective identifications—both pathological and nonpathological—a function through which, once again, the analyst may implicitly benefit.

As for the influence of countertransference in these areas, these may derive from undue or pathological (instinctualized: aggressivized or sexualized) holding needs, and an unconscious fear of, or need to repudiate, the patient's hold, a dread of the patient as container, and an excessive need to utilize the patient's containing capacities. These countertransference influences are manifested through the analyst's mismanagement of the frame, his erroneous interventions, his failures to intervene, and, overall, through conscious and unconscious deviations in the analyst's central commitment to the therapeutic needs of the patient. The analyst who inordinately requires a rigid and unmodified frame will be intolerant of his patient's alterations of that frame; these may take the form of latenesses, missed sessions, necessary requests to change the time of an hour because of changed life circumstances, unnecessary requests for such changes in schedule, and a variety of gross and subtle efforts to alter the basic ground rules of analysis—such as efforts to engage the analyst in conversation after an hour.

It is my empirically derived conclusion (Langs 1975c, 1976a,c) that it is the analyst's main responsibility to maintain, to the extent feasible, the framework intact in the face of all inappropriate efforts at deviation. I am therefore in no way advocating conscious—or unconscious—participation in inappropriate modifications of the frame. I wish to stress, however, that analysts with pathological needs for a rigid frame—in contrast to the necessary rigorous frame (Sandler, in Langs et al., in press)—will have difficulty in recognizing those rare valid indications for an alteration in the framework (e.g., a suicidal emergency), a change that is in essence a revised version of the basic framework without its destruction or defective reconstitution. In addition, such an analyst will have a great deal of difficulty in dealing with his patient's efforts to modify the framework and in recognizing such endeavors as a crucial adaptive context for the organization of the analysand's subsequent material. He also will have major problems in understanding the unconscious implications of these intended or actual alterations in the frame, and in carrying out effective, relevant analytic work. Further, he will dread those interpretations to his patient that might generate moments of hostility and rejection, and which might unconsciously prompt the patient to modify in some way his usual, implicit hold of the analyst.

Those analysts for whom the patient's inevitable hold generates a threat, whether related to fears of intimacy, instinctualization of the patient's holding capacities in terms of seductive and aggressive threats, or the dread of the necessary and therapeutic regression evoked by such a hold, unconsciously will make efforts to disturb the patient's holding capacities. It seems evident that the patient derives a degree of implicit and necessary gratification in regard to his capacity to safely hold the analyst, a satisfaction that is not unlike those derived from his unconscious curative efforts on the analyst's behalf (Searles 1965, 1975, Langs 1975b, 1976a,c). Thus, the repudiation on any level of the patient's appropriate holding capacities not only generates active countertransference-based inputs into the bipersonal field, but also denies the patient a form of growth-promoting gratification that forms an important complementary means of achieving adaptive structural change, in addition to the more generally recognized means derived from affect-laden insights and inherent positive introjective identifications. It is evident too that the analyst's need to repudiate the patient's appropriate hold will prompt him to generate interventions and mismanagements of the framework designed unconsciously to disturb that holding function, create artificial and undue distance, and erect pathological and inappropriate barriers between himself and the patient.

Every analyst at some time in the course of an analytic experience, and a number of analysts in the course of much of their work with all of their patients, will be burdened by countertransference pressures that prompt the inappropriate use of the patient as what I have termed a *pathological container* for his own disturbed inner contents (Langs 1976a). At such junctures, the analyst's interventions are not primarily designed for the meaningful insight of the patient and for the appropriate maintenance of the framework, but instead unconsciously function as efforts at projective identification as a means of placing into the patient the analyst's burdensome psychopathology and inappropriate defensive needs. And while, as I have mentioned above, the patient can indeed accrue adaptive benefit from his own unconscious capacities to function as a pathological container for the analyst's projective identification and from his curative efforts on the analyst's behalf, such gains are dangerously intermixed with the destructive aspects of such interactions. These include the overburdening of the patient with the analyst's pathology to a degree that evokes a pathological regression that not only will be difficult to manage and interpret, but also may be essentially misunderstood by the analyst who has unconsciously evoked the regressive process and who maintains his unconscious disturbed needs for the patient's containing ability. Failures by the patient to contain the analyst's pathological projective identifications, and to metabolize them, however unconsciously, toward insights for the analyst, will be unconsciously resented by the analyst, and will considerably complicate the analytic interaction. The influence on the patient of the pathological introjects generated by the analyst also may be quite destructive, and may in a major way reinforce the patient's own pathological introjects and defenses. In large measure, such an interaction may constitute the repetition of an important past pathogenic interaction which helped to generate the patient's emotional problems in his formative years.

On the other hand, the analyst may dread any even momentary and limited use of the patient as a container—not only for his pathological projective identifications, but for his valid interventions as well. Under these conditions he will experience an extreme constriction in his capacity to interpret to the patient and excessive anxiety in communicating freely to him, however consciously these interventions are founded on a wish to be appropriately helpful. Often, the dread of containing the patient's projective identifications is based on conscious and unconscious fears of being driven crazy by the patient, and related fears of psychic disintegration or loss of control; fears of similar effects

on the patient may inhibit the analyst's necessary projective
communications to the analysand.

*Postulate 3: Countertransferences have a significant influence on the
communicative properties of the bipersonal field, and on both the
analyst's and the patient's style of communicating.*

It is evident that the communicative style of the analyst (and of the
bipersonal field of which he is a part) is a function of a wide range of
factors, the most immediately obvious being inborn tendencies; acute
and cumulative genetic experiences; personality and character
structure; ego resources; ego dysfunctions; intrapsychic conflicts;
unconscious fantasies, memories, and introjects; and the overall extent
of emotional health or psychopathology. The focus here on the
influence of countertransference is, then, an attempt to delineate
simply one vector among many that coalesce to effect a particular
communicative style and field.

Initial clinical evidence suggests that the ideal analyst basically
employs the Type A mode of communication, with its essential
symbolic qualities, and that he has a capacity to manage the
framework of the analytic situation in order to create with the patient a
potential field for a Type A communicative interaction. Such an
analyst would undoubtedly, from time to time, and based on many
factors, momentarily shift to the Type B, action-discharge mode of
communication and to the Type C, barrier-negation mode. He would,
however, through his own awareness and through communications
from his patient, be capable of recognizing these shifts in communicative style, of self-analyzing their underlying basis, of rectifying their
influence on the patient and the therapeutic bipersonal field, and of
interpreting to the patient his conscious and unconscious perceptions
of this communicative shift and its unconscious meanings and
functions.

In contrast to the Type A therapist, the Type B therapist experiences
repeated difficulty in deriving symbolic formulations of his patient's
associations and in generating symbolic interpretations. While his
conscious intentions may well be to offer such interventions—there is
considerable lack of insight within analysts in regard to their
communicative mode—his use of language will be unconsciously
aimed at projective identification into the patient and internal relief-
producing discharge. While at times patients may undoubtedly derive
some type of symptom relief from such therapeutic interactions—

based primarily on relatively benign projective identifications from the analyst and on positive self-feelings derived from unconscious curative efforts and containing responses to his pathology—such gains are not embedded in valid cognitive insights and modulating, positive introjective identifications. As a result, they are quite vulnerable to regression and are without the necessary substantial foundation characteristic of lasting adaptive structural change. In addition to their use of verbal interventions that function interactionally as pathological projective identifications, these analysts are quite prone to unneeded modifications of the framework which similarly serve their needs for pathological projective identification, action, and discharge. Elsewhere (Langs 1976a,c) I have designated as *misalliance and framework cures* the noninsightful, unstable symptom relief, in either patient or analyst, that may be derived in a Type B communicative field.

The analyst who is prone to a Type C communicative style will seldom be capable of a truly symbolic interpretation. His verbal interventions make use of language not primarily as communication, but as a form of noncommunication and as an effort to destroy meaning. These analysts make extensive use of the psychoanalytic cliché and, unconsciously, their interventions and mismanagements of the framework are designed to destroy the communicative qualities of the bipersonal field and to render it frozen and static. Based on the massive defensive barriers and falsifications offered by these analysts, patients will from time to time experience symptom relief through reinforcement of their own Type C communicative style or through the development of impermeable defensive barriers that momentarily serve as a protection against disruptive underlying contents—fantasies, memories, and introjects. This type of *misalliance cure* (Langs 1975b, 1976a,c) may well account for a large percentage of symptom relief among present-day psychotherapeutic and psychoanalytic patients, and within their therapists and analysts as well.

The Type A therapist will, of course, tend to be rather comfortable with a Type A patient, and will be capable of interpreting his communications. Countertransference-based anxieties may occur because of the regressive pressures that he experiences in a Type A field and, in addition, will arise when the communications from the Type A patient touch upon areas of continued vulnerability. With a Type B patient, he will be capable of contining, metabolizing, and interpreting his patient's projective identifications, though countertransference difficulties may intrude when these projective identifications are massive or touch upon areas of excessive sensitivity. Some Type A analysts experience discomfort with the action-prone, projectively identifying Type B patient, and will experience difficulties in containing, metabolizing, and interpreting their interactional projections.

A Type C patient may be quite boring to the Type A analyst, who will consciously and unconsciously experience the envy, destruction of meaning, and attack on the analyst's ability to think and formulate that is characteristic of these patients. The Type A analyst may be vulnerable to these qualities of the negative projective identifications of these patients, and he may also have difficulty in tolerating their use of massive, impenetrable, and uninterpretable defensive barriers. Still, he is in the best position to identify the qualities of a Type C communicative style and to patiently interpret the primary defensive aspects. In addition, he is best prepared to tolerate, contain, and interpret the underlying psychotic core of these patients.

While clinical evidence indicates that it is possible to conduct a successful analysis with a Type B or Type C patient (Langs 1978a), it appears likely that the reverse is not true: Type B and Type C analysts cannot be expected to generate bipersonal fields characterized by an openness of communication, the use of symbolic language, the rendering of symbolic interpretations that lead to cognitive insight and mastery, and the interactional experience of positive projective and introjective identifications—all culminating in adaptive structural change and growth for the patient. While, as I have noted above, Type B and Type C analysts may indeed afford their patients periods of symptom relief, and while these may on occasion structuralize and lead to the disappearance of symptoms, the underlying basis for these symptomatic changes are infused with pathological mechanisms and are quite vulnerable to regressive pressures. There can be no substitute for a personal analysis and for the self-analytic efforts designed to master a given analyst's propensities for the Type B and Type C communicative modes.

In concluding this delineation of interactional postulates related to countertransference, two points implicit to this discussion deserve to be specified. First, in virtually every countertransference-based intervention there is a nucleus of constructive intention and effect.

While in general, this kernel of valid effort is by no means sufficient to compensate for the hurt and damage done by a countertransference-based intervention—effects that may range from the relatively modifiable to the quite permanent—this positive nucleus often can be used as the center of constructive therapeutic work during the therapeutic interludes evoked by the consequences of an unconscious countertransference fantasy or introject. Second, it follows from this observation, and from more general clinical impressions, that considerable insightful analytic work can prevail throughout the rectification-analysis phase of such countertransference-dominated interludes. Thus, we must maintain a balanced view of the effects of the analyst's countertransferences: to some degree, they damage the patient and reinforce his neurosis (a term I again use here in its broadest sense), and thereby perpetuate or even intensify his psychopathology; in addition, however, so long as the countertransference-based effects are recognized, rectified, and fully analyzed with the patient—and of course, subjected to self-analysis by the analyst—these experiences also can provide extremely moving, insightful, positive introjective moments for both patient and analyst.

CLINICAL VIGNETTE

I will now present a single condensed clinical vignette as a means of illustrating these postulates. Because of my commitment to total confidentiality regarding my direct work with patients, this material will be drawn from a supervisory seminar. While this approach is somewhat limiting in the area of countertransference, the interested reader will find additional data in several recent and pending publications (Langs 1976a,b, 1978a); most important, he should have ample opportunity to clinically document these postulates in his own therapeutic endeavors.

Mr. A. was married, in his mid-thirties, depressed, and afraid of growing old and dying. Early in his analysis, during sessions in which his analyst took notes and intervened largely in terms of questions and reflections of the patient's anxiety about initiating treatment, the patient seemed concerned with a certain deadness in the analytic situation: it was, he said, like talking into a tape recorder. He spoke a great deal of tennis, of the homosexual discussions of his closest male friend, and of his fears of divorce, despite feelings that his marriage was killing him. His wife, he said, often loses control and acts crazy; she is overdependent on him. He also expressed wishes that he could invent a machine that could do psychoanalysis. He spoke of friends who fared poorly in analysis, and the analyst suggested that the patient had doubts about his own treatment. The patient disagreed, but said, however, that he wanted it to be quiet and peaceful, like smoking pot. He was not afraid of talking about homosexuals, though he felt that a physician who worked for him had many such fears.

In the next session, he reported a dream in which he found himself in bed with two women. Earlier that day, he had lingered at his tennis club after one of the members had died of a heart attack or sudden stroke. Mr. A. had fantasies of dropping dead on the tennis court, but spoke instead of feeling quite alive and interested in some medically related research in which he and a male friend were engaged.

The analyst asked the patient how he felt in the dream and inquired about other details. The twosome reminded the patient of a harem and of how he often thinks of other women during intercourse with his wife. He thought of a madam in a movie who had been destructive toward the girls who worked for her, and added that he never understood women and feared them. Further questions along these lines by the analyst led to additional allusions to discussions with friends about homosexuality and to curiosity about what was going on in the analyst's mind. When he plays tennis, the patient said, he thinks of nothing—his mind is blank. The analyst pointed out that the patient seemed frightened of his thoughts concerning homosexuality, but that having two women at one time could hardly be called "homosexual." In response, Mr. A. wondered why he comes to analysis at all. When his friends told him that homosexuals hate women, he panicked; these women were his slaves. He spoke of his hatred for his mother and of his close relationship with a research physician, and wondered what he saw in him; he was always involved with other men; it would be awful to be homosexual.

In the next hour, Mr. A. reported a dream of being late for his session. He was standing outside his analyst's office. The analyst came out to move his car and everybody started to laugh. His tire hit a rock, which then hit a taxicab and disabled it. A black woman got out of the cab and called the analyst crazy; he then pushed the cab around because it couldn't go. In associating, the patient alluded to the previous session and how analysis was a dangerous field because the wrong people can influence you. He feels constricted in what he says while on the couch. The dream followed tennis. He can't be close with anyone; he fights with his wife; everything he does brings him unhappiness.

The analyst asked a series of questions related to the manifest dream, and the patient spoke of how his friends and father think that he is crazy for coming to analysis, though in the dream people are calling the analyst crazy. His father accuses him of trying new things and dropping them. After some rumination, the patient spoke of feeling constricted in the sessions and of possible envy of the analyst; he had to arrange his life in keeping with the analyst's schedule. The analyst responded that the patient skips out in the dream, but the patient rejoined that it was the analyst who had been late—not he. He said he recognized that he is not the analyst's only patient and that the analyst's life doesn't center around him, as is true for himself in relation to the analyst. If he missed an appointment, he mused, would the analyst lie down? That would be reversing their roles and would make the analyst the crazy one. The analyst responded that the patient seemed afraid of being laughed at, and the patient agreed, suggesting again that the whole thing was a big reversal. The analyst emphasized again that the dream reflected the patient's fears of being laughed at, criticized, and going crazy.

The patient was late for the next session and spoke of a friend who had become a college professor; the patient felt guilty that he had not taken the right path for his own life. There were further references to being crazy, to being in analysis, and to the static qualities of his marriage. The research center at which the patient had done his postgraduate work was probably going to close because it could not get enough funds or students. Many of the staff had died, and the patient spoke of a fear of cancer that he had felt since beginning his analysis. He had had gastrointestinal symptoms; his mother was always preoccupied with gynecological problems; and at his engagement party he had suffered food poisoning. When his father had had his recent surgery, the patient had experienced an intense fear of dying. His father was seldom available when Mr. A. was a child and would never play tennis with him. Mr. A. recalled several accidents in his childhood, and spoke considerably of his father's disinterest, coldness, and lack of care; if he had been different, the patient would have realized his potential far more than he had. His mother, on the other hand, would get hysterical to the point that no one could talk to her; she was only concerned when he was hurt.

At this point, the analyst suggested that the patient write a short biography of himself for the analyst. Without responding directly, the patient continued to associate: he could always make his mother cry and yet she never hated him as did his father, who held grudges.

In the next hour the patient reported that he had not written the biography; he hadn't had time. He spoke of his research physician friend who had come to Mr. A's office to get some downers (sleeping pills) that the patient kept on hand. This doctor was a man worried about aging, and yet Mr. A still idealized him. He was, however, beginning to see new things and maybe this doctor friend was becoming more human. He felt at any rate that he was more honest with himself than this other man was, and Mr. A was thinking of leaving the area. He wondered if he should get a nursemaid for his infant daughter and spoke again of his tennis club. He wished his wife would be more aggressive and wondered how women ever develop into good mothers. If he left her, he said, she'd fall apart, and all the time he spends with his men friends interferes with his love for her. So much of this had happened since he started analysis, and it came up too because he'd been talking to his physician friend about that analytic jargon about homosexuality and castration anxiety. His friend felt that analysis is actually insignificant and that one day Mr. A would have a gnawing pain somewhere, and they'd open him up and find something that would mean that everything would soon be over. Mr. A would sometimes think about childhood and sex, but not about his parents in that respect. He said he felt he should have read more before he came into analysis, and here the analyst noted that the patient seemed to be looking for some kind of guidelines. The patient said that analysis is like an examination, and he spoke of his secret purchase of nudist magazines. His parents never talked about sex. He had his first sexual relations quite late in life; it was a difficult experience and he had trouble getting an erection and had considered turning on with some kind of drug.

I will focus here solely on those aspects of this material that are pertinent to this discussion. The early fragments of this material are in part an unconscious response to the analyst's note-taking and questions—nonanalytic work with manifest contents. At the time this material was presented, the supervisee indicated some sense of confusion with this patient and stated that the note-taking was an effort to get a better idea about what what was going on in this analysis; it was also based on a wish to discuss this case with colleagues. The patient's unconscious perceptions and experiences of the note-taking serve us well in attempting to define its unconscious implications, especially those related to the analyst's countertransferences: the analyst is not alive, but a tape recorder and analytic machine; his wife loses control and acts crazy; craziness is connected with homosexuality; his wife is excessively dependent; and there is worry about a physician who worked for the patient.

I will take this as sufficient commentary on the note-taking, and will not attempt to trace out its implications in the additional clinical material. We can therefore pause here and suggest that the note-taking did indeed serve as a significant adaptive context for the patient's associations. It is a meaningful organizer of these communications from the patient, which may be viewed as symbolic in nature and largely in terms of Type Two derivatives: disguised unconscious perceptions of, and fantasies about, the analyst. Much of this falls into the realm of unconscious perceptiveness, and conveys possibly valid unconscious fears, motives, and needs within the analyst that have prompted him to take notes—motives of which the analyst was largely unaware, if we are to take his justifications as reflecting the extent of his insight into himself. It would be difficult here to identify and establish the patient's own unconscious homosexual anxieties and fantasies, fears of losing control and going crazy, and needs for mechanical protective devices, since he can justifiably project and conceal them within the analyst's own evident similiar anxieties, efforts at inappropriate gratification, and pathological defenses, expressed, however unconsciously, through the note-taking.

In terms of the postulates developed here, I also would suggest that this patient is making extensive efforts at Type A communication and toward the development of a Type A bipersonal field. The analyst, for his part, both through the alteration in the framework reflected in his note-taking and through his use of noninterpretive interventions— questions directed at the surface of the patient's associations—is utilizing a Type C mode of communication and is endeavoring to create a static, surface-oriented, falsifying communicative field. While there are, in this material, occasional efforts by the analyst at projective identification which I will soon consider, many of his interactional projections are attempts to place a sense of emptiness and void into the patient, and to develop impenetrable, cliched defenses—the negative type of projective identification characteristic of the Type C field. The main hypothesis, then, is to the effect that the note-taking and the surface-oriented interventions are unconsciously designed by this analyst to satisfy his own needs for a Type C barrier and, actually, to destroy the patient's openness to symbolic communication—to the expression of anxiety-provoking contents that are too disturbing for this analyst.

This hypothesis is supported by the patient's material, and while under other conditions these associations might well reflect the patient's own need for a Type C field, here the data suggest that this is not at all the case: the patient seems to be making repeated efforts at Type A communication, and his allusions to Type C mechanisms appear to be based on introjective identifications with the analyst.

The patient's associations, then, support the formulation that the note-taking and questioning unconsciously reflect impairments in the analyst's capacity to safely hold the patient and to contain the patient's projective identifications. The analyst's behaviors also convey his inappropriate needs to be held by the patient and for the patient to contain his anxieties—implications to which the patient is quite sensitive. On a communicative level, these intervention's reflect an unconscious effort by the analyst to modify this potential Type A field into a Type C field in which he would feel better held and safer, especially in regard to disturbing communications and projective identifications from the patient.

The very act of writing down every word from the patient, with its striking containing and incorporative qualities, reflects a dread of actually containing in an affective way the patient's projected contents and a distinct incapacity to metabolize them toward interpretation. Instead, much as the patient unconsciously perceives the therapist's interventions—in respect to the frame and verbally—the note-taking is an effort to deaden the analytic situation, to make it mechanical, and to render it static. The mention of the tape recorder, and the later reference to a psychoanalytic machine, are metaphors of the analyst's containing functions rendered inanimate, probably because of inordinate fears of the patient's projective identifications—the container's fear of the contained (Bion 1962). To state this another way, in terms of the patient's unconscious perceptions and Type Two derivative communications, the therapist fears being driven crazy by his patient and his material, and attempts a Type C mode of expression and set of defenses in a massive effort to seal off this potential craziness and to prevent the contained contents from destroying him—a formulation quite in keeping with an earlier delineation of the Type C field and its function (Langs 1978a).

Among these terrifying contents and projective identifications, those related to latent homosexual themes, uncontrolled destructiveness, and annihilation seem most prominent. While, as I pointed out earlier, the patient may well have intense anxieties in each of these areas, for the moment these formulations apply very directly to the analyst. These countertransferences and their manifestations must be rectified in actuality, and the patient's responses to them analyzed, before the latter's own disturbances could surface in derivative and analyzable form in this bipersonal field. The patient himself refers to the conditions of this field, in which the communicative interface, and the elements of psychopathology it contains, has shifted toward the analyst by referring to efforts to put himself in the analyst's shoes and the reference to role reversal. The analyst's unneeded deviations in the frame and inappropriate interventions unconsciously express his countertransferences and his wish to have the relevant contents contained by the patient and in a sense, therapeutically modified.

In this context, the analyst's intervention that the patient seemed to have many doubts about treatment may be seen as what I have termed a *psychoanalytic cliché*—a psychoanalytically derived generalization based on manifest content or Type One derivatives that primarily serves to destroy the true underlying meaning of the patient's communications, and to substitute a defensive falsification (Bion 1965, 1970, Langs 1978a). The patient's response to this intervention, in which he referred to feeling peaceful when he smoked pot, reflects again the unconscious obliterating qualities of the analyst's interventions—a characteristic of almost all the interventions described in this vignette—and suggest in addition that the patient's own propensities toward the Type C mode are being intensified in this therapeutic interaction. The patient rather wisely concludes this hour with a further allusion to the underlying homosexual anxieties unconsciously shared by both himself and the analyst.

In a general way, the analyst confirmed aspects of this formulation in indicating that he was having a difficult time understanding this patient's material and that he was feeling somewhat anxious about the patient's pathology and the initial course of this analysis. These conscious feelings and thoughts are related to the analyst's difficulty in holding this patient and in containing his projective identifications; they also suggest a countertransference difficulty related to the patient's hold of the analyst. In some way, this patient's material and reactions were not providing the analyst a sense of safety. But rather than tracing out the sources of the analyst's discomfort, he turned to note-taking as a means of artificially and mechanically (how well the patient senses this!) providing himself with a holding device and a containing substitute that will protect him from the postulated dreaded inner destruction—denudation and annihilation, as Bion (1962, 1970) terms it.

In addition, it may well be that the analyst's sense of dissatisfaction regarding the hold that he is experiencing in this analytic interaction has been intensified, rather than reduced, by his own alteration in the framework: his note-taking. Unconsciously, analysts tend to have anxieties in regard to their need to take notes, their anticipation of presenting such material to colleagues and exposing their vulnerabilities, and their use of what I have termed *framework cures* (Langs 1975c, 1976a,c) to resolve underlying countertransference problems. The note-taking itself is often distracting. The entire constellation, conscious and unconscious, actually disrupts the analyst's sense of security rather than enhancing it.

In evaluating the next hour, it would appear that in addition to continuous specific precipitants (the analyst's note-taking and erroneous interventions—questions and generalizations) there was a specific and related adaptive context in the patient's outside life: the death of a member of his tennis club. This day residue can be readily related not only to the patient's fears of death, but also to his unconscious perception of similar anxieties in the analyst—based on earlier material not presented here. However, in the actual session, these day residues were not integrated with the dream, which appears to have been a response to these precipitants; instead the analyst chose to focus on the manifest content of the dream and to its postulated role as a defense against homosexual fantasies and anxieties.

Keeping to ideas relevant to this presentation, it would appear that interventions of this kind, offered without a specific adaptive context and in terms of manifest content and Type One derivatives—the direct reading of a manifest dream and limited associations for latent content, rather than the use of an adaptive context to generate dynamically meaningful Type Two derivatives—characteristically serve to reinforce the Type C, falsified and static qualities of the bipersonal field. As this session illustrates, such interventions almost always are designed to avoid a specific adaptive context which connects on some level to the patient's relationship with the analyst, and usually they are designed to cover over the patient's unconscious perceptions of the analyst's countertransference-based interventions. This approach facilitates an emphasis on the patient's pathology, and on his unconscious fantasies rather than his unconscious perceptions, and often deals with anxieties extraneous to the analytic relationship; they are a major form of defensiveness in respect to the influence of the analyst's countertransferences on the analytic interaction, the bipersonal field in which it occurs, and the analysand.

Interventions of this type are experienced by patients in terms of an impaired sense of holding, and especially as a reflection of the analyst's refractoriness in regard to his containing functions. Here, the unconscious communication from the analyst is to the effect that death, and especially sudden death, is to be denied, rendered nonexistent, and split off into a bastion of the bipersonal field (Baranger and Baranger 1966). A more general and widespread effort at obliteration may follow, creating a Type C field.

To some extent, these hypotheses are supported by the patient's response to the analyst's general interpretation of the patient's concerns about homosexuality and the dream of the two women as defensive in this regard. The patient rightly wonders why he comes to analysis at all, implying that if important meanings are to be destroyed in the analytic bipersonal field, effective analytic work will be impossible. There are also further indications of his doubts regarding the analyst's capacity to contain, manage the frame, and interpret, and, in respect to his stress on underlying homosexual anxieties, it might be asked whether these are primarily the analyst's concerns, and whether as such they serve as a deflection from more disturbing worries.

In the following hour, the patient had a dream that he immediately linked to the previous session. In terms of the patient's associations, it alludes to the analyst's craziness and his fear of doing damage—and by implication, of being damaged. The patient comments on the dangers of being an analyst, a point quite pertinent to the present discussion. He also describes his sense of constriction in the sessions, conveying both the extent to which the Type C mode is being imposed upon him and his unconscious perceptions of the analyst's own needs to constrict. It is then that the patient refers to his envy of the analyst and his security. On one level, this alludes to the analyst's massive defensiveness and the protection it affords him; while on another level, it is an introjective identification of the analyst's envy of the patient, who feels secure enough to communicate his unconscious fantasies, introjects, memories, and anxieties—a communicative mode that is quite difficult or perhaps even impossible for this analyst.

It is also noteworthy that when the analyst attempts to suggest that the dream reflects the patient's wish to leave analysis, the patient points out that it is the analyst who had the problem in the dream—a formulation in keeping with the assessment of this material being offered here. It is in this context that the patient implies the projection into himself by the analyst of the wish that patient become therapist in this bipersonal field—the reversal of roles. The analyst's rejoinder is to emphasize the patient's paranoid feelings and anxieties, partially, it seems, to deny his own concerns and partially to projectively identify them into the patient as well.

In the next hour, the patient was late and the analyst felt concerned about the course of the analysis. Patients frequently respond to failures in the analyst's holding, containing, and interpretive capacities with disruptions in the framework that impart to the analyst a sense of being held poorly and a related sense of disturbance.

The hour itself begins with direct and indirect allusions to having made a mistake in entering analysis. The patient then returns to the theme of death and his own fear of cancer—an image that would suggest, in the context of this discussion, both the patient's dread of contaning the analyst's pathological projective identifications and the analyst's comparable fear. It is a metaphor of the container's fear of the contained, and is the reprojection of the analyst's pathological projective identification in a form that is further imbued with toxicity and destructiveness. The patient's reference to food poisoning conveys similar implications.

The interactional qualties of this material is supported by the patient's reference to his own fears, as well as those of his mother, and his allusion to his father's surgery. Unconsciously, he then reprimands the therapist for his insensitivity and distance, but sees it as an alternative to utter loss of control—hysteria.

It was at this point in the session that the analyst experienced an intense sense of disquietude and concern about the patient's pathology and asked him to write a biography. Consciously, he had been concerned about the dream of the previous hour, in which he had appeared undisguised, and while he wondered whether this was an indication of some type of countertransference difficulty, most of his thoughts related to anxieties about serious underlying pathology in the patient. The request for the biography was made by the analyst as another effort to learn more about the patient in order to understand his pathology more clearly.

Once again, we will allow the patient's response to guide us in evaluating this intervention—another alteration in the frame. First, he did not write the biography, and he soon spoke of a physician friend who asked him for some sedatives. This consciously idealized physician was now being seen as human and vulnerable, and in some sense, as dishonest with himself. Here we have a metaphor for the analyst's projective identification into the patient of his own anxieties and need for noninsightful, artificial, drug-based relief. It is the patient who is to offer a healing reprojection—the pill or the biography—to relieve the analyst of his inappropriate anxieties. The danger, as the patient puts it in Type Two derivative form, is that the analyst might fall apart; the dread is of something deadly inside. Exhibitionism, voyeurism, sexual impotence, and homosexuality are all implied as related anxieties and themes.

At this point in his presentation, the analyst was able to describe some unresolved anxieties regarding death. He soon realized that the request of the patient that he write a biography was an effort to undo these anxieties by creating a permanent, 'ndestructible record of the patient with which he—the analyst—could reassure himself. It is interesting that this patient refused to serve as a pathological container for the analyst's anxieties, at least on this level, and that he also refused to join in the sector of misalliance and in the framework cure offered by the analyst. Apparently recognizing unconsciously that the biography was an effort at artificial communication and an effort to erect a barrier to the disturbing contents that were emerging in this analysis, the patient unconsciously communicated these perceptions to the analyst and became engaged in additional unconscious efforts at cure—largely through a series of insightful unconscious interpretations related to the analyst's need to obliterate, his wish for the patient to serve him as a nursemaid and good mother, his homosexual and bodily anxieties, and his fears of death, containing, and sexuality.

While considerably more could be said in regard to this vignette, I will conclude this discussion by suggesting that only a series of self-insightful efforts directed toward resolution of the analyst's underlying countertransference difficulties, and the actual rectification of his difficulties in holding, containing, interpreting, and creating a Type A rather than a Type C communicative field—and the full interpretation of the patient's unconscious perceptions, introjections, and reactions to these inputs by the analyst—could redirect the interface of this bipersonal field to the pathology of the patient, and provide him a Type A communicative medium and an opportunity for insightful therapeutic work.

CONCLUDING COMMENTS

I will not attempt a comprehensive discussion of these postulates regarding countertransference, nor will I endeavor to delineate further the special advantages of viewing countertransference as an interactional product of the bipersonal field. I shall conclude by simply emphasizing the importance of an adequate and full listening process, of a validating clinical methodology, and of self-knowledge in applying these concepts regarding countertransference in the clinical situation, and more broadly in the expansion of psychoanalytic knowledge.

As many other analysts have noted (Langs 1976a), transference was first seen by Freud as the major enemy and obstacle to psychoanalysis, and only later recognized as its greatest ally—a quality that is by no means fully appreciated even to this day, so that the patient as the enemy and as resisting dominates the analyst's unconscious images, while the patient as ally and as curative is still far less appreciated. Similarly, with an even greater sense of dread, countertransference was first viewed as an enemy to analytic work; and while Freud never specifically acknowledged its constructive aspects, later analysts have indeed attempted to do just that. There has been a recent trend toward identifying the constructive dimensions of countertransference, and these very much deserve to be put into perspective.

However, it is well to conclude this discussion with a recognition that despite the many parallels between transference and countertransference (in their narrowest sense), there are important differences. While both are inevitable in the course of an analysis, transference manifestations are absolutzly vital to the analytic work and are bound to be a major component of the patient's constructive experiences with the analyst and of his unconscious communications to him. By contrast, it is essential that countertransference expressions be kept to a reasonable minimum, that they not dominate the experiences and communications of the analyst, and that they not overfill the bipersonal field. However human such expressions are, and however meaningful their rectification and analysis with the patient may be, countertransference-based communications do traumatize the patient to some degree and these effects must be fully appreciated. It can be seen, then, that a properly balanced view of countertransference is extremely difficult to maintain. It is my hope that the present paper has enabled the reader to develop a more sensitive conception of this most difficult subject.

NOTE

1. The clinical observations and formulations to be developed in this paper are equally pertinent to psychotherapy and psychoanalysis. Since almost all the prior literature on this subject is derived from the psychoanalytic situation, I will adopt that as my model for this presentation.

REFERENCES

Baranger, M., and Baranger, W. (1966). Insight and the analysic situation. In *Psychoanalysis in the Americas,* ed. R. Litman, pp. 56–72. New York: International Universities Press.

Bion, W. (1959). Attacks on linking. *International Journal of Psycho-Analysis* 40:308–315.

———(1962). *Learning from Experience.* New York: Basic Books.

Reprinted in W. Bion, *Seven Servants.* New York: Jason Aronson, 1977.

————(1963). *Elements of Psycho-Analysis.* New York: Basic Books. Reprinted in W. Bion, *Seven Servants.* New York: Jason Aronson, 1977.

————(1965). *Transformations.* New York: Basic Books. Reprinted in W. Bion, *Seven Servants.* New York: Jason Aronson, 1977.

Greenson, R. (1972). Beyond transference and interpretation. *International Journal of Psycho-Analysis* 53:213-217.

Grinberg, L. (1962). On a specific aspect of counter-transference due to the patient's projective identification. *International Journal of Psycho-Analysis* 43:436-440.

Langs, R. (1973a). The patient's view of the therapist: reality or fantasy? *International Journal of Psychoanalytic Psychotherapy* 2:441-431. [Chapter 4, this volume]

————(1973b). *The Technique of Psychoanalytic Psychotherapy* Vol. I. New York: Jason Aronson.

————(1974). *The Technique of Psychotherapy* Vol. II. New York: Jason Aronson.

————(1975b). Therapeutic misalliances. *International Journal of Psychoanalytic Psychotherapy* 4:77-105. [Chapter 6, this volume]

————(1975c). The therapeutic relationship and deviations in technique. *International Journal of Psychoanalytic Psychotherapy* 4:106-141. [Chapter 7, this volume]

————(1975a). The patient's unconscious perception of the therapist's errors. In *Tactics and Techniques in Psychoanalytic Therapy, Vol. II: Countertransference,* ed. P. Giovacchini. New York: Jason Aronson. [Chapter 5, this volume]

————(1976a). *The Bipersonal Field.* New York: Jason Aronson.

————(1976b). On becoming a psychiatrist: discussion of "Empathy and intuition in becoming a psychiatrist" by Ronald J. Blank. *International Journal of Psychoanalytic Psychotherapy* 5:255-279. [Chapter 12, this volume]

————(1976c). *The Therapeutic Interaction.* 2 vols. New York: Jason Aronson.

————(1978a). Some communicative properties of the bipersonal field. *International Journal of Psychoanalytic Psychotherapy* 7:89-161. [Chapter 15, this volume]

———(1978b). Validation and the framework of the therapeutic situation. *Contemporary Psychoanalysis* 14:98–124. [Chapter 14, this volume]

Langs, R. et al. (in press). *Psychoanalytic Dialogues III: Some British Views on Clinical Issues.* New York: Jason Aronson.

Reich, A. (1960). Further remarks on counter-transference. *International Journal of Psycho-Analysis* 41:389–395.

Searles, H. (1965). *Collected Papers on Schizophrenia and Related Subjects.* New York: International Universities Press.

———(1975). The patient as therapist to his analyst. In *Tactics and Techniques in Psychoanalytic Therapy, Vol. II: Countertransference,* ed. P. Giovacchini. New York: Jason Aronson.

Chapter Eighteen

Dreams in the Bipersonal Field

[1978]

It is by no means coincidence that one of the most compelling means through which Freud illuminated the structure and function of neuroses (a term used here in its broadest sense to allude to the entire gamut of psychopathological syndromes) was derived through his remarkable insights into dreams and dreaming (Freud 1900). As private internal experiences which occur during an altered state of consciousness and are remembered subsequently in the waking state, dreams are, as Freud so convincingly demonstrated, a special form of communication. They possess distinctive features on the one hand, and yet have qualities that are shared on some level with virtually all other means of expression—memory, thought, narrative, action, and the like.

Dreams are therefore both unique and representative creations. They embody nonneurotic expression and yet are among the most exquisite representations of a communicative mode that is the hallmark of the neuroses—one characterized by a predominance of primary process mechanisms or by what I have termed *derivative, convoluted communication* (Langs 1978c). As a result, the clinical study of dreams provides an unusual opportunity for the understanding and application of the basics of the listening process (Langs 1978c), especially as it relates to interpretive interventions and efforts to manage the ground rules or framework of the therapeutic situation.

Having recognized, then, that dreams have a special place in clinical practice and yet are merely one representative realm of effective work within the clinical situation, we will be able to maintain a perspective on the present study of dreams in psychotherapy. We can view this exploration largely as a ready means of representing effective psychotherapeutic practice. In this way, we can set aside the debate as to whether the therapist should respond in any special way to dream material or should simply treat it as he would all other communications. The answer appears to be that both are true: he should respond somewhat differently because dreams have certain special qualities, and yet he should use the same basic principles of technique because dreams are merely one among many means of communicating the unconscious fantasies, memories, introjects, and perceptions on which neuroses are founded, sustained, and, with proper therapeutic work, modified.

I will develop my discussion by first providing a framework for my exploration of dreams: I will offer an outline of the main features of the therapeutic situation and interaction (see also Langs 1973, 1974, 1976a, b, 1978b, c, d). I will then define and discuss two broad and basic principles for listening to and interpreting dreams in psychotherapy. Finally, I hope to venture into a number of relatively unexplored realms pertinent to the understanding and analysis of dreams in psychotherapy.

THE BIPERSONAL FIELD IN PSYCHOTHERAPY

In brief, I shall offer a basic conception of the therapeutic situation—and I allude here to psychoanalytically oriented or insight psychotherapy—that is founded on an adaptational-interactional approach. The treatment situation is viewed as a bipersonal field with a given set of boundaries and a frame, with the patient and therapist at opposite poles (for details, see Langs 1976a, b, 1978b, c, d). The field is defined by a set of ground rules, implicit and explicit, that affords the therapeutic relationship its special communicative and potentially therapeutic qualities (Langs 1975b). Treatment unfolds on the basis of the therapeutic commitment of the therapist and the therapeutic needs of the patient.

Among the essential tenets that create this unique situation are the patient's free associations and the therapist's capacities to establish and manage the framework, and to develop verbal interventions geared toward interpretations. Basic to the process of cure is the patient's experience of an adequate therapeutic hold; the therapist's ability to contain and metabolize the patient's projective identifications so as to process them toward cognitive understanding; the specific cognitive insights, conflict resolution, and adaptive resources derived from the therapist's valid interpretations and reconstructions; and the inevitable positive introjective identifications that accrue to the patient from a therapeutic interaction with a therapist who is effective in each of these spheres (for details, see Langs, 1976a, b, 1978d).

Within the bipersonal field, every experience and communication receives vectors from both participants. The unfolding interaction is a spiraling one, in which the therapist and patient each respond adaptively to the other's communications. Translated into terms most relevant to the present paper, the patient's communications to the therapist are prompted by intrapsychically significant adaptive contexts, the vast majority of which pertain to the therapeutic relationship. He responds to these precipitants with derivative communications that contain his unconscious fantasies, memories, introjects, and perceptions as mobilized by the particular primary adaptive tasks (Langs 1972, 1973, 1976a, 1978b). Of considerable importance in this sequence is the patient's unconscious perceptions and introjections of the therapist, based on the latter's unconscious communications within the therapeutic interaction, conveyed through his silences and interventions. For his part, the major adaptive context for the therapist's responses to the patient is that of the latter's communications; the therapist's interventions are therefore viewed as conscious and unconscious adaptive responses within the framework of the therapeutic situation.

The material from the patient may be organized in three ways (Langs 1978b, c, d): in terms of *manifest contents,* which contain surface meanings that are essentially without dynamic meaning for his neurosis; in terms of *Type One derivatives,* which are readily available inferences from the manifest content and which provide important clues to unconscious processes, without defining them with sufficient specificity for definitive interpretive work; and in terms of *Type Two* derivatives, which are organized around a specific adaptive context, usually within the therapeutic interaction, and which affords definitive and dynamic meaning to the material from the patient to a degree that fosters definitive interpretive interventions.

On the basis of the foregoing distinction, and through consideration of a number of additional factors, it is possible to define three basic types of communicative bipersonal fields in psychotherapy. The *Type A field* is one with a well-defined frame and is a field in which illusion, play, transitional space, and symbolic communication are characteristic. It involves a patient who is capable of communicating through Type Two derivatives and whose resistances can ultimately be interpreted on that basis. It fosters the delineation and interpretation of specific unconscious fantasies, memories, introjects, and perceptions, as well as their genetic underpinnings. This field requires a therapist capable of abstracting and particularizing, and of symbolic understanding and interpreting.

The *Type B field* is one that is characterized by projective identification and the use of action-discharge. Verbal and nonverbal communications are not designed for symbolic expression and representation, but instead are utilized as a means of getting rid of accretions of psychic tension and of interactionally and psychologically placing contents and mechanisms into the object. Such a communicative field may develop when the framework is modified, when the patient is prone to the use of projective identification, or when the therapist is so inclined. Effective therapeutic work in a Type B field requires a therapist capable of introjecting the patient's projective identifications, and of metabolizing and detoxifying them through cognitive understanding and interpretation, thereby returning the projected contents and mechanisms to the patient in a less toxic and mastered form.

The third and final communicative field, the *Type C field,* is characterized by the use of action and language to destroy the interpersonal links between patient and therapist, and to erect impenetrable barriers designed to seal off the chaotic parts of their inner mental worlds and personalities. It is a field characterized by nonmeaning, lies and falsifications, destruction of the links between patient and therapist, and efforts at noncommunication. Patients who utilize a Type C communicative mode will tend to ruminate emptily, to describe recent and past events in great detail without linking them to a significant, current adaptive context (the *Type C narrator;* Langs 1978b, c), or will allude to a meaningful adaptive context without producing interpretable Type Two derivatives. As a rule, these patients will, on occasion, communicate isolated metaphors of the Type C field and mode, and it is these that must be interpreted initially. For his part, the therapist who contributes to this type of communicative field tends repeatedly to utilize the psychoanalytic cliche. This kind of intervention purports to be dynamically meaningful but in actuality serves an unconscious need to create an impenetrable barrier, a falsification designed to cover over underlying thruths that would generate catastrophe and chaos—usually for himself as well as the patient (for further details, see Langs 1978c).

There are many other attributes of the essential psychotherapeutic situation, but I will not attempt a full delineation. I would, however, stress that psychotherapy should take place within a well-defined field and frame, that it should include the fundamental rule of free association, that it may or may not take place with the patient on the couch, and that it entails the therapeutic functions of containing, metabolizing, managing the frame, and interpreting (for details, see Langs 1973, 1974, 1976a, b, 1978b, c).

PRINCIPLES OF LISTENING TO AND INTERPRETING DREAMS IN PSYCHOTHERAPY

Throughout the course of my clinical investigations of the psychotherapeutic situation, I maintained a special eye on the nature and function of dreams, and the techniques necessary for their analytic comprehension and use (see Langs 1971, 1973, 1976a, 1978b). Here, I will offer a distillate of the major concepts that have emerged through this work. While clinically founded, much of this is also in keeping with, and in a sense derives from, Freud's remarkable efforts (1900, 1905, 1911, 1923) in this area. In this context, it is well to note the dirth of literature on dreams in psychotherapy; most investigations and books in this area confine themselves to the psychoanalytic situation. In part, this lack reflects the belief that little of unique value can be derived from such investigations, and that dreams play a less significant role in psychotherapy than in psychoanalysis—positions I would dispute.

If I may be permitted a general impression, the prevailing view regarding the place of dreams in psychotherapy might be characterized as follows. In the therapy situation, it is often impossible to obtain meaningful associations to dream elements, and there is seldom sufficient time to permit a detailed or thorough analysis of the unconscious meanings of a dream. Instead, the therapist must often work with the manifest content, or sometimes, with evident symbols and inferences. At times, dreams will have to be set aside in favor of interpretive work with other material in areas more pertinent to psychotherapy—often, pertaining to outside relationships rather than to the therapeutic relationship itself.

In all, the prevailing belief seems to be that the psychotherapeutic situation is not especially conducive to what has loosely been termed *dream analysis* and that, in particular, dreams cannot be used in therapy as a special means of analyzing resistances and core unconscious fantasies-memories—especially as they pertain to the therapeutic relationship (mistakenly alluded to as "the transference" or "transference neurosis"; see below, and Langs 1976a, b, 1978b).

This viewpoint is essentially derivative of a conception of psychotherapy that sees it as considerably different from psychoanalysis, and far more restricted in the use of free association and interpretation-reconstructions. It is also importantly related to the usual companion belief that the psychotherapist cannot meaningfully or consistently analyze material related to the therapeutic relationship (transference and nontransference), largely because a so-called transference neurosis or analyzable transference constellation does not emerge in the psychotherapeutic situation (see Langs 1976b: Chapter 18). Such a position holds that this dimension of the patient's experience and material can be interpreted only sporadically, and that the main work of psychotherapy must focus on the patient's outside relationships.

As implied in the brief delineation of the psychotherapeutic situation offered above, my own empirical observations do not support this view of the psychotherapeutic experience. It is my own contention that every communication from the patient in psychotherapy alludes on some level to his relationship with the therapist, in terms of transference and nontransference—pathological unconscious fantasies, memories, and introjects, on the one hand, and nondistorted unconscious perceptions and introjects on the other. While the manifest content of the patient's associations may refer either to aspects of the therapeutic relationship or to outside interactions, on an unconscious level and in terms of derivative communication, there is a consistent thread that relates the material to the therapeutic interaction. It follows, then, that the interpretation of the unconscious fantasies, memories, introjects, and perceptions that pertain to this interaction is by far the most meaningful vehicle of therapeutic work in the psychotherapeutic situation, and that the material from the patient has to be consistently monitored and understood in this regard—whatever additional elements are also present. These findings are especially pertinent to the two clinical principles that I wish to state and briefly discuss in regard to dreams in psychotherapy:

1. *In psychotherapy, it is possible to make full use of dreams so long as the therapist maintains the basic framework of the therapeutic situation, and the usual principles of listening and intervening.*

In principle, dreams have special communicative qualities which are, nonetheless, potentially available in all other forms of material. It is widely accepted that dreams may be reported primarily in the service of either resistances or the communication of core unconscious fantasies, memories, and introjects. Similarly, it is generally acknowledged that the report of a dream can be taken as an implicit signal that the patient is prepared to communicate in some meaningful manner—again, either in terms of resistance or important revelation.

While I shall attempt in the final section of this paper to refine these general concepts, I would stress here that dreams are, indeed, a sign of a distinctive wish to communicate, though I would add that recognition of this quality need not call for any special variation in technique. In the clinical situation, dreams appear to have a particularly evocative quality that fosters a special type of receptivity in the therapist, though much of this type of listening actually should be maintained in attending to all of the material from the patient (for a full discussion of the listening process, see Langs 1978b).

In the main, the purpose of this tenet is to establish the position that there is available to the psychotherapist a full range of possibilities in listening to, processing, and interpreting dreams. While there may well be particular limitations in the degree to which a dream can be interpreted in the therapeutic situation as compared to psychoanalysis, these restrictions should derive solely from the relative infrequency of the sessions and from the use of the face-to-face mode where it is applied. It should be recognized, however, that the therapeutic setting is only one of a number of variables that influence the analytic work with dream material. Other factors include the personality of the patient, the nature of his psychopathology, various qualities in his dream report, as well as in his ability to associate and work with dreams; the nature of the day residue or precipitant of the dream; and a wide range of factors within the therapist, involving both countertransference and noncountertransference capacities. In a given therapeutic situation, some of these elements may enhance the therapeutic work with dreams, while others will prove restrictive. Still, the goal should be to work as meaningfully as possible with dreams, as one would with any other material from the patient, and to adhere to an essentially in-depth interpretive effort.

2. *In listening to and formulating a dream, the fundamentals of the listening process are consistently applied.*

Most of the detailed efforts made by Freud (1900, 1905) in developing the listening process (a term used here to allude to all aspects and avenues of taking in the communications from the patient, and to efforts at formulating and synthesizing such data—verbally and nonverbally, consciously and unconsciously; see Langs 1978b) unfolded through his ivestigations of dreams. Because of this, and partly because dreams themselves, as definable and often meaning-laden communications, lend themselves to a definition of the listening process, much of the psychoanalytic understanding of listening and formulating has been developed through models based on the analysis of dreams.

Freud (1900) himself first discovered the basic interaction between reality and fantasy in his study of the relationship between the day residue and the dream—more precisely, the external stimulus and the intrapsychic response, pathological or nonpathological. This basic adaptive model is essential to our understanding of neuroses to this day and is far from fully appreciated.

In some ways, it is unfortunate that in a sense Freud discovered the dream and its latent content first, and the day residue secondarily. This occurred largely because his focus was on the intrapsychic aspects of psychopathology (unconscious fantasies, and ultimately unconscious transference fantasies), far more than on the interplay between reality and fantasy—although, clearly, he took cognizance of this aspect as well. However, if his theory of dream formation and analysis had established the day residue as its cornerstone, rather than a peripheral element, considerable misunderstanding might well have been avoided.

Much of the confusion to which I refer stems from the initiation of the investigation of dreams with the manifest dream content, and tracing out from there the day residue in one direction, and in the other, the intrapsychic latent content. While the structure of the dream implied by this approach is essentially the same as that I will outline here, a delineation of unconscious meanings and functions that begins with the external precipitant will permit greater conceptual clarity and will demonstrate that the basics of the listening process as applied to dreams are the same as those applied to any other material from the patient.

In essence, then, a dream is prompted by some reality stimulant or day residue (Freud 1900, Langs 1971). These adaptive contexts have manifest and latent content, and in psychotherapy the latter are, as a rule, pertinent to the therapeutic interaction. The dream itself is an adaptive effort in response to the day residue, and constitutes a working over, directly and indirectly, of its conscious and unconscious implications.

As a conscious communication, however, the manifest dream is *by itself* a form of direct and linear communication, not a form of convoluted and neurotic communication. Still, the manifest content organized around the significant adaptive context for the dream reveals a variety of Type Two derivatives—latent content—that do involve convoluted, neurotic communication. It is the day residue, along with the dream itself and the prior and subsequent associations to the dream, that together may constitute a convoluted communicative network. It is this network, with the day residue (adaptive context) as its nodal point, that yields unconscious meanings—latent contents—and functions in the form of Type Two derivatives.

The stress, then, is on the adaptive sequence initiated by the day residue, reflected in the manifest dream, and extended through the patient's additional associations. Without knowledge of the adaptive context, the therapist is restricted to readily available inferences, his understanding of symbols, and to the monitoring processes to be described below—the level of Type One derivatives. In the presence of a significant adaptive context, however, it is possible to generate from the dream-associational network dynamically meaningful Type Two derivatives whose specific nature and function are revealed in terms of their relationship with the day residue. There is a spiraling interaction between the day residue and the intrapsychic reaction, and the latter includes unconscious selection, interpretation, and evocation (Arlow 1969, Langs 1971).

In its essentials, the steps in the listening process as applied to dreams are as follows (Langs 1978b): taking in freely and without organization; searching for the specific adaptive context for all the material, including the dream; applying the abstracting-particularizing process to the ongoing material: identifying first-order manifest themes, generating meaningful abstractions, deriving specific second-order themes; monitoring all of the material in terms of the therapeutic interaction and the me-not-me interface; deriving a series of Type One derivatives in the absence of an adaptive context, while generating a series of Type Two derivatives in the presence of the primary adaptive task; and finally, evaluating all derivatives for mixtures of reality and fantasy, distortion and nondistortion, transference and nontransference.

This approach permits the processing of all the material from the patient, including his dreams, for both unconscious fantasies and unconscious perceptions, and for significant defenses-resistances and contents. It is an organized means of arriving at the latent content of the dream, in a fashion comparable to that used with all types of communications from the patient. It fosters the identification of defenses, and permits the recognition that the primary process mechanisms first described by Freud (1900) as the means through which the latent content of a dream is transformed into the manifest content—condensation, displacement, symbolization, and considerations of representability—allude more broadly to all of the ego's unconscious defenses and cognitive capacities as brought into play in response to a significant adaptive stimulus and in the generation of a manifest dream.

It may well be that it has been impediments and confusion in regard to the listening process as applied to dreams that have led many therapists to believe that there are extensive limitations in the analyzability of dream material from patients in psychotherapy. As one is able to refine and broaden the listening process itself, it is possible to recognize that the dream-associational network is often rich in derivative communication, and that it lends itself in psychotherapy to an extensive application of a basic interpretive approach. It seems without question that therapeutic efforts of this kind offer the patient the best opportunity for insightful, adaptive inner change and symptom relief.

With these as the basic tenets for the exploration, analysis and interpretation of dreams in psychotherapy, I will now turn to a number of specific refinements and realtively new conceptions pertinent to work with dreams in psychotherapy. In so doing, I will offer several clinical vignettes and attempt to demonstrate the clinical referents of the listening process I have just outlined. At that point, I hope to resolve any possible confusion generated by this relatively abstract delineation.

SOME UNIQUE CONSIDERATIONS OF DREAMS IN PSYCHOTHERAPY

In the course of recent researches into the bipersonal field, a number of insights relevant to dreams have unfolded. Here, I will present those that have been most extensively validated and which seem most important to clinical practice.

1. *In each type of communicative bipersonal field, there are important differences in the ways in which patients report and associate to dreams, and in the techniques required for their processing and interpretation.*

A consideration of the role and function of dreams in each of the three types of communicative bipersonal field described above sheds considerable light on individual styles of dream reporting and associating. It is only in the Type A field, illusory and symbolic, that the prevailing conception of dream communication and analysis applies.

Patients who use the Type A communicative mode tend to report dreams rather frequently. More often than not, their associations will reveal the day residue for the dream and its unconscious links to the therapeutic interaction. The patient's associations to the dream may take the form of material directly linked to one or the other dream element (direct associations), or may involve associations seemingly unrelated to the manifest elements which nonetheless contain important latent meanings when organized around the adaptive context (indirect associations). While both direct and indirect associations may be used primarily to serve the ego's defenses and as resistances against the progress of therapeutic work in the face of some type of anxiety and inner conflict or disturbance, the dream network (by which term I denote the complex of day residues, manifest dream, and all associations to either or both) will generally tend to reveal the unconscious meanings and functions of these resistances through derivative communication. At other times, this network permits the interpretation of specific, meaningful, pathology-related unconscious fantasies, memories, introjects, and perceptions.

While the dream network may not yield analyzable latent meaning in a particular session, Type A patients will soon shift to communicative constellations, with or without dreams, that are open to interpretation: they do not maintain periods of projective identification or noncommunication over many sessions. For these patients, dreams serve as a means of representing and symbolizing their inner mental world, past and present, in a manner that lends itself to interpretation through the development of Type Two derivatives that can be organized around immediate adaptive contexts. The latter tend, as I said, to involve the therapeutic interaction, and eventually the adaptive response can be traced out to its important genetic antecedents—whether primarily in the transference sphere or largely related to aspects of nontransference (see below). These patients are able to use the therapeutic situation and their own communications, including dreams, as a means of conveying illusion and in an effort to generate cognitive understanding. In all, then, they meet the usual criteria for dream communication and its analysis.

It should be noted, however, that therapeutic work of this kind requires a therapist who is capable of establishing and maintaining a secure, well-defined bipersonal field (Langs 1975b, 1976a, b). He must also be able to fully apply the listening process, of abstracting and formulating, and of imparting meaningful, symbolic-illusory interpretations. The latter include the identification of the specific immediate adaptive context for the dream-associational material, and the definitive unconscious fantasies, memories, introjects, and perceptions that constitute the patient's intrapsychic response. Such a therapist must also be capable of detecting communications related to the genetic antecedents of such associations, and of meaningfully relating this material to the unconscious nature and functions of the patient's symptomatology. To do this, he must be able to enter each session without desire, memory or understanding (Bion 1970, Langs 1978b), and to allow the patient to communicate in some form the derivatives through which he can build a meaningful, well-timed, affective interpretation or reconstruction. Countertransference-based disturbances in this regard will significantly influence the patient's communications of, and work with, dreams in psychotherapy (see below).

In the Type B field, dreams are not communicated by the patient in an essentially symbolic, illusory mode, but are utilized as a means of projective identification and action-discharge (Bion 1977, Segal, in press). In essence, these patients utilize their dream experiences and communications as a means of discharge and of placing disturbing inner contents and defenses, and—more rarely—good contents, into the therapist for processing, for proxy evocations (Wangh 1962), and as a means of managing such mental products outside of themselves. At times, dreams are also used as a vehicle for disturbing or disrupting the functioning of the therapist.

Type B patients tend to report relatively few dreams compared to the Type A patient, and their dreams are often fragmented, quite blatant or primitive, and responded to with intense aversion. In contrast to the Type A patient, who generates a relatively meaningful dream network, the Type B patient will characteristically isolate his dream or report them in rather divergent fragments. The day residue is often unclear, and even when it is available it proves difficult to meaningfully relate the dream associational material to the adaptive context. Nonetheless, at times the recognition of the dream stimulus does permit a better appreciation and metabolism of the prevailing projective identifications.

Type B patients also tend to produce few direct associations to their dreams, and those that are reported are largely an effort to read some meaning or inference from the surface of the dream. This type of association, which is even more common in the Type C field, tends to be highly defensive rather than dynamically meaningful. In addition, the indirect associations of the Type B patient tend to be relatively unrelated to the dream network, and the result is a relatively fragmented overall associational network that is difficult to contain, netabolize, or interpret.

The Type B patient, despite his statements to the contrary, has little deep interest in deriving understanding from the dream network, and he concentrates his efforts on projective identification and discharge. Endeavors by the therapist to cognitively interpret the contents of these dreams and associations, even in terms of a particular adaptive context, without alluding to their use for projective identification, tend not to be validated (see Langs 1976b, 1978b). The focus on meaning is generally experienced by the patient as a failure in containing and metabolizing, and the erroneous intervention often constitutes a projective counteridentification (Grinberg 1962)—the unconscious reprojection into the patient of poorly metabolized contents and mechanisms.

A more valid intervention is derived from the introjective identification and containing of the patient's projective identifications and efforts at discharge, working them over in light of the associational material, identifying both the adaptive context and the threads of cognitive communication, and processing all of these inputs toward a cognitive interpretation of the projective function of this particular type of dream communication. It is quite crucial for the therapist, in formulating such subjective interactional experiences, to validate the impressions derived on this basis through his own subsequent subjective experiences, and especially through the patient's cognitive material (see Langs 1976a, 1978b, c, d).

It is the patient in a Type C communicative field who seldom reports dreams, and when he does, they tend to be quite limited, realistic, and often replications of actual events. A significant adaptive context is seldom available, and associations are sparse. The dream network is filled with gaps and is, as a rule, lacking in depth and convoluted, derivative meaning. The dream serves as a relatively opaque barrier to therapeutic relatedness and to underlying catastrophic truths which exist within the patient and, sometimes, within the therapist and the therapeutic interaction.

In a Type C field, the therapist may be confronted with the other extreme: a patient who reports extended and detailed dreams, either without a clear-cut significant adaptive context or with so many details it is not feasible to derive essential unconscious meanings and functions from the totality of the patient's communications. Such patients might be termed *Type C dream narrators*; they utilize extensively detailed associations as barriers and as means of breaking meaningful ties between themselves and the therapist. These patients often associate in terms of Type One derivatives, repeatedly suggesting implicit and often obvious meanings for the many dream elements reported. They approach their own dreams as detached observers who attempt, without any adaptive context and in the absence of any meaningful indirect associations, to intellectually read off a variety of implied meanings based on the manifest content. As a result, the dream network is highly intellectualized, filled with endless details, and lacking in any significant crystallization of meaning.

Unconsciously, this mode of communication is designed as an attack upon the therapist's listening and integrating capacities, and ultimately serves as another form of impenetrable barrier to underlying chaos. To the extent that there are qualities of projective identification in the Type C communicative mode, the barren communicator generates what I have termed a *negative projective identification* (Langs 1978c)—a destructive void. The Type C narrator may also overtax the therapist's containing capacities to the point of destruction and denudation (Bion 1962).

In the midst of these fragments and efforts to destroy meaning, the Type C patient will from time to time communicate metaphors of a Type C field. Sometimes these will occur as isolated dream images related to walls and barriers, to voids and vacuums, to impenetrable barriers, to the destruction of relatedness, and to lies and falsifications. It is these metaphors which must be interpreted to these patients, either as Type one derivatives or, whenever feasible, as Type Two derivatives around a specific adaptive context that has evoked the Type C defensiveness (Langs 1978b, c). The material from the patient usually does not permit an analysis of the underlying fantasies, memories, introjects, and perceptions, as is the case in the Type A field. Often, however, interventions of the type just described are followed by an alteration in the rigidity and intensity of the Type C barriers, to the point where some of the underlying chaos emerges in derivative form and is momentarily analyzable.

Efforts to interpret the contents of dream communications from Type C patients also are uniformly met with nonvalidation. They convey the therapist's failure to understand the essential function of the patient's associations and tend to reveal the therapist's need to find meaning in the midst of its essential absence. Technically, such interventions also represent a failure to deal with communicative modes before other resistances and contents, a variation on the principle of interpreting resistances before core unconscious fantasies and memories. Such interventions are aptly characterized as the use of psychoanalytic cliches; unfortunately, much clinical work with dreams in psychotherapy (and in psychoanalysis) entails the therapist's use of this mode. Its hallmark is the use of dynamic formulations developed from diverse segments of the patient's associations, as a basis for an interpretation which, upon deeper analysis, is revealed primarily to serve as a barrier to more compelling and anxiety provoking underlying truths.

2. *The dream network is an important source of information regarding the ongoing therapeutic relationship. This network provides important revelations regarding the state of the transference component of the patient's relationship to the therapist, but in addition, contains unconscious perceptions and essentially valid introjects derived from that relationship; further, it makes available important insights into the status of the framework and the communicative properties of the bipersonal field (Langs 1976a, 1978b).*

In my conception of the psychotherapeutic relationship and of the nature of psychotherapy, I have stressed the crucial role played by the conscious and (especially) the unconscious aspects of the communicative therapeutic interaction. The patient's relationship with the therapist is viewed as having transference and nontransference elements, and the transference component is seen essentially in terms of unconscious fantasies, memories, introjects, and interactional mechanisms; it is viewed adaptively as being evoked by some aspect of the current therapeutic interaction which prompts a distorted, albeit adaptive, response in the patient.

Dreams are, of course, often among the most analyzable of these adaptive reactions. Their implications can readily be interpreted so long as the therapist is able to identify the specific adaptive context— the precipitant within the therapeutic relationship, often in the form of unconscious implications conveyed in his interventions—and is then able to trace out, using the manifest dream, the additional associations, and the distorted unconscious fantasies, perceptions, and pathological defenses with which the patient has responded. In addition, as the dream network permits, interpretation of the relevant genetic aspects is necessary ultimately as a means of offering a complete intervention. It should be noted, however, that this characterization of therapeutic work with dreams in terms of transference-based components implies the presence of a Type A communicative field, the relative absence of countertransference-based inputs from the therapist, and a predominance of the patient's pathological reactions.

Quite often, however, the actual therapeutic situation is considerably different than implied in this first model. I have already alluded to the implications of the presence of a Type B or Type C communicative field, and noted that in these fields the comprehension and interpretation of dreams is developed somewhat differently than in the Type A field.

There is, in addition, a very crucial, relatively overlooked aspect of the therapeutic relationship regarding which dreams are often a vital means of communication: the primarily nontransference sphere—the patient's valid unconscious perceptions of, and reactions to, the therapist, and the resultant introjects. While such responses characteristically have a valid core, they may be extended subsequently into pathological fantasies, thereby reaching into the realm of transference.

Nonetheless, it is essential to recognize the nondistorted aspects of these responses, since they involve major sectors of healthy and adaptive functioning in the patient, and even unconscious curative efforts on the therapist's behalf (Searles 1975, Langs 1975a, 1976a). In this respect, it is to be stressed that the dream network will, as a rule, contain the relevant unconscious perceptions and introjects in the form of Type Two derivatives when organized around a specific adaptive context. On this basis, we might rephrase and extend Freud's well-known dictum (1900), that dreams are the royal road to the unconscious: not only are they a royal approach to transference, but also to nontransference—and to countertransference and noncountertransference as well.

Another dimension of the therapeutic situation regarding which the dream network bears strong commentary is that of the ground rules or framework. It is not uncommon, in situations where any degree of deviation has occurred at the prompting of either patient or therapist, for this event to serve as a crucial adaptive context and day residue for a patient's dream (see especially Langs 1975b, 1976a). The dream-associational response is characteristically imbued with pertinent unconscious perceptions and introjects of the unconscious implications of the therapist's deviation, to which the former may add distorting elements. Organized as Type Two derivatives around the adaptive context of the alteration in the framework, the dream network characteristically serves as the vehicle for the development of important insights, and, further, as a guide toward the necessary rectification of the frame (Langs 1975b, 1976a, b, §978s). In fact, one of the more remarkable findings in this regard relates to the discovery that it is characteristic of patients with all three communicative styles to respond in the Type A mode, often through meaningful dream networks, to unneeded alterations in the frame.

In terms of the listening process, then, it is especially important to monitor all the material from the patient in a session in which a dream has been reported in terms of the therapeutic relationship and along the me-not-me interface—as referring simultaneously to both patient and therapist (Langs 1978b). When the day residue and adaptive context are known, the monitoring can take place through Type Two derivatives referring to both participants, can be tested for elements of distortion and nondistortion, and can generate important interpretations keyed to the therapeutic relationship—transference and nontransference. A similar process in the specific context of an alteration in the framework will lead to both the necessary rectification of the frame and the interpretations of the relevant unconscious fantasies, memories, and perceptions. In actual clinical practice, a great deal of meaningful therapeutic work is carried out along the lines just described.

3. *There is a multilevel interplay between the patient's dreams and the analyst's essentially valid, noncountertransference-based functioning and the effects of his countertransference-based inputs as well.*

Both the therapist's assets and sensitivities and his unresolved residuals of psychopathology and countertransference influence the extent to which his patients report dreams and the extent to which these are analyzable. A Type A therapist, who has a capacity to effectively hold the patient, contain his projective identifications, and fully interpret his commuinications, will create a field with the potential for symbolic and illusory communication. Under these conditions, patients are likely to report dreams, and to do so through a Type A communicative mode. With a Type A therapist, Type B and Type C patients have an opportunity to experience the adequate containing, metabolizing, and cognitive interpretations of the actual functions of the patient's dream reports, and under these conditions, they will tend, from time to time, to describe more frequent dreams in a form that favors their analyzability.

A Type B therapist will have difficulty containing and metabolizing toward cognitive understanding his patient's symbolic dreams and those dreams that are used for projective identification or which are part of a Type C barrier. He will tend to experience dream communications as disturbing projective identifications into himself, and will tend to have considerable difficulty in working cognitively with the dream network. As a rule, these problems generate unconscious pressures on his patients to either not remember and report their dreams, or to use dreams themselves for pathological projective identification and discharge.

The Type C therapist will essentially be unable to meaningfully interpret his patient's dreams, will have little capacity to contain and metabolize those dreams that are used for projective identification, and will prefer to drain the dream network of vital meaning. He will tend to use cliched interventions as a means of creating major barriers against inner mental contents and true relatedness, and falsifications designed to seal off his own underlying chaos, as well as that of the patient. On the whole, his patient will seldom dream and will gradually restrict their associations to such dreams, moving closer themselves toward the use of dream material for Type C barriers.

In all, then, within the bipersonal therapeutic field, the patient's report of a dream, and the associational matrix within which it is embedded, is an interactional product. It is influenced by vectors from both patient and therapist that relate to virtually every dimension of their respective inner mental lives and their shared relationship. The extent to which dreams are embedded in efforts at resistance, and the degree to which they serve to meaningfully communicate Type Two derivatives related to the unconscious dimensions of the patient's psychopathology—as well as that of the therapist—are also under constant interactional pressure. This conception implies that resistances to dream reporting, the use of dream networks for resistance, and any other problem related to dream usage calls for an examination of contributions from both therapist and patient.

These last comments touch upon another relationship between the therapist's functioning—pathological and nonpathological—and the patient's dreams. As Little (1951) pointed out, the patient is a mirror for the therapist, to which we may add that the patient is also a container for the therapist's projective identifications and unconscious communications. These inputs, received usually on an unconscious level, generate introjects imbued with valid unconscious sensitivities, whatever the additional distortions. Patients will characteristically react to such pathological introjects, on the one hand attempting to exploit them for the maintenance of their own neurosis, and on the other engaging in unconscious efforts designed to cure the introject and the therapist from whom it has been derived (Searles 1965, 1975, Langs 1976a, b).

The development of a dream network in response to a countertransference-based intervention by the therapist is a relatively frequent occurrence in psychotherapy, and a greatly overlooked communication and resource. The sensitive therapist who is capable of recognizing the manifestations of his unconscious countertransference fantasies and interactional mechanisms can learn a great deal about himself from the patient's responses—and especially from his patient's dreams. These dreams are filled with Type Two derivatives pertinent to unconscious perceptions and introjections of the therapist and his pathology, and can be understood and implicitly interpreted on that basis. It is here that monitoring the patient's material along the me-not-me interface for self- and object-representations, and for communications related to the inner mental world of both participants, takes on its clearest meaning. While Freud (1900) noted that every figure in a dream is a representation of the dreamer, it can now be added that every figure in a dream (and in a dream network) is a representation of both patient and therapist—the "me" and the "not me," as stated from the patient's vantage point (Langs 1978b).

Often, in response to the influence of the therapist's countertransference-based interventions, patients will have what I have termed *curative dreams* (1976a). These are powerful unconscious efforts by the patient, through a dream network, to alert the therapist to the presence of a disturbance, to the need to rectify a damaged frame, and to a need to insightfully modify an underlying countertransference difficulty. In addition, such an associational matrix will pinpoint the general nature of the therapist's disturbed communications, and will include efforts at unconscious interpretation (Little 1951, Langs 1976a, b), based on whatever the patient has been able to unconsciously experience and on his curative wishes toward the therapist. While there may be extensions of these efforts into the transference and distorted sphere, much of this is valid and should be understood and interpreted as such.

On the other hand, in response to a sound intervention, the patient's dream network will reflect positive, constructive, and ego-enhancing unconscious perceptions and introjects. In all, then, the dream network, understood in terms of the multitude of sequential adaptive contexts that unfold in each session with the patient, is an important means of detecting and resolving countertransferences.

THE WRITTEN DREAM

Recognition of the Type B and Type C communicative fields and modes sheds a good deal of light on the written dream (Blum 1968). While the literature as summarized by Blum, and as represented by Blum's own findings, suggests that the writing down of dreams is in the service of both resistance and communication, my own findings indicate that the recording of a dream is an attempt to modify the framework of the bipersonal field. This effort therefore actually diminishes the Type A qualities of the patient's communicative mode, and provides either a Type B or Type C vehicle for dream communication.

The written dream is a modification of the fundamental rule of free association, and as an alteration in the framework it tends to be invoked in the service of some type of framework or misalliance cure (Langs 1975a, 1976b). It must therefore be viewed primarily as a resistance, in terms of the alteration in communicative mode. Stated along the lines being developed in this paper, writing down a dream can be used as a means of action and discharge, fostering the use of the dream as a projective identification—the Type B mode. More usually, it is an effort to gain distance from the dream and the chaotic world within patient or therapist that it touches upon. As such, the practice of writing down a dream very often serves as a form of Type C barrier, transforming the alive and threatening dream experience into a relatively dead and empty psychological cliché.

It is here, once again, that the principle of analyzing the medium before content is essential: the functions of the communicative mode must be interpreted and the mode itself modified before the contents of the dream can be effectively analyzed. It follows too that the latter cannot be dealt with under the conditions of a written dream. Interestingly, quite often such dreams contain some representation of the action-discharge Type B communicative mode or of the Type C barrier, and it is here that the interpretive work must be concentrated.

CLINICAL MATERIAL AND TECHNICAL ISSUES

I will conclude with several vignettes derived from the supervision of psychoanalytically oriented psychotherapy. My discussion of this clinical material will be designed almost entirely to illuminate the therapeutic understanding and approach to dreams; little will be said of other issues even though they may well be important to the specific clinical situation under study. The material will also provide an opportunity to comment more specifically on the techniques involved in working with dreams (see also Langs 1978a).

Miss A. was a young woman in twice weekly psychotherapy for depression and difficulty in relating to men. At the point in therapy to be described, she had started dating a man who had been rather seductive. While there were evident indirect links to the patient's unconscious perceptions of the therapist, and to some distortion of these perceptions into the realm of transference, the therapist had had considerable difficulty in understanding and interpreting the material. He had attempted to link the patient's sexual anxieties to her relationship with himself, but had done so with considerable confusion, quickly shifting to comments about the boyfriend that had to do with the patient's surface feelings and fantasies.

In the following session, the patient began by stating that just when things seemed to be under control something terrible had happened. She alluded to her fears of trains, which had intensified in recent days, based on a fear of riding in dilapidated commuter cars and in anything but new and modern equipment. She spoke of preferring to be alone and wishing to avoid people, and described standing up to her boss so that she had been given an important editorial assignment in which she had acquitted herself well. Yet she felt different, stigmatized, and defeated. She wanted to go home, where she lived with her parents and a sister, to sleep and withdraw. Just prior to the session, a man had seen her head for her commuter train only to pass it by, and she felt he must have thought her absurd.

The therapist intervened, stating that in the previous session the patient had brought up a number of sexual issues regarding her new boyfriend. He added that he had responded to these issues with a great deal of uncertainty as to whether sexual matters had to do with himself or with the boyfriend. He linked his confusion to the patient, saying that she felt good in some respects and yet bad in others; that she felt absurd, and needed to avoid other people. He suggested that her fear of the man who watched her at the commuter station implied that she felt that if she brought her sexual feelings toward the therapist into the session he would laugh at her. The patient responded that she did not feel that the therapist had vacillated in the previous session, and that she had left feeling helped and good. For now, she didn't feel like talking about closeness and spoke again about wanting to go home in order to retreat into bed.

In the following hour, the patient described a continuation of her fear of dilapidated trains. She had been out with her boyfriend, who had suggested that they visit friends and had arranged it without telling her. She felt badly and had asserted her wish that he had told her about his plans; he had responded by saying that he hadn't expected her to be upset. She wondered why he judged her by himself, and then described visiting a couple with two little children. The patient felt panicky, unable to love anyone, and sad, and asked the therapist what she should do. She disparaged herself and felt there was something missing inside of her.

She then described a nightmare: she was going into her old apartment house, and was being chased by a gang of boys. She got to her apartment, but her mother wasn't there. She was just able to open the door and woke up with a persistent image of running and having to lock the door.

The patient indicated that this was a recurrent dream, one she had not dreamt in some while. She often dreamt of running from someone and locking her doors. She spoke again of feeling incapable and empty, but wanting a man. She thought of an earlier boyfriend with a violent temper and of how she could not contemplate marrying him.

The therapist intervened, and said that the patient was being chased in the dream, and was locking the doors; she also was talking of feeling empty and unable to love. He suggested that he had, in the previous session, brought up their earlier discussion of the sexual feelings she was experiencing, and he went on to suggest that the dream and what she was talking about were attempts to avoid that material—a reflection of the patient's wish to feel nothing and to lock the doors. The patient responded that she thought again of nothingness, and of drowning in oneness. When she fell silent, the therapist brought up the couple and their two children, and asked what images came to mind. The patient said that she knew the couple, thought they were depressed, and now discovered they weren't. She wondered how they managed to support their children, even though both were working.

The therapist spoke of the couple and their two children; he suggested that in some way they were connected to the patient's mother and father, indicating that her misperceptions of the couple's boredom and coldness fit in with her perception of her parents. The patient saw this as a marvelous intervention, because, after all, how could she ever think of escaping her parents? The apple doesn't fall far from the tree. Still, she felt depressed and unable to love, and she suggested that her parents had destroyed her ability to love; her sense of hope had been extinguished.

Before adding an important addendum to these two sessions, we may discuss this material with a central focus on the dream. It seems evident that this therapist was experiencing countertransference-based anxieties and fantasies in response to the patient's introduction of her sexual experiences and fantasies, and that these underlying problems are reflected in his premature interventions in that area. Thus, in the initial session described here, the therapist introduced his previous intervention and the patient's sexual material without related derivatives from the patient in that particular hour. However sensitive this comment may have been, it was his own fantasies and associations that led him to suggest that the patient's discomfort about the man who witnessed her behavior at the commuter station contained a conscious or unconscious concern that the therapist would laugh at her if she mentioned her sexual feelings toward him. In many ways, the therapist's initial intervention has the qualities of a pathological projective identification into the patient of his own sexual fantasies and anxieties, and his use of repressive and fragmenting defenses.

The patient's response was ruminative and not validating, and was characterized by a sense of denial. She seems to have had little wish to contain the projective identification from the therapist, and described a reluctance to talk about the issue of closeness; instead, she ruminated and thought of retreating.

The portion of the next session that precedes the dream can best be formulated for the moment in terms of the adaptive context of the therapist's interventions in the previous hour. The material has the qualities of what I have termed *transversal communication* (Langs 1978b), in that it contains a condensation of both valid unconscious perceptions and neurotic distortions. In essence, in the adaptive context of the therapist's interventions, the material regarding the patient's boyfriend and the couple with two children suggest an unconscious perception of the therapist as controlling and provocative, and as judging the patient in terms of himself rather than in the light of her own needs and communications. Along the me-not-me interface, the patient's anxieties about having children and her feelings that something is missing within herself refer on one level to her own sexual conflicts and fantasies. On another level, however, this material conveys a perception of similar problems in the therapist, whom the patient is suggesting tends to intervene in a penetrating and impregnating manner, largely out of a fear of silences and a need to fill his own inner emptiness.

In the sequence of the patient's associations, the dream appears after the patient had spoken about her date and her fear of having children. In essence, in the dream the patient is being chased by a gang of boys, flees to her old apartment, finds her mother absent, and is just able to open the door and is struggling to lock it.

At this point, one could characterize the usual approach to a session in which a dream appears in the following way: the patient is, on the surface, implying that the dream has been prompted by her date and by some thoughts regarding her fears of having a baby. While the manifest content of the dream had to do with being chased by a gang of boys, the latent content as developed from these associations would suggest that the patient feels threatened by her new boyfriend, endangered by his sexual overtures, and in dread of impregnation. She wishes to find protection with her mother, who is unavailable. She tries instead to lock the door, and to thereby shut out her boyfriend.

To elaborate a bit further, the patient then mentioned that this is a recurrent dream and spoke at some length of feeling empty, wanting a man, wishing to marry, but not having a suitable suitor. These associations suggest that the dream is an effort to deal with repetitive conflicts and anxieties about dating, about her fear of men, and the like.

However appealing such a formulation may be, in the terms presented in this paper and in my recent discussion of the listening process (1978b), these formulations actually take a rather direct and linear course. They are based on relatively undisguised and direct associations, and on an adaptive context outside of the therapeutic relationship which in no way specifically illuminates the nature of the patient's intrapsychic conflicts and pathological unconscious fantasies, memories, and introjects.

For example, the patient is suggesting that her boyfriend is insensitive to her feelings, and that she resents it. She sees a couple with a baby, and vaguely describes a dread of emptiness, and yet a fear of having a child. There is some image of threat and pursuit, but it is not defined in terms of specific unconscious contents. There is a passing reference to a boyfriend with a temper, and therefore a vague suggestion of fears of violence, but there is no sense of coalescence and little sense of specificity or depth. Elsewhere (Langs 1978b) I have termed this *linear, nonneurotic communication,* and have found that it is consistently developed around a manifest (direct) adaptive context outside the therapeutic relationship, and that while it touches upon aspects of the patient's psychopathology, it does not communicate or illuminate the underlying pathological factors.

In contrast, if we recognize that the manifest day residue of the experiences with the boyfriend contain in latent form the patient's experiences with the therapist in the previous session or two, and that the external day residue serves as a disguised and derivative expression for a more latent (indirect) day residue related to the therapeutic relationship, we discover that the material, including the manifest dream, organizes in a meaningful, convoluted, derivative way around specific unconscious perceptions and fantasies that relate to the psychopathology of both patient and therapist. If we proceed to organize this material in terms of the therapist's premature intervention regarding the patient's sexual feelings toward himself, the second session reveals a series of Type Two derivatives related largely to the patient's unconscious perceptions of the therapist, though it also includes some quality of her own pathological sexual fantasies and wishes—although the latter will be difficult to identify so long as the therapist has intruded his own pathological needs into the situation.

As a response to the therapist's interventions, the patient's material indicates that she found herself in trouble again, and that she felt under pressure from the therapist, who was treating her like a girlfriend, and toward whom she had feelings similar to those felt toward a boyfriend. Further, she experienced the therapist as confusing himself with her, and as attributing to her fantasies and anxieties that actually resided with him—an unconscious allusion not only to a blurring of self-object boundaries by the therapist, but also to a projective identification.

In some way, the patient had experienced this thrust by the therapist as an unconscious effort to impregnate her, and as a reflection of his incapacity to love and his hatred for himself (Type Two derivatives organized along the not-me part of the interface). It is in this sequence of associations that she then recalled her dream, which can, at this level, be seen as a special communication of the patient's adaptive responses—unconscious perceptions and fantasies—to the premature intervention. In it, the patient conveys her sense of being pursued, her feeling unprotected (in addition, a possible allusion to a theme that had come up previously in regard to the fact that the therapist shares his waiting room with two other therapists), and her need to protect herself by shutting herself off to the therapist's communications and projective identifications—an extension of the patient's initial response to the intervention in the previous hour, and an indirect form of Type Two derivative validation of the hypotheses generated here in evaluating that initial reaction.

Next the patient comments upon this having been a recurrent dream. This permits an approach to the understanding of recurrent dreams as reported in psychotherapy—a relatively neglected topic. This material has a bearing on the relationship between such dreams and countertransference. The clinical data suggest that this patient is indicating unconsciously that she has been exposed to assaults and threats of this kind from the therapist—and others—on previous occasions. The repetition of the dream may therefore be connected to recurrent and similar day residues (adaptive contexts), as well as to a certain degree of fixity both in the patient's unconscious perceptions and fantasies and, more broadly, in her response to these traumatic stimuli. This suggests that the recurrent dream, unless it actually varies in important ways from one version to another, may imply a stalemated situation in which both the therapist's countertransferences and the patient's responses to them—both transference and nontransference—have been relatively unmodified.

The recurrent dream also provides us an opportunity to recognize that the same material—manifest content—may be the carrier of somewhat different unconscious fantasies and perceptions, depending on the prevailing adaptive stimulus. Elsewhere (Langs 1978b) I have termed this the *functional capacity* of a manifest sequence, a concept designed to take into account the presence of distinctly different latent contents within virtually identical manifest material.

It was at this point in the session that the therapist intervened. He identified the latent adaptive context for this material, although he did so without bridges from the patient that would have linked the relationship and experiences with the boyfriend to the therapeutic interaction; he therefore once again spoke prematurely (see Langs 1978a). However, his intervention essentially was an attempt to interpret a transference resistance, while it appears that the patient's communications could more accurately have been described in terms of interactional resistances to which both therapist and patient had contributed, and within which important unconscious perceptions prevailed. In a manner that is characteristic of the work of many therapists, and this is especially true of their work with dreams, the material is treated largely as a reflection of the patient's fantasies and resistances, and valid unconscious perceptions and introjections are excluded.

The patient's response, her feeling that she was drowning in oneness, seems to reflect her own idiosyncratic elaboration of the therapist's efforts to overwhelm her with his own countertransference-based needs and fantasies. There is little evidence of validation, and the therapist suddenly shifts to asking the patient to associate to having a baby. She then talks about her own uncertainty as to what is real and what is illusion, and wonders how this couple manages. Monitored around the adaptive context of the therapist's new intervention, these associations seem to reflect an introjection of the therapist's sense of confusion and his own difficulties in managing the material from the patient. The therapist responds with additional associations of his own, attempting now to relate the material to the patient's parents, largely, I would suggest, as an effort to create a barrier against that level of meaning that pertains to the patient's relationship to the therapist and the turmoil it is generating in him—and in the patient. The patient accepts this common psychoanalytic cliché—the defensive use of a genetic link—as a momentary barrier to her own inner turmoil, but ends the hour feeling quite depressed and with a further unconscious commentary on the therapist's interventions: they reflect his own incapacities to love (as a therapist) and destroy her hope to develop such a capacity in herself.

If we were to attempt, as a contrasting exercise, to formulate this material by maintaining the dream as the focal point, we would begin with the manifest themes of being chased, the absence of her mother, and having to lock out her pursuers. On a sophisticated level, one might derive Type One derivatives pertaining to the therapeutic relationship simply as a monitoring exercise, and wonder whether the patient was experiencing rape fantasies (the most common type of formulation, one that is generated in the cast of transference) or that on some level she felt that she was actually being endangered and pursued by the therapist (the much neglected nontransference elements). If we thought of this material in terms of a transversal communication, we might conclude that the therapist had indeed been pursuing the patient, and that the patient unconsciously believed that the underlying basis for this was an unresolved sexual countertransference. We might also suspect that these unconscious perceptions and introjects were evoking unresolved pathological sexual fantasies and related needs within the patient.

With the dream as the focal point, the prior associations would suggest latent sexual anxieties and fears of impregnation. The subsequent associations involve a sense of emptiness and a boyfriend with a severe temper. They hint at isolated latent themes, but the entire formulation remains at the level of Type One derivatives without a special day residue (adaptive context). Once the context is established in terms of the therapist's intervention in the prior session, the material takes on the specific Type Two derivative meaning already outlined.

It may well be a matter of preference and style of listening as to whether the therapist would begin with the dream, develop the associational network, and then seek out the day residue, or would instead begin with the day residue and trace out the dream network from there. Both approaches, if applied sensitively and in terms of both transference and nontransference, reality and fantasy, would ultimately lead to the same formulations. In my own study of the listening process (Langs 1978b), it has appeared more effective to begin the formulation with the day residue when it is available. In contrast, in those situations in which the adaptive context is lacking, there develops a search for the primary adaptive task that would best fit the dream associational matrix.

In terms of the communicative styles outlined above, it would appear that this patient is attempting to express herself in a Type A mode, and to use the dream network to generate Type Two derivatives which convey interpretable unconscious perceptions and fantasies. For his part, the therapist's interventions have qualities of the Type B and Type C communicative modes. The former is evident in his use of interventions to place into the patient his own sexual anxieties and defenses, and several of his own conscious, defensive fantasies (e.g., his effort to connect the material to the patient's parents). The Type C style is evident in his use of questions and is another quality of his intervention about the patient's parents; these appear to be designed as Type C barriers to the underlying sexual fantasies and anxieties existing within both himself and the patient in regard to one another.

There is a final irony. In the following session, the patient felt extremely depressed and hopeless. She began to think about terminating treatment, saying that she felt sorry for a therapist who had a patient like herself; she was so miserable and so often gave him the business. She didn't want to talk, but she denied that her evil came from therapy. She described how she couldn't handle the boyfriend who had so often lost his temper and how angry she was at her present boyfriend, who had become such a burden.

It was at this point in his supervisory presentation that the therapist suddenly remembered that for the past two weeks he had been taking very brief notes in the sessions. This was a practice he had stopped with this patient some time earlier, but he had resumed it again in response to the sexual material he found so confusing. With this recollection, he immediately suggested that the dream of the gang of boys in pursuit of the patient must have been a response to the note-taking.

It is evident, then, that this modification in the framework had a significant impact upon the patient. The second session described earlier, including the dream, was clearly a response to several interrelated adaptive contexts, especially the note-taking and the therapist's premature intervention. The day residue that had been repressed by the therapist becomes a significant organizer of the dream network, and serves as a selected fact (a new truth that provides integrated meaning to previously unorganized material; Bion 1962).

In light of this new information, we could suggest that the boyfriend who did not tell the patient of his plans and brought her together with his friends is a derivative allusion to the therapist who unexpectedly began to take notes that he may well be presenting to others. The patient wished to assert herself and to protest, but was unable to do so directly with the therapist.

Continuing, the reference to having a baby alludes unconsciously to the therapist's concrete need to take something in from the patient and to place it on paper—giving it substance and constituting a form of impregnation and birth. Such a communication has the qualities of a transversal association in that it has unconscious validity, and yet may contain distortions which are, however, quite difficult to determine at this point. In actuality, note-taking may very well unconsciously represent for a therapist the gratification of fantasies of impregnation; how then can we determine whether the patient herself is sexualizing and distorting? These are the uncertainties that prevail within a modified frame and in the presence of a therapist's countertransference expressions.

The patient sees the therapist, then, as panic-stricken and uncertain as to what to do. The note-taking is a form of pursuit, and it also entails the loss of the therapist as a protective mother figure (both his holding and containing capacities are impaired). The patient wishes to shut herself off from the therapist and from communicating meaningfully to him, since the note-taking represents the gratification of pathological fantasies and endangers the total confidentiality and one-to-one qualities of the treatment situation.

In terms of the subsequent associations, the note-taking is also seen as a loss of control and as a destructive attack upon the patient. It is an attempt to repair the therapist's sense of emptiness and to manage his own dread of losing control—it is a way of locking the door. The patient's reference to oneness conveys the extent to which the note-taking is validly perceived as an effort to merge with the patient, as a kind of exciting form of merger and defense, but, ultimately, as a means of destroying the therapeutic and openly communicative qualities of the bipersonal field, and with it all sense of therapeutic love and hope.

The preceding formulation demonstrates the extent to which the dream network indirectly alludes to the therapeutic relationship, and how, in the presence of an alteration in the basic framework of the bipersonal field, it constitutes an intense working over of the unconscious meanings of the deviation for both therapist and patient. In this context, the patient's efforts to bar the door against the group of boys who are in pursuit of her can be taken as a model of the necessary rectification of the frame required in this situation: the therapist should desist from his note-taking and exclude the outside observers for whom these notes may have been written. To put this another way, he should stop in order to no longer pursue, threaten, and attack the patient. Both the rectification of the frame and the necessary interpretations of the patient's unconscious perceptions and fantasies as evoked by that alteration could be undertaken on the basis of this dream network.

The note-taking itself is also an effort at projective identification, in the sense that the therapist is putting into the patient his own sense of confusion, his difficulties in managing, his inability to deal with his own and her conscious and unconscious sexual fantasies and anxieties, his need to introjectively incorporate the patient, and his need for inappropriate barriers—to identify just a few of the projected contents and mechanisms. It is also a form of Type C barrier in which the material from the patient is recorded, rendered nonhuman, and extruded from within the therapist, and in which the patient is warned that she should not communicate too meaningfully lest it be put down on paper and exposed publicly.

The patient, however, responded in a Type A mode to these threats from the therapist, incorporating and metabolizing his projective identifications only up to a point, and returning them to the therapist relatively undetoxified and filled with anxiety and panic. The dream itself serves as a projective identification on this level, though the dream network suggests less an effort at discharge than an endeavor to communicate symbolically to a therapist who is expressing himself nonsymbolically—in terms of efforts at direct and inappropriate gratification and defense.

In some ways, then, this is a potentially curative dream network, and the depression in the final session briefly described here may be seen, on one level, as the patient's sense of hopelessness in response to the therapist's failure to rectify the frame and to appreciate her curative efforts on his behalf. I will add only that the therapist did soon stop his note-taking, and had a later opportunity to interpret the patient's unconscious perceptions and fantasies, doing so to a degree that helped to restore some positive therapeutic qualities to this particular treatment situation.

Another patient, Miss B., was in twice weekly psychotherapy at a clinic with a male therapist. She was in her early thirties and homosexual, and worked as a gym teacher. She had been in therapy for about a year for episodes of depression. At times, she had been suicidal, especially after breaking up with a recent homosexual lover.

I will present two sessions that followed a two-week vacation by the therapist. These hours occurred some four months before the expected termination of this patient's therapy, and, although the patient had been told vaguely of the duration of therapy, termination and disposition had not been specifically introduced by the therapist.

The patient began the first session by describing several telephone calls with a former woman lover who had moved to the West Coast. The girlfriend would write daily letters for a week or so, and then not communicate for days on end. Miss B. felt that the girlfriend had found a new lover, and no longer cared for her; the patient was angry but forgiving. She was tired of pursuing the friend, who seldom returned her calls. The girlfriend had said that Miss B. seemed to treat her as a weak, sick asshole who could come in and out of her life whenever Miss B. wished. The patient viewed the relationship as a battle, but felt that it was no longer important who won.

Throughout this session, the therapist had asked a number of detailed questions about the incidents the patient was describing. He attempted to establish who was rejecting whom, and to clarify the patient's feeling about this former girlfriend. Toward the end of the hour, he offered an extended intervention about how the patient felt out of touch with this girlfriend, and how angry she seemed, linking the resentment to her feelings toward the therapist for his vacation, and suggesting that the anger had been reflected in the fact that the patient had missed the session just prior to the vacation. He also connected her disillusionment with the girlfriend to feelings revealed in other sessions prior to that vacation, to the effect that therapy was becoming an unfulfilled promise; the therapist added that the patient seemed to feel that he was not doing enough for her. He concluded that there remained within her a lot of unresolved feelings about her relationship with him. The patient responded by denying that her depression and interaction with the girlfriend had anything to do with his vacation. Instead she described her resentment that, in the last session she had attended prior to the vacation, the therapist had been silent. She was angry and depressed when he didn't speak.

In the next session Miss B said that she was angry with a female teacher who had canceled a dinner date. She thought of visiting this friend at her apartment and described an unexpected visit from another woman from California, who was probably living with the patient's former girlfriend. The patient had had a strange dream: her mother was standing in front of her and she squirted her mother with water from a plant sprayer until her mother's hair was all wet. The patient didn't know why she did it.

The therapist asked the patient her thoughts about the dream, and Miss B. recalled that it had been dreamt while the therapist was on vacation. She had had another dream during the current week: her father was alive (in actuality, he had died several years earlier) and her mother was dead. Her father didn't know that her mother was dead and the patient had to tell him. There was a sense of strangeness that the patient experienced in regard to not having been home for a long time, but not in regard to having to tell him that her mother had suddenly died.

Miss B. went on to say that she had conscious fantasies of killing her mother because of arguments that they have been having over her father's will. The patient had been thinking a great deal about her father. The night before the session, she had dreamt about the therapist. She was seeing him and another therapist, a woman, and didn't remember her therapist saying much. The woman had done all the talking.

The patient stated that she was afraid to expect too much from the therapist for fear of being disappointed. She found her dreams interesting and felt that the dream about the therapist had something to do with his remarks in the previous hour. The therapist suggested that there was a great deal to all of these dreams, and the patient said that the first dream was silly, but she wasn't hurting her mother. Here the therapist suggested that the patient wanted her mother to prove she cared for her, and that the patient experienced the relationship with her mother as a hopeless struggle which left her feeling hurt and angry, and wanting revenge. Still, the patient didn't hurt her mother, because she also really loves and cares about her. He tied this conflict of feelings to the patient's relationship to her homosexual girlfriend and to her feelings toward himself, saying that in general the patient wanted people to care for her and yet felt hurt, angry, and vengeful when they did not. This was in conflict with her wish to feel close to others, and created considerable confusion.

The patient felt that the therapist had identified the issue, and that this was why she did not treat herself better. She saw herself as too concerned with getting back at others and with wishes to shout and scream her mother's guts out. As a result, she said, she would hurt herself and tend to overeat. The therapist said that this went back to her feeling that she needed someone to care about her, and he suggested that to the extent he offered her advice he fostered that particular search. He felt that the patient experienced his efforts as attempts to help her with specific situations in her life by encouraging her to look for somebody to take care of her, rather than caring for herself. He also noted that the patient did not understand why she hurt herself and was looking to him to help her solve that riddle, but that she seemed to sense that this would not work.

In response, the patient talked in some detail about her own sense of defensiveness, and how she feels one way but tries to tell herself to feel another. She often feels jealous and takes on the feelings of others toward herself, and then feels guilty and goes against herself. The therapist agreed that all of this was true and suggested that the greatest problem was that when she got good feelings toward others, they were mixed up with bad feelings, and she felt confused. He then linked this to a number of confusing incidents in her childhood.

In this clinical situation, we have a series of dreams and several day residues. On the most superficial level, there is the patient's struggle with her former lover, while on the level of the therapeutic relationship there is the therapist's vacation, his silence in an hour prior to that vacation, his interventions in the session prior to the dream report, and the much-neglected anticipation of a forced termination in midyear— an expectation that would undoubtedly be aroused by the therapist's vacation.

In the session prior to the dream, the patient described in some detail, with the therapist's encouragement, her conflicted feelings toward her former lover. The therapist, without adequate bridges in the patient's material, attempted to link this in a rather general way to the patient's reaction to his vacation and to some sense of dissatisfaction with the treatment situation. The patient's response was rather flat; she denied feelings about the vacation, but stated that she felt deprived when the therapist was silent. Without the details of the session in question, it is impossible to evaluate the latent content of that particular complaint.

The following session began with the patient's talk of pursuing a woman who had canceled a dinner appointment. Next was the dream of spraying her mother's hair and the therapist's query as to the patient's thoughts about it. In this context, it should be stressed that, technically, when a patient reports a dream it is best to allow him to continue to free associate. It is quite common for relatively inexperienced therapists to ask patients their thoughts about a dream or what they think a dream means. In addition, it is generally accepted practice to ask the patient for day residues (what do you think prompted the dream?) or for associations to particular dream elements.

One may define a series of interconnected technical principles (Langs 1976a, 1978a, b), which begins with entering each session without desire, memory, or understanding (Bion 1970), and extends to allowing the patient to create the meaning of each session and to put the necessary interpretations and rectifications of the framework into the therapist (de Racker 1961, Langs 1978b). On this basis, the preferred technique in response to a dream report is to allow the patient his own unfolding. Since most questions interfere with the therapist's neutrality and often serve defensive purposes (Langs 1978a, b), it is best to work with the material as expressed by the patient. This approach also enables the therapist to observe the extent to which the patient permits dream reports to be part of meaningful communication, as well as the extent to which dreams are used to generate either meaningful resistance or confusion and nonmeaning. The latter is extremely common when patients present more than one dream, or a single lengthy dream (for an illustration, see Langs 1978b: chapter 10). Therapists tend consistently to search for meaning, an effort that is accentuated when a patient communicates a dream. However, we should not overlook the use of dreams to place into the therapist a sense of confusion and for the destruction of meaning, often as a response to comparable projective identifications by the therapist.

This particular dream network has some of these qualities, as I will demonstrate below.

Further, by allowing the patient to freely associate to the dream, the therapist can ascertain his communicative mode. If the patient does not allude to an adaptive context, it is likely that the Type B or Type C mode is in use. On the other hand, if a day residue is evident in the material, it is likely that the therapist will be able to generate Type Two derivatives and that he is dealing with Type A communication. By being silent, the therapist also has an opportunity to observe the links between the patient's prior and subsequent associations and the manifest dream, and the extent to which connections are either evident or lacking. In this way he can determine to what extent the patient uses splitting and fragmentation or, by contrast, generates derivatives that tend to coalesce around meaningful, unconscious nodal points.

The therapist's silence also permits him to assess the extent to which the dream network either serves resistance or is designed (unconsciously, of course) to reveal latent meaning. What is often termed the patient's style of working with dreams is, as a rule, a representation of the patient's basic associative style and communicative mode. Premature interventions by the therapist tend top generate pressures toward the utilization of Type B and Type C modes, and greatly interfere with the expression of the patient's own communicative preferences, defenses, and inner contents, whether fantasies or perceptions. In essence then, the report of a dream does not call for any basic modification in the therapist's essential approach to the patient's communication. Allowing the patient to lead the way, an attitude of neutrality and efforts to understand in order to generate interpretive interventions remain essential (for further details, see Langs 1978a).

Finally, it should be noted that the practice of asking the patient his impression of a dream, his thoughts about it, or what he believes it to mean creates a significant thrust toward a Type C field. It asks the patient to intellectualize and speculate about her own dream, an effort that is bound to be defensive and have qualities of a Type C barrier. It stands in contrast to the patient's spontaneous associations, which may or may not be imbued with direct and indirect meaning. Many of the questions asked of the dreamer are based on an erroneous conception of the nature of neurotic communication, and on a failure to appreciate the importance of indirectly communicated derivatives (see Langs

1978a, b).

Returning to this material, the patient went on to say that she had and the dream of her mother while the therapist was away. She then reported the dream in which she was to tell her father that her mother had died. There followed thoughts about killing her mother and the dream about the therapist and the second female therapist. This last dream touches upon the fact that this patient had previously been seen by another therapist in the clinic and, in addition, had from time to time been suicidal—to a point where the therapist felt it essential to give her his home telephone number. This she had called on several recent occasions.

In the session, however, the patient spoke of her fears of wanting too much from the therapist, and her associations then became ruminative. The therapist intervened at some length, making almost no specific use of the manifest dream elements as bridges to their possible specific latent meanings. His comments lacked any specific adaptive context, and the dream network was shorn of its specific derivatives and utilized in a most vague and nonspecific way. The patient responded by accepting the Type C barriers offered by the therapist in his intervention, and by unconsciously conveying her perception and introjection of the therapist's extended intervention as a kind of screaming his guts out, his hurt. The therapist then intervened again at some length, introducing a number of his own impressions and associations, and the patient responded by ruminating about defensiveness. The therapist concluded the hour with another rather general intervention.

Before briefly tracing out the implications of this dream network, I would like to comment upon the therapist's interventions in the presence of dream reports. First, it might actually suffice to say that the basic principles of intervening apply to all sessions, including those in which the patient has reported a dream; no new principles are needed. This could then be followed by a discussion of the therapist's interventions, which I provide in a separate communication (Langs 1978a). Still, many therapists experience a disposition to intervene when the patient reports a dream, and a few comments are therefore in order, particularly with regard to common errors in this clinical situation.

It is strongly implied throughout this paper that the listening process is the key to proper interventions and that we are in need of some reconceptualization of the therapist's interventions—their nature, implications, and consequences. Though in the present study it will not be possible to develop these principles in any detail, I would stress in brief that identifying the formal nature of the therapist's interventions (e.g., silences, questions, clarifications, confrontations, interpretations, and reconstructions) is only an initial step in evaluating an intervention. More important in any such consideration of the therapist's interventions are their unconscious functions and nature, implications unconsciously perceived and introjected by the patient. Based on extended empirical studies, I have concluded that there are six essentially valid interventions by the therapist (Langs 1978a): silences; managements of the framework; interpretations-reconstructions; the playing back of derivatives in the absence of an acknowledged adaptive context (usually one that pertains to the therapeutic relationship); the metabolism of projective identifications; and the identification of metaphors of the Type C communicative mode. In a Type A field, when the frame is secure, interpretations-reconstructions and sometimes the playing back of derivatives are the essential tools. It is to be stressed, however, that such interventions should be as specific as possible and should include all possible instinctual drive representations and unconscious fantasies and perceptions, as reflected in the dream network.

In the presence of meaningful communication, it is not uncommon for therapists to neglect the specific derivatives communicated in a manifest dream and the related associations, and to fail to interpret them as Type Two derivatives around a specific adaptive context. Even when the dream network is devoid of any adaptive context, and the therapist elects to play back selected derivatives in search of that context, it is important to be as specific as possible. In general, dreams will often be the special vehicle of meaningful derivatives of unconscious fantasies and perceptions, and any tendency by the therapist to drain away the definitive contents reflected in a dream is an effort toward the development of a Type C barrier designed to obliterate underlying instinctual drive fantasies and conflicts. Such interventions are a misuse of the concept of interpreting upward (Loewenstein 1957), and reflect a defensive need on the part of the therapist. They constitute the offer of a sector of misalliance (Langs 1975a) and of interactional obsessive defenses (Langs, 1976a,b)—which this patient momentarily accepted—and efforts to destroy the meaning of the patient's material for both herself and the therapist, a directive toward a Type C field (Langs 1978c).

Returning to this material, if we take first—as an exercise—the adaptive context of the patient's conflicts with her homosexual lover, the dream of the mother suggests that in some unconscious way the homosexuality expresses sexual fantasies about the mother, and possibly has some meaningful relationship to earlier actual sexual experiences with her. In actuality, the patient had reported incestuous contact with her father, of which her mother was ignorant for some years, but which was later discovered by the mother. Following this, the sexual involvement was stopped.

The second dream serves as a further response to that particular day residue and, on one level, as a further association to the first dream, reflects the patient's destructiveness toward her mother, a constellation readily seen as ambivalent. The third dream, of the therapist and a woman therapist, quickly brings the therapeutic relationship into the picture, and at this level suggests that the presence of the woman lover was designed as a protection against underlying sexual feelings toward the therapist—here, I make use of the dream network to generate a formulation in need of validation. However, if we continue to organize the material around the adaptive context of the patient's relationship with her girlfriend, her fantasies about the therapist and her fears of expecting too much of him have to be seen as displaced from the girlfirend—the central object who is related genetically to both her mother and her father.

It is difficult to formulate this line of thought beyond this point, because of the therapist's interventions and the ruminative qualities of the balance of the session. However, there is once again a rather linear quality to this particular dream network; and while it has a bearing on the patient's psychopathology, it offers no unique insights into that situation. Let us therefore turn to the alternative formulation which would organize material around a series of adaptive contexts related to the therapeutic relationship.

In this regard, the main day residues are the therapist's vacation, his intrusive interventions, his alternating periods of silence (perhaps at times when interventions were needed) and overactivity, and his silence regarding the pending forced termination. In light of these several adaptive contexts, the material about the girlfriend, who writes often and then disappears, immediately takes on indirect meaning in terms of an unconscious perception of the therapist. Here too the contents related to mutual sexual involvement must be formulated as alluding to unconscious perceptions of the therapist and to needs of the patient—a transversal communication—and the two could not be adequately sorted out until the therapist's countertransference-based contributions are rectified.

There follows in this first session indirect representations of the patient's anger at the therapist and the patient's feeling that she is weak and being manipulated, a communication that may allude to her unconscious perception of the therapist's weakness as well (a formulation afforded us by application of the me–not-me interface). The intervention in that hour attempts to relate the material, which is quite general and superficial, and all too evident for a neurotic communication, to the therapist's recent vacation and to some general discontent with treatment. As such it is inadequate, and the patient responds with some degree of denial and with her complaint about the therapist's silence, which may well have a great deal to do with what is being left out and missed currently, including the pending forced termination.

In the next hour, there are initial derivatives related to the theme of sudden cancellation and the undoing of separation. The dream of the mother is difficult to decipher within this adaptive context, though it suggests an unconscious perception of the inadequacy and sexual qualities of the therapist's interventions, and their use to deny underlying destructive impulses. The therapist's question interfered with further spontaneous associations, and we are left with a sense of an unfinished associational network. The patient did, however, indicate that the dream was somehow related to the therapist's absence, and the material suggests a genetic link to the patient's relationship with her mother. It is impossible, however, to determine whether this is a transference-based distortion or a primarily nontransference communication related to some way in which the therapist has in actuality repeated a trauma that the patient experienced at the hands of her mother.

The next dream involves the father coming to life and the mother being dead. It is a theme that has an evident bearing on the pending forced termination, and at this point much of the fragmentation and vagueness may well be related to the fact that the therapist himself has completely avoided this subject despite its intense importance to the patient. We are experiencing here, I believe, a fragmented dream network based on defensive needs in both patient and therapist.

Next are the patient's thoughts of killing her mother. These have to do with the struggle over the inheritance left by the father—again, the final separation theme. The dream of being with two therapists can be seen as the wish to be protected against loss, though more specific associative links are once again lacking. Still, we may note here that once a meaningful adaptive context is established, the manifest dream itself will often reflect meaningful Type Two derivatives—which may then be enriched by other associations. The patient does go on to express her fear of wishing for too much from the therapist and later comments about feeling better because she doesn't hurt her mother in the dream.

This last association may very well be the key: the patient is attempting to fragment her associations and to generate some degree of nonmeaning, a narrative form of Type C barrier, in an effort to spare the therapist her rage and murderous feelings toward him over the pending forced termination and his erroneous interventions (a tentative hypothesis that I will be unable to validate from this material, although I can state that subsequent sessions offered strong support for this hypothesis).

It is at this point that the therapist began the series of interventions that took the patient quite a distance from the dream network, and deprived the material of its specific unconscious meanings. I would view this as in part a reflection of defensive needs within the therapist, and in part as an unconscious response to the relative absence of meaning in the patient's material. It would appear that the patient's associations are an effort to reproject back into the therapist the mixture of confusion, sexual anxieties, and concern about the therapeutic relationship which the patient had introjected from the therapist himself. In this sense, these dreams serve as a form of projective identification in addition to their function, for the moment, as a kind of Type C barrier. As a result, I would postulate that any effort to interpret the contents of these dreams, either in the adaptive context of the relationship with the girlfriend (which would be highly defensive) or in an adaptive context related to the therapeutic relationship, would be met with nonconfirmation.

The one intervention most needful at this juncture would entail the processing of the patient's projective identifications. I would not in fact have positively intervened here at all, but would have sat back and allowed the material to settle and then blossom. Such silence might well have permitted a far more meaningful intervention in this session; if not, I would have waited for subsequent sessions and for more definitive material.

Still, in an effort to offer a model intervention related to dealing with the Type B and Type C communicative qualities of a particular series of dreams, I would propose the following hypothetical *silent intervention* (Langs 1978a, b): "You seem quite confused about the therapeutic situation: the nature of our transactions, as reflected in the way in which you spray your mother's hair with water; the conditions of the treatment, as seen in the presence of a woman therapist in the session; and the nature of what's actually happening, as expressed by the uncertainty about whether your father is dead or alive." (Since I am attempting to build my intervention on the material placed into the therapist by the patient, I could not as yet allude to the pending forced termination.) "It's not clear what is specifically evoking this confusion, though it may well have something to do with separation and death— since you refer to a cancelled dinner engagement and undo the death of your father." This is an attempt to indicate to the patient an awareness of a crucial adaptive context that had been omitted; here, I am playing back selected derivatives in search of the pertinent adaptive context. "As a result, you present a series of dreams that seem rather unrelated and fragmented, and designed, it seems, as an effort to generate some degree of confusion, some of which you may have been experiencing from me." (I would only impart this to the patient if she herself brought up the theme of confusion, and would add the part related to the therapist when the patient has referred to his silences or to concerns about his being able to help her.) "In a way, then, all of this seems designed to place your sense of confusion into me and to make it impossible to decipher its underlying basis." (This is the metabolism of her projective identification, and the interpretation of the metaphor for the Type C barrier.)

I have most reluctantly offered this model intervention in order to illustrate some of the techniques that I have described on a more abstract level. The intervention itself is extremely unsatisfactory because the patient was not permitted sufficient time to free associate in order to build the necessary elements, and because I have had to introduce some of my own impressions without sufficient basis in the material from the patient. However, in the course of listening, therapists will make silent hypotheses (Langs 1978b) of this kind again and again, though they should not be expressed to the patient unless they have been silently validated by the patient's ongoing associations, which in addition provide adequate bridges to the therapeutic relationship and adequate derivatives of the essential components needed for the intervention.

The manifest dream of the therapist permits a few comments about that class of dreams. I will not here enter the debate concerning manifest dreams of the analyst reported in first sessions, except to note that such dreams in particular, as I have attempted to demonstrate for all dreams, call for careful examination for contributions from the therapist as well as from the patient. The conditions under which this dream was reported suggest that it may well pertain to important countertransference-based inputs from the therapist, and from the uncertainty regarding the pending forced termination. Such circumstances, in which the therapist's inappropriate needs are being directly gratified, are often, in my experience, evocative of dreams in which the therapist appears directly. Similarly, such dreams often occur when the patient is experiencing needs for direct and inappropriate gratification from the therapist, satisfactions that extend beyond those afforded to him through valid interpretations and management of the framework. These latter situations are often characterized in terms of the presence of an erotized transference, but more often they constitute the presence of an erotized misalliance and interactional syndrome (see Langs 1976a).

The manifest appearance of the therapist in a dream of the patient, then, calls for a detailed examination of the unconscious therapeutic interaction, and often signals the presence of pathological inputs from both patient and therapist. In addition, it is important to recognize that such a communication is a manifest element, and that in terms of the patient's neurosis, it is the latent, derivative contents and functions that are crucial. Often, therapists will intervene on a manifest level in the presence of such dreams, suggesting—fusing the material here by way of example—that the patient wishes to have someone else present in the treatment situation, or that the patient feels that the therapist is not being sufficiently helpful and so brings in a second therapist to assist. Such interventions are based on direct readings of the manifest content and have a minimal Type One derivative quality—they constitute very evident inferences from the manifest material. As such, they do not meet the criteria of valid interpretations (Langs 1978a), and will tend to be countertransference-based and over defensive, generating Type C barriers. The meaning of such dream elements can be ascertained only through a full assessment of the dream network, and must include the derivation of Type Two derivatives around a specific adaptive context related to the therapeutic interaction, through which the manifest dream elements take on specific unconscious meaning—whether fantasy or perception or a mixture of both.

I will not attempt a further description of various types of dreams in other communicative fields. The reader will undoubtedly be familiar with massive dream reports that unconsciously are designed as assaultive projective identifications on the therapist, although he must be certain to examine his own interventions as a possible means of evoking such dream communications. Type C patients who rarely report dreams, or who report only quite realistic ones, or only primitive ones to which they provide virtually no meaningful associations, are easily recognized and fairly common (for an illustration, see Langs 1978c). The variations are infinite and it is my hope that the basic discussion and the two illustrations offered here will enable the reader to develop some general principles of listening and intervening that will serve in all situations.

CONCLUDING COMMENTS

I hope to have demonstrated, at the very least, that dreams reported in psychotherapy are as a rule part of a rich and interpretable associational matrix or (more specifically here) dream network, and that they can be understood and interpreted in the therapeutic situation. I have left room for the recognition of resistances and the use of dreams for pathological projective identifications and for the establishment of Type C barriers, but have tried to stress the extent to which the psychotherapist should strive toward a maximal understanding and interpretation of the network. Implicit in this discussion is the principle that dreams should not be treated in isolation, but entirely as part of an associational matrix which includes, of course, the dream's day residues and associations. What I have termed the *dream network* in this paper thus reveals itself as no different in kind from an associational matrix lacking a manifest dream as one of its sets of elements. We therefore need no new principles of technique in responding to dreams, but should in their presence apply the basics of the listening process and of intervening.

I have offered as a basic thesis, and tentatively documented, the concept that every dream network has a significant bearing on the therapeutic relationship, and is best understood and interpreted in that context. Possessing both special and ordinary qualities, dream communication should evoke special and ordinary reactions within the therapist. As signals of particular needs to communicate, whether in terms of resistance or of meaning, the report of a dream can heighten the therapist's listening capacity and sharpen his interpretive and framework management endeavors. Dreams offer an elegant opportunity to comprehend the therapeutic process and interaction, and to provide the patient adaptive insight and inherently positive introjective identifications. The mastery of the technique of dream interpretation, as it is called, is tantamount to the mastery of the psychotherapeutic situation. It is an ideal well worth seeking.

REFERENCES

Arlow, J. (1969). Unconscious fantasy and disturbances of conscious experience. *Psychoanalytic Quarterly* 38:1–27.

Bion, W. (1962). *Learning from Experience.*   In W. Bion *Seven Servants* New York: Jason Aronson, 1977.

—— (1970). *Attention and Interpretation.* In W. Bion, *Seven Servants.* New York: Jason Aronson, 1977.

—— (1977). *Seven Servants.* New York: Jason Aronson.

Blum, H. (1968). Notes on the written dream. *Journal of the Hillside Hospital* 17:67–78.

Grinberg, L. (1962). On a specific aspect of counter-transference due to the patient's projective identification. *International Journal of Psycho-Analysis* 43:436–440.

Freud, S. (1900). The interpretation of dreams. *Standard Edition 4/5.*

—— *(1905). A fragment of an analysis of a case of hysteria. Standard Edition* 7:1–122.

—— (1911). The handling of dream-interpretation in psycho-analysis. *Standard Edition* 12:89–96.

———— (1923) Remarks on the theory and practice of dream interpretation. *Standard Edition* 19:109–124.

Langs, R. (1971). Day residues, recall residues, and dreams: reality and the psyche. *Journal of the American Psychoanalytic Association* 19:499–523. [Chapter 2, this volume]

———— (1972). A psychoanalytic study of material from patients in psychotherapy. *International Journal of Psychoanalytic Psychotherapy* 1(1):4–45. [Chapter 3, this volume]

———— (1973). *The Technique of Psychoanalytic Psychotherapy,* Vol. I. New York: Jason Aronson.

———— (1974). *The Technique of Psychoanalytic Psychotherapy,* Vol. II. New York: Jason Aronson.

———— (1975a). Therapeutic misalliances. *International Journal of Psychoanalytic Psychotherapy* 4:77–105 [Chapter 6, this volume]

———— (1975b). The Therapeutic relationship and deviations in technique. *International Journal of Psychoanalytic Psychotherapy* 4:106–141. [Chapter 7, this volume]

———— (1976a). *The Bipersonal Field.* New York: Jason Aronson.

———— (1976b). *The Therapeutic Interaction.* 2 Vols. New York: Jason Aronson.

———— (1978a). Interventions in the bipersonal field [Chapter 20, this volume; to appear in *Contemporary Psychoanalysis* 15, 1979]

———— (1978b). *The Listening Process.* New York: Jason Aronson.

————(1978c). Some communicative properties of the bipersonal field. *International Journal of Psychoanalytic Psychotherapy* 7:89–161. [Chapter 15, this volume]

———— (1978d). Validation and the framework of the therapeutic situation. *Contemporary Psychoanalysis* 14:98–124. [Chapter 14, this volume]

Little, M. (1951). Countertransference and the patient's response to it. *International Journal of Psycho-Analysis* 32:32–40.

Loewenstein, R. (1957). Some thoughts on interpretation in the theory and practice of psychoanalysis. *Psychoanalytic Study of the Child* 12:127–150.

deRacker, G. (1961). On the formulation of the interpretation. *International Journal of Psycho-Analysis* 42:49–54.

Searles, H. (1965). *Collected Papers on Schizophrenia and Related Subjects.* New York: International Universities Press.

––––– (1975). The patient as therapist to his analyst. In *Tactics and Techniques in Psychoanalytic Therapy, Vol. II: Countertransference.* ed. P. Giovacchini. New York: Jason Aronson.

Segal, H. (in press). On dreams. In H. Segal, *A Kleinian Approach to Clinical Practice.* New York: Jason Aronson.

Wangh, M. (1962). The "evocation of a proxy": a psychological maneuver, its use as a defense, its purposes and genesis. *Psychoanalytic Study of the Child* 17:451–469.

Chapter Nineteen

A Model of Supervision: the Patient as Unconscious Supervisor

(1978)

This paper is an attempt to outline a basic and specific model of supervision founded on clinically derived principles. Its main thrust is that there is a set of fundamental tenets through which the supervisory situation may be established and explicated, and within which a given supervisor and supervisee may work in keeping with their respective therapeutic styles and the particular needs of the patient under supervision. Once the basic model is delineated, I will discuss a series of important but relatively neglected supervisory issues, with an eye toward their resolution. Stress will be placed on a methodology founded on prediction and validation. A brief clinical illustration will be offered, and the interested reader may turn to a series of publications in which I have discussed some of my views on supervision and presented in detail my own interpretation and application of the principles to be described here (see Langs 1973, 1974, 1976c, 1978b, in press).

A BASIC MODEL OF PSYCHOTHERAPY

It is self-evident that a supervisor's model of supervision—and hence his functioning as a supervisor—is founded on his conceptualization of the psychotherapeutic situation.[1] In brief (see also Langs 1973, 1974, 1976a, c, 1978b, d, e), insight-oriented or psychoanalytic psychotherapy may be conceptualized as taking place within a bipersonal field which is defined by the ground rules or framework that establishes the therapeutic situation and the conditions of its unfolding. With the patient at one pole and the therapist at the other, their communicative interaction takes place along an interface which ideally is determined primarily by the psychopathology of the patient, and by the adequate interpretive and management capacities of the therapist, although not infrequently, the patient's (largely unconscious) valid functioning and the therapist's psychopathology play a major role, as they do in some small measure throughout the treatment. Most vital is a spiraling and unfolding communicative interaction, in which unconscious processes and mechanisms play a central role. These unconscious transactions provide the central adaptive stimuli and contexts for the two participants, and is the major realm of the therapist's interpretive work—to which are appended links to outside relationships and to the significant genetic past.

Basic to the therapeutic situation is the establishment and maintenance of the framework, which is essential for a sound therapeutic alliance, and which establishes the therapist's basic hold and containing capacities, as well as the communicative properties of the bipersonal field: the nature, function, and implications of the behaviors and verbalizations of each participant. In addition to managing the framework, the therapist strives to offer essentially interpretive and reconstructive interventions which are determined by the patient's communicative style, the nature of the communicative field, and the available derivatives of the patient's pathological unconscious fantasies, memories, introjects, and the conflicts to which they are related. The basic goal of psychotherapy is that of adaptive, inner structural change, based on cognitive insights and the inevitable positive introjective identifications that accrue to the patient by virtue of the therapist's adequate management and interpretive functioning.

Both the therapist's silence and his application of the listening process (Langs 1978b) are among his most fundamental tools. The material from the patient may be organized in the cognitive sphere in terms of manifest and latent content. The latter may be classified as Type One derivatives, readily available inferences postulated from the manifest content, and as Type Two derivatives, which are organized dynamically and interactionally around the prevailing neurotic adaptive context (which usually refers to some aspect of the therapeutic interaction). On this basis, three communicative styles and fields can be identified: Type A, which is symbolic, illusory, and uses an imaginative play space; Type B, in which projective identification and action-discharge pervail; and Type C, in which intrapsychic and interpersonal barriers, falsifications, clichés, and impenetrable defenses are characteristic. Listening must be geared to the nature of the patient's prevailing communicative style, and must be directed to both the cognitive contents of the patient's material and to its interactional aspects: identification of role and image evocations (the object relational sphere), and recognition and processing of interactional projections or projective identifications (the interactional mechanism sphere). In addition to yielding understanding on the cognitive and interactional levels, these conceptualizations permit the identification of six types of interventions, which together constitute a complete armamentarium (Langs 1978a): silences; establishing and managing the framework; interpretations and reconstructions; the playing back of derivatives in the absence of an identified adaptive context related to the therapeutic interaction; the interpretive processing of projective identifications; and the interpretive playback of metaphors of the Type C communicative style and field.

THE BASIC MODEL OF SUPERVISION

The structure and nature of the supervisory situation is determined by its ground rules and framework (cf. Langs 1975, where these are set out for the therapeutic situation). To be specific, supervision should be defined in terms of set fees, hours, and length of sessions, though there is latitude and flexibility with each of these aspects. The discussion of the supervisory situation here is based primarily on individual supervision, though clearly supervision is feasible within a group format; it should, however, be realized that the presence of even necessary and agreed upon observers influences the supervisory interaction between supervisor and supervisee. The relative anonymity of the supervisor is a valid tenet for supervision, though minimal and carefully selected personal revelations are acceptable as long as they are pertinent to the clinical work and are not unduly self-exposing. On the other hand, total confidentiality is a sine qua non and should be strictly observed; it is vital to a sound supervisory alliance in which the supervisee is safely and securely held and may freely speak and expose his difficulties, and is equally necessary for the supervisor, who must be candid, though tactful, and able to speak without fear of the public misuse of his teaching efforts.

The counterpart in supervision to the fundamental rule of free association in therapy is the structuring of the supervisory experience around the *strictly sequential, direct presentation* of the process notes of the therapeutic transactions of the sessions under consideration. This method, for which there is no viable alternative, provides the supervisor the opportunity to experience the unfolding therapeutic interaction with some sense of how it actually took place, and in a manner that fosters his empathic understanding of its influence on both patient and therapist. More important, however, this procedure is essential to the predictive, validating approach that is basic to the supervisory model proposed here.

It is a procedure that requires either a remarkable capacity for remembering on the part of the supervisee, or the writing of notes immediately after each therapy session as a means of providing the necessary material for the supervisory process. While note-writing does indeed alter one of the basic aspects of the optimal approach to each therapy session—characterized by Bion (1970) as entering each hour without desire, memory, or understanding—it is nontheless one of the necessary alterations in the fundamental framework of the therapeutic situation that arises under conditions of supervision, along with modifications in confidentiality and the one-to-one relationship (the supervisor becomes a third party to treatment).

These changes, justified by the fact that psychotherapy cannot be learned without supervision, will affect the psychotherapy, and both patient and therapist, in major ways that are as a rule difficult for supervisees to appreciate and handle interpretively. As modifications of the frame, however, they come up repeatedly in derivative form throughout such a therapy, and constitute a major adaptive context for the listening process of both supervisor and supervisee (see Langs 1975, 1976a, c, 1978b).

The conditions of the supervisory bipersonal field (see Langs in press) preclude the psychotherapy of the supervisee: the situation does not call for or permit his free associations, nor is a framework created that would permit analysis of his manifest and derivative communications. On the other hand, conditions are established for supervisory interventions directed toward the analysis and understanding of the therapeutic interaction under study, and toward the theoretical and technical education of the supervisee. To this end, each supervisory session should begin without direct recall of the prior therapy sessions or supervisory hour—the equivalent in supervision to approaching the treatment hour without desire, memory, or understanding.

One final quality of the supervisory alliance must be mentioned: the supervisor's commitment must be primarily to the patient in therapy and only secondarily to the trainee; physicianly responsibilities precede all else in any type of therapeutic situation. Supervisory interventions for which the supervisee may be unprepared are thus at times indicated, in the interests of securing for the patient a sound therapy situation. As might be expected, it is therefore especially crucial for the supervisor to be patient, tactful, careful in his explanations, and even, at times, directly supportive, because of the difficult discussions and confrontations he often must have with the supervisee.

Within this basic framework, I must again stress a predictive approach is essential. Virtually all of the supervisor's interventions should be derived directly from the process notes of the supervised therapeutic interaction, should be couched as formulations with definitive and predictive qualities, and must be open to validation from the subsequent material from the session—from both patient and therapist. While incidental comments from the supervisee, or his unanticipated recollection of previously repressed aspects of a session or of forgotten information about the patient, may be taken as second-order validation, first-order validation must always take the form of the communication of Type Two derivatives from within the therapeutic situation under study.

A first type of supervisory situation arises when the supervisor develops a formulation before the supervisee has offered any intervention that might suggest, or have been predicted by, the formulation in question. If the formulation is correct, subsequent material from the patient should, in indirect, derivative, and coalescing form, provide otherwise unanticipated illumination and elaboration of the conception. As a rule, a correctly developed supervisory assessment should be "echoed" by the patient in the form of Type Two derivatives which communicate in disguised form (and the patient's own language) the supervisor's ideas and their implications. Ultimate validation occurs when the supervisee reports having intervened to the patient in a manner seen as consistent with the supervisor's formulation and when the patient, in response, provides an appropriate Type Two derivative. Optimally, this takes the form of a selected fact (Bion 1962) which organizes the known material in a new and unforeseen manner that reveals its latent meaning.

The same principles as apply to the supervisee's interventions to the patient apply as well to any additional formulations he might offer during supervision. This predictive, validating methodology is so essential to supervision that it must be applied without exception to every clinical formulation developed; further, it must be taught to the trainee in order to help him master the listening process and all its components—including the validating process (Langs 1978b).

As with interventions in the therapeutic situation (see Langs 1973, 1976a, 1978a), there is for supervisory interventions a definitive hierarchy of indications. Virtually without exception, and in marked contrast to the principles governing interventions in therapy, the supervisor should be prepared to intervene one or more times in any supervisory hour. Though the subject merits considerable empirical investigation, I propose the following order of precedence for problems calling for definitive supervisory interventions (with a full understanding that patience and tact should prevail, and that these interventions should be derived in specific fashion from the process notes at hand): first, indications in the direct supervisory interaction, or, more indirectly, in the therapeutic situation, of the presence of countertransference difficulties in the supervisor (defined here as any expression of his psychopathology)—including any crisis in supervision; second, any indication of countertransference difficulties in the supervisee, including any crisis in therapy; third, any major issue regarding the framework of the supervisory or therapeutic situations; fourth, any major accumulation of resistances within the patient, or any stalemate in the therapeutic interaction; and fifth, the appearance in the material from the patient of derivatives related to core pathological unconscious fantasies, memories, and introjects. This hierarchy should serve as a rough guide in respect to the order of importance of supervisory issues, and as a framework for the supervisor's decisions on intervening.

In general, the supervisor should, at the beginning of each

supervisory hour, allow the description of the session at hand to unfold for a while. At a point when he is able to develop a pertinent formulation related to any of the issues just described (or any other important aspect of the material or interaction), he should voice his conceptualization in a form comparable to the silent hypotheses made by the therapist in the opening phase of each session. These formulations are then open to validation from the subsequent material.

The next major juncture for supervisory comments occurs when the supervisor spots an indication for intervention that the supervisee has missed. In order of precedence, this would occur in the presence of countertransference difficulties unconsciously introjected by the patient from the supervisee; the appearance of related interactional resistances; a major rupture in the therapeutic alliance; any basic alteration in the framework; or the presence of coalescing derivatives related to resistances and core fantasies, memories, and introjects. The supervisor's formulation and proposed intervention (the latter should be stated in the actual language that would have been used with the patient) are then open to subsequent Type Two validation in the material that follows. Implicit here is an assessment that the therapist's silence reflects a countertransference-based failure to intervene—a topic that can be introduced through the material that follows from the patient, who will, as a rule, respond to such errors with unconscious supervisory communications (see below).

A third point of supervisory intervention occurs whenever the supervisee has himself intervened. In principle, this is a vital moment for definitive supervisory work. It is crucial here first to define the formal nature of the intervention (beyond silences, this includes questions, clarifications, confrontations, interpretations, reconstructions, and managements of the framework; see Langs 1978a); and, second and more important, to delineate the unconscious communicative qualities of the intervention. It is these qualities that will be most critical to the patient's responses, as they define the underlying nature of the adaptive context the patient will be working over—consciously and unconsciously, validly and with distortions—in the associations that follow an intervention. An appreciation of this material, which is best viewed as a *commentary* on, and *transversal communications* related to, the therapist's effort (see Langs 1978b), of this material, is feasible only if these unconscious elements have been identified and stated as a means of predicting the patient's response—a step then open to Type Two validation.

All supervisory interventions should, then, be as specific and clinically definitive as possible. Validation from the subsequent therapeutic interaction is vital and should be evaluated independently by both supervisor and supervisee. It is through his own application of the validating process (Langs 1976c, 1978b,e) that the supervisee should assess the quality of the supervisor's interventions—and of his silences or failures to comment, as well. In addition to this basic clinical foundation, the first priority in supervision, the supervisor should, as a second priority, feel free to allude to the pertinent literature, to suggest relevant readings, and to discuss briefly the broader issues raised by the material of the therapeutic interaction.

Last in order of precedence in supervisory teaching, though somewhat overlapping with the priorities already described, is attention to a basic teaching program, outlined for the one or two year period over which most supervisory experiences are extended. In general, with many exceptions based on the requisites of the therapeutic interaction under study and the immediate needs of the patient and the supervisee, teaching should begin with the listening and validating processes (Langs 1978b), since this is fundamental to the understanding of every transaction in both the therapeutic and the supervisory situations. In this respect, the application of what I have termed *listening exercises* (1978b) is a basic teaching vehicle well worth repetition in early supervisory sessions.

These exercises entail listening to a segment of material from the patient, identifying the central adaptive context, formulating the manifest content and Type One and Type Two derivatives, and monitoring them in terms of the ongoing therapeutic interaction, especially along the me-not-me interface, recognizing that every communication from the patient refers on some level to the therapeutic experience, and quite specifically to both patient and therapist. Each formulation so derived is then evaluated for its veridical and valid, and its fantasied and distorted, elements. Full use is made of the abstracting-particularizing process, as well as the self-knowledge of the therapist.

Perhaps most overlooked in this regard is the importance of applying the listening process to the patient's unconscious perceptions and introjections of the therapist's communications. Even more neglected are the patient's unconscious perceptions and introjections of the *supervisor's* interventions as they are consciously and unconsciously communicated to the patient through the supervisee. There has been a great tendency among therapists and analysts to focus on the "me" part of this interface—the patient's self-representations and projections onto the therapist (mainly transference and distortion) and to neglect the "not me" part—the usually valid, though sometimes distorted, introjections of qualities of the supervisee and supervisor, and the patient's object-representations and introjective experiences vis-a-vis the therapist. In the supervisory situation, it is this not-me dimension that proves most difficult and yet critical to formulate in regard to both the therapeutic and the supervisory interactions; it is of course the essential realm of countertransference-based influences, from both supervisor and supervisee, and the most likely arena for blind spots and other cognitive difficulties.

After the listening and validating processes, the nature, functions, and implications of the ground rules of therapy deserve emphasis, since the therapist's establishment and maintenance of the framework expresses his holding and containing capacities, and provides the essential conditions and medium for the interactional expression of the patient's neurosis (a term used here in its broadest sense to allude to all psychopathology) in a manner that is analyzable and open to shifts toward adaptive mastery. The therapist's explication of these basic tenets is rich in unconscious communication and determines, as well, the basic communicative properties both of the therapeutic situation and of supervision. Next, the supervisor should concentrate on the therapeutic relationship, especially the unconscious communicative interaction, and, finally, on a study of interventions (Langs 1978a). With this as the fundamental model of the supervisory situation and its transactions, let us now turn to a number of clinically relevant and relatively neglected problems that may arise in the course of supervision.

SOME COMMUNICATIVE PROPERTIES OF THE SUPERVISORY BIPERSONAL FIELD

Depending on a wide range of factors within the supervisor, the supervisee, and the patient under supervision, as well as in the structure and maintenance of the framework, the supervisory bipersonal field will acquire communicative characteristics which may, however, fluctuate. The ideal supervisor, of course, uses predominantly the Type A communicative mode, through which he formulates, abstracts and particularizes, uses language symbolically, and maintains the framework of supervision in a manner permitting full play to illusion and fantasy, while promoting understanding and learning.

Unfortunately, many supervisors are quite unaware of their usual communicative style; in addition, a particular supervisee or patient may prompt the supervisor to a shift to the Type B or Type C modes. It is, of course, the responsibility of each supervisor to be aware of his propensities toward these latter modes of communication and supervision, and to undertake the necessary self-analytic work that will enable him to become primarily a Type A communicator. In addition to self-awareness, a monitoring of the supervised therapeutic bipersonal field for its communicative qualities, which often mirror those within supervision, may provide clues that should then prompt the necessary investigation of the supervisory bipersonal field for Type B and Type C trends.

Almost always without his conscious awareness, the Type B supervisor uses the supervisory situation for unburdening himself of his own inner mental disturbances and for pathological projective identifications into the supervisee. He may tend to fragment the framework of the supervisory field and will intervene in a manner, despite his conscious intentions to the contrary, that satisfies his own pathological needs for action-discharge far more than the needs of the supervisee for understanding and guidance.

The Type C supervisor, by contrast, may just as likely maintain a rigid framework as one that is fragmented, but his supervisory work will be characterized by frequent failures to intervene, by the use of psychoanalytic clichés, and by relatively superficial formulations that are dynamically irrelevant or of only peripheral pertinence to the material being presented. His main efforts will be toward maintaining intrapsychic and interpersonal barriers designed to seal off any threat of inner disturbance or of the arousal of the psychotic part of his own personality, as well as that of the supervisee and the patient. While the Type A supervisor makes consistent and elaborate use of the listening and validating processes, and of the predictive methodology described here, neither the Type B nor the Type C supervisor will apply these processes with any sense of regularity, depth, or meaning. The Type B supervisor is likely to flit about, preferring to dump into the supervisee a variety of pressured formulations, while the Type C supervisor will hardly be concerned at all with validation or with the complexity of the material at hand; he will tend to oversimplify.

For his part, the supervisee capable of using the Type A mode of communication is able to present from process notes that are neither overly long nor too condensed. His formulations of the material from the patient is in the symbolic mode, and he has a strong capacity to understand the symbolic implications of the supervisor's communications. The Type B supervisee, by contrast, usually presents fragmented and disorganized notes, and becomes engaged in intense efforts to relieve himself of inner tension and to projectively identify pathological contents and mechanisms into the supervisor. In response, the supervisor must be capable of metabolizing these interactional pressures toward understanding, so that he may intervene in a manner that reflects a true capacity for reverie (Bion 1962). These supervisees often evoke crisis situations in therapy and supervision that will require direct discussion in addition to the usual supervisory efforts.

Finally, the Type C supervisee will tend to produce either extremely terse or overly lengthy notes, which serve primarily as a barrier to an affective, symbolic, meaningful understanding of the therapeutic interaction. His formulations will be abbreviated, clichéd, mechanical, and lacking in dynamic pertinence, and will as a rule tend to neglect the ongoing therapeutic interaction. Initial teaching efforts must therefore be directed toward the supervisee's pathological style of communication and presenting, in order to create the necessary conditions of the supervisory bipersonal field within which true learning and growth can occur. In general, then, the teaching approach of the supervisor should be greatly influenced by the communicative mode of the supervisee.

As part of the interaction between the supervisory and therapeutic bipersonal fields, the communicative style of the patient may have considerable influence on the supervisory dyad. The Type A patient opens both therapist and supervisor to regressive pressures and exposes both to the psychotic parts of each of the three principals. While this may foster a therapeutic regression and a very constructive supervisory learning situation, this generally will not occur without a strong measure of anxiety and threat, which entails a risk of the use of pathological defenses in either supervisor or supervisee.

The Type B patient may reinforce comparable communicative propensities, if present in both supervisor and supervisee. At times, such a patient may even prompt the use of Type C barriers by either the therapist or his mentor, based largely on their inability to metabolize and understand the prevailing interactional pressures. The Type C patient may promote the use of a comparable communicative mode in the supervisor or supervisee, or may evoke provocative countertransference-based projective indentifications. Patients of this type often contribute to very hollow and stalemated supervisory experiences.

As a fundamental component of the supervisory bipersonal field, the communicative styles of supervisor and supervisee, as well as of the patient, deserve first-order attention in the supervisory experience. Any trend toward the use of a pathological communicative mode in the supervisor must be identified, recitified, and subjected to self-analysis, while such disturbances in the supervisee must be a matter of fundamental supervisory concern. Communicative mode is basic to the nature and function of the supervisee's presentation, and therefore to the material available from the therapeutic situation for teaching purposes. Since the supervisee's communicative style will be reflected in his work with both the patient and the supervisor (an aspect of the reflection process described in Searles 1955), it is, as a rule, feasible to use the presentation of process notes to confront and discuss disturbances in communicative style in the supervisee. Every effort should be made to carry out such discussions on this basis, though at times of crisis a more direct confrontation may be necessary. It is here, by the way, that some of the limitations of the supervisory situation become evident.

THE SUPERVISOR'S COUNTERTRANSFERENCES

There has been a rather striking neglect in the literature of the supervisor's countertransferences, the expressions of his psychopathology as they are manifested in the supervisory interaction. Since they are, however, a first-order influence on the nature of the supervisory field, work, and experience, they deserve systematic consideration, especially with regard to how they are expressed and detected. In fact, the supervisee himself should be taught to make efforts to apply the listening and validating processes to the supervisor's interventions, and to be prepared to express his disagreement and, especially, to point out situations in which Type Two validation does not appear. All supervisory errors must be considered to contain significant elements of countertransference, as indeed every supervisory intervention, successful or not, inevitably includes some such ingredient (these principles are parallel to those that apply to the therapist's interventions; see Langs 1978a).

The supervisor must carefully though silently monitor all transactions in the supervisory and therapeutic bipersonal fields for expressions of his countertransferences. Evidence should be sought in all pertinent spheres: his own subjective reactions, the material from the patient (serving here as an unconscious supervisor for the supervisor), and the communications from the supervisee—both to his patient and in supervision. It is to be stressed, however, that the supervisor's countertransferences, while they should at times be directly acknowledged to the supervisee, should not be overstated or worked over in the supervisory bipersonal field. They are matters for the private self-analysis of the supervisor, or for his personal therapy, and should not become the direct burden of the supervisee.

In terms of the principles being established in this paper, any deviation from standard supervisory practices should be investigated for significant countertransference-based inputs. The supervisor, who can never be free of countertransference, has a responsibility to attempt to be aware of its presence and expressions, and especially of its influence on what would otherwise be unrecognized biases in his approach to the therapeutic material. These may take many forms, including a preference to work with certain types of derivatives and material, a need to focus almost exclusively in one communicative sphere, a tendency to shift to manifest content, a preference to work with one of the three macrostructures (id, ego, superego), and so on. The ultimate goal is, of course, to recognize these prejudices, to modify them through self-analysis and, especially, to exercise sufficient care in monitoring the transactions in both bipersonal fields, the therapeutic and the supervisory, to detect the unanticipated introduction of a countertransference-based difficulty into the supervisory work.

THE SUPERVISORY INTROJECT

There has been some discussion of the literature of parallel and reflectional processes in supervisory and therapeutic bipersonal fields (see for example Arlow 1963, Searles 1955), much of it focused on the manner in which the supervisee plays a pivotal role in evoking comparable responses in both the patient and the supervisor. As a consequence, the latter may make special use of his subjective reactions to the supervisee and his presentation, thereby accuring information (this information is, of course, open to validation in the presentation itself) regarding the therapeutic interaction that may not for the moment be imparted directly in the process notes.

In contrast, little has been written in respect to the influence of the supervisor on the therapeutic bipersonal field, and especially in regard to the development of what I shall term a *supervisory introject* within the supervisee (Langs, in press). This introject, which is a precipitant of the supervisory interaction, includes the conscious and unconscious communications of the supervisor and its implications as they are selectively introjected by the supervisee on both a conscious and an unconscious level, and then processed in keeping with the latter's pathological and nonpathological needs. It is an important interactional amalgam with crucial kernels of truth and valid conscious and unconscious perceptiveness, intermixed as a rule with some degree of pathological elaboration, which then exerts a significant influence on the supervisee's work with his patient.

In brief, this introject may be primarily either pathological or nonpathological, a fairly complete representation of the supervisor's communication or a rather constricted selection. It may be adequately processed and metabolized by the supervisee, and then integrated into his self-representation and ego functioning, or it may remain a poorly metabolized, ego-alien introject identified with the supervisor and not experienced to any significant extent as part of the supervisee's self-representation and own capacities. The latter alternatives apply whether the introject, as derived from the supervisor's interventions, are primarily pathological and disruptive, or nonpathological and constructive.

Failures to metabolize and integrate essentially constructive supervisory interventions are related to learning blocks, to the supervisee's countertransference difficulties, and to problems in his functioning as a therapist. The overinclusion of pathological and countertransference-based interventions from the supervisor has similar implications, although one must take into account the enormous pressures toward conformity and even blind acceptance that are exerted upon some supervisees by certain supervisors. On the other hand, an adequate metabolization of a pathological supervisory introject would entail the conscious understanding of the supervisor's error and the decision on the part of the supervisee to largely dispute or disregard that particular intervention.

It is, of course, the supervisory introject that serves as the vehicle through which the supervisor influences the therapeutic bipersonal field and indirectly communicates with the patient. Because the patient is consciously and unconsciously exposed to this introject, his own communications are under the sway of the supervisor's efforts. In this regard, the patient too has the usually unconscious choice of refuting or containing these pathological and nonpathological introjects, and of metabolizing them in keeping with his own appropriate or inappropriate needs. Under most circumstances, positively toned introjects will be accepted and will have a therapeutic effect when communicated to the patient through the supervisee's largely valid interventions, whether interpretations or management of the framework.

Pathological supervisory introjects are communicated through the supervisee's erroneous interventions and are usually introjected by the patient and worked over in terms of his own inner needs. The most common response is the patient's initial exploitation of the introject for the maintenance of his own pathology, and then the undertaking of unconscious curative efforts directed first and foremost toward the supervisee as therapist, though clearly, when a pathological supervisory introject is involved, these efforts are ultimately directed toward the supervisor himself. It is this type of interactional sequence, occurring between the supervisory and therapeutic bipersonal fields, that renders useful the supervisor's monitoring of the presented process notes for unconscious commentaries—mixtures of valid and distorted perceptions and fantasies—on his supervisory work, as they are reflected in both the supervisee's interventions and the patient's behavioral responses and verbal associations. It is on this level that the patient serves in an important manner as supervisor to the supervisor.

DEALING WITH THE SUPERVISEE'S
COUNTERTRANSFERENCES: THE PATIENT
AS UNCONSCIOUS SUPERVISOR

In addition to failures to establish a basic predictive, validating methodology, the single most unresolved problem in supervision may well be how to deal with indications or expressions of the supervisee's countertransferences as they emerge in the therapeutic situation and, at times, in the supervisory experience. Recommendations have ranged from using the supervisee's therapist or analyst as his supervisor, to ignoring these phenomena or treating them as learning difficulties to which the supervisor should respond with educational measures. My own resolution of this particular dilemma has followed from an understanding of the therapeutic interaction itself, through which it is discovered that the expressions of the supervisee's countertransferences lie mainly in essentially erroneous attitudes and interventions (inappropriate silences—which constitute failures to intervene—verbal misinterventions, and mismanagements of the frame). These errors entail unconscious communications that are, in a complex way, introjected by the patient in terms of their manifest and latent meanings and functions, and the resultant pathological *therapist introject* is then worked over in a variety of ways by the patient.

In the presence of a significant countertransference-based input into the therapeutic bipersonal field from the therapist, the interface of that field shifts toward the working over of the expressions of his pathology. As a rule, the patient unocnsciously becomes preoccupied with this disturbance, and becomes involved in its exploitation and resolution. At such times the patient will embed or conceal his own usually related psychopathology within that of the therapist, so that it is not, for the moment, available for interpretation. Instead, the unconscious focus of the therapeutic work within the bipersonal field shifts momentarily to the identification, rectification, and under-standing of the therapist's pathology and the patient's responses to it, to which the therapist himself must add self-analyst endeavors undertaken privately without burdening the patient.

Lest this description (derived from actual clinical observation) be misunderstood, let me repeat that the therapeutic bipersonal field is not designed for the therapy of the therapist, that it should be no more than minimally occupied with such endeavors, and that the therapeutic work in which these countertransference difficulties are resolved is in no way comparable to that undertaken on behalf of the patient. That such considerations arise is simply an inevitability which should, however, always be kept secondary, and which may, if properly understood and resolved, provide the therapist incidental gain. The patient in such situations is himself offered a special opportunity for unconscious and, ultimately, conscious insights and gains, based on his unconscious therapeutic functioning and on the analysis of his inappropriate responses.

During these countertransference-dominated interludes, the patient responds in part with unconscious interpretations and other corrective efforts directed toward the therapist himself and the introjected disturbance (Langs 1976a). The recognition of these endeavors, however, depends on a correct evaluation of the unconscious communicative qualities of the technical error, and a recognition that the patient's responsive material is to be taken as Type Two derivatives—commentaries and transversal communications with both perceptive and inappropriate qualities—in response to that particular adaptive context. These corrective and therapeutic efforts, which tend to be expressed on a rather general level but which rather often are quite perceptive, constitute on one level the patient's unconscious efforts to supervise the therapist (and his supervisor). A sensitive therapist can therefore benefit from these communications as long as he truly understands their implications. Similarly, the supervisor needs only tune in on the patient's unconscious supervisory efforts and play them back to the supervisee in his own teaching idiom in order to initiate his own corrective efforts in supervision. Thus the patient truly functions as the key unconscious supervisor in both the therapeutic and the supervisory fields.

Often the supervisor will already have discussed a particular intervention with the supervisee, and will have identified its unconscious communicative qualities. It therefore becomes feasible to anticipate or predict the patient's unconscious responses; validation occurs when the patient, through Type Two derivatives, indirectly works over in his own idiom the erroneous intervention of the therapist in a manner that confirms and elaborates the supervisor's predictive assessment. Failure to obtain such validation should lead the supervisor to reassess and reformulate; it suggests that his own countertransferences may be active and may be influencing both his supervisory interventions and the therapy at hand.

Among the many implications of these findings and formulations, many of which are beyond the scope of this paper (see Langs, in press), this understanding of the therapeutic interaction gives considerable emphasis to nondistorted and introjective processes within the patient, while according projective and distorting processes their due. Since these observations indicate that in the presence of a countertransference based intervention, the therapeutic work of the bipersonal field and the responses of the patient are momentarily preoccupied with those inputs, this view suggests that the supervisor must of necessity deal with these countertransferences and the patient's reactions to them; he has no choice but to focus his teaching here. In effect, it is not a question of whether he will comment on or ignore the supervisee's countertransferences; he must do his teaching in this area because it is what both patient and therapist are dealing with and need from him.

This approach also offers a definitive means of dealing with the supervisee's countertransferences in the supervisory situation. In principle, the supersivor makes use of his assessment of the unconscious communications in the therapist's interventions, and very specifically employs the patient's unconscious perceptions and fantasies (introjections) of these interventions as a means of identifying their presence and of stating, within the limits possible in the supervisory situation, their underlying basis. The identified unconscious elements, then, are discussed almost entirely in terms of the communicative qualities of the therapist's interventions and the patient's unconscious commentaries. In this way, the supervisor relies on the patient's unconscious supervisory and curative efforts, understands them to contain valid and perceptive elements in addition to whatever distortions are present, and translates these communications into conscious understanding. He uses the patient's unconscious perceptions, interpretations, and teaching efforts in response to the supervisee's countertransferences, while at the same time he carries out his supervisory work in the main area of concern for both patient and therapist. Because of the conditions of the supervisory bipersonal field, it is, by and large, inappropriate for the supervisor to add any significant remarks to the patient's unconscious formulations; he should maintain the principle of doing his teaching from the process notes of the therapy. On occasion, when there is evidence of a major countertransference problem, a brief extraneous comment may be in order, though it should not, as a rule, be an attempt at interpretation; rather, it should be confined to a gentle and tactful confrontation.

COMMON SUPERVISORY PROBLEMS

It would be helpful if supervisors could develop a literature on the most common problems seen in supervisees and their therapeutic work, and in supervision itself. Preliminary efforts of this kind (see especially Langs in press) suggest the lack of a consensus, despite the likelihood that there are patterns of difficulties shared by therapists-in-training (for a different approach to this problem, see Langs, 1976b). Evaluations in this area clearly relate to the supervisor's model of therapy and to his conceptions of the listening process, the therapeutic interaction, and interventions.

To offer some brief preliminary impressions, it seems to me that the single most overriding difficulty in supervisees (and the same applies, by and large, to more experienced therapists as well) is learning how to listen to derivatives, and how to organize them specifically as Type Two derivatives around a significant adaptive context. The tendency in therapists is overwhelmingly toward attention to manifest content and Type One derivatives, and this is largely derived from a related trend, namely, to divorce the patient's material from the ongoing therapeutic interaction. This second pitfall is prevalent because therapists-in-training fail to monitor the patient's associations for unconscious perceptions and fantasies related to the actualities of the therapeutic experience, constructive or destructive, as they evoke mixtures of transference-based and nontransference-based responses. Especially neglected are the principles that every communication from the patient refers on some level to the therapeutic interaction, and to both himself and the therapist (the *me–not–me interface;* Langs 1978b), and that every intervention must on some level be connected to the actualities of this interaction in terms of both the reality stimuli and their unconscious, communicative, and intrapsychic meanings.

Thus, supervisees tend to work manifestly and to avoid the therapeutic interaction except when the patient directly refers to it or in the face of an obvious and blatant countertransference-based input—and even then dealing with it only in terms of the surface of the material rather than through derivatives organized around the usually covered-over and defended-against countertransference-related adaptive context. Another common problem in supervisees is really just another dimension of these trends: the tendency to treat the patient's communications as largely distorted and transference-based, as primarily displaced from past pathogenic experiences, and as occurring largely in the projective mode. The patient's functioning is viewed almost entirely in terms of intrapsychic fantasies, memories, and introjects that are placed by him into the therapeutic situation or projected onto the therapist, thereby distorting his image and the patient's responses to him. In keeping with this, transference resistances and fantasies tend to be interpreted almost entirely in terms of their supposed genetic basis, in a manner that vitually denies any actual pathological contribution from the therapist despite the finding that an element of countertransference is present in every intervention (Langs 1978a). Genetic interpretations are therefore frequently used as a defense against the pathogenic actualities of the current therapeutic interaction, especially as a means of consciously and unconsciously denying the therapist's pathological contributions to the patient's experience and responses. Overemphasis on the projective aspects of the patient's communications is used to deny their very crucial introjective dimensions and the countertransferences which contribute to intorjects. Instead, a balanced approach should be taught, one that recognizes cycles and intermixtures of introjective and projective processes in both patient and therapist, and that allows for a sensitive appreciation of the constructive and disturbed functioning of both.

In general, then, it has not been my experience that most supervisees tend to become involved in wild analysis or therapy, nor that they tend to prematurely shift to overly deep id interpretations. Quite to the contrary, they tend to remain rather superficial and, in addition, to offer a variety of unconscious interactional defenses and Type C barriers designed to seal off the more chaotic aspects of their linkage and interaction with the patient, and of their respective inner mental worlds.

SUPERVISORY CRISES

There are two major types of crises in supervision. The first arises when there is an emergency or critical period in the therapy situation, such as a threat by the patient to terminate, an uncontrolled regression, a danger of suicide, or the like. The second involves a major difficulty in supervision itself, such as the supervisee's conscious dissatisfaction with supervision and his wish to terminate it, or a feeling by the supervisor that his teaching efforts are falling on deaf ears. In the first type of crisis, there is no need to modify the basic supervisory field and methodology, since the understanding of a therapeutic crisis must derive from a study of the process notes of the session. Under these conditions it is quite crucial for the supervisor to identify the critical adaptive contexts that appear to be evoking the disruptive responses in the patient or therapist, and to think of the severe resistance or regression as an interactional syndrome with contributions from both participants. He should allow the material from both members of the therapeutic dyad—especially the derivative communications of the patient—to generate the necessary understanding of the critical interlude. The supervisor should not, under these conditions, succumb to the tendency in many therapists to forgo the complexities of the listening process, and to shift to manifest content-based interventions and modifications in the framework; instead, he should recognize that such crises have important and pivotal unconscious foundations and that his task is to identify the unconscious contributions of both patient and therapist.

In virtually every crisis situation in therapy there are significant countertransference-based inputs; these will be revealed in the process notes through the therapist's interventions and the patient's associations and behaviors, and should not be neglected. A supervisor who, with relative calm, is able to contain, metabolize, and conceptualize the unconscious basis for a therapeutic crisis affords his supervisees both essential cognitive insights into the source of acute disturbances and the measures necessary for their resolution—whether these are rectifications of unneeded deviations or offers of necessary interpretations. He affords them also the opportunity to incorporate a supervisory introject that will provide them positive introjective identifications that embody a sense of control and understanding and an appreciation for the analytic approach.

Supervisory crises are also interactional amalgams, with inevitable contributions from both participants (although as a rule either the supervisor or supervisee will bear the brunt of the responsibility for the urgent situation). Undoubtedly, the major blind spot under these circumstances is the failure of the supervisor to fully recognize and comprehend his own contributions to the crisis at hand, and his likely tendency to blame the supervisee and to exonerate himself. In addition, the supervisory crisis is to be viewed in interaction with the therapeutic situation; whenever possible, the material from the process notes should be used as a guideline in determining the unconscious basis for the critical issues in supervision, and the role played by both the student and his mentor.

The supervisor's contribution to the crisis will vary depending on a wide range of factors, including his psychological liabilities and assets, his communicative style, his specific response to the supervisee and to the patient under study, and the like. A supervisor who uses a Type A communicative mode is likely to threaten any poorly defended supervisee. His sensitive formulations and capacity to identify the patient's unconscious perceptions of, and interpretations to, the supervisee can generate intense anxiety and threats of regression in the latter. An especially fragile supervisee will respond with thoughts of interrupting or terminating the supervision; still, efforts to validate these factors as the main source of the problem are essential. A shadow of doubt should always cross the supervisor's mind; with fragile supervisees, he must attempt to slow down his teaching efforts and must offer considerable direct support. His own role in a crisis must never be denied.

One the other hand, the Type A supervisor may repeatedly offer the same incorrect formulations, and this can create a more valid wish on the part of a supervisee to end the supervision. Critical to this general distinction between appropriate and inappropriate wishes in the supervisee to end supervision is the use of the validating process by both participants in assessing the material from the therapeutic interaction and the supervisor's formulations; this should serve as the basic means of determining the extent to which the student's complaints have some realistic, cognitive basis. Here too, the self-knowledge of the supervisor plays an important role.

The supervisor who uses the Type B mode will tend to projectively identify into the supervisee intensely pathological communications—both contents and mechanisms—that can generate an intense crisis and wishes to terminate supervision. A Type C supervisor can so stalemate the teaching situation that it becomes virtually useless to the supervisee, and at some point of urgent need a supervisee may decide to terminate. As a perspective on these possibilities, however, it is well to recognize that often supervisees do not allow themselves to be consciously aware of their valid dissatisfactions with supervision and, for a variety of countertransference-based defensive and inappropriately gratifying needs, continue in nondestructive supervisory situations. The supervisor himself should therefore monitor the quality of his teaching efforts and the progress or lack of progress of both the supervisee and his patient.

A supervisor may feel that a particular supervisory experience has reached crisis proportions when he finds his supervisee unable to learn and unable to modify intensely countertransference-based defenses and interventions. On the whole, it is the responsibility of the supervisor to explore the process note material and his own interventions for contributions to the supervisee's difficulties and, beyond that, to patiently continue with his teaching efforts, focusing on the supervisee's countertransferences and their expressions in his therapeutic work. Even when the situation reaches crisis proportions and the therapy is endangered, the supervisor must remember that he has made a basic and physicianly commitment to the supervisee; in general, the chronic pathology of the supervisee is not a sound basis for interrupting supervision. In fact, such a step generates a very destructive supervisory introject which would only further traumatize the supervisee and intensify his countertransferences. A period of months or even years of patient work is indicated under such circumstances, and from time to time, especially when material from the therapeutic interaction suggests it, the supervisor may point to the supervisee's need for personal therapy.

An acute supervisory crisis may call for brief comments from the supervisor that are divorced from the process notes of the psychotherapy under supervision. This may occur when the supervisee directly confronts the supervisor with complaints about his work, attitude, teaching method, or the like. The supervisor's response to such complaints should be offered with great restraint and tact, should be kept to an absolute minimum, and should always include an appreciation for the valid aspects of the supervisee's criticisms—no matter how inappropriate they may seem to be after intense evaluation and self-analysis by the supervisor. At such times, the supervisor should take care to avoid a sense of criticism and hostility toward the supervisee, and yet should feel free to patiently establish some of the inappropriate factors in the supervisee's dissatisfaction with supervision, as long as these can be documented in both the supervisory and therapeutic situations, and as long as the supervisor's own contributions are acknowledged. In general, a brief and direct discussion of this kind should end on a note of new resolve to work cooperatively.

LIMITATIONS TO SUPERVISION

As might be expected, the results of a supervisory experience have most definite limitations, established by the framework and nature of the supervisory bipersonal field, and by the assets and psychopathology of both supervisor and supervisee. Although the framework precludes an insightful therapeutic experience for the supervisee, it does not eliminate opportunities for isolated segments of conscious insight and growth which may at times extend into unconscious working over. Nonetheless, the supervisee's psychopathology will, in various ways, prove to be a major, definitive limiting factor to the outcome of a supervision, and much will depend upon his motivation for supplementary therapy and the actual treatment he obtains.

In this last respect, important complications and limitations develop for the supervisory situation when the supervisee's own therapist is using poor technique and has established a therapeutic situation with major drawbacks. The presence of such flaws in the works of the supervisee's therapist often has drastic consequences for the outcome of supervision; it may, in addition, contribute to supervisory crises, especially under two conditions: first, when the supervisor's work is far more valid than that of the supervisee's therapist, raising major questions regarding the latter situation which tend to generate extensive turmoil in all participants and in the three bipersonal fields involved; and second, when the supervisor's work is quite inadequate as compared to the therapist's abilities, leading to supervisory crises based on the actuality of poor supervision.

The literature has tended to neglect the interaction between the three bipersonal fields now under consideration: between the supervisee and his patient; between the supervisee and his therapist; and between the supervisee and his supervisor. To these a fourth may be added when the supervisor himself is in some form of psychotherapy or psychoanalysis. Clearly, there is an extensive interaction among these bipersonal fields in which both projective and introjective processes play a crucial role, and whereby a disturbance in any of the four can create a ripple effect that influences the other three.

Also to be considered here are disturbances and limitations to supervision that arise from the countertransferences not only of the supervisor, but also of the supervisor's therapist or analyst, whether past or present. Here once again, it is ultimately the application of self-analysis leading to in-depth self-knowledge, as well as the use of the listening and validating processes in respect to communications within each of these bipersonal fields, that provides the supervisor the necessary methodology for investigating these issues and for identifying the limits of the teaching experience.

The presence of limitations to supervisory outcome, however difficult they may be to define precisely, should not, however, be a source of discouragement for the supervisor. They must be accepted as inevitable restrictions on any teaching effort and especially to the teaching of psychotherapy, which so intensely impinges upon the personal assets and pathology of the participants. As the material from the process notes permits, the supervisor may point to specific sources of limitations in a given supervisory situation, in the hope that, when they apply mainly to the supervisee, such confrontations will motivate him toward personal therapy or self-analysis. Those restrictions that derive from problems within the supervisor himself may also be modified through self-analysis and personal therapy, though recognizing and accepting the residuals of one's limitations in this regard is also ultimately a necessity.

SUPERVISION AND CREATIVITY

For quite some time I felt apologetic, even lacking in insight, because I realized that most of my ideas were developed in the course of supervisory work. While some new concepts arose, though in a primarily tangential way, in the course of my work with patients, and while it proved necessary to validate the concepts derived from supervision in my own therapeutic endeavors. I was nevertheless faced with that realization and the fact that my colleagues seemed to devalue psychoanalytic understanding founded on the supervisory situation.

Yet in time my attitude changed. I began to realize that there is considerable validity to the use of supervision as an arena for creativity. The supervisor does not have, as does the primary therapist, the intense and overriding responsibility to think and respond to the greatest extent possible to the patient's therapeutic needs, and to set all other considerations aside. While responsible for teaching the supervisee and for safeguarding the therapy of the patient, the supervisor nevertheless enjoys a good deal of room in which to generate original insights and conceptualizations based on the material presented him. In fact, such use of the supervisory situation for discovery and innovation, as long as it is not the overriding purpose of supervision and does not detract from the teaching of the supervisee or the management of the therapy, finds support in the work of Freud. After all, Freud's basic discovery of transference was greatly facilitated by the fact that he in a sense served as supervisor to Breuer (Breuer and Freud 1983–1895). The very fact that the supervisor has some distance on the patient, and is functioning as an observer, facilitates the creative process in the supervisor, despite the obvious deficiencies that arise from the crucial absence of direct emotional contact and interaction with the patient.

Another benefit of supervision in this regard accrues to therapists and analysts who recognize the need for total confidentiality in their own therapeutic work and who, like myself (see Langs 1975, 1976a,c), will make no use of material from patients—past or present—for any purpose other than the therapy of the patient within his sessions. For them, material from supervision offers a means of clinically documenting new psychoanalytic ideas. Since the clinical material of these therapy sessions has already been made "public," in the interests of the patient, whose therapy with an inexperienced practitioner must be monitored, and of the supervisee, who cannot learn to do therapy except through the detailed presentation of his own work, the use of such material, totally disguised, is a reasonable means of serving the needs of the therapeutic community at large, while safeguarding the rights of patients.

SELF-SUPERVISION

Ultimately, of course, responsibility for supervision, an attitude and a formal process essential to every therapeutic situation, must rest upon the therapist himself. With the assistance of the ever-present unconscious supervisory efforts of the patient, every therapist must, in the course of each session, maintain a silent and continuous level of self-supervisory work. Such an attitude is inherent to the conception of the therapeutic bipersonal field presented above, and is one way of characterizing the listening and validating processes—the predictive methodology—that is at the heart of this presentation and, I make bold to say, of valid psychotherapy. It is an aspect of the therapist's essential therapeutic attitude which calls for a continuous monitoring of countertransference-based influences, as well as for sound formulations and interventions. It implies continual efforts at self-understanding and self-analysis.

In keeping with the principles that the therapist should enter each session without desire, memory, or understanding, and that each session should be its own creation, these self-supervisory undertakings, as a rule, should be confined to the session with the patient and should not spill over into sessions with other patients or into efforts at self-reflection after hours. However, when a therapist is faced with a stalemate or crisis in therapy, such after-hours efforts to review the material from the session, and to search for pathological contributions from the therapist himself and from the patient, may prove necessary. In extreme circumstances, direct consultation with a supervisor may be necessary, and such a step is preferable to referring the patient to another therapist for an evaluative consultation. The latter option shatters the framework of the original therapeutic bipersonal field and has disastrous unconscious implications and consequences. As a rule, if an impasse or crisis has proven unresolvable, referral to a new therapist (but never to one who has supervised the particular case, as this would be a major contamination of the second bipersonal field) is to be preferred.

A CLINICAL VIGNETTE

I will present a brief vignette through which some of the issues and processes outlined in this paper can be illustrated.

Mr. A. had been in therapy in a clinic with Dr. B., a woman therapist in the middle phase of her training. He sought treatment for depression and for feelings that he was getting nowhere in his life; he was in his twenties. The early sessions had been characterized by extensive activity on the part of the therapist, who asked many questions, made frequent noninterpretive interventions, including self-revelations, and who had failed to establish any semblance of a secure frame for the treatment. Just before the session excerpted here, Dr. B. had changed both the hours of the patient's sessions and her office, because of her professional advancement. Much of this therapist's work could be characterized as a mixture of seductiveness and hostility: she tended to tease and chide this patient, who responded in kind.

In the session to be described here, the patient began by saying that he had recently become involved with two girls who worked in another department of the factory at which he worked. The girls had been quite seductive and teasing with him, and they had really stirred him up sexually; he had responded with a great deal of teasing of his own that they in turn seemed to find quite exciting. During his coffee breaks and lunch hours, he would go over to their department and banter with them. Their boss, who was quite seductive himself, seemed to object and spoke to Mr. A., implying that he was coming on too strong and didn't know his place. He seemed to want to get rid of Mr. A. and was quite demeaning in his attitude. The patient said maybe this boss was right, that maybe he *was* overdoing it, but he was still furious with this fellow and imagined all sorts of ways of getting revenge. His favorite fantasy was of writing fake love letters to him, as if he were some girl who was arranging a date, coming on strong to him, and then standing him up.

At this point, evidently struck by the therapist's relative silence (in fact, under the influence of an initial supervisory session, this was the longest period of silence the therapist had yet maintained with Mr. A.), the patient remarked that Dr. B. seemed very quiet today. He began to tease her and to plead with her to ask him a question—to say something. He laughed nervously and thought about his wishes to take vengence on the supervisor of the two girls he had recently met. It occurred to him that he himself tended to be very impulsive, and that it really took a lot of strength to control oneself—to let tension build inside of you without acting impulsively.

The therapist now intervened and said that the patient seemed to be talking a great deal about levels of relationships. Mr. A. said that he was puzzled by what she meant, and he then went on to ruminate a great deal about how he likes to be in control of situations and how insecure he feels at times. He went on and on in this vein, and the therapist interrupted him, pointing out that he had been on a date the previous weekend and that he had not said anything about it. The patient said that the date had been fine, described some of the details, and tried to shrug off the subject. In response to another question, he thought of a terrible neighborhood he and his date had wandered into, and how dangerous the situation had seemed. In the balance of the session, the therapist asked a series of detailed questions, introduced a number of subjects that she wished the patient to discuss, and again became involved in a series of self-revelations. The patient's material became rather disorganized and bleak, and included a reference to how, when he gets depressed and feels isolated, he likes to flit about from one bar to another. He ended the session feeling rather discouraged with treatment.

The material described here was presented in a second supervisory session. The first hour of supervision had been devoted to supervisory efforts at identifying the details of the listening process and at showing the therapist the patient's unconscious perceptions and introjections of her seductive, hostile, and self-revealing interventions—all of which had generated frightening and critical, yet somewhat excitingly gratifying, introjects which the patient had been working over in derivative form—his own unconscious supervisory efforts. The supervisee had responded to these supervisory interventions with a sense of relief, since she had herself felt that the treatment situation was chaotic and that her interventions had been relatively uncontrolled and lacking in a much-needed neutrality.

The supervisor had been guided by the principle of initiating supervision with major attention to the listening process, though within that framework he responded to the acute needs of both the supervisee and the patient. These needs dictated a discussion of the meanings and functions of the framework and the need for its definition and rigorous maintenance, as well as a tactful and tentative effort to help this therapist to an awareness of the extent to which her interventions were countertransference-based and disruptive of the therapeutic interaction and work. Stress was therefore placed on slowing the supervisee down, so to speak, and helping her to sit back, listen to her patient, and appreciate the complexitities of the therapeutic interaction. Some initial reading, all related to the listening process, was recommended, though it was mentioned that if the supervisee had additional time, a number of articles related to the ground rules and framework of psychotherapy would serve her well.

The opening segment of the session just described demonstrates the influence of a positive supervisory introject on a supervisee who was relatively amenable to its constructive qualities. The supervisor had been quite patient, had been able to contain, metabolize, and understand the unconscious implications of the communications from both the supervisee and her patient, and had imparted some of his insights, along with some direct support, to the supervisee; he had then validated them from the subsequent process note material. These capacities, along with his more direct teaching efforts, through which he encouraged the therapist to sit back and listen, had had a salutory effect. Due to limitations inherent in the early stages of supervision, however, these effects were maintained for only half the session. Still, this is an extremely positive response in a supervisee who had initially been so active and disorganized; it augured well for the future of this particular teaching situation.

In this second supervisory hour, the supervisor had been silent until the supervisee had made her first intervention. At that point, he undertook a series of *listening exercises* through which the therapist was encouraged to identify the adaptive contexts for the session, as well as the available first-order, general, and second-order themes (see Langs 1978b), which were then to be organized around the most significant adaptive contexts. All of this was then to be related to the ongoing therapeutic interaction, considered along the me-not-me interface, and assessed for elements of reality and fantasy. Listening exercises of this kind are basic to the teaching of psychotherapy and, if not spontaneously produced by the supervisee, should be introduced as an essential component in the evaluation and formulation of the process note material. It is on this basis that hypotheses can be generated, predictions made, and validation sought.

In this situation, the supervisee suggested that the main adaptive contexts for this session were the move of her office, the change in hours, and her hostile and demeaning interventions to the patient. She was then asked to review the material for indications of any additional qualities to the therapeutic interaction to which the patient might unconsciously be responding; at this point she recognized the derivative allusions to her seductiveness—especially since, she now added, the patient, in describing the seductive boss, had said directly to her: "You know the type."

It is not uncommon for supervisees (and therapists in general) to be far more readily aware of the derivatives of their unconscious aggressive fantasies toward their patients than they are of the derivatives of their unconscious sexual fantasies. Still, this therapist was able to organize this material as Type Two derivatives around the adaptive contexts now identified, and to recognize the patient's unconscious perceptions and introjections of her teasing, provocative, hostile, and seductive interventions. The supervisor was then able to extend these formulations by pointing out that the patient unconsciously viewed these interventions as efforts to get rid of him, especially in light of the recent changes in his hours and in her office, which seemed to make him feel that he was in her way. However, the supervisor did not voice his impression that these interventions, as unconsciously perceived and introjected by the patient, had qualities of disruptive and pathological projective identifications into the patient, and that these had created pressures toward a Type B communicative field. Nor did he suggest that there was a manic-like and unreal quality to all this excitement which the patient experienced as a lie and falsification that would lead ultimately only to hurt and disappointment (the fake letters and the jilting fantasy). Instead, because it was so early in supervision, the supervisor confined himself to some general comments on how disruptive, hurtful, and detrimental Dr. B.'s interventions had been; he stressed also how sensitive Mr. A. had been to these effects.

Next, the supervisor introduced a more positive note and discussed the influence of the therapist's temporary rectification of the frame—the momentary creation, through Dr. B.'s initial silence, of a necessary sense of distance, modulation, neutrality, and anonymity. In this regard, the supervisor might well have commented earlier on this part of the session, doing so once it had become clear that the supervisee had changed her style of work. He could then have predicted the appearance of a positive introjective identification within the patient, and would have had his prediction validated through Type two derivatives in the patient's reference to the value of controls and restraint when under pressure. This would have offered the supervisee a living model of the predictive-validating approach to psychotherapy and supervision that the supervisor was trying to develop with her. As the actual supervision unfolded, these aspects were discussed in retrospect and has a less powerful effect. While unfamiliarity with the supervisee's therapeutic style played a role in this oversight, the supervisor also looked to his countertransferences for possible influences; he felt that he might have been too focused on the patient's negative introjects of the therapist and on her countertransferences, and that this may have led him to fail to fully appreciate the change in Dr. B.'s style of work.

The therapist's initial silence, as I indicated, reflected a positive supervisory introject which was then unconsciously communicated to the patient, who rather sensitively incorporated some of its most helpful attributes. We see here the influence of the supervisory bipersonal field on that of therapy, and the effects and validation of the supervisor's constructive efforts, which had been derived primarily from the unconscious supervisory efforts of the patient (these were reported in the first supervisory hour and are not detailed here). In this therapeutic situation, the positive supervisor-therapist introject may well have been especially welcomed by this patient, who, in the initial part of the present situation was (1) intensely involved in unconscious supervision of his own (offering a series of derivative commentaries and transversal communications related to the inappropriate aspects of the therapist's work and its negative consequences—derivatives which also alluded to aspects of his own pathology which later could be analyzed once the pathological contributions from the therapist were analyzed and rectified) and (2) expressing his hope for supervisory interventions that could, in part to his regret, set some limits and establish some controls for both himself and the therapist (clinic patients implicitly or explicitly expect that their therapists will be supervised—note the reference to the modulating boss).

In the actual therapy and supervision, both supervisee and supervisor drew upon the patient's unconscious introjection of the supervisee's erroneous interventions and aspects of their underlying basis, and on his efforts at unconscious confrontation, interpretation, and supervision. These efforts were essential guiding factors in the supervisor's interventions, and had also helped the therapist remain silent in the opening part of this session. She stated rather directly that as she began to understand the material from the patient as derivative communications around the adaptive context of her recent interventions, she has experienced a considerable need to sit back, to control these inputs into the bipersonal field, and to understand both herself and the patient. She was also quite aware that when her initial intervention, which was an attempt to provide a bridge between the experiences at work and the therapeutic situation, evoked a ruminative response in the patient, she has become quite discouraged and confused, and no longer felt certain of the derivative meaning of the material. She then experienced a rather sudden urge to actively search for new associations and to ask questions. She was well aware of the loss of control involved and of some of the technical errors that these interventions reflected.

Relying on the patient's unconscious supervisory efforts, the supervisor was now able to show the therapist that the tone of the patient's derivatives had then changed from positive to negative, and that her nonneutral interventions had created a threatening and dangerous atmosphere once again—the reference to the bad neighborhood. At this point, the supervisor added, the patient himself became depressed, partly out of disappointment with the therapist and partly through an introjection of her own underlying depression, and he endeavored to join in with her manic defenses and to unconsciously suggest (interpret) that the therapist's need for activity was a defense against distance, separation, and depression. At this point, sensing a need for further clarification of the functions of the framework, and for the understanding of the nature of interventions, the supervisor briefly outlined some basics in these two areas and suggested some pertinent readings for the supervisee.

In the main, this vignette reflects a supervisory situation in which clear-cut ground rules had been established, including the need for sequential process notes. The supervisor was capable of utilizing the Type A communicative mode and of cognitively understanding the communications from the patient and the therapist; he also had the capacity to contain and metabolize the projective identifications from both of these parties as they were communicated in the initial supervisory hour. The supervisee communicated in a mixed fashion that had qualities of both the Type A and the Type B styles. She was clearly capable of symbolic communication and understanding, though there was in addition an overintensity and an overdetailed quality to her presentation that reflected a need to projectively identify into the supervisor her sense of disorganization, her manic defenses, and her manic-like fantasies. The patient's unconscious cognitive processing and understanding of these efforts—reflecting a type of supervisory reverie (Bion 1962)—had served this supervisee well, despite the subsequent setback. As early as this second supervisory session, there were indications that she was shifting toward a greater use of the Type A communicative mode with both her patient and her supervisor.

In the supervisory session described here, the supervisor attempted to ascertain whether his countertransferences had contributed in any way to the therapist's difficulty in maintaining her distance and neutrality once her initial intervention had failed—not unexpectedly— to evoke a confirmatory response. He had briefly reviewed the intervention with the supervisee, stressing its nonspecific and superficial qualities, the failure to use day-dreaming (fantasy) language, and the need to wait for bridges to the therapeutic situation from the patient rather than trying to promote their expression. (At this point, he decided against a more extensive discussion in this area.) As for his own countertransferences, he considered the possibility of his having been stimulated or titilated by the supervisee's seductive style, taking his cue from the patient's allusion to flitting around from bar to bar; this was seen as a possible reference to a need in him to share the manic defenses of both patient and therapist as a defense against his own possible depressive trends. He wondered whether he should have been more definitive in recommending the use of silence and in suggesting a limit, except in an emergency, of but one or two interventions. It proved possible for him to subjectively validate the presence of a countertransference-based input, though it was clear that the major countertransferences lay within the supervisee. This recognition is comparable to the recent realization (Langs 1978a) that every intervention from the therapist contains at least some measure of countertransference-based input. The same principle applies to every supervisory intervention, and the supervisor has the responsibility for monitoring his work in order to detect its influence and to become engaged in subsequent self-analytic work designed with its rectification and resolution in mind. Such endeavors may be described as the self-supervision of the supervisor, another level of supervisory work that needs continuous attention.

CONCLUDING COMMENTS

The supervisory situation is filled with complexities and is the scene of a critical, and often moving, communicative interaction. In general,

writers on the subject have failed to recognize many of the practical
and difficult issues or the pitfalls that pertain to the supervisory
experience, and in addition, have neglected its creative potential.

My most recent observations of the unconscious communicative
interaction between patient and therapist has led me to a more
balanced view of both participants. Until now, the patient was viewed
as primarily sick and the therapist as essentially healthy, and the
constructive functioning of the patient as well as the pathological
functioning of the therapist had been relatively neglected. In this
connection, the realization that, unconsciously, the patient is capable
of extensive, valid, and perceptive understandings of the therapist, and
that in addition—still largely on the unconscious level—he is capable
of significant therapeutic and supervisory efforts, has led to an image
of the patient as someone who is significantly disturbed or
dysfunctional on a behavioral and conscious level, while rather gifted
and sound in certain sectors of his unconscious functioning. In
addition, the patient's exquisite sensitivity to the therapist's errors, as
well as his own use of largely unconscious yet sound validating process
(Langs 1976c, 1978c) and his unconscious capacities to understand his
therapeutic needs and whether they are being met, suggests that every
human being is, in some perhaps inherent as well as unconsciously
developed way, a capable therapist and supervisor. This thesis is a
variation on Searles's point (1975) regarding the newborn infant's
almost innate therapeutic tendencies in his relationship with his
mother.

This conception has meaning for the supervisory situation: it implies
that each of us is, in a sense, a natural born (and subsequently
developed) therapist, though many of these therapeutic qualities exist
on an unconscious level and within the realm of our unconscious
functioning. It is other, more disruptive sectors of our personalities,
and the major obstacles that develop in trying to make these abilities
conscious and directly available for expression, that make it necessary
for us to formally learn how to do psychotherapy (or to undergo a
personal therapeutic experience). Still, our conception of supervision
and the nature of a supervisor's work takes on a particular valence
when these actualities and potentials are recotnized, the main problem
in supervision, then, is not so much a matter of teaching and
developing new techniques and ideas, as it is to find the ways of freeing
up the supervisee's unconscoius sensitivities and capabilities.

This line of thought also implies that there is hope for every supervisee, no matter how grossly disturbed or disruptive his therapeutic work may at first seem. It should foster a positive attitude in the supervisor as he approaches work with each of his supervisees. It also should prompt us to remember, as supervisors, that we too once were supervisees and that through the efforts of our own supervisors (and, as a rule, personal therapy or analysis) we have experienced many constructive, however painful, transformations and periods of growth. We too, then, once were neophytes, confused and disturbed; today, presumably, we are far more integrated and capable. It is now our responsibility to create the conditions and to offer the supervisory interventions through which such constructive growth may be afforded to each and every supervisee who comes to us to learn and mature.

NOTE

1. The principles discussed in this paper are, by and large, equally applicable to both psychotherapy and psychoanalysis. Since most of my previous studies and reported supervision are drawn from the former situation, I will use therapy as my model for this paper.

REFERENCES

Arlow, J. (1963). The supervisory situation. *Journal of the American Psychoanalytic Association* 11:576–594.

Bion, W. (1962). *Learning from Experience.* W. Bion, in *Seven Servants.* New York: Jason Aronson, 1977.

———(1970). *Attention and Interpretation.* W. Bion, in *Seven Servants.* New York: Jason Aronson, 1977.

Langs, R. (1973). *The Technique of Psychoanalytic Psychotherapy,* Vol. I. New York: Jason Aronson.

———(1974). *The Technique of Psychoanalytic Psychotherapy,* Vol. II. New York: Jason Aronson.

———(1975). The therapeutic relationship and deviations in technique. *International Journal of Psychoanalytic Psychotherapy.* 4:106–141. [Chapter 7, this volume]

————(1976a). *The Bipersonal Field.* New York: Jason Aronson.

————(1976b). On becoming a psychiatrist: discussion of "Empathy and intuition in becoming a psychiatrist," by Ronald J. Blank. *International Journal of Psychoanalytic Psychotherapy* 5:255–279. [Chapter 12, this volume]

————(1976c). *The Therapeutic Interaction.* 2 vols. New York: Jason Aronson.

————(1978a). Interventions in the bipersonal field. [Chapter 20, this volume]

————(1978b). *The Listening Process.* New York: Jason Aronson.

————(1978c). Reactions to creativity in psychoanalysts. *International Journal of Psychoanalytic Psychotherapy* 7:189–207. [Chapter 15, this volume]

————(1978d). Some communicative properties of the bipersonal field. *International Journal of Psychoanalytic Psychotherapy* 7:89–161. [Chapter 15, this volume]

————(1978e). Validation and the framework of the therapeutic situation. *Contemporary Psychoanalysis* 14:98–124. [Chapter 14, this volume]

————(in press). The *Supervisory Experience.* New York: Jason Aronson.

Searles, H. (1955). The informational value of the supervisor's emotional experiences. *Psychiatry* 18:135–146.

————(1975). The patient as therapist to his analyst. In *Tactics and Techniques of Psychoanalytic Therapy, Vol. II: Countertransference,* ed. Q. Giovacchini. New York: Jason Aronson.

Chapter Twenty

Interventions in the Bipersonal Field

(1978)

It is my purpose in this paper to reconceptualize the nature and function of interventions, consequent to a study of their effects within the bipersonal field. I will take an adaptational-interactional approach to the unconscious communicative interaction between patient and therapist or analyst,[1] in contrast to existing studies of interventions, which appear based upon a classification founded on their manifest properties, rather than on their implications within the therapeutic interaction.

THE PREVIOUS LITERATURE

The literature related to the analyst's interventions has confined itself almost entirely to the sphere of verbal efforts designed to generate cognitive insight within the patient. This tone was set by Freud, who, with the exception of his paper on reconstructions (1937), did not offer a systematic study of the analyst's interventions. There are virtually no references to interpretations in the Standard Edition; these are confined to a few brief remarks on the importance of the interpretation of transference resistances (see especially Freud 1913), and scattered efforts at dream interpretation (perhaps best illustrated in his analysis of the two dreams reported by his patient, Dora; Freud 1905). Implicit in Freud's endeavors is the important role of unconscious fantasies, especially transference fantasies, in the patient's symptoms and neurosis, and the use of interpretations of their derivative expression, especially at times of resistance, as a means of making unconscious contents and the related defensive mechanisms conscious to the patient. Throughout these writings, however, there is consistent evidence for Freud's grasp of the need for validation from the patient of both interpretations and reconstructions, essentially through what he termed *indirect material* (Freud 1937).

Perhaps the single paper most often referred to in discussions of intervening is that of Bibring (1954), who synthesized the scattered writings on this subject by distinguishing five techniques, verbal and nonverbal, expressed in the behaviors of the therapist and intended to affect the patient in the direction of the goals of analysis. These techniques he designated suggestive, abreactive, manipulative, clarifying, and interpretive.

In brief, suggestion refers to the therapist's induction of ideas, impulses, emotions, and actions in the patient, to the relative exclusion of the latter's rational or critical thinking. Abreaction alludes to emotional discharge and reliving, through which intense feelings and responses to traumas are ventilated. Manipulation includes advice, guidance, directives, efforts to neutralize certain emotional forces, the mobilization of certain conflicts, and a wide range of comparable measures. Clarification is any effort by the therapist to enable the patient to see more clearly the nature of his feelings, thoughts, and other communications; it is generally developed on a conscious level and alludes to contents or implications of which the patient is not sufficiently aware. Finally, interpretations are an attempt to identify unconscious material, defenses, and warded-off instinctual drive tendencies, related to the hidden meanings of the patient's behaviors and their unconscious interconnections. Interpretations include constructions and reconstructions of unconscious processes assumed to determine manifest behavior. They are the essential vehicle through which the patient is afforded insight, and become effective through the process of assimilation, which is related to working through, and which leads to reorientation and readjustment.

Virtually every work on psychoanalytic technique has regarded interpretation and working through as the ultimate expression of the analyst's interventions, the means through which the patient gains insight and adaptive structural change. Greenson (1967) is representative in this regard, and he leaned heavily on the contribution of Bibring (1954). He suggested that the analysis of transference or the transference neurosis is the central therapeutic effort in psychoanalytic treatment. It involves demonstrating the transference through confrontations and the use of evidence; clarification of the transference, which includes at times, a pursuit of the transference trigger; interpretation of the transference in terms of the relevant affects, impulses, and attitudes, which entails tracing the antecedents of the transference figure and a full exploration of the transference fantasy; and the working through of transference interpretations. For Greenson, to interpret means to make an unconscious phenomenon conscious. In addition, he commented on the necessity for validation, and, while not exploring this aspect in any detail, he did note that verification is essential in determining the correctness of an interpretation and that it often takes the form of the patient's adding some new embellishing material.

My own clinical delineation of the therapist's interventions (1973) used and expanded the basic contributions of Bibring and Greenson. However, certain additional trends are evident. First, I included silence among the therapist's basic interventions, to which I added questions, clarifications, confrontations, interpretations, and reconstructions. Second, while maintaining the usual psychoanalytic focus on the formal characteristics and conscious intentions of these interventions, I also alluded to a variety of unconscious meanings and communications inherent in both valid and essentially erroneous interventions. For perhaps the first time in the literature, there was specific consideration of the misuses of the various interventions and of the influence of the therapist's countertransferences in this regard. Third, I offered an extended discussion of confirmation and nonconfirmation of interventions, and attempted to develop specific clinical criteria for the validity of an intervention.

Finally, in a chapter that in many ways is the forerunner of the findings and hypotheses to be described here, I reexamined the therapist's so-called supportive (supposedly positive, though noninterpretive) interventions (Langs 1973: Chapter 16). Through an investigation of the patient's unconscious (indirect and derivative) responses to such measures, it became evident that they were experienced as destructive manipulations, invasions of privacy, infringements upon the patient's autonomy, and the like, and that despite conscious acceptance on the part of the patient, the unconscious repercussions were uniformly negative.

In the five years since publication of the technique books, my studies of the analytic and therapeutic situations have evolved more and more in terms of adaptive and interactional considerations. With the use of the metaphor of the bipersonal field, the unconscious interaction between patient and analyst, and their unconscious communicative exchange, began to take on increasingly greater importance. As this perspective widened, the formal attributes and goals of an intervention, while still critical, were viewed as but one dimension of the therapist's communications to the patient, and their unconscious communicative qualities and functions became the subject of extensive investigation.

The bipersonal field concept also led to an elaborate study of the nature and functions of the ground rules or framework of the therapeutic and analytic situations. This led to the specific delineation of a major sphere of interventions that previously had not been separated from the therapist's interpretive endeavors: the establishment, management, and rectification of the frame. Many new hypotheses were generated and validated, leading to fresh perspectives on the therapeutic interaction (Langs 1976a,b, 1978a,b,c,d). In the course of this work, new insights were developed in regard to many aspects of the therapist's interventions, and these form the substance of this paper.

BASIC METHODOLOGY: THE LISTENING AND VALIDATING PROCESS

The listening process itself entails the first application of the validating process. In the course of listening and formulating, the analyst generates *silent hypotheses* which must be silently validated from the patient's continued associations—e.g., through a coalescence of unconscious meaning—before the analyst intervenes. The second application of the validating process occurs after the intervention, and entails a search for confirmation in both the cognitive and the interactional spheres (see Langs 1976b, 1978b,d for details).

Two basic propositions must be stated: first, that the full application of the listening process consistently reveals that the most significant unconscious communications and adaptive reactions within the patient derive from his relationship with the analyst. This implies that this relationship and interaction must be the essential realm of the analyst's interventions, and that interventions based on outside adaptive contexts and unconscious reactions must in some way be related to the therapeutic relationship (Langs 1978b).

The second proposition involves the essential methodology for the present study of the analyst's interventions. This may be stated in general as the complete application of the full range of the listening and validating processes. Beyond that, however, a particular aspect of these processes plays a major role: the role of every intervention by the analyst, whatever its nature, as the essential adaptive context for the patient's subsequent communications. These responses are considered as validating or nonvalidating on one level but, on another, are viewed as a rich *commentary* (Langs 1978b) on the unconscious implications of the intervention at hand.

In distinction from the usual view of the patient's material as essentially transference-based and distorted, and as falling largely in the realm of fantasy, attending to such material as a commentary implies that the patient's associations and behaviors will be organized as Type Two derivatives in the adaptive context of the analyst's intervention, taking fully into account its unconscious implications. Here, the me–not–me interface is fully applied, revealing the manner in which the patient has unconsciously experienced and introjected these unconscious qualities of the analyst's intervention (Langs 1978b,c,d).

In keeping with principles already stated, the patient's manifest and latent response is seen as a mixture of reality and distorted fantasy, of veridical perception and pathological misperception. This material therefore contains both truths and falsifications regarding analyst and patient alike; it is essential to sort out the different components of this mixture. As is true with every aspect of the listening process, which is greatly influenced by the whole gamut of factors within the analyst, this crucial step in the listening process—the distinction of the veridical from the distorted—relies on the self-awareness of the analyst, his capacity to maintain perspective, and his understanding of internal and external reality as it applies to both himself and the patient. By maintaining an openness for valid unconscious perceptions and introjects based on the patient's internal processing of the therapist's interventions (in addition to investigating these reactions for their pathological components), the analyst has a rich opportunity to ascertain the unconscious qualities of his therapeutic endeavors. This basic resource is supplemented by the analyst's own subjective responses to his interventions, his reconsideration of what he has said or done, his thoughts and feelings about it, and the like—his own conscious commentary and efforts at validation, which can themselves be processed for unconscious meaning.

The evaluation of an intervention, then, is based on the totality of these applications of the listening and validating processes. Validating sequences tend to confirm the analyst's conscious intentions, and to reflect minimal disturbing inputs on the unconscious communicative level—an aspect that is, of course, always present, though it need not be essentially pathological. Nonvalidating responses contain derivatives related both to the correct intervention required for the moment and to the unconscious, countertransference-based inputs reflected in the erroneous intervention. A revised formulation—silent hypothesis—that is subsequently subjected to silent validation can then be interpreted to the patient, and the entire sequence subjected to a second effort at interactional validation.

It is evident that this methodology has little use for an assessment as to whether a given intervention is designed as an interpretation, a question, or whatever. It treats all interventions as conscious and unconscious communications, identifies their conscious form and purpose, and then extensively explores the unconscious intentions, functions, and communicative roles. It does so in a manner that is repeatedly subjected to validation, and it is efforts of this kind that have yielded the findings and hypotheses to which I will now turn.

SIX BASIC INTERVENTIONS

On the basis of this clinical research, I will propose an armamentarium for the analyst (or therapist) of six basic interventions (I will discuss below those interventions excluded from this classification): silence; the establishment, management, and rectification of the framework; interpretations-reconstructions; the playing back of derivatives in the absence of a clear-cut adaptive context (one usually related to the therapeutic relationship); the metabolization of a projective identification; and the identification of metaphors for the Type C field and their function. The latter four interventions reflect what I would broadly term the *interpretive efforts* of the analyst, and occur in two basic forms: *definitive interventions* and *transversal interventions*.

I will comment briefly on these fundamental tools.

1. *Silence* is, of course, absolutely basic to the analyst's repertory of interventions. It is filled with nonverbal and unconscious implications, which may vary from moment to moment and from session to session, within the context of the dynamic interaction between patient and analyst. It implies holding the patient, containing his communications and projective identifications, and permitting him to build the analyst's interventions out of fragments that need only be synthesized and organized. It implies entering each session without desire, memory, or understanding (Bion 1970, Langs, 1978b), and permitting the patient to create unconsciously the analyst's understanding and intervention. It implies too a capacity for the adequate management of internal conflicts, tensions, and the like within the analyst, and it certainly conveys a wish to understand and help the patient. It represents the analyst's free-floating attention (Freud 1912), free floating role-responsiveness (Sandler 1976), and openness to the metabolism of projective identifications (Langs 1976a, 1978b). It embodies the analyst's wish to listen, contain, understand, and offer constructive help in keeping with the patient's appropriate needs.

It is also self-evident that silence can be misused and inappropriately extended in the service of countertransference-based needs within the analyst. This occurs in all situations that call for a positive intervention from the analyst, at which point his silence no longer serves the therapeutic needs of the analysand. However, with the exception of preliminary efforts in the technique book (Langs 1973; see also Langs 1976a, for additional references), there has been little effort to empirically delineate the characteristics of appropriate silence and the definitive properties of moments at which its maintenance is no longer tenable. The matter is extremely complex, though it can be definitively stated that the evaluation of the functions of the analyst's silences calls for full use of the validating process. Silence is by far the best way of facilitating the patient's free association, communication of indirect, derivative contents and mechanisms, and unconscious interactional thrusts; it is the optimal means through which expressions of the patient's neurosis become available for interpretation.

There are, then, two major indications for the use of silence: first, the need to wait and allow the patient to build up a neurotic communicative network, to communicate the role evocations, cognitive derivatives, and interactional pressures that provide the substance through which a positive intervention can be made; and second, the absence of truly analyzable material, of interpretable derivatives, role pressures, and interactional processes. There is a tendency among analysts to intervene more actively under the latter conditions, with the expectation that such interventions ultimately will promote derivative expression by the patient; my own observations indicate that this is a deceptive rationalization and that active interventions under the conditions just described have no such effect. Silence, then, is the preferred intervention in the absence of interpretable material. Inappropriate silences lead to the problem of failures to intervene, a subject that will be discussed in the section on countertransference-based influences.

2. *Establishing, managing, and rectifying the framework, and analyzing infringements* constitute a major group of relatively unrecognized and consistently crucial interventions. Included here is the series of interventions through which the analyst establishes the analytic contract and the conditions of treatment (Langs 1973, 1976b). Interventions in this area also involve responses to efforts by the patient to modify the framework, and in addition, any necessary steps involved in rectifying an alteration in the ground rules. Included here, too, is the announcement of any change in the usual course of the sessions (e.g., a vacation by the analyst), and any other major or minor modification in the basic agreement and tenets of the psychoanalytic situation.

Elsewhere (Langs 1975a,b, 1976a,b, 1978a,b,c), I have rather extensively defined the basic framework of psychoanalysis and psychoanalytic psychotherapy, and have clinically demonstrated and discussed its multiple meanings and functions for both patient and analyst. In essence, the framework contributes to the basic ego-enhancing therapeutic hold offered by the analyst to the patient, a security that permits therapeutic regression and the unfolding of analyzable expressions of the patient's intrapsychic pathology—

primarily within the analytic interaction. Similar support is inherently afforded the analyst by these conditions, and both patient and analyst have available a secured container for pathological projective identifications and other pathological communications. In addition, the framework is the single most essential factor in determining the nature of the communicative medium and whether language will be used for insight and understanding, or instead for pathological projective identifications, for inappropriate and pathological forms of defense and gratification, and as massive defensive barriers.

Since the conditions of the analytic situation as constituted by the framework are one of the most basic actualities of treatment, the patient is extremely sensitive to the most minor alteration in the frame; deviations will consistently function as traumatic adaptive contexts engendering intense unconscious reactions. Deviations in the frame, no matter what the reason (even in emergencies), are experienced unconsciously as in part disruptive and threatening, and as filled with danger and countertransference (when the analyst has participated). They consistently disturb the communicative properties of the bipersonal field and tend to shift the field from a Type A mode, if present, to a Type B or Type C modality.

As an essential determinant of the communicative medium of psychoanalysis, responses to alterations in the framework are among the most crucial indications for intervention. Interventions in such situations should be designed to restore a secure frame in actuality—rectification—and should include the interpretation of the extensive implications that both the alteration and the rectification have had for the patient. These efforts are productive of extensive insight and positive introjective identifications, and are a major vehicle of adaptive structural change and cure.

It is the analyst's responsibility in the first hour to establish the analytic contract with clear and firm definition. Such an approach cannot be characterized as rigid, though it is rigorous, since it is designed for the patient's therapeutic needs (and has been extensively validated in the clinical situation as offering the best medium for the patient's analysis).

As a matter of principle, then, the analyst endeavors to maintain the framework as defined in the initial hour, without exception. For example, the unexpected need on his part to be absent for a session will entail its cancellation without the offer of a make-up appointment; similarly, vacations are taken as anticipated and hours are not made up. In all other ways, the analyst strives to maintain the frame—a point also made by Viderman (1974).

Any effort on the part of the patient to modify the basic framework (e.g., the wish to change an hour, to have an insurance form filled out, to take a unilateral vacation, etc.) is met with the basic response of silence (the absence of any direct reaction), permitting the patient to continue to free associate. When under pressure, the analyst must avoid both participation and direct refusal to participate, and must maintain his basic analytic attitude: it is essential that the patient continue to free associate. On that basis, the patient's subsequent material serves as a commentary on his proposal, and will reveal in derivative form both its unconscious meanings and the appropriate response for the analyst, which, remarkably enough, always turns out to be—adherence to the established frame. The analyst is then in a position to use the material from the patient as a means of deriving his management response—adhering to the principle of permitting the patient to shape every intervention—and to interpret the unconscious meanings for the patient. The latter interventions take the form of the interpretation of Type Two derivatives around the adaptive context of the proposed alteration in the frame, and are almost always expressed in the Type A mode. Such work clearly entails additional communications beyond the analyst's interpretive efforts; he has no choice but to establish his position regarding the frame in reality, although I must stress again that this can always be done at the prompting of the patient's unconscious communications.

In situations in which there has been a deliberate or inadvertent alteration of the frame, it is essential to both rectify the frame and interpret the entire experience. Rectification is the essential first step, since it is vital to the restoration of the therapeutic alliance and the positive communicative properties of the bipersonal field, as well as to the necessary interpretive work. When the frame has been altered, unconsciously the analyst is seen as dangerous, the boundaries are unclear, the implications of his verbal and behavioral communications are uncertain, and the patient feels endangered. Rectifying measures— e.g., no longer signing insurance forms, shifting hours, or extending sessions, and desisting in nonneutral interventions—should always be accompanied by interpretive efforts. Examples will be provided and discussed in the clinical section of this paper.

3. *Interpretations-reconstructions* allude to the analyst's basic efforts to make unconscious contents, processes, defenses, interactional mechanisms—fantasies, memories, introjects, self- and object-representations, and the like—conscious for the patient within a dynamic and affective framework. It is well beyond the scope of this presentation to discuss the mechanics of interpretation and reconstruction, or to explore many issues involved in the development and offer of an interpretive and reconstructive intervention (see Kris 1947, Loewenstein 1951, 1957, Ekstein 1959, Greenson 1960, Shapiro 1970, Fine, Joseph, and Waldhorn 1971, Zac 1972, Levy 1973, Langs 1973, Rosen 1974, Viderman 1974, Edelson 1975, Davis and O'Farrell 1976). Here my focus will be on certain properties of interpretations and reconstructions (I will offer my discussion mainly in terms of the former) which are brought to the fore by the adaptational-interactional approach. While these two interrelated interventions play a central role in generating cognitive insight and adaptive structural change as the basis for symptom alleviation, interpretations can serve their intended function only if the bipersonal field has a secure frame. In its absence, intended interpretations consistently serve as vehicles for the analyst's pathological projective identifications or as a means of creating Type C barriers.

Within the bipersonal field, then, every interpretation should be developed around an adaptive context and in terms of Type Two derivatives. These interventions must in addition be appended to the therapeutic interaction, even in the presence of a central outside adaptive context (even here, the outside adaptive context will allude on some level to an aspect of the patient's therapeutic experience). Further, the analyst must be prepared to interpret both unconscious fantasies and unconscious perceptions, since the neglect of either or the confusion of one with the other is disruptive of the analytic process. Much so-called analytic work is carried out in disregard of these essential principles, and is maintained through a suspension of the validating process and a denial of the patient's unconscious perceptions and their elaboration.

Clearly, then, the formal classification of a particular intervention says relatively little about its communicative properties. Every interpretation contains inputs both from the analyst's countertransferences and from his noncountertransference functioning. A valid interpretation minimizes the former, while an erroneous intervention is relatively saturated with the latter.

In preparing an interpretation and in listening to it as it is spoken, the analyst can initiate a process through which he endeavors to become aware (of necessity, partly in retrospect) of the essential unconscious communications it contains. He should begin by identifying the manifest content of his effort; next he should attempt to identify the particular adaptive context, and to monitor the patient's responses for unconscious fantasies, introjects, defenses, and interactional efforts. At times he will be able to relate this delineation to a particular therapeutic context—symptoms, resistances, etc.—and, in addition, to introduce from the patient's material specific genetic links.

However, beyond the analyst's conscious intentions, the range of unconscious communication is infinite. As is well known, much is conveyed in the tone, style, wording, affective investment, timing, tact, and other verbal and nonverbal qualities of an intervention. In undertaking to restructure the relatively dispersed or fragmented communications from the patient into a meaningful whole organized around a particular adaptive context, the analyst will inevitably be selective. There is a need for him to be definitive and to be understood without becoming overrepetitive or confusing; if he is to succeed in this, he must deal not with too many facets of the complex communicative networks he faces. This danger of being overinclusive is of course countered by that of being too restrictive. The proper balance falls within a rather ill-defined range, and errors in either direction may be viewed as communicative blind spots.

The possibilities for error here are endless. The analyst may identify a wrong adaptive context or attempt to intervene without having identified the primary adaptive task. There may be interventions based largely on the analyst's associations rather than on the patient's: fragment's of the analyst's own fantasies may be introduced, or, more subtly, material from other sessions which for the moment is quite dormant within the patient (every session should, in its entirety, be its own creation). Other instances of error are the need to exclude particular types of derivatives, and the failure to be sufficiently selective, giving the impression of disorganization and uncertainty.

Any fragment or thread that extends beyond the patient's own unconscious communications tends to be derived from the analyst's countertransferences. In subjectively reviewing an intervention, the analyst must be able to identify relatively quickly his own idosyncratic contributions. He will be guided in this task by the associations from the patient, which will often address the countertransference-based aspects of the analyst's communication before those elements that are essentially valid and helpful. While this is an aspect of the listening process that is beyond the scope of this paper (see Langs 1978b), it is to be stressed that these commentaries from the patient occur almost always in derivative form. Subsequent interventions from the analyst must therefore address the patient's introjection and processing of any pathological communication from the analyst, though not to the exclusion of other aspects of the patient's material. A fully balanced, perceptive interpretive approach is difficult to achieve, but an important ideal to strive for.

As for reconstructions my concern lies, first, in the possibility of the analyst's introducing countertransference-based elements because of the climate of uncertainty in these interventions and the consequent need to postulate; second, in the tendency to invoke a genetic reconstruction primarily in the service of countertransference-based defenses and needs within the analyst. Clinically, it is not uncommon to discover that an analyst has introduced a genetic reconstruction entirely divorced from the present analytic interaction, or one that treats current experience almost entirely in terms of the patient's distortions and fantasies. Such reconstructions serve defensive needs in the analyst and are often invoked when he has placed disturbing, countertransference-based interventions into the analytic bipersonal field, and the patient has introjected and perceived them unconsciously, and is working them over in a rather disturbed climate. The shift to genetics and the past becomes a major invitation to the patient to desist in his conscious and unconscious responses to the analyst's countertransference-based interventions. In this context, when a reconstruction evokes new memories and genetic material, these communications must be understood as having *functional meaning* (Langs 1978b) that pertains not only to the past, but to the current analytic experience. In principle, then, reconstructions should be offered in terms of prevailing adaptive contexts within the therapeutic interaction, and in a manner that accords meaning to both past and present.

4. *The playing back of selected derivatives* is an important technical measure that is often used in the absence of an adaptive context acknowledged by the patient, a context almost always related to the therapeutic interaction. The analyst is aware of the adaptive context (e.g., the patient has been absent the prior hour, the analyst has announced his vacation, there has been some extraanalytic contact, etc.), but the patient has not alluded to it or provided any clear-cut bridge to it in his associations in the hour. Such an omission reflects significant intrapsychic, and sometimes interactional, defenses, and efforts at pathological instinctual drive gratification; these should not be bypassed or gratified by the introduction of the missing element by the analyst. The analysis of such defenses is fostered by the analyst's silence until the relevant material has surfaced. At times, however, the missing adaptive context is also a crucial therapeutic context; here there are important reasons to intervene.

In a session of this kind, while maintaining an openness for additional adaptive contexts, the analyst organizes the patient's material around the unmentioned primary adaptive task. Virtually always, the patient's indirect communications will convey a commentary on that context, in terms of both unconscious fantasies and unconscious perceptions. They will be filled with unconscious implications and Type Two derivatives related to the context, and in the later part of the session, sound technique calls for the playback of these selected derivatives in a form that leaves open the possibility of fantasy and perception, as well as allusions to both patient and therapist. This is a quality that is essential to what I term a *transversal intervention,* which alludes equally to seemingly contradictory possibilities.

This type of playback is designed to create a tension state or preconception (Bion 1962) in the patient, which can be alleviated or saturated into a conception only through an identification of the organizing adaptive context. Quite often, the patient responds in a way that fulfills this expectation, permitting subsequent interpretive work around the now identified adaptive context.

It is evident that the technique of playing back selected derivatives can be seen as a form of confrontation, but I prefer to discard the latter term largely because of its many destructive implications and misapplications. In general, confrontations address the surface of the patient's communications, while the playing back of derivatives is a transversal communication that embodies both manifest and latent contents. It is designed as a bridge to the patient's unconscious communications and is not fixated at the surface. It fosters expression of the necessary missing communicative elements, including the unconscious basis for the patient's resistances. Further, it minimizes the possibility of countertransference-based inputs from the analyst at a time when he is frustrated in not having sufficient material from the patient for interpretation. It is an extremely useful technique, and I will illustrate its use in the section on clinical material.

5. *The interventional processing—or metabolization—of a projective identification* is related to each of the four interventions I have so far identified, and is based on listening and experiencing the communications from the patient in terms of interactional pressures and projections (Langs 1978b). All formulations built on subjective experiences of this kind must be considered *silent hypotheses* to be validated largely through the cognitive material from the patient. The insightful metabolism of a projective identification from the patient will yield cognitive understanding that ultimately can be conveyed to the patient through an interpretation.

These considerations are equally applicable to interventions in the object relational sphere, as they pertain to unconscious efforts on the part of the patient to evoke role responses, self-images, and other reactions in the analyst in keeping with the patient's unconscious transference fantasies and the real or imagined behaviors of earlier objects—as well as of the analyst in the present (the countertransference aspect; see Langs 1978b). Because of the major element of subjectivity, the need for silent validation is again essential.

In intervening in regard to a projective identification or role evocation, the analyst should maintain the principle of initiating his comments with an adaptive context whenever possible. In the absence of such a context, his remarks should be modeled on the playing back of derivatives, though these must be expressed largely in the interactional sphere. In general, though he should be aware of the adaptive context, however disguised, in the face of massive efforts at interactional projection he may find it necessary to intervene without a clear-cut precipitant. In so doing, he must either state or hint that the adaptive organizer is lacking, and he must make every effort to use Type One derivatives and unconscious inferences; there is a major danger of adhering to the surface of a projective identification rather than delving into its unconscious contents and functions.

When an adaptive context is available, the interactional projection elements are organized as Type Two derivatives and interpreted in terms of the analytic interaction. In the absence of an adaptive context, it is necessary to minimize the introduction of idiosyncratic elements that are open to significant countertransference-based inputs. The patient's projective identifications often impinge upon the framework of the analytic situation, and maintenance of the frame is essential for their effective processing.

6. *Identifying metaphors related to the Type C field and their function* is a special intervention designed to cope with patients who make use of the Type C communicative style. The material from these patients is flat and lacking in derivatives, and as a rule lends itself neither to interpretations nor to the playing back of selected derivatives. It is only after interventions related to the patient's unconscious metaphorical representation of his communicative style and defenses that derivative material, usually quite chaotic and regressive, becomes momentarily available for interpretive work. With such patients, long periods are spent in silent listening and in the occasional presentation of these metaphors (see also Langs 1978b,c).

Wherever possible, the metaphorical representation should be linked to an adaptive context and its defensive-barrier function hinted at or directly stated. Such barriers often serve as massive defenses against an active psychotic disturbance. Unconsciously, the patient is aware of his defensiveness and will from time to time permit a metaphor to communicate this awareness. Typical metaphors of this sort include allusions to safes, tanks, walls, dead ends, voids, unrelatedness, lies and deceptions.

TRANSVERSAL INTERVENTIONS

Finally, I wish to discuss an aspect of intervening that may apply to interpretations-reconstructions, the playing back of selected derivatives, and the interpretive processing of projective identifications. I refer to the *transversal* quality or form of an intervention, a necessary aspect of technique with which the analyst responds to the patient's *transversal communications* (Langs 1978b). Such communications are characterized by the manner in which they traverse two realms: reality and fantasy, patient and analyst, transference and nontransference, or perception and distortion. Every communication, whether from patient or analyst, has dormant transversal qualities in that it condenses opposite elements of one kind or another (a possible exception occurs in the Type C field, where apparent communications are actually attempts to destroy meaning; but even this is only a tendency, as the attempt is often betrayed by the appearance of Type C metaphors). We will reserve the term *transversal communication,* however, for those associations and behaviors whose heavy investment with ambiguity makes itself felt; when a communication is so experienced, it is almost always found to arise from and to express a specific adaptive context; where this is not found, the experience must itself be examined, in the case of the analyst, for countertransference inputs.

Often, when the patient has unconsciously perceived and introjected the countertransference-based aspect of an intervention from the analyst, the working over and commentary by the analysand will be heavily invested in both veridical perceptions and pathological distortions. In intervening, it is essential that the analyst acknowledge the validity of the patient's perceptions, while not neglecting the distorted aspects that derive from the patient's own pathological unconscious fantasies and the like. Similar considerations apply to associations that meaningfully though unconsciously allude to both the patient himself and the analyst—both must be acknowledged through a transversal interpretation.

This position is in contrast to the usual approach to interpretations, especially those related to transference and resistances, which are based on the premise that the patient's communications are essentially distorted and based on pathological fantasies. Such an approach, while it might acknowledge an occasional reality element or adaptive context, views the patient's communications as usually related to himself alone, and to the realm of fantasy. In contrast, other analysts will adhere to the manifest content of the patient's associations, and will deal only with realistic and nondistorted elements. Occasionally, when there is an acute countertransference-based input, the focus will be on the analyst's inappropriate communications, often with the neglect of the patient's distorting addenda.

In contrast to all of these attitudes, the *transversal intervention* consistently acknowledges all aspects condensed in the patient's communications—both reality and fantasy. This concept will become clearer, I trust, when illustrated in the final section of this paper.

THE VALIDATION OF INTERVENTIONS

Elsewhere (Langs 1976b, 1978b,d), I have offered rather extended comments on the validating process in psychoanalytic psychotherapy and psychoanalysis. It has become increasingly evident that many analysts and therapists make little or no effort to validate either their silent formulations or their actual interventions to the patient. I will stress here only the importance of taking each intervention as the adaptive context for the patient's subsequent associations, and the need to listen to this material, first, as a *commentary* on the intervention—an amalgam of unconscious fantasy and perception, valid and invalid responses offered in derivative form (a variety of *transversal communication*)—and, second, as the means through which the correctness of an intervention is assessed.

In this latter regard, true validation is seen in the cognitive sphere by the report of new, previously repressed associations that lend genuinely new meaning to the prior material. This constitites the appearance of a *selected fact* (Bion 1962), a realization that reorganizes the previous material so that it yields up a meaning not previously evident. Lesser validation is seen in associations which, in some genuinely new manner, add to the richness of the material under analysis. Direct confirmation of an intervention, its general surface acceptance, comments that extend it in ways already known, and the repetition of earlier material—all are linear and nonvalidating. They call for reformulation and a renewed period of silence on the part of the analyst, so that the patient may assist him in the search for the prevailing adaptive context, the crucial unconscious meanings and functions of his communications, and the working over of the countertransference elements and bias in the analyst's error.

In the interactional sphere, validation is expressed through the report of positive introjects, usually in terms of some outside figure who has functioned constructively or of some reference to a positive attribute of the patient himself. Both cognitive and interactional validation can be achieved only by organizing the subsequent material around the analyst's intervention, thereby throwing into relief the critical Type Two derivatives. Every meaningful and curative intervention from the analyst, whether interpretations or managements of the ground rules and frame, should find validation through Type Two derivatives from the patient, and any intervention not so confirmed must be considered in error and explored for countertransference-based inputs.

DISCARDED INTERVENTIONS

The six interventions I have described should serve all the therapeutic needs of the patient. They are to be maintained even in situations of emergency, although it is more than evident that in some crises, in part because of the usual presence of countertransference-based inputs, the analyst will be at a loss for a valid interpretive intervention and may have to resort to emergency directives. Nonetheless, even though used as a lifesaving measure (and the emergency should be of such proportions), there are uniformly negative repercussions within the patient, many of them expressed in derivative form under the guise of conscious gratitude. Since I have elsewhere established my position on the detrimental consequences of most of the interventions I have discarded (Langs 1973, 1975b, 1976a, 1978b), my discussion here will be brief.

As for methodology, my position is based on repeated empirical tests of the unconscious functions, communications, and meanings conveyed in the actual interaction between patient and therapist or analyst by each of the interventions to be described. Each application was taken as an adaptive context, and the patient's responses studied in terms of Type Two derivatives as commentaries in terms of both meaning and validity. I shall now briefly indicate my findings.

Questions and clarifications are used largely because of confusion as to the nature of neurotic communications and the best means of obtaining derivatives from patients. Rather than recognizing that silence and a secure frame offer the conditions that best facilitate the patient's expressing himself in derivative and analyzable form, some analysts mistakenly believe that pertinent questions and clarifications foster these expressions. This attitude also reflects basic confusions regarding the listening process and particular difficulties in identifying adaptive contexts and Type Two derivatives (see Langs 1978b).

Both questions and clarifications direct the patient toward manifest content and the surface of his communications. A remarkable number of these interventions occur at a point in a session in which the patient is unconsciously working over, through displaced and disguised derivatives, an aspect of his relationship with the analyst—usually a countertransference-based input. Typically, the analyst intervenes with a question or clarification directed toward an outside relationship or an aspect of the manifest content. These interventions constitute the offer of Type C barriers to the patient (Langs 1978b), and serve to defend both patient and analyst against more meaningful derivatives related to a more catastrophic aspect of the analytic interaction. Empirically, these interventions almost never foster the expression of analyzable derivatives (see Langs 1978b); they tend instead to detract from that level of communication (for earlier discussions, see Olinick 1954, 1957, Langs 1973).

Confrontations have been replaced in the present delineation by the technique of playing back selected derivatives organized around an unspoken adaptive context and by the identification of metaphors of Type C barriers and falsifications. The very term *confrontation* conveys a sense of forcefulness and attack that, unfortunately, characterizes all too well a major unconscious function that this intervention serves for many analysts (see Adler and Myerson 1973, Langs 1973). In addition, despite the conscious intention to use this intervention as a means of developing derivative communication, observations of actual clinical interactions indicate that this seldom proves the case.

Confrontations tend to address the surface of the patient's material, to elicit direct and manifest responses, and to fix the patient on a relatively superficial level of communication. In addition, their use, all too common, without an adaptive context entails the risk of major countertransference-based inputs, largely designed to gratify the analyst's unconscious pathological fantasies and defensive needs; often harshly seductive, punitive, and attacking qualities prevail. As a result, the patient's material will unconsciously center around the introjection and working over of the analyst's countertransferences and the disruptive elements of his confrontation, rather than constructively and unconsciously elaborating in a new and meaningful manner those themes, contents, and defenses relevant to the analyst's manifest intervention.

There are a wide range of noninterpretive and nonneutral interventions that may be classified under such rubrics as supportive, directly responsive, self-revealing, gratuitous, and extraneous. In my previous writings (1973, 1975a, b, 1978b, d), I have, based on repeated empirical documentation, demonstrated that such seemingly well-meaning interventions evoke responses in the patient that are, as a rule, split: manifestly and consciously, the patient is grateful, while unconsciously—in his derivative communications—he uniformly experiences the unconscious communications contained in these interventions as seductive, destructive, and nonsupportive, and as a violation of his autonomy, an assault on his ego- and self-boundaries, and a reflection of the analyst's lack of faith in the patient's ego capacities. These interventions are essentially in the service of the analyst's unresolved countertransferences. Sometimes, though quite rarely, a direct response to the patient is needed (for example, when a patient forgets the date of the analyst's vacation); even then, clarification must be delayed until a full analysis and working through of the unconscious implications of the analysand's failure to remember has been completed.

Finally, there are a wide range of inappropriate alterations in the ground rules and framework of the analytic interaction, implicit and explicit, that entail interventions that consistently reflect the analyst's countertransferences and which find nonvalidating responses from the patient. Similarly, repetitions or elaborations by the analyst of an intervention without clear-cut validation are in the service of pathological needs within the analyst, and will evoke further nonvalidating reactions in the patient.

These comments should serve as a reminder that seemingly innocuous interventions are filled with significant unconscious implications and are not to be treated lightly.

INTERVENTIONS: INDICATIONS AND TIMING

At present, analysts have an extremely loose conception of when they should intervene. In general, the principle has been to maintain an interpretive focus on transference resistances, expecting to clear the way for the revelation of core unconscious transference fantasies, memories, and introjects—so-called contents—which are then subjected to both interpretation and reconstruction. This led to the maxim that one interprets defenses and resistances before contents, a tenet usually supplemented by some vague recognition that interventions are indicated also by ruptures in the therapeutic alliance, acting out, and unexpected symptomatic and regressive episodes.

In an early paper (Langs 1972), I labeled all such indications for intervening *indicators.* Later I termed these indicators the *therapeutic context* (Langs 1973). This term implies that there are specific communications and behaviors on the part of the analysand that create conditions under which the analyst should be inclined to intervene—in keeping with the needs of the patient. In addition, the term suggests that once the material in the session has been organized around a specific adaptive context and identified for Type Two derivatives, the entire constellation should be reorganized around the therapeutic context as a means of revealing the unconscious meanings and functions of the particular indicator.

The major therapeutic contexts, as generally accepted, are resistances; ruptures in the therapeutic alliance; living out; acute regressions, symptoms, or crises within the patient; and any other disturbance within the analysand or the analytic situation. A second, seldom identified group of therapeutic contexts derive from the behaviors of the analyst, and pertain to his erroneous interventions—whether mismanagements of the frame or verbal misinterventions. In keeping with the principles described below, there is a hierarchy of therapeutic contexts: the analyst must interpret the patient's responses to his own errors before responses to essentially internally derived psychopathological reactions. Still, it is important to remember that every disturbance within the bipersonal field, whether within the patient or the analyst, receives vectors from both participants. Sound interpretive work takes into account the contributions of each, and often entails the use of transversal interpretations.

The presence of a therapeutic context, however, does not place the analyst under a total obligation to intervene. It expresses a need within the patient for an intervention, to which the analyst responds if the material permits. The analyst must maintain a sense of balance and proportion, and must evaluate the acuteness of the therapeutic context. He is likely to intervene even in the face of material that is not clearly formulated if the situation is one of emergency proportions or has been evoked by an error in technique; he is less likely to do so in the absence of an acute therapeutic context, since he then has time to allow the material to unfold to the point of permitting a clear-cut interpretive intervention.

It is well to stress that initially, even in a crisis, it is best to maintain the basic listening process, in order to identify the crucial adaptive context and to be able to intervene in terms of Type Two derivatives. The analyst should also safeguard his interpretive efforts by consistently developing silent formulations and searching for silent validation before intervening to the patient.

This said, we may state as a principle that every intervention should be placed into the analyst by the patient. The latter conveys derivatives or scattered fragments that require organization by the analyst around a particular adaptive context. Interventions should be confined to the material from the session at hand, since each session should be allowed to be its own creation (see also de Racker 1961, Bion 1970, and Langs 1978b).

In keeping with the observation that, almost always, the major unconscious and neurotic communications from the patient are organized around the analytic interaction, another important principle of intervening may be stated as follows: the analyst should not intervene unless he has identified the prevailing adaptive context, organized the material in terms of Type Two derivatives along the me–not-me interface as it pertains to the analytic relationship, and has obtained a definitive manifest bridge from the patient's indirect, derivative communications to the therapeutic relationship itself. While there are occasions in which the analyst will, because of an acute therapeutic context, have no choice but to intervene in terms of Type One derivatives or without a direct bridge to the analytic relationship, these situations should be extremely rare. They occur at times of crisis or when the patient is in acute distress, when he communicates relatively intense, often primitive projective identifications, or when he is involved in disruptive behaviors in the analytic situation itself—the so-called acting in (Zeligs 1957, Langs 1976b).

The presence of massive projective identifications may require a processing intervention not included in my list of six. The analyst's first goal here should be to validate his subjective experiences and to deal with the material in terms of derivative communication to the greatest extent feasible. It is a common technical error under these conditions, largely because of the patient's disruptive interactional projections and the analyst's countertransference responses, to respond either with inappropriate silence or with premature interventions, many of them in terms of manifest content. The patient will find such comments the reflection of a failure to properly metabolize his projective identifications, and often he will use them as intellectualized material with which to form interactional obsessive defenses. The patient then continues to communicate on a manifest level in a manner consistent with the invervention, and true validation through Type Two derivatives is lacking.

Another indication for intervening occurs when the analyst has identified an adaptive context, related it to the analytic interaction, and formulated a series of relevant unconscious memories and fantasies in terms of Type Two derivatives. He then silently validates his formulation by finding additional coalescing derivatives. There is in such a process a point of saturation, a shift from preconception to conception (Bion 1962), and the fullness of the communicative network and the presence of silent confirmation serve as an indication to intervene. This is best done, again, when there is a bridge to the analytic relationship.

Finally, there are a number of priorities for interventions, which I would state as follows: resistance before content, interactional resistance before intrapsychic resistance, defense before content, framework before all other material (content or defense), medium before content, communicative style before content, reality before fantasy, analyst before patient.

INTERVENTIONS WITHIN THE THREE BASIC COMMUNICATIVE FIELDS

In the Type A field, both patient and analyst use language and behavior for symbolic communication, illusion, and transition (Langs 1978c). The patient communicates essentially through Type Two derivativesorganized around sequential adaptive contexts. Whether the prevailing attitude is resistance or revelation, in very little time the derivatives necessary to interpret the unconscious fantasies, memories, introjects, and perceptions on which the defensiveness or core fantasy is based become available. In this field, the analyst offers the patient a secure hold and container by defining and maintaining the framework. He then interprets the patient's behaviors and verbal associations, whether they impinge upon the ground rules or serve as a communicative medium. The analytic work takes place mainly in the cognitive sphere, though there may be occasional episodes of interactional projection and efforts at role evocation. There is a general sequential alteration between periods of resistance and revelation, with interpretive resolution of the inevitable obstacles and insight into their unconscious sources and meanings, supplemented by similar insight into core fantasies and memories and the like.

The Type A field, then, is one in which silence, interpretations-reconstructions, and occasional management responses to infringements by the patient on the framework prevail. At times of acute anxiety or conflict, these patients may repress allusions to important adaptive contexts within the analytic relationship, and the playing back of selected derivatives pertinent to that adaptive context proves a valuable intervention.

In the Type B field, established largely through the patient's use of projective identification and action-discharge, the analyst's main function is to receive, contain, and metabolize toward cognitive understanding the patient's interactional pressures. The silent hypotheses developed in this way should consistently be subjected to validation both through the reception of further interactional pressures from the patient, and through the latter's cognitive material. The major intervention in this field is that of processing a projective identification, and of interpreting the implications of role and image evocations. At times the playing back of selected derivatives can be important, and quite often management and interpretation of impingements on the framework will also require responses from the analyst.

It is well to remember that projective identification may serve both defensive and revealing functions, and often expresses efforts at resistance. Still, this is a valid mode of communication for the patient, and should be accepted as such so that the analyst can intervene in an interpretive manner. Often the analyst is under considerable pressure to intervene with these patients, and, while he must develop the capacity to silently tolerate interactional pressures until they can be cognitively understood, there will be a need to intervene more frequently with these patients at times of crisis.

In the Type C field, silence is an essential tool for the analyst. While there may be efforts to modify the frame from time to time, characteristically these patients accept the frame as established and make few impingements in any direction. There is little or no use in playing back apparent derivatives to these patients in the hope of identifying a hidden adaptive context, since they maintain their opaque defenses and interpersonal distance quite intensely and will seldom provide missing links—in part, because such a revelation would reestablish the link between patient and analyst.

A limited form of interpretation proves the primary verbal tool for the analyst in this type of field, and can be characterized as identification of the patient's metaphors for the barriers, void, destruction of meaning, falsifications, and destruction of relatedness that prevails in the Type C field. Using sometimes minor bridges to the therapeutic interaction, these metaphors must be interpreted in terms of the nature of the patient's communicative style. Validation is generally found in momentary expression of the tumultuous inner mental world that these defenses serve to seal off.

Work with Type C analysands requires much patience of the analyst. There are long periods of uninterpretable resistance and noncommunication, and the communicative mode itself functions to conceal the underlying basis for these resistances rather than to reveal them in the form of Type Two derivatives. The analyst must tolerate the Type C narrator (Langs 1978b,c) and must recognize that his elaborate communications serve essentially to destroy meaning. He must refrain from attempting to interpret the contents of the material; his doing so would be met with nonvalidation and, sometimes, a sense of triumph over the analyst, who has permitted himself to be fooled by these nonmeaningful series of verbiage. It is in this sphere that the analyst's tolerance and capacity to contain a void—what I term *negative projective identifications* (Langs 1978b)—proves crucial.

As mentioned, the occasional modification of a Type C barrier will lead to an interlude during which the inner chaos—the psychotic core within patient, analyst, or bipersonal field—that has been sealed off by the Type C barrier will emerge in the material from the analysand. At such moments, interpretations-reconstructions, playing back selected derivatives around an unmentioned adaptive context, and even the metabolizing and processing of projective identifications will be required. The patient will, however, soon restore the Type C barriers and the analyst must shift back to the use of interpretations of the patient's metaphorical representations of the Type C communicative mode.

In all, the analyst's interventions are distinctive for each communicative bipersonal field or particular style of communication by the patient. The timing, pace, and nature of these interventions will vary considerably for each field, and it is essential to identify the patient's communicative mode and work accordingly (see Langs 1978c for details).

THE ROLE OF NONCOUNTERTRANSFERENCE AND COUNTERTRANSFERENCE

It is beyond the scope of this paper to identify and fully discuss the multitude of factors within the analyst that influence his style of intervening (see Langs 1976a,b, 1978a,b,c). Here, to be brief, it is well to note that every analyst has his own style of listening and intervening. Some analysts prefer the cognitive mode and tolerate poorly the Type B and Type C communicative styles in their patients. Others prefer to process interactional projections and are less responsive to symbolic communication. Clearly, the variations are considerable (see Langs 1978c), and it is essential for the analyst to be aware of his preferences in this regard. He must be aware of his capacity or incapacity to tolerate ambiguity or closeness, as well as for synchronized and discordant communication, holding, and containing—to name but a few of the important aspects that deserve fuller discussion.

The analyst must carefully examine through self-analysis, and through his understanding of his patient's commentary responses to his interventions, the true unconscious nature and function of his verbal interventions and efforts to manage the framework. He must be prepared to discover in himself the presence of unconscious projective identifications and Type C barriers—psychoanalytic clichés (Langs

1978b,c). These aspects are mentioned specifically because they extend beyond the usual discussions of the influence of the analyst's unconscious countertransference fantasies on his interventions, in which stress is placed on unresolved conflicts, special areas of vulnerability, the misuse of interventions for seductive and hostile purposes, the presence of defensive blind spots, and unconscious wishes for inappropriate gratification (see, for example, Langs 1974).

I wish to emphasize in this discussion a single tenet which, once stated, will seem self-evident. It is a principle, however, that has taken several years to develop, and that required a departure from the usual view of interventions as essentially correct or incorrect. It is as follows: every intervention made by the therapist—interpretively or in terms of the management of the framework—contains some element of countertransference-based expression.

To my knowledge, this principle and its many implications, most of which cannot be traced out here, has not been explicitly stated in the literature. It implies a continuum of interventions, ranging from those with only a modicum of countertransference to those in which its influence is overridingly significant. It suggests too that the timing of an intervention, the material selected for comment, the associations that are not picked up on, the therapist's linguistic style and tone, his use of innuendo or of concrete thinking, and many other dimensions of intervening leave extensive room for the expression of countertransference no matter how essentially valid a particular intervention may be. This implies too that both countertransference and noncountertransference are ever-present in the therapeutic interaction, as are, of course, both transference and nontransference on the patient's part.

There is therefore an element of countertransference in every moment of the communicative interaction, and the patient will respond continuously to this aspect along with his reactions to the noncountertransference elements in the therapist's interventions, including his silences. It becomes essential now to recognize that when we have spoken of a valid intervention we have been characterizing its predominant qualities, just as when we have considered erroneous interventions we have been stressing major countertransference-based influences—to which, quite often, there has been an added acknowledgement of what I have called a valid core or noncountertransference element (Langs 1976a).

In evaluating a therapist's intervention, then, it becomes essential to identify both its valid and invalid aspects, and to at least be aware of any measure of error in an essentially correct intervention. It seems likely that it is this continuous stream of countertransference-based inputs that provides the patient a greater or lesser degree of external and interactional pathology to which he responds in terms of his own both distorted and valid repertory of reactions. This tenet becomes another means through which the crucial importance of therapeutic work within the framework of the therapeutic interaction is established. On the one hand, the countertransference-based inputs serve on some level as a repetition of past pathogenic experiences and in the actual therapeutic interaction constitute a means, however modified, through which the patient's neurosis is actually restimulated in the present—in a form that is open to analysis only so long as (1) the therapist ultimately becomes aware of the true nature of the unconscious communicative interaction, and (2) these inputs are, by and large, relatively small. On the other hand, the valid, constructive, and essentially noncountertransference-based components of the therapist's interventions provide the patient previously unavailable adaptive resources, cognitive insights, and inevitable adaptive introjective identifications crucial to analytic cure.

Under those conditions in which countertransference factors take on major proportions, a traumatic repetition of the pathological past will prevail, as will an offer of interactional defenses and resistances, of inappropriate and pathological gratification and sanction, and of misalliance and bastion formations (Langs 1975a, 1976a). It is the use of the validating process and of self-knowledge that provides safeguards in this respect, and offers a means through which the therapist may detect these elements in his intervening—making use both of the patient's unconscious communications and of self-analysis.

In this context, it can be stated again that every erroneous intervention contains its constructive nucleus, and that the rectification and analysis of therapeutic interludes related to essentially erroneous interventions may provide both the patient and the therapist significant opportunity for insight, adaptive inner change, and growth—so long as the situation is identified and corrected, and is not part of a repetitive, countertransference-dominated interaction. Clearly, the optimal therapeutic work takes place in a situation in which the countertransference-based elements are, most of the time, a relatively minor component of the therapist's interventions. This provides a setting within which the analyst's constructive interpretations and management of the framework provide a predominantly positive tone to the therapeutic interaction and to the vital work that centers around the patient's introjections of the therapist's pathology and his projection of his own inner disturbances.

THE PATIENT'S INTERVENTIONS

The usual study of the analytic situation has considered only the analyst's interventions, while neglecting those of the patient. It is supposed that the patient simply free associates, and that these communications are designed to reveal his inner conflicts, unconscious fantasies, defenses, projections onto the therapist, and the like. A careful investigation of the analytic interaction reveals, however, that this characterization is limited, and that the patient will from time to time, depending on the underlying nature of the analytic interaction, offer major conscious and unconscious interventions to the analyst. Since we now realize that countertransference is ever present, activities of this kind undoubtedly occur at a low level of intensity throughout the therapeutic experience. Major inputs of this type occur when the analyst has placed significant aspects of his own countertransferences into the bipersonal field and patient; they may also occur when the patient wishes unconsciously to offer a model intervention to the analyst, one that neither participant has been able to generate consciously.

As a rule, the patient's valid interventions—i.e., those that the analyst is able ultimately to confirm through Type Two derivatives organized around the adaptive context of the patient's intervention—are offered in derivative form, unconsciously (Little 1951, Searles 1975, Langs 1975a, 1976a). On occasion, the patient will consciously and directly rectify the frame or confront the analyst with an aspect of the latter's implicit psychopathology or explicit errors. A conscious, valid interpretation is extremely rare. However, unconsciously the patient will consistently offer interpretations in derivative form in response to the analyst's pathological inputs; he will also convey models of valid functioning to the analyst, directives toward the rectification of the frame, and the like. The unconscious resourceful-ness of the patient has been insufficiently appreciated. These efforts should be silently accepted by the analyst as offering ameliorating insights and directives. This is feasible, however, only if he tries to be aware of the unconscious communications contained in his own interventions, and if he is prepared to treat his patient's responses to his therapeutic endeavors as commentaries filled, as a rule, with rich and valid understanding—this in addition to their pathological qualities.

CLINICAL MATERIAL

I shall present several condensed clinical vignettes to illustrate the basic techniques of intervening. My formulation will center around these issues, and little effort will be made to discuss other apsects of the material.

Mr. A was in once-weekly psychotherapy with a therapist who had offered family therapy to his brother, sister, and parents. He was now the only member of his family seeing the therapist, and these excerpts took place after a year and a half of treatment for periods of depression, problems in dating, and fears of becoming a homosexual. The patient was twenty-seven and single.

In the first session of this sequence, the patient spoke in great detail of feeling criticized at work, especially by a woman supervisor who had called him irresponsible for allowing a grade-school class that he taught a free period in the schoolyard. This assistant principal had quarreled with another assistant principal, who had attempted to protect the patient, and of whom the patient had had some homosexual thoughts.

After hearing many details, the therapist suggested that the patient was talking about women and men, feelings of irresponsibility, and two people who are fighting over him. The patient felt accused of being irresponsible by the therapist, and stated that he had not behaved in any such manner. The therapist responded by apologizing, saying that he had not meant to imply that he believed the patient irresponsible; he then attempted to clarify that he had meant to imply that the patient himself was concerned about taking responsibility. The patient agreed that this was a possibility, and he ruminated about his responsibilities at work.

To comment briefly on these interventions: this is a session in which the therapist was unable to identify a specific adaptive context related to the therapeutic interaction, and with some lack of certainty he took as the context the accusation made against the patient at work. In our supervisory discussion, the therapist felt in retrospect that he had probably intervened in the previous hour in a manner that was critical of the patient and irresponsible; this may well have been the primary adaptive task that had evoked this material, which could then be seen as Type Two derivatives related to the patient's unconscious fantasies and perceptions in response to the intervention.

This therapist quite consistently alternated between rather effective and helpful interventions, and sudden lapses during which he became noninterpretive, critical, and confused in his responses. The material suggests the possibility that the two assistant principals represent the patient's unconscious split image of the therapist. Considered along the me–not-me interface, the allusions to homosexuality may be a form of unconscious perception and interpretation to the therapist regarding the underlying basis for his problems in intervening—his unconscious homosexual anxieties and countertransferences. These difficulties serve to mask the patient's own homosexual conflicts and divided self, and would have to be rectified before the patient's pathology could clearly emerge within this bipersonal field.

The unconscious perception of the therapist as having homosexual conflicts which are expressed in the therapeutic interaction appears, based on my knowledge of his work, to be a transversal communication that contains valid perceptiveness and some minor degree of internal distortion—a mixture of reality and perception, nontransference and transference. These comments are of course quite tentative in light of the brief extract offered here, and are offered primarily as models for the type of clinical referents that pertain to the formulations offered in the theoretical and discussion sections of this paper.

If we turn now to the therapist's first intervention, which lacked a definitive adaptive context (Langs 1978b), we can identify it as a type of confrontation with the manifest content of the patient's outside relationships. It was not organized as a playback of selected derivatives around a known unmentioned adaptive context that exists within the therapeutic interaction. The confrontation is designed unconsciously to steer the patient away from that interaction, and to place the burden of prevailing difficulties within the patient—the therapist's contributions are totally set aside. The patient's nonvalidating response seems to allude to the therapist's efforts to blame the patient for the sense of difficulty, and to the irresponsible qualities of this intervention, which failed to take into account derivatives and unconscious communication.

In the face of direct negation, it is well for the therapist to sit back, become silent, listen, and reformulate. The therapist's efforts at apology and clarification are noninterpretive interventions which treat the patient's disclaimer in terms of its manifest content, rather than as a derivative communication which serves as a commentary on the therapist's intervention, and which contains both unconscious fantasies and perceptions—especially the latter. It shifts the patient and the therapist to the surface of their respective communications, offers the patient an interactional obsessional defense and misalliance, and creates a bastion which seals off derivatives and more direct communications related to the therapeutic interaction. Rumination follows within the patient, as a representation of these interactional defenses.

In the next session, the patient began by saying that he hated to talk about his sister (the one whom the therapist had treated); he thought it a waste of time. However, she had threatened suicide because her fiancé had been critical of her and she felt that no one could help her. His mother had said that his sister was fine and the patient had seen her. She told him a dream in which her leg is injured and bleeding; she turns to her mother, who walks away. The dream was depressing, and later his parents fought and the patient felt quite helpless. He remembered times when his father would not allow him to help at work.

The therapist intervened and suggested that the patient had been counseling his sister. He noted that in the dream someone was not being helped, and he pointed out that this sister had been in treatment with him and that the dream must have implications regarding therapy. In fact, he suggested, the image of someone not getting help could tie into treatment, and he pointed out that after the patient had talked to his sister he had become depressed. He also had been unable to help his mother and father, and had recalled his father not allowing the patient to help him. With his sister, he had also been in a helping situation and ended up feeling inadequate and helpless.

The patient agreed that he had been counseling his sister, and thought he deserved a handsome fee. He now felt like crying and remembered a time at supper when he started to wheeze at the dinner table and left for a moment. When he returned, his sister had been given the steak that he wanted and his protests were to no avail—his parents thought he had finished dinner.

In evaluating this session, we must take the prior hour, and in particular the therapist's interventions, as the initial adaptive context for this material. It is striking that the patient began the hour by talking about how he had been wasting his time in therapy—a relatively valid commentary on the prior sesssion and the therapist's interventions. His sister's suicide threat and dream represents, on one level, something of the patient's own depression and bodily anxieties, to which he rather directly adds his own sense of helplessness and the failure of his father to call on him for assistance at work.

However, if we monitor this material along the me–not–me interface in the context of the ineffective interventions made by the therapist in the previous hour, and if we keep in mind the possibility of a latent adaptive context related to the modification in the framework of this therapy that compromised the one-to-one relationship between patient and therapist, it is possible to suggest tentatively that the patient experienced the therapist's need to treat multiple family members as a defense against depressive and suicidal feelings, and as a reflection of his own helplessness. The images certainly convey a disturbance in the working relationship between patient and therapist, and as commentary on the altered frame the patient seems to be suggesting that under these conditions there is no sense of therapeutic hold and no protection against suicidal fantasies.

As for the therapist's interventions, there was a failure to wait for a bridge to the therapeutic relationship and to identify a specific adaptive context in that area. Had the therapist played back a series of seemingly pertinent Type One derivatives related to the general context of therapy not being helpful, the patient might well have revealed a more specific adaptive context and clearer, Type Two derivatives. In general, however, I would recommend continued silence, offering a secure hold, and allowing the patient an opportunity for meaningful derivative communication.

Rather than adhering to the principle of permitting the patient to build the therapist's intervention in its entirety, the therapist rather dramatically introduced the fact that the patient's sister had been in treatment with him; it was also he who suggested the bridge between the allusions to failures to be helpful and the treatment situation. The intervention also has a transversal quality, in that the therapist alludes both to certain realities regarding conditions of treatment, and to the patient's experience of not being helped—without suggesting that the latter is either well founded or distorted.

Still, the focus is almost entirely on the patient's experience, without any indication of specific contributions from the therapist—a point that I make in assessing the intervention, and not as a suggestion for a proposed intervention. (For the moment, technically, I would have allowed the derivatives to build further in the hope of obtaining a bridge to the treatment situation; failing that, I would have played back selected derivatives taken from the material from the patient with the expectation that he would then communicate with less disguised derivatives, in terms of both unconscious fantasies and perceptions.) Finally, we should note that the therapist intervened in a rather confused manner, scattering his comments and shifting back and forth from one theme to another. This type of disjointed intervention is not uncommon in the absence of a reference to an organizing adaptive context, and in itself suggests an underlying sense of helplessness, rather than mastery.

The patient's response to this intervention (which was partially correct, though premature) has another type of transversal quality: it seems both confirmatory and nonconfirmatory. In the main, however, it lacks definitive validation. On the positive side, it may be seen as containing Type Two derivatives related to the prevailing problems in the therapeutic situation; these imply that under conditions in which the one-to-one relationship is altered, the patient is open to illness, and further, that the particular deviation is experienced as favoritism toward the sister and deprivation. As a model, an intervention made on the basis of such a formulation would constitute an effort at interpretation—the identification of a specific adaptive context and the patient's derivative unconscious perceptions and fantasies. In this respect there is a transversal quality in that there is truth to the patient's appreciation of his actual vulnerability under these conditions, and to his sense of favoritism and deprivation, although the oral qualities of his fantasies seem to derive at least in part from within himself. It is an open question as to whether it would be possible for the therapist to be analytically helpful to the patient after having seen the siblings and parents previously.

It is, as I have indicated, a fundamental principle that each intervention should be treated as the adaptive context for the associations that follow, and that the latter be treated as a commentary on the intervention—an unconscious appraisal with mixtures of perceptiveness and distortion. In this context, the patient's acknowledgment of his counseling efforts, and his comment that he deserved a high fee, seem to be a response to the positive elements in the therapist's comment. In supervision, I had previously suggested that the intervention had a valid core; that is, it was an effort to approach the truth of what was really disturbing the patient, though it was undertaken rather prematurely and with some sense of confusion. The patient's response appears to appreciate that mixture: there are the positive elements just noted, an appreciation of the positive endeavors of the therapist which hint at a new understanding of the consequences of the altered frame. On the other hand, the memory of deprivation implies that there is something lacking in the intervention and that the patient has not been adequately fed—a transversal, oral model of the analytic interaction that contains both unconscious truth and unconscious fantasy.

In the next hour, the patient began by saying that he had little on his mind, but was glad to be at the session. He had begun to think about women sexually (a new development), and was masturbating less. He felt he might be responding to the pressures of his mother, who kept insisting that he was doing much better of late—and it was true.

The patient had talked with a young man who was serving as his assistant teacher. He had had homosexual fantasies about being in bed with this man and embracing him, though without having an orgasm. He imagined this student needing help, and helping him sexually. He stopped the fantasy, lest he imagine actual sexual contact.

The patient had been with a friend who had also been a patient of the therapist. For the first time since early in therapy, he described the overt homosexual relationship between the two of them, and how it had developed when they had been classmates and their parents had become friends. Initially, the friend had been the aggressor and the patient had eventually stopped him, only to reinitiate the sexual contact later on. The friend had resisted stimulation to orgasm, but the patient had insisted to the point where they performed mutual fallatio.

The patient was pleased to have told all of this to the therapist, and stated that he now had the wish to go out with a woman. The therapist responded by pointing out that the patient had had a daydream about the assistant teacher which did not reach closure and that he had prevented himself from imagining orgasm. He noted that the patient had gone on to talk about women, fears of exposure, fears of being found inadequate, and a need to cover up. He also pointed out that the patient had stressed how his friend would not look at his penis and denied having had an orgasm, stressing once again the qualities of hiding and secretiveness.

The patient responded by saying that the image of secrets stirred him up, and he then recalled a series of childhood secrets: finding his father's pictures of nude women and having an erection; not being able to undress in the locker room in high school in front of the guys; having nocturnal emissions that his mother commented on in a humiliating way; being bathed by his mother; and first masturbating with great fears of damaging himself.

We may note that in the adaptive context of the therapist's intervention in the previous session—which entailed an attempt to rectivy the frame (in actuality, the therapist had stopped all contact with other family members and had also desisted from such practices as note-taking and answering the telephone during sessions(and to interpret the implications of the previously impaired frame to the patient—the patient indicated that he was doing well and described both homosexual fantasies and a previous homosexual relationship with a former patient of the therapist. This material too has a transversal quality, in that it suggests that the patient now feels safe enough to reveal and explore his homosexual relationships and fantasies, largely in the form of an effort to resolve the underlying pathology and to move toward heterosexuality. At the same time, these communications serve as Type Two derivatives in the adaptive context related to the framework, and suggest that the patient had experienced the alterations in the frame as a seduction and as an expression of unresolved homosexual fantasies and needs within the therapist.

The therapist attempted to play back derivatives around the unmentioned adaptive context of the alterations in the framework, though once again he did so in a confusing manner which impaired his efforts to stress the patient's concern about secret sexual contact and needs to cover up. The intervention was stated in a manner that left no room for the patient's unconscious perceptions of the therapist, and did not constitute a definitive interpretation. It is therefore especially interesting to review the many new memories that emerged subsequently. While they undoubtedly reveal aspects of the patient's psychopathology—his overstimulation as a child, the seductiveness of his mother, his intense castration anxiety—it must be recognized also that they function as unconscious communications related to the qualities of the therapeutic situation as experienced under the conditions of this therapy.

Any isolated intervention related to this material, one directing itself entirely toward the patient's earlier experiences in an effort to help him understand the unconscious basis for his homosexuality and fears of women, would include a major defensive element: it would deny the patient's unconscious perceptions of the therapist and the therapeutic interaction, perceptions which have served as the immediate adaptive context for this material, and to which it is also attached. A more appropriate interpretation would have a transversal quality:it would take the conditions of treatment, both past and present, as the adaptive context, would attempt to show the patient that he is currently experiencing the earlier deviant conditions as a repetition of the pathogenic past, and would detail the relevant unconscious perceptions and their extension into fantasy. The material might then permit an interpretation of the patient's awareness of the differences that have been developing with the restructuring of the framework. The therapist could then delineate some of the patient's anxieties within the more clearly defined therapeutic situation—his fears of a therapeutic regression (Langs 1976a). Technically, however, such an intervention could not be made until the patient provided a clear-cut bridge to the therapeutic interaction. To develop such a communication, the selected playing back of derivatives would serve well, including some allusion to the friend in a way that might hint at the fact that he too had been in treatment with the therapist.

It is, of course, the revelations regarding the homosexual relationship with the friend that are the closest derivatives of the patient's unconscious perceptions and fantasies of his relationship with the therapist. As a major transversal communication, these derivatives contain elements of truth and distortion, of transference and nontransference: there is indeed a seductive aspect to family treatment, and the hypothesis that it satisfies and protects against the therapist's unconscious homosexual fantasies would probably be validated if it could be tested out. On the other hand, the therapist had never been directly seductive, was not overtly homosexual, and had made every effort to manage and master expressions of his unresolved homosexual countertransferences. We would therefore have to see this material as containing both kernels of truth and extensive distortions based on the patient's own unconscious homosexual fantasies and conflicts, and their genetic sources. An intervention designed to interpret the implications of this material would have to take into account the diametrically opposed qualities of these associations from the patient—it would have to be stated in transversal form.

In the following hour, the patient described his discomfort in the waiting room (which was in the hospital at which the therapist was associate director), stating that there were too many sick people around. He felt better for what he had discussed in the previous session, and described how well he was doing at work, where he was receiving admiration and was now ready for either a promotion or for a new job at a higher level. His main concern was leaving his job and having a farewell party, during which he might break down emotionally. He had been praised by the principal of the school and had had homosexual thoughts about him. He wondered if he should leave or not.

The therapist pointed out that the patient had said that he felt strange and uptight in the waiting room, and that this was connected to some ambivalence regarding change and his concern about public exposure. He suggested that there were various meanings to the themes the patient was talking about. The patient responded that he had no thought of leaving treatment, if that's what the therapist had in mind, and he reviewed again his concern about leaving his job and becoming too upset and crying at a farewell party. His mother had once attended the funeral of a near stranger and had made a fool of herself by carrying on. He thought of his sister's depression and how he still gets somewhat upset when he has to speak in front of his class. There's no place where he can cry—not at home, not with friends, and not in treatment.

The therapist said that the patient had now brought up his mother and sister, and that they were somehow related to facing a problem in changing jobs, speaking in public, and speaking freely. He added that the patient seemed to feel a similar problem here in therapy, where he is unable to cry. The patient responded that actually therapy had changed considerably since the therapist had stopped being a friend. At first the patient hated it and felt betrayed, but now it was working out well. Before, the therapist was a member of the family, but now there seemed to be a change and the patient felt safer. He could talk and he felt more secure when, as just a moment ago, the therapist no longer answered the telephone. Still, there was his fear of revealing himself, and he wondered now if it had been induced by the therapist and if he then took it outside. The therapist said that there might well be a kernel of truth in that, and the patient went on to talk about the recent differences in the therapist, and his own improvement of late. He thought then of his anxieties and of his hand-shaking, and how he controlled it with strangers. He feels like he keeps up a facade. He is two people living in a shell: one part is a stranger, but confident and liked, and now top dog and interested in women, and doing well; while the other part is the little boy under the covers, masturbating and afraid of exposure.

The therapist said that the patient had mentioned his—the therapist's—involvement with his family and had gone on to talk of exposure, adding that there were two parts to himself: one strong and the other immature. The therapist added that he thought that the patient was referring to therapy, and that he was feeling better about it and safer, and was now revealing more. This was related in part, the therapist said, to his involvement with the patient's sister and mother, which had been inappropriate and not right.

The patient said that he had been flooded by a number of additional thoughts, but there was time to share only one: he had stopped going to pornographic movies and to the backrooms of pornographic shops where he used to masturbate. He felt he no longer needed them because he now had privacy in treatment.

In brief, the patient appears to be working over his reactions to both the previously modified frame and the currently secured one. The therapist, in his first intervention, played back a series of themes expecting to hear from the patient that he was, indeed, having some thoughts about terminating. It should be noted that the therapist's use of the word *ambivalence* runs the risk of intellectualization and carries with it a certain clichéd quality. It is best to intervene using the patient's language, and to do so without technical terms.

The playback of derivatives was clearly organized around the therapeutic situation and made use of the material from the patient. It may have been a bit premature, since the adaptive context was not as yet clear, and there was still a good deal of time available to allow the patient the freedom of direct and indirect expression.

The patient responded by denying thoughts of leaving treatment, although the therapist felt that there had been improvement to the point where such an issue might soon appropriately arise. The expressed fears of humiliation and exposure now appear to relate to the patient's dread of his own inner mental world, which would emerge within the therapeutic situation as secured by the frame. The therapist again played back derivatives, attempting to develop further the patient's insight into his feelings about the previous family therapy and the current therapeutic situation. This led to entirely new material about the patient's experience of the rectification of the frame, associations that reveal considerable conscious appreciation of the differences between the two treatment situations.

The therapist's acknowledgment that he may have contributed to the patient's symptoms, while clearly a constructive and honest effort, nonetheless addresses itself to the manifest content and serves as a kind of confession. This could more adequately have been done within the context of a more definitive interpretation. If we now take this intervention as the adaptive context for the associations that follow, it appears that the patient is unconsciously perceiving striking variations in the therapist's capacity to intervene: one moment rather effectively, the next moment based on anxieties. According to the patient's unconscious interpretation, the latter is based on continued unresolved sexual countertransferences.

The intervention—the therapist's acknowledgment of error—is an attempt to address the adaptive context of the alterations in the freamework; it alludes to both the patient's unconscious perceptions and his unconscious fantasies. It is somewhat confused once again, and while addressing the contributions of the therapist, it stresses the split within the patient without clearly relating it to the distinct alterations—the split—in the therapist's interpretations and manage-ments of the framework. Still, it seems clear that the patient appreciated the valid efforts contained in this intervention (and they certainly stand in contrast to earlier interventions that failed to appreciate the implications for the patient of the family therapy). The patient's response appears validating in that it reflects an unconscious positive introject of the therapist, who had secured the frame and brought under control a major segment of his unconscious sexual countertransferences. This introject helps modify an earlier pathological introject that had, as the associations reveal, actually contributed to the patient's homosexuality and other perversions. The material suggests that the patient's voyeurism and masturbation had been an interactional symptom based in part on the therapist's countertransferences as expressed in the family therapy situation, and in part derived from the family interaction and the patient's intrapsychic conflicts and pathology.

The therapist's final intervention, then, implies the rectification of the framework, and a transversal interpretation of the unconscious fantasies and perceptions involved in the patient's experience of the altered frame. The patient's allusion to his renunciation of pornography validates the intervention through Type Two derivatives that derive special transversal meaning in the adaptive context of the intervention. It serves too, as a selected fact (Bion 1962) that provides new meaning to the previous material; it reveals the unconscious sexual implications, both reality and fantasy, for both patient and therapist, of the altered framework.

Let us turn now to another brief vignette:

Mr. B. was a young man in psychotherapy for about a year on a once-weekly basis. He was afraid that he might be crazy and had intense homosexual fantasies and anxieties; he had been impotent with women. The therapist was aware that he was having considerable difficulties in treating this patient and found that his interventions consistently seemed to miss the mark and to evoke responses within the patient that reflected a view of the therapist as monstrous and destructive.

The patient began one hour by saying that he felt he was not getting anywhere in therapy. He was ruminating about the daily events of his life without getting into things, as the therapist had pointed out in the previous hour. He bullshits, as the therapist had said, and the therapist was also right when he told the patient that he accuses everyone else of being crazy, when he is really the one who is struggling with these feelings (a gross distortions of the therapist's intervention).

The patient was bothered because he can't really get into what bothers him. He had had a bad scene with his sister and brother-in-law. He had been critical of how his sister had dressed, and she had then told her husband, who became angry with the patient. The patient tried to apologize, but it wasn't accepted. He had been less depressed in the past week, and felt that his sister and brother-in-law had overreacted and had been too attacking in their comments.

The therapist intervened and said that the patient was relating things to the session in the previous week, that he was indicating that the therapist had made him apprehensive and upset, just as his brother-in-law was trying to do.

The patient responded by becoming ruminative again, talking about how immature and selfish he is, how bad he is, and how he did bad things as a child and got his mother angry again and again. When he came to therapy he thought he'd be able to get rid of all the bad things inside himself and become clean and pure, walking the streets free of the bad things inside of him. He thought the therapist would sweep out all of that bad stuff. The therapist responded by saying that he now felt a sense of disorganization as the patient spoke. He suggested that it must relate to the patient's comment about bad things in himself; the bad stuff had somehow gotten out of him, into the room and into the therapist. The therapist went on: he was now coping with a sense of fear, helplessness, and disorganization, which he felt existed in the patient and was now within himself—in the room. The patient responded that he had always been frightened of being crazy and sick, and had always thought of others as nuts. He constantly thinks the other person is crazy so that he himself won't feel crazy.

Briefly, this is a Type B communicative field, which reflects a therapeutic situation in which the patient is engaged in efforts at pathological projective identification, to which the therapist is responding with efforts at metabolism and cognitive interpretation, though it seems evident that he is unable to maintain this level of functioning and ultimately responds with unconscious pathological projective identifications of his own. As a result, the therapeutic situation appears stalemated and disturbed.

The patient's initial associations allude not only to his own difficulties in communicating meaningfully, but to the nature of the therapist's interventions as well (a point confirmed, in part, by the therapist's own subjective awareness). The patient's recollection of the previous hour was filled with distortions to the point where the therapist felt attacked, angry, crazy, and under pressure to see himself as bad. The shift in the patient's associations to the sister and brother-in-law provided a moment of relief for the therapist, but he nonetheless intervened in an effort to process the material in terms of the interactional pressures that seemed to prevail. Much of the intervention, however, is stated in terms of manifest content, and to some extent is an effort to blame the patient for distorting everything the therapist says and for feeling attacked when the therapist has no such intention.

A more adequate intervention might well have been derived if the therapist had continued to process the patient's projective identifications in terms of efforts to destroy his grasp on reality, attack him, and drive him crazy—a transversal communication that unconsciously alludes to both patient and therapist, and that has some representation in the cognitive material. This intervention could have been related to the adaptive context of the therapist's specific interventions in the previous session, which although unreported here, did indeed have qualities of attacking the patient, disturbing his grasp of reality, and driving him crazy.

We can see then that this material is part of a spiraling exchange of pathological projective identifications between patient and therapist. Any intervention that would adequately process this material would have to allude to this spiraling interaction, to the patient's experiences of the therapist's interventions, and to the patient's attempts to place these disturbances back into the therapist. It would have to be stated in transversal form, alluding to patient and therapist, reality and fantasy, nontransference and transference, and noncountertransference and countertransference.

Such an intervention should not be offered to the patient until silently validated in the cognitive material. The associations to the sister and brother-in-law provide validation to some degree, but it is wise to wait for the patient's associations to form a new bridge back to the therapeutic interaction. There is a danger here of intervening prematurely in a way that would consitutute a further unconscious attack on the patient and a further projective identification of disruptive defenses and contents into him. Granted this bridge, however, the therapist could have pointed out that the patient seems to be experiencing the therapeutic interaction in a manner not unlike what had happened with his sister and brother-in-law: there is a sort of spiraling interaction without relief in which both himself and the therapist are being seen as attacking, blaming, and accusatory. The patient is experiencing the therapist as provocative and destructive, and as placing crazy and destructive contents into him, and he responds in kind by overreacting, distorting as had the brother-in-law, and by attempting to disturb the therapist in turn.

Such a transversal intervention, initiated in terms of a specific adaptive context, draws upon both Type One and Type Two derivatives. It is an attempt to understand the nature of the unconscious interactional mechanisms as they exist in this bipersonal field, and in both patient and therapist. The therapist might add, if the material permitted, that the patient seems to feel he is being cast in the role of someone who is sick and crazy, someone to be demeaned, and that in turn he attempts to have the therapist feel and behave similarly. To the extent that this interpretive processing is valid, the patient would then respond cognitively with new material and, quite likely, with important genetic links; interactionally, there would be a positive introjective identification based on the therapist's valid containing and metabolizing functions, and his ability to interpret this unconscious exchange of pathological interactional projections.

In response to the rather mixed intervention that actually was offered, the patient describes an accusatory relationship between himself and his mother, one that it seems is unconsciously being repeated in the therapeutic interaction, rather than interpreted. The patient then alludes to fantasies of projectively identifying and discharging his bad inner stuff into the therapist. In the adaptive context of the antecedent intervention, this is an acknowledgment of some of the inappropriate qualities of the therapy, as it is being misused by both participants, though this is conveyed largely on a manifest level. It also contains, as Type Two derivatives along the me–not-me interface, an unconscious perception of the therapist who is using his own interventions as a means of attempting to get rid of the bad stuff within himself. In a sense, too, the patient's comments appear to convey a refusal to contain the therapist's badness and an effort unconsciously to interpret the therapist's unconscious projective identifications.

The therapist's final intervention is a direct self-revelation which has no place in the techniques being described here. The therapist's attempt to use his subjective experiences and to hold the patient responsible for them reveals no effort to understand the basis for his own subjective responses. As is true of all such noninterpretive interventions, his comments serve as a confession of his own disorganization and as an effort to further attack the patient to engender gult, and to blame him for the therapist's pathology. The therapist presents himself as a victim of the persecutions of the patient, in a form that now makes the patient a victim of the therapist's persecutions. The patient's responsive expression of his own fears of being crazy and his need to think of others as nuts, organized as Type Two derivatives in the adaptive context of this intervention, presents a compelling introject of this therapist's unconscious communications.

We turn now to a final vignette:

Mr. C. was in once-weekly psychotherapy at a point when the therapist had brought up the possibility of termination. He had apparently decompensated during an earlier period in his life, and now had secured powerful barriers against this psychotic part of his personality. In the session to be described, he reported a dream of a man who seemed to be chasing him out of his own apartment. There was the danger of rape, but the patient then found himself in an empty vault with the door closed, safe and protected.

In associating, Mr. C. spoke of mistrusting his banker, and conveyed thoughts of changing his bank because he no longer felt appreciated as a customer; still, he put the matter out of his mind. When conflicted, he makes his mind a blank and feels relief. The therapist pointed out that the patient has a tendency to seal himself off from dangers and to seek safety in voids, and suggested that this is reflected not only in his dream, but in the way in which he was communicating in the session. In response, the patient recalled childhood fears of bombs and explosions, and recent fantasies of attacking his boss for firing a friend whom the patient very much liked. He then wondered if this had anything to do with the recent discussion of the termination of his therapy, and recognized that he felt much better and that perhaps it was time to think about it after all.

In this brief excerpt, the therapist attempts to interpret several metaphors of the patient's use of Type C barriers, doing so, of course, without identifying a specific adaptive context since one was not available in the material. The intervention is confirmed through Type Two derivatives, through which the patient expresses his need for vaults and blankness as a protection against inner disintegration; on another level, validation is reflected in the recollection of the fantasies of attacking the boss who had fired a friend. This latter derivative led the patient directly to termination, and to a continued working through of his anxieties and reactions to the therapist's proposal in this regard.

CONCLUDING COMMENTS

Despite the lengthy clinical material, it has been possible to discuss within that context only a limited number of aspects of the intervening process. The main thrust of this paper has been to offer a series of basic postulates, to selectively illustrate them, and to point toward future studies.

In concluding, it seems appropriate to reflect upon the need for some rather major alterations in the prevailing conception of the analyst's interventions. The current approach stresses the formal nature of interventions and addresses only the rather gross contradictory unconscious communications contained in them. It neglects the continuous unconscious inputs from the analyst. If one shifts instead to a study of the unconscious communicative interaction, a new and more sensitive appreciation of the analyst's work emerges. It confronts us as therapists with our continual countertransference-based inputs, however major or minor, but fosters their mastery and a more effective approach to the therapy of the patient.

NOTE

1. The observations, tenets, and principles to be developed in this paper are equally applicable to both psychotherapy and psychoanalysis. Because most of the relevant literature has addressed itself to the psychoanalytic situation, I will use that as my basic model.

REFERENCES

Adler, G., and Myerson, P. (1973). *Confrontations in Psychotherapy.* New York: Jason Aronson.

Bibring, E. (1954). Psychoanalysis and the dynamic therapy. *Journal of the American Psychoanalytic Association* 2:745-770.

Bion, W. (1962). *Learning from Experience.* In W. Bion, *Seven Servants.* New York: Jason Aronson, 1977.

—— (1970). *Attention and Interpretation.* In W. Bion, *Seven Servants.* New York: Jason Aronson, 1977.

Davies, G., and O'Farrell, V. (1976). The logic of transference interpretation. *International Review of Psycho-Analysis* 3:55-64.

Edelson, M. (1975). *Language and Interpretation in Psychoanalysis.* New Haven: Yale University Press.

Ekstein, R. (1959). Thoughts concerning the nature of the interpretive process. In *Readings in Psychoanalytic Psychology*, ed. M. Levitt, pp. 221-247. New York: Appleton-Century-Crofts.

Fine, B., Joseph, E., and Waldhorn, H. (1971). *Recollection and Reconstruction: Reconstruction in Psychoanalysis.* New York: International Universities Press.

Freud, S. (1905). Fragment of an analysis of a case of hysteria. *Standard Edition* 7:3-122.

—— (1912). Recommendations to physicians practicing psychoanalysis. *Standard Edition* 12:111-120.

—— (1913). On beginning the treatment (further recommendations on the technique of psycho-analysis III). *Standard Edition* 12:121-144.

—— (1937). Constructions in analysis. *Standard Edition* 23:255-270.

Greenson, R. (1960). Problems of dosage, timing, and tact in interpretation. *Bulletin of the Philadelphia Association of Psychoanalysis* 10:23-24.

—— (1967). *The Technique and Practice of Psychoanalysis*, Vol. I. New York: International Universities Press.

Kris, E. (1947). The nature of psychoanalytic propositions and their validation. In *Freedom and Experience*, ed. S. Hook and M. Konwitz. Ithaca, N.Y.: Cornell University Press.

Langs, R. (1972). A psychoanalytic study of material from patients in psychotherapy. *International Journal of Psychoanalytic Psychotherapy* 1(1):4-45. [Chapter 3, this volume]

—— (1973). *The Technique of Psychoanalytic Psychotherapy*, Vol. I. New York: Jason Aronson.

———— (1974). *The Technique of Psychoanalytic Psychotherapy*, Vol. II. New York: Jason Aronson.

———— (1975a). Therapeutic misalliances. *International Journal of Psychoanalytic Psychotherapy* 4:77–105. [Chapter 6, this volume]

———— (1975b). The therapeutic relationship and deviations in technique. *International Journal of Psychoanalytic Psychotherapy* 4:106–141. [Chapter 7, this volume]

———— (1976a). *The Bipersonal Field.* New York: Jason Aronson.

————(1976b). *The Therapeutic Interaction.* 2 vols. New York: Jason Aronson.

———— (1978d). Validation and the framework of the therapeutic situation. *Contemporary Psychoanalysis* 14:98–124. [Chapter 14, this volume]

———— (1978c). Some communicative properties of the bipersonal field. *International Journal of Psychoanalytic Psychotherapy* 7:89–161. [Chapter 15, this volume]

———— (1978a). The adaptational-interactional dimension of countertransference. [Chapter 17, this volume]

———— (1978b). *The Listening Process.* New York: Jason Aronson.

Leavy, S. (1973). Psychoanalytic interpretation. *Psychoanalytic Study of the Child* 28:305–330.

Loewenstein, R. (1951). The problem of interpretation. *Psychoanalytic Quarterly* 20:1–14.

———— (1957). Some thoughts on interpretation. *Psychoanalytic Study of the Child* 12:127–150.

Olinick, S. (1954). Some considerations of the use of questioning as a psychoanalytic technique. *Journal of the American Psychoanalytic Association* 2:57–66.

———— (1957). Question and pain, truth and negation. *Journal of the American Psychoanalytic Association* 5:302–324.

de Racker, G. (1961). On the formulation of the interpretation. *International Journal of Psycho-Analysis* 42:49–54.

Rosen, V. (1974). The nature of verbal interventions in psychoanalysis. *Psychoanalysis and Contemporary Science* 3:189–209.

Zac, J. (1972). An investigation of how interpretations arise in the analyst. *International Journal of Psycho-Analysis* 53:315–320.

Sandler, J. (1976). Countertransference and role-responsiveness. *International Review of Psycho-Analysis* 3:43–47.

Shapiro, T. (1970). Interpretation and naming. *Journal of the American Psychoanalytic Association* 18:399–421.

Viderman, S. (1974). Interpretation in the analytic space. *International Review of Psycho-Analysis* 1:467–480.

Zeligs, M. (1957). Acting in. *Journal of the American Psychoanalytic Association* 5:685–786.

Chapter Twenty One

Continuing Transitions

(1978)

At the very moment that this book is about to go to press, a number of new conceptions have emerged in my thinking that seem an apt way of completing this volume on a note of continued evolution. These ideas will be stated in terms of four postulates and briefly clarified as blueprints for later and more definitive presentations. They are, in the main, further spin-offs from the transition in technique and theory that has brought me now to view the spiraling conscious and—especially— unconscious communicative interaction between patient and therapist as the central organizing conception of the therapeutic experience.

COUNTERTRANSFERENCE AS EVER-PRESENT

The first postulate is self-evident, though its implications have not previously been fully traced out. To state it here: *There is an element, however small or large, of countertransference in every communication from the therapist—his silences, management of the ground rules (setting and hold), and his other verbal interventions.*

A full appreciation of this thesis leads first to a classification of this aspect of countertransference as (1) *inevitable countertransference,* the minimal residuals of pathology to be found in any therapist, and (2) *preponderant countertransferences,* those aspects of his pathology which extend beyond that minimum. There is a continuum here, perhaps best stated as follows: each intervention by a therapist falls somewhere on a continuum with, at one end, relatively minor (but ever-present) countertransference-based inputs; at the other extreme, distinctly major pathological qualities; and, between the two, a gray area of somewhat equally mixed valid and distorted elements. The determining factors in this regard are interactional, residing in both therapist and patient, though clearly the ultimate responsibility for these expressions is with the former. Further, the effects of a given intermixture of countertransference-based and nonpathological elements are also interactional in nature, and depend in important ways on a variety of propensities and sensitivities within the patient.

Second, this precept leads to a major revision in the basic conception of the therapeutic interaction and process of cure. It implies that there is a never-ending cycle of varying degrees of countertransference-based influence on the patient, who is constantly, and largely unconsciously, responding to these fluctuations as a sequence of specific and central adaptive contexts. The continuous presence of inevitable counter-transference means that in some form and on some level, the patient is always being confronted with an actual experience that replicates in some way the critical past pathogenic interactions which were the soil in which his "neurosis" developed, and that expresses and confirms pathological aspects of his own inner mental world.

This understanding places the actual unconscious communicative interaction at the heart of the therapeutic experience. No expression from the patient, or its management (if related to the frame) or interpretation, can be divorced from that transaction. Further, we can see now that inevitable countertransference is an inherent stimulus for, and part of, the cure of the patient. However, this positive outcome is feasible only if the therapist, through his own self-scrutiny and by monitoring the material from the patient for pertinent derivatives (unconscious responses to the therapist's pathology, ranging from efforts at exploitation to those at cure), consciously recognizes the elements of disturbance in his intervention, attitude, or silence. With this as his adaptive context, he can then recitify his errant contribution, subject it to self-analysis on his own so the underlying basis can be resolved (lest there be new manifestations in his work with the patient), and interpret the patient's responsive unconscious perceptions and fantasies. In this way, the interlude leads to both cognitive insight and a positive introjective identification with the analyst by the patient.

It is this type of sequence that truly characterizes sound therapeutic work. We are dealing here with a naturalistic description, not with a brief for unmanaged countertransference or for the exploitation of the patient. It is now that we can see that countertransference is an inevitable component of the cure of the patient—and therapist—as long as its presence is detected, worked over, and both resolved and interpreted. Effective therapeutic work consistently derives from the recognition and analysis of the continuous cycles of the ascending presence of countertransference and its subsequent resolution—only to appear again in need of new identification, modification, and interpretation.

NEWLY DISCOVERED ASPECTS OF RESISTANCE

The concept of resistance, defined as any interference in the work of analysis derived from the intrapsychic defenses of the patient, is fraught with unclarified difficulties and wanting clinically in many ways. It has already been demonstrated that evaluations the patient resists are founded on important subjective elements within the analyst or therapist, and that resistances whose presence have been validated and resolved through interpretations are always interactional products, with greater or lesser contributions from the therapist— which must be recitified first as a prerequisite for adaptive change within the patient. Studies of the three communicative styles and fields (see chapter 15) have shown too that the nature and structure of resistances are distinctive for each mode; thus their adaptive resolution requires special intervention in keeping with their particular manifestations, functions, and properties.

While these interactional considerations are in need of further elaboration, the focus here will be on aspects of resistances that are revealed and clarified by a consideration of the unconscious communicative interaction—as illuminated by a full application of the listening and validating processes. The main thesis that emerges in this regard may be stated as follows: *the ideal meaningful communication from a patient includes a neurotic adaptive context pertaining to the therapeutic interaction and a group of scattered Type Two derivatives that coalesce by unconsciously illuminating distinctly different dimensions of that context. Resistances, then, may be defined communicatively as the presence of any flaw in this basic communicative entity.*

This tenet leads to an empirical, interactionally founded approach to resistances that is readily open to psychoanalytic validation. It provides also a secure means of identifying these obstacles and dealing with them through recitifying and interpretive means. It fosters the recognition of previously uncharted forms of resistances and promotes insight into additional motives for these defenses that previously were neglected.

In brief, it is, of course, the adaptive context that gives vital meaning to the patient's derivatives; in its absence, there are only isolated Type One derivatives and manifest content which serve as interpersonal and intrapsychic barriers and, often, as deceptions (lies in the nonmoral sense) designed for defensive protection, action (discharge, and noninsightful pathological projective identifications—rather than for meaningful symbolic communication generated in the quest for cognitive insight and inevitable growth) promoting introjects. Under the unconscious control of the patient in keeping with his own inner needs for both defense and meaningful expression, and with the influence of his unconscious perceptions and introjections of the therapist, the patient may for example, totally exclude references to the organizing adaptive context for his behaviors and associations. Under the sway of lesser defensive needs, he may allude to the context indirectly, through disguised derivatives.

Another common resistance is seen in the break of the link between the derivatives which carry potential meaning (always a mixture of perception and fantasy) and their *specific* adaptive context of precipitant in the recent therapeutic interaction. Often this is done by offering seemingly rich associations but excluding either the pertinent adaptive context or a functional bridge between the derivatives and the therapeutic relationship. One variation of this type of communicative dispersal or fragmentation occurs when the patient talks at length and manifestly about the therapist and the relationship, while excluding the currently pertinent precipitant for his pathology-related unconscious responses. Clearly, failure to allude to the adaptive context in the course of associating is a major form of resistance. Similarly, the links between context and derivatives, on which identifying meaning and offering an interpretation depend, can be broken by the patient's alluding to the adaptive context but surrounding it with uncoalescing, scattered, and therefore unilluminating derivatives.

Resistance, then, may take the communicative form of (1) omitting the key context, (2) not including meaningful derivatives in the presence of an identified adaptive context, and (3) breaks in the link between the context and relevant derivative responses, so that the connection between the two cannot be meaningfully identified and interpreted.

Finally, clinical data viewed in this light indicate that in addition to commonly known motives for resistance, unconscious perceptions and introjections of the therapist's defenses, anxieties, needs, and unconscious fantasies, memories, and introjects—as communicated through his behaviors and words—play a critical role, as does the need to defend against the psychotic part of the patient's (and therapist's) personality. Further, in addition to known gross behavioral forms of resistance (e.g., silences, conscious avoidance, premature termination) and the communicative forms identified here, a major manifestation of resistance is that of alterations in the basic analytic agreement, setting, hold, and boundaries. These changes—or efforts in this direction—are filled with unconscious defensive meaning and powerfully serve the anti-insightful forces within the patient—and often the therapist. The study of the spiraling therapeutic interaction promises to greatly clarify the typology and functions of resistances and to reinforce their place among the major indications—therapeutic contexts—for interventions.

TRUTH THERAPY—LIE THERAPY

With the growing understanding of the unconscious communicative interaction and especially the unconscious nature of the therapist's and analyst's interventions, there has been a mounting need to reclassify and reconceptualize the basic forms of psychotherapy, the means by which they effect symptom resolution and the degree of stability to such effects, and their detrimental consequences. This problem is so complex and enormous that it seems to defy meaningful resolution of even a single sector, though such nihilism can serve only to perpetuate questionable therapeutic practices. The matter must be approached descriptively, without prejudice or moralizing, and with scientific rigor and compassion. We need, too, some new terms to free us to whatever degree possible from the considerable biases already so prevalent in this area.

Toward this end I propose a continuum of one fundamental characteristic of treatment procedures, with what I will term *truth therapy* at one end, and *lie therapy* at the other. I will comment here on the definition of each extreme of this continuum and on the following proposition: *all therapists and analysts, whatever their avowed intentions, have powerful needs to offer major segments of lie therapy to their patients—in addition to some measure of truth. In actual clinical practice, there is strong evidence, however, that varieties of lie therapy are by far the prevailing form of treatment in use in all quarters—psychoanalytic and otherwise.*

Truth therapy may be defined as the sensitive and tactful pursuit of the most critical and essential unconscious meanings and functions of both the patient's and analyst's communications. It is the search for the dynamic apogee of layers of conscious and unconscious implications, and for the most pertinent implications of each interactive moment. Truth in this sense is ever changing, and one moment's truth may well be the next moment's barrier to veracity.

In clinical practice, the truth pertains to the psychopathology of both patient and analyst—their expression and unconscious basis. This is so because the therapeutic situation is designed specifically for symptom alleviation as it pertains to the emotional ills of the patient. In truth therapy, this derives from the identification and working through of inner and outer truths and their implications. Clinical truth, then, always pertains ultimately to the psychotic and neurotic parts of the personality of both members of the therapeutic dyad, and to a hierarchy of persecutory, depressive, sexual, and aggressive anxieties, dangers, fantasies, and memories, and the related introjects.

First and foremost, truth therapy can unfold only under a particular set of conditions—a stable background object relationship, defined setting, secure boundaries, and an open and safe communicative field. Thus, the ground rules must be clearly defined and maintained, the hold secured, the conditions for containing established, and the sense of security clearly conveyed on all levels—not only for the patient, but also to a lesser degree, for the therapist. The latter must hold the setting (frame) steady; deviations virtually always shift the situation toward lie therapy in greater or lesser proportions.

Within this space, the patient free associates or is silent, in keeping with the fundamental rule, and the therapist manages impingements on the setting and intervenes interpretively as the material permits. Such work may be pragmatically characterized as founded on a search for all pathologcial expressions stemming from patient or therapist, and as based on a consistent understanding of the ongoing communicative-therapeutic interaction. Present evidence points unmistakably to the tenet that clinical truth can be stated only in terms of an adaptive context and Type Two derivatives involving the spiraling therapeutic interaction. All other formulations are in the service of lie therapy, as attested for by the absence of true validation of interventions so derived. Truth therapy, by contrast, finds consistent verification through Type Two derivative validation of interventions, often in the presence of a response that offers a compelling selected fact.

Truth therapy involves the analytic modification of Type A derivative resistances, of the defensive use of the Type B communicative mode, and especially of Type C barriers—the break of interpersonal links, and impervious inner defenses founded on empty clichés, lies, and falsifications. It entails, too, the experience of momentary chaos out of which understanding and growth may emerge. It requires much of therapist, of which least recognized appears to be a capacity to tolerate and master, and to contain and interpret, the primitive and psychotic parts of his own and his patient's inner mental world.

Lie therapy may be seen as a curative effort through bastion formation, misalliance, and, more broadly, the offer of essentially pathological defenses and barriers to the current and dynamically prevailing meanings in the therapeutic interaction, and within both participants. It is founded in large measure on the therapist's offer to the patient of interactional defenses, especially in the form of Type C barriers, which tend to be fragile, vulnerable to inner and outer pressures, and inimical to growth.

Lie therapy is characterized by a wide range of modifications in the basic setting and hold—the ground rules—which unconsciously create conditions for the defensive use of falsifications and clichés, and which communicate the therapist's propensities in this direction. In addition, it is a factor in any intervention that is not linked meaningfully to the specific and most pertinent adaptive context within the therapeutic interaction, or which fails to tie that context to relevant unconscious responses—Type Two derivatives. Isolated so-called interpretive work and reconstructions, and almost all confrontations, clarifications, questions, and noninterpretive interventions (e.g., so-called supportive comments) are typical of lie therapy.

Much can be said about truth therapy and lie therapy. Each has its form of protection for both patient and therapist, and each has its own set of positive and negative attributes. Discussion of these dimensions is not feasible here, but there can be no question that every therapist has the responsibility to his patient—and to himself—to identify the form of therapy he is engaged in, and to try to use that system of treatment which, in truth, is best for his patient—and, secondarily for himself.

THE BACKGROUND OF SAFETY: THE THERAPEUTIC SETTING AND HOLD

The transition from a stress on the bipersonal field concept to that on the conscious and unconscious communicative interaction has led to some revision of my thinking on the ground rules and therapeutic setting. The bipersonal field idea fostered a much-needed shift from a view of the ground rules as merely an often ill-defined set of tenets, applied with flexibility and designed to "safeguard the transference," to an understanding of the holding and containing functions implicit to their application, and their critical role in determining the communicative properites of the therapeutic firld—the concept of a functional framework for the therapeutic space.

Nonetheless, in keeping with the origins of analytic thinking in this area in terms of a set of ules—a strongly mechanistic conception—the frame concept carried with it a burden of nonhuman and rigid qualities which could limit our understanding in this area. The focus on the communicative interaction, then fosters a humanistic and transactional view of this aspect of the therapeutic interaction. It leads to a division of that interaction into *background communications and experiences* (related to the ground rules, setting, boundaries, sense of hold and containment, etc.) and *foreground communications and experiences* (spiraling specific, sequential adaptive contexts and both conscious and unconscious response). The former may, of course, come to the foreground, thereby serving the immediate interpretive work, but by and large they constitute a set of relatively stable functions and communications from the therapist—and, at times, from the patient—that create the basic conditions and foundation for interpretative work with foreground sequences—unconscious meanings and genetic links.

The adequate management of the therapeutic setting and background may be thought of as providing the patient a growth-promoting hold, a therapeutic symbiosis essential for truth therapy. These efforts by the therapist are, of course, filled with unconscious meanings and functions, and are always an admixture of noncountertransference and countertransference elements—the latter creating a requisite for essential background-foreground analytic work (rectification and interpretation) related to the most fundamental part of the therapeutic experiences.

There is, too, a powerful correlation between deviations of all kinds and the therapist's countertransferences. To turn this around, modifications in the basic setting and hold are a notable means through which therapists and analysts express their pathology within the therapeutic interaction. In fact, it appears that these erroneous though well-intended measures remain to this day the single most overlooked vehicle for pathology-based interventions by the analyst. Further studies of the unconscious communicative interaction between patient and therapist should serve to clarify this problem as well as many other pressing clinical issues.

GLOSSARY

Abstracting-Particularizing Process, the. That aspect of the listening process in which first-order, manifest themes are used to derive more general or abstract themes, from which second-order specific themes are generated. The latter are often monitored in terms of the therapeutic relationship and the me–not-me interface

Adaptational-Interactional Viewpoint, the. A clinical-meta-psychological approach to the patient and therapeutic interaction which takes into account both intrapsychic and interactional processes, conscious and unconscious in both spheres.

Adaptive Context, the. The specific reality stimulus that evokes an intrapsychic response. *Direct* or *nonneurotic* adaptive contexts are those stimuli which evoke linear intrapsychic reactions and nonneurotic communicative responses; in essence, they are unrelated to psychopathological reactions and mechanisms. *Indirect* or *neurotic* adaptive contexts are those precipitants that evoke convoluted, derivative intrapsychic responses that contain pathological unconscious fantasies, memories, and introjects; they are related to psychopathology and to neurosis. Often an adaptive context outside of the therapeutic relationship will have a direct context within its manifest content, and an indirect context in its latent content. The latter is, as a rule, a derivative of a significant adaptive context within the therapeutic situation itself, communicated in disguised form. On the whole, the major indirect and neurotic adaptive contexts derive from the therapeutic interaction. The term *primary adaptive task* is a synonym for adaptive context.

Bastion. A term first used by Baranger and Baranger (1966) to allude to a split-off part of the bipersonal field which is under interactional repression and denial, so that the contents involved are avoided by both patient and therapist or analyst.

Bipersonal Field, the. A term first used by Baranger and Baranger (1966) as a metaphor for the therapeutic situation. It stresses the interactional qualities of the field, and postulates that every experience and communication within the field receives vectors from both patient and therapist or analyst. The metaphor requires the concept of an *interface* along which communication occurs between the two members of the therapeutic dyad, and points to the need to conceptualize the presence, role, and function of a framework for the field.

Commentary. A term used to describe the patient's responses to an intervention from the therapist (management of the framework or verbal). These associations and behaviors contain validating and nonvalidating communications, and they are to be viewed as a mixture of fantasy and reality, accurate perceptiveness and distortion. Often, commentaries take the form of *transversal communications*; unconsciously, they convey the patient's evaluation of the intervention.

Communication, Convoluted. An image used to describe the presence of derivatives and the indirect expression of pathological unconscious fantasies, memories, introjects, and interactional contents and mechanisms. It is one of the hallmarks of neurotic communication. See *Neurotic Communications*.

Communication, Linear. A sequence evoked by an adaptive context in which the intrapsychic response is relatively logical, readily apparent or easily inferred, directly responsive, and relatively undisguised. It is a form of reaction that characterizes the direct adaptive context and nonneurotic communication. See *Nonneurotic Communication.*

Communicative Field. The amalgam from patient and therapist that characterizes the dominant mode of communicative interaction in a given bipersonal field. See *Bipersonal Field, Type A Field, Type B Field, Type C Field.*

Communicative Space. A metaphor for the interior of the bipersonal field and for the realm in which communication occurs between patient and therapist or analyst. The image suggests that there are a number of possible communicative spaces, each with a set of defining attributes. It allows, too, for the recognition that patient and therapist may be in separate communicative spaces, rather than sharing the same mode.

Communicative Style or Mode. The form of communicative expression that characterizes the interactional thrusts and form of relatedness of the patient and therapist or analyst. See *Type A Field and Mode, Type B Field and Mode, Type C Field and Mode.*

Conception. A term first used by Bion (1962, 1977) to describe the outcome when a preconception mates with appropriate sense impressions. More broadly, the term may be used to describe the saturation of a preconception through a realization that satisfies its inherent expectations.

Confirmation, Primary. A term used to describe the patient's initial response to an intervention, often in the form of direct affirmation or negation. In general, direct agreement has little bearing on the validity of the intervention, while negation often suggests nonvalidation, though, in exceptional circumstances, it will constitute a defensive response that emerges prior to secondary confirmation.

Confirmation, Secondary. The extended response to the therapist's interventions (management of the frame and verbal) which contain selected facts, uniquely original and previously unknown communications from the patient that extend the intervention, especially in the form of Type Two derivatives. Psychoanalytic confirmation of an intervention requires the presence of truly unexpected Type Two derivatives. In general, their absence constitutes nonconfirmation.

Contained, the. A metaphor first used by Bion (1962, 1977) to allude to the contents and psychic mechanisms that are projectively identified by an infant into his mother, and by a patient into his analyst. More broadly, they allude to the contents and functions of a projective identification emanating from a subject toward an object.

Container, the. A metaphor first used by Bion (1962, 1977) for the recipient of a projective identification. The container may be open to containing such projective identifications, or may be refractory. The metaphor also implies the processing or metabolizing of the introjected contents and functions. An adequate container is seen as being in a state of *reverie.*

Containing and Containing Function. A metaphor used to describe the taking in and processing of projective identifications. An adequate containing function has been described by Bion (1962, 1977) as a state of *Reverie* in the mother or analyst, and may also apply to the therapist or patient. Containing function alludes to the receptiveness to projective identifications, and to an ability to metabolize and detoxify *pathological interactional* projections, returning them to the subject in appropriately modified form. For the therapist or analyst, this process implies the metabolizing of a projective identification to conscious insight, imparted to the patient through a valid interpretation and through the maintenance of a secure framework and hold.

Countertransference. A term used in this volume to allude to all inappropriate and pathological responses of the therapist to his patient. These reactions are founded on pathological unconscious fantasies, memories, introjects, and interactional mechanisms (see Langs. 1976b).

Day Residue. A term first used by Freud (1900) to allude to the reality stimulus for the dream. More broadly, it may be seen as the external stimulus, filled with latent and unconscious meaning, that evokes any intrapsychic response. In that sense, it is virtually synonymous with the *adaptive context.*

Denudation. A term used by Bion (1962, 1977) to metaphorically represent one type of effect that the contained may have on the container, and the reverse: the generation of a disruptive and destructive experience and set of affects, leading to some form of inner disturbance that often is characterized by the destruction of function and meaning.

Derivatives. Manifest communications, verbal and nonverbal, which contain in some disguised form expressions of unconscious fantasies, memories, introjects, and perceptions. These are, then, the communicative expressions of neuroses, and the basis on which they are maintained. See *Type One Derivatives, Type Two Derivatives.*

Derivatives, Embedded. A representation of an unconscious fantasy, memory, introject, or perception that is communicated as a seemingly irrelevant component of a sequence of manifest contents, in a form that seems peripheral to the main conscious intention and to the major first-order and general themes.

Detoxification. A term used to describe the metabolism of a projective identification so that its relatively primitive and destructive qualities are altered through some appropriate means, usually through cognitive understanding directed toward insight. This process is an essential quality of reverie.

Empathy. A form of emotional knowing and noncognitive sharing in, and comprehending, the psychological and affective state of another person. Empathy involves both affect and cognition, and is based on a relatively nonconflicted interplay of introjective and projective mechanisms, and a variety of forms of unconscious sharing. It is a temporary form of immediate ingagement and understanding,, which must then be processed and validated along the lines designated for any subjective experience by the therapist or analyst—or patient.

Faith. A term used by Bion (1972) to describe a form of passive listening or intuiting by the therapist or analyst that is founded upon entering each session without desire, memory, or understanding. It implies a fundamental belief that the patient will put into the therapist or analyst all that he needs for his own cure, and all that that the latter requires for his interventions. It also implies an appreciation of the principle that each session should be its own creation, and that, unconsciously, the patient will provide the therapeutic situation with all that is necessary for his cure, except for the therapist's or analyst's interpretive interventions and management of the framework, which are themselves based on the ingredients provided by the patient.

First-Order Themes. See *Themes, First-Order.*

Frame. A metaphor for the implicit and explicit ground rules create a basic hold for the therapeutic interaction, and for both patient and therapist, and that they create a distinctive set of conditions within the frame that differentiate it in actuality and functionally from the conditions outside the frame. The metaphor requires, however, an appreciation of the human qualities of the frame and should not be used to develop an inanimate or overly rigid conception.

Framework. A term used synonymously with *frame*, usually as a means of referring to the ground rules of the bipersonal field.

Framework Cures. The maladaptive alleviation of symptoms through an inappropriate modification in the frame.

Functional Meaning. Synonymous with *Functional Capacity*. A term used to indicate that associations never exist as isolated mental products, and that among their most essential dynamic implications are the unconscious communications contained within the material as they pertain to the therapeutic relationship and interaction. In essence, it is a concept that stresses that all associations have some dynamic relevance to the therapeutic interaction.

Ground Rules. The implicit and explicit components of the analytic or therapeutic situation which establish the conditions for treatment and the means through which it shall be undertaken (for details, see Langs, 1975b, 1976a,b).

Holding. A term used to describe the therapist's or analyst's establishment and maintenance of a secure and safe therapeutic situation. The result is a holding environment that is created through the implicit and explicit delineation of the ground rules, explicated through their maintenance, and significantly elaborated through valid interpretive efforts. The holding capacity of the therapist or analyst may be likened to his containing capacity, although the former is a more general concept, while the latter specifically refers to the taking in of interactional projections.

Identification. An intrapsychic process through which the self-representations and other aspects of the subject's internal mental world and defenses are unconsciously modified in keeping with a model derived from an external object.

Interactional Defenses. Intrapsychic protective mechanisms which are formed through vectors from both patient and therapist. This type of defense may exist in either participant to the therapeutic dyad, and has both intrapsychic and interactional (external) sources.

Interactional Projection. A synonym for projective identification (Langs, 1976a).

Interactional Resistances. Any impediment to the progress of therapy that receives vectors, usually on an unconscious level, from both patient and therapist.

Interactional Symptoms. An emotional disturbance in either participant to the therapeutic dyad with significant sources from both participants (Langs, 1976b).

Interactional Syndrome. Clusters of interactional symptoms. Langs, 1976b).

Interface, Me–Not–Me. See *Me–not–Me interface.*

Interface of the Bipersonal Field. A metaphor used to describe a hypothetical line along which the communications between patient and therapist take place within the bipersonal field. It implies that vectors which determine this interface are derived from both patient and therapist, and that these may be contained in relatively fixed intermixtures or may vary considerably. Among the determinants of the qualities and location of the interface, pathological inputs from both patient and therapist are especially significant.

Introject. An intrapsychic precipitate which stems from the process of introjective identification. Among its qualities is the extent to which it is transient or becomes structuralized, the degree to which it is incorporated into the self-image and self-representations or maintained as separate from them, the extent to which it is pathological or nonpathological, and the degree to which it is constructive or benign rather than destructive or malignant. In addition, these internal representations of conscious and unconscious traits and interactions have a variety of specific qualities in keeping with the nature of the object, the subject, their relationship, and the qualities of their separate and shared experiences. See *Unconscious Introject.*

Introjective Identification. The interactional process through which introjects are formed. As a rule, it is invoked by a projective identification from the object, although it may also entail active incorporative efforts by the subject. The process is influenced both by the nature of the object, the contents and processes that are being taken in, and the inner state of the subject.

Intuition. An immediate form of knowing, understanding, or learning developed without the conscious use of reasoning and knowledge.

Latent Content. The hidden dimension of the patient's associations contained in disguised form within the surface of that material. The term is used to refer to readily available inferences from the manifest content—disguised specific unconscious fantasies, memories, introjects, and perceptions.

Listening Process, The. A term used in the broadest possible psychoanalytic sense to refer to all conscious and unconscious intaking and organizing processes within both patient and therapist. For the therapist, the term includes all available cognitive and interactional sources of information about the patient, verbal and nonverbal, and his own use of sensory and nonsensory, conscious and unconscious, sensitivities. Included too are efforts at synthesizing and formulating cognitive material, the experience of role pressures and image evocations, and the metabolism of projective identifications. The process culminates in conscious understanding or insight, in proper holding and containing, and in the formulation of a valid intervention. Similar processes take place within the patient, although, as a rule, much of it on an unconscious level.

Manifest C Content. The surface of the patient's associations and the therapist's interventions. The term refers to the direct and explicit meanings so contained.

Me–Not-Me Interface, the. An imaginary interface of the patient's communications so designed that every aspect refers on one level to the patient himself, while on another level to the therapist or analyst. The me–not-me is stated from the patient's vantage point and indicates that every communication contains allusions to both himself and the therapist or analyst.

Metabolism, or the Metabolism of Projective Identifications. A term first used by R. Fliess (1942) to describe the processing by the analyst of temporary trial identifications with the patient. The concept is used more broadly to refer to all efforts to work over sensory and nonsensory inputs from the patient, and in another specific sense to refer to the introjective identification and containing of a projective identification from the patient, ultimately processed toward cognitive understanding and insight. This last sense of the term may also be applied to the patient's efforts to introjectively identify and contain projective identifications from the therapist, so long as efforts are made toward understanding.

Misalliance. A quality of the basic relationship between patient and therapist, or of a sector of that relationship, which is consciously or unconsciously designed to bypass adaptive insight in favor of either some other maladaptive form of symptom alleviation or the destruction of effective therapeutic work (see Langs, 1975c).

Neuroses. A term used in a special sense to allude to all forms of psychopathology, ranging from symptomatic disturbances to character disorders, from neurotic disturbances to borderline syndromes and narcissistic disorders to psychoses, and from psychosomatic disorders to addictions, perversions, and other emotionally founded syndromes. In essence, then, the term refers to all types of syndromes based on intrapsychic and interactional emotional disturbances and dysfunctions.

Negative Projective Identification. A term used to describe an empty or voidlike interactional projection designed to destroy meanings within the bipersonal field and to disrupt the mental capacities of the object or recipient of the interactional projections.

Neurotic Communication. That form of behaving and conveying meanings that is related to the neuroses, and which is characterized by the use of derivative and convoluted sequences, related ultimately to pathological unconscious fantasies, memories, introjects, and perceptions.

Nonconfirmation. See *Nonvalidation.*

Noncountertransference. The essentially nonconflicted sphere of the therapist's or analyst's functioning expressed in his appropriate capacity to relate to the patient, listen, intervene, manage the framework, and the like.

Nonneurotic Communication. A means of conveying conscious and unconscious meaning that is essentially unrelated to neuroses. It is characterized by manifest messages, readily available inferences, and linear causal sequences.

Nontransference. The essentially nonconflicted areas of the patient's valid functioning within the therapeutic relationship. It is exemplified by validatable conscious and unconscious perceptions and reactions to the therapist, and by other spheres of adequate functioning and interacting.

Nonvalidation. A response to an intervention by the therapist or analyst (management of the framework or verbal) that is flat, lacking in unique contents or a selected fact, repetitious, linear, and without surprise. It is an indication that the intervention has been erroneous, and is largely in the sphere of secondary confirmation—here constituting secondary nonconfirmation.

Preconception. A term first used by Bion (1962, 1977) to represent a state of expectation and more broadly a state of need, a quality in need of fulfillment or closure, an unsaturated state, which, once saturated, would generate a conception.

Precipitant or Reality Precipitant. A synonym for *day residue*, and a term synonymous with *adaptive context* when used to refer to the evocation of an intrapsychic response.

Predictive Clinical Methodology. A mode of psychoanalytically oriented therapy founded on the validating process, and especially on efforts at prediction so designed that validation takes the form of Type Two derivatives.

Primary Adaptive Task. A synonym for *adaptive context* (Langs, 1973a).

Projective Counteridentification. A term coined by Grinberg (1962) to allude to all countertransference-based responses within the analyst to the patient's projective identifications. The term implies a failure to metabolize the relevant interactional projections and the reprojection into the patient of nondetoxified contents and mechanisms.

Projective Identification. An interactional effort by a subject to place into the object aspects of his own inner mental state, inner contents, and unconscious defenses. The term identification is used here in the sense of remaining identified with the externalized contents and wishing to evoke in the object an identification with the subject.

Proxy, Evocation of a. A form of projective identification described by Wangh (1962) which stresses an interactional effort to place into the object areas of malfunctioning and disturbance, largely as a means of evoking adequate responses which can then be introjected.

Psychoanalytically Oriented Psychotherapy, or Insight Psychotherapy. A form of psychotherapy which takes place within a well-defined bipersonal field and which is designed to provide the patient symptom relief based on cognitive insights and the inevitable positive introjective identifications that derive from the therapist's capacity to hold the patient, contain and metabolize his projective identifications, establish and manage the framework, and interpret the neurotic communications and expressions from the patient.

Psychoanalytic Cliche. An intervention based on psychoanalytic theory and on the material from the patient at a point at which it is communicated in a nonneurotic form. It is a statement of apparent psychoanalytic meaning or truth which is essentially and functionally false in light of the prevailing sources of inner anxiety and turmoil, conflict and disturbance within the patient and or the therapist. It is therefore unconsciously designed to serve as a barrier to the underlying catastrophic truths and as a means of disrupting the meaningful relationship links between patient and therapist.

Regression, Nontherapeutic. A shift toward more primitive communication and expression of derivatives of unconscious gantasies, memories, introjects, and perceptions that takes place under conditions of unneeded modifications in the framework and in response to other errors in technique by the therapist or analyst. The impairments in the framework render such regressions difficult to analyze and resolve, and the restoration of the frame is essential to a shift from a nontherapeutic to a *therapuetic regression.*

Regression, Therapeutic. An adaptive form of re-regression that takes place within a secure bipersonal field and is a means of describing the constructive emergence of unconscious fantasies, memories, introjects, and perceptions related to the patient's neurosis as mobilized by the therapeutic interaction and based on earlier genetic experiences and traumas. This emergence of relatively primitive material occurs in a form and under conditions that render the neurotic components analyzable and modifiable through insight (Langs, 1967a).

Resistance. A term used to describe any impediment within the patient to the work of therapy or analysis. It is a conception that is based on a subjective evaluation by the therapist or analyst. In its narrow clinical sense, these obstacles are founded on defenses against intrapsychic conflicts and anxieties, as they are expressed within the therapeutic relationship. See *Interactional Resistances*.

Reverie. A term used by Bion (1962, 1977) to describe the state of the mother, therapist, or analyst who is capable of receiving the projective identifications from the infant or patient, appropriately metabolizing them, and returning them to the subject in a relatively detoxified form. In a psychotherapeutic situation, this implies a correct interpretation and appropriate management of the framework.

Second-Order Themes. See *Themes, Second-Order*.

Selected Fact, the. A term used by Bion (1962), borrowed from Poincaré, to describe a newly discovered formulation, finding, or fact that introduces order and new meaning into, and unites into a whole, previously disparate elements. It is the realization, then, that links together elements not previously seen to be connected.

Silent Hypothesis. A formulation derived from the various avenues of the intaking aspect of the listening process, developed, as a rule, around a specific adaptive context. Its development relies too on the abstracting-particularizing process, monitoring material around the therapeutic interaction, and utilizing the me–not-me interface, as well as all other means available to the therapist or analyst for generating dynamic, adaptive conceptions of the most pertinent unconscious meanings of the patient's material. In its most complete form, it will entail the identification of the most active unconscious fantasies, memories, introjects, and perception within the patient's material. In its most complete form, it will entail the identification of the most active unconscious fantasies, memories, introjects, and perception within the patient, and will relate these to the present therapeutic interaction, to important genetic experiences for the patient, and to his psychopathology. While these hypotheses may be developed at any point in a session, they are especially common in the opening segments of each hour, and are maintained by the therapist without intervening.

In principle, they should be subjected to silent validation before the therapist or analyst intervenes, doing so most often at a point when there is a relevant bridge between the silent hypothesis itself and the communications from the patient.

Silent Question. An issue that arises within the mind of the therapist as he listens to the patient, leading him to raise it subjectively while not directing it to the patient. When pertinent, such queries will, as a rule, be answered in some derivative form by the patient's ongoing associations. In principle, silent questions are to be preferred to direct queries of the patient, which tend to serve a variety of defensive and countertransference needs within the therapist or analyst, and to impair the patient's use of indirect, derivative communication.

Silent Validation. An aspect of the evaluation of the material from the patient that follows the development of a silent hypothesis. When subsequent material further coalesces with the initial hypothesis, and supports it through the communication of Type Two derivatives, the silent hypothesis is seen as confirmed. See also *Validation*.

Themes, First-Order. The general contents and specific subject matter that can be derived from an examination of the manifest content of the patient's material.

Themes, Second-Order. Derivative contents developed through the use of the abstracting-particularizing process. First-order manifest themes are identified and general thematic trends are then formulated: inference derived on that basis are considered second-order themes. As a rule, such themes are developed in terms of the ongoing relationship and interaction, and take on specific form and meaning when related to pertinent adaptive contexts within that relationship.

Therapeutic Context. Any communication from the patient that suggests a need for understanding and resolution. As an indication for interventions, the therapeutic context is an important organizer of the patient's material. This material is first organized around the prevailing adaptive contexts; it is then reorganized around the therapeutic context in order to reveal its unconscious meanings and functions. Among the more common therapeutic contexts are disturbance within the patient, and on the part of the therapist, countertransference-based errors in intervening both in the interpretive sphere and in his establishment and management of the framework.

Therapeutic Interaction. A term used to describe the conscious and unconscious communicative interplay between the patient and therapist or analyst.

Therapeutic Misalliance. An attempt to achieve symptom alleviation through some means other than insight and the related positive introjective identifications with the therapist. See *Misalliance,* an essentially synonymous term.

Therapeutic Relationship. A term that embraces all components, conscious and unconscious, pathological and nonpathological, of the interaction between patient and therapist. For the patient, the therapeutic relationship involves both transference and nontransference components, while for the therapist it involves countertransference and noncountertransference elements. The term is strongly preferred to "transference" when describing the patient's relationship with the therapist, and equally preferred to "countertransference" when describing the therapist or analyst's relationship to the patient. See *Transference, Nontransference, Countertransference,* and *Noncountertransference.*

Transference. The pathological component of the patient's relationship to the therapist. Based on pathological unconscious fantasies, memories, and introjects, transference includes all distorted and inappropriate responses and perceptions of the therapist derived from these disruptive inner mental contents and the related mechanisms and defenses. These distortions may be based on displacements from past genetic figures, as well as on pathological interactional mechanisms. Unconscious transference fantasies and mechanisms are always communicated in some derivative form, while the manifest communication may allude to either the therapeutic relationship itself (disguised, however, in regard to the latent content) or to outside relationships. Transference responses are always maladaptive adaptive and can only be understood in terms of specific, indirect adaptive contexts (see Langs 1976b).

Transfersal Communication. Associations from the patient that bridge, and therefore simultaneously express, both fantasy and reality, transference and nontransference, uncosncious perception and distortion, truth and falsehood, self and object. Such communications are, on one level, entirely valid, while on another level, essentially distorted.

Transversal Intervention. A particular type of communication from the therapist or analyst to the patient which is shaped in keeping with the presence of a transversal communication. In essence, such interventions, usually in the form of interpretations, although sometimes developed through the playback of derivatives related to an unidentified adaptive context, take into account the dual qualities of transversal communications, and are stated in a manner that is open to the contradictory elements contained in the patient's associations.

Trial Identification. An aspect of the listening process especially developed by Fliess (1942) as an important means of empathizing with and cognitively understanding the communications from the patient. It entails a temporary merger with, or incorporation of, the patient and his material in the presence of distinct self-object boundaries in most other respects. It is a temporary form of being and feeling with the patient, and the cognitive-affective yield from such experiences must then be processed toward insightful understanding and subjected to the validating process.

Type A Field, the, and Type A Communicative Mode, the. A bipersonal field and communicative style in which symbolism and illusion play a central role. Such a field is characterized by the development of a play space or transitional space witin which the patient communicates analyzable derivatives of his uncosncious fantasies, memoreis, introjects, and perceptions, ultimately in the form of Type Two derivatives. Such a field requires a secure framework, and a therapist or analyst who is capable of processing the material from the patient toward cognitive insights which are then imparted through valid interpretations. Such endeavors represent the therapist's capacity for symbolic communication. The Type A communicative mode is essentially symbolic, transitional, illusory, and geared toward insight.

Type B Field, The, and Type B Communicative, Mode the. A bipersonal field characterized by major efforts at projective identification and action-discharge. The field is not essentially designed for insight, but instead facilitates the riddance of accretions of disturbing internal stimuli. The Type B communicative mode is one in which efforts at projective identification and action-discharge prevail.

Type C Field, the, and Type C Communicative Mode, the. A field in which the essential links between patient and therapist are broken and ruptured, and in which verbalization and apparent efforts at communication are actually designed to destroy meaning, generate falsifications, and to create impenetrable barriers to underlying catastrophic truths. The Type C communicative mode is designed for falsification, the destruction of links between subject and object, and for the erection of barriers designed to seal off inner and interactional chaos.

Type C Narrator, the. A patient who utilizes the Type C communicative mode through the report of extensive dream material or the detailed description of events and experiences within his life or in regard to the therapeutic interaction. Such material is characterized by the absence of a meaningful adaptive context, the lack of analyzable derivatives, and the use of these communications essentially for the generation of nonmeaning and the breaking of relationship links. It is not uncommon for the Type C narrator to interact with a therapist or analyst who makes extensive use of psychoanalytic clichés, generating a therapeutic interaction falsely identified as viable analytic work, while its primary dynamic function falls within the Type C communicative mode.

Type One Derivatives. Readily available inferences derived from the manifest content of the patient's associations, without the use of an adaptive context. These inferences constitute one level of the latent content, arrived at in isolation and without reference to the dynamic state of the therapeutic interaction and to the adaptive-dynamic function of the material at hand.

Type Two Derivatives. Inferences from the manifest content of the patient's material that are arrived at through the abstracting-particularizing process when it is organized around a specific adaptive context. These disguised contents accrue specific dynamic-adaptive meaning when so organized, and are the main medium for the therapist's or analyst's interpretation, primarily in terms of the therapeutic interaction.

Unconscious Fantasy. The working over in displaced form of a particular adaptive context. The relevant contents are outside of the patient's awareness and are expressed in derivative form in the manifest content of his associations. This is a type of daydreaming without direct awareness of the essential theme, and may be either pathological or nonpathological. The derivatives of unconscious fantasies are an essential medium of interpretive work and have important genetic antecedents. Among the most crucial unconscious fantasies are those related to the therapist, and when they are distorted they fall into the realm of transference, while those that are nondistorted belong to nontransference. These daydreams include representations from the id, ego, superego, self, and from every aspect of the patient's inner mental world, life, and psychic mechanisms.

Unconscious Interpretation. A communication from the patient to the therapist, expressed in disguised and derivative form, and unconsciously designed to help the therapist understand the underlying basis for a countertransference-based intervention. These interpretations can be recognized by taking the therapist's intervention as the adaptive context for the material from the patient that follows; hypothesizing the nature of the therapist's errors; and accepting the patient's material as reflecting an introjection of the error, and an effort to heal the disturbing aspects of that introject. Put in other terms, the patient's responses are viewed as a commentary on the therapist's intervention, and are found to contain unconscious efforts to assist the therapist in gaining insight in regard to the sources of his errors.

Unconscious Introject. A network of intrapsychic precipitants derived from interactions between the subject and object, in the past and present. They are derived from the process of introjective identification, and depend on the nature of the contents and mechanisms involved, as well as qualities within both subject and object. Introjects may be short lived or relatively stable, pathological and nonpathological, incorporated into the self-image and self-representations or isolated from them, and may involve any of the structures of the mind, id, ego, and superego. In psychotherapy, an especially important form of introjection occurs in response to the therapist's projective identifications, either helpful or traumatic, nonpathological or pathological, which generate alterations in the inner mental world of the patient. Such a process is continuous with the therapeutic interaction and may, in addition, occur within the therapist as a result of projective identifications from the patient. See also *Introjects.*

Unconscious Memory. Derivative precipitates of past experiences— mixtures of actuality and distortion—expressed through indirect communication and inner representations of which the subject is unaware. Such reminiscences without awareness may be pathological or nonpathological, and the former are an important aspect of the genetic basis of the patient's psychopathology.

Unconscious Perception. A term used to describe evidence of valid perceptiveness of another person's (an object's) communications and cues of which the subject is unaware. These may be identified through a correct appraisal of the nature of an adaptive context, including an accurate understanding of the object's unconscious communications. While outside the subject's awareness, his derivative communications demonstrate an essentially verdical perception in terms of the prevailing underlying realities. When the adaptive context is known, unconscious perceptions are reflected in Type Two derivatives. They are the basis for nondistorted introjects.

Validated Hypothesis. A silent hypothesis that has been confirmed via Type Two derivatives, and especially an interpretation or management of the frame that has been communicated to the patient and which is affirmed through the development of Type Two derivatives and the appearance of a selected fact.

Validation, Indirect, See *Validation via Type Two Derivatives,* with which it is essentially synonymous.

Validation Via Type Two Derivatives. A form of confirmation that is synonymous with the development of a selected fact, and with the modification of repressive barriers. This type of indirect, derivative validation is the essential proof of the truth of a spychoanalytic clinical formulation and intervention. Every clinical psychoanalytic hypothesis can be accepted as a general truth only if it has been subjected to this type of validation.

Validating Process, the. A term used to describe conscious and unconscious efforts within either patient or therapist to affirm, support, and substantiate conscious or unconscious formulations and hypotheses. It is a crucial component of the listening process, receives its ultimate test in the patient's responses to the therapist's interpretations and management of the framework, and must take the form of confirmation via Type Two derivatives and the development of a selected fact (see Langs, 1976b, 1978a).

Additional Publications

by Robert Langs

1959

A Pilot Study of Aspects of the Earliest Memory. Read before the Section on Neurology and Psychiatry of the New York Academy of Medicine and the New York Neurological Society, Joint meeting, May 22, 1958. Abstract: *Archives of Neurology and Psychiatry* 81:709.

1960

A Method for the Clinical and Theoretical Study of the Earliest Memory. *Archives of General Psychiatry* 3:523–423 (with M. Rothenberg, J. Fishman, and M. Reiser).

1962

Subjective Reactions to Lysergic Acid Diethylamide (LSD-25). *Archives of General Psychiatry* 6:352–368 (with Harriet Linton).

Placebo Reactions in a Study of Lysergic Acid Diethylamide (LSD-25). *Archives of General Psychiatry* 6:369–383 (with Harriet Linton).

1964

Empirical Dimensions of the LSD-25 Reaction. *Archives of General Psychiatry* 10:469–485 (with Harriet Linton).

Retrospective Alterations of the LSD-25 Experience. *Journal of Nervous and Mental Diseases* 138:409–423 (with Harriet Linton and I. H. Paul).

1965

Individual Differences in the Recall of a Drug Experience. *Journal of Nervous and Mental Diseases* 140:132–423 (with Harriet Linton-Barr and I. H. Paul).

Earliest Memories and Personality: A Predictive Study. *Archives of General Psychiatry* 12:379–390.

Manifest Dreams From Three Clinical Groups, *Archives of General Psychiatry* 14:634–643.

1967
First Memories and Characterologic Diagnosis. *Journal of Nervous and Mental Diseases* 141:318–320.

1966
Stability of Earliest Memories Under LSD-25 and Placebo. *Journal of Nervous and Mental Diseases* 144:171–184.

Manifest Dreams in Adolescents: A Controlled Pilot Study. *Journal of Nervous and Mental Diseases* 145:43–52.

1968
Lysergic Acid Diethylamide (LSD-25) and Schizophrenic Reactions. *Journal of Nervous and Mental Diseases* 147:163–172 (with Harriet Barr).

1969
Discussion of "Dream Content in Psychopathologic States," by Milton Kramer. In *Dream Psychology and the New Biology of Dreaming,* ed. Milton Kramer. Springfield, Ill.: Charles C. Thomas.

1971
Altered States of Consciousness: An Experimental Case Study. *Psychoanalytic Quarterly* 40:40–58.

1972
LSD: *Personality and Experience.* New York: John Wiley (with H. Barr, R. Holt, L. Goldberger, and G. Klein).

1973
The Technique of Psychoanalytic Psychotherapy, Volume I, New York: Jason Aronson.

1974
The Technique of Psychoanalytic Psychotherapy, Volume II. New York: Jason Aronson.

1976
The Bipersonal Field. New York: Jason Aronson.

1977
The Therapeutic Interaction. Volume I: Abstracts of the Psychoanalytic Literature; Volume II: A Critical Overview and Synthesis. New York: Jason Aronson.

1978
The Listening Process. New York: Jason Aronson.

INDEX